The Bible and the Pursuit of Happiness

The Bible and the Pursuit of Happiness

What the Old and New Testaments Teach Us about the Good Life

Edited by

BRENT A. STRAWN

OXFORD
UNIVERSITY PRESS

OXFORD
UNIVERSITY PRESS

Oxford University Press is a department of the University of Oxford.
It furthers the University's objective of excellence in research,
scholarship, and education by publishing worldwide.

Oxford   New York

Auckland   Cape Town   Dar es Salaam   Hong Kong   Karachi
Kuala Lumpur   Madrid   Melbourne   Mexico City   Nairobi
New Delhi   Shanghai   Taipei   Toronto

With offices in

Argentina   Austria   Brazil   Chile   Czech Republic   France   Greece
Guatemala   Hungary   Italy   Japan   Poland   Portugal   Singapore
South Korea   Switzerland   Thailand   Turkey   Ukraine   Vietnam

Oxford is a registered trade mark of Oxford University Press in the UK and certain other countries.

Published in the United States of America by Oxford University Press
198 Madison Avenue, New York, NY 10016

© Oxford University Press 2012

Library of Congress Cataloging-in-Publication Data
The Bible and the pursuit of happiness /edited by Brent A. Strawn.
p.   cm.
Includes bibliographical references (p.) and index.
ISBN 978-0-19-979573-4 (hardcover: alk. paper)—ISBN 978-0-19-979574-1 (pbk.: alk. paper)
1. Happiness—Religious aspects—Christianity. 2. Happiness—Biblical teaching.
3. Bible—Psychology. I. Strawn, Brent A.
BV4647.J68B53   2012
220.6—dc23   2011052866

1 3 5 7 9 8 6 4 2

Printed in the United States of America
on acid-free paper

For Reese E. Verner, Esq.
Father-in-law and Friend

Contents

PART THREE
Beyond the Bible:
Continuing the Conversation into Other Disciplines

Preface

THE ESSAYS IN this collection originated in a conference held in Atlanta during December 11–13, 2009. That conference and, indeed, the project as a whole emerged out of a larger, five-year project devoted to the Pursuit of Happiness hosted by Emory University's Center for the Study of Law and Religion (CSLR) and funded by the John Templeton Foundation. The larger Pursuit of Happiness project was chaired by my Emory colleague Philip L. Reynolds, who at several key junctures lent expert advice to this related, though much smaller project. I am thankful to Philip and to the director of the CSLR, John Witte, Jr., for inviting me to take up this task, which proved, happily (!), to be an enjoyable one. I should also register my thanks to my colleagues Carol A. Newsom and Carl R. Holladay—both of whom participated in the original Pursuit of Happiness project—for recommending me for the job. The lion's share of my thanks go to the contributors, of course, for their excellent work as well as their patience and good humor during the editorial process. I'm thankful also to several of them for taking time to read and comment on my own contributions to the volume. I would be remiss if I did not also acknowledge the hard work of the indefatigable Linda B. King, without whom, I'm quite sure, the original conference would not have happened. Anita W. Mann also helped with details surrounding the conference, as did my research assistant Michael J. Chan, who offered help both then and at numerous points since—all in addition to contributing a very useful appendix to the volume that will be of great help to future studies on the Bible and happiness. Both Michael and another research assistant, Josey Bridges Snyder, provided crucial assistance in the final stages of editorial work. My most recent assistant, Henry M. Huberty, deserves thanks for producing the index.

Lastly, given this work's relationship to the CSLR, it seemed only right that I dedicate it—or at least my efforts on it—to the best lawyer I know, Reese E. Verner. Reese has always showed great interest in my work and has often offered to help me, though, thankfully, he has never billed me for his hours. In addition to being an honest lawyer, he is also, all things considered, a quite happy one. I suspect this is due in no small part to the fact that he is a deeply compassionate and profoundly thankful person—qualities that the positive psychology litera-ture shows correlate directly with happiness.[1] I admire these qualities in Reese and I am thankful to have experienced them firsthand, but most of all I'm thankful for the fact that he is both my father-in-law and friend.

Brent A. Strawn
Associate Professor of Old Testament
Candler School of Theology, Graduate Division of Religion, and
Department of Middle Eastern and South Asian Studies
Senior Fellow, Center for the Study of Law and Religion
Emory University

---

1. See, e.g., Richard Layard, *Happiness: Lessons from a New Science* (New York: Penguin, 2005), 8, 191–193, 235; Philip C. Watkins, Michael Van Gelder, and Araceli Frias, "Furthering the Sci-ence of Gratitude," in *Oxford Handbook of Positive Psychology* (eds. C. R. Snyder and Shane J. Lopez; Oxford: Oxford University Press, 2009), 437–45; Eric J. Cassell, "Compassion," in Sny-der and Lopez, eds., *Oxford Handbook of Positive Psychology*, 393–403; Robert A. Emmons and Michael E. McCullough, eds., *The Psychology of Gratitude* (New York: Oxford University Press, 2004); and Robert Emmons, *Thanks! How the New Science of Gratitude Can Make You Happier* (Boston: Houghton Mifflin, 2007).

Contributors

William P. Brown
Professor of Old Testament
Columbia Theological Seminary

Greg Carey
Professor of New Testament
Lancaster Theological Seminary

Michael J. Chan
Doctoral candidate in Hebrew Bible, Graduate Division of Religion
Emory University

Ellen T. Charry
Margaret W. Harmon Professor of Historical and Systematic Theology
Princeton Theological Seminary

Terence E. Fretheim
Elva B. Lovell Professor of Old Testament
Luther Seminary

Joel B. Green
Professor of New Testament
Associate Dean for the Center for Advanced Theological Studies
Fuller Theological Seminary

Carl R. Holladay
Charles Howard Candler Professor of New Testament Studies
Candler School of Theology, Graduate Division of Religion,
and Center for the Study of Law and Religion
Emory University

Jacqueline Lapsley
Associate Professor of Old Testament
Princeton Theological Seminary

Thomas G. Long
Bandy Professor of Preaching
Candler School of Theology and Graduate Division of Religion
Emory University

Nathan MacDonald
Leader of the Sofja-Kovalevskaja Research Team
University of Göttingen
and Reader in Old Testament
University of St Andrews

Carol A. Newsom
Charles Howard Candler Professor of Old Testament
Candler School of Theology, Graduate Division of Religion,
and Center for the Study of Law and Religion
Emory University

Steven J. Sandage
Professor of Marriage and Family Studies
Bethel University

Colleen Shantz
Associate Professor of New Testament
St. Michael's College
Toronto School of Theology
and Department of Religion
University of Toronto

Brent A. Strawn
Associate Professor of Old Testament
Candler School of Theology, Graduate Division of Religion,
Department of Middle Eastern and South Asian Studies,
and Center for the Study of Law and Religion
Emory University

List of Abbreviations

BT	*The Bible Translator*
BTB	*Biblical Theology Bulletin*
BZ	*Biblische Zeitschrift*
BZAW	Beihefte zur Zeitschrift für die alttestamentliche Wissenschaft
BZNW	Beihefte zur Zeitschrift für die neutestamentliche Wissenschaft
CBQ	*Catholic Biblical Quarterly*
CBQMS	Catholic Biblical Quarterly Monograph Series
CC	Continental Commentaries
CEB	Common English Bible
CEJL	Commentaries on Early Jewish Literature
ChrCent	*Christian Century*
Contemp Fam Ther	*Contemporary Family Therapy*
Couns Val	*Counseling and Values*
Cult Div Ethn Min Psychol	*Cultural Diversity and Ethnic Minority Psychology*
Curr Dir Psychol Sci	*Current Directions in Psychological Science*
Europ J Soc Psychol	*European Journal of Social Psychology*
EvT	*Evangelische Theologie*
HALOT	L. Koehler, W. Baumgartner, and J. J. Stamm, *The Hebrew and Aramaic Lexicon of the Old Testament* (trans. M. E. J. Richardson; 5 vols.; Leiden: Brill, 1994–2000)
HB	Hebrew Bible or Heavenly Being (the latter only in the Appendix)
HBT	*Horizons in Biblical Theology*
HTR	*Harvard Theological Review*
HTS	Harvard Theological Studies
HUCA	*Hebrew Union College Annual*
IBS	*Irish Biblical Studies*
ICC	International Critical Commentary
IEJ	*Israel Exploration Journal*
Int	*Interpretation*
Int J Intercult Rel	*International Journal of Intercultural Relations*
Int J Psychol Relig	*International Journal for the Psychology of Religion*
IRT	Issues in Religion and Theology
ITQ	*Irish Theological Quarterly*
JBL	*Journal of Biblical Literature*
J Couns Psychol	*Journal of Counseling Psychology*

J Exper Soc Psychol	*Journal of Experimental Social Psychology*
J Happiness St	*Journal of Happiness Studies*
J Humanist Psychol	*Journal of Humanistic Psychology*
JPS	Jewish Publication Society
J Pers Soc Psychol	*Journal of Personality and Social Psychology*
J Psychol Theol	*Journal of Psychology and Theology*
JR	*Journal of Religion*
J Res Pers	*Journal of Research in Personality*
JSFSC	*Journal of Spiritual Formation and Soul Care*
JSNT	*Journal for the Study of the New Testament*
JSNTSup	Journal for the Study of the New Testament Supplement Series
J Soc Clin Psychol	*Journal of Social and Clinical Psychology*
JSOT	*Journal for the Study of the Old Testament*
JSOTSup	Journal for the Study of the Old Testament Supplement Series
KJV	King James Version
LCL	Loeb Classical Library
LHBOTS	Library of Hebrew Bible/Old Testament Studies
LUÅ	Lunds universitets årsskrift
LXX	The Septuagint/Greek version of the Old Testament
MHRC	*Mental Health, Religion, and Culture*
MT	The Masoretic Text/Hebrew version of the Bible
NETS	New English Translation of the Septuagint
NIB	*The New Interpreter's Bible* (12 vols.; eds. Leander E. Keck et al.; Nashville: Abingdon, 1994–2004)
NIBC	New International Biblical Commentary
NIDB	*The New Interpreter's Dictionary of the Bible* (5 vols.; eds. Katharine Doob Sakenfeld et al.; Nashville: Abingdon, 2006–2009)
NIGTC	New International Greek Testament Commentary
NIV	New International Version
NJB	New Jerusalem Bible
NJPSV	New Jewish Publication Society Version (Tanakh)
NovT	*Novum Testamentum*
NovTSup	Novum Testamentum Supplements
NRSV	New Revised Standard Version*
NT	New Testament
NTL	New Testament Library
NTS	*New Testament Studies*

OBO Orbis biblicus et orientalis

OBT Overtures to Biblical Theology

OECT Oxford Early Christian Texts

OED *The Oxford English Dictionary* (2nd ed.; 20 vols.; Oxford: Clarendon, 1989)

OT Old Testament

OTL Old Testament Library

OTS Old Testament Studies

OTT Old Testament Theology

Pers Indiv Differ *Personality and Individual Differences*

PRS *Perspectives in Religious Studies*

PSB *Princeton Seminary Bulletin*

Psychol Inq *Psychological Inquiry*

Psychol Relig Spir *Psychology of Religion and Spirituality*

Psychol Rev *Psychology Review*

Psychol Sci *Psychological Science*

RB *Revue biblique*

Res Aging *Research on Aging*

Rev Gen Psychol *Review of General Psychology*

RHPR *Revue d'histoire et de philosophie religieuses*

RSV Revised Standard Version

SBL Society of Biblical Literature

SBLDS Society of Biblical Literature Dissertation Series

SBLRBS Society of Biblical Literature Resources for Biblical Study

SBLSymS Society of Biblical Literature Symposium Series

SBS Stuttgarter Bibelstudien

SBT Studies in Biblical Theology

ScrB *Scripture Bulletin*

SNTSU Studien zum Neuen Testament und seiner Umwelt

STDJ Studies on the Texts of the Desert of Judah

Tanakh See NJPSV

TB Theologische Bücherei

TDNT *Theological Dictionary of the New Testament* (eds. G. Kittel and G. Friedrich; trans. G. W. Bromiley; 10 vols.; Grand Rapids: Eerdmans: 1964–1976).

TDOT *Theological Dictionary of the Old Testament* (eds. G. J. Botterweck et al.; trans. J. T. Willis et al.; 15 vols.; Grand Rapids: Eerdmans, 1974–2006)

TJT	*Toronto Journal of Theology*
TPINTC	TPI New Testament Commentaries
TRu	*Theologische Rundschau*
TU	Texte und Untersuchungen zur Geschichte der altchristlichen Literatur
VT	*Vetus Testamentum*
VTSup	Supplements to Vetus Testamentum
WBC	Word Biblical Commentary
WMANT	Wissenschaftliche Monographien zum Alten und Neuen Testament
WW	*Word and World*
ZAW	*Zeitschrift für die alttestamentliche Wissenschaft*
ZNW	*Zeitschrift für die neutestamentliche Wissenschaft*
ZThK	*Zeitschrift für Theologie und Kirke*

Sigla:

x	times—e.g., 2x = twice, 3x = three times, etc.
√	before a term designates a word root (Hebrew or Aramaic)
Yhwh	The Divine Name, often translated "Lord" in English version of the Bible

Note:

Biblical citations are from the NRSV unless otherwise indicated.

The Bible and the Pursuit
of Happiness

INTRODUCTION

The Bible and . . . Happiness?

Brent A. Strawn

And don't some people fall in love with their heart's desire,
marry, and live reasonably happy lives?
Some. For a while. Maybe. I can't say.
Don't you believe in love?
Yes, but the word has been polluted. Beware of people who go
around talking about loving and caring.

—WALKER PERCY[1]

1. Introducing the Bible and . . . Happiness

Publications on "The Bible *and . . .*" are in no short supply these days, comprising nothing less than a rather large "cottage" industry. But this is nothing new. For centuries, millennia even, people have looked to the Bible for help in navigating life, and the overstuffed shelves in the religion aisle of our local bookstores only demonstrate that the trend isn't letting up. Today, however, the range of life concerns people bring to the Bible is possibly even larger than it was in the past: people look to the Bible not only for spiritual help, but also for advice and life-strategy on childrearing, beauty secrets, making money, even dieting. Countless books treat these and many other topics, with some collating all the answers the Bible gives, from A–Z, in conveniently priced and handy sized portable paperbacks.[2]

---

1. Walker Percy, *Lost in the Cosmos: The Last Self-Help Book* (New York: Picador, 1983), 187.

2. See, e.g., Ken Anderson, *Little Book of Where to Find it in the Bible: The Ultimate A to Z Resource Fully Illustrated, Hundreds of Contemporary Topics, For Users of KJV, NIV, NKJV, CEV, LB, NRSV, and Other Popular Translations* (Nashville: Thomas Nelson, 2001).

Given this trend, *The Bible and the Pursuit of Happiness* could be viewed rather skeptically as the latest in a never-ending line of publications of rather dubious utility (new "Bible-help" books keep getting published, after all, but life seems pretty much the same, if not worse). It could be seen as "just another" book designed to pick up on the perennial appeal of the Bible by applying it to "yet another" topic—one that may even be tangential to the Bible's main concerns, but one that, regardless, has some decent marketing potential (recall the Bible's "perennial appeal," after all). One could even wonder if this book has been mis-shelved. Does it belong instead in the self-help section? Or, perhaps worse, in light of the conjunction in "the Bible *and* ...," is this a book that lays only the thinnest veneer of religion over what might otherwise be an important topic (happiness), but which is now—given that seemingly innocuous but oh-so-sinister "and"—seriously watered-down? Is it the literary equivalent of a sparkling new Range Rover with a license plate reading "Psalm 1"? Wouldn't it be better to put this book back and walk down to the self-help aisle after all?

Well, not necessarily, though the subject following the conjunction in "The Bible *and* ..."—namely, "the Pursuit of Happiness"—might just fuel the disdain. This is not to say that happiness itself is to be sniggered at; quite to the contrary, happiness and its associated themes or states (health, flourishing, well-being, and so forth) are quite the rage today, comprising no small cottage industry themselves. The bookshelves at our local bookstores are equally if not more overstuffed with happiness "Product," and these are at most only an aisle or two away from the packed shelves on health, self-improvement, diet, and the like. Television, too, is full of information (and infomercials!) about health, fitness, and fashion, all with the promise that losing a few pounds or those skin blemishes or that outdated wardrobe will translate directly into a happier affect and/or increased success with the object of one's affection. Or, to relate these developments more closely to religious groups that care deeply about the Bible, one need only think of the so-called "Prosperity Gospel," the power of positive thinking, and/or mega-church preachers who promise "your best life" in the very imminent future, if not, in fact, right now.[3]

The happiness sought for in the culture generally, the happiness prized in certain popular forms of Christianity, and the happiness depicted within the Bible are not exactly the same thing, of course, but neither are they completely unrelated. If they are kin, then the relation is probably no farther than first cousins,

---

3. The not-so-subtle allusion is to Joel Osteen, *Your Best Life Now: 7 Steps to Living at Your Full Potential* (New York: FaithWords, 2004). Just as the current volume went to the publisher, Osteen's newest book on happiness was released: Joel Osteen, *Every Day a Friday: How to Be Happier 7 Days a Week* (New York: FaithWords, 2011). The "classic" on positive thinking is, of course, Norman Vincent Peale, *The Power of Positive Thinking* (New York: Fireside, 2003 [orig: 1952]).

and it may be a good bit closer than that. What's more—and this gets directly to the concerns of the present volume—the Bible is frequently summoned as a source that contributes to these "pursuits" of happiness, especially of the religious variety, and most particularly, of course, the *Christian* variety. Setting aside forty days of purpose, for instance, which will improve your life all around, will also involve a good bit of Bible reading.[4] The same may be true in order to have your best life now, or for any number of other, similar approaches.[5]

Of course, all such approaches—whether religious or not—typically dissatisfy precisely when they fail to produce "authentic happiness."[6] Thoughtful—not to mention unhappy!—people are thus severely tempted to throw the Bible out along with the rest of the quick fixes that have turned sour. Indeed, a number of important arguments have been proffered that turn the tables on happiness altogether, arguing that what human beings (including, presumably, human beings that give some attention to the Bible) need right now is a strong dose of sobriety and seriousness—dare one even say sadness?[7] The authors of these "antihappiness"

---

4. Here the allusion is to Rick Warren's bestseller: *The Purpose Driven Life: What On Earth Am I Here For?* (Grand Rapids: Zondervan, 2002). Warren's endnotes are almost all references to the Bible, the vast majority coming from the New Testament. In an appendix, he explains why he uses so many different English translations of the Bible, citing no less than fifteen.

5. Osteen's *Your Best Life Now* was critiqued in some circles for its *lack* of biblical engagement. In point of fact, with only four exceptions, the endnotes refer to the Bible exclusively (again, mostly the New Testament) but the references are few in comparison with Warren's volume (see the previous note). Other books besides Warren's and Osteen's could be mentioned, but these two are the far-and-away blockbusters, with millions of copies in print, and come replete with extensive support apparatus: study guides, devotional journals, videos, curricula, and so on and so forth (see, e.g., Warren, *The Purpose Driven Life*, 323, and www.purposedrivenlife.com).

6. Here I invoke the work of Martin E. P. Seligman, the founder of the positive psychology movement (see further §3 below), especially his *Authentic Happiness: Using the New Positive Psychology to Realize Your Potential for Lasting Fulfillment* (New York: Free Press, 2002). See also his recent work *Flourish: A Visionary New Understanding of Happiness and Well-being* (New York: Free Press, 2011).

7. See, e.g., Eric G. Wilson, *Against Happiness: In Praise of Melancholy* (New York: Sarah Crichton Books/Farrar, Straus and Giroux, 2008); Ronald W. Dworkin, *Artificial Happiness: The Dark Side of the New Happy Class* (New York: Carrol and Graf, 2006); and Julie K. Norem, *The Positive Power of Negative Thinking: Using Defensive Pessimism to Harness Anxiety and Perform at Your Peak* (New York: Basic, 2001). Barbara S. Held, "The Negative Side of Positive Psychology," *J Humanist Psychol* 44 (2004): 9–46, takes up the critique from within psychology, appealing to the work of William James, who spoke of two religious temperaments, one being the "the sick soul," and who pointed out that unhappy or negative life experiences can often be very meaningful. This is not unrelated to the much earlier spiritual notion of "the dark night of the soul," familiar from the mystical writer St. John of the Cross (1542–1591). For an application of John's (and Teresa of Ávila's) work to contemporary psychology, see Gerald G. May, *The Dark Night of the Soul: A Psychiatrist Explores the Connection Between Darkness and Spiritual Growth* (San Francisco: HarperSanFrancisco, 2004). Note also the essay by Steven J. Sandage and the Epilogue in the present volume.

arguments would no doubt resonate deeply with Walker Percy's quotation on love used as the epigraph above: "Beware," they would say, "of people who go around talking about loving and caring"—or, in our case, "authentic happiness"—especially with Bibles in tow!

At issue, then, is a fundamental question: does the Bible really support the pursuit of happiness as that is popularly understood, whether culturally or religiously? Or, to put the matter somewhat differently, we might ask the following question: What, if anything, does the Bible contribute to the contemporary obsession, whether religious or not, with happiness?

2. The Pollution of "Happiness"

Before addressing these large questions, a logically prior one must be asked: What is happiness anyway? To begin answering that question, as well as its relationship to the question of the Bible's contribution to the study of happiness, a brief side-trip into the study of language is in order.

Consider again Percy's statement on love: "don't some people fall in love with their heart's desire, marry, and live reasonably happy lives?" Despite Percy's devolution toward ultimate uncertainty, he admits that at least "some" people really do "live reasonably happy lives"—"for a while" at any rate. At the very least, Percy has to allow for the *potential* for such happiness: "maybe"! Then he punts: "I can't say."

But then comes the most important part of Percy's remarks, when he answers his own question about believing in love: "Yes," he says, "but the word has been polluted." Maybe the problem with so many discussions about happiness, not to mention self-help literature more generally, especially according to the nay-sayers, is exactly this: perhaps "happiness," like "love," has become polluted. Part of the issue, that is, is that words like "love," "happiness," and the like are consistently and constantly *ill*-defined. In the face of no clear, agreed-upon definition, the words become super-injected with whatever personal content and meaning are at hand, regardless of context or situation—even suitability, for that matter. One "loves" a cereal just as (though presumably not as much as) one "loves" a spouse. One is "happy" because breakfast was yummy, and one is "happy" to be cancer free. Or then there is Tom Cruise, who on the Oprah show once said that he wanted his children to be happy, which he then immediately glossed with, "You know, enjoy their jobs." In each of these examples, the word in question ("love" or "happiness") hasn't changed but our understanding of the word's meaning and content *must* or else the word becomes flat, stale, ruined—in a word, "polluted."

"Happiness," Semantic Drift, and Word Pollution

Linguists, those scholars who devote their lives to studying languages, wouldn't want to call all such instances of ill-definition clear-cut cases of "word pollution." Words have histories, after all—etymologies—and it is a linguistic fact that words, especially important and popular words, tend to change meaning, even if only slightly, due to frequent and repeated use in numerous and diverse contexts, not to mention through the normal march of history. Linguists call this lexical development "semantic drift."[8] Information about semantic drift and word-histories (etymologies) can be found in any number of studies, but the most impressive and exhaustive repository for the English language is housed in the *Oxford English Dictionary (OED).*[9] There one learns, for instance, that the word "silly" once meant "helpless, defenseless"—as, for instance, in Shakespeare's *Two Gentlemen of Verona* (1623)[10]—or that "to make love" meant, until the twentieth century, and specifically in twentieth-century US usage, "to pay amorous attention; to court, woo."[11] In both cases, then, "silly" and "to make love" have drifted a good bit over the years.

The first definition of "happiness" in the *OED* is "good fortune or luck in life or in a particular affair; success, prosperity."[12] The earliest instance of such meaning is traced to 1530, in John Palsgrave's (d. 1554) explanation of the French language, where "Happynesse" is glossed with "*prosperité.*"[13] The *OED*'s second definition, which is first attested not too much later (1591), is: "The state of pleasurable content

---

8. For a nice overview, see John McWhorter, *The Power of Babel: A Natural History of Language* (New York: Perennial, 2001), 31–32. McWhorter points out that semantic drift (or "change," as it is often called) can result in either narrowing or broadening of the original meaning of a word, or even both.

9. *The Oxford English Dictionary* (2nd ed.; 20 vols.; Oxford: Clarendon, 1989; online version June 2011).

10. *OED* online (2nd ed., 1989; online version June 2011), s. v. "silly," accessed August 19, 2011. McWhorter, *The Power of Babel*, 32, points out that still earlier, in Old English, "silly" meant "blessed," but eventually came to mean "innocent" around 1400, then "deserving of compassion" a bit later (as in a 1470 writing), then later "weak" (in a text from 1633), and later still, "simple" or "ignorant," until it finally came to mean "foolish"—a far cry indeed from its initial meaning as "sanctified by God."

11. *OED* online (3rd ed., March 2008; online version June 2011), s. v. "love," accessed August 19, 2011.

12. *OED* online (2nd ed., 1989; online version June 2011), s. v. "happiness," accessed August 19, 2011.

13. John Palsgrave, *Lesclarcissement de la langue francoyse* (1st ed.; London: J. Haukyns, 1530), 229/1.

of mind, which results from success or the attainment of what is considered good."[14] The third definition, dating from 1600, is "[s]uccessful or felicitous aptitude, fitness, suitability, or appropriateness; felicity."[15]

These definitions, now nearly five hundred years old, are not much different from contemporary uses. Semantic drift in the case of "happiness," it seems, has been nearly as slow as the continental variety. Or, one might ask, is it the case that the pollution of happiness is as old as the sixteenth century?

As everyone knows (or should), the Bible wasn't originally composed in English, but in the ancient languages of Hebrew, Aramaic, and Greek. That's proof enough that the Bible stems from times and cultures far removed from our own. So, if the question at hand is what *the Bible* says about happiness, then, as important as the *OED* is, English simply won't do. The sixteenth century isn't going back nearly far enough. Instead, we must access the biblical texts in their original languages and their original contexts if we want to know what the Bible says about "the pursuit of happiness." "Happiness" in English—whether that is the English of the sixteenth or the twenty-first-centuries—may be too ill-defined, if not already too polluted, to afford insight on the meaning of happiness in the Bible.[16]

The essays in this volume are very much an attempt to set the record straight on happiness when it comes to the Bible. In many ways, this book is the first of its kind, not because it looks to the Bible with an eye toward happiness—many books have attempted to do that to some degree or the other, with greater or lesser success—but because it tries to define biblical happiness, first, emically or inductively, from the Bible itself, utilizing the best tools of critical biblical scholarship, rather than by means of an over-, under-, or predetermined definition of "happiness." This "Bible first" approach is crucial because, without careful investigation and definition, the "happiness" that one finds generally available (whether

---

14. *OED* online (2nd ed., 1989; online version June 2011), s. v. "happiness."

15. Ibid.

16. In her essay in this collection, Ellen T. Charry traces one unhelpful notion of happiness all the way back to Augustine, "who saw the contingencies of life as so prevalent that he concluded that happiness in this life was an unrealistic expectation," and whose writings set the course for what Charry calls the "eschatological view" of happiness ("The Necessity of Divine Happiness: A Response from Systematic Theology," 232). Charry notes that this "narrow and fragile vision of happiness"—one that is largely pathology-driven—seeped into later systematic theology and is "implied ... even when it is not explicitly discussed" (ibid., 234). It seems obvious in Aquinas's later work (see Stephen Wang, "Aquinas on Human Happiness and the Natural Desire for God," *New Blackfriars* 88 [2007]: 322–34). Whatever the case, the thicker meanings of happiness explicated in the present volume show the deficiencies of any and all "narrow and fragile" perspectives, and also demonstrate that the pollution of (at least) biblical happiness is as early as Augustine in the fourth century.

in bookstores or on television) is often the polluted, flat kind, which will only go so far and which will typically not go nearly far enough—especially when the going gets rough. More on all that in due course.

The present volume is also the first of its kind because it conducts this investigation of biblical happiness with an eye toward and with help from the positive psychology movement and the recent and significant scholarly attention to happiness that has emerged from it. I turn to that movement and scholarship below (§3), but want to underscore here that while the present book models a "Bible *first*" kind of approach, it definitely does not model a "Bible *only*" sort of approach. This is definitely a "Bible *and . . .*" kind of book; in this case, it is the Bible "*and* the Pursuit of Happiness." Both elements in the title are crucial, then, but so is their sequence.

The Pollution of the "Pursuit" of Happiness

Before discussing positive psychology, one final caveat is in order and concerns the specific phrase "the Pursuit of Happiness." This phrase is perhaps most familiar, in the United States at any rate, from its appearance in the Declaration of Independence of July 4, 1776. The second paragraph of the Declaration states

> We hold these truths to be self-evident, that all Men are created equal, that they are endowed by their Creator with certain unalienable Rights, that among these are Life, Liberty, and the Pursuit of Happiness—

While a famous and familiar clause, it is important to observe that "the Pursuit of Happiness" in the Declaration does not mean simply the "pursuing" or "seeking" of happiness. While that is a common assumption, Arthur M. Schlesinger has demonstrated that it is, in fact, quite wrong.[17] Instead, the Declaration proclaims "the *practicing* rather than the *quest* of happiness as a basic right equally with life and liberty."[18] Schlesinger proves his case by citing similar use of the word "pursuit" in then-contemporary documents, all of which show that "the pursuit of happiness" has the sense "of the actual practicing" of happiness and "no other."[19] In fact, the immediate continuation of the very same sentence in the Declaration,

---

17. Arthur M. Schlesinger, "The Lost Meaning of 'The Pursuit of Happiness,'" *The William and Mary Quarterly* 31 (1964): 325–27. Wilson's attempt to make "the pursuit of happiness" equivalent to the ownership of property and thus make of the Declaration of Independence an endorsement of happiness via acquisition is thus mistaken (*Against Happiness*, 13–14).

18. Schlesinger, "The Lost Meaning of 'The Pursuit of Happiness,'" 325.

19. Ibid., 326.

though not as well-known or oft-cited, makes the point clear and is entirely in line with the other documentation Schlesinger has collected (picking up at the dash at the end of the preceding citation):

> —That to secure these Rights, Governments are instituted among Men, deriving their just Powers from the Consent of the Governed, that whenever any Form of Government becomes destructive of these Ends, it is the Right of the People to alter or to abolish it, and to institute new Government, laying its Foundation on such Principles, and organizing its Powers in such Form, as to them shall seem most likely to effect their Safety and Happiness.[20]

So, contrary to common (mis)understandings, the point was never that happiness was "something a people were entitled simply to strive for but as something that was theirs by natural right."[21]

This brief digression on "the Pursuit of Happiness," which would be better glossed, with the Virginia Convention's Declaration of Rights of June 12, 1776, as the "pursuing and obtaining" of happiness, is instructive for several reasons. For one, it represents something analogous to the pollution of the word "happiness" described above, only that, in this case, the pollution is of the word "pursuit," or perhaps of the whole phrase "the Pursuit of Happiness." Either way, the pollution has taken place in a relatively brief period of time, within the same language, and in the same country. If that can happen, even with such a foundational document as the Declaration of Independence and within the same cultural and linguistic context, we should not be surprised to find similar problems besetting the over-, under-, or predetermined word, "happiness," especially when we investigate that concept in ancient texts that come from cultural and linguistic contexts far different than our own.

Schlesinger's work also showcases something of the method and import of such historical-linguistic "reclamation projects." Methodologically, Schlesinger goes back to the sources and to the historical contexts of those sources, to find out what "pursuit" meant there, as far as that is possible. He also pays close attention to the literary context of the Declaration of Independence, pointing out what should have been obvious from the start: that the two parts of the sentence must be read together. "Life," "Liberty," and "Safety," when considered as unalienable political rights, are not quests or pastimes. So, "the Pursuit of Happiness," in the first instance, or more simply just "Happiness," in the second, should be understood in the same way.

---

20. See ibid., 327.

21. Ibid., 326.

In terms of the importance of this kind of investigation, Schlesinger observes that, properly understood, the pursuit of happiness in the sense of the obtaining and practicing of happiness has a "more emphatic meaning" than simply the "quest" of happiness.[22] Even more importantly, the Declaration makes that obtaining and practicing of happiness a matter of government and public policy, not simply one of individual leisure or pleasure. That the idea of happiness is about more than personal satisfaction and that the pursuit of happiness has profound public policy ramifications, and thus real connections to social justice, are points that go back all the way to Aristotle's *Nicomachean Ethics*, which was a preface to his *Politics*—even earlier still, as the present collection of essays shows—and they are also points that have been echoed in more recent happiness literature, especially in work based on the insights of positive psychology.[23] Positive psychology is important at this point because in recent years it has been the primary arena in which the question "What is happiness anyway?" has been repeatedly asked and answered, even empirically. Before turning to positive psychology proper, a consideration of ancient studies of happiness that have both led up to positive psychology and have informed it is in order.

3. *"Pursuits" of Happiness: Ancient and Modern*

The question "What is happiness anyway?" is deceptively simple because, as we all know, happiness is often an all-too-elusive prey, which means, among other things, that it is hard to trap long enough to subject to it to the appropriate tests that would reveal where it lives, what it is made of, and how it procreates.

---

22. Ibid., 327.

23. See, e.g., Richard Layard, *Happiness: Lessons from a New Science* (New York: Penguin, 2005); and Peter H. Huang and Jeremy A. Blumenthal, "Positive Institutions, Law, and Policy," in *Oxford Handbook of Positive Psychology* (eds. C. R. Snyder and Shane J. Lopez; Oxford: Oxford University Press, 2009), 589–97; as well as the following essays, all of which appear in P. Alex Linley and Stephen Joseph, eds., *Positive Psychology in Practice* (Hoboken, NJ: Wiley, 2004): David G. Myers, "Human Connections and the Good Life: Balancing Individuality and Community in Public Policy," 641–57; Ruut Veenhoven, "Happiness as a Public Policy Aim: The Greatest Happiness Principle," 658–78; William Pavot and Ed Diener, "Findings on Subjective Well-Being: Applications to Public Policy, Clinical Interventions, and Education," 679–92; Felicia A. Huppert, "A Population Approach to Positive Psychology: The Potential for Population Interventions to Promote Well-Being and Prevent Disorder," 693–709. Note also Sandage's essay in the present volume and Patricia Walsh, "Well-being," in *The Oxford Companion to Philosophy* (2nd ed.; ed. Ted Honderich; Oxford: Oxford University Press, 2005), 955–56. The Himalayan kingdom of Bhutan actually measures the country's Gross National Happiness (GNH) and uses it as a basis for making policy decisions. See Black Dog Institute, "Fact Sheet: Happiness," 3, www.blackdoginstitute.org.au/docs/Happiness.pdf, accessed September 23, 2011.

That has not stopped many people from pursuing the game, however. And, in the case of happiness, the hunt has a long and venerable tradition running back, famously, to Aristotle (384–322 BCE). But, as Aristotle himself notes, the search preceded his own work. Among the predecessors he mentions is Solon.

Solon vs. Croesus

According to Herodotus's (ca. 484–ca. 425 BCE) *Histories*, King Croesus of Sardis, after learning that the sagely Solon had traveled "much of the world in the search for knowledge," says: "I really can't resist asking you now whether you have seen anyone who surpasses all others in happiness and prosperity?"[24] Croesus assumes that he himself is this "happiest man in the world," but Solon sets him straight with a lesson from the life of the Athenian Tellus who was most blessed because

> [f]or one thing, he lived in a famous city, and had good and noble children, and he saw all his children and grandchildren surviving him. Besides, he was well off, at least by our standards of living, and he ended his life in the greatest glory, for he came to the aid of the Athenians in a battle against their neighbors in Eleusis and forced them to flee before he died most nobly on the battlefield. The Athenians buried him at public expense in the very place he fell and gave him great honors.[25]

Solon's remarks begin to line out a profile of happiness—at least according to Greek thought at that time. It includes matters of *place* (city), *descendants* and *health* (seeing children and grandchildren), *resources* (being "well off, at least by our standards of living"), and *ending life well* in terms of sacrificial service on behalf of others and an honorable death and burial. Solon underscores these points by describing Cleobis and Biton as the next "most happy" (*eudaimonia*) men. These brothers "had enough resources to live on and in addition were physically fit, as is shown by the fact that they both won prizes at athletic contests."[26] They also performed a heroic and sacrificial feat on behalf of their mother, and died peacefully in a sanctuary almost immediately thereafter.

---

24. Herodotus, *Histories*, 1.30; the translation is from Robert B. Strassler, ed., *The Landmark Herodotus: The Histories* (New York: Pantheon Books, 2007), 19. I thank Michael J. Chan for first drawing my attention to this passage.

25. Herodotus, *Histories*, 1.30; Strassler, *The Landmark Herodotus*, 19.

26. *Histories*, 1.31; Strassler, *The Landmark Herodotus*, 19.

What is not to be missed in this exchange is that Croesus expects Solon to identify him as the happiest person, or at least as runner-up in case the happiest person can't fulfill his or her duties, *only after* escorting Solon on a tour of his treasuries and all his riches. In the Croesus-Solon exchange, then, one sees the clash of two different views of the happy or blessed life—the hedonic and eudaimonic—and begins to learn how these are not quite the same. The former view can be defined as a transitory state of pleasure (Greek *hēdonē*), which is dependent on external accoutrements of various sorts, especially wealth;[27] the latter is an enduring state of well-being (*eudaimonia*).[28] But in ancient Sardis, no less than nowadays Vegas, money can't buy happiness.[29] Solon explains:

> You see, the man who is very wealthy is no more happy and prosperous than the man who has only enough to live from day to day, unless good fortune stays with him and he retains his fair and noble possession right up until he departs this life happily. For many wealthy people are unhappy [ἀνόλβιοι], while many others who have more modest resources are fortunate [εὐτυχέες]. The man who has great wealth but is unhappy outdoes the fortunate man in only two ways, while the fortunate man outdoes him in many ways. . . . [T]he fortunate man, although he does not have the same ability to sustain himself in adversity or passion, avoids these anyway by virtue of his good fortune. Moreover, he has no injury, no sickness, no painful experiences; what he does have is good children and good looks. Now if, in addition to all these things, he ends his life well, too, then this is the man you are looking for; he alone deserves to be called happy and

27. See, e.g., James A. Montmarquet, "Hedonism," in *The Cambridge Dictionary of Philosophy* (2nd ed.; ed. Robert Audi; Cambridge: Cambridge University Press, 1999), 364–65; and J. C. B. Gosling, "Hedonism," in *The Oxford Companion to Philosophy* (2nd ed.; ed. Ted Honderich; Oxford: Oxford University Press, 2005), 363–64.

28. Note, however, that Epicureanism also identified *eudaimonia* with pleasure. See Richard J. Norman, "Happiness," in *The Oxford Companion to Philosophy* (2nd ed.; ed. Ted Honderich; Oxford: Oxford University Press, 2005), 358–59.

29. The happiness literature is remarkably consistent on this point in part due to the notions of adaptation and what is often called "the hedonic treadmill" (namely, that people get used to what they have so it no longer satisfies as it once did; they want more). See, e.g., Mihaly Csikszentmihalyi, "If we are so rich, why aren't we happy?" *American Psychologist* 54 (1999): 821–27; Seligman, *Authentic Happiness*, 49–55, 60–61; Christopher Peterson, *A Primer in Positive Psychology* (Oxford: Oxford University Press, 2006), 94; Layard, *Happiness: Lessons from a New Science*, 3, 7, 35–44, 229. At the most, more money and material prosperity provides a slight bump in happiness, but the effect is not long term and the very rich are only slightly happier (if at all) than the nonrich. In fact, the richer people become, the less extra income increases their happiness (ibid., 230).

prosperous [ὁ ὄλβιος]. But before he dies, refrain from calling him this—
one should rather call him lucky [εὐτυχέα].[30]

Solon didn't convince Croesus, who is said to have "dismissed him, thinking
him worthless and extremely ignorant for overlooking the good things right
before his eyes and telling him [i.e., Croesus] instead to look to the end [τελευτὴν]
of every matter."[31] The vignette is instructive nevertheless as it shows that the
meaning, let alone pursuit and practice, of happiness was vexed and debated even
in ancient times. Croesus's hedonic view operates with a definition of happiness
not unlike John Palsgrave's "*prosperité*" two thousand years later, but Solon's
eudaimonic perspective begins to redefine for him what, precisely, constitutes
said "prosperity." Who is right?

Aristotle on Happiness

Aristotle's work is critical at this point, not only given his importance in the history of philosophy, but also because his thoughts on happiness have become the
touchstone for much subsequent reflection on the topic—with the present collection of essays no exception.[32] We might begin with Aristotle's *Rhetoric*, where
he states that there is one goal (*skopos*) for both individuals and people more generally that motivates what they do and what they do not do: "Summarily stated,
this is happiness [*eudaimonia*] and its parts."[33] He continues:

> Let happiness be [defined as] success [*eupraxia*] combined with virtue, or
> as self-sufficiency [*autarkeia*] in life, or as the pleasantest life accompanied
> with security, or as abundance of possessions and bodies, with the ability
> to defend and use these things; for all people agree that happiness is pretty
> much one or more of these.[34]

Aristotle then defines the "parts" of happiness as follows:

---

30. *Histories*, 1.32; Strassler, *The Landmark Herodotus*, 20–21.

31. *Histories*, 1.33; Strassler, *The Landmark Herodotus*, 22.

32. See, for instance, the essays by Nathan MacDonald, Jacqueline Lapsley, Carol A. Newsom, and Carl R. Holladay in the present volume.

33. Aristotle, *Rhetoric*, 1.5 (1360b); the translation is from George A. Kennedy, *Aristotle: On Rhetoric: A Theory of Civic Discourse* (2nd ed.; New York: Oxford University Press, 2007), 56.

34. Aristotle, *Rhetoric*, 1.5 (1360b); Kennedy, *Aristotle: On Rhetoric*, 57.

good birth, numerous friendships, worthy friendships, wealth, good children, numerous children, a good old age, as well as the virtues of the body (such as health, beauty, strength, physical stature, athletic prowess), reputation, honor, good luck, virtue.[35]

In this account, there are both "internal" and "external" goods that relate to happiness: "Internal goods are those relating to the mind and the body, while good birth and friends and wealth and honor are external."[36] Also, Aristotle adds, one shouldn't forget "the power to take actions and good luck."[37] Happiness itself, regardless, is the greatest good, and necessarily so, because "it is both desirable in itself and self-sufficient, and we choose other things to obtain it."[38]

Aristotle's remarks in the *Rhetoric* appear to be a "more popular, and probably earlier, version" of his thoughts on happiness which receive fuller form in his *Nicomachean Ethics*.[39] Aristotle famously begins that work by stating that everything has some *telos*, some intended purpose: "Every art and every inquiry, and similarly every action as well as choice, is held to aim at some good."[40] Since everything has its purpose, Aristotle inquires after the highest good for human beings. Everyone would agree, he states, that "happiness" (*eudaimonia*) and "living well" (*eu zēn*) are precisely that (*Nicomachean Ethics*, 1.4 [1095a]). But given his teleological starting point, Aristotle believes that this highest human good of happiness must be intrinsically related to what it means to be human. For Aristotle, what separates human beings from other species and thus constitutes the human *telos* of happiness is the capacity to reason (*Nicomachean Ethics*, 1.7

---

35. Ibid. Kennedy thinks this listing of happy parts "reflect[s] varying popular understanding[s] of happiness" (*Aristotle: On Rhetoric*, 57 n. 99).

36. Aristotle, *Rhetoric*, 1.5 (1360b); Kennedy, *Aristotle: On Rhetoric*, 57.

37. Ibid. Note Aristotle's definition of "good luck" a bit later: "*Good luck* [*eutykhia*] means to get and keep those good things of which chance [*tykhē*] is the cause, either all or most or the most important" (*Rhetoric*, 1.5 [1361b–1362a]; Kennedy, *Aristotle: On Rhetoric*, 60). For more on Aristotle's views on good luck, see his *Eudemian Ethics*, 8.2. Note also the extensive study by Martha C. Nussbaum, *The Fragility of Goodness: Luck and Ethics in Greek Tragedy and Philosophy* (rev. ed.; Cambridge: Cambridge University Press, 2001 [orig.: 1987]).

38. Aristotle, *Rhetoric*, 1.6 (1362b); Kennedy, *Aristotle: On Rhetoric*, 62.

39. So Kennedy, *Aristotle: On Rhetoric*, 56. Following the lead of most scholars of Aristotle's ethics, I leave aside the *Eudemian Ethics* as well as the *Magna Moralia*. See, among others, Richard Kraut, "Aristotle's Ethics," in *Stanford Encyclopedia of Philosophy*, last modified March 29, 2010, http://plato.stanford.edu/entries/aristotle-ethics/, accessed September 2, 2011.

40. Aristotle, *Nicomachean Ethics*, 1.1 (1094a); translation from Robert C. Bartlett and Susan D. Collins, *Aristotle's Nicomachean Ethics* (Chicago: University of Chicago, 2011), 1. Subsequent citations will be parenthetical and are from Bartlett's and Collins's translation.

[1098a]; 10.7 [1178a]). So, in the end, Aristotle defines the goal of human life, which is happiness, as "a certain activity of soul in accord with complete virtue" (*Nicomachean Ethics*, 1.13 [1102a]). This "activity of the soul" involves both *living* well and *doing* well, which, for Aristotle, means living and doing *virtuously* (see *Nicomachean Ethics*, 1.8 [1098b]; 10.9 [1179a–b]).

As Richard Kraut has observed, Aristotle's conclusions about the nature of happiness are "uniquely his own"[41]—especially given his emphasis on philosophical contemplation (*theoria*) as the highest form of human happiness (*Nicomachean Ethics*, 10.8 [1178b]), a point that "seems much too narrow" and "too rigid,"[42] not to mention self-serving for a philosopher. Aristotle's perspective is also one that conflicts a good bit with contemporary understandings of happiness since his is a highly objective view and we tend to think of happiness in terms of subjective personal experience (including someone's current goals), not objective criteria (such as someone's ideal life, however defined).[43] Even when we do think of objective criteria—money, for instance—we tend to be wrong. Recall Croesus and Solon![44]

While we may emphasize the subjective side of happiness more than Aristotle did, his emphasis on the eudaimonic life, which can be defined as the good, flourishing, and virtuous life as opposed to simply the pleasurable life filled with enjoyable sensations, has been seminal ever since he wrote. So, while the concept of "happiness"—whether in English or Greek—may lean in two directions "sometimes referring to the *feeling* of happiness, sometimes to the kind of *life* that is happy,"[45] Aristotle's work, while not completely neglecting the former, resolutely

---

41. Kraut, "Aristotle's Ethics." Among other critiques (see further below), one might note that, in the Bible, the book of Ecclesiastes would challenge Aristotle's notion that the life of wisdom is the happiest and can be practiced free of fatigue. See, e.g., Eccl 1:18; 12:12; and Newsom's essay in the present volume.

42. Richard Kraut, "Two Conceptions of Happiness," *The Philosophical Review* 88 (1979): 191–92.

43. See Kraut, "Two Conceptions of Happiness," 167–97. Objective criteria are not, of course, completely to be ruled out, esp. in the study of ancient peoples and their literature where access to *feelings* proper may prove impossible to obtain. See Gary A. Anderson, *A Time to Mourn, A Time to Dance: The Expression of Grief and Joy in Israelite Religion* (Pennsylvania: Pennsylvania State University Press, 1991). Ellen T. Charry argues that the term "happy/blessed" in the Psalms (אשרי) is in fact an objective criteria (*God and the Art of Happiness* [Grand Rapids: Eerdmans, 2010], 198–99). See also the essay by William P. Brown in the present volume.

44. Consider further the hedonistic paradox, which observes that "[m]any of the deepest and best pleasures of life (of love, of child rearing, of work) seem to come most often to those who are engaging in an activity for reasons other than pleasure seeking. Hence, not only is it dubious that we always in fact seek (or value only) pleasure, but also dubious that the best way to achieve pleasure is to seek it" (Montmarquet, "Hedonism," 364).

45. Kraut, "Two Conceptions," 179.

focuses our attention on the latter, all the while emphasizing that the happiest life is marked by virtuous action.

Laudable though this vision of happiness may be (and is), not everyone would agree. As already indicated, most popular conceptions of happiness nowadays include both subjective well-being and personal pleasure—and both to a far greater degree—than Aristotle's view would allow. But who is to say that our modern definitions of "happiness" aren't already infected or polluted somehow? So, we must ask once more: who is right about happiness? And, further, how would we know?

Positive Psychology

Enter positive psychology and the new "science of happiness."[46] Positive psychology came on the scene around 1998, the year Martin E. P. Seligman was elected president of the American Psychological Association and began meeting with like-minded scholars to form the Positive Psychology Network.[47] Since then, the movement has exploded and can now boast of centers for research,[48] scholarly monographs and reference works,[49] histories,[50] undergraduate- and

---

46. Note esp. Stefan Klein, *The Science of Happiness: How Our Brains Make Us Happy—and What We Can Do to Get Happier* (trans. Stephen Lehmann; Philadelphia: Da Capo, 2006 [German orig: 2002]); Layard, *Happiness: Lessons from a New Science*; and Sonja Lyubomirsky, *The How of Happiness: A Scientific Approach to Getting the Life You Want* (New York: Penguin, 2008). Also Claudia Wallis, "The New Science of Happiness" in *Time* (Sunday, January 9, 2005), online at www.time.com/time/magazine/article/0,9171,1015902,00.html, accessed September 20, 2011.

47. See Ed Diener, "Positive Psychology: Past, Present, and Future," in *Oxford Handbook of Positive Psychology* (2nd ed.; eds. Shane J. Lopez and C. R. Snyder; New York: Oxford University Press, 2011), 7–11. Diener points out that certain aspects of positive psychology are thousands of years old (witness Solon, Aristotle, the Bible, etc.) and that in the last hundred years, behavioral scientists often studied positive topics like altruism, personality strengths, and happiness. What was needed, however, was "an integrated network to bring . . . scholars together in a common mission" (7) and that is precisely what Seligman provided. Cf. further Peterson, *A Primer in Positive Psychology*, 4–6.

48. Particularly the Positive Psychology Center, located at the University of Pennsylvania. See further below.

49. E.g., Corey L. M. Keyes and Jonathan Haidt, *Flourishing: Positive Psychology and the Life Well-Lived* (Washington, DC: American Psychological Association, 2003); Shane J. Lopez, ed., *The Encyclopedia of Positive Psychology* (2 vols.; Malden, MA: Wiley-Blackwell, 2009); Shane J. Lopez and C. R. Snyder, eds., *Oxford Handbook of Positive Psychology* (2nd ed.; New York: Oxford University Press, 2011).

50. See, e.g., the following items, though these are focused not on positive psychology so much as happiness more generally: Darrin M. McMahon, *Happiness: A History* (New York: Grove, 2006); and Nicholas White, *A Brief History of Happiness* (Malden, MA: Blackwell, 2006). For the ancient philosophical material see also Julia Annas, *The Morality of Happiness* (New York: Oxford University Press, 1993).

graduate-level textbooks,[51] even journals devoted to the topic.[52] Positive psychology has birthed several bestselling popular books written from various angles by psychologists,[53] economists,[54] and business leaders,[55] among others. Yes, there's even a reference "for the rest of us": *Positive Psychology for Dummies*.[56] There are books on positive psychology in practice,[57] teaching positive psychology,[58] positive psychology at work,[59] positive psychology and religion,[60] "applied" positive

---

51. In my judgment, the two best are Peterson, *A Primer in Positive Psychology*; and C. R. Snyder, Shane J. Lopez, and Jennifer Teramoto Pedrotti, *Positive Psychology: The Scientific and Practical Explorations of Human Strengths* (2d ed.; Los Angeles: Sage, 2011).

52. E.g., *The Journal of Positive Psychology* (2006–) and *Journal of Happiness Studies* (2000–).

53. E.g. (by date of publication): Daniel Gilbert, *Stumbling on Happiness* (New York: Vintage, 2006); Jonathan Haidt, *The Happiness Hypothesis: Finding Modern Truth in Ancient Wisdom* (New York: Basic, 2006); Tal Ben-Shahar, *Happier: Learn the Secrets to Daily Joy and Lasting Fulfillment* (New York: McGraw-Hill, 2007); Ed Diener and Robert Biswas-Diener, *Happiness: Unlocking the Mysteries of Psychological Wealth* (Malden, MA: Blackwell, 2008); Lyubomirsky, *The How of Happiness* (2008); and Samuel S. Franklin, *The Psychology of Happiness: A Good Human Life* (Cambridge: Cambridge University Press, 2010). Note also the earlier work by David G. Myers, *The Pursuit of Happiness: Discovering the Pathway to Fulfillment, Well-Being, and Enduring Personal Joy* (New York: Avon, 1992).

54. E.g., Layard, *Happiness: Lessons from a New Science*.

55. E.g., Shawn Achor, *The Happiness Advantage: The Seven Principles of Positive Psychology that Fuel Success and Performance at Work* (New York: Crown, 2010).

56. Averil Leimon and Gladeana McMahon, *Positive Psychology for Dummies* (Chichester: John Wiley and Sons, 2009). Note also W. Doyle Gentry, *Happiness for Dummies* (Hoboken, NJ: Wiley, 2008), which was evidently not yet simple enough—the audio version released later the same year was abridged!

57. P. Alex Linley and Stephen Joseph, eds., *Positive Psychology in Practice* (Hoboken, NJ: John Wiley and Sons, 2004).

58. See, e.g., Ryan M. Niemiec and Danny Wedding, *Positive Psychology at the Movies: Using Films to Build Virtues and Character Strengths* (Cambridge, MA: Hogrefe and Huber, 2008); and the essays in Linley and Joseph, eds., *Positive Psychology in Practice*, 181–237.

59. E.g., Sarah Lewis, *Positive Psychology at Work: How Positive Leadership and Appreciative Inquiry Create Inspiring Organizations* (Oxford and Malden, MA: Wiley-Blackwell, 2011); P. Alex Linley, Susan Harrington, and Nicola Garcea, eds., *Oxford Handbook of Positive Psychology and Work* (Oxford: Oxford University Press, 2010); also the essays in Linley and Joseph, eds., *Positive Psychology in Practice*, 241–302.

60. E.g., Sidney Callahan, *Called to Happiness: Where Faith and Psychology Meet* (Maryknoll: Orbis, 2011); and Robert Rocco Cottone, *Toward a Positive Psychology of Religion: Belief Science in the Postmodern Era* (Winchester, UK: O-Books, 2011), though the "religion" in the latter case is something of a conglomeration of Cottone's own making. The role of happiness in Buddhism is well known. See His Holiness the Dalai Lama and Howard C. Cutler, *The Art of Happiness: A Handbook of Living* (New York: Riverhead Books, 2009 [orig: 1998]). The role of meditation and mindfulness in Buddhism (especially), has made a large impact on positive psychology. See, e.g., Haidt, *The Happiness Hypothesis*, 35–37.

psychology,[61] positive psychology and counseling[62]—even positive psychology and coaching.[63] No less than two of the bestsellers boast connections to Harvard University's popular undergraduate course on Happiness (which enrolls over a thousand students),[64] and some of the books are accessorized with associated paraphernalia—workbooks, journals, and the like[65]—which constitutes still more proof that positive psychology is no small industry. Quite to the contrary, happiness is big business these days.

This is precisely the sort of thing that gets the ire of the more melancholy among us—"the only thing worse," they mutter, "than one dopily happy person is a whole slew of them"—and so before immersing ourselves in the happy flood of work that has emerged out of positive psychology, we need to delve further into what it is, especially given the backlash to happiness that has emerged in recent years.

The first thing to say is that positive psychology isn't solely about "happiness," not, at least, as that term is thinly used or understood.[66] Instead, positive psychology is helpful precisely in the way it has helped (re)define happiness in a thick, robust way. A convenient articulation is found on the website of the Positive Psychology Center, housed at the University of Pennsylvania—the home institution of the field's founding father, Martin Seligman:

> Positive Psychology is the scientific study of the strengths and virtues that enable individuals and communities to thrive. . . . This field is founded on the belief that people want to lead meaningful and fulfilling lives, to cultivate

---

61. See Stewart I. Donaldson, Mihaly Csikszentmihalyi, and Jeanne Nakamura, eds., *Applied Positive Psychology: Improving Everyday Life, Health, Schools, Work, and Society* (New York: Routledge, 2011).

62. E.g., Collie Wyatt Conoley and Jane Close Conoley, *Positive Psychology and Family Therapy: Creative Techniques and Practical Tools for Guiding Change and Enhancing Growth* (Hoboken, NJ: John Wiley and Sons, 2009). Note also the essay by Sandage in the present volume.

63. E.g., Robert Biswas-Diener and Ben Dean, *Positive Psychology Coaching: Putting the Science of Happiness to Work for Your Clients* (Hoboken, NJ: John Wiley and Sons, 2007); Robert Biswas-Diener, *Practicing Positive Psychology Coaching: Assessment, Activities, and Strategies for Success* (Hoboken, NJ: John Wiley and Sons, 2010).

64. Ben-Shahar, *Happier*; and Achor, *The Happiness Advantage*.

65. See, e.g., Tal Ben-Shahar, *Even Happier: A Gratitude Journal for Daily Joy and Lasting Fulfillment* (New York: McGraw Hill, 2010); and Martin Seligman's website "Authentic Happiness" (www.authentichappiness.org).

66. See, e.g., Peterson, *A Primer in Positive Psychology*, 7–8, on how positive psychology is not "Happiology"; and Lewis, *Positive Psychology at Work*, 2–6, on how positive psychology is not positive thinking.

what is best within themselves, and to enhance their experiences of love, work, and play.

Positive Psychology has three central concerns: positive emotions, positive individual traits, and positive institutions. Understanding positive emotions entails the study of contentment with the past, happiness in the present, and hope for the future. Understanding positive individual traits consists of the study of the strengths and virtues, such as the capacity for love and work, courage, compassion, resilience, creativity, curiosity, integrity, self-knowledge, moderation, self-control, and wisdom. Understanding positive institutions entails the study of the strengths that foster better communities, such as justice, responsibility, civility, parenting, nurturance, work ethic, leadership, teamwork, purpose, and tolerance.

Some of the goals of Positive Psychology are to build a science that supports:

- Families and schools that allow children to flourish
- Workplaces that foster satisfaction and high productivity
- Communities that encourage civic engagement
- Therapists who identify and nurture their patients' strengths
- The teaching of Positive Psychology
- Dissemination of Positive Psychology interventions in organizations & communities.[67]

At least four important aspects of positive psychology are obvious here. (1) First and foremost, given its prominent placement at the very start of the description, is that positive psychology is understood as "scientific study." From the beginning of the movement Seligman placed major emphasis on a scientific approach to the flourishing life.[68] Among other things, that means that the experiments and interventions are all measurable, even if, as we would expect, debate continues over which are the best instruments for data-gathering and so on and so forth.[69] (2) Second, positive psychology emphasizes human goodness (strengths, virtues) as opposed to the "old" psychology's focus on human

---

67. Positive Psychology Center homepage, accessed August 10, 2011, http: www.positivepsychology. org.

68. See Diener, "Positive Psychology: Past, Present, and Future," 8.

69. See Peterson, *A Primer in Positive Psychology*, 80, 86–91.

pathologies.[70] Positive psychology is thus not a disease-based or pathology-driven model but rather one based on what is good about life. As Seligman has put it elsewhere, whereas the "old" psychology focused on relieving misery so as to get miserable people from minus five to zero, positive psychology is about getting people from zero to plus five.[71] (3) So, third, one finds in the preceding definition of positive psychology a marked emphasis on people living thriving, meaningful, and fulfilling lives. Aristotle's influence on positive psychology is especially evident here (though it is also evident in the second point with its accent on virtue), since the movement's more robust understanding of "happiness" or "flourishing" is largely appropriated from Aristotle's notion of *eudaimonia*.[72] That said, there remain important differences between positive psychology and Aristotle's view of the happy life. Two of the most important of these are that positive psychology pays significant attention to subjective (as opposed to Aristotle's objective) well-being and to experiences of pleasure.[73] (4) Finally, the above definition indicates the importance positive psychology places on the context(s) of and for happiness—namely, the "positive institutions" (families, organizations, communities, etc.) that permit and facilitate happiness as that is robustly understood. To be sure, Aristotle, too, thought about the good life in terms of the good society (recall that the *Ethics* were prefatory to the *Politics*), but not as directly or as extensively as positive psychology given Aristotle's ultimate valuation of contemplation. By realizing

---

70. Peterson prefers to call the "old" psychology "business-as-usual psychology" (*A Primer in Positive Psychology*, 16). Note that Peterson and Seligman coauthored a book that is the positive psychology alternative to the standard diagnostic manual, *Diagnostic and Statistical Manual of Mental Disorders* (4th ed., text revision; Arlington, VA: American Psychiatric Association, 2000). See Christopher Peterson and Martin E. P. Seligman, *Character Strengths and Virtues: A Handbook and Classification* (New York: Oxford University Press, 2004). Note also Nansook Park, Christopher Peterson, and Martin E. P. Seligman, "Strengths of Character and Well-Being," *J Soc Clin Psychol* 23 (2004): 603–19.

71. See Wallis, "The New Science of Happiness."

72. See, e.g., Peterson, *A Primer in Positive Psychology*, 78–80; Seligman, *Authentic Happiness*, ix, 112, 289–90; Franklin, *The Psychology of Happiness*; and note the entries on "Aristotle" by Michelle Mason and Valerie Tiberius, and on "Eudaimonia" by Tiberius and Mason in Lopez, ed., *The Encyclopedia of Positive Psychology*, 1:63–64 and 1:351–55, respectively.

73. See Tiberius and Mason, "Eudaimonia," 352, who emphasize the componential (as opposed to all-encompassing), subjective (as opposed to objective), and fluctuating (as opposed to a whole life perspective) understandings of happiness in positive psychology vs. classical *eudaimonia*. Seligman, *Authentic Happiness*, discusses three types of happy life: the pleasurable life, the engaged life, and the meaningful life. Pleasure has the lowest positive correlation with overall life satisfaction. Recently, Peterson has added a fourth kind of happy life: the victorious life (*A Primer in Positive Psychology*, 78–80).

(and studying) the significance of "the facilitating environment" (to borrow a term from D. W. Winnicott),[74] positive psychology is thus a significant advance over most previous theories of happiness, especially hedonic ones, which have tended to be highly and overly egoistic.[75]

4. Overview of the Volume

If positive psychology has made of happiness a science, then, like any science, "the happiness hypothesis"[76] must be tested to see if it is accurate. The (re)testing should take into account what Aristotle called "the facts of life" (*Nicomachean Ethics*, 10.8 [1179a]), which include, for present purposes, "the *religious* facts of life" or "the facts of the *religious* life." In the pages that follow happiness is also examined by means of the ancient and sacred texts of the Bible—a book that has contributed profoundly not only to Western civilization, religion, philosophy, and so on, but also, and because of all that, to notions of happiness and the good life.

While positive psychology abounds in empirical studies, the academic study of the Bible is of a different sort. It is obviously not the work of this volume, then, to engage in any kind of measurable "experimentation." Even so, the authors of the essays collected here kept two major points in mind as they worked—namely, (1) the pollution of "happiness," on the one hand, and (2) developments in positive psychology and the study of happiness, on the other.[77] Moreover, not unlike Schlesinger's work on the meaning of "the Pursuit of Happiness" in the Declaration of Independence, the authors went back to the sources and to the historical contexts of those sources, to find out what the Bible meant by happiness, as far as

---

74. D. W. Winnicott, *The Maturational Processes and the Facilitating Environment: Studies in the Theory of Emotional Development* (London: Karnac and the Institute of Psycho-Analysis, 2004 [orig: 1965]).

75. See, e.g., Diener, "Positive Psychology: Past, Present, and Future," 9, who points out that positive psychology, too, has suffered the same critique. Gosling believes the connection between hedonism and egoism is not a necessary one: there is no inherent reason why the pleasure sought shouldn't be of humans or sentiment beings more broadly ("Hedonism," 363). David Trent Devereux notes that egoism also marks ancient theories of eudaimonism, but states that ancient egoism isn't the same as the modern variety because "according to the ancients, at least some of the virtues are dispositions to act from primarily other-regarding motives" ("Eudaimonism," in *The Cambridge Dictionary of Philosophy* [2nd ed.; ed. Robert Audi; Cambridge: Cambridge University Press, 1999], 291).

76. The language is borrowed from Haidt, *The Happiness Hypothesis*, of course. Haidt means by the term his own synthesis of happiness hypotheses—namely that happiness comes from both within and without (xii and *passim*). See similarly Layard, *Happiness: Lessons from a New Science*, 230, 235.

77. See above, §§2–3, respectively.

that is possible. Remember, this is a "*Bible* (first) and . . ." kind of book. The studies offered here also pay close attention to the literary contexts wherein biblical notions of happiness are found. Like Schlesinger's work on the Declaration, the results of the present essays are instructive about the nature of biblical happiness, specifically, but also about the nature of happiness more generally given the Bible's contribution to so many varieties of (at least religious) happiness. Thus, even though they are not empirical in nature, these studies nevertheless contribute valuable "data" on happiness, especially since positive psychology has been keen to draw on insights from both ancient texts and religious traditions in understanding human flourishing.[78]

As noted in the Preface, the essays in this volume were first presented at a conference entitled "The Bible and the Pursuit of Happiness" held in Atlanta in December 2009. That conference, in turn, emerged out of a larger, five-year consultation devoted to the Pursuit of Happiness housed in the Center for the Study of Law and Religion at Emory University and funded by the John Templeton Foundation. Nine biblical scholars were invited to the Atlanta conference—five specializing in the Old Testament/Hebrew Bible, four specializing in the New Testament—along with three scholars from the fields of systematic theology, practical theology, and counseling psychology. Over the course of three days, each scholar presented on happiness from their respective areas of expertise, with a formal response offered by another participant, which was then followed by general group discussion. After the conference, the participants had time to revise their papers in light of the common work that was done at the Atlanta meeting.

Part I collects the five papers devoted to the Hebrew Bible/Old Testament. It begins with Terence E. Fretheim's wide-ranging paper on God, creation, and happiness in which he argues not only that God is happy—a severely underappreciated point in theological circles (see also Ellen T. Charry's essay in Part III)—but also that divine happiness affects the created world and is in turn affected by the created world. Next, Nathan MacDonald considers happiness in the Torah, where, admittedly, much *un*happiness is found. Employing happiness as a hermeneutical lens, MacDonald finds points of similarity and difference between the Torah, on the one hand, and Aristotle, on the other. Perhaps the most interesting point of connection is that the Torah, too, in its current canonical shape, is teleological in terms of happiness. In the next essay, Jacqueline Lapsley looks at happiness in the Prophets, focusing on the book of Isaiah. Despite the many judgment oracles that appear throughout the prophets, Lapsley finds a "happy blend" of happiness in

---

78. See esp. Haidt, *The Happiness Hypothesis, passim*; Peterson, *A Primer in Positive Psychology*, 80–88, 310 n. 3; Snyder, Lopez, and Teramoto Pedrotti, *Positive Psychology*, 19–35.

Isaiah—a blend made up of both hedonic and eudaimonic elements. William P. Brown turns his attention to happiness in the Psalms, where a host of "happy" notes are sounded, though not to the neglect of the more somber and sorrowful tones that are also heard there. Despite those famous sad notes, the psalmists somehow chart a happy life *through* misery, not around it (see also the Epilogue). Finally, Carol A. Newsom considers the eudaimonic and hedonic versions of happiness that are located in the Wisdom books of Proverbs and Ecclesiastes, respectively. While both types of happiness are clearly attested in these books, Newsom argues cogently that the hedonic version can only work—or, at least, it can only work best—when it is encompassed within a eudaimonic framework. More information on each of these essays is found in the Introduction to Part I.

Part II contains four papers focusing on the New Testament. Carl R. Holladay studies what is probably the most famous biblical text on happiness, Jesus's beatitudes. Holladay treats the several interpretive problems that beset the beatitudes, and also offers a fascinating look into how these makarisms were received by later interpreters. What the beatitudes *originally* meant, Holladay argues, is inextricably connected to what they have meant *ever since*. In the next essay, Joel B. Green considers the "topsy-turvy" nature of happiness in Luke-Acts, which enabled the apostles to rejoice when they suffered persecution (Acts 5:41). Their joyful response is only understandable and facilitated, Green argues, by the world- and worldview-changing event that is Jesus's birth, life, ministry, and death. Colleen Shantz shows how Jesus's death is equally paradigmatic for Paul's life and teaching, as those are known from the apostle's letters. Without the transformation of Paul's prior "honor script"—a transformation that is directly related to Jesus's death and resurrection—Paul would not have been able to experience his trouble-filled life as "happy," nor would he have been able to provide a compelling vision for the early Christian communities he founded. The fact that he is able to do both of these things shows that Paul found in his experience of Jesus a meaningful way to live, and so could face his own death "not only resolutely, but, extraordinarily, with what might properly be called happiness."[79] Finally, Greg Carey considers happiness in apocalyptic literature. Although one might be tempted to see apocalyptic happiness as so much "pie-in-the-sky" futurism, Carey points out that suffering and trauma mark the apocalypses literarily if not also in terms of their sociohistorical origins. Apocalyptic literature is able to help people survive such experiences and even thrive thereafter (see also William P. Brown's essay in Part I, as well as the Epilogue), in no small part because these texts provide people with

---

79. Colleen Shantz, "'I Have Learned to Be Content': Happiness According to St. Paul," 200.

a narrative identity and something to commit to—points that resonate with Shantz's work on Paul and Green's work on Luke-Acts. Further information on each of these essays can be found in the Introduction to Part II.

Part III has three contributions by experts in fields beyond biblical studies proper. Although they are framed as "responses," and each does respond to selected essays from Parts I and II, these three chapters are perhaps better termed "projections": they take up the textual insights offered by the biblical essays and extend them much further into other fields. Ellen T. Charry, writing from the perspective of doctrinal theology, offers a vigorous critique of prior theological treatments of happiness as solely an eschatological phenomenon. These previous treatments are deficient in no small way, she argues, because of their inattention to God's own happiness (see also Terence E. Fretheim's essay in Part I) and to the importance of pleasure (see also the essays by Jacqueline Lapsley and Carol A. Newsom in Part I). In his essay, Thomas G. Long, a practical theologian, takes up the distinct notions of happiness as a futuristic, eschatological ideal and as an everyday, mundane reality, arguing that *both* must proceed *together*. This is no easy task, but Long, himself a famous preacher, draws inspiration for such an approach from the ancient "Preacher" known as Qoheleth (see also Newsom's essay in Part I and the Epilogue). Last but not least, Steven J. Sandage, a positive psychologist with both an academic post and a private practice, takes up the themes of the volume with reference to counseling psychology. As one would expect, Sandage draws heavily from the happiness research of positive psychology, paying particular attention to the study of the virtues and to the idea of spiritual maturity. He argues that, taken as a whole, the biblical essays argue for a transformed or reoriented view of happiness (see also the Epilogue)—one that has significant contributions to make back to positive psychology in terms of the latter's research foci (especially the crucial importance of positive institutions) and its appreciation "for the spiritual dimensions of the definitions and theoretical understandings of happiness and virtue," which in turn might "lead to more robust measures for scientific research."[80] Sandage thus points out that the work done in this volume is an example of "the tremendous advantages of a constructive triangulation of disciplinary resources of interpretation in the hermeneutical study of happiness and well-being."[81] Such triangulation is never easy—methodologically or otherwise—but the results are well worth the risk. Once again, additional information about each of these essays is provided in the Introduction to Part III.

---

80. Steven J. Sandage, "The Transformation of Happiness: A Response from Counseling Psychology," 282.

81. Ibid.

After the essays of Parts I–III, I offer an epilogue entitled, "The Triumph of Life: Towards a Biblical Theology of Happiness." In this essay, I summarize and synthesize the findings of the other essays, supplementing them with further considerations, which in many ways come back to the central questions posed in this introduction—most especially, the meaning(s) of (biblical) happiness—all with an eye on the implications of this research for a larger, biblical theology of happiness.

Finally, the volume is rounded out by two items that will be useful for future research on the Bible and happiness. The first is an Appendix by Michael J. Chan, "A Biblical Lexicon of Happiness," which presents the fullest listing of biblical happiness terms ever amassed. This lexicon is broken down by specific term and language (Hebrew, Aramaic, Greek), and is presented in two different datasets. The first presents all the lexical data; the second (re)presents only those verses where a specific subject for the happiness in question can be identified. Readers who are primarily interested in *who* or *what* is happy in the Bible should thus start with Set 2, though Set 1 remains the invaluable comprehensive collection. The second item that will prove useful for future research is the cumulative bibliography.

5. Once Again, the Bible and Happiness

A careful perusal of the essays collected here will reveal that much of the Bible resonates with many aspects of positive psychology and the study of happiness. On the one hand, that is not surprising. Raymond E. Brown once quipped that saying "The Bible says x, y, or z" is like saying "The Public Library says x, y, or z."[82] The library has a lot of books that say lots of different things, and the Bible, too, is a library (the English term "Bible" derives, after all, from Greek τά βιβλία, "the books"—*plural*), and so it also says a lot of different things. This means, of course, that not everything in the Bible does resonate with the happiness literature—and certainly not with any polluted versions of "happiness"—but a key point to remember is that positive psychology is no monolith either. It is a decent sized library itself! The goal, regardless, is not prooftexting—the worst aspect of so many "Bible *and* . . ." books—but rather the *definition* or, better, the *re*definition of "happiness" by means of "The Bible and the (Positive Psychological) Pursuit of Happiness." This redefinition project is important because of the high stakes of the game, which are nothing less than human flourishing itself. But this work is

---

82. Raymond E. Brown, *An Introduction to the New Testament* (ABRL; New York: Doubleday, 1997), xxxiii.

also essential in light of the pollution of happiness, even, it must be admitted, its pollution *in* religious arenas and *from* readers of the Bible itself. This crucial redefinition of happiness will take some time, though, and more than a few pages.

So . . . what *does* "happiness" mean anyway? And what does the Bible have to say about that?

Sit back, relax, and happy reading.

PART ONE

Hebrew Bible/Old Testament

Introduction to Part I

Part I collects five essays focusing on the Hebrew Bible or Old Testament. Terence E. Fretheim, Elva B. Lovell Professor of Old Testament at Luther Seminary, begins the book with a wide-ranging study on "God, Creation, and the Pursuit of Happiness." Throughout his career, Fretheim has devoted a great deal of his work to creation and the biblical construal of God. In this essay, he highlights an oft-neglected theme—namely, that happiness is a characteristic of the divine life of God according to the Old Testament. This divine happiness is not simply an ontological possession of God; it is also, if not equally, a divine outcome: the result of the genuine effect that the created world has on God. Simply put, what happens in creation can (and does) make God happy (or not). Seen in this light, creation itself is a playful, joy-filled activity of God and realm that is in turn dependent on God's continuing joy. It is not surprising, then, that God gifts human beings with happiness and that even nonhuman creatures—insofar as they, too, are part of God's joyful creational activity—are capable of happiness and joy, which is often manifested in praise of their creator. Happiness, in this way, is a means of talking about the flourishing of all creation.

Nathan MacDonald, of the Universities of Göttingen and St Andrews, takes up a wide swath of text—the entire Pentateuch—to ask if there is happiness in the Torah. MacDonald conducts this investigation with reference to the Greek discussion of happiness, especially Aristotle's classic definitions in his *Nicomachean Ethics* and *Rhetoric*. Interestingly, according to many scholars, the Pentateuch was reaching its final form at approximately the same time that Greek philosophical discussions of happiness were flourishing. The comparison is thus apt and reveals points of both similarity and dissimilarity. In terms of dissimilarity, the happy life in Israel comes from obedience to Torah not from Aristotelian virtue (though the two are not completely unrelated), and luck has very little, if indeed anything, to do with it. But happiness in the Torah, as also in Aristotle, has to do with "mundane realities" such as family life, children, land, fruitfulness, and so forth. Perhaps most importantly, the shape of the Torah means that happiness is oriented toward a *telos* and is open-ended. In many ways God's people are *on their way* to happiness.

In the next essay, Jacqueline Lapsley, associate professor of Old Testament at Princeton Theological Seminary, turns to the prophets to see how they contribute to the study of happiness. Focusing on Isaiah, Lapsley discerns an overall emphasis on flourishing—what Aristotle called *eudaimonia*—as opposed to pure hedonism. That said, the line is blurred in the prophets insofar as human flourishing includes many of the "little things" that are of only secondary importance in Aristotle's understanding. So, "for Isaiah, true human flourishing is not possible without the consistent pleasure of a good meal and a fine glass of wine." This mixture of and blurring between the hedonic and eudaimonic visions has significant ethical payoff according to Lapsley. On the one hand, the presence of eudaimonic aspects—most especially the notions that the truly good human life is one of obedience to God's Torah and that it inescapably involves the life of the other/neighbor—means that life is not to be lived according to the nihilistic, market-driven worldview that is so familiar in our own culture. At the same time, the presence of hedonic aspects means that the happy life isn't solely one of self-sacrifice or self-emptying as is so often the case in certain, particularly ascetic, versions of Christianity. Instead, happiness in Isaiah and beyond is a "happy blend" of eudaimonic and hedonic aspects of the life well-lived with God and others.

William P. Brown, professor of Old Testament at Columbia Theological Seminary, begins his essay with the obvious fact that the Psalms are full of the righteous experiencing deep pain and suffering. In the words of Ps 77:3: "I think of God, and I moan." Moreover, according to Psalm 73, the only people who live lives filled with ease are the wicked! In light of the Psalter's sober realism, it presents an "oblique but remarkably thick portrayal of happiness." Brown begins by focusing on the *'ašrê-*, or "happy," sayings, which highlight that happiness is the result, alternatively, of divine agency, human agency, or the complex mixture of both—the latter nicely exemplified in the "twin" psalms, Psalms 111–112. Next, Brown considers the shape of the book of Psalms as a whole—a shape that reveals the "broad dynamic of happiness" in the book (see also the Epilogue). He concludes that happiness in the Psalms "is reached in a certain way; it is neither a packaged given nor a static state." The Psalms' greatest contribution to the study of happiness may, in fact, be the way these ancient poems shape human desire. In the case of the Psalms, that is, happiness "is found in a life passionately lived in commitment to God, a life lived *coram deo*."

Finally, Carol A. Newsom, the Charles Howard Candler Professor of Old Testament at the Candler School of Theology, Graduate Division of Religion, and Center for the Study of Law and Religion at Emory University, takes up ancient Israelite wisdom literature in light of positive psychology. Much misunderstanding surrounds positive psychology, she notes, precisely because of "the confusing semantics of the word happiness" (see also the Introduction to the present volume). The Bible's wisdom literature, especially Proverbs and Qoheleth, have much that is of direct pertinence to positive psychology's concerns with happiness and human flourishing. In Proverbs, a eudaimonic vision of happiness is presented. It seems that this vision is predicated in no small way on "the belief that the structures of the world, including human nature, have been created in a stable and regular fashion that is intelligible to the human mind." The book of Qoheleth, on the other hand, is a very different story. There, one must reckon with the author's perspective that, even if some sort of cosmic order exists, it is largely unknowable. So, the problem and certainty of death along with one's inability to control the future "is the precondition for his embrace of a distinctive kind of (hedonic) joy." Without an intelligible order, Newsom argues, people will give up on eudaimonism and embrace something more immediate, individual, and hedonic. While that is not all bad, and it may well have its time and place, one must beware that such a move does not eventuate in behaviors that are ultimately nihilistic and (self-)destructive—what Newsom calls "the hedonism of despair" (see also Lapsley's essay). Newsom's work on Proverbs and Qoheleth also highlights the crucial role played by healthy institutions and social structures in the creation and maintenance of happiness. This insight is important for any definitions of happiness—even within positive psychology—that focus overmuch on individualistic aspects of happiness (cf. also Steven J. Sandage's essay in Part III). Ancient Israelite wisdom literature, that is, may actually "aid the positive psychology movement in its reflection on the fundamental conditions that permit and encourage persons to see happiness in both its hedonic and eudaimonic dimensions as realized within an encompassing eudaimonic framework."

I

God, Creation, and the Pursuit
of Happiness

Terence E. Fretheim

1. Introducing (Hebrew) Happiness

In this essay I will address happiness as it relates to God and to creation in the witness of the Old Testament. This will entail reflections on the happiness of God (in creation and more generally), the happiness given to those who are created in God's image, and the happiness of nonhuman creatures, especially when they praise God.

There are many Hebrew words belonging to the semantic field of "happiness."[1] These words may connote differences in the intensity of happiness, and may stem from different traditions,[2] but from what I can discern, little study has been devoted to this issue.[3] Words specifying the absence or diminishment of happiness (e.g., the brokenhearted or crushed in spirit in Ps 34:18) and the exercise of certain dispositions (e.g., mourning or anger) also need attention. Whatever the case, a word study

---

1. See the Appendix by Michael J. Chan in the present volume.

2. It might be fruitful to study which traditions use more happiness language (e.g., Isaiah 40–55), which use less (e.g., 1–2 Kings after Solomon's death), and why this should be the case (e.g., the nature of the historical events reflected).

3. For example, William P. Brown claims that the verb *śāmaḥ* "signals ... a more heightened, ecstatic level of emotion" ("Joy and the Art of Cosmic Maintenance: An Ecology of Play in Psalm 104," in *"And God Saw That It Was Good": Essays on Creation in God in Honor of Terence E. Fretheim* [eds. F. Gaiser and M. Throntveit, St. Paul: Luther Seminary, 2006], 24). He claims that this language of "unabashed joy" is rarely attributed to God in the OT. I have suggested that, of the words used in Prov 8:31," delighting" (*śa ʿăšù ʿîm*) may refer to internal pleasure, while "rejoicing" (*śāḥaq*, usually translated "laugh" or "play" [e.g., 2 Sam 6:5; Zech 8:5] for both adults and children) may designate more external indications that one is pleased (Terence E. Fretheim, *God and World in the Old Testament: A Relational Theology of Creation* [Nashville: Abingdon, 2005], 216).

approach is not sufficient to uncover the passages that pertain to (un)happiness. A range of human activities must be included since many of these reflect happiness, even when no explicit joy language is found. Such activities include: singing, shouting, making noise (with an uproar or loud voice), praising, feasting, dancing, clapping hands, leaping, stamping the feet, whirling, playing musical instruments (e.g., Exod 15:20–21), and so forth. Even without this sort of verbiage, a text may describe a (conventional) situation wherein the participants are clearly happy, for example: communal worship, some sort of personal or communal triumph, recovery from sickness, or a moment of surprise or amazement (e.g., Gen 2:23).[4]

2. *God Is Happy*

Happiness is, first of all and most importantly, *a characteristic of the divine life.*[5] God is happy—or pleased, delighted, joyful.[6] The following list collates a few of these texts, in part because they tend to be neglected. The more specific creation texts are treated in the next section.

> Numbers 6:25–26: The LORD *make his face to shine* upon you, and be gracious to you;
> The LORD *lift up his countenance* upon you, and give you peace.
> Deuteronomy 30:9: the LORD will again *delight* in you and make you prosperous, just as he *delighted* in your fathers.
> 1 Chronicles 28:4: [God] *took delight* in making me [David] king over all Israel.
> 1 Chronicles 29:17 (cf. 16:25–27): I know, my God, that you search the heart, and *take pleasure* in uprightness.

---

4. See Mayer I. Gruber, "Nonverbal Display of Joy and Happiness," in idem, *Aspects of Nonverbal Communication in the Ancient Near East* (2 vols.; Studia Pohl 12; Rome: Biblical Institute Press, 1980), 2:554–614. Among the several nonverbal examples he gives, the following is especially important: the face/eyes of "the happy individual is perceived to shine or light up" (555). Among biblical texts, Gruber cites various Hebrew expressions for the human face—see 1 Sam 14:27, 29; Job 29:24; Pss 13:3; 19:8; 38:10; 104:15; Prov 16:15; Isa 60:1. For the divine face, see Num 6:25; Pss 4:6; 31:16; 34:5; 44:3; 67:1; 80:3, 7, 19; 89:15; 119:135; Isa 31:12; Dan 9:17. Of Isa 60:1–3, he states: "the Lord's smile is cause for Jerusalem to smile" (563). The expression "lift up the head" is also pertinent (see 1 Sam 2:1; Pss 3:3; 110:7). Gruber also cites many ancient Near Eastern parallels.

5. One of the few studies working on this theme is that of Brown ("Joy and the Art of Cosmic Maintenance"). Dictionaries occasionally have a sentence about divine joy. A "happy" exception is the entry "Pleasure" in *Dictionary of Biblical Imagery* (eds. L. Ryken, J. Wilhoit, T. Longman III; Downer's Grove, IL: InterVarsity Press, 1998), 651–54.

6. On God *not* being happy with someone or something, see Ps 5:4; Isa 1:11; 65:12; Amos 5:21; Mal 1:10. See also note 50 below.

Psalm 35:27: Great is the LORD, who *delights* in the welfare of his servant.

Psalm 44:3: for not by their own sword did they win the land,

nor did their own arm give them victory;

but your right hand, and your arm,

and the *light of your countenance,*

for you *delighted* in them.

Psalm 51:18–19: Do good to Zion in *your good pleasure;*

Rebuild the walls of Jerusalem,

Then you will *delight* in right sacrifices.

Psalm 147:11 (cf. 149:4): The LORD *takes pleasure* in those who fear him,

in those who hope in his steadfast love.

Proverbs 15:8 (cf. 11:1, 20; 12:22): The sacrifice of the wicked is an

abomination to the LORD,

but the prayer of the upright is his *delight.*

Isaiah 42:1: Here is my servant, whom I uphold,

my chosen, in whom my soul *delights.*[7]

Isaiah 62:4–5: You [Jerusalem] shall be called My *Delight* is in Her . . .

For the LORD *delights* in you . . .

and as the bridegroom *rejoices* over the bride

so shall your God *rejoice* over you.

Jeremiah 9:24: I act with steadfast love, justice, and righteousness

in the earth,

for in these things I *delight,* says the LORD.

Jeremiah 31:20: Is Ephraim my dear son?

Is he the child I *delight in*? . . .

Therefore I am deeply moved for him.

Micah 7:18: Who is a God like you, pardoning iniquity . . .?

He does not retain his anger forever,

because he *delights* in showing clemency.

Zephaniah 3:17–18a: [God] will rejoice over you with *gladness* . . .

he will *exult* over you *with loud singing* as on a day of festival.[8]

Haggai 1:8: build the house, so that I may *take pleasure* in it.

---

7. With "personal affection," Second Isaiah "dares to talk about Yahweh's 'I,' his 'soul'" (*nepeš*). God commonly responds in this way to sacrifices, but here "it is the response to a person instead" (Klaus Baltzer, *Deutero-Isaiah: A Commentary on Isaiah 40–55* [trans. M. Kohl; ed. Peter Machinist; Hermeneia; Minneapolis: Fortress, 2001], 127).

8. The calls to Israel to rejoice (Zeph 3:14) find their parallels in God's promise to join them in rejoicing. The verb *gyl* is used almost exclusively for human beings in contexts of worshipful response to God's saving actions.

The following may be offered as an initial response to these texts: God is joyful in taking actions that issue in positive developments for God's people (1 Chr 28:4; Mic 7:18). Joy is God's reason for acting in a positive way on behalf of the people (Ps 44:3; Jer 9:24). The unalloyed joy at the relationship between God and people is likened (by God!) to the joy between a bride and a bridegroom (Isa 62:4–5)[9] and between a parent and a child (Jer 31:20). Divine happiness is evident when the relationship between God and the people is thriving (Ps 147:11), including when prayers are offered (Prov 15:8), when faithfulness (Prov 12:22) and uprightness (1 Chr 29:17) are exhibited, and when justice is practiced (Prov 11:1). What people do can bring pleasure to the divine life (Hag 1:8). Generally, God is happy over the good and constructive things that happen to people (Ps 35:27), in their life rather than their death (Ezek 18:23, 32), and this joy extends across the generations (Deut 30:9). These texts also suggest that, while happiness is an ongoing characteristic of the divine life (not least in view of internal divine relationships), things can happen in relationship with human beings that bring more intense pleasure to God—and intense displeasure.[10]

These texts raise issues relating to divine emotion and, more generally, divine affectivity and/or affectability.[11] The Old Testament contains many texts where God is genuinely affected by what happens in God's world.[12] For example, the flood is introduced by a grieving God (Gen 6:6–7), or God is provoked to anger (e.g., 2 Kgs 22:13 and often), or God laments over what has happened to Jerusalem's people and environment (e.g., Jer 9:10), or God, in a salvific move, "cries out" like a woman in labor (Isa 42:14). Then too are passages recounting the divine change of mind in the wake of human prayer (e.g., Exod 32:14; Jer 26:19;

---

9. Cf. Elizabeth Achtemeier who writes that God is "like a young man with a new wife—solicitous, adoring, enraptured . . . pictures of God that are breathtaking in the love they portray" (*The Community and Message of Isaiah 56–66* [Minneapolis: Augsburg, 1982], 98). The emotional element seems especially strong in this text.

10. See note 50 below for texts where people's actions occasion displeasure for God. For issues of differing intensities in God, see Terence E. Fretheim, *The Suffering of God: An Old Testament Perspective* (OBT; Philadelphia: Fortress, 1984), 60–65.

11. "Happiness" is not limited to emotion; it can refer more broadly to a life that is functioning well (to be content). This angle suggests that happiness can persist through times of unhappiness (cf., e.g., many parent-child relationships).

12. For details, see Fretheim, *The Suffering of God*; and idem, *God and World*.

Jon 3:10). Such perspectives stand over against views that God is impassible and immutable in some simplistic or absolute sense.[13]

It may be claimed that language that ascribes emotions or changes to God is "only" anthropomorphic or anthropopathic, and hence has no "real" relationship to God. But we should be alert to the fact that biblical language for God is almost always anthropomorphic (e.g., God speaks, God acts, God thinks, God hides). As with all analogical language, then, such expressions need to be examined for the "yes" and "no" of the reference to God.[14] For example, one might say that God's emotions are never "out of control." Generally, theologians seem to have much less difficulty speaking of God's mind or God's word than God's emotions/feelings. Our culture seems to be much more comfortable with a left-brain God and a male God ("big boys don't cry," after all). The stereotypical female, by contrast, cannot control her emotions very well!

What difference does it make for our theological reflection and pastoral practice that God is happy? That God enjoys the world and all of its creatures? That human joy occasions a joyful response in the divine life? That human happiness is a gift from God and how we respond to that gift can have a negative or positive effect on the shape of the life of faith? It is probably true to say that the church has stressed the unhappiness of God—most famously in God's anger at human sin—more than the divine happiness. Does such an emphasis have a negative effect on how people think of God and live their lives? On how they value themselves and creation more generally? Does the lack of attention to *divine* happiness contribute to the often dour and stern countenance of so many Christians? How might increased emphasis on divine joy positively affect the teaching and preaching of the church and the well-being of Christians? Might we enjoy life more than we do?[15]

---

13. It is important to note that God *is* immutable in several respects, e.g., God's love is immutable. It is often thought that change is a category that is not applicable to God—can change be characteristic of a perfect being?—and hence God cannot be affected by creatures in any way. But if the Scriptures bear witness that God is affected by what happens in the world of creatures, then this classical understanding of God needs at least some revision.

14. See, e.g., Paul Ricouer, *The Rule of Metaphor: Multi-Disciplinary Studies of the Creation of Meaning in Language* (trans. R. Czerny et al.; Toronto: University of Toronto Press, 1977 [French orig: 1965]). Among texts to consider on this matter, see Prov 3:11–12, where God is likened to a father who "delights" in his son. How is God like and unlike such a father? It might be noted that Jesus Christ is not an exception in the life of God; Jesus reveals who God essentially is and this God is revealed in the Old Testament in remarkable ways.

15. See also the essay by Jacqueline Lapsley in this volume; as well as Ellen T. Charry, *God and the Art of Happiness* (Grand Rapids: Eerdmans, 2010).

3. God's Creative Work and the Joy that Accompanies It

In creation God expresses joy and other creatures join in God's joy. The joy language used at creation is, in turn, also used to describe the new creation. Creation is a joy-filled task and a joy-filled result for both Creator and created—in the beginning, in the ongoing, and in the new creation.

> Genesis 1:31: God saw everything that he had made, and indeed,
>> it was *very good*.
>
> Job 38:4–7: Where were you when I laid the foundations of the earth? . . .
>> when the morning stars *sang together* and all the heavenly beings
>>> *shouted for joy*.
>
> Psalm 104:26: The sea . . . Leviathan whom you made to *sport with*. (NJB)
>
> Psalm 104:31, 34: May the Lord *rejoice* in his works. . . .
>> May my meditation *be pleasing* to him [i.e., God],
>> for I *rejoice* in the LORD.
>
> Proverbs 8:30–31: Then I [i.e., Woman Wisdom] was daily beside him . . .
>> and I was daily his *delight*,
>> *rejoicing* before him always,
>> *rejoicing* in his inhabited world
>> and *delighting* in the human race.
>
> Isaiah 65:17–19: For I am about to create new heavens and a new earth. . . .
>> But *be glad* and *rejoice* forever in what I am creating;
>> for I am about to create Jerusalem as a *joy*
>>> and its people as a *delight*.
>> I will *rejoice* in Jer.usalem, and *delight* in my people.[16]
>
> Jeremiah 32:41: I [i.e., God] will *rejoice* in doing *good* to them
>> [i.e., Israel], and I will plant them in this land in faithfulness,
>> with all my [God's!] heart and all my soul.[17]

Three creation texts deserve closer analysis: Genesis 1–2, Psalm 104, and Proverbs 8.

---

16. This new creation issues in a joy/delight that is shared by God and people alike (the same two verbs, *gîl+śûś*, are used for both). What is God creating? God is creating Jerusalem and its people *as* a joy/delight. So, human happiness is a creative act of God. There will be no more weeping or the cry of distress (which was an effect of judgment in Jer 7:34; 25:10). God will in turn respond to this new creation by rejoicing and delighting in what God has created. Claus Westermann (*Isaiah 40–66: A Commentary* [OTL; Philadelphia: Westminster, 1969]) states: "It is not just that the inhabitants of Jerusalem are summoned to rejoice; God, too, can take joy in his new creation . . . There can be no doubt that Deutero-Isaiah is also the origin of the accumulation of words for joy" (409).

17. The repeated "good" in Jer 32:39–44 suggests the creational themes of Genesis 1 (see Terence E. Fretheim, *Jeremiah* [Macon: Smyth & Helwys, 2002], 467).

Genesis 1–2

It is often noted that Genesis 1 has a doxological character. These verses may have been shaped in and through liturgical usage and the regular round of the community's praise of God the Creator.[18] Praise language is fundamentally evaluative language, discerning and then voicing the praiseworthiness of something or someone: their beauty, purposefulness, and correspondence with the intention of the one who created. The rhythmic use of the evaluative word "good" in Genesis 1 (with a follow-up in 2:18 and its aftermath) fits with the praise character of these verses.[19] To evaluate the creation as "good" is *to be happy with* the results, *to delight in* the "final product."[20] And because it is *God* who declares that each creature is good, God can be said to be happy with the results. Such a divine evaluation conveys a sense of value to each and every creature—both in the sense of value in itself and its value for others—that cannot be matched by any human evaluation. Both human and nonhuman are given the same language of valuation: good.[21]

Some brief reflections on the divine "us" (Gen 1:26–27; 3:25; 11:7) may be helpful at this point.[22] A majority of scholars understand that "us" in these texts refers to a council of heavenly beings of which God is a part.[23] In other words, God is a social being, functioning within a divine community that is rich and complex.

---

18. See the helpful discussion in Samuel E. Balentine, *The Torah's Vision of Worship* (OBT; Minneapolis: Fortress, 1999), 81–95.

19. On the image of God as evaluator in Genesis 1–2, see the discussion in Fretheim, *God and World*, 40–42.

20. Note the scare quotation marks. As I have argued elsewhere, I believe God made the world "good" not "perfect," and thus "final product" is something of a misnomer. See my *God and World*, *passim*, also my *Creation Untamed: The Bible, God, and Natural Disasters* (Grand Rapids: Baker Academic, 2010).

21. It is striking that the valuation by God of the goodness of creation in Genesis 1 is a valuation returned to God in praise: "O give thanks to the Lord, for he is *good*" (emphasis mine; Pss 106:1; 107:1; 118:1; 136:1). In other words, the creatures reflect the goodness of their createdness back to God and thereby become a witness to God, reflecting that created goodness toward the entire world.

22. For a recent study of Gen 1:26–28, see Paul Niskanen, "The Poetics of Adam: The Creation of *'adam* in the image of *'elohim*," *JBL* 128 (2009): 417–36. Note also Brent A. Strawn, "Comparative Approaches: History, Theory, and the Image of God," in *Method Matters: Essays on the Interpretation of the Hebrew Bible in Honor of David L. Petersen* (eds. Joel M. LeMon and Kent Harold Richards; SBLRBS 56; Atlanta: Society of Biblical Literature, 2009), 117–42.

23. See, for example, Patrick D. Miller, Jr., *Genesis 1–11: Studies in Structure and Theme* (JSOT-Sup 8; Sheffield: JSOT Press, 1978); J. Richard Middleton, *The Liberating Image: The* Imago Dei *in Genesis 1* (Grand Rapids: Brazos, 2005), 55–60. See also Isa 6:8. The later witness that God is one (e.g., Deut 6:4) is not compromised by this recognition of the sociality of God, for the divine beings in the assembly are not other gods on par with Yahweh.

God is therein engaged in a relationship of mutuality. And so relationship is integral to the identity of God prior to and independent of God's relationship to the world (see also texts such as Jer 23:18–22).

Such a "good" evaluation by God makes clear that God is not removed from the creation once the creature comes into being. In order to evaluate, one must *experience* that which has been created and one will therein *be affected by* what has been experienced. A remarkable imaging of God! Readers may wonder why God would evaluate God's own work. Would it not be good just by being a creature of God's own making? But a clue to this evaluative process may be found in Gen 2:18, where God observes what has been created and declares that "it is *not* good." That is, God's creation of human beings to this point does not fulfill the purpose God intends for them (God is not "happy with" the human situation at this point); further creative work will be needed.

Consider again the language of Gen 2:18: "It is not good that the man should be alone." To whom is God speaking? It is likely that here again (see 1:26–27) the reader is permitted to overhear the inner-divine reflective process. This would suggest that the 'adam-creature's not-being-alone is correlated with God's not-being-alone. Or, in different terms, it is not good for the human being to be alone because it would not be good for God either. Only the human being as social and relational to other human beings is truly correspondent to the sociality of God (and to being in the image of God).[24] If so, one might then claim that, given the joyful response of the 'adam to the creation of the woman in 2:23, the inner-divine relationship is also comparably characterized by joy. Such a perspective is reinforced by the "us" and "our" language in Gen 1:26–27.

This not-good evaluation of God's own work in Gen 2:18 suggests that creation is not conceived in static terms. Rather, it is understood in terms of a *process* wherein the divine response to what has been created leads to further development

---

24. These plural references to God have often been interpreted by Christians as Trinitarian. But it is historically more accurate to say that these Old Testament perspectives regarding the social nature of God provided a theological matrix for the development of later theological perspectives. See Terence E. Fretheim, "Christology and the Old Testament," in *Who Do You Say That I Am? Essays on Christology* (eds. Mark A. Powell and David Bauer; Louisville: Westminster, 2000), 201–15. That is to say, the early Christian reflections about God that led to Trinitarian thought were not grounded solely in claims about Jesus and the Holy Spirit but also rooted in the complexity of the Godhead witnessed in the Old Testament. See further, Patrick D. Miller, "A Strange Kind of Monotheism," in *Theology Today: Reflections on the Bible and Contemporary Life* (Louisville: Westminster John Knox, 2006), 44–46; Brent A. Strawn, "And These Three Are One: A Trinitarian Critique of Christological Approaches to the Old Testament," *PRS* 31 (2004): 191–210; and Benjamin D. Sommer, *The Bodies of God and the World of Ancient Israel* (New York: Cambridge University Press, 2009).

of the creation and of intracreaturely relationships.[25] It is striking that in Genesis 2:23 it is the human who, finally, responds to God's creation of the woman in a joyous way, delighting in what God has created in response to the divinely discerned creational need. This human evaluative response may be understood as parallel to God's "good" evaluation in Genesis 1.

This textual analysis raises the question as to whether God's vision of human happiness changes over time.[26] That is to say, if God's creative work is understood in terms of process rather than the maintenance of a once-for-all given creation, what it means to be human and what it means to be a happy human will be on the move. Such an understanding suggests that, even within the relatively brief time of the life of Israel (let alone human history), the nature of human happiness may change in view of new times and places.

Moving now to texts concerning the *new creation*, the language of Isa 65:17–19 suggests that, just as God created human happiness in the initial creation, so also God will create human happiness in the creating of the new heaven and earth. In other words, God's rejoicing and delighting in the results of the new creation will correspond to the "good" of the original creation in Genesis 1 (and 2). Not to be missed here is the fact that, for this comparative language to "work," God's rejoicing and delighting must be just as real as the people's joy.

Psalm 104

Psalm 104:31 is a particularly important text.[27] As William P. Brown cogently argues, this verse reflects the "frightful possibility" that if

> the creator were to *stop* enjoying creation, the cosmos would suffer collapse . . . The possibility of cosmic demise in the psalm is attributed not to divine wrath against a resistant or hostile creation but to something seemingly more benign, namely, to God's abstaining from joy.[28]

Creation is not only brought into being by God *but is sustained by the joy of God.*

---

25. Correlatively, Genesis 1–2 do not present the creation as precisely or finally ordered. For example, Gen 1:28 recognizes that God's creation needs to be "subdued." See note 20 above.

26. I thank Carl Holladay for pressing my thinking on this point.

27. See Brown, "Psalm 104"; also idem, *Seeing the Psalms: A Theology of Metaphor* (Louisville: Westminster John Knox, 2002), 172–75.

28. Brown, "Psalm 104," 26–27.

Psalm 104:34 repeats the verb *śāmaḥ*, "to rejoice," but this time with a human subject, namely, the author of the psalm, "May I rejoice in the LORD." The psalm itself is thus "an act of creativity intended to bring pleasure to God. God's joy and the psalmist's joy (vv. 31 and 34) are in some sense parallel: as the psalmist rejoices in God, so God is to rejoice in creation"—further: "God's delight provides a model for human interaction with the world and God.... counter[ing] all manner of treating the world in terms of utility.... Ecology is at root an exercise in joy."[29]

Psalm 104:26 (cf. Job 41:5) speaks of "Leviathan that you [God] formed to sport with [in the sea]." Leviathan is "God's playmate!"[30] Brown continues: "Leviathan brings out God's playful side, but such play is no isolated moment in God's engagement with the world."[31] Rather, "it supports all creation." God finds pleasure in the creation by the very process of its being brought into existence, and the world's future is dependent upon God's continuing enjoyment.

Proverbs 8

What are we to make of the delighting and rejoicing reported in Prov 8:30–31?[32] The fourfold reference to these themes in four successive lines is striking and emphatic. It strongly suggests that the creation of the world was a moment of great joy for all involved. Moreover, the two words, "delighting" and "rejoicing," seem to be used as near-synonyms, with the basic idea of "taking pleasure in" (see Jer 31:20; 31:4: "merrymakers"). These words imply an evaluative stance, thinking so highly of what is happening that delight is the only proper response. (An analogue would be parents being delighted at the birth of a baby.) These words thus have reference to joy and wonder both with respect to the creative process itself and to the effects of that process (see also Job 38:7). Basic to this responsiveness is

---

29. Ibid., 27, 31.

30. Ibid., 30. See also Kathryn Schifferdecker, *Out of the Whirlwind: Creation Theology in the Book of Job* (HTS; Cambridge, Mass.: Harvard Divinity School, 2008).

31. Brown, "Psalm 104," 31. Brown notes, in contrast to Jon D. Levenson (see his *Creation and the Persistence of Evil: The Jewish Drama of Divine Omnipotence* [Princeton: Princeton University Press, 1988], 17), that Leviathan is "neither a rubber ducky nor a subjugated beast, but a fitting playmate for the divine. For genuine play to occur, Leviathan must be fully alive and functioning."

32. The following paragraphs depend on my work in *God and World in the Old Testament*, 216–18. See also the reflections on this text by William P. Brown, *The Ethos of the Cosmos: The Genesis of Moral Imagination in the Bible* (Grand Rapids: Eerdmans, 1999) 271–316. See also the chapter by Carol A. Newsom in this volume.

the ongoing close relationship among all involved: God, Wisdom (personified), and the creation itself, especially humanity.[33]

To speak of wisdom being God's daily delight is, most fundamentally, to make a claim about *God*. God is not passive or aloof to the daughter who has been birthed but so enters into this relationship that it has a dynamic and interactive character. Integral to such a relationship is a delighting in the other; wisdom is a source of pleasure to God.[34] Inasmuch as *delight* is an evaluative word, it is parallel to God's evaluating of the creation as "good" in Genesis 1. Woman Wisdom does not introduce joy and delight into the creative process, God does. But Wisdom as the offspring of God continues that divine commitment and response.

From another angle, God delights in Woman Wisdom because Wisdom has *enabled God* to make the world such a dynamic place. God's creating would not have had such extraordinary effects without Woman Wisdom. Then, evincing the genuine character of the relationship, Wisdom delights in God and what God is creating. Notably, their mutual delighting does not take place simply at the completion of the "construction" of the creation; delight is a "daily" matter, occurring all along the way as the creation comes into being.[35] Together God and Wisdom take pleasure in each other, in what has been created, and in what continues to be created.

This mutual delight is taken a step further in Prov 8:31, perhaps climactically so. Here Wisdom's delighting no longer simply relates to God as Creator; it relates also to the *effects* of God's creative work, namely God's "inhabited world"— human beings in particular. Even more, as human beings live out their proper role in the world, Wisdom delights in who they are and what they are doing; she has the best interests, the good pleasure of human beings at heart. Then, as 8:32–36 makes clear in the repeated reference to human happiness, Wisdom's delighting in humanity will be matched by the delight of human beings in keeping Wisdom's ways. God, Wisdom, and humanity, interrelated as they are, are each represented as delighting. When this happens, God's purposes for the creation are being realized: The world is a delight!

More can be said about this mutuality of delight. Delight is not amusement in the sense of an activity different from work but a dimension of the relationship

---

33. See Gale Yee, "The Theology of Creation in Proverbs 8:22–31," in *Creation in the Biblical Traditions* (eds. Richard J. Clifford and John J. Collins; CBQMS; Washington, D.C.: Catholic Biblical Association, 1992), 94.

34. Wisd 8:3 sharpens the point: "The Lord of all loves her."

35. A widespread pattern in ancient and modern cultures is an expression of joy at the completion of a construction project. See Raymond C. van Leeuwen, "The Book of Proverbs," in *NIB* 5:95. But this text reports a rejoicing that does not wait for completion; it is expressed all along the way (so also Job 38:7).

itself, including work and all participants—God, Wisdom, and creation. Delight and work must remain integrated with each other; happiness is as much associated with work as with play (so also Eccl 5:18–20).[36] Another way of putting the matter is that pleasure and playfulness are built into the very structure of things, enabling all of life, including God's own life, to be what God intended it to be.[37] The pleasure evident in the God-Wisdom relationship becomes a dimension of all of creation, dancing into every creature's life as they are brought into being over time.[38] As Woman Wisdom delights both before God and before humankind in an *ongoing* relationship, there is a sense in which "wisdom functions as an intermediary between God and man [*sic*], between God and his world."[39] Wisdom belongs both in the world and with God; as we have noted, Wisdom is both creature and divine. It is not simply a quality "immanent in creation" or "an attribute of the world," but remains alongside God.[40] Wisdom delighting with human beings carries the implication of divine immanence—direct presence and involvement in creation. God not only created the world but, in and through the figure of Wisdom, chooses to dwell among creatures in terms that are described as delightful.

Because delighting and rejoicing demonstrate the dynamic character of this relationship, this text "excludes any theological view that the universe is a closed system operating according to fixed laws, of either nature or human destiny, which determine every occurrence."[41] That Wisdom is not a fixed order will become evident in Proverbs 10–31 by the way individual proverbs sometimes contradict

---

36. This point could be contrasted with the common American conviction that happiness is to be associated with play and not work. These texts refuse to separate these dimensions of life and what makes for happiness.

37. See Michael V. Fox, *Proverbs 1–9: A New Translation with Introduction and Commentary* (AB 18A; New York: Doubleday, 2000), 288–89. Fox's emphasis that "Wisdom's play expresses the joy of intellect: exploring, thinking, learning" should not be stressed at the expense of other dimensions of a genuine relationship. Note that in Psalm 119 (vv. 14, 16, 24, 70, etc.) the psalmist takes pleasure in the law because of the way in which it gives shape to a life of joy and gladness.

38. Karl Löning and Erich Zenger, *To Begin with, God Created . . .: Biblical Theologies of Creation* (Collegeville, MN: Liturgical, 2000) speak helpfully of the image of God as an artist who forms the world "in a kind of euphoric 'creative high'" (62).

39. Helmer Ringgren, *Word and Wisdom: Studies in the Hypostatization of Divine Qualities and Functions in the Ancient Near East* (Lund: Ohlssons, 1947), 55.

40. See Gerhard von Rad, *Wisdom in Israel* (trans. James D. Martin; Nashville: Abingdon, 1972 [German orig: 1970]), 156.

41. Ellen F. Davis, *Proverbs, Ecclesiastes, and the Song of Songs* (Westminster Bible Companion; Louisville: Westminster John Knox, 2000), 68.

themselves, depending on the life situation. Hans-Jürgen Hermisson also points out that, given the nature of the proverbial literature and its varied contents, "creation did not only happen at the beginning of the world, but takes place continuously; therefore, the orders have not become rigid, but necessarily remain flexible."[42] Wisdom does not set absolute standards or norms. Wisdom does not fix life in place. The wise and discerning human response may, indeed must, vary from situation to situation if it would be true to Wisdom's intention. The authority of Wisdom, and the limits of which one might speak, are of such a nature that much freedom of life and expression is allowed. That means that Woman Wisdom opens up the world rather than closes it down: she is always ready to take new experience into account, recognizing that God may be about new things for new times and places. Such is the life of a genuine Creator.

Finally, the presence of irregularities and ambiguities in the order of things means that discernment has to be open to new perceptions and shifts in understanding regarding what is wise. Wisdom is more dynamic than static in view of such changes and perceptions of reality. "These relationships, however, were always extremely variable and could certainly never be evaluated unambiguously. Behind the teachings of the wise men there lies, therefore, a profound conviction of the ambivalence of phenomena and events."[43] Close attention to actual experience means learning to live with ambiguity. And rejoicing in that reality!

4. Happiness as a Creational Gift of God to Human Beings

Happiness as God's gift to human beings is perhaps most evident in thinking about the human as created in the image of God. Because God's life is characterized by happiness, those made in God's image are also so gifted. Happiness may be a specific creational step in light of Gen 2:18, "It is not good that the man should be alone." God moves to resolve this identified problem in God's own creation, and, with creaturely help (Gen 2:19–22), does so by the creation of the woman. The creational situation thereby moves from "not good" to "good" and the *'adam* responds with a joyous exclamation (Gen 2:23). God's action in creation produces human joy. Supporting such an understanding is the parallel depiction of the new creation in Isa 65:18, wherein God will "create Jerusalem *as a joy* and its people *as a delight*" (emphasis mine). Joy is a gift of God in creation and hence it is God's will for human beings that they be happy.

---

42. So H.-J. Hermisson, "Observations on the Creation Theology in Wisdom," in *Creation in the Old Testament* (ed. Bernard W. Anderson; IRT 6; Philadelphia: Fortress, 1984), 122.

43. Von Rad, *Wisdom in Israel*, 311.

The joyful response of the '*adam* to God's gift of the woman (Gen 2:23)—the first human words in the Bible—in effect identifies human happiness as integral to what "good" is (and "backfills" into the meaning of "good" in Genesis 1).[44] If so, such happiness is integral to what it means to be truly human. At the same time, the text suggests that a close relationship with at least *one other human being* is considered essential for the '*adam* to be happy (and that nonhuman creatures are insufficient, though there is a link between human and nonhuman joy).[45] In other words, *human interrelationships* are essential to the happiness of the human being. In its most fundamental sense, happiness has a relational element (as noted above, this is true of God as well). To be clear, I do not think that the text suggests that one cannot, say, be happy living alone or even thrive in times of aloneness; rather, it is to recognize that such "happiness in isolation" is possible because human others have played an integral role along the way in one's becoming.[46] It would seem, then, that happiness is an innate quality of life (perhaps like personality itself) that is drawn out in relationship to others and "matures" over time as one relates to self and others.

On the other hand, happiness can diminish as relationships fail. The testimony of Genesis 1–11 is that human failure has profoundly negative effects on relationships—with God, with other human beings, with nonhuman creatures (including the ground and animals), and with one's own self (e.g., issues of shame). The negative effects of human behaviors suggest that, at the most basic level, the vision of human well-being (happiness) in the opening chapters of Genesis focuses on well-functioning relationships at all levels of existence.

This way of putting the matter suggests that happiness is, at least initially, *a gift of creation, not redemption*.[47] Another way of putting the matter: people who are not Christians, nor religious, or who have never experienced redemption, can be happy by virtue of (and within) their humanity in relationship to others. It might even be said that many nonreligious people are happier than many religious individuals!

---

44. See above. Also, Jer 32:41 brings the language of "good" into close proximity with God's happiness.

45. See below. Notably, God's presence does not resolve the issue of human aloneness either.

46. In the psychological literature, one might compare the work of D. W. Winnicott—esp. his *Playing and Reality* (London: Routledge, 2005 [origl: 1971]).

47. Such a perspective may stand over against the claim of Aquinas that "a perfect happiness . . . cannot be found in this life and can only be found in union with God" (see Stephen Wang, "Aquinas on Human Happiness and the Natural Desire for God," *New Blackfriars* 88 [2007]: 322). One might quarrel over what the word "perfect" means or what "union with God" entails, both of which are ambiguous at best. Another way of making the point is that human beings do not become something other than (or more than) human in their relationship with God. Their humanity may be enhanced in such a relationship, but they remain finite human beings.

This creational dimension of happiness is evident in that the experience of happiness often does not have explicit religious connections. A remarkable variety of God's good gifts in the creation have the capacity to generate happiness, including the birth of children (Ps 113:9), a birthday (Job 3:7), one's continuing years of life—from youth to old age (Eccl 11:8–9), good wine and oil (Judg 9:13; Ps 104:15), a good word (Prov 12:25; 15:23), sexual love (Song 1:4), married life (Prov 5:18), a good harvest (Isa 9:3), and, more generally, the capacity to eat, drink, and enjoy one's work (Eccl 3:13; 5:18–20; 8:15). Many, if not all, of these gifts are a part of human life because they are *creational* gifts. Moreover, most such gifts entail relationships with other people either directly or implicitly. Happiness, that is, is often generated by the daily rhythms in our interrelationships with others.

That these gifts are creational suggests that happiness is a regular feature of life for many people, if not all. These gifts demonstrate that it is a mistake to think that "real" joy comes only in or from a redemptive context. It might be further suggested that this more primal or foundational set of joyful experiences in "regular," created life becomes a metaphor for the happiness of life in relationship with God, with much "yes" to the analogy![48] An explicit example would be Isa 9:3:

> You [i.e., God] have multiplied the nation, you have increased its joy;
> they rejoice before you *as* with joy at the harvest,
> *as* people exult when dividing plunder. (My emphases)

A contrasting example is Ps 4:7:

> You have put gladness in my heart
> more than when their grain and wine abound.

The latter text may suggest that the issue is a matter of the depth and breadth of gladness.

It might be asserted that being or becoming a member of a community of faith makes some people happier, but this is certainly not necessarily so. *Creational issues are always in play*, from the nature of the personality involved to the character and quality of the relationships with others. At the same time, "happy" does not have a single definition, as if every human being would be "happy" if precisely the same state of affairs came to be in or for each. "Happy" varies from individual to individual.

---

48. It is noteworthy that God and human beings are often the subjects of the same words for joy and happiness. The one possible exception may be the image of the shining face in Num 6:25, but cf. 1 Sam 14:27, 29 (of Jonathan's eyes). See further the Appendix by Michael J. Chan in this volume.

Despite the importance of creation, there are several texts that suggest that happiness is a gift from God that moves beyond the creational sphere.[49] At the same time, just exactly what it is that distinguishes these expressions of happiness

---

49. Note the following listing:

> 1 Kings 8:66: The people . . . *joyful and in good spirits* because of all *the goodness* that the LORD had shown.
>
> Nehemiah 12:43: They offered great sacrifices that day and rejoiced, *for God had made them rejoice with great joy*; the women and children also *rejoiced*. The *joy* of Jerusalem was heard far away.
>
> Psalm 30:11: You have turned my mourning into *dancing*; you have taken off my sackcloth and *clothed me with joy*.
>
> Psalm 32:1–2: *Happy* are those whose transgression is forgiven, whose sin is covered.
>
> Psalm 51:12: Restore to me *the joy* of your salvation.
>
> Psalm 90:14: *Satisfy* us in the morning with your steadfast love, so that we may *rejoice and be glad* all our days. Make us *glad* as many days as you have afflicted us.
>
> Psalm 94:19: When the cares of my heart are many, your consolations *cheer* my soul.
>
> Psalm 119:111: Your decrees are my heritage forever; they are the *joy* of my heart.
>
> Isaiah 12:6: *Shout aloud* and *sing for joy*, O inhabitant of Zion, for great in your midst is the Holy One of Israel.
>
> Isaiah 29:19: The meek shall *obtain fresh joy* in the LORD and the neediest people shall exult in the Holy One of Israel.
>
> Isaiah 35:10 (cf. Isa 51:11): And the ransomed of the LORD shall return, and come to Zion with *singing*; *everlasting joy* shall be upon their heads; they shall obtain *joy and gladness*, and sorrow and sighing shall flee away.
>
> Isaiah 51:3: For the LORD will *comfort* Zion . . . *joy and gladness* will be found in her, *thanksgiving* and the voice of *song*.
>
> Isaiah 60:15: Whereas you have been forsaken and hated . . . I will make you majestic forever, a *joy* from age to age.
>
> Isaiah 61:1–3: he [i.e., the Lord GOD] has sent me to bring good news . . . to bind up the brokenhearted . . . to provide for those who mourn in Zion— to give them a *garland* instead of ashes, the *oil of gladness* instead of mourning, the *mantle of praise* instead of a faint spirit.
>
> Jeremiah 15:16: . . . your [i.e., God's] words became to me a *joy* and the *delight* of my heart.
>
> Jeremiah 31:13: Then shall the young women *rejoice* in the *dance*, and the young men and the old shall *be merry*. I will turn their mourning into *joy*, I will *comfort* them, and give them *gladness* for sorrow.
>
> Jeremiah 33:9: And this city shall be to me a name of *joy, a praise and a glory* before all the nations of the earth who shall hear of all the *good* that I do for them.

from the creational is not altogether clear. Is it a deeper quality or intensity of happiness? Is it a more realistic view of happiness? Being assured of forgiveness of sin may be the most evident factor at work in these texts—does it gift one with a kind of happiness that has a special quality? Again and again these passages indicate that human joy is something that is endangered, or withered, or perhaps even lost.[50] On the other hand, various aspects of God's work among the people can take away sorrows, cares, brokenheartedness, and "hates." So it is that happiness can include healing. New dimensions of joy and life (e.g., "fresh joy" in Isa 30:19) are created by divine action, including God's goodness, forgiveness, salvation, comfort, steadfast love, law, and presence. What do such "new dimensions" include? Perhaps redemption reinvigorates or revitalizes creational happiness that has been diminished in one way or another and gives it new energy in view of newly shaped purposes for life. Whatever the case, whether in creation or redemption, joy is seen to be a gift of God (see Eccl 5:18–20).

It is clear, regardless, that it is not helpful to speak of "total" or "perfect" happiness (except perhaps as a momentary exclamation!).[51] Human beings are gifted with happiness, but that gift is never something that is realized in life in some comprehensive or totalizing way. This is the case not simply because of human sin (though that is often asserted), but also because of the limits entailed in human finitude.[52] Hence, happiness is not only something that is *given*; it is also something that may be (1) *enhanced*, when, say, relationships thrive; (2) *diminished*, when, say, relationships fail; and (3) *stymied* or *frustrated* in its development, when, say, limits have been reached. Once gifted with happiness, what we do with the gift will make a difference for ourselves and for others—often a great deal of difference.

5. The Happiness Expressed by Nonhuman Creatures

Does the Bible witness to the happiness of nonhuman creatures? If so, how might we appropriately speak of, say, animals being happy or contented or delighted? And, of what importance is such a reality for understanding and enabling human

---

50. God is also one who *takes joy away* or is *not delighted*. See Deut 28:63; Hos 2:11; Eccl 5:4; Jer 7:34; 16:9 (25:10; cf. 33:11); Ezek 35:14–15; Mal 1:10; Amos 5:21; Ps 5:4; Isa 1:11; 9:16; 65:12; Ezek 18:23, 32; 33:11.

51. See further my book *Creation Untamed*, esp. chap. 1.

52. Finitude is a neglected theme in Old Testament theological studies. Even in the new heaven and new earth, human beings will not be static, where no change or no new development is possible. Such a place of stasis would better be described as hell.

happiness?[53] Anyone who has loved a dog knows that that love is returned (perhaps the same cannot be said for cats!). Given the relationships that human beings often have to pets, household plants, and even trees and other natural elements, we dare not suggest that God is incapable of similar relationships.

One of the more remarkable features of Old Testament creation theology is the extent to which nonhuman creatures are imaged as joyful and happy and engaged in the praise of God.[54] God is said to draw nonhuman creatures out or call them forth, and they are said to be responsive in some sense to the work of God within them. This is already true in the opening chapters of Genesis, where God's call to the waters and the earth to participate in creative activity (Gen 1:11, 20, 24) suggests that a response is expected and, indeed, is forthcoming (Gen 1:13). The natural order is certainly not understood to be passive; to the contrary, it is a *coparticipant* in God's creative activity.

The extensive list of texts on the interresponsiveness of God and nonhuman creatures is remarkable (see, e.g., Job 37:6; 38:35, 39–41; Ps 19:1; 50:4; Ps 104:21; Ps 145:10, 15–16; 147:4, 9; 148; Isa 40:26; 45:8; Hos 2:21–22; Hag 1:11).[55] Specific examples of happiness on the part of nonhuman creatures follows:

> Job 38:7: When *the morning stars* sang together
>   and all the heavenly beings *shouted for joy.*
> Psalm 19:5: *The sun* like a strong man runs its course *with joy.*
> Psalm 65:8: You [i.e., God] make *the gateways of the morning*
>   and the evening *shout for joy.*
> Psalm 65:12–13: *The pastures* of the wilderness *overflow,*
>   *the hills* gird themselves *with joy,*
>   *the meadows clothe themselves* with flocks,
>   *the valleys deck themselves* with grain,
>   *they shout and sing together for joy.*

---

53. For a beginning on these important questions, see Marc Bekoff, *The Emotional Lives of Animals: A Leading Scientist Explores Animal Joy, Sorrow, and Empathy—and Why They Matter* (Novato, CA: New World Library, 2007).

54. For analysis of this and related phenomena, see Terence E. Fretheim, "Nature's Praise of God in the Psalms," *Ex Auditu* 3 (1987): 16–30; and idem, *God and World*, 249–68. For iconographical evidence related to nature's praise, see Brent A. Strawn and Joel M. LeMon, "'Everything That Has Breath': Animal praise in Psalm 150:6 in the light of ancient Near Eastern iconography," in *Bilder als Quellen/Images as Sources: Studies on ancient Near Eastern artefacts and the Bible inspired by the work of Othmar Keel* (eds. S. Bickel, S. Schroer, R. Schurte, and C. Uehlinger; OBO Sonderband; Fribourg: Academic Press and Göttingen: Vandenhoeck & Ruprecht, 2007), 451–85 and Pls. XXXIII–XXXIV.

55. For a full listing of texts regarding nature's praise of God (ca. 40 total), see Fretheim, *God and World*, 267–68.

Psalm 69:34: Let *heaven and earth praise* him [i.e, God],
   the seas and everything that moves in them.

Psalm 89:5: Let the *heavens praise* your wonders, O LORD.

Psalm 89:12: [The mountains] *Tabor and Hermon joyously praise*
      your [i.e., God's] name.

Psalm 96:11–12 (=1 Chronicles 16:31–33): Let the *heavens be glad,*
      and let *the earth rejoice*;
   let *the sea roar*, and *all that fills it*;
   let *the field exult*, and *everything in it.*
   then shall *all the trees of the forest sing for joy*
   before the LORD; for he comes to judge the earth.

Psalm 98:8–9a: Let the *floods clap their hands*;
   let the *hills sing together for joy*
      at the presence of the LORD, for he is coming to judge the earth.

Psalm 100:1 (cf. 66:1; 98:4): Make a *joyful noise* to the LORD, *all the earth.*

Isaiah 32:14: The populous city . . . will become . . . the *joy of wild asses.*

Isaiah 35:1–2: The *wilderness and the dry land shall be glad,*
   the desert shall rejoice and *blossom*;
   like *the crocus* it *shall blossom abundantly,*
   and *rejoice with joy and singing.*

Isaiah 44:23: *Sing, O heavens*, for the LORD has done it;
   shout, O depths of the earth;
   break forth into singing, O mountains,
   O forest, and every tree in it!
   For the LORD has redeemed Jacob . . .

Isaiah 49:13: *Sing for joy, O heavens*, and *exult, O earth*;
   break forth, O mountains, into singing!

Isaiah 55:12: For you shall go out in joy,
   And be led back in peace;
   the mountains and the hills before you
   shall burst into song,
   and *all the trees of the field shall clap their hands.*

Jeremiah 51:48: Then *the heavens and the earth,*
   and all that is in them,
   shall shout for joy over Babylon;
   for the destroyers shall come against them out of the north.

Joel 2:21: Do not fear, *O soil*;
   be glad and rejoice, for the LORD has done great things!

Note also that in Job 39:18, 22; and 41:29 the (nonhuman!) creatures
      of God *laugh.*

A key question arises from such texts: What kind of thinking about God and about nature could have occasioned this kind of "happiness" language? In response, it might be offered that it is God's creational activity that enables these nonhuman creatures to flourish. Happiness and joy is thus a way of saying that these creatures are flourishing, which is to say that they are being what God created them to be.

Interestingly, nature's praise of God is a theme that never appears in narrative material. Found only in poetry, it is almost exclusively associated with hymnic literature (primarily Psalms and Isaiah). This genre specificity gives no little credence to the oft-suggested notion that what we have here is merely poetic fancy or license or just "highly poetic language." Or, perhaps one might say that the language of personification is obviously employed: nature is simply *represented* as a human being. But this issue is more complex than such sentiments would suggest. Consider the following judgments by Luis Stadelmann: "Certainly we have here more than a mere poetical personification of the cosmos when it is invited to rejoice";[56] Hermann Gunkel: "Such exhortation of creatures to praise of God was not simply a 'poetic figure' in Israel; the concept of nature as animate still was lodged" in human minds at that time;[57] and H. Wheeler Robinson: "objects of nature were conceived as having a psychical life of their own. . . . with [their] own psychical possibilities, and their own capacity to be indwelt or made instrumental . . . by Yahweh himself."[58] It is important at this point to remember that nonhuman creatures can really and truly communicate with other nonhuman creatures in various ways and at differing levels of depth and breadth.[59] Why then, in a theistic framework, would they not be able to communicate with God?

To be sure, natural phenomena must be of such a kind that God is able to sustain a close relationship with them. The nature of such relationships is complex and the evidence ambiguous, but the texts suggest that these creatures have a certain interiority so that more than external relationships with God are possible.

---

56. Luis I. J. Stadelmann, *The Hebrew Conception of the World* (AnBib 39; Rome: Pontifical Biblical Institute, 1970), 7.

57. Hermann Gunkel, *Die Psalmen* (5th ed.; Gottingen: Vandenhoeck & Ruprecht, 1968), 618. Quoted with approval by Delbert R. Hillers, "Study of Psalm 148," *CBQ* 40 (1978): 334.

58. H. Wheeler Robinson, *Inspiration and Revelation in the Old Testament* (Oxford: Clarendon, 1946), 12, 15–16, 47. Comparably, G. Ernest Wright, *The Old Testament Against Its Environment* (SBT 2; London: SCM, 1950), 36; Walther Eichrodt, *Theology of the Old Testament* (2 vols.; OTL; Philadelphia: Westminster, 1961), 2:152. For further discussion and possible ancient Near Eastern parallels, see Fretheim, *Word and World*, 253–55; and Strawn and LeMon, "Everything That Has Breath," 451–85.

59. How this communicating reality is related to issues of "consciousness" would be important to explore. See note 53 for the emotional lives of animals.

That is to say that the possibilities for *an internal relationship* between God and nonhuman creatures must be left open.[60] Indeed, the texts seem to require it (see, among other texts, Psalm 148).

In fact, that the joy of nonhuman creatures comes in response to what God has done for all creation gives evidence of the interresponsiveness of God and these beings. Moreover, creaturely response demonstrates that God's action in the world has to do with much more than simply human well-being; it extends to the well-being of the larger, indeed entire, environment. God's work in the world is not just about the salvation of *people*, but is also about the salvation of *the whole (human and nonhuman) world*. That human joy and nonhuman joy join each other in response to what God has done is witness again to a deeply interconnected world. And the joy of the nonhuman world is not simply over what God has done for human beings, but witnesses also to what God has done for nonhuman beings and for the larger environment of which they are a part. Seen in this way, the joy of nonhuman creatures, though independent of human beings, can nevertheless become a human vocation: how might we relate to these nonhuman creatures in such a way that the effect of our relationship is joyful for them?[61]

It is noteworthy that nature metaphors are often used for God: God is light, water, rock, fire, wind, as well as a few birds and animals—most especially the lion.[62] What might this kind of creational language for God suggest? If God is a rock or a mother eagle, for example, then rocks and mother eagles can be understood to reflect the identity of God in some sense. That is, there is a "yes," and not simply a "no," to be discerned between some aspects of these creatures and the reality of God (see, e.g., Ps 36:6; Jer 31:35–36). Such creatures reflect the reality of God in their being what they are.

Nature's praise of God and its associated joyfulness is thus to be related to and understood in light of the larger discussion about metaphors for God. In my judgment, it is basically in terms of their intrinsic rather than instrumental value that nonhuman creatures function as metaphors for the divine. In themselves and all by themselves they are capable of showing forth the strength, care, glory, faithfulness,

---

60. To speak in this way does not necessarily lead to panpsychism or vitalism, but it does suggest a greater continuity between the animate and the inanimate than many moderns have been willing to allow.

61. See further the insightful study by Ellen F. Davis, *Scripture, Culture, and Agriculture: An Agrarian Reading of the Bible* (New York: Cambridge University Press, 2009).

62. See, e.g., Brent A. Strawn, *What Is Stronger than a Lion? Leonine Image and Metaphor in the Hebrew Bible and the Ancient Near East* (OBO 212; Fribourg: Academic Press and Göttingen: Vandenhoeck & Ruprecht, 2005).

majesty, and so on, of their creator. Generally speaking, the use of natural metaphors for God opens up the entire created order (even maggots, Hos 5:12!) as a
resource for depth and variety in our God-talk. In the process, such language tem-
pers a certain anthropocentricity in our reflections about God and our discussions
of human happiness.[63]

The praise of nonhumans offers an example, even a model, for human praise.
As these creatures are what they were created to be, so human beings should offer
their joyful praise to God. Moreover, the natural order provides raw material for
human praise. Without the natural order, the praising metaphors at the disposal
of the human would be fewer in number; we would be without much praise-ful
painting, joy-filled music, and nature-inspired literature. Without these creatures, the witness of the human would not be what it has the potential of becoming. From the human side, human beings are the secretaries of nature's praise
(George Herbert), giving voice to nonhuman praise, and making its genuine happiness articulate for the use and benefit of human beings and their ethics.

6. Conclusion

In closing, the following may be said as a summary of the preceding points:

1. Happiness is characteristic of the life of God, ranging from divine well-being
   to particular experiences of joy in the course of the God-world relationship.
   Israel's God is genuinely affected by what happens in these relationships; what
   creatures say and do brings pleasure (or displeasure) to the divine life.
2. More particularly, creation is a pleasurable task for God with ongoing
   joy-filled effects for both Creator and creature. Pleasure and playfulness are
   built into the very structure of things, enabling all of life, including God's own
   life, to be what God intended it to be. God delights in the results of the divine
   creative work in and through Wisdom, and the world's future is dependent
   upon God's continuing pleasure.
3. The life of those who are created in the image of God is gifted with happiness.
   Essential to such human happiness are relationships with other human beings.
   Even more, a remarkable variety of God's good gifts in the creation have the
   capacity to generate happiness. At the same time, once gifted with happiness,
   what is done with the gift will make a difference in life.

---

63. See Strawn, *What Is Stronger*; also Hilary Marlow, *Biblical Prophets and Contemporary
Environmental Ethics: Re-Reading Amos, Hosea, and First Isaiah* (Oxford: Oxford University
Press, 2009).

4. God's work in redemption can revitalize diminished creational happiness.

5. Nonhuman creatures are imaged as engaged in the praise of God. Their happiness and joy is a way of saying that these creatures are flourishing as God's good creation and in their ongoing relationship with God and other creatures. The use of nonhuman creatures as resources for depth and variety in our God-talk has the capacity of tempering anthropocentricity in our discussions of God and human happiness.

2

Is There Happiness in the Torah?

Nathan MacDonald

1. Introduction: (Un-)Happiness in the Torah?

On first appearances the Pentateuch (Torah) seems to make for rather unpromising material for those wishing to study the human pursuit of happiness. Looking elsewhere in the Hebrew canon, the book of Psalms famously begins with the affirmation "Blessed [אשרי/ *'ašrê*] is the man who does not walk in the counsel of the ungodly,"[1] and many modern translations seek to capture the sense of the Hebrew *'ašrê* with the English translation "happy" (so NRSV).[2] The situation in the Pentateuch is quite different, however. With the exception of Leah's joyous acclamation at the birth of Asher (אשר/ *'āšēr*)—which could easily be taken as a later explanation of a traditional tribal name—the same Hebrew word, *'ašrê*, is only found as the Pentateuch approaches its final words:

> Happy are you, O Israel.
> Who is like you, a people saved by Yʜwʜ,
> your helpful shield and glorious sword?
> Your enemies will fawn before you;
> you shall trample on their backs. (Deut 33:29)

Not only are Israel's happiness and someone else's misery intermingled (and a similar thing could be said of Leah's shout of joy), but this happiness occurs right at the end of the Pentateuch so as to have almost not made it in at all. Indeed,

---

1. Translations are my own unless otherwise indicated.

2. See further the essays by William P. Brown and Ellen T. Charry in the present volume.

Moses's blessing speaks not so much of Israel's present happiness, but of its future happiness, which is anticipated by him as he speaks in prophetic mode. Happiness thus slips beyond the Pentateuch's boundary into the history that will follow in Joshua and onward. We might say, as one of my students remarked as I mentioned my assignment to write on happiness in the Pentateuch: "There's only *un-happiness* in the Pentateuch." That statement is not entirely true, but, as we will see, it nevertheless grasps something accurate of the nature of this collection of writings.

A word study of *'ašrê*, though, can only take us so far.[3] Thus, it might be objected (not unfairly) that I have omitted another word that might be rendered "happy" or something similar in English translation: the Hebrew word שׂמח/ *śāmaḥ* ("to rejoice").[4] This, together with other cognate words, provides a much more promising prospect since it occurs in a number of places and is used in a particular manner by the book of Deuteronomy. In addition, it has long been observed that, valuable as they are, word studies have various limitations.[5] This is for a whole variety of reasons, not least of which is that the lack of a word does not mean the absence of the idea. Thus, one of the most exuberant expressions of happiness in the Pentateuch, if not in the whole of the Old Testament, is to be found in the Song of the Sea following the defeat of Pharaoh and his horsemen (Exod 15:1–21) where no trace of *'ašrê* or *śāmaḥ* appears. Nevertheless, even taking into account these caveats, we should have to confess that the Pentateuch seems to offer thin soil for reflection on human happiness. Even in Exodus 15, for example, the songs of rejoicing have hardly finished reverberating before they are replaced by the sounds of grumbling (Exod 15:22–27).

To think about happiness in the Pentateuch, then, is not in the first instance an act of exegetical recovery. It is not that there is something to discover that centuries of Jewish and Christian interpretation, or even historical-critical interpretation, have obscured. We will not be able to set forth the Pentateuch's theology of happiness as we might, say, seek to understand its presentation of the Law or covenant. Instead, we are engaging a hermeneutical issue. In what ways might it be useful and enlightening to use "happiness" as a lens by which to read the Pentateuch? How might our reading of the Bible be improved, and how might our understanding of this most elusive of human ideas—happiness—be deepened in the process?

---

3. Again, see the essays by Brown and Charry in this volume.

4. See the Appendix by Michael J. Chan in this volume.

5. See, famously, James Barr, *The Semantics of Biblical Language* (London: Oxford University Press, 1961).

2. Israel and Greece

To come to the biblical texts with the question of happiness at the foremost of our minds is to bring to the text our own set of issues. This much is apparent in the title of the present volume with its reference to the "pursuit of happiness." This way of putting things has a rather obvious allusion to the United States' Declaration of Independence and is something that I, as a British scholar, perhaps inevitably feel to be a distinctively American way of expressing this human concern. That granted, in one sense such an approach and modern set of questions is not entirely inappropriate because it was around the same time that the Pentateuch was being composed that, a little further around the Mediterranean coast, Greek dramatists and philosophers were beginning to contemplate in a more systematic fashion the problem of human flourishing and the possibility of securing happiness.

To raise the question of the similarities between happiness in Greek thinkers and the Bible is to approach the Bible from the perspective of one particular way of reflecting on happiness. Although this leaves to one side the advantages that might accrue from applying, for example, the insights of the positive psychology movement, the Greek tradition is a rich one that has had a deep influence on Western thought, including Western Christian thought. It is necessary, though, to remind ourselves that when Greek thinkers reflected upon happiness they had in mind something different from what we might today mean by "happiness." Happiness for these Greek thinkers was not a subjective state, but a way of characterizing the whole of life. The happy life was a life well lived, but also a life in which external events had brought good fortune. Aristotle, one of the most significant thinkers on the question of happiness, could describe these different sides of happiness as the internal and external goods. In his *Rhetoric*, for example, he defines the constituent parts of happiness as follows: "good birth, numerous friendships, worthy friendships, wealth, good children, numerous children, a good old age, as well as the virtues of the body (such as health, beauty, strength, physical stature, athletic prowess), reputation, honor, good luck, virtue."[6] Virtue and honor jostle alongside good birth and plenty of children. This is a rich vision of the happy life, but one that raises a significant question with which many Greek thinkers wrestled. How might such a happy life be secured? Is there a good life that is not vulnerable to the slings and arrows of outrageous fortune?

Tertullian's famous question, "What has Athens to do with Jerusalem?" (*Quid ergo Athenis et Hierosolymis*), might rightly be raised here. Less than eight hundred

---

6. Aristotle, *Rhetoric*, 1.5 (1360b); the translation is from George A. Kennedy, *Aristotle: On Rhetoric: A Theory of Civic Discourse* (2nd ed.; New York: Oxford University Press, 2007), 57.

miles separate them, and yet at the time of the sixth and fifth centuries BCE there is a yawning gap between the literature to which each city gave birth. How might we account for this difference? Darrin M. McMahon suggestively draws attention to the ground upon which the frail flower of contemplating happiness first took root:

> Although it would be reductive to say that Athenian democracy was the *cause* of the emergence of happiness as a new and apparently realizable human end, it was nevertheless in Athens, democratic Athens, that individuals first put forth that great, seductive goal, daring to dream that they might pursue—and capture—happiness for themselves. Surely we must admit some connection between context and concept, between a society in which free men had grown accustomed, through rational inquiry and open deliberation, to decide matters for themselves.[7]

Certainly there was in Greece a confidence, or at least a strong desire, to overcome the capricious motions of fate and the gods and to secure in a decisive manner human happiness. The social and political environment that shaped the intellectual reflections of the Jerusalem elite was quite different. At that time, their political world was determined by the great imperial power of Persia, the successor to empires that had destroyed the independent power of the kingdoms of Israel and Judah many years before. As often observed, the pressing intellectual and political questions were how to square the catastrophic defeat of the two kingdoms with the tradition of beliefs about YHWH the national deity and how to reconstitute the people's social, political, and religious life in light of that brutal and all-encompassing reality. It is perhaps for this reason most especially that one detects more about unhappiness, or as Carol A. Newsom puts it, the Old Testament "is a prolonged meditation on the sense of flaw or brokenness that prevents human flourishing."[8] The exilic and postexilic context that was crucial to the Pentateuch's final compilation and composition draws attention to a further and related distinction from ancient Greece. Ancient Jewish beliefs were strongly corporate and were less focused on the happiness of the *individual*. The burning questions revolved around *the nation, its* failure and *its* reconstitution. In this we might detect a

---

7. Darrin M. McMahon, *Happiness: A History* (New York: Grove, 2006), 23.

8. Carol A. Newsom, oral communiation; conference on the Bible and the Pursuit of Happiness (December 2009).

contrast to later biblical texts, such as Ecclesiastes, that show a stronger influence of Hellenistic thinking.[9]

Despite these significant differences I will seek to examine the Pentateuch in light of Greek reflections about happiness. It is hardly possible to do justice to such a rich and complex text as the Pentateuch in one short essay; that granted, I will attempt to provide an overarching perspective on happiness in the Pentateuch, rather than focusing on one or two texts that may or may not be representative of the rest of the Pentateuch. As we shall see, there are points where the Pentateuch offers a not entirely dissimilar vision of human flourishing to that found among Greek thinkers, yet as we have already had reason to note there are also significant differences.

3. Aristotle's Tabernacle (The Priestly Texts)

To approach the question of happiness in the Pentateuch, I want to begin at the beginning with Genesis 1. The creation story in Genesis is widely considered to be a programmatic introduction to the priestly material specifically and to the Pentateuch more generally.[10] This rich chapter sets out a vision of the world with everything formed and ordered by God. As Jon D. Levenson observes, God acts like a priest in Genesis 1, making divisions and assigning everything to its proper place.[11] As each part of the world is ordered, God recognizes it as "good": "and God saw that it was good" (Gen 1:4, 10, 12, 18, 21, 25). At the end of creation with humanity created in the divine image, God affirms that the whole creation is "very good" (Gen 1:31). As Claus Westermann observes, this clause of affirmation is difficult to translate exactly, not least because it incorporates two related ideas:

> The procedure in itself is quite clear: a craftsman has completed a work, he looks at it and finds that it is a success or judges that it is good. The Hebrew sentence includes the "finding" or "judging" in the act of looking. He regards the work as good. The work was good "in the eyes of God," it exists as good in God's regard of acceptance. The light is good simply because

---

9. Though there is debate over the dating of Ecclesiastes, see conveniently Martin Hengel, *Judaism and Hellenism: Studies in Their Encounter in Palestine during the Early Hellenistic Period* (trans. John Bowden; Philadelphia: Fortress, 1981), 1:115–30.

10. See, e.g., S. Dean McBride, Jr., "Divine Protocol: Genesis 1:1–2:3 as Prologue to the Pentateuch," in *God Who Creates: Essays in Honor of W. Sibley Towner* (eds. William P. Brown and S. Dean McBride Jr. (Grand Rapids: Eerdmans, 2000), 3–41.

11. Jon D. Levenson, *Creation and the Persistence of Evil: The Jewish Drama of Divine Omnipotence* (2nd ed.; Princeton: Princeton University Press, 1994), 127.

God regards it as good; the light and its goodness cannot be separated from God's attentive regard.[12]

The work is good, that is, because it is good in God's eyes.[13]

The good in Genesis 1 is that which has been ordered. This includes not just the physical space of heaven and earth, but also time. Importantly, the first story of creation does not end until an account of God's resting on the seventh day is given. Although the Sabbath is not mentioned, the seventh day is set apart and hallowed. This concern with time also explains the considerable attention given to the fourth day wherein the celestial luminaries are created to order the times and seasons (Gen 1:14–19).[14]

The subsequent history of the world sees a dismantling of this structure and order. In the canonical form of the Pentateuch this begins already in Genesis 3.[15] Adam and his wife take from the tree of the knowledge of good *and evil*, moving beyond the perspective of Genesis 1. The common flourishing of humans among themselves and together with the created world more broadly disintegrates, and, prior to the Flood, the world becomes characterized by violence (Genesis 4–6). After the Flood, new boundaries are erected in an attempt to contain this tendency to violence. Humans are not to be killed and animals may only be killed if the blood is drained away (Gen 9:3–6).

In its canonical form, the Pentateuch, strongly impressed by priestly theology, sees the world to be in a distressed state. The present, that is, is a continuation of the primeval history.[16] The answer to this problem is the construction of the Tabernacle in the center of Israel's communal life and the careful fulfillment of all its attendant rules and regulations.[17] As has often been observed, the conclusion of

---

12. Claus Westermann, *Genesis 1–11* (trans. John J. Scullion; CC; Minneapolis: Augsburg, 1984), 113.

13. See further the essay by Terence E. Fretheim in this volume, also his volume *Creation Untamed: The Bible, God, and Natural Disasters* (Grand Rapids: Baker Academic, 2010).

14. Although it is very common to see the fourth day explained as a polemic against astral deities, Jan Gertz has recently shown how this is highly problematic. See his "Antibabylonische Polemik im priesterlichen Schöpfungsbericht?" *ZThK* 106 (2009): 137–55.

15. The term "canonical form" is used here simply as shorthand to distinguish the Pentateuchal text as it has been received within Judaism and Christianity from the documents and recensions that underlie it. That the term skates over a number of complexities is obvious; nevertheless, it has certain advantages.

16. See Norbert Lohfink, "The Priestly Narrative and History," in idem, *Theology of the Pentateuch: Themes of the Priestly Narrative and Deuteronomy* (trans. Linda M. Maloney; Minneapolis: Fortress, 1994), 136–72.

17. For a convenient summary, see Jacob Milgrom, *Leviticus: A Book of Ritual and Ethics* (CC; Minneapolis: Fortress, 2004).

the Tabernacle account has a number of similarities with the priestly story of creation.[18] Here the divine and priestly work of ordering by making division(s) can be continued: "You are to separate between the holy and the profane, and between the unclean and the clean" (Lev 10:10). Here, too, the ordering of time can occur with the setting apart of the seventh day (Exod 31:12–17; 35:1–3) and the celebration of the festivals (e.g., Leviticus 23; Numbers 28–29).

The Pentateuch is itself centered around the Tabernacle and centers Israel around it. In doing so it offers a return to what creation was at the beginning, God's original purpose for the world. According to this vision, doing good results in being good. That is, doing what is right by Torah, whether in cultic worship or in social relationships, results in the state that brings the divine affirmation: God saw that it was good. In the Tabernacle and in Israel, rightly observing Torah rightly orders everything and there is a way of atoning for sin.

The notion that the Pentateuch's vision of the "good" can only be fully realized in the land of Canaan, not in the wilderness, is what provides the setting and forward movement of the Pentateuch from Exodus 15 onward. This is apparent if we examine that frustratingly elusive expression "the image of God," which comes toward the end of the creation account in Genesis 1.[19] As is well known, the exact wording "image of God" is limited to Genesis 1–9; nevertheless there are other echoes of the associated language found in Gen 1:26–28 elsewhere in the early books of the Old Testament. These mark out decisive moments in Israel's story as Israel realizes part of what it means to *image* God. One turning point occurs in Exod 1:7 when Israel is "fruitful and prolific" (cf. Gen 1:22, 28; 9:1) such that Israel is a nation in waiting, although still oppressed on the banks of the Nile. A second turning point occurs at Josh 18:1 where Israel has conquered the land of Canaan, which is now said to be "subdued" (cf. Gen 1:28). It is significant that this text indicates not only that the land has been brought under Israelite control, but also that the Tabernacle has received its fixed abode at Shiloh.[20]

How did the authors of the Pentateuch imagine this vision would be realized? In a seminal essay, Norbert Lohfink raises this question in the context of

---

18. See Levenson, *Creation*, 78–99.

19. For recent studies, see J. Richard Middleton, *The Liberating Image: The* Imago Dei *in Genesis 1* (Grand Rapids: Brazos, 2005); and Brent A. Strawn, "Comparative Approaches: History, Theory, and the Image of God," in *Method Matters: Essays on the Interpretation of the Hebrew Bible in Honor of David L. Petersen* (eds. Joel M. LeMon and Kent Harold Richards; SBLRBS 56; Atlanta: Society of Biblical Literature, 2009), 117–42.

20. Cf. A. Graeme Auld, "Creation and Land: Sources and Exegesis," in idem, *Joshua Retold: Synoptic Perspectives* (OTS; Edinburgh: T & T Clark, 1998), 63–68; and Norbert Lohfink, "'Subdue the Earth?' (Genesis 1:28)," in idem, *Theology of the Pentateuch*, 1–17.

the composition of the original priestly document (P).[21] In giving so much attention to the Tabernacle, is P offering a perspective on what Israel might be, or what it actually is? Is the priestly writer offering us a utopian vision composed in exile or a portrayal of the postexilic community in Yehud?

It seems to me that Lohfink's contrast of utopia versus reflection obscures other possibilities.[22] In particular, the Pentateuch's description of the Tabernacle is projected into Israel's distant past in such a way that it looks strongly realistic, but not easily or obviously realizable. Thus, a portable shrine with twelve tribes assembled around it, three on each side, fits the literary context of Exodus to Numbers well, but it is not clear how this would be practicable in Yehud. In other words, *contra* Lohfink, the text is not transparent to a postexilic context. The biblical text requires close engagement—that is, interpretation—and a form of analogical reasoning in order to determine what realizing it might entail for Jews who are in exile or have returned to Persian Yehud.

Whatever the case, the idea of the "good"—Israel becoming what humanity was created to be—may be fruitfully compared to Aristotle's view of the world. For Aristotle everything has some *telos*, some intended purpose. "Every art and every inquiry, and similarly every action as well as choice, is held to aim at some good."[23] The purpose of an acorn is to become an oak, the ship to sail. Everything has its purpose, its good. But what of the purpose of human beings? Their special end is happiness, which "is a certain activity of soul in accord with complete virtue."[24] This would seem to be not so very far from what we have been exploring in the Pentateuch, though there are also significant differences. First, obedience to Torah stands in place of Aristotle's virtue. The end of Israel in the Pentateuch is to restore order to the world through the construction of the Tabernacle and careful obedience of the Pentateuch's laws (both of which must ultimately take place in the land). In this sense, the initial verses of Psalms 1 and 119 offer Aristotelian readings of the law when they connect obedience of Torah with blessedness or happiness.[25] Second, individual pleasure or feelings of happiness, which are not excluded in Aristotle's

---

21. Lohfink, "Priestly Narrative."

22. For a similar contrast in relation to the Covenant Code and arguments against it, see Bernard Jackson, *Wisdom Laws: A Study of the Mishpatim of Exodus 21:1–22:16* (Oxford: Oxford University Press, 2006), 3–4.

23. Aristotle, *Nicomachean Ethics*, 1.1 (1094a); translation from Robert C. Bartlett and Susan D. Collins, *Aristotle's Nicomachean Ethics* (Chicago: University of Chicago, 2011), 1.

24. Aristotle, *Nicomachean Ethics*, 1.13 (1102a); Bartlett and Collins, *Aristotle's Nicomachean Ethics*, 23.

25. See Brown's essay in the present volume.

account, are far from apparent in the pentateuchal material we have examined. Indeed, the priestly laws can sometimes be intent on overruling the emotions. Thus, Aaron is forbidden to mourn after the death of Eleazar and Ithamar (Leviticus 10).

Now, Aristotle's account of happiness is not focused only on virtue, but also on those elements that were commonly taken to constitute the happy life. As we have seen, Aristotle defines the constituent parts of happiness in *Rhetoric*, 1.5 (cited above). Although the Pentateuch offers almost no overlap with the list of bodily excellences and little with the final list of "reputation, honor, good luck, [and] virtue," it shares much with the first part of the list. The fact that the "image of God" is realized in fruitfulness and in living in the Promised Land is ample evidence that mundane realities are not excluded from the Pentateuch's vision of the good. They are, in fact, rather fully treated in material that we have to this point passed over—namely, the patriarchal (and, indeed, matriarchal) material in Genesis.[26]

4. The Good Life and the Virtuous Life (Genesis 12–50)

The presentation of the lives of the ancestors is found in Genesis 12–50. It is rather distinctive material in many respects. Chronologically, it is set historically in the time before there was an Israelite people and, consequently, before there was an Israelite religion. When read together with the rest of the Pentateuch—or the rest of the Old Testament—it demands that its readers work with imaginative analogies. One cannot simply read in a transparent manner from the patriarch's experiences to those of later Israel. Nowhere is this more apparent than in the case of the call that Abraham sacrifice his only son.[27]

Because they are in some sense "pre-Israel," the patriarchal texts are rather unique in portraying ordinary life, especially family life.[28] The structures and concerns of

---

26. Scholars have traditionally referred to this material as the "patriarchal narratives." The briefest acquaintance with the book of Genesis is enough to confirm that they have much to say about the matriarchs. Nevertheless, biblical texts frequently refer to the ancestors as "the fathers" (e.g., Deut 1:8) or as "Abraham, Isaac and Jacob." The traditional scholarly nomenclature thus reflects the text's own patriarchal assumptions. Nevertheless, our present concern with happiness is to bring a different set of concerns to the biblical text: the happiness of both men *and* women. Again, the latter is not unknown in these texts: see, e.g., Gen 18:12; 21:1–7.

27. For a recent treatment, see R. W. L. Moberly, *The Theology of the Book of Genesis* (OTT; Cambridge: Cambridge University Press, 2009), 179–99.

28. They are not entirely unique, of course, since the book of Ruth also portrays ordinary life. This raises the question, though, of the exact relationship that Ruth has to the patriarchal texts. That is, we may wonder whether Ruth is composed in imitation of Genesis 12–50. For the early dating of Ruth, see Edward F. Campbell, *Ruth: A New Translation with Introduction, Notes, and Commentary* (AB 7; New York: Doubleday, 1975).

nation, kingship, and cult, which so dominate Joshua through 2 Kings, are conspicuously absent. Even when they might be expected, Genesis 12–50 seems to studi-
ously avoid them, such that one could almost get the impression, with the exception
of one or two chapters, that the land of Canaan of the patriarch's day was an empty
space, entirely devoid of social and political structures. This, then, is *ordinary* family
life. Yet, despite that admission, it is not just *ordinary* because in these stories God
frequently, even casually, appears giving promises and making covenants with the
ancestors.

We might note, first, that happiness does literally appear in these ancestral
accounts. When Leah's maidservant Zilpah equals Rachel's maidservant Bilhah
in bearing Jacob two sons, Leah declares herself happy and names the child Asher.
This appearance of "happy," though rare, is representative because the good and
happy life in Genesis 12–50 would seem to focus especially around the family.[29]
As R. Norman Whybray observed, "the importance of family life is particularly
stressed in the history of Abraham and his family."[30] When Abraham is called by
Yʜᴡʜ, he is promised that he will become a great nation (Gen 12:2). As the story
progresses this becomes one of the central themes, for it all turns on the question
of whether he and his wife will have a child. The desire for children and the threat
to them is a scarlet thread running throughout the patriarchal stories—the promise of a son to Abraham and Sarah, the near-sacrifice of Isaac, the departures of
Esau and Jacob, the desires of Jacob's wives for children, the loss of Joseph.

There are other elements to the patriarchal stories that should also be mentioned. God promises to Abraham that he will be blessed and his name will be
great (Gen 12:2). This is impressively realized in Genesis 12–14 as Abraham finds
himself becoming extremely wealthy—albeit at Pharaoh's expense—and respected
and honored by others. The story of Jacob finds him prospering in the east—albeit
at Laban's expense. In the Joseph story, the favored son is eventually elevated to
the highest position in Egypt below Pharaoh—albeit at his brothers' expense.
However, despite the ancestors' wealth, there is one aspect of the flourishing life
that is not realized for them in Genesis: the possession of property. The importance of property is hinted at already in the promise to Abraham that if he leaves
his ancestral land and goes to the land that God will show him he will become a
great nation (Gen 12:1–2). Nationhood implies land as later elaborations of the
promise make clear (see, e.g., Gen 13:14–17; 15:7, 18–21; 17:8; 26:3–4; 28:4, 13–14;
35:12; 48:4). For the ancestors—as indeed for the Pentateuch—however, this is
always beyond the horizon. Finally, whether a life could be judged good or not

---

29. See David L. Petersen, "Genesis and Family Values," *JBL* 124 (2005): 5–23.

30. R. Norman Whybray, *The Good Life in the Old Testament* (London: T & T Clark, 2002), 15.

could only be ascertained at the very end. Abraham, Isaac, Jacob, and Joseph die "old and full of years," with their family around (see Gen 25:8; 35:29; 49:33; 50:26). The family is crucial not only because they represent the progeny that is so important to Genesis' view of the good life, but also because death is when one moves from one sphere of family life to another: from the descendants with which one's been blessed to the ancestors who preceded one into the afterlife.[31]

The good life that Genesis envisages maps well to the good life as perceived by many in ancient Greece and incorporated into Aristotle's vision of happiness:

> Let happiness be [defined as] success [*eupraxia*] combined with virtue, or as self-sufficiency [*autarkeia*] in life, or as the pleasantest life accompanied with security, or as abundance of possessions and bodies, with the ability to defend and use these things; for all people agree that happiness is pretty much one or more of these.[32]

The patriarchs, with their rich households, fit this vision of the good life well. They also exemplify the components of Aristotle's good life: "good birth, plenty of friends, wealth, good children, plenty of children, a happy old age." The very nature of these blessings means it is only possible to judge a life to be "happy" at its very end. Here, Aristotle and Genesis agree. Where they would differ is the question of whether that can be determined beforehand. In Aristotle's account of the happy life, good luck, εὐτυχία/*eutuchia*, has an important role; in Genesis luck plays no role.[33] Instead, behind the patriarchal lives is God who as the creator can promise and bestow blessings. As Whybray observes concerning the different components of the good life in Genesis: "all these things are presented as due to the benevolent care of God, without whom there would have been no good life, or indeed any life at all."[34]

---

31. See the essay by Herbert Chanan Brichto, "Kin, Cult, Land and Afterlife—A Biblical Complex," *HUCA* 44 (1973): 1–54, esp. this summary: "We believe that the evidence deduced from earliest Israelite sources through texts as late as the exilic prophets testifies overwhelmingly to a belief on the part of biblical Israel in an afterlife, an afterlife in which the dead, though apparently deprived of material substance, retain such personality characteristics as form, memory, consciousness and even knowledge of what happens to their descendants in the land of the living. They remain very much concerned about the fortunes of their descendants, for they are dependent on them, on their continued existence on the family land, on their performance of memorial rites, for a felicitous condition in the afterlife" (48).

32. Aristotle, *Rhetoric*, 1.5 (1360b); Kennedy, *Aristotle: On Rhetoric*, 57.

33. Note, e.g., the famous testimony to God's providence by Joseph in Gen 50:20.

34. Whybray, *Good Life*, 25.

The problem that Genesis's construal of the good life raises is that of the relationship between virtue and happiness. In the Greek dramatic and philosophical tradition, virtue, happiness, and luck coexist in an uneasy relationship with one another. The quests of the different philosophical schools can be seen as attempts to bind happiness strongly to virtue, all the while loosening the grip of luck. Whether their philosophical programs successfully achieved this is a matter of continued debate.[35] The monotheistic setting of Genesis is quite different, but raises its own acute set of problems.

As those who lived before the giving of Torah at Sinai, the patriarchs fail to fit easily into later Israelite models of virtue.[36] The good life, it would seem, does not necessarily come to those who *are* or *do* good. But neither is it merely a matter of chance. While the ancestors appear vulnerable to some elements of chance—for example, the failure of Abraham and Sarah to beget a child prior to Isaac's miraculous birth—their stories are now overwhelmingly set within the context of promise. Yes, this promise is, as David J. A. Clines reminds us, partly fulfilled and, therefore, partly unfulfilled;[37] nevertheless, the ancestors flourish under the covenant. They come to their end full of years and, however torturous it may have been to get there, with children and grandchildren surrounding them. Thus, the fragility of life, the often arbitrary motions of τύχη/tyche, "luck," and the possibility of hedging oneself against misfortune through virtue are nowhere in evidence as they are among the Greek philosophers and tragedians. The subsequent and unarticulated question, of course, is how this bears on those whose lives do not so directly touch upon the continuation of the covenant or who do not live under the security of the divine promise—that is, those who are not the blessed ancestors themselves. The question is only raised beyond the Pentateuch's borders, but interestingly when it is raised it is done so in patriarchal dress. Job, for instance, looks very much like a contemporary of Abraham, Isaac, and Jacob, as was well appreciated by earlier commentators who dated the book of Job to the same time period as the ancestors. But Job does not live under the divine covenant, for he dwells in the land of Uz. It is thus the book of Job, not Genesis, that raises the question of the virtuous man, to whom God is not beholden by promise. Ultimately, even Job does not resolve the problem, but pushes it back into the territory of Genesis 1–11—back to the hidden wisdom of God at creation (cf. Job 28; 38–41).

---

35. See, e.g., Martha C. Nussbaum, *The Fragility of Goodness: Luck and Ethics in Greek Tragedy and Philosophy* (rev. ed.; Cambridge: Cambridge University Press, 2001).

36. See the study by R. W. L. Moberly, *The Old Testament of the Old Testament: Patriarchal Narratives and Mosaic Yahwism* (OBT; Minneapolis: Fortress, 1992).

37. David J. A. Clines, *The Theme of the Pentateuch* (2nd ed; Sheffield: Sheffield Academic Press, 1997).

5. Dependence of Life (Deuteronomy)

The patriarchs fit well Aristotle's definition of happiness as "independence of life" (αὐτάρκεια τῆς ζωῆς/*autarkeia tēs zōēs*). They wander freely around Canaan, rarely touching upon the lives of others. As the narrative progresses, the family of Abraham, Isaac, and Jacob are separated from the families of Lot, Ishmael, and Esau, all of whom find their home beyond the boundaries of the Promised Land. This is why Balaam saw Israel as a "people living alone, and not reckoning itself among the nations" (Num 23:9). This might well be an attractive vision of the happy life, especially for some in the Western world, but it would be a narrow one that failed to do justice to the entirety of the Pentateuch. It would be to embrace a version of happiness that is, in the words of Aleksandr Solzhenitsyn's Shulabin, the idol of the marketplace.[38] As an alternative, Deuteronomy points us to Israel's communal life, in particular communal meals.

In Deuteronomy, happiness is not so much described as demanded. Repeatedly, the book deploys the verb *śāmaḥ*, "to rejoice," to describe the kind of response that the Israelites should exhibit at their communal celebratory meals.[39] "You shall eat there before YHWH, your God, and you and your households shall rejoice in all the undertakings in which YHWH, your God, has blessed you" (Deut 12:7; cf. 12:12, 18; 14:26; 16:11, 14, 15; 26:11; 27:7). The demand to rejoice is strange to our ears, but is not unusual in Deuteronomy, which constantly intertwines new versions of traditional commandments (cf. Exodus 20–23) with exhortation and is deeply concerned for an inward disposition that matches outward obedience. As the book's literary context suggests, this is not just Moses's bequeathing the divine law, but is also a valedictory sermon.

These communal celebrations take place on three significant axes: *vertically*, they take place before YHWH; *horizontally*, they are communal events; and *chronologically*, they link present celebration to past salvation. First, the communal meal is to take place "before YHWH." A key component of Deuteronomy's message is that worship is only to take place at the sanctuary chosen by YHWH. In this context, "before YHWH" is the briefest way of indicating that this feast is to take place at this chosen sanctuary and not at home or at another illicit sanctuary. It is more than that, however, because the "rejoicing" is directed to YHWH. The feast is the occasion to offer some agricultural produce to YHWH (Deut 26:1–11), for it is only because of YHWH's past acts of salvation and continued

---

38. Aleksandr Solzhenitsyn, *Cancer Ward* (New York: Noonday, 2001), 447.

39. The connection is so close in Deuteronomy that the book often indicates the celebration of a communal meal simply with the verb "to rejoice."

blessing of the land in the present that the Israelites have a harvest to eat. Indeed, in Deuteronomy the characteristic form of cultic worship is the celebratory meal.[40]

Second, the meal is a communal event. The book of Deuteronomy is composed for male Israelites who have land and a household. Their celebration of the harvest is to include not only their households, but also the disenfranchised poor in Israel, such as the Levites, the widows, and the orphans. The communal aspect is further underlined by the address of the book to "Israel," rather than to individuals. It is *all of Israel* that is to assemble at the chosen sanctuary during the festivals and together celebrate the goodness of YHWH. The book acknowledges no distinctions among the descendants of Jacob.

Third, the meals are a means of structuring memory of the past. Deuteronomy anticipates a time of rejoicing in "the land flowing with milk and honey." The book itself is set at a liminal point just outside the Promised Land. From this perspective, the landless past stretches backwards and the landed future forwards. The feasts themselves celebrate this transformation. At the beginning of the year, during the combined feast of Passover-Unleavened Bread, the Israelites eat the "bread of affliction" (Deut 16:3). In the harvest feasts of Weeks and Tabernacles, however, they celebrate with feasting and rejoicing (Deut 16:10–15).[41]

Similar to what we saw in the ancestral narratives of Genesis 12–50, Deuteronomy's vision of the happy life is one of happiness in and through the physical world gifted by God. Happiness is found in the mundane realities of life—the food one has produced, family, communal life—enjoyed under the beneficent gaze of a deity whose generosity must be acknowledged. Here the Reformed tradition of Protestant Christianity could find much inspiration for its vision of the "sanctification of ordinary life"[42] as well as the central importance of rejoicing within the Christian life.[43]

---

40. It is often observed that the Deuteronomic cult is surprisingly sparse. Worship takes place at the chosen sanctuary and there is little evidence of the usual cultic apparatus known from other texts in the Bible or from elsewhere in the ancient Near East. Indeed, according to Deuteronomy 12, much of the familiar cultic apparatus is prohibited. Worship is focused instead around these communal meals. It is thus difficult to determine whether Deuteronomy might presuppose other cultic realities. Possibly not, since its vision of Israelite life appears to be intended as unified and comprehensive.

41. For detailed discussion, see Nathan MacDonald, *Not Bread Alone: The Uses of Food in the Old Testament* (Oxford: Oxford University Press, 2008), 70–99.

42. See Charles Taylor, *Sources of the Self: The Making of the Modern Identity* (Cambridge, MA: Harvard University Press, 1992), 226.

43. See, e.g., the discussion of John Calvin in Ellen T. Charry, *God and the Art of Happiness* (Grand Rapids: Eerdmans, 2010), 114–17.

In Deuteronomy's vision of the happy life there is a direct connection between virtue and happiness secured by the covenant. If Israel obeys Torah, it will be blessed by YHWH in all it does (Deut 28:1–14). Israel will enjoy agricultural prosperity, large families, and international repute. This direct relationship between virtue and happiness is particularly apparent on a national level. On an individual level luck seems to play some role, although Deuteronomy is not entirely consistent on this question. According to Deut 15:4 "there will be no one in need among you," while Deut 15:7 enjoins generosity to those who are poor and needy. It seems that the vicissitudes of fortune may bring some into poverty, but the communal meals and communal generosity are the answer to this problem. Thus, Deuteronomy offers a vision of the dependence of some on others for their happiness—of the physical sort at any rate—not "independence of life."

6. "We Few, We Happy Few"?

In Deuteronomy and the ancestral material we encounter the problem of the limits of happiness. Happiness, it seems, is a zero-sum game: there are winners and there are losers. Happiness in the ancestral narratives is often at someone else's expense, or so it seems to the human actors. Leah's exclamation is something of a paradigm: her happiness comes at Rachel's expense (Gen 30:13). The patriarchal blessing—closely related to the good and the happy life—seems limited in its application. It is for Isaac not Ishmael, for Jacob not Esau, for Ephraim not Manasseh. In this world, Esau's anguished cry is, indeed, great and bitter: "Have you not reserved a blessing for me?...Have you only *one* blessing?" (Gen 27:36, 38). This is part of the dynamic of election, it seems, and is also reflected in Deuteronomy in different ways. The land of Canaan offers no end of blessings to the Israelites, but they receive it only once it is wrested from the grasp of the Canaanites, who must be finished off in full fashion (see, e.g., Deut 7:1–6). Here, as in Genesis, God seems to collude with preferential treatment.

But to stop there would be to give only one side of the issue, and not the most important one. In point of fact, the reality of happiness' distribution in the Pentateuch is complicated. In particular, the world seems large enough for all peoples. Thus, in Genesis there is little hint of Israel's latter conquest of the land; Lot and Abraham go their separate ways; Ishmael is blessed; Esau possesses Seir; and Jacob has twelve sons, not just Joseph and Benjamin. Similarly, in Deuteronomy there are God's "other stories," the stories of Edom and Ammon, which are hinted at in Deuteronomy 2–3, but receive little further reflection.[44] Nor should we forget the

---

44. See Patrick D. Miller, "God's Other Stories: On the Margins of Deuteronomic Theology," in *Realia Dei: Essays in Archaeology and Biblical Interpretation in Honor of Edward F. Campbell Jr. at His Retirement* (eds. Prescott H. Williams, Jr. and Theodore Hiebert; Atlanta: Scholars

vision of Israel centered around the Tabernacle. Exodus 25–Numbers 10 shows little concern for the wider world, but seen in the context of the whole of the Pentateuch, the Tabernacle has the purpose of bringing not just Israel, but the whole cosmos, into a state of orderly relations. What is good for Israel is thus good for the world.[45]

This more generous account of the divine election is not a minor theme, but is integral to how the Pentateuch envisions God's relationship to Israel and the nations. The promise to Abraham in Gen 12:1–3 has long been recognized as a key account of these relationships, occurring as it does at a significant canonical location—the beginning of the patriarchal narratives. Although the final clause in 12:3 is probably best understood as the nations using the name of Abraham as a blessing, rather than being passive recipients of a blessing,[46] the promise to Abraham nevertheless does highlight the divine propensity to blessing. The nations can also participate in blessing through their response to the elect; the alternative response of despising Abraham and his descendants and being subject to the curse is clearly viewed as the exception.[47] The Pentateuch never envisages Israel's election being eviscerated, and its elect status is a privilege that others do not share. Even so, within this account of God's differentiated relationships to the nations of the world, blessing or happiness is the dominant note. Thus, the human perspectives, whether from Jacob or Esau, Leah or Rachel, do not adequately capture or reflect the extent of generosity of the divine promise.

7. Conclusion: The Rest of/beyond the Pentateuch

In our study of happiness in the Pentateuch we have again and again bumped up against the artificial boundary that is key to the Pentateuch as a discrete collection. And yet the Pentateuch does not have a satisfactory end. Instead, it is open-ended, embracing a future not yet realized. This is apparent in the different

Press, 1999), 185–94, reprinted in idem, *Israelite Religion and Biblical Theology: Collected Essays* (JSOTSup 267; Sheffield: Sheffield Academic Press, 2000), 593–602; also Brent A. Strawn, "Deuteronomy," in *Theological Bible Commentary* (eds. Gail R. O'Day and David L. Petersen; Louisville: Westminster John Knox, 2009), 66–67.

45. For intelligent and perceptive accounts of election in the Pentateuch, see Joel Kaminsky, *Yet I Loved Jacob: Reclaiming the Biblical Concept of Election* (Nashville: Abingdon, 2007); and Joel N. Lohr, *Chosen and Unchosen: Conceptions of Election in the Pentateuch and Jewish-Christian Interpretation* (Siphrut 2; Winona Lake: Eisenbrauns, 2009).

46. See Moberly, *The Theology of the Book of Genesis*, 141–61.

47. See discussion in Patrick D. Miller, "Syntax and Theology in Genesis XII 3a," *VT* 34 (1984): 472–76; reprinted in idem, *Israelite Religion and Biblical Theology*, 492–96.

but complementary visions of the good and the happy that we have examined. Ellen T. Charry rightly observes that "[a]ncient philosophies of happiness are teleological: life reaches toward an achievable goal,"[48] and this is no less true of those found in the Pentateuch. The ordered creation, the land flowing with milk and honey, the communal meal, the Tabernacle established in the land—fulfillment of all of these lies behind the Pentateuch's boundary.

In my judgment, what unites these different visions of happiness in the Torah is a *sense of rest*, which is where the good creation of Genesis 1 originally concluded on the seventh day, before its disruption in the chapters that follow. What we find otherwise is a sense of restlessness. Thus, if there is anything that summarizes the Pentateuch's vision of the good and happy life it is rest. Rest at the end of a life well lived, rest together at the communal meal at the end of the harvest, rest in the Promised Land.[49]

I have already indicated my unhappiness with Lohfink's arguments that the priestly writer has a utopian vision that reflects the fact that he writes during the exile. The Pentateuch is projected into the past, but opens into a future that includes its readers. The past insists on being realized, but how that is to take place is unclear. In particular, the open-ended vision of the Pentateuch means that Israel is *not there yet*. Thus, the readers find themselves in a time-between-the-times; they are between the "very good" world of Genesis 1 and the vision of the reordered creation. They are *on the way* to rest.

It was early Christian readers' receptiveness to the Pentateuch's vision of the good and happy life that caused them to see in the Pentateuch's images signs of the heavenly rest (see Hebrews 4). It was only at this point that creation was going to be rightly ordered as a new heaven and new earth, only here that all humanity would feast together around a table flowing with milk and honey, only here that the true Tabernacle was to be found. For later Christian faith, as also for the Pentateuch, true happiness is always one step ahead in God's future. "So then, a Sabbath rest still remains for the people of God" (Heb 4:9; NRSV).

---

48. Charry, *God and the Art of Happiness*, 3.

49. This might be compared fruitfully with the notion of *katastematic* pleasure—pleasure that comes from lack of disturbance of the soul—as found in Epicurianism, or with aspects of neo-Platonism. Both ideas were to be taken up by Augustine, through whom they influenced western Christian thinking (Charry, *God and the Art of Happiness*, esp. 25–62). Cf. the famous opening line to Augustine's *Confessions*: "our heart is restless until it rests in you" (1.1; translation from Henry Chadwick, *Saint Augustine: Confessions* [Oxford: Oxford University Press, 1991], 3).

3

A Happy Blend

ISAIAH'S VISION OF HAPPINESS (AND BEYOND)

Jacqueline Lapsley

*The reason you haven't felt [love] is because it doesn't exist.
What you call love was invented by guys like me, to sell nylons.
You're born alone and you die alone and this world just drops
a bunch of rules on top of you to make you forget those facts.
But I never forget. I'm living like there's no tomorrow, because
there isn't one.*[1]

1. Introducing Happiness in Isaiah

In his book *Happiness: A History*, Darrin M. McMahon, after surveying Socrates, Plato, and Aristotle, but before he tackles the New Testament, briefly discusses the way "happiness" appears in the Hebrew Scriptures. Not surprisingly, he arrives at a necessarily very general overview of what happiness means in the Hebrew Bible by examining occurrences of the Hebrew root אשׁר/ *'šr* ("happy, blessed"). From this, McMahon tells us that the Psalms have much to say about what makes a person or nation happy (e.g., Ps 40:4: "Happy are those who make YHWH their trust"), and that Proverbs, too, has much to contribute to our understanding of happiness (e.g., Prov 14:21: "Happy are those who are kind to the poor").[2]

---

1. Don Draper, advertising executive, in episode one, season one of AMC's *Mad Men*.

2. See Darrin M. McMahon, *Happiness: A History* (New York: Grove, 2006), esp. 77–81. For the Psalms and Proverbs, see the chapters by William P. Brown and Carol A. Newsom in this volume, and, further, the contribution of Ellen T. Charry as well as her larger work, *God and the Art of Happiness* (Grand Rapids: Eerdmans, 2010). Biblical translations are my own.

By this measure, however, the prophets have next to nothing to say about happiness because *'šr*, when bearing connotations of happiness, occurs only five times in the entire prophetic corpus.[3] Indeed, this relative lack of "happiness" language would seem to confirm for many—including many biblical scholars—that the prophets were not only profoundly unhappy themselves (!), but also out to make others equally unhappy! The prophetic view thus seems more in line with Eric G. Wilson's rebuttal of the now trendy pursuit of happiness: Wilson argues that there is something seriously wrong with relentless efforts to be happy in a world so full of sorrow.[4]

How then to proceed? One could work backwards, inferring conceptions of happiness from what is implied in the outpourings of prophetic unhappiness, and indeed such an approach could prove quite fruitful. One might justly infer from the prophets' fulsome denunciations of behaviors that violate God's instruction or Torah (broadly understood), for example, that they believe happiness inheres in participation in a community centered on Torah.[5] That granted, we might nevertheless hope for a more detailed and nuanced picture. So a further possibility would be to examine some of the eschatological prophetic visions because, though they are designed to give us a glimpse of the future, and in some cases what we might even call future "happiness," they may well tell us as much about a prophetic understanding of happiness in the present, were that possible under the prevailing historical circumstances.[6]

For several reasons, the book of Isaiah is a promising place to start such an endeavor. First, there are several eschatological visions that promise a blessed, albeit distant, future in the book, and second, a constellation of words that cluster around the general theme of happiness ($\sqrt{}$ *'šr*, $\sqrt{}$ *śmḥ*, $\sqrt{}$ *ṭwb*, $\sqrt{}$ *'ng*, $\sqrt{}$ *šlm*, $\sqrt{}$ *š''*, $\sqrt{}$ *śwś*, $\sqrt{}$ *gyl*, $\sqrt{}$ *ḥpṣ*, $\sqrt{}$ *rnn*)[7] occur plentifully throughout the book as a whole (and especially in the eschatological texts), thus providing the vocabulary for a thicker description of happiness than we might get if we restricted ourselves to one vision

---

3. Isa 30:18; 32:20; 56:2; Mal 3:12, 15. I will return to some of these occurrences below. For further lexical information, see the Appendix by Michael J. Chan in the present volume.

4. Eric G. Wilson, *Against Happiness: In Praise of Melancholy* (New York: Farrar, Straus, and Giroux, 2009).

5. See the essay by Nathan MacDonald in the present volume.

6. For more on happiness in eschatological and apocalyptic modes, see the essay by Greg Carey in the present volume.

7. These terms are discussed and defined below. For more on these, and the many others that belong to the Bible's "lexicon of happiness," see also the Appendix by Michael J. Chan in the present volume.

alone, or if we turned to the other prophets more reticent to employ the idioms of happiness. While there are surely differences of meaning among these various terms, I will only be concerned with such nuances insofar as they affect Isaiah's understanding of happiness; indeed, in many cases the semantic overlap among these words is significant. Then too some texts express something we might call "happiness" without employing any of this vocabulary.

Taking the book of Isaiah as a whole as the object of analysis in this investigation is justified by its overall thematic and theological coherence, although, to be sure some attention to the different historical circumstances underlying the major sections of the book will have to be paid in order to avoid too flat and homogenous a picture. So, while there are other ways of proceeding, I propose here to examine the eschatological vision in Isa 65:17–25 for its implied understanding of happiness, with considerable reference to the ways other passages in Isaiah further illumine what we might tentatively consider an "Isaianic vision of happiness."[8]

These days it is nearly de rigueur among those happy scholars who, from a wide variety of disciplines, write on happiness, to grant at least a passing nod to Aristotle, who articulated a particularly potent vision of happiness, which is now a touchstone of the discussion. It is appropriate to do the same here, at least to the extent that Aristotle's account is relevant to our purposes. Aristotle argues that happiness entails both the practice of virtue through the exercise of reason and external goods (friends, family, wealth, good birth, etc.). Aristotle's vision is thus *eudaimonic* (oriented to long-term flourishing based on what is truly worthwhile) as opposed to *hedonic* (oriented to pleasure and present experience). While Isaiah is a long way from Aristotle in nearly every way, some elements in the prophetic vision brush up against what Aristotle articulates—for example, happiness is exercised through a virtuous life (for the prophets, a life lived in obedience to Torah), and is thus fundamentally eudaimonic in character.[9] While obviously alien to the biblical material, the vocabulary of eudaimonic/hedonic is heuristically useful in thinking about Isaiah's vision of happiness.

So, what does Isaiah say about happiness? The simplest thing to say is that happiness for Isaiah is grounded in God. Several implications unfold from this basic premise. First, Israel's happiness is predicated on YHWH's happiness—that

---

8. Some have explored the connections between Isa 65:17–25 and Genesis 1–3 (the snake eating the dust in Isa 65:25, etc.). See, e.g., Odil Hannes Steck, "Der neue Himmel und die neue Erde: Beobachtungen zur Rezeption von Gen 1–3 in Jes 65, 16b–25," in *Studies in the Book of Isaiah: Festschrift Willem A. M. Beuken* (eds. J. van Ruiten, M. Vervenne; BETL 132; Leuven: Leuven University Press, 1997), 349–65.

9. For both Aristotle and the prophets, happiness is an *activity*, the exercise of a virtuous life, not a state of being.

is, humanity shares in and imitates the divine joy.[10] Second, happiness means living a life centered on YHWH, in obedience to YHWH's Torah, in a Torah-centered community with YHWH's people. To live in this way, oriented and faithful to God and embedded in the covenantal community, is to flourish and so, be happy. Again, in Aristotelian categories, happiness for Isaiah is fundamentally eudaimonic. But I will also argue that Isaiah's understanding of happiness blurs the line between eudaimonic and hedonic, folding significant elements of the hedonic into what is predominantly a eudaimonic vision. Or, to put it in different words, for Isaiah, true human flourishing is not possible without the consistent pleasure of a good meal and a fine glass of wine. Yet practicing happiness is not easy, and certainly not in Third Isaiah (Isaiah 56–66), the context for the final eschatological vision of 65:17–25. One complication stressed in Third Isaiah but also widely present in the prophetic corpus is that happiness involves *choice*: you decide whether to align yourself with YHWH. And, even after having made this crucial choice, you are *not* guaranteed a hedonically happy present since the conditions of being in a community centered on YHWH are not easily controlled. That is to say that Third Isaiah offers a *promise* of *future* happiness, the hope of which, in turn, partially constitutes present happiness.

Even as I describe below how Isaiah blends hedonic and eudaimonic dimensions of happiness, I want to press the implications of this vision in two different directions:

1. First, the vision of happiness that Isaiah offers (and I daresay this might well be true for most of the Hebrew Scriptures) resists an (over)emphasis on selflessness, the pouring out of oneself for others, which is so apparent in some strains of Christian ethics and which is derived in turn from selected New Testament traditions. As we shall see, Isaiah understands the good of the self and the other as inextricably bound together: my well-being, my happiness, is partly determined by the happiness of others, and vice versa. So if the well-being of others in the community is significantly diminished, then my own well-being is also of necessity diminished. But the opposite is equally true: if my own happiness is diminished, the happiness of the larger community is also at risk. Indeed, the idea that God wants us to be "happy" at all is in some tension with certain Christian emphases on self-denial as the greatest virtue in Christian life.

2. The second direction that Isaiah's vision forces us to consider relates to the epigraph used at the start of this chapter. Don Draper, the advertising executive

---

10. See the essay by Terence E. Fretheim in the present volume.

from the television drama *Mad Men*, offers an extreme example of an attitude prevalent, if often unconscious, in our culture: the idea that ultimate meaning, happiness, even love, are fabricated, that they are mechanisms to cope with a world devoid of meaning, or are deceptions used to sell things, or both. If Isaiah's vision resists an overemphasis on self-denial, it equally resists the pure nihilism of Draper, but also the quasi-nihilism that undergirds so much of our cultural practice. Happiness in Isaiah is neither the altruistic emptying of the self for others (as in some versions of Christian ethics), nor the pouring out of others for the self (as in Don Draper's philosophy and business practice). Rather, it offers a vision of the self deeply and meaningfully connected with other selves, living in a community marked by profound relationship to God and to one another.

2. Isaiah's Vision of Happiness

Now to the specific nuts and bolts of happiness in Isaiah: in both the book as a whole, and in the vision of Isa 65:17–25, we see true happiness as comprised of four key elements:

1. a life of intimate, harmonious relationship with God;
2. a secure, prosperous, and joyous home life, including robust eating and drinking;
3. a peaceful and just community in which to live; and
4. hope for the future (preservation in the memory of those to come after).

To be sure, we could understand this vision of happiness as merely the flipside of the very difficult conditions prevailing in the postexilic community, which was marked by scarcity, fear, and the like. Yet this would surely be too reductionist because these four elements appear not only in the eschatological vision in 65:17–25, but also elsewhere throughout the book—not all of which stem from those same dire sociohistorical circumstances. In the rest of this study, I will take up these features in turn, and, at the end, briefly contemplate to what extent we may consider Isaiah's vision of happiness as representative of a prophetic vision more generally.

Before turning to the four elements just named, however, a few comments are in order to address (a) two aspects of the vision in 65:17–25 that do *not* appear elsewhere in Isaiah, as well as (b) one important theme found elsewhere in the book that does not appear in the vision. The two aspects that are significant for the vision, but not found explicitly elsewhere in the book, are the importance of meaningful work (even, let it be noted, in the eschatological future!) and the absence of contingency (probably because unpredictable events can destroy happiness). The theme that is important throughout most of the book of Isaiah but absent in the eschatological vision of chapter 65 is obedience to Torah (again, broadly understood; hence: prophetic injunctions against idolatry, injustice, and so forth). In some passages in Isaiah Torah obedience is an important part of an intimate, harmonious relationship with God (the first of the four key elements of happiness). But Third Isaiah is strikingly *un*interested in Torah obedience apart from Sabbath observance. With these differences in mind, we are now ready to turn to the four elements of happiness that appear both in the vision and widely in Isaiah as a whole.

Joy in the Life with God

In the new creation depicted in Isa 65:17–25,[11] God's happiness and human happiness are related:[12]

> But be glad and rejoice forever
>   in what I am creating!
> Indeed, I am about to create Jerusalem a joy,
>   and its people a delight!
> I will rejoice in Jerusalem,
>   and delight in my people. (65:18–19)

God's joy in creating Jerusalem anew engenders human joy at being so recreated. Joy inheres, naturally enough, in the prospect of God's deliverance of the people from the present travails of restoring community life after the exile. Thus the emotional life of God, if one may speak in this way, is intimately connected to the emotional life of the people.[13] Human beings model their happiness on God's happiness: as in the moral life (e.g., loving the stranger, Deut 10:18–19), so also in the happy life, it is a matter of *imitatio dei*. The idea appears, albeit negatively, in 65:12:

---

11. The Hebrew verb √*br'* ("to create") is repeated twice in Isa 65:18; elsewhere in the Hebrew Bible, it is used only with God as subject.

12. Regarding the various redactional theories concerning the relationship among chapters 63–66, I am agnostic. For a review of the major proposals, see Brevard S. Childs, *Isaiah* (OTL; Louisville: Westminster John Knox, 2001), 532–34. Childs makes the sensible suggestion that "in the ancient hearing and reading of scripture . . . the resonance set up from repeated themes played a more important role in interpretation than the modern concerns with establishing exact literary units." On the question of dating the vision of Isaiah 65, Childs is equally sensible: there is not enough evidence to be precise about the dating of any of the material in Third Isaiah beyond the general affirmation that the setting is post-539 BCE (ibid., 534).

13. Again, see Fretheim's essay in the present volume.

I will destine you to the sword . . .
because I called, but you did not answer;
   I spoke, but you did not listen.
Rather you did evil in my eyes,
   and that which I did not delight in, you chose.

Israel is judged for failing to delight in that which delights God. Here, then, the moral life expands to encompass that which induces delight, joy, and happiness: Choosing what is "good" means choosing what makes for happiness.

A second feature of v. 12 is also noteworthy: God's desire for intimacy with Israel went unrequited. A poignant divine lament appears earlier in 65:1–2 as well:[14]

I desired to be sought by those who did not ask,
   I desired to be found by those who did not seek me,
I said, "Here I am, here I am"
   to a nation that did not call[15] on my name.
I spread out my hands all day long to a stubborn people
   who walk in the way that is not good, following their own inclinations.

God's vulnerability to Israel's lack of interest in, even hostility to, the divine desire for relationship is movingly expressed here. "Here I am" (Hebrew *hinnēnî*) is the customary response of one called by God who wishes to express openness to the deity and to the divine call in particular (see, e.g., Abraham in Gen 22:1, 11; Jacob in Gen 46:2; Moses in Exod 3:4; Samuel in 1 Sam 3:4). The roles are reversed, however, in Isaiah 65: here, *God* expresses openness to the people and to *their* call (cf. also Isa 52:6; 58:9)—but it is a call that never comes. Furthermore, nowhere else in the Hebrew Bible is *hinnēnî* repeated twice in immediate succession as it is here—thus intensifying the expression of divine longing for relationship with a people who are manifestly disinclined.

In the vision that follows in 65:17–25, God promises not only to do for Israel what Israel has failed to do for God—that is, to seek and nurture relationship—but to go one step further, moving beyond verbal communication to a kind of wordless communion:

---

14. Odil Hannes Steck, among others, argues that chapters 65–66 respond to the lament in 63:7–64:11. See his "Beobachtungen zur Anlage von Jes 65–66," *BN* 38/39 (1987): 103–16.

15. The Pual perfect verb form in the MT is difficult here. So, following the LXX, I read the Qal perfect 3ms verbal form *qārā'* ("he called").

> Before they call I will answer,
>   and while they are still speaking, I will hear. (65:24)

A significant component of happiness is here conceived as a nearly wordless relationship with God, in which we are known and understood without needing to communicate with spoken words.

The same vocabulary that is employed in 65:18–19 expresses the joy evoked from pondering God's salvation elsewhere in Isaiah.[16] God's multiplying of the nation is compared to "exulting" (Hebrew *yāgîlû*) over plunder (Isa 9:3 [Heb 9:2]), for example; and the appropriate response to divine deliverance is to rejoice (25:9: "let us be glad [*nāgîlâ*] and rejoice [*wĕniśmĕḥâ*] in his salvation").[17] The root is principally found in Third Isaiah and Psalms, and it too expresses the joy of salvation (here in conjunction with *gyl* again): "I will greatly rejoice [*śôś 'āśîś*] in YHWH, my whole being shall exult [*tāgēl*] in my God; for he has clothed me with the garments of salvation" (61:10).[18] While the happiness fostered by contemplating God's salvation is often expressed in this general way, it is also often associated (using a variety of words) with the specific act of returning the people from exile and God's accompanying return to Zion (so 35:10; 51:11, 12; 52:8, 9; 55:11). In other instances it is God's compassion on the suffering of God's people that elicits joy (44:23; 49:13; 61:7, 10). So, in all of the book's several historical contexts an important element of happiness is the hope that God is acting to deliver God's people from present suffering.

A slightly less pronounced, but still important, element in happiness is the way the people's relation to God is sustained in worship. Waiting on YHWH (Isa 30:18: "Happy ['*ašrê*] are all who wait on him"), worshiping (30:29; 56:7, √*śmḥ*, "to rejoice"), drawing near to God (58:2, √*ḥpṣ*, "to delight"), and contemplating the majesty and glory of God (24:14: "exult" [√*rnn*] and "shout" [√*ṣhl*]) all arouse deep and presumably enduring joy in the worshipers, including even foreigners (see 56:7). As mentioned above, fulfilling the commandments of Torah does not figure prominently in Third Isaiah (save for Sabbath observance), but is important elsewhere in Isaiah as a fount of lasting happiness. The notion appears in Second Isaiah, for example (48:18, 22: peace [*šālôm*] belongs to those who fulfill the commandments), as does the broader notion that the word of the prophet—the divine

---

16. Especially, √*śwś* and √*gyl*. See further the appendix in the present volume.

17. See also similar occurrences of √*gyl* in Isa 29:19; 35:1–2; 41:16; 49:13; 61:10; 66:10. Some of these occur in contexts of the joy of seeing God's justice enacted (29:19; 41:16) or the transformation of the desert into fecund landscape (35:1–2).

18. Other occurrences of √*śwś* in Isaiah: 35:1; 62:5; 64:4; 66:10, 14.

message communicated by the prophet—is itself a source of delight that nourishes the spirit and inspires joy in the hearer (55:1–2).[19]

For Third Isaiah, Sabbath observance especially is a source of enduring delight. For example, the sapiential saying of 56:2 indicates that the one who keeps Sabbath and refrains from doing evil is "happy" (*'ašrê*). Or again, in 58:13–14 careful and sincere Sabbath observance, as contrasted to self-serving Sabbath observance, is connected to joy: if you call it your delight (*'oneg*), it will become a delight (*tit'annag*). The sequence here is important—one does not derive happiness from Sabbath observance unless one already understands it to be a gift that produces happiness. Fasting, on the other hand, is not advocated per se, but is subject to reinterpretation. So 58:6: "Is not this the fast that I choose: to loose the bonds of injustice?"

In sum, then, though Third Isaiah's interest in Torah is restricted to Sabbath observance, in contrast to other parts of Isaiah, intimacy with God, often achieved through worship as well as obedience to Torah, is of vital importance throughout the book as a whole. A close relationship with God is a key component of enduring happiness in all corners of Isaiah.

A Joyous Home Life Centered on Good Food and Drink

A second feature of happiness in the vision of chapter 65, as well as in Isaiah more broadly, is a secure sense of home. "They shall build houses and dwell in them; they shall plant vineyards and eat their fruit," Isa 65:21 asserts. It is perhaps not unexpected to see an image of house building in 65:17–25, set as it is against a backdrop of the uncertainties of rebuilding the community in Judea. Happiness involves building your own house, living in it, cultivating the land around it, and eating and drinking at home. The imagery of the vineyard, moreover, points to the importance of rootedness. Vines must be tended over many years to produce their fruit. The literal rootedness of the vines thus points to the metaphorical rootedness of the people: a secure home means cultivating and dwelling in the land over the long term. From its importance elsewhere in Isaiah it is clear that this sense of a bountiful, secure home is as essential to happiness as an intimate relationship with God. In its emphasis on the everyday pleasures of eating and drinking, Isaiah folds what is usually understood as primarily if not exclusively hedonic into the eudaimonic. The regular, quotidian rhythm of having plenty to eat and drink, and enjoying that safe and sound in one's own home, are part of what is truly worthwhile, part of the life that is well lived and truly happy.

---

19. Note that the metaphor relies on an abundance of food and drink to convey the joy of "ingesting" the word of God.

Chapter 66 continues the imagery of abundance and satiety as the people are urged to rejoice in Jerusalem so that they may nurse and be sated at her breast, "delighting [*wĕhit'annagtem*] in the abundance of her glory" (66:11). The image of nursing at a breast full of milk is understood to mean that prosperity and peace will flow like a river, or more aptly, like breast milk. Anyone who has seen the face of an infant who has just come off the breast—eyes drowsily closed, milk dribbling from the mouth, emitting a little sigh of supreme satisfaction brought on by perfect satiety—can imagine the kind of deep, hedonic pleasure conjured by the image here. The "milk" of this consoling breast is provided by the wealth of the nations coming to the once impoverished Jerusalem (66:12). Still nursing, the people are envisioned as borne along in her arms, and delighting (*tĕšo'ŏšā'û*) in sitting on her lap.[20] Surrounding this imagery of overflowing breast milk, which is already marked by the language of joy and delight (√ *'ng* and √*š''*), are yet more expressions of joy:

> Rejoice [*śimḥû*] with Jerusalem, and be glad [*wĕgîlû*] in her,
>   all you who love her;
> rejoice [*śîśû*] with her joy [*māśôś*]
>   all you who mourn over her—
>
> ...
>
> You shall see, and your heart shall rejoice [*wĕśāś*];
>   your bones will flourish like the grass. (66:10, 14a)

This last phrase prevents us from thinking that the happiness envisioned here is somehow "only" affective or "merely" an emotion. As with the nursing imagery, it is clear that this happiness pervades *the body* as well as the spirit. Even the prophet's language "runneth over"—so overwhelming is the contemplation of such joy that language itself seems to fail (so the repetitions of √*śwś*). This happiness seems to break the very bonds of language itself.

Throughout Isaiah the grape harvest is associated with joy. Indeed, the joy associated with the harvest (*kĕśimḥat baqqāṣîr*, 9:3 [Heb 9:2]) is used as a standard by which to understand other, less familiar, sources of joy in the book, like the rarer joy of God's in-breaking deliverance in 9:2–3 (Heb 9:1–2). The grape harvest even has its own specific shout of joy, such that the destruction of Moab, envisioned as the destruction of its vineyards, eliminates all joy:

---

20. This same word is used in another Isaianic vision—that of the child "playing/delighting" over a snake's hole (Isa 11:8).

> Joy and gladness [*śimḥâ wagîl*] are taken away
>> from the fruitful field;
> and in the vineyards no songs are joyously sung,
>> no shouts are raised;
> no treader treads out wine in the presses;
>> the vintage-shout [*hêdād*] is hushed. (Isa 16:10; cf. 5:1–7)

These texts from chapters 9 and 16 speak to the elemental joy associated with the grape harvest, and the product it portends: the wine itself. The "vintage-shout" of joy is the vehicle for understanding the tenor of other kinds of joy, or lack thereof. For example, in Isa 65:8 a harvest song is cited as a metaphor for separating the apostate from the faithful in the community.[21]

In a different vision, this one belonging to the apocalyptic nightmare conjured in chapter 24, we might be tempted to see the loss of wine as a purely hedonic motif—the loss of the only available anesthetic precisely when it is most needed:

> The wine dries up,
>> the vine languishes,
>> all the joyful of heart [*śimḥê lēb*] sigh.
> The joy [*māśôś*] of the timbrels is stilled,
>> the noise of the jubilant has ceased,
>> the joy [*māśôś*] of the lyre is stilled.
> No longer do they drink wine with singing;
>> beer is bitter to those who drink it.
> The city of chaos is broken down,
>> every house is shut up so that no one can enter.
> There is an outcry in the streets for lack of wine;
>> all joy [*śimḥâ*] has reached its eventide;
>> the gladness [*māśôś*] of the earth is banished. (Isa 24:7–11)

But the image as a whole is not simply about the loss of wine to alleviate the pain of the moment; it is more importantly about the loss of the deep, enduring joy associated with the rhythm of the grape harvest, of its role in the ongoing life of the community over time. Music, also a source of joy, is connected to the bounty of the grape harvest, and it too comes to an end in the so-called "little apocalypse" of Isaiah (chapters 24–27).

---

21. See Childs for an interpretation that "Don't destroy it, there's still a blessing in it" is a harvest song (*Isaiah*, 536).

So, wine is a source of joy—within limits. Just before the apocalypse of chapter 24, Isaiah warns against pouring out wine in inappropriate contexts. Celebration requires discernment:

> In that day the Lord, Yhwh of hosts
>   called to weeping and mourning,
>   to baldness and putting on sackcloth;
> but instead—joy and rejoicing,
>   killing oxen and slaughtering sheep,
>   eating meat and drinking wine!
> "(Let us) eat and drink,
>   for tomorrow we die." (22:12–13)

The historical context of "in that day" is not entirely apparent, though it may refer to the destruction by, and slim deliverance from, Sennacherib in the late eighth century.[22] Whatever occasion is in view, the problem here is not that the people are so despairing that they resort to drink to numb the pain (as v. 13 has come to signify colloquially); rather, they have misinterpreted their survival as victory and so celebrate inappropriately.[23] The cost of war and its destruction is high, though Jerusalem itself may be spared this time around. The prophet suggests that celebrating victory in this instance is premature, and the failure to take a longer view blinds the people to the city's destruction that lies ahead.

In addition to criticizing wine consumption on inappropriate occasions, Isaiah also condemns two other approaches to alcohol: overconsumption and drinking as a purely hedonic pleasure (the first entails the second, but the second does not quite require the first). Overconsumption is addressed in 28:1–14, where the drunken behavior of Israel's leaders ("scoffers who rule this people in Jerusalem," v. 14) is vividly and forcefully skewered:

> These also reel with wine
>   and stagger with beer;
> priest and prophet reel with beer,
>   they are confused with wine,
>   they stagger with beer;

---

22. See, e.g., John Goldingay, *Isaiah* (NIBC; Peabody, MA: Hendrickson, 2001), 128–29.

23. The statement, "Let us eat and drink, for tomorrow we die" is thus not a verbatim citation of the people, but the prophet's interpretation of their behavior. The people do not realize that they celebrate inappropriately—they fail to see that destruction is looming. See Goldingay, *Isaiah*, 128–29.

> they reel in vision,
> > they stumble in judgment.
> All tables are covered with filthy vomit;
> > no place is clean. (28:7–8)

Priests are of course responsible for teaching Torah to the people, and prophets to convey the word of God to the community (cf. Jer 18:18)—so this distressing picture portrays the reason for the total breakdown of the community's covenantal relationship with God. Are we to take the image at face value: that the priests and the prophets were really drunk most of the time? Or does the image function metaphorically to convey their overall failures of leadership, as the result, perhaps, of the intoxications of power? While it is clearly unwise to take too narrow a view (e.g., that it is *only* when they are drunk that they "reel in vision and stumble in judgment"), the repeated depictions of these religious leaders as reeling and staggering suggest that actual and consistent drunkenness is a problem that provokes an overall failure of leadership.[24]

Overconsumption is also in view in Isa 5:11–13 ("Ah, you who rise early in pursuit of beer ..." v. 11), as is a purely hedonic orientation to drinking: the prophet rails against those whose "feasts consist of lyre and harp, tambourine and flute and wine, but who do not regard the deeds of YHWH, or see the work of his hands!" (v. 12). In other words, sure it's a great party, but it is completely disconnected from the eudaimonic vision of happiness that emphasizes long-term flourishing with God. The irony is pointed: because the leaders are endlessly drinking, the people are dying of thirst (v. 13). So, it is one's *approach* to wine that is important: when it is part of a faithful life lived before God, is consumed in moderation and at the appropriate moments, it is one of the sources of genuine human happiness in Isaiah's eudaimonic vision. But at other times or with different uses, it is unwise and subject to God's judgment.

A Communal Life Marked by Security, Peace, and Justice

It will come as no surprise to those with even a passing acquaintance with the Hebrew Scriptures that a happy life is only possible as part of a wider, happy community.[25] Isaiah stresses three characteristics of the happy community: justice,

---

24. See John Barton, "Ethics in the Book of Isaiah," in *Writing and Reading the Scroll of Isaiah: Studies of an Interpretive Tradition* (eds. C. Broyles and C. Evans; 2 vols.; VTSup 70; Brill: Leiden, 1997), 1:69.

25. Perhaps the palpable isolation of Qoheleth helps to explain his unhappiness? See further the essay by Newsom in the present volume.

peace, and abundance. The last of these bears similarity to things already discussed above—especially the second element—but with more emphasis on the abundance that characterizes the entire community.

In the vision of chapter 65 that we have been using as a focal point for our study, the happy future is devoid of violence, even the usual violence associated with the "natural" order.

> The wolf and the lamb shall pasture together as one,
>> the lion shall eat straw like the ox;
>> and the serpent—dust will be its food!
> They shall not hurt or destroy
>> on all my holy mountain, says YHWH. (65:25)

This is an eschatological vision, to be sure, such that a return to the early chapters of Genesis where everyone ate plants (Gen. 1:30; 9:2–3), lions and tigers and bears included, can be seen as utopian. Nevertheless, the implications for happiness in this vision are provocative: the reversal of the (debased) "natural" order, which seems to function metonymically for a world devoid of violence in general,[26] suggests that violence in all its forms, even "natural" ones, destroys happiness.[27]

The emphasis on "peace" (usually though not always conveyed by šālôm) in the community appears throughout the rest of Isaiah as well. In the eschatological vision of Isaiah 32, for example, peace and security come to the fore, no doubt because the preceding verses have conjured the specter of impending war. The passage is addressed to the affluent women of the community (Isa 32:9) and announces that armies will ravage the landscape (including the vineyards!) in which these women presently take their ease (vv. 10–14). Yet, after that, when the "spirit from on high" descends upon "us" peace will envelop the land, bringing security:

> The effect of righteousness will be peace,
>> and the result of righteousness, quietness and trust forever.
> My people will abide in a peaceful habitation,
>> in secure dwellings, and in quiet resting places. (32:17–18)

---

26. This is true even for the snake (contrast Gen 3:14–15). Following a suggestion by Jeremy Hutton (private communication), and against many translations, I choose not to read the *waw* as disjunctive. The snake, like the other animals, experiences a change in diet.

27. Scholars have long noted that 65:25 alludes to 11:6–9. See, e.g., J. T. A. G. M. van Ruiten, "The Intertextual Relationship between Isaiah 65:25 and Isaiah 11:6–9," in *The Scriptures and the Scrolls* (eds. F. García Martínez, A. Hilhorst, and C. J. Labuschchagne; VTSup 49; Leiden: Brill, 1992), 31–42.

In an oft-quoted phrase, Isaiah links peace to justice: the effect (or "work," Heb *ma ʿăśeh*) of righteousness, that is, of living in a community that lives by Torah, will be peace. And one of the few occurrences of *ʾăśēr* appears precisely here in a bucolic vision: "Happy [√ *ʾšr*] are you who sow by every stream, and graze cattle and donkey freely" (32:20). Peace and security appear in numerous other passages in Isaiah, as well, thus underscoring their significance in his understanding of the good and happy life (see, e.g., Isa 9:5, 6; 26:3, 12; 52:7). Peace and security may seem an obvious necessity for happiness to flourish, but peace and security are strikingly absent from the lives of many in the world today, and their lack is cited by many children in distress as one of the major sources of their unhappiness.[28] For that reason alone it is worth lifting up the attention that the biblical witness gives to the (safe) quality of our corporate life as intrinsic to happiness.

It may seem obvious to those familiar with the prophetic corpus that justice is a fundamental feature of the happy community, just as acting justly is a fundamental characteristic of those who would be happy, and yet a brief discussion is nonetheless warranted. The eighth-century prophet Isaiah is famous for his indictment of Israel, especially its leaders, for abandoning their responsibilities to the widow and the orphan, the poor and the needy. They are specifically accused of profiting from widows and orphans by making them their "spoil" and "prey" (Isa 10:2; see also 1:16–17, 23). In the eschatological future envisioned in chapter 29, however, when the ones who do evil are cut off, "the oppressed shall again have joy [*śimḥâ*] in Yhwh, and the poorest of humanity shall rejoice [*yāgîlû*] in the Holy One of Israel" (29:19; see also 41:16, where "joy," √*gyl*, is the effect of injustice overturned; and 59:8, where injustice is associated with a lack of "peace," *šālôm*). Justice is a mark of a joyous community, and it produces joy in the ones who practice it.

Abundant food was one of the elements needed for happiness, as mentioned above, especially in connection with Isa 65:17–25. On this score, we may note that many other passages in the book associate abundance with the good life, especially through images of barren landscapes transformed into lush, Edenic gardens. When foes are vanquished and the redeemed Israel returns to the land, the landscape blossoms and joy overflows:

> The wilderness and the dry land shall be glad,
>> the desert shall rejoice and blossom;
> like the crocus it shall blossom abundantly,
>> and rejoice with joy and singing. (35:1–2; see also 51:3).

---

28. Steven J. Sandage (private communication) at the "Bible and the Pursuit of Happiness" Conference in Atlanta, December 11–13, 2009. For the global context, see the United Nations' report "Status of the Convention on the Rights of the Child" (August 2, 2010).

A common theme of Second Isaiah, especially, is the joy at the prospect of Israel's return from exile, a joy expressed by creation itself:

> For you shall go out in joy,
>   and be led back in peace;
> the mountains and the hills before you
>   shall burst into song,
>   and all the trees of the field shall clap their hands. (55:12)

Whereas the emphasis in 65:17–25 is on abundance close to home, on the vineyards that are lovingly tended over years and over generations, in these other passages the accent falls on the abundance of the *whole land* for the *whole people*, and the joy that inheres in a lush and fruitful landscape.

Hope for the Future

For Isaiah, as elsewhere in the Old Testament, having children who will remember you when you are dead is a significant blessing and a primary source of long-term hope. In the vision of chapter 65, hope presents itself as children who live to have their own children, each generation passing down the memory of the previous one to the next.

> They shall not labor in vain,
>   or bear children for horror;
> for they shall be offspring blessed by YHWH—
>   and their descendants with them. (65:23)

Contrary to Qoheleth's lament, the work of one's life will not be in vain, but will have purpose.[29] Labor will bring happiness both because it is an intrinsic pleasure (Isa 65:22) and because it forges ties across generations, strengthening the generation that follows. The knowledge that one's own children have a future marked by blessing and hope (they will not "bear children for horror") is a profound source of happiness.

Similarly, in a moving passage in Isaiah 56, eunuchs are promised that they will be remembered forever, even though they have no biological children:

> I will give to them, in my house and within my walls,
>   a monument and a name [*yād wāšēm*]
>   better than sons and daughters;

---

29. See, e.g., Eccl 1:14; 2:11, 15, 18–23, and, further, Newsom's essay in the present volume.

> an everlasting name I will give them,
> that shall not be cut off. (56:5)[30]

In general, sons and daughters are the very best hope for the future—their flourishing is a major component of happiness in this life—but here even that happiness is surpassed by the promise to faithful eunuchs that they will be remembered. Another dimension is added to future hope as an element of happiness when the promise is made that the offspring and descendants of the faithful will be publicly recognized ("among the nations") as blessed by God (61:9). In all these cases, happiness comes from imagining a future of blessing for one's descendants and their active remembering of the deceased, since the one doing the imagining will not be present when it all unfolds. Once again, a future of hope may seem like a rather obvious component to happiness. After all, individuals in distress, cut off from supportive communities, often lack precisely this capacity to imagine a future marked by hope and blessing. In some cases, the problem may be one of imagination (mental illness, etc.), but in others, the problem is that reality truly offers little raw material by which the imagination might conjure a future of blessing and hope.

3. Prophetic Happiness Beyond Isaiah

Does Isaiah's vision of happiness resonate with other prophetic books? It may be that some prophets, like Jeremiah and Amos, resist happiness through and through,[31] but the book of Ezekiel, for one, may not be as resistant to happiness as it appears on first read—though one suspects the prophet himself would not have done well on the motivational speaking tour. Despite containing some of the most disturbing and unhappy texts in the Bible (see, e.g., Ezekiel 5, 6, 16, and 23, for starters), the canonical shape of the book *points toward happiness*. Roughly the first half of it is nearly all pure judgment—first against Israel, then against other nations—but then, beginning especially in chapter 33, the book takes a decisive turn toward a future of hope, culminating in the vision of a restored and verdant land, revivified by the life-giving water that flows from the temple where YHWH is forever present (chapters 40–48).

Thus two of Isaiah's key elements reappear in Ezekiel: a veritable cornucopia of the fruits of the land—food for everyone! (the second element)—and the

---

30. This text has been famously appropriated as the name for the "living memorial to the Holocaust" in Jersualem: Yad Vashem.

31. Even if this is so, the "inverse method" of inferring happiness from what makes for unhappiness, may yet yield constructive results, even when applied to these prophetic books.

promise of God's sustaining presence (the first element). These two are connected; indeed, the latter causes the former in chapters 40–48. It is God's presence in the temple, in the midst of the land, that makes life not only possible, but also good and happy. For Ezekiel, life in such a land is surely deeply happy, even if often difficult to fully envision.[32] To illustrate the point: There are hardly any people in Ezekiel's vision, and one might conclude that the potential for happiness in such a land may well depend on the *relative absence* of human beings (!). Perhaps so, but the vision is all the happier for its haziness. Regardless, the prominence of the concrete (good food to eat), the corporate (oriented around communal worship in the temple), and the transcendent (the life-giving presence of God) in Ezekiel's vision point to significant commonalities shared by both this prophet and Isaiah. They both affirm the incorporation of hedonic elements of happiness within a larger eudaimonic understanding of what it means for human beings to flourish, and so be happy.

4. Ethical Implications of Prophetic Happiness

In closing, I want to draw out three implications for ethical reflection from this foray into Isaianic happiness:

1. First, as mentioned briefly at the start of this essay, the happy life is to some extent a matter of *choice*. In Third Isaiah this is clear in the way the text presents the "servants" as those who have *chosen* to be faithful to YHWH, as opposed to others who have not.[33] And for Third Isaiah it is clearly the servants who will receive the benefits of divine favor that fund happiness (see, e.g., 65:13–16, but also throughout Third Isaiah). Even so, as we have seen, since a significant component of happiness is intimate connection to YHWH through worship and prayer, it is not so much that happiness *is the result of* faithfulness, as it is that true happiness *inheres in* the life faithfully lived.

---

32. For a fuller interpretation of the ending of Ezekiel, see Jacqueline Lapsley, "Doors Thrown Open and Waters Gushing Forth: Mark, Ezekiel, and the Architecture of Hope," in *The Ending of Mark and the Ends of God: Essays in Memory of Donald Harrisville Juel* (eds. Beverly Roberts Gaventa and Patrick D. Miller; Louisville: Westminster John Knox, 2005), 139–53.

33. According to Third Isaiah, those who do not choose YHWH are destined for the sword and divine mocking (e.g., 65:12; 66:4). For further discussion of the implications of the community divisions and Israel's election see, Joseph Blenkinsopp, *Isaiah 56–66: A New Translation with Introduction and Commentary* (AB 19B; New York: Doubleday, 2003), 273–79.

2. This leads to the second implication for ethics: even what appear to be external goods, like the just and peaceful community described in 65:17–25, are not truly external insofar as they flow out of lives faithfully lived. Justice and peace, after all, characterize the communities in which people live by Torah.[34] Ellen T. Charry makes this point forcefully in her *God and the Art of Happiness*: In the Tanakh, "there is no excellent living apart from God's way for Israel that is to become the way for all people."[35] Yet what are we to make of the insistent fact that, in some important respects, the "servants" in Third Isaiah seem manifestly unhappy? That is to say that in Third Isaiah the temple has not yet been rebuilt, towns are devastated, people are in distress, and there is considerable conflict among the community (see 64:9–10, the end of an extended lament beginning in 63:7). At such times the most prominent feature of happiness may well be its *futurity*—the future hope that God will deliver on the divine promise that the life of faith is not lived in vain. The eschatological vision funds present (eudaimonic) happiness—even in the midst of present (hedonic) unhappiness.

3. Finally, I want to return to the two perspectives that I mentioned at the beginning of the paper, which Isaiah implicitly challenges. First, there is no room for the nihilistic—or less starkly, the market-driven—worldview articulated by Don Draper in the epigraph above. Genuine happiness is possible, Isaiah affirms, but not by any means Draper has ever imagined. Second, the Isaianic vision of happiness traced here (and which may be true too for a larger prophetic vision, if not for the entirety of the Old Testament) is *not* predicated on an orientation to the other at the expense of self, as certain kinds of overly sacrificial Christian ethics would have it. In the Isaianic vision, the well-being of the self is inextricably tied to the well-being of others, and vice versa, because all are woven into communal life, the character of which determines to a significant degree the happiness of all. So, in the Isaianic vision—and here I dare to generalize—in the *biblical* vision, true happiness for the individual is not really possible apart from a happy communal life. The (over)emphasis in some Christian ethics on the emptying of self, derived from particular interpretations of some New Testament texts, does not do justice to the larger claim in the Hebrew Scriptures, and the New Testament as well, that one's own flourishing—which is to say, one's *happiness*—cannot

---

34. To be sure, and as noted previously, Third Isaiah does not emphasize Torah obedience but the point is supported by other prophetic texts in spades.

35. See Charry, *God and the Art of Happiness*, 201. I thank Charry for sharing her work with me prior to its publication.

be uncoupled from the flourishing of the neighbor.[36] Thus, in addition to challenging Christianity's discomfort with hedonic conceptions of happiness by incorporating these elements into a larger view of the flourishing life, the Old Testament also presses against Christianity's unease even with eudaimonic conceptions of happiness.[37]

36. On this point, see Patrick D. Miller, "The Good Neighborhood: Identity and Community Through the Commandments," in *Character and Scripture: Moral Formation, Community, and Biblical Interpretation* (ed. William P. Brown; Grand Rapids: Eerdmans, 2002), 55–72.

37. Charry traces the modern movement in Christian theology away from a eudaimonic vision toward an aversion to "self-love": "if Pascal is the 'first modern Christian,' it is not difficult to see why and how less religious souls turned away from a 'Christian' vision of happiness to embrace a secular hedonist interpretation of happiness as immediate, short-term pleasure detached from the love of God" (*God and the Art of Happiness*, 130). According to her, modern Christian theologians are uncomfortable with both hedonic and eudaimonic conceptions of happiness.

4

Happiness and Its Discontents in the Psalms

William P. Brown

1. Misery and Happiness in the Psalms

The physicist Steven Weinberg shares a joke told by scientists in Moscow about how the "anthropic principle" explains not the mystery of life but the misery of life:

> There are many more ways for life to be miserable than happy; the anthropic principle only requires that the laws of nature should allow the existence of intelligent beings, not that these beings should enjoy themselves.[1]

In this light, perhaps "misanthropic principle" is more apt! Although the course of evolution is devoid of purpose, it is not without certain directional trends, according to biologist Jeffrey Schloss.[2] One trend is the "intensification of life," which includes a deepening capacity to suffer.[3]

If Russian scientists, or readers of any nationality, were to search the Psalms for suffering, they would not have far to look. The Psalter, perhaps like life itself, seems filled with more misery than happiness. The language of lament, the Psalter's dominant genre, exceeds the language of praise in both variety and

---

1. Steven Weinberg, *Dreams of a Final Theory* (New York: Pantheon Books, 1992), 221–22.

2. Jeffrey P. Schloss, "From Evolution to Eschatology," in *Resurrection: Theological and Scientific Assessments* (eds. Ted Peters et al.; Grand Rapids: Eerdmans, 2002), 72.

3. Ibid., 78.

volume. Disease, persecution, isolation, shame, deprivation, poverty, abuse, betrayal, debilitation, and death all take up residence in the Psalms, and relief from any one of them seems at best temporary.[4] Consider the following psalmic passages:

> I am poised to fall,
>   and my pain is ever with me. (Ps 38:18)

> For my soul is filled with distress,
>   and my life has reached the brink of Sheol. . . .
> Afflicted I am, dying since youth;
>   I have endured your terrors; I am lifeless. (Ps 88:3, 15)

> O Lord, what are human beings that you should know them,
>   or mortals that you consider them?
> Humans are like a breath;
>   each one of their days passes away like a shadow. (Ps 144:3–4)[5]

Pain, distress, affliction, terror, death: all are omnipresent and all are intimately related. Like death itself, pain has no cure, and relief comes only temporarily:

> When anxieties within me are many,
>   your consolations cheer my soul. (Ps 94:19)

But such "consolations" come and go: anxiety remains constant, ever poised to proliferate and overwhelm the carrier. Moreover, a life filled with ease draws not the psalmist's commendation but his condemnation, because freedom from pain is associated not with the righteous, but with the *wicked*:

> For I was envious of the arrogant;
>   I saw the prosperity of the wicked.
> For they have no pain;
>   their bodies are sound and sleek.

---

4. A masterful treatment of pain in the Psalms is given in Kristin M. Swenson, *Living through Pain: Psalms and the Search for Wholeness* (Waco, TX: Baylor University Press, 2005). Swenson helpfully distinguishes between "cure" and "healing/wholeness," only the latter of which is treated in the Psalms.

5. All translations are my own, unless otherwise indicated. Versification follows the Hebrew text.

They are not in trouble as others are;
>   they are not plagued like other people.…
Such are the wicked;
>   always at ease, they increase in riches. (Ps 73:3–5, 12; NRSV)

Thus the claim that the Psalter is "a guide to a blessed life"[6] seems, on the face of it, patently absurd. The one who speaks the Psalms is no "happy camper." Indeed, a frequent form of self-designation in these ancient prayers is "poor and needy," perhaps better translated as "wretched and miserable" (*'ānî wĕ'ebyôn*).[7] Regardless of its specific nuance, this near formulaic expression is "a confession that existence is structured by finitude and fallibility,"[8] and, one should add, beset by misery. The Psalms, it would seem, are more about "pain seeking understanding" than about the pursuit of happiness.

That said, the book of Psalms nevertheless opens with an extended saying about happiness—an *'ašrê*-saying (Ps 1:1: "How happy …!")—that commends a certain salutary state of being. Its placement at the very start of the Psalter powerfully orients the reading of the Psalms as a whole. Likened to a flourishing tree transplanted beside flowing channels, this happy/*'ašrê* individual is one who refuses to follow the way of the wicked but instead finds delight in YHWH's Torah or "teaching" (1:1–3). Twenty-four additional *'ašrê*-sayings are dispersed throughout the Psalter, each one commending a certain aspect or example of human flourishing, whether individual or communal. Together these sayings suggest that well-being in the Psalms entails more than temporary relief from the manifold conditions of misery—the conditions that provoke constant complaint and plea from the speaker's lips. Well-being, rather, is an object of human desire that is met by the God who saves and sustains, delivers and protects. It is, in fact, the God of the Psalms who provides refuge and well-being—or, to use other language, flourishing and happiness.

On the one hand, the Psalter does not embrace misery as an essential feature of the well-lived life, as some modern dissenters of happiness would insist on doing.[9] The psalmists, after all, typically implore God to relieve their misery and restore them to a better life. On the other hand, the Psalms acknowledge the

---

6. So James L. Mays, *Psalms* (Interpretation; Louisville: John Knox, 1994), 40. But see Mays's sentiment quoted at note 8 below.

7. See, e.g., 40:17; 70:5; 86:1; 109:16, 22; cf. 37:14; 74:21.

8. James L. Mays, *Preaching and Teaching the Psalms* (eds. Patrick D. Miller and Gene M. Tucker; Louisville: Westminster John Knox, 2006), 56.

9. See, e.g., Ronald W. Dworkin, *Artificial Happiness: The Dark Side of the New Happy Class* (New York: Carroll & Graf, 2006); and Eric G. Wilson, *Against Happiness: In Praise of Melancholy* (New York: Farrar, Straus and Giroux, 2008).

reality of misery as a pervasive feature of life, as the essential backdrop as it were to happiness. Within this polarity of weal and woe the psalms yield their cry and praise, and it is within this polarity that the variegated contours of happiness are forged.

To explore the Psalter's oblique yet remarkably thick portrayal of happiness, I begin with the most obvious locus, the happy or 'ašrê-sayings. These scattered sayings point to various facets of human flourishing that together establish an encompassing framework for happiness in the Psalms. In the center of this framework is a pair of "twin" psalms that profile happiness in a substantially theological way and thus deserve separate treatment. Widening the scope of our investigation, I then explore how the overall shape of the Psalter reveals something about the broad dynamic of happiness. Happiness in the Psalms, that is, is reached in a certain way; it is neither a packaged given nor a static state. Probing more deeply, I conclude this study with perhaps the most basic issue underlying happiness in the Psalms: the shaping of desire.

2. The 'Ašrê-*Sayings*

The 'ašrê-sayings of the Psalms stand resolutely behind the beatitudes of Jesus in Matthew and Luke.[10] They describe more an ostensible state of being than a subjective feeling or emotion.[11] Rhetorically, they bear a certain show-and-tell quality that points to something deemed worthwhile and appealing. In fact, Waldemar Janzen has gone so far as to suggest that the label 'ašrê conveys a sense of envy.[12] Put more positively, the 'ašrê-saying commends a condition, practice, or virtue considered eminently desirable. In some cases, the saying takes on a distinctly prescriptive force by highlighting a particular virtue or commendable mode of conduct. In other instances, it highlights a fortunate circumstance enjoyed by an individual or a community, such as prosperity and divine protection. In various ways, then, the 'ašrê-saying in the Psalms points to a discernible state of well-being, for which it elicits desire.

Such is the performative force of 'ašrê; the interpretive challenge lies in the actual translation of 'ašrê: "happy," "blessed," "fortunate," and "felicitous" are a few of the suggestions proffered. Some fit certain passages better than others. The translation "fortunate" smacks too much of chance (Latin *fortuna*).[13] Though

---

10. See the essay by Carl R. Holladay in the present volume.

11. Cf. Carol A. Newsom's discussion in the present volume.

12. Waldemar Janzen, "'Ašrê in the Old Testament," *HTR* 58 (1965): 215–26. For more extensive discussion, see Edward Lipiński, "Marcismes et Psaumes de congratulation," *RB* 75 (1968): 321–67.

13. My thanks to Ellen T. Charry for pointing this out.

semantically related to *'ašrê*,[14] "blessed" derives from an altogether different Hebrew root, *brk*. Moreover, the designation *'ašrê* need not directly presuppose divine agency. "Felicitous" may come closer to the Hebrew *'ašrê*, since it suggests a sense of appropriateness. A felicitous choice of words, for example, occurs not by luck but by the skill or intuition of the communicator. Nevertheless, the *'ašrê*-sayings cover a spectrum of salutary conditions that extends far beyond matters of communicative skill. For all its inadequacies, "happy" fits best if one keeps in mind that *'ašrê* bears a wider range and richer nuance of meaning than is typically reflected in contemporary English usage.[15] "Happiness" in the Psalms presumes an externally observable objective condition of well-being as much as it suggests an inwardly felt experience of joy and satisfaction. In the Psalms, "happiness" is a demonstrable state of being. In the *'ašrê*-sayings, happiness has a profile.

Divine Agency

That profile covers a wide range in the Psalms, wider than what one finds in Proverbs, for example.[16] Nevertheless, the *'ašrê*-sayings can be grouped together according to theme and orientation. Take the following examples:

> How happy is the one whose transgression is forgiven,
>   whose sin is covered.
> How happy is the person to whom YHWH imputes no guilt;
>   and in whose spirit[17] there is no deceit. (Ps 31:1–2)

> How happy is the nation whose God is YHWH;
>   the people whom he has chosen for his heritage. (Ps 33:12)

> How happy is the one you choose and bring near,
>   the one who dwells in your courts.
> We are satisfied with the goodness of your house,
>   the holiness of your temple. (Ps 65:5)

> How happy, YH,[18] is the man whom you discipline,
>   and teach with your law,

---

14. See, e.g., the coordination of *'ašrê* ("happy") and *yĕbōrak* ("blessed") in Ps 128:1–2, 4.

15. See the introduction to the present volume by Brent A. Strawn.

16. For more on Proverbs, see the essay by Newsom in this volume.

17. The LXX reads "mouth," apparently drawing from a tradition different from the MT.

18. A short form of the divine name YHWH.

> providing him respite from calamitous days,
> > until a pit is dug for the wicked. (Ps 94:12–13)

Each saying highlights *divine agency*: *God's* forgiveness of sins, *God's* election of a nation, *God's* education and protection of an individual. None commends human achievement or activity per se. The focus is on God, who is, in these sayings, the true agent of happiness. Instead of affirming certain modes of human conduct, these *'ašrê*-sayings convey a sense of gratitude for certain blessings from God, at least for the reader who has experienced such blessings. For the reader who has not experienced them, then perhaps envy is what is elicited (see above). In either case, specific warrant for such blessings is absent. Below is a parade example.

> May our sons be like plants full-grown in their youth,
> > our daughters like corner-pillars carved
> > > according to the model of the palace.
> May our granaries be full, supplying produce of all kinds;
> > may our flocks be in the thousands,
> > > in the ten thousands in our fields.
> May our cattle be heavy laden;[19]
> > may there be neither breach nor exile,
> > > nor outcry in our streets.
> How happy are the people who have it so!
> > How happy are the people whose God is YHWH! (Ps 144:12–15)

This *'ašrê*-saying concludes a jussive-laden petition that envisions abundant familial and agricultural prosperity. YHWH is the agent behind such blessing.

Human Agency

Another group of *'ašrê*-sayings highlights a different kind of agency, one that is primarily human rather than divine. Psalm 1, as noted above, equates the happy person with the righteous individual, the one who refuses contact with the wicked and finds delight in the study of Torah. Here, happiness presupposes righteousness. Like the opening psalm of the Psalter, the following passages highlight human agency.

---

19. The line is elliptical: the domestic animals are either laden with pregnancy or able to bear heavy loads.

How happy are the people who know the festal shout;
>   Yhwh, they walk in the light of your countenance. (Ps 89:16)

How happy are those who guard justice,
>   who practice[20] righteousness at all times. (Ps 106:3)

How happy are those whose way has integrity,
>   those who walk in Yhwh's *torah*.
How happy are those who keep his testimonies;
>   they seek him wholeheartedly. (Ps 119:1–2)

How happy is the man who fears Yhwh,
>   who greatly delights in his commandments. (Ps 112:1)

How happy are all who fear Yhwh,
>   who walk in his ways. (Ps 128:1)

How happy is the one who has regard for the poor.
>   On the day of disaster Yhwh will deliver him. (Ps 41:2)

How happy is the man who makes Yhwh his trust,
>   who does not turn to the proud,
>   to those who go astray after false gods. (Ps 40:5)

Yhwh gives, and does not withhold, good things
>   for those who walk in integrity.[21]
Yhwh of hosts,
>   how happy are those who trust in you! (Ps 84:12b–13)

Human agency takes center stage among these sayings, though not entirely apart
from divine agency: God is the object of reverence and trust, God's salvific power
is readily acknowledged, and God's instruction sets the occasion for happiness.
Nevertheless, these sayings paint a broad picture of virtuous conduct and faithful
practice on the level of human agency. The one who leads a life of integrity, which
includes justice and compassion for the poor, and who trusts and fears God, is the
one who leads a happy life. The life of happiness is exemplified even at the most

---

20. Reading a plural form (*'ōśê*) for the MT's singular *'ōśeh* ("the one who practices").

21. Despite scholarly redivisions of this verse, the MT is understandable as it is.

concrete liturgical level: those who "know the festal shout"[22] are deemed happy
(89:16). Commending specific modes of human conduct as they do, these 'ašrê-
sayings exhibit their own prescriptive force. As they point to examples of embodied happiness, they implicitly convey the message: "Go and do likewise!" Here,
happiness has an ethos.

Joint Agency

The last text cited above couches the value of trust within the context of YHWH's
beneficence (84:12b). Although most of the 'ašrê-sayings fall primarily on one
or the other end of the divine—human agency spectrum, a few acknowledge
joint agency in equal fashion.

> How happy are all who take refuge in him [i.e., God]. (Ps 2:12b)
>
> How happy is the man who takes refuge in him [i.e., God]. (Ps 34:9b)

"Taking refuge" (Hebrew √ḥsh) a widespread motif in the Psalms,[23] acknowledges, on the one hand, the divine provision of protection and, on the other, the
human decision to rely upon God, to cast one's allegiance to YHWH, as confirmed
in the following verse:

> See the man who would not make God his refuge,
> > but instead trusted in his abundant riches,
> > > taking refuge in his own ruin.[24] (Ps 52:9)

Wealth offers a refuge that is only temporary at best; seeking security in riches
ultimately leads to ruin. Refuge in God, however, is another matter. Following this verse, the psalmist presents the evocative image of the "green olive
tree in the house of God" as emblematic of the speaker's well-being (52:10). It
is no accident that this metaphor mirrors the arboreal image featured in 1:3,

---

22. Hebrew tĕrû 'â, a term for a loud shout of joy, though it can also be used for a cry of alarm.

23. For a full study of this theme in the Psalter, see Jerome Creach, *Yahweh as Refuge and the
Editing of the Hebrew Psalter* (JSOTSup 217; Sheffield: Sheffield Academic Press, 1996). See
also William P. Brown, *Seeing the Psalms: A Theology of Metaphor* (Louisville: Westminster
John Knox, 2002), 15–30.

24. *BHS*, in accordance with Peshitta and Targum, reads bĕhônô ("in his wealth") at the end of
the line, against MT's bĕhawwātô ("in his own ruin") which makes good sense as it stands. The
verb is likely derived from √'wz (and so translated here: "taking refuge") rather than √yzz
("grow strong"), although a wordplay cannot be ruled out.

which designates the "happy" individual whose delight is found in Yʜwʜ's Torah (see also 92:13–16). In both cases, the divine agency of (trans)planting is presupposed.[25]

The final *'ašrê*-saying in the Psalter, perhaps not coincidentally, captures well the duality of human-divine agency:

> How happy is the one whose help[26] is the God of Jacob,
> whose hope is in Yʜwʜ, his God. (Ps 146:5)

This psalm of praise is concerned with identifying the proper object of trust: "Put no trust in princes, or in mortals, in whom there is no salvation," the speaker exhorts in v. 3. The *'ašrê*-saying combines God's "help," connected earlier in the psalm with "salvation," and the individual's "hope." Happiness denotes a salutary state of being that is both achieved and granted, received and attained. Happiness is where "hope" and "help" meet, where human disposition and divine grace intersect. The relationship between the "happy" individual and God is further explicated in a deliberate pairing of psalms that mirror each other and, in so doing, reflect the divine in the human: Psalms 111 and 112.

3. *Psalms 111–112*

As is commonly recognized, Psalms 111 and 112 are compositionally aligned.[27] Both are acrostic in form, and a number of verbal and thematic correspondences can be discerned across their distinctive genres.[28] Psalm 111 is a thanksgiving song that opens with a command to praise and an expressed desire to give thanks for God's "works" and "wonders" (vv. 1–4a). The psalm instantiates such "wonders": God provides food (v. 5a), establishes an eternal covenant (vv. 5b, 9b), grants Israel an "international heritage" (v. 6b), establishes "precepts" (vv. 7b–8), and redeems "his people" (v. 9a). God's "work" is characterized by "splendor and majesty" (v. 3) and

---

25. For further discussion, see Brown, *Seeing the Psalms*, 75–78; also Brent A. Strawn, "Psalm 1," in *Psalms for Preaching and Worship: A Lectionary Commentary* (eds. Roger E. Van Harn and Brent A. Strawn; Grand Rapids: Eerdmans, 2009), 50–55, esp. 51–52.

26. Read *'ezrô* ("whose help") for the MT's *bě'ezrô* ("*in* whose help"), which is the result of dittography.

27. See Walter Zimmerli, "Zwillingspsalmen," in idem, *Studien zur alttestamentlichen Theologie und Prophetie: Gesammelte Aufsätze 2* (TB 51; Munich: Kaiser, 1974), 263–67.

28. For a recent discussion, see Raymond C. Van Leeuwen, "Form Criticism, Wisdom, and Psalms 111–12," in *The Changing Face of Form Criticism for the Twenty-First Century* (eds. Marvin A. Sweeney and Ehud Ben Zvi; Grand Rapids: Eerdmans, 2003), 71–81.

is described as "faithful and just" (v. 7a). In addition to the deity's deeds, YHWH (specifically YHWH's "name") is described as "gracious and merciful" (v. 4b) and "holy and fearsome" (v. 9b). The psalm concludes with a proverbial saying (v. 10a):

> The fear of YHWH is the beginning of wisdom;
>   comprehension of the good is for all who perform them.[29]

While the first colon of this couplet appears in variant forms in Prov 1:7; 9:10; and Sir 1:14 (cf. also Job 28:28), its association here with the performance of *God's* "precepts" (see v. 7b) is unusual from a sapiential perspective. Indeed, the second line qualifies the first: wisdom is evidenced in fulfilling the divine commandments (cf. Deut 4:5–6). The exercise of wisdom, moreover, is contextually related to the capacity to praise and give thanks (Ps 111:1b, 10b). To "fear YHWH" is to give due praise and thanks, which is a wise thing to do in the psalmist's estimation. This proverbial saying makes for a fitting transition to the following psalm, which profiles the happy individual.

As the sequel to Psalm 111, Psalm 112 is often regarded as a "wisdom psalm," even though its preceding partner is one that features the proverbial saying noted above. Proverbial sayings are lacking in Psalm 112, but, regardless of generic distinction, both psalms contain numerous thematic and verbal correspondences. Psalm 112 opens with an identical "hallelujah" command, immediately followed by an *'ašrê*-saying: "How happy is the one who fears YHWH, who delights greatly in his commandments" (v. 1b). James L. Mays regards this psalm as an "extended beatitude."[30] If so, Psalm 112, especially in relation to its partner, says something theologically significant about happiness.

Together, these two psalms effectively join the theocentric and the anthropocentric. Whereas Psalm 111 describes YHWH's character and power, Psalm 112 characterizes the individual who acknowledges YHWH in reverence ("fear"). The "Lord-fearer" prospers (112:3a), is altogether righteous (vv. 3b = 9b, 6a; cf. 111:3b), is generous and just (vv. 5, 9a), is renowned (v. 6b; cf. 111:4), has a "firm" and "steady" heart (vv. 7b, 8a), is not afraid (vv. 7a, 8b), and receives honor (v. 9b; cf. 111:3a). Like YHWH's own character, which is described in 111:4b, the righteous individual is also "gracious and merciful" (112:4b). Both deity and human being are defined by their comparable deeds: they share an identity marked by righteousness,

---

29. The antecedent of the masculine plural suffix "them" in the MT is a crux. The LXX and Peshitta feature a feminine singular ("who perform her"), presupposing "wisdom." The MT, however, bears the more difficult reading, whose antecedent is apparently the "precepts" mentioned earlier in v. 7b.

30. Mays, *Psalms*, 359.

grace, mercy, and renown, not to mention power. In content, too, the psalms are veritable mirror images. Raymond C. Van Leeuwen argues that these two psalms, by forming a conceptual whole, make the case that "humanity is image and imitator of God."[31] Although the essentialist language of the *imago dei* found in Gen 1:26–27 is not explicitly present in Psalm 112, *imitatio dei* well captures the nexus of these two psalms. And it is within that nexus where happiness is found. To be happy is, in the estimation of Psalms 111–112, to be godly.[32]

4. *The Pilgrimage of Happiness*

As much as happiness in the Psalms is found at the vertical intersection of human and divine agency, it also reflects a distinctive dynamic on the horizontal plane, a movement whose route is not altogether obvious or straightforward. Happiness does not come out of the blue, nor is it something acquired as a possession. Happiness is a process, a journey set by the overarching "plot" of the Psalter.

This "plot" is found in the overall movement of the Psalms from beginning to end. The Psalter begins with Psalm 1 and its profile of the happy individual dedicated to the study of Torah, the way of righteousness. The book of Psalms ends with the symphonic exhortation that every breathing thing give praise to God (150:6).[33] The connection between the first and last psalms forms, as it were, an existential inclusio that envelops the Psalter in an aura of joy. But the journey from Psalm 1 to Psalm 150, from joyful obedience to ecstatic praise, proceeds in fits and starts, with wild oscillations between despair and joy—a veritable roller-coaster ride of emotions.[34] The cultivation of happiness is somehow found amid these bipolar swings in the Psalter.

---

31. Van Leeuwen, "Form Criticism," 77, 80. See also Beth LaNeel Tanner, *The Book of Psalms through the Lens of Intertextuality* (Studies in Biblical Literature 26; New York: Peter Lang, 2001), 144.

32. This ethical nexus also suggests that happiness is ultimately a divine virtue. For God's happiness, see the essay by Terence E. Fretheim's in the present volume.

33. See the iconographical study by Brent A. Strawn and Joel M. LeMon, "'Everything That Has Breath': Animal praise in Psalm 150:6 in the light of ancient Near Eastern iconography," in *Bilder als Quellen/Images as Sources: Studies on ancient Near Eastern artefacts and the Bible inspired by the work of Othmar Keel* (eds. S. Bickel, S. Schroer, R. Schurte, and C. Uehlinger; OBO Sonderband; Fribourg: Academic Press and Göttingen: Vandenhoeck & Ruprecht, 2007), 451–85 and Pls. XXXIII–XXXIV.

34. See Walter Brueggemann, "Bounded by Obedience and Praise: The Psalms as Canon," *JSOT* 50 (1991): 63–92, reprinted in idem, *The Psalms and the Life of Faith* (ed. Patrick D. Miller; Minneapolis: Fortress, 1995), 189–213.

It is also found in the Psalter's complex structure or shape. The Psalter is a divided whole consisting of five "books," each concluding with a doxology:

> Book I: Psalms 1–41
>
> Book II: Psalms 42–72
>
> Book III: Psalms 73–89
>
> Book IV: Psalms 90–106
>
> Book V: Psalms 107–150

According to rabbinic tradition, the Psalter's fivefold structure finds its precedence in the Pentateuch, the Torah of Moses, as noted in the *Midrash Tehillim*: "As Moses gave five books of laws to Israel, so David gave five books of Psalms to Israel."[35] The statement claims David as the source of the entire Psalter. As the first five books of the Bible came to be attributed to Moses, the Psalter became, in turn, the Davidic Torah, or at least David's counterpart to the Mosaic Torah. Either way, given their common fivefold form, the Pentateuch and the Psalter form the two poles of ancient Israel's faith: God's word and deed, on the one hand, and Israel's response in prayer and praise, on the other.

If, as Psalm 1 claims, the righteous, happy individual is the one who finds delight in the study of Torah (v. 2), and if Torah has anything to do with the Psalter, as evidenced in its fivefold division, then perhaps one may find the pathway to happiness by studying the Psalms. That pathway is forged within the irregular yet discernible movement from lament to praise. In Book I a string of laments or complaints in Psalms 3–13 is broken by only one hymn (Psalm 8); in contrast, the last five psalms of Book V burst forth with uninterrupted, all-encompassing praise (Psalms 146–150).

The Psalter's overall movement or "plot" can also be read thematically, not just generically. As is often noted, Books I–III (Psalms 1–89) reflect thematic and editorial features that set them apart from Books IV–V (Psalms 90–150). Interpreters have observed that Psalms 2–89 reflect a primarily Davidic or *earthly* view of kingship. Gerald H. Wilson has noted the strategic placement of "royal psalms" at the "seams" of the first three books (Pss 2, 72, and 89) as well as their absence in the transition from Book IV to Book V.[36] This movement is also paralleled to some degree with the decreasing number of psalms attributed to David (95 percent in Book I; 32

---

35. See the translation in William G. Braude, *The Midrash on Psalms* (2 vols.; Yale Judaica Series 13; New Haven: Yale University Press, 1959), 1:5.

36. Gerald H. Wilson, *The Editing of the Hebrew Psalter* (SBLDS 76; Chico, CA: Scholars Press, 1985), 207.

percent in Book V).[37] Taking their cue from Psalm 2, some interpreters refer to Books I–III as the "messianic collection," in contrast to the "theocratic collection" of Books IV–V, which develop the theme of *divine* kingship over all creation.[38]

The pivot behind the thematic shift from earthly to divine kingship is found at the end of Book III, specifically in Psalm 89, which recounts God's "eternal" covenant with David and his dynasty in vv. 1–37 (cf. 2 Samuel 7). But in an abrupt about face, the latter half of the psalm delivers a blistering protest against God's abandonment of the earthly monarchy (vv. 38–51). The so-called "eternal" covenant, the psalm attests, has utterly failed. By documenting its demise, Psalm 89 paves the way for subsequent psalms to laud God's exclusive kingship over Israel, the nations, and the cosmos. Psalm 90 marks the shift with a psalm attributed to Moses (as opposed to David) that, on the one hand, focuses resolutely on the "power of [God's] wrath" (v. 11) and the eternity of God's reign (vv. 1–2) and, on the other, laments the fragile finitude of human existence (vv. 3–10). This psalm, along with the remaining sixteen psalms that constitute Book IV, has been called the "answer" to the failure of God's covenant with David and the "editorial center" of the Psalter's final form.[39] At the juncture of Book IV and Book V, Psalm 106 concludes Book IV with a plea for Israel's deliverance from exile (v. 47), to which Psalm 107 responds with testimony of the ingathering of exiles.[40] The Davidic psalms that sparsely populate Book V profile David as the king who "bows to the kingship of YHWH."[41]

Such a reading of the Psalter, with many details still to fill in, suggests a meta-narrative that begins with the Davidic monarchy and ends in hope for returning exiles. It is a story that, as Nancy deClaissé-Walford argues, gives shape to Israel's identity, making possible its very survival in a postexilic age without a king and court.[42] Or

---

37. The final Book of the Psalter actually marks a minor resurgence of the Davidic psalms, compared to only one psalm in Book III attributed to David (Psalm 86) and two in Book IV (Psalms 101, 103). Nevertheless, the contrast with Book I remains marked. See Nancy L. deClaissée-Walford, *Introduction to the Psalms: A Song from Ancient Israel* (St. Louis: Chalice, 2004), 116.

38. Such thematic and editorial distinctions find a measure of convergence with the compositional history of the Psalter. In light of evidence gained from Qumran, it appears that Books I–III of the Hebrew Psalter were actually stabilized before Books IV and V, since the order of the latter differs markedly in some of the Dead Sea Scrolls from the one reflected in the Masoretic tradition. See Peter W. Flint, *The Dead Sea Psalms Scrolls and the Book of Psalms* (STDJ 17; Leiden: Brill, 1997), esp. 135–49.

39. Wilson, *The Editing of the Hebrew Psalter*, 215.

40. Ibid., 220.

41. Ibid., 227.

42. See deClaissé-Walford, *Introduction*, 129.

as V. Steven Parrish puts it, the Psalms lift up a story of "emergence" (Psalms 1 and 2), "establishment" (Books I–II), "collapse" (Book III), and "reemergence" (Books IV–V).[43] Happiness in this scheme is reached most fully in the "reemergence" of a new identity marked by praise. In praise, happiness is consummated.

The Psalms in their canonical arrangement suggest, therefore, a dynamic of happiness that finds a way *through* misery rather than around it, a way that moves from "orientation" through "disorientation" to "new orientation."[44] Happiness is false if it is not reached through the lived experience of affliction and deprivation, if it does not signal a process and transformation. Again, the Psalms insist, only the wicked live a life devoid of pain (see Psalm 73). The righteous, by contrast, know pain all too well as they cry out for deliverance, and, once delivered or in anticipation of deliverance, convey their gratitude and joy to God. Praise and thanksgiving are the form-full, psalmic expressions of happiness.[45] They confirm that happiness is not a possession but an activity and a gift. Happiness is a gift received and sustained in God's ongoing work of salvation and edification. It is also an activity, a human striving toward praise. Happiness, in short, is found in the fulfillment of right desire.

5. Shaping Desire

The Psalter's shape—its overarching movement from petition to praise, pain to joy, crisis to hope—can be seen as a way of shaping desire. In his discussion of Thomas Aquinas, Stephen Wang notes that happiness is constituted by the fulfillment of desire.[46] Further, Richard Kraut argues that for Aristotle the "complete fulfillment of desire is a necessary condition of *eudaimonia*, but not a sufficient one. For on Aristotle's theory, those desires must be directed at worthwhile

---

43. V. Steven Parrish, *A Story of the Psalms: Conversation, Canon, and Congregation* (Collegeville, MN: Liturgical Press, 2003), 16–17. Parrish suggestively pairs Israel's story profiled in the Psalms with the "story of the church," specifically the rise and fall of Christendom.

44. To borrow from Walter Brueggemann's typology of function for the Psalms. See his *The Message of the Psalms: A Theological Commentary* (Augsburg Old Testament Studies; Minneapolis: Augsburg, 1984), as well as the article-length study where he originally laid out the program: "Psalms and the Life of Faith: A Suggested Typology of Function," *JSOT* 17 (1980): 3–32, reprinted in idem, *The Psalms and the Life of Faith*, 3–32.

45. Cf. the work of Walter Brueggemann in the previous note, to which one might add his essays "Praise and the Psalms: A Politics of Glad Abandonment," *The Hymn* 43/3 (1992): 14–19; 43/4 (1992): 14–18; and "The Formfulness of Grief," *Int* 31 (1977): 263–75, both reprinted in idem, *The Psalms and the Life of Faith*, 112–32 and 84–97, respectively.

46. Stephen Wang, "Aquinas on Human Happiness and the Natural Desire for God," *New Blackfriars* 88 (2007): 322–34, esp. 322.

goals."[47] Combining Aquinas and Aristotle, one finds that happiness is gained from the fulfillment of *right* desires, desires directed toward ethically worthy objects or goals. In the Psalms, the direction of desire leads ineluctably to God.

> As a doe longs for ravines of water,
>   so my soul longs for you, O God.
> My soul[48] thirsts for God, the living God.
>   When shall I come and see the face of God? (Ps 42:2–3)

> O God, my God, you are the one for whom I search;
>   my soul thirsts for you.
> My flesh grows faint for you
>   in a dry and wearied land, with no water.
> So I have looked for you in the sanctuary,
>   to behold your power and glory. (Ps 63:2–3)

> My soul longs, indeed it faints, for the courts of Yhwh;
>   My heart and my flesh cry aloud to the living God. (Ps 84:3)

> Whom else do I have in the heavens?
>   Besides you there is nothing I desire [*ḥāpaṣtî*] on earth.
> Though my flesh and my heart may fail,
>   God is the rock of my heart and my portion forever. (Ps 73:25–26)

Whether as consuming passion or unquenchable thirst, the desire for God in the Psalms is inscribed as the most intense and worthy of desires. The intensity of poetic expression serves to augment the worthiness of the desideratum. God is deemed the ultimate object of desire, captivating both *nepeš* and flesh, heart and soul. By inscribing God as *the* object of desire, the Psalms articulate the deepest of all desires, thereby unveiling desire's true meaning. As Susan Griffin notes, "[T]his is the meaning of desire, that wanting leads us to the sacred."[49]

The sacred, moreover, *has a place*, a home. The yearning for God's presence in the Psalms is coupled with the longing to dwell in God's temple or "house" (see,

---

47. Richard Kraut, "Two Conceptions of Happiness," *Philosophical Review* 88 (1979): 167–77, esp. 176.

48. Here and below, "soul" translates Hebrew *nepeš*.

49. Susan Griffin, *Pornography and Silence: Culture's Revenge against Nature* (New York: Harper & Row, 1981), 262.

e.g., 65:5; 84:11), heightened all the more by the intensely aesthetic descriptions of God and God's holy residence.

> One thing I ask of Yhwh, which I seek:
>> to dwell in Yhwh's house all the days of my life,
> to gaze upon Yhwh's beauty
>> and inquire in his temple. (Ps 27:4)

God's aesthetic appeal is localized in the Psalms. "From Zion, the perfection of beauty, God shines forth," intones Ps 50:2. "His holy mountain, beautiful in elevation, is the joy of all the earth," the psalmist rhapsodically declares (48:2–3; see also 26:8).

God's locality in the Psalms is an expression of God's intimacy, hence the ardent language of love that permeates the psalmist's orientation to God, matching the depth of expressed desire:

> I love you, Yhwh, my strength. (Ps 18:2)

> Yhwh, I love the beauty of your abode,
>> the dwelling place of your glory. (Ps 26:8)

> May all who seek you rejoice and be glad in you,
>> and may those who love your salvation say continually,
>>> "Great is God!" (Ps 70:5)

These three passages present three interrelated objects of desire: Yhwh, Yhwh's abode, and Yhwh's salvific work.

Desire, however, is by no means one sided; it is not the sole property of the human heart. The psalmist's longing for God's abode is, at least in two psalms, met by God's desire for the same.

> For Yhwh has chosen Zion;
>> he desired it ['iwwāh] for his residence.
> "This is my resting place forevermore;
>> here I shall reside, for I have desired it ['iwwitîhā]." (Ps 132:13–14)

> O mountain of God, O mountain of Bashan;
>> O many-peaked mountain, O mountain of Bashan!
> Why do you gaze with envy, O many-peaked mountains,
>> at the mountain that God desires [ḥāmad] for his enthronement,

where YHWH himself dwells forever?
God's chariots are twice ten thousand, thousands ad infinitum,
The Lord is with them, the One of Sinai, in the sanctuary. (Ps 68:16–18)

Divine desire finds its fulfillment in divine residing, suggesting that God's "happiness" is realized in and through a particular locus. God desires resting space, communion space. So does the psalmist:

For better is a day in your courts than a thousand elsewhere;
I would rather stand[50] at the threshold of the house of my God,
than dwell in the tents of wickedness.
For YHWH is a sun and shield;
God is favor and glory.
YHWH gives, and does not withhold, good things
for those who walk with integrity.[51]
YHWH of hosts,
how happy [*'ašrê*] are those who trust in you! (Ps 84:11–13)

Happiness, in short, has a *Sitz im Leben*, and it is the house of God. The *'ašrê*-saying in 84:13 extends the sanctuary setting to include all (not just temple doorkeepers) who "trust" in God, the God of all "good things" (84:12).

In addition to God and God's abode, God's Torah is cast as an object of love. The longest psalm of the Psalter, for example, is also the most passionate of the psalms:

O how I love your Torah!
All day long it is my deliberation! (Ps 119:97)

And I find delight in your commandments,
which I love.
And I shall lift up my hands to your commandments,
which I love,
and deliberate on your statutes. (Ps 119:47–48)

Therefore, I love your commandments
more than gold, even fine gold. (Ps 119:127)

---

50. Literally, "choose to stand." The syntax suggests that the verb √*bḥr* is to be conjoined with the following Hiphil infinitive from √*spp* despite the Masoretic division.

51. Despite scholarly redivisions of this verse, the MT is perfectly understandable as it stands.

> I hate falsehood, indeed, I abhor it;
> it is your law that I love. (Ps 119:163)

In this mystical meditation, the speaker is love-struck over God's "law." As Torah elicits the speaker's ardent love, it awakens, in turn, the speaker's desire for righteousness and understanding (vv. 40, 106, 144). So, again, Psalm 1's beatitude rings clear: "How happy is the one ... whose delight is in Yhwh's Torah!" (1:1–2). In Psalm 19, which could be aptly called "The Joy of *Lex*," Yhwh's Torah is deemed a source of happiness and the object of unsurpassed desire.

> The Torah of Yhwh is perfect,
>   reviving the soul.
> The testimony of Yhwh is sure,
>   imparting wisdom to the simple.
> The precepts of Yhwh are upright,
>   gladdening the heart.
> The commandment of Yhwh is lucid,
>   giving light to the eyes.
> The fear of Yhwh is pure,
>   enduring forever.
> The ordinances of Yhwh are firm,
>   all of them righteous.
> They are more desirable than gold,
>   more than abundant fine gold,
>   sweeter also than honey, the drippings of the honeycomb. (Ps 19:8–11)

Torah has the effect of "reviving the soul" and "gladdening the heart." It is the medium of happiness. Happiness, thus, is set squarely within the ethos of wisdom and obedience, within the ethos of Torah piety.

According to Thomas Aquinas (via Stephen Wang), "Perfect happiness ... can only be found in union with God."[52] Although the language of divine union is not to be found in the earthy, poetic discourse of the Psalms, God does play an indispensable role in the embodiment of happiness. Although Psalms 111 and 112 do not speak of a union between the divine and the human, as if God's presence can be merged, metaphysically or otherwise, with the human, happiness is nevertheless gained by those who "walk in God's ways" (128:1) or "walk in the light of

---

52. Wang, "Aquinas on Human Happiness," 322.

[YHWH's] face" (89:16) or "walk in YHWH's Torah" (119:1). Put more prosaically, obedience is key to happiness; obedience is next to *imitatio.*

But the way to psalmic happiness involves more than just obedience to God or imitation of God. The psalmist also speaks of being in God's very presence (literally "face").

> You make known to me the path of life;
>> in your presence is abundant joy;
>> in your right hand are delights forevermore. (Ps 16:11)

In this psalm of trust, happiness has its home before God's countenance. How appropriate! The face is the one part of the body that can communicate happiness. So God's "face," in particular, is the source of joy. And it is before God's lifted, radiant "face" (cf. Num 6:25–26) that the speaker is filled with gratitude for God's many blessings ("delights"), the blessings of prosperity and security. God's presence, in short, bears human happiness.

In order to speak of God's presence in proximity to (rather than in union with) the individual, the psalmist frequently refers to being "before" the deity, often conjuring the setting of worship (e.g., 22:27; 95:6). However, being "before" God can be a decidedly mixed blessing because God's presence can also bring about harsh judgment (9:3), destruction (18:12; 50:3), defeat and dismay (66:3; 81:15). Being in proximity to God may not be desirable or an occasion for happiness at all (e.g., 39:13)! "You, yes you, are awesome; who can stand before you when you are enraged?" (76:8). It all depends on God's disposition, for joy and exaltation are also felt "before" God:

> Let the field exult and all therein;
>> then shall all the trees of the forest rejoice aloud,
> before YHWH, for he is coming,
>> for he is coming to judge the earth. (Ps 96:12–13a)

> Sing praise to YHWH with the lyre,
>> with the lyre and the sound of song.
> With trumpets and the *shofar* blast,
>> shout for joy before YHWH the king! (Ps 98:5–6)

Joyful worship, both human and nonhuman, is exhorted as the proper response to being in God's presence, the divine king, even as the deity approaches to render judgment. As happiness has its source in God's manifest beneficence, it also has its derivation in human conduct. Happiness is something that can be commanded and cultivated.

> Delight yourself in Yʜwʜ,
> > and he will give you the desires of your heart.
> Direct[53] your way to Yʜwʜ;
> > trust in him and he will act.
> And he will bring forth your vindication like the light,
> > and your cause like noonday.
> Be still before Yʜwʜ,
> > and wait restlessly for him. (Ps 37:4–7)

In Psalm 37, the language of delight and desire meets the rhetoric of commitment and trust. The result is a mixture of restraint and restless anticipation "before Yʜwʜ." Can one call this happiness? If so, it is more than a matter of fulfilled desire and far from a life of blissful contentment. Happiness according to this psalm is found in a life passionately lived in commitment to God, a life lived *coram deo*.

6. Conclusion

Happiness has many faces in the Psalms. In the "pursuit" or practice of happiness, divine and human agency are highlighted in various ways. Happiness is both a prescription or mode of human conduct and a matter of reception rooted in God's grace. Happiness is where human yearning and divine fulfillment meet; it is the intersection of hope and help, of desire and gift. But happiness is also a process, a movement directed toward its consummation, with misery as its point of departure, ever lurking in the background. Unlike in Proverbs, the righteous suffer in the Psalms while the wicked remain immune from pain. Yet the righteous, not the wicked, are the ones deemed happy. While the wicked "boast of their desires" (10:3), the righteous pray and wait, meditate and trust—restlessly. Happiness in the Psalms has more to do with one's passionate reliance on God, come what may, than with material prosperity and freedom from pain.[54] "I think of God, and I moan" (77:3) certainly does not suggest bliss and contentment. Nevertheless, orientation to God, painful as it may be, is key to happiness. Happiness is found in a passion for God.[55]

---

53. Literally, "roll" (from √*gll*). See Pss 22:9; 119:22; Prov 16:3. The LXX reads "reveal," which reflects √*glh*.

54. See J. Clinton McCann Jr., "The Shape of Book I of the Psalter and the Shape of Human Happiness," in *The Book of Psalms: Composition and Reception* (eds. Peter W. Flint and Patrick D. Miller; VTSup 99; Leiden: Brill, 2005), 343.

55. For the importance of passion in biblical theological reflection, see David M. Carr, "Passion for God: A Center in Biblical Theology," *HBT* 23 (2001): 1–24.

Happiness in the Psalms is a matter of anguished, confident trust in God. It is also a matter of leading a morally credible life in relation to God, evidenced in obedience to God's Torah, in the practice of justice, and in compassion for the poor (see, e.g., 41:2; 106:3). The joy-filled presence of God is embodied in the joy-filled imitation of God. Happiness, moreover, points to a distinct setting, one in which God and human dwell together, a refuge that rests upon God's providential care. As much as happiness is a matter of piety, it is also a gift of God in blessing, the outworking of God's *ḥesed* or benevolence, which is frequently referenced in petition and praise. As for those who engage God in petition in the Psalms, they are the "poor and needy," the wretched and the miserable (*'ānî wě'ebyôn*). They do not deny their need for God. Total self-sufficiency and complete independence are delusions conjured by the wicked. For the righteous in the Psalms, the need for the Lord is the beginning of happiness, a distinctly wise happiness. The abject need mentioned so often in the Psalms reflects a world wracked by misery and disillusionment, finitude and deprivation, in other words, a *real* world. And real happiness charts a rocky path through that pain, never around it.

5

Positive Psychology and Ancient Israelite Wisdom

Carol A. Newsom

1. The Positive Psychology Movement

The positive psychology movement, which developed in quiet and respectable scientific obscurity for a number of years, has recently become a popular culture phenomenon, with best-selling books like Daniel Gilbert's *Stumbling on Happiness* and Martin E. P. Seligman's *Authentic Happiness: Using the New Positive Psychology to Realize Your Potential for Lasting Fulfillment*, just to mention two of the best known.[1] Considerable misunderstanding surrounds the field, in part because of the confusing semantics of the word "happiness." Popularly understood, "happiness" refers to a subjective affective state or an emotion. One might say, "That was one of the happiest days of my life" or "Happiness is a warm puppy." In these sentences, happiness is a subjective feeling, and one of the concerns of positive psychology has indeed been to study subjective well-being, including the "hedonic capacity" of persons—that is, their ability to experience pleasure.[2] More broadly, however, positive psychology is concerned with multiple dimensions of

---

1. Daniel Gilbert, *Stumbling on Happiness* (New York: Knopf, 2006); Martin E. P. Seligman, *Authentic Happiness: Using the New Positive Psychology to Realize Your Potential for Lasting Fulfillment* (New York: Simon and Schuster, 2002).

2. See, e.g., Ed Diener, Richard E. Lucas, and Shigehiro Oishi, "Subjective Well-Being: The Science of Happiness and Life Satisfaction," and David Watson, "Positive Affectivity: The Disposition to Experience Pleasurable Emotional States," both in *Handbook of Positive Psychology* (eds. C. R. Snyder and S. J. Lopez; New York: Oxford University Press, 2002), 63–73 and 106–19, respectively.

human flourishing, as is reflected in the definition from the website of the Positive Psychology Center at the University of Pennsylvania:

> Positive Psychology is the scientific study of the strengths and virtues that enable individuals and communities to thrive. . . . This field is founded on the belief that people want to lead meaningful and fulfilling lives, to cultivate what is best within themselves, and to enhance their experiences of love, work, and play.
>
> Positive Psychology has three central concerns: positive emotions, positive individual traits, and positive institutions. Understanding positive emotions entails the study of contentment with the past, happiness in the present, and hope for the future. Understanding positive individual traits consists of the study of the strengths and virtues, such as the capacity for love and work, courage, compassion, resilience, creativity, curiosity, integrity, self-knowledge, moderation, self-control, and wisdom. Understanding positive institutions entails the study of the strengths that foster better communities, such as justice, responsibility, civility, parenting, nurturance, work ethic, leadership, teamwork, purpose, and tolerance.[3]

In this more encompassing understanding, positive psychology is concerned not just with the hedonic dimensions of well-being but also the eudaimonic aspects of the same. The term "eudaimonic" is appropriated from the ancient Greek philosophical reflection on the nature of the good life considered as a whole and how one should pursue it. In this view, the result of a life well lived would be *eudaimonia* ("happiness").[4] The Greek philosophical schools disagreed among themselves, however, as to how one best goes about achieving *eudaimonia*, and the Epicureans even made the pursuit of "pleasure" (*hedonia*) the goal, though their definition of pleasure is more akin to what one might today call "tranquility" or "contentment."[5] As positive psychology has appropriated the term *eudaimonia*, it is largely in the Aristotelian sense of the pursuit of the good life through the cultivation of virtues.[6]

---

3. Positive Psychology Center homepage, accessed August 10, 2011, http://www.ppc.sas.upenn.edu.

4. See Julia Annas, *The Morality of Happiness* (New York: Oxford University Press, 1993), 329–33.

5. See the discussion by Annas (ibid., 238).

6. This connection has been made most explicitly by Samuel S. Franklin, who has integrated the findings of positive psychology and Aristotelian virtue ethics in his work, *The Psychology of Happiness: A Good Human Life* (Cambridge: Cambridge University Press, 2010).

2. *The Wisdom Tradition*

While it is evident that there is a natural affinity between Aristotelian philosophy and positive psychology, in this essay I would like to investigate the extent to which the Israelite wisdom tradition also provides an insightful conversation partner for positive psychology, and in particular wish to explore whether the wisdom tradition can shed light on the different contexts within which eudaimonic and hedonic aspects of happiness may be emphasized. Within biblical literature, the wisdom tradition is distinctive in that here specific and sustained attention is given to the nature of human well-being and how that is to be secured. This is most clearly the case with the book of Proverbs, though the issue also preoccupies Qoheleth.[7] To understand why the wisdom tradition seems to have been so different from so much of the rest of Israelite literature in its preoccupation with achieving a happy life one needs to reflect briefly on two dimensions of its social location: its folk substratum and its professional scribal context.

As many ethnographic studies have shown, folk proverbs across the globe are deeply practical bits of wisdom designed to help persons negotiate the vicissitudes of life by maximizing the good and minimizing the bad. Moreover, they are regularly used in the education of the young for the purpose of teaching insights and values that benefit both the individual and the social group.[8] While the stock of proverbs in any society will reflect aspects of its distinctive culture, they share this fundamental human concern of enhancing one's well-being and negotiating social conflict through acting wisely. Thus one should not be surprised that Israel's proverb collections, even though they are preserved in sophisticated literary form rather than directly as a folk tradition, also give evidence of this concern for securing well-being.

At the same time, the fact that wisdom literature *as literature* is part of an international scribal culture may also help account for why its specific focus on the human condition differs somewhat from other Israelite literary traditions. The wisdom instruction, often couched as advice from a highly placed father to his son on how to succeed in life and at court, is not only the oldest known literary

---

7. The book of Job could also be said to pursue the issue, but it does so by exploring a life made unbearable through the loss of family, wealth, health, and meaningfulness. Such an exploration would thus be a negative one. Cf. the essay by Jacqueline Lapsley in the present volume for the possibilities of extrapolating positive prospects of happiness even from prophetic negativity. The project is thus not impossible, but rather circuitous and certainly not direct.

8. Wolfgang Mieder, *Proverbs: A Handbook* (Westpoint, CT: Greenwood Press, 2004), 146. MaximsNet, a research initiative developed by the Templeton Foundation, funds research on the teaching of maxims for character education in schools and other contexts (www.maximsnet.org; accessed, August 10, 2011).

genre in the ancient Near East, but was also an international genre, attested in Mesopotamia, Egypt, and Israel.[9] It apparently served as a part of the first stage of the scribal curriculum and in this way was an important element in constructing the scribal ethos and identity.[10] In fact, the section of Proverbs entitled "The words of the wise" (Prov 22:17–24:34) is in part an adaptation of the Egyptian Instruction of Amenemope.[11] Although traces of the court setting remain discernible in Proverbs (in particular in the short instruction to King Lemuel by his mother in Prov 31:1–9 and perhaps in the Solomonic persona adopted in Eccl 1:1, 12), the instructions in Proverbs 1–9 simply have the framing of a father's advice to his son concerning the dispositions, disciplines, and actions that will lead to a flourishing life. Thus the combination of proverb collections and instructions that are represented in the book of Proverbs derive from oral and literary traditions that have as their primary concern the transmission of knowledge that enables the one who appropriates it to live a good life both in the moral sense of the term and with respect to one's own personal satisfaction.

Since the literary wisdom tradition is literature cultivated by the intellectual scribal elites for their own study and reflection, it is also the place where ideas were vigorously debated and challenged. Thus it also contains a skeptical tradition, represented in biblical canon by the books of Job and Qoheleth. For the purposes of asking how the biblical wisdom tradition might engage with positive psychology concerning the nature, possibility, and conditions for human happiness, the books of Proverbs and Qoheleth form a particularly instructive contrast. Proverbs is deeply committed to what we would call the eudaimonic understanding of happiness, whereas Qoheleth emphasizes the hedonic understanding as the only kind of happiness available to humans.[12] In what follows, I want to make a case for this distinction and to look at the different assumptions about the world and the place of human beings in it that led to such different assessments of how one finds happiness.

---

9. See the survey of ancient Near Eastern wisdom literature in Michael V. Fox, *Proverbs 1–9: A New Translation with Introduction and Commentary* (AB 18A; New York: Doubleday, 2000), 17–27.

10. Fox, *Proverbs 1–9*, 6–12.

11. See Roland E. Murphy, *Proverbs* (WBC 22; Nashville: Thomas Nelson, 1998), 290–94.

12. My use of the terms "eudaimonic" and "hedonic" is closer to their general use in positive psychology than to their technical use in Greek philosophy. Most Greek philosophers would have been rather dismissive of the particular goods identified by the book of Proverbs as the rewards of a life of wisdom and virtue. They generally argued that virtue was its own reward and was superior to the material and social goods that Proverbs so frequently mentions.

3. The Eudaimonic Ideal: Proverbs
The Dominant Tropes

The book of Proverbs is not a unified composition but rather a collection of collections, and the explicit preoccupation with the eudaimonic ideal is not evenly represented in the different parts of the book.[13] It is least evident in the oldest strata (e.g., the proverbs of the men of Hezekiah in Proverbs 25–29, which may date from the eighth through seventh centuries BCE) and most prominent in the introductory and concluding sections (Proverbs 1–9; 31), which are generally considered to date from the Persian period (fifth through fourth centuries BCE). The eudaimonic ideal is also strongly present in Proverbs 10–15, however, which probably dates from the time of the monarchy. Why there should be differences in the distribution of proverbs and instructions that feature the eudaimonic ideal is not immediately evident, but perhaps it has to do with the changing function of the proverb collections and instructions over time, or perhaps with different literary preferences that shape the various collections. In any event, the positioning of Proverbs 1–9 at the beginning of the book makes its concern for the eudaimonic understanding of wisdom the hermeneutical lens through which the entire book of Proverbs is presented.

One way of examining the eudaimonic ideal in Proverbs is to look at the motivational rhetoric by which the acquisition of wisdom is commended to the reader. The term "wisdom" here is a shorthand for a set of related terms, since "wisdom" (ḥokmâ), along with its synonym "understanding" (bînâ), is the preferred terminology in Proverbs 1–9. In Proverbs 10–15 the comparable concept is "righteousness" (ṣĕdāqâ). While there certainly are differences in meaning between "wisdom" and "righteousness," for present purposes, I take these terms to be functionally equivalent as signifiers of what one must embody in order to experience the eudaimonic ideal.[14]

The range of tropes used to commend wisdom provides a good indication of the values associated with it. Without question, the fundamental underlying trope for recommending wisdom to the reader is a life/death contrast. Wisdom and righteousness are repeatedly associated with life, whereas folly and wickedness are

13. The usual divisions are as follows: Prov 1:1–9:18; 10:1–15:33; 16:1–22:16; 22:17–24:22; 24: 23–34; 25: 1–29: 27; 30: 1–9; 30:10–33; 31:1–9; 31:10–31.

14. Knut M. Heim (*Like Grapes of Gold Set in Silver: An Interpretation of Proverbial Clusters in Proverbs 10:1–22:16* [BZAW 273; Berlin: Walter de Gruyter, 2001], 77–82) has demonstrated that the antitheses "wise/foolish" and "righteous/wicked," though not technically synonymous, are coreferential. That is to say, they refer to the same sets of persons, and, along with antitheses from additional semantic domains, serve to fill out the characterization of those persons.

associated with death (e.g., 2:18–19; 4:4; 11:19). Sometimes wisdom is said to give one a *long* life (3:2), but most often the term is used without a qualifier. In addition, the mythic image of wisdom as a "tree of life" occurs several times (3:18; 11:30; 13:12; 15:4). Although imagery of flourishing plants (i.e., life as vital, growing matter) occurs only sporadically in Proverbs (11:18), it is the dominant image in the wisdom psalm, Psalm 1.[15] Perhaps also related to the "life" cluster is the trope of healing (3:8; 4:22; 12:18), which is used both to describe the rewards of wisdom and the effect of the wise on others.

What does it mean to associate wisdom with "life"? Insofar as wise and prudential behavior means engaging in less risky and antisocial behavior and in following various practices (e.g., diligent work) that enhance the likelihood of well-being, one could say that wisdom literally results in a net advantage in terms of duration and quality of life. Much of the advice in chapters 10–30 has this pragmatic quality. But the life/death contrast that occurs frequently throughout the book, and the mythic imagery associated with wisdom and its opposite in chapters 1–9, suggests that references to life often have more than just a literal or pragmatic meaning (see further below).

To continue the analysis of tropes, it is quickly evident that even more numerous than the motivational images of life are those that are cast in terms of the ability of wisdom or righteousness to prevent something negative from happening. Wisdom is a shield (2:7), a protection (2:11–12), a prevention from stumbling (4:12; 6:22). Righteousness saves from death (10:2). The righteous person is not shaken (10:30), is delivered from trouble (11:21), suffers no harm (12:21), experiences security (10:25), and has a house that endures (12:7). This listing could be easily extended. These images lend an important nuance to the life/death contrast. As micro-narratives, they imply a perception of the world as a place of danger, threat, and insecurity, in which surviving intact is a great good. Thus the good that wisdom secures is envisioned as a kind of confident stability, a freedom from anxiety in the face of turmoil.

Wisdom is not simply about security, of course, but also is positively associated with material prosperity. The connection between wisdom and wealth is also one of those aspects of the wisdom literature that evokes criticism from some biblical scholars.[16] Proverbs, however, is quite clear that prosperity is a good, even though a relative good (as suggested by the sequences of "better than" sayings in

---

15. See the essay by William P. Brown in the present volume.

16. See the discussion of the ambiguity of wealth and poverty in Proverbs in Timothy J. Sandoval, *The Discourse of Wealth and Poverty in the Book of Proverbs* (BIS 77; Leiden: Brill, 2006), 31–39.

15:16–17; 16:8; 17:1; 19:1; etc.). Moreover, in the society in which the wisdom literature developed, extremes of wealth and poverty were not common.[17] Prosperity in Proverbs is thus rather to be understood in the context of freedom from want. As such, it is closely related to the cluster of tropes that feature security and life.

Slightly different is the association of wisdom with social approbation, both from the community and from the deity. In contrast to some modern individualistic rhetorics of happiness, well-being in ancient Israel was understood to be a socially dependent phenomenon. To enjoy the esteem of one's peers and to be honored by God were deeply satisfying aspects of existence, just as shame and contempt were associated with misery.[18] Significantly, wisdom is not only understood to be a benefit to the one who possesses it but is also a benefit to the community. As Gerhard von Rad demonstrated, good and bad are envisioned as active principles.[19] Good action creates good for others and for the one who does it (e.g., 10:11; 11:30; 14:25). Bad action similarly does harm to others and ultimately to the one who acts badly (25:18–19; 26:27–28).

One category of motivation, however, is strikingly absent from the description of wisdom and human flourishing in Proverbs. Only seldom are terms used that have to do with the emotions. The expression "happy" (*'ašrê*, 3:13; 8:34), though it can refer to subjective experience (Gen 30:13), more often describes an objective condition (e.g., fortunate, blessed; see Psalm 128).[20] Similarly, the experience of *šālôm* ("peace," "well-being," 3:17) straddles the objective/subjective line. Occasionally, the terms "pleasantness" (*nōʿam*, 3:17; cf. 2:10) and "joy" (*śimḥâ*, 10:28) occur, but they are not the primary vocabulary for describing the one who possesses wisdom. Virtually nowhere in Proverbs is there a sense of hedonic pleasure as a desired good in itself. Indeed, Proverbs goes out of its way to stress the nonhedonic aspects of acquiring wisdom through its repeated descriptions of the discipline (*mûsār*) to which the individual must submit (3:11; 4:1; 8:33, etc.). The term *mûsār* occurs some twenty-three times in Proverbs and is regularly associated with the term "reproof" (*tôkaḥat*, 10:17; 12:1; 13:18, etc.) and with the imagery of beating with a rod (*šebeṭ*). The acquisition of wisdom is thus depicted as something that does not come easily to an individual and that is acquired only through resisting one's natural inclinations to seek immediate pleasure.

---

17. David Jobling, "Wealth," in *NIDB* 5:826–27.

18. F. Gerald Downing, "Honor," in *NIDB* 2:884–85.

19. Gerhard von Rad, *Wisdom in Israel* (trans. James D. Martin; Nashville: Abingdon, 1972), 77.

20. See Brown's essay in the present volume, as well as the chapter by Ellen T. Charry. For *'ašrê* and the other happiness terms mentioned below, see also the Appendix by Michael J. Chan.

Proverbs is primarily focused on the satisfactions that come from the nexus that connects disciplined and virtuous character, diligent work, and the rewards these will bring (6:6–11; 12:11). It has often been suggested that the concluding acrostic poem of the book in Prov 31:10–31 is a portrait of the ideal of wisdom as embodied in a woman—the "woman of strength" ('ēšet ḥayil). She is in many respects the embodiment of quasi-mythic Woman Wisdom of Proverbs 8, or, as Michael V. Fox puts it, "she does not personify wisdom; she *instantiates* it."[21] Perhaps modeled on the well-to-do Jewish women of the Persian period,[22] she is presented as, above all, a capable businesswoman and household administrator, a model of industriousness and accomplishment. Prosperity, flourishing life, and security are closely associated with her. But she is also associated with charity toward the poor, with piety, and with instruction in wisdom in her household. Her children have apparently turned out well. Moreover, she enjoys the esteem of her children, her husband, and the community. She embodies a model of the eudaimonic ideal that is highly oriented to security, economic well-being, social connectedness, virtue, and reputation. The connection between knowledge, technical expertise, and diligence, on the one hand, and successful accomplishment of goals, on the other, is central to the poem's imagination. These are the satisfactions of wisdom. This is what it means to have and get "life."[23]

The Metaphysical Assumptions

Wisdom is frequently described by scholars as the search for regularities within the world of practical experience, the recognition of which can enable one to live successfully.[24] Fundamental to this project is the ability to trace out the relationship between acts and their consequences. In the older strata of Israelite wisdom, such as Proverbs 25–29, there is little theoretical speculation but much acute observation of human social and psychological behavior (e.g., 14:20; 25:13–23). The wisdom literature does recognize certain limits to the regularity of experience (16:1–2, 25); but in general, it judges reality to be sufficiently regular and

---

21. Fox, *Proverbs 1–9*, 915.

22. See Christine Roy Yoder, *Wisdom as a Woman of Substance: A Socioeconomic Reading of Proverbs 1–9 and 31:10–31* (BZAW 304; Berlin: Walter de Gruyter, 2000). Yoder's argument pertaining to this poem can also be found in her essay "The Woman of Substance ('ēšet ḥayil): A Socioeconomic Reading of Proverbs 31:10–31," *JBL* 122 (2003): 427–47.

23. Notably, the woman of strength is described from a male perspective. She herself does not speak nor does she indicate whether she ever suffers from burnout!

24. See, e.g., Leo G. Perdue, *Wisdom and Creation: The Theology of Wisdom Literature* (Nashville: Abingdon, 1994), 34–48.

sufficiently transparent to human understanding to be mastered by those who engage in the disciplines of wisdom.

Despite the occasional recognition of the contingent in the sphere of human experience, wisdom's rhetoric sometimes seems so absolute as to bring upon it the charge of failing to accurately observe reality. Sayings such as "No harm happens to the righteous, but the wicked have their fill of misfortune" (12:21) or "Treasures acquired by wickedness do not profit, but righteousness delivers from death" (10:2) do have the ring of complacency about them. Perhaps, however, one should engage in a slightly more generous hermeneutic. When a statement in a generally insightful writing appears stupidly false, one may need to look for meaning on a deeper level. What do the terms "harm" and "death" mean in these sayings? While it is possible that Israelite wisdom makes an assumption somewhat akin to what one finds in Stoic thought that to the truly wise person no *real* evil can occur, the terse aphoristic style of these wisdom texts leaves one uncertain.

Later strands of wisdom develop the theological and speculative implications of the worldview implied in the aphorisms, and in doing so help to shed light on what underlies the tropes of life, security, and prosperity beyond their everyday dimensions. Two passages in Proverbs 1–9 are especially instructive, 3:13–26 and 8:1–36. Proverbs 3:13–26 begins and ends with the term "happy" ('*ašrê*). This word introduces a *makarism* or beatitude, an exclamation of the good fortune of the person who possesses the quality named. Performatively, it is similar to a blessing.[25] Notably, this important passage and chapter 8 account for most of the occurrences of '*ašrê* in Proverbs. The recommendation of wisdom found in 3:13–20 uses the familiar tropes (the promise of long life, riches, and honor, even of something better than literal riches), as well as the more rare ones of pleasantness and peace.

Verses 16–18 introduce imagery of a different order, however. The depiction of Wisdom as holding long life in her right hand and riches and honor in her left is evocative of the way in which many Egyptian gods were represented, holding the *ankh* symbol (life) in one hand and the *wa'as* scepter (prosperity, dominion) in the other.[26] Whether this is a specific allusion to the Egyptian goddess Ma'at, who is often compared with biblical wisdom, is uncertain.[27] A second mythic motif occurs with the identification of wisdom as the tree of life. This motif,

---

25. Fox, *Proverbs 1–9*, 161.

26. Ibid., 156.

27. This connection is argued by Christa Kayatz, *Studien zu Proverbien 1–9* (WMANT 22; Neukirchen-Vluyn: Neukirchener Verlag, 1966), 105.

widespread in ancient Near Eastern art and literature, is associated with abundance, fertility, and even eternal life.[28] These mythic images, used rhetorically here, provide a transition to the opening of the next section, which has to do with the role of wisdom in divine creation. Here wisdom, understanding, and knowledge are apparently used instrumentally in God's creation of the physical world (vv. 19–20). This same wisdom is then urged upon the reader (v. 21; cf. v.13), suggesting that through the disciplines of wisdom instruction one has access to the structuring and life-giving qualities (v. 22) that are the imprint in the world of God's creative activity. The concluding section then describes the result of the acquisition of this wisdom in a series of images all having to do with security, freedom from fear, and confidence (vv. 23–26).

The passage in Proverbs 8 featuring personified wisdom also examines the nexus among the insights provided by wisdom instruction, the place of wisdom in the structures of creation, and the access to life provided by wisdom. In the first part of the poem (vv. 1–21), where Wisdom is introduced in the guise of a public wisdom teacher, many of the familiar tropes are present, especially those having to do with riches (vv. 10–11, 19–21), along with some less common ones. A notable section in vv. 15–16 connects wisdom with the all-important social role of just governance.

The central and most mythic part of the poem (vv. 22–31) is Wisdom's account of being "present at the creation." Unfortunately, several ambiguous or difficult words affect the understanding of the relationship between wisdom, God, and the act of creation, and these difficulties have given rise to considerable scholarly debate. But whether God creates, begets, or acquires wisdom (v. 22),[29] God is, in any event, represented as the first sage. In contrast to Prov 3:13–26, where wisdom is explicitly instrumental, in Proverbs 8 personified wisdom is present but is given a different role. The key words are "delight/delighting" (ša ʿăšū ʿîm, 8:30) and "laughing" or "playing" (měśaheqet, 8:30). Wisdom is first described in this relationship vis-á-vis God (v. 30b: "I was daily his delight, rejoicing before him always," NRSV) and then in this relationship to the world and humankind (v. 31: "rejoicing [měśaheqet] in his inhabited world and delighting [wěša ʿăšū ʿay] in the human race," NRSV).[30] Two things are noteworthy. First, Wisdom's facing in two directions—God and the created world—underscores what was evident also

---

28. Nancy deClaissé-Walford, "Tree of Knowledge, Tree of Life," in *NIDB* 5:660–61.

29. The Hebrew verb *qānâ* is frequently used in Proverbs 1–8 with the sense "acquire" (cf. 4:5). Given the context of Proverbs 8, many scholars prefer to translate the verb as "create," as in Gen 14:19. The sense "beget" is similar to the usage in Gen 4:1 and would be appropriate if one understands wisdom as God's daughter.

30. Translations are my own, unless otherwise indicated, as here.

in Prov 3:13–26, namely, that wisdom serves as a kind of mediator between the wise creator, the creation, and the wise sage who thus understands and locates himself in relation to this intelligible and life-giving order. Second, there is a place within the eudaimonic vision of Proverbs for the role of joy and playfulness. This appears, however, to be a kind of intellectual joy, as the image occurs just at the point where the reader has been given a view of God's creation of the structures of the world. Moreover, it is personified Wisdom herself who plays and delights. Thus the poem appears to suggest that understanding itself is a kind of joy. Here, one might note that for Aristotle, too, contemplation was the best form of *eudaimonia*.[31]

The concluding section of the poem is Wisdom's renewed appeal to the reader as teacher and perhaps as lover (v. 34b). As in Prov 3:13–18, the word "happy" (*'ašrê*) figures prominently (vv. 32, 34). Most significant, however, is the fact that the reason that one who seeks wisdom is happy is expressed in the life/death trope: "For whoever finds me finds life and obtains favor from Yʜᴡʜ; but whoever misses me does himself violence; all who hate me love death" (vv. 35–36). Having examined these passages, one is in a better position to understand the depth of the terms "life" and "death" and thus what one receives through wisdom. The promise of life from wisdom includes but is not limited to the likelihood of a longer and better quality of existence. To know wisdom is to root oneself in the creative forces and orderly structures that give rise to the generativity of the world. Although Hebrew thought in its developing monotheism does not preserve full mythic expression of the notion, the opposition between life and death is the same opposition articulated in Canaanite myth as that between Baal and Mot as the forces of generativity and sterility. The imagery that best captures the relationship is that of Psalm 1, which, perhaps not coincidentally, also begins with the word *'ašrê*.[32] There the one who finds pleasure (*ḥepeṣ*) in "the *torah* of Yʜᴡʜ" is compared to a tree whose roots have access to life-giving water and so consequently has both fruit and unwithered foliage (v. 3). But the wicked are like dry chaff that is cut off from earth and water and so do not have access to life and consequently "perish" (*'ābad*).

To summarize: the wisdom tradition as represented in Proverbs embraces a eudaimonic ideal of human flourishing. The possibility for this type of happiness is grounded in the belief that the structures of the world, including human nature, have been created in a stable and regular fashion that is intelligible to the human mind. To perceive these structures and to attune one's attitudes and actions with

---

31. See Aristotle, *Nichomachean Ethics*, §10.7–8.

32. Again, see Brown's essay in this volume.

them is to experience life, security, and even material well-being—but perhaps above all a kind of serenity that comes from understanding itself. The wise person is rooted in the structures of creation. Acquiring wisdom may well be a hard and lifelong pursuit, but the rewards clearly make it worthwhile.

4. From the Eudaimonic to the Hedonic: Qoheleth

If the eudaimonic ideal characterizes the book of Proverbs, one encounters a very different picture in the book of Qoheleth. Rightly characterized as a pessimistic book, it is also emphatic in its recommendation of a certain type of hedonic plea- sure. Although firm dating is elusive, it is generally agreed that the book of Qohe- leth is somewhat younger than the final edition of Proverbs, and is probably a product of the early Hellenistic period.[33] It is debated whether the sharp differ- ence between Qoheleth and Proverbs is to be attributed to the changing interna- tional political and cultural circumstances (i.e., the impact of the centralized Ptolemaic economic system and of Hellenistic culture in general) or whether Qoheleth simply represents the skeptical voice that was always an option within wisdom traditions. Very likely, the book of Qoheleth owes something to both factors.

The very opening words of Qoheleth's teaching indicate the nature of the problem: *hăbēl hăbālîm hakkol hābel* (Eccl 1:2b). While the phrase defies ade- quate translation, I find the most persuasive English equivalent for what Qohe- leth tries to convey in his image that everything is (literally) a "puff of air" (Hebrew *hebel*) to be the term "futility." Thus, the opening motto can be rendered "Utter futility! Everything is futile!" As many have noted, Qoheleth employs a remark- able amount of terminology that has economic and commercial overtones[34]— perhaps this is an ironic nod to the wisdom tradition's traditional concern with prosperity. Thus, in 1:3 Qoheleth asks, *mah yitrôn*, literally, "what is left over?" or "what is the profit"? The rest of the verse plays on the double nuances of the Hebrew root √ *'ml*—the verbal form meaning "to work, exert oneself," and the noun variously meaning both "acquisition, gain" and "trouble, anxiety, harm." So what is the net profit to a person in all the gains she makes for herself, or in all the anxiety with which she exerts herself? Somehow, all of the effort that a person

---

33. Choon-Leong Seow (*Ecclesiastes: A New Translation with Introduction and Commentary* [AB 18C; New York: Doubleday, 1997], 20–21) argues for a Persian period date for Ecclesias- tes, but most scholars think that the evidence points more likely to an early Hellenistic date (see, e.g., Roland E. Murphy, *Ecclesiastes* [WBC 23A; Dallas, TX: Word, 1992], xxii), though either date is possible.

34. See Seow, *Ecclesiastes*, 21–22.

puts forth and all of the pain involved results in nothing but insubstantial puffs of air—futility indeed!

Clearly, Qoheleth differs from the perception of the sages of Proverbs who had confidence in the ability of diligent work to produce reliable and valuable rewards. Such assumptions were at the center of their vision of the eudaimonic ideal. The difference, however, does not lie in the metaphysical question of whether or not there is an underlying orderliness to creation, as one might suppose, because Qoheleth is even more eloquent than Proverbs in describing order. But he does so with a devastatingly sardonic twist. The famous poem on the times in Eccl 3:1–8 may well be a traditional wisdom poem cited by Qoheleth.[35] Traditional wisdom would have drawn the conclusion that the wise person understands the times and adjusts his or her actions accordingly in order to produce the most reliable results. Qoheleth, however, having recited the list of paired opposites, concludes with the familiar question, "what profit is there?" (again, *mah yitrôn*)—that is, "what is left over for the worker from all at which he toils?" (3:9). To translate the balanced opposites of the poem into mathematical terms: "+ 1 and -1 = 0." Despite the orderly pattern of the times, the efforts of a person's life cancel each other out. There is nothing "left over," nothing that profits.

One can see a similar observation in the first poem of the book as well (1:3–8), where an observation of regularity in nature is set in relation to a claim that nothing is accomplished by all of this regular activity. The regular rising and setting of the sun (v. 5), the regular and perhaps seasonal rotation of the winds (v. 6), and the regular path of the rivers to the sea (v. 7) all appear to be evidence of nature's order. Yet if looked at as purposive activity, these repeated motions accomplish nothing, for "the sea is never filled" (v. 7). The beginning and end of the poem describe the nature of human experience of this order. "A generation goes and a generation comes, but the earth remains forever" (v. 4). The human presence changes nothing. Moreover, human comprehension and human speech are rendered futile by this order. "All words are wearisome; there is nothing one can say. The eye is not satisfied by seeing, nor the ear filled by hearing."[36]

Thus it is not the absence of an order but the absence of a *usable* order that troubles Qoheleth, and the problem is described in the book in several related ways. The wisdom project as it is represented in Proverbs is very "results oriented." One orients oneself within a dependable and intelligible order so as to accomplish

---

35. See Addison G. Wright, "'For Everything There is a Season': The Structure and Meaning of the Fourteen Opposites (Ecclesiastes 3,2–8)," in *De la Tôrah au Messie: Mélanges Henri Cazelles* (eds. J. Dore et al.; Paris: Desclée, 1981), 321–28.

36. The translation here is Murphy's (*Ecclesiastes*, lxxi, 5).

certain outcomes. The order that Qoheleth perceives in the natural world is not at all concerned with achievements, outcomes, and accrued results. Thus the suspicion arises that though the world may be orderly, it is not an order built to the human scale or appropriable for human purposes. A similar suggestion occurs in the enigmatic line that follows the poem on the times. The translation is debated, but is most often understood as follows: "He [i.e., God] has made everything fitting (*yāpeh*) in its time. Also he has put the duration of ages (*hā ʿōlām*) into their mind, but without a person's being able to find out what God has done from beginning to end" (3:11).[37] This verse is a notorious crux, but what Qoheleth is apparently saying here is that people can not only recognize the (futile) times of seasonality but can even have a sense of the vastness of past and future. Qoheleth was contemporary with the early stages of apocalyptic speculation, which often attempted to comprehend the events of the world over long ages of time and to grasp the divine intention for history. But Qoheleth asks whether this knowledge does a person any good. The answer is no, in his perspective, because one cannot in fact figure out what it is God is doing from beginning to end (*contra* the apocalypticists). Thus both on a small scale and on a large scale human beings can see the order of the world but not in a way that makes it usable for purposeful action.

What has changed between Proverbs and Qoheleth is not a belief in the orderliness of creation but rather the developing sense that the order is just beyond intelligibility, or, to put it more forcefully, the recognition that creation's patterns are finally inhuman patterns of order. In this regard, even though Qoheleth and the divine speeches in Job are in many respects the products of different questions, they both converge on the intuition that human desires and projects are an ill fit with the cosmos.[38] For Qoheleth, above all, the futility of human existence is the inability to exert reliable control over outcomes. One may amass wealth but cannot assure that the person who inherits it will not be foolish (2:18–21). One may do good and yet not experience good (8:14). Whereas Proverbs had a modest recognition of the contingent as an element of human experience (14:12; 16:25), for Qoheleth the contingent is the foreground of experience itself. "Time and chance happen to all. A person cannot even know his time. Like fish that are caught in a

---

37. See the translations and discussions in Murphy, *Ecclesiastes*, 29, 34–35; Seow, *Ecclesiastes*, 158, 172–73; and Thomas Krüger, *Qoheleth: A Commentary* (trans. O. C. Dean, Jr.; ed. Klaus Baltzer; Hermeneia; Minneapolis: Fortress Press, 2004), 80, 86–87.

38. For a discussion of the divine speeches in Job 38–41 as embodying a tragic sublimity, see Carol A. Newsom, *The Book of Job: A Contest of Moral Imaginations* (New York: Oxford University Press, 2003), 241–56. Although Qoheleth focuses on the topic of time, in Job it is the exorbitant and mysterious extremities of the cosmos and the undomesticability of so much of creation that communicates the book's denial that the orders that make human life meaningful are the orders by which creation is organized.

cruel net, and as birds are caught in a snare, just like them human beings are snared in a cruel time, when it falls upon them suddenly" (9:11b–12; NJPSV; cf. 8:16–17).

Not surprisingly, the collapse of the sense of the ability to exert control over one's situation through wisdom leads Qoheleth to a morbid revaluation of the traditional trope of life and death. Whereas Proverbs had associated wisdom with life, Qoheleth observes that both the wise person and the fool alike die. His conclusion? "And so I hated life" (2:17). When he does give the advantage to life, it is with tongue firmly in cheek, as when he tropes on a traditional saying, and observes that "a live dog is better than a dead lion—for the living know that they will die; but the dead know nothing" (9:4b–5a).

One can begin to see why Proverbs' eudaimonic ideal would be utterly impossible for Qoheleth. Without the confidence that actions more or less reliably produce anticipated consequences, there is no sound basis for planning and pursuing goals or for engaging in the hard work of the disciplines one needs in order to achieve wisdom and the other skills of living. Thus it is logical that Qoheleth would instead champion hedonic pleasure. His embrace of hedonic pleasure, however, is more subtle than one might anticipate. Early in the book, in chapter 2, Qoheleth makes a test of pleasure, including merriment, wine, beautiful houses and watered gardens, servants, property of all kinds—indeed, anything his heart desired (2:1–10). Yet at the beginning of this description he declares that it, too, was *hebel*, futile (2:1). His conclusion at the end of the passage initially sounds disjointed but actually holds the key to an important distinction. Having declared his experiment with pleasure to be *hebel*, he now says "I got enjoyment out of all my *ʿāmāl* [i.e., his wealth and/or work]; and this was all I got out of my *ʿāmāl*" (translation adapted from NJPSV).[39] What Qoheleth is saying is that the *pursuit* of happiness is doomed. One cannot pursue it as a project, because all projects qua projects are doomed. The pursuit of anything is "a chasing after wind" (4:6)—which is to say unreachable, unattainable. If the work itself is enjoyable, that is all you get. There will be nothing left over or secured as a lasting good.

To understand finally what Qoheleth means one has to examine his analysis of temporality. There is, of course, no control over the past. Memory, which the ancient Israelites considered to be the bridge between present and past, Qoheleth deems to be unreliable and even illusory:

> There is no memory now of those who came before, and as for those who will come after them—there will be no memory of them either among those who will come afterwards. (1:11)

---

39. As noted above, the noun *ʿāmāl* can refer both to work and to the rewards of work.

Nor is there control over the future, as Qoheleth's repeated dismantling of the act-consequence relationship demonstrates (see, e.g., 2:11–12; 7:15; 8:14). That leaves only the present and the experience of pleasure in the present. But the relentless Qoheleth will not even allow that one has control of the present moment. Even the ability to enjoy the present moment is in the hands of God, not the individual:

> There is an evil that I have seen under the sun, and a serious one for humanity. God gives a person riches and possessions and honor, so that he has no need of anything that he might desire. But God does not give him the ability to enjoy it; instead, a stranger enjoys it. (6:1–2)[40]

And yet, pleasure remains a human possibility. For this possibility, Qoheleth employs the tropes of "gift" and "portion" (i.e., "inheritance"):

> Also, whenever a person is given riches and property by God, and is also permitted by him to enjoy them and to take his portion and get pleasure for his gains—that is a gift of God. (5:18; adapted from NJPSV)

Just as pleasure cannot be made into a project, so work itself is to be valued not for what it accomplishes but for the pleasure that comes from the exercise of it, independent of its outcome: "all that your hand finds to do, do it with all your strength" (9:10).

Qoheleth's most eloquent articulation of this hard-won wisdom occurs in the familiar passage in 9:7–11, which is worth quoting in full:

> Go, eat your bread with joy
> > and drink your wine with a happy heart,
> > for God has already approved of what you do.
> Let your clothes always be white,
> > and never lack oil for your head.
> Enjoy life with a woman whom you love,
> all the days of your futile life that has been given to you under
> > the sun—all your futile days—
> > for that is your portion in life
> > and in the work that you do under the sun.
> All that your hand finds to do, do it with all your strength,
> > for there is no deed or thought or knowledge or wisdom in
> > > Sheol to which you are going.

---

40. In Hebrew the verb translated "enjoy" is literally "to eat" ($\sqrt{}$ '*kl*).

The shadow of death that hangs over life in Qoheleth does not, however, mean that happiness in the hedonic sense cannot be experienced. Rather, the certainty of death, like the knowledge of an individual's inability to control the future, is the precondition for his embrace of a distinctive kind of (hedonic) joy.

5. The Ecology of Eudaimonic and Hedonic Ideals of Happiness

This investigation of two key texts in the Israelite wisdom tradition has suggested that the key to the prominence of the eudaimonic or hedonic ideal of happiness is closely tied to the sense of a person's ability to exercise control over his or her circumstances. For this to be possible, not only must there be an order rather than a chaos, but that order must be intelligible to the person. Qoheleth seems also to add the important qualifier that even an intelligible order is of little use unless it is of a human scale and appropriable for human purposes. To be able to perceive an order that is inhuman in scale only adds to the misery. Where one can exercise control, then pleasure is to be found in projects planned and executed, material security provided for, relationships developed and maintained, justice and good governance envisioned and enacted, the mishaps of life avoided or minimized. At least this is the vision of the book of Proverbs. Hedonic pleasure may be part of the package, but it can be a danger as well as a good if it is allowed to dominate. The deepest satisfaction comes from understanding oneself as embedded not only within but as an active and constructive part *of* a moral order. This is what it means that wisdom "gives life."

There is no question but that Qoheleth would like to live in this kind of a world, but he perceives that the world is not like this, and his frustration brings him to the brink of bitterness. As a sage, he is relentlessly honest and relentlessly analytical. He names what he sees as the truth and then he explores the implications of this truth. If the act-consequence relationship is unreliable, if one cannot exercise even a measure of control over one's situation, if even enjoyment is something that is not in one's own power—then how should one live? For Qoheleth, the fundamental trope becomes that of the gift—not the gift of anthropological analysis in which complex social networks are tied together in mutuality, but the gift of a mercurial sovereign. Qoheleth's wisdom is the wisdom of the radically disempowered. What chance brings one's way should be enjoyed to the fullest—but without any sense of claim upon it. All that one can bring to the situation is receptivity (again, cf. 3:1–15).

6. Concluding Reflections

What might this analysis of eudaimonic and hedonic ideals in the wisdom tradition suggest for a conversation between biblical studies and positive psychology? It is helpful to return to the description of positive psychology from the Positive

Psychology Center of the University of Pennsylvania. Their understanding of the project of positive psychology is primarily eudaimonic, as is demonstrated in their threefold focus on positive emotions (which they describe as contentment, happiness, hope), positive individual traits (strengths and virtues: capacity for love and work, as well as integrity, moderation, self-control), and positive institutions that have as their strengths justice, work ethic, teamwork, and similar values. What I think the comparison of Proverbs and Qoheleth illumines is the vital nature of the institutional component. And this would perhaps present a challenge to certain approaches to positive psychology that tend to focus largely on the individual or simply on interpersonal elements in happiness.

Although both Proverbs and Qoheleth assume that they are talking about the nature of reality itself, the difference between Proverbs' confidence in the plausibility of the eudaimonic ideal and Qoheleth's despair over it probably has much to do with changing socioeconomic and political realities as one moved from Persian period Yehud, which still retained many of the autonomous and small-scale aspects of culture that had characterized Israelite society for centuries, to Ptolemaic-era Judea, which increasingly came under the authority of a highly centralized and exploitative bureaucratic state. Whether or not that is historically accurate, I would suggest that these two books certainly *imply* different kinds of societies. Proverbs and its eudaimonic ideal make sense in a small-scale, healthy society where people in fact are able to affect the circumstances of their lives through their own actions. In such a society the value of the cultivation of the virtues is evident and the emotions that flow from the exercise of those virtues result in a sense of well-being. Qoheleth implies a society in which people are *not* able to reliably affect the circumstances of their lives through their own actions. In such a context the cultivation of the virtues, especially those requiring nonhedonic discipline, simply makes less sense. And positive emotions such as "contentment" and "hope" are more difficult to achieve. That is not to say that happiness is not possible. Qoheleth convincingly shows that even in such a disempowered condition, intense hedonic joy is nevertheless possible. In fact, although he does not put it this way, the hedonic joy he describes could be seen as an important act of resistance against oppressive conditions, since it refuses to let the human spirit be crushed.

To the extent that positive psychology is a fundamentally eudaimonic project, then I would suggest that it needs to highlight the fundamentally important nature of healthy social structures—families, workplaces, communities, societies.[41] To the extent that individuals see themselves as part of a coherent, intelligible, and

---

41. Cf. Christopher Peterson, "Enabling Institutions," in idem, *A Primer in Positive Psychology* (New York: Oxford University Press, 2006), 275–304. My thanks to Charlotte Witvliet for pointing this work out to me.

just moral order to which their own actions contribute but which in an important way transcends them, they will likely find their happiness primarily through participation in that order. Where that order is still embraced as a normative ideal but is not consistently validated in experience, they will be critics and rebels (as is Job). But if the very plausibility of such a coherent, intelligible, and just moral order comes into question, then rational people will give up the eudaimonic ideal and will embrace a more individualistic experience of pleasure, as and when the opportunity offers. This may be still an individually and even socially positive response, as in the advice of Qoheleth to enjoy life with the spouse whom you love, but it can also lead to behaviors that are nihilistic—both destructive and self-destructive. This is the hedonism of despair, so often exemplified in the cultures of the urban underclass across the globe, but not only there. The hedonic principle as such— that is, the valuing of pleasure for pleasure's sake—does not appear to possess a clear rationale for preferring one type of pleasure over the other. So, while the hedonic ideal has an important role to play in negotiating the vicissitudes of any human life, in that it retains the possibility of happiness even for those who lack substantial control over their lives, the eudaimonic ideal and the conditions that make it possible should rightly remain the primary focus for positive psychology. A conversation with Israelite wisdom literature in turn may aid the positive psychology movement in its reflection on the fundamental conditions that permit and encourage persons to see happiness in both its hedonic and eudaimonic dimensions as realized within an encompassing eudaimonic framework.[42]

---

42. For similar points made from the perspective of the Hebrew prophets, see Lapsley's essay in this volume.

PART TWO

New Testament

Introduction to Part II

Part II contains four essays devoted to the New Testament's contribution to the study of happiness. Carl R. Holladay, Charles Howard Candler Professor of New Testament Studies at the Candler School of Theology, Graduate Division of Religion, and Center for the Study of Law and Religion at Emory University offers a wide-ranging study of Jesus's beatitudes in the first essay. Holladay shows that the beatitudes are not nearly as simple as they seem, and notes that their interpretation is complicated by a number of factors, not the least of which is the fact that they appear in slightly different forms in two distinct places in the New Testament (Matt 5:3–12 and Luke 6:20–26). The differences between the Matthean and Lukan accounts are related to what Holladay calls "each Evangelist's distinctive frame of reference." This means that one must pay close attention to even fine distinctions between the two sets of beatitudes—asking why, for instance, Matthew uses "kingdom of heaven," while Luke uses "kingdom of God"; or why Matthew uses the word "righteousness" twice, but Luke not at all. Through a brief but evocative exploration of the beatitudes in the history of interpretation from Gregory of Nyssa through Augustine, Holladay also demonstrates that what the beatitudes *originally meant* is inextricably bound up with what they have meant *ever since*. The constant (re)reading and (re)studying of a beloved passage of Scripture shows "how different levels or registers of meaning can emerge." Given the complexity and depth of the beatitudes as well as their interpretive flexibility, it is no wonder that they "have connected with Christians in every time and place."

In the next contribution, Joel B. Green, professor of New Testament at Fuller Theological Seminary, investigates happiness in a major part of the New Testament: the Gospel of Luke and its sequel, the book of Acts. As is clear from the title of Green's essay, the view of happiness in Luke-Acts confounds expectations. A different kind of happiness appears there, as evidenced, for example, in the fact that the apostles actually rejoice when they are treated dishonorably (Acts 5:41).

Through an analysis of three key junctures where the language of happiness is particularly heightened—namely, the stories about the births of John and Jesus in Luke 1–2; the parables of the lost sheep, lost coin, and lost son in Luke 15; and the Sermon on the Plain in Luke 6—Green demonstrates that the topsy-turvy happiness found in the narrative is "defined by God's eschatological intervention to bring salvation in all its fullness to all and, then, by the invitation to persons to order their lives accordingly." Jesus's coming, his message, his death, and his resurrection fundamentally change what happiness means, undercutting then-current understandings and calling for a new construal of "what constitutes and cultivates happiness." Those who would live their lives oriented to God's work in Jesus must thus redefine human flourishing and experience it in radically differently ways.

Colleen Shantz, who is associate professor of New Testament at St. Michael's College, Toronto School of Theology, and cross-appointed to the Department of Religion at the University of Toronto, turns her attention to the apostle Paul. Paul's letters afford a rather unique perspective on happiness in the Bible, since in this correspondence we hear from Paul directly, in his own voice. According to Paul's testimony, his life contained no small amount of suffering, and this leads Shantz to wonder how Paul could be happy when the facilitating conditions for happiness were so often absent from his life. After considering the details of Paul's hardships from the perspective of Martin Seligman's typology of the three kinds of happy lives, Shantz argues that both the pleasurable life and the good life were largely beyond Paul's reach. What Paul found instead was the *meaningful* life. That meaning, derived from the pattern of Jesus Christ, was precisely one that turned conventional notions of honor on their heads. It was this transformed understanding of happiness that enabled Paul to establish and nurture early communities of Christ-followers. These groups, then, provided the social cohesion needed to generate further happiness. This is what kept Paul from turning bitter, and this is what enabled him to face the worst circumstances, even the possibility of his own violent death, "with what might properly be called happiness."

In the last essay, Greg Carey, professor of New Testament at Lancaster Theological Seminary, considers happiness in apocalyptic literature. Apocalyptic is commonly associated with violent and cataclysmic end-time scenarios, but Carey finds a remarkable diversity among ancient Jewish and Christian apocalyptic writings. This means, not only that apocalyptic literature knows happiness, but also that "Apocalyptic happiness comes in different flavors." Positive psychology has demonstrated that identity and commitment are essential to human flourishing, and Carey finds both to be prominent in apocalyptic literature. Indeed, it is precisely these elements that enabled people to flourish despite the difficult times that are described in the apocalyptic texts, that lie behind them (in terms of their social location and historical origins), and that are foretold within them. Armed with these insights, Carey is able to delineate a profile of apocalyptic happiness: it is not primarily subjective or individualistic but is rather "judged according to publically articulated values and behaviors"; humans have some agency in the "pursuit of happiness," but within limits because some things are simply out of one's control; happiness is not primarily about attitude but about favored behavior; and, finally, happiness "involves a divine perspective." Apocalyptic happiness need not be restricted solely to the world to come, according to Carey. Rather, the crucial combination of narrative identity and commitment are profoundly relevant to all human flourishing. A basic sign of human happiness is found precisely in "the sense that one's life is oriented toward a greater, compelling good." That is what is offered in apocalyptic literature, which "promotes happiness by unmasking deception and summoning people to fidelity and purpose."

6

The Beatitudes

HAPPINESS AND THE KINGDOM OF GOD

Carl R. Holladay

1. Getting the Beatitudes in View

Given the prominence of the beatitudes in the New Testament and their extraordinary influence in shaping Christian sensibility through the centuries, they occupy a central place in the biblical vision of happiness.[1] That granted, determining how the beatitudes relate to the pursuit of happiness is complicated for several reasons.

---

1. From the vast literature on the beatitudes, the following are especially worth noting (in chronological order): Chester S. McCown, "The Beatitudes in the Light of Ancient Ideals," *JBL* 46 (1927): 50–61; Denis Buzy, "Béatitudes," in *Dictionnaire de Spiritualité* 1 (1937): 1298–1310; Ernst Percy, *Die Botschaft Jesu: Eine traditions-kritische und exegetische Untersuchung* (LUÅ, n.f. Avdeeling 1, vol. 49.5; Lund: Gleerup, 1953), 40–108; G. Braumann, "Zum traditionsgeschichtlichen Problem der Seligpreisungen Mt V 3–12," *NovT* 4 (1960): 253–60; David Flusser, "Blessed are the Poor in Spirit ..." *IEJ* 10 (1960): 1–13; Charles H. Maahs, "The Makarisms in the New Testament: A Comparative Religions and Form Critical Investigation" (PhD diss, Tübingen, 1965); Jacques Dupont, *Les Béatitudes* (vol. 1, 2nd ed.; Bruges: Abbaye de Saint-André, 1958; vol. 2, Paris: Gabalda, 1969; vol. 3, Paris: Gabalda, 1973); Ernest Best, "Matthew V.3," *NTS* 7 (1960–1961): 255–58; F. Hauck and G. Bertram, "*makarios* ktl," *TDNT* (1967), 4:362–70; J. Merle Rife, "Matthew's Beatitudes and the Septuagint," in *Studies in the History and Text of the New Testament in Honor of Kenneth Willis Clark* (eds. Boyd L. Daniels and M. Jack Suggs; Salt Lake City, Utah: University of Utah Press, 1967), 107–12; C. H. Dodd, "The Beatitudes: A Form-Critical Study," in idem, *More New Testament Studies* (Manchester: Manchester University Press, 1968), 1–10; Christine Michaelis, "Die π-Alliteration der Subjektsworte der ersten 4 Seligpreisungen in Mt v 3–6 und ihre Bedeutung für den Aufbau der Seligpreisungen bei Mt., Lk., und in Q," *NovT* 10 (1968): 148–61; Nikolaus Walter, "Die Bearbeitung der Seligpreisungen durch Matthäus," in *Studia evangelica IV–V: Papers Presented to the Third International Congress on New Testament Studies Held at Christ Church, Oxford, 1965* (2 vols.; ed. F. L. Cross; TU 102–3; Berlin: Akademie-Verlag, 1968), 1:246–58; S. Agouridès, "La tradition des béatitudes chez Matthieu et Luc," in A. Descamps and A. de Halleux, eds.,

First, the New Testament contains two distinct versions of the beatitudes. Most well known are the Matthean beatitudes (Matt 5:3–12), which constitute the first main section of the Sermon on the Mount in the Gospel of Matthew (chaps. 5–7).[2]

Mélanges bibliques en hommage au R. P. Béda Rigaux (Gembloux: Duculot, 1970), 9–27; Walter Käser, "Beobachtungen zum alttestamentlichen Makarismus," *ZAW* 82 (1970): 225–50; Hubert Frankenmölle, "Die Makarismen (Mt 5,1–12; Lk 6,20–23): Motive und Umfang der redaktionellen Komposition," *BZ* n.f. 15 (1971): 52–75; Georg Strecker, "Die Makarismen der Bergpredigt," *NTS* 17 (1971): 255–75; R. Kieffer, "Wisdom and Blessing in the Beatitudes of St. Matthew and St. Luke," *StEv* 6 (TU 112; Berlin: Akademie-Verlag, 1973), 291–95; Eduard Schweizer, "Formgeschichtliches zu den Seligpreisungen Jseu," *NTS* 19 (1973): 121–26; Christoph Kähler, "Studien zur Form- und Traditions-geschichte der biblischen Makarismen," (PhD diss., 2 vols.; Jena, 1974); Barclay M. Newman, "Some Translational Notes on the Beatitudes. Matthew 5.1–12," *BT* 26 (1975): 106–20; Robert Guelich, "The Matthean Beatitudes: 'Entrance Requirements' or Eschatological Blessings?" *JBL* 95 (1976): 415–34; R. Kieffer, "Weisheit und Segen als Grundmotive der Seligpreisungen bei Mattäus und Lukas," in *Theologie aus dem Norden* (ed. A. Fuchs; SNTSU; Linz: SNTSU, 1977): 29–43; G. Schwarz, "'Ihnen gehört das Himmelreich'? (Matthäus V.3)," *NTS* 23 (1977): 341–43; David Flusser, "Some Notes on the Beatitudes (Matt 5:3–12, Luke 6:20–26)," *Immanuel* 8 (1978): 37–47; Walther Zimmerli, "Die Seligpreisungen der Bergpredigt und das Alte Testament," in *Donum Gentilicium: New Testament Studies in Honour of David Daube* (eds. E. Bammel, C. K. Barrett, and W. D. Davies; Oxford: Clarendon, 1978), 8–26; Neil J. McEleney, "The Beatitudes of the Sermon on the Mount/Plain," *CBQ* 43 (1981): 1–13; Robert Guelich, *The Sermon on the Mount: A Foundation for Understanding* (Waco: Word, 1982), 62–118; Rudolf Schnackenburg, "Die Seligpreisung der Friedensstifter (Mt 5,9) im mattäischen Kontext," *BZ* 26 (1982): 161–78; George W. Buchanan, "Matthean Beatitudes and Traditional Promises," in *New Synoptic Studies* (ed. William R. Farmer; Macon: Mercer University Press, 1983), 161–84; Christopher M. Tuckett, "The Beatitudes: A Source-Critical Study; with a Reply by Michael M. Goulder," *NovT* 25 (1983): 193–216; Georg Strecker, *Die Bergpredigt: Ein exegetischer Kommentar* (Göttingen: Vandenhoeck & Ruprecht, 1984); Hans D. Betz, "The Beatitudes of the Sermon on the Mount (Matt. 5:3–12): Observations on Their Literary Form and Theological Significance," in idem, *Essays on the Sermon on the Mount* (trans. L. L. Welborn; Philadelphia: Fortress, 1985), 17–36; Hans Weder, *Die 'Rede der Rede': Ein Auslegung der Bergpredigt Heute* (Zurich: Theologischer Verlag, 1985); Ingo Broer, *Die Seligpreisungen der Bergpredigt: Studien zu ihrer Überlieferung und Interpretation* (BBB 61; Bonn: Peter Hanstein, 1986); Martin Hengel, "Zur matthäischen Bergpredigt und ihrem jüdischen Hintergrund," *TRu* 52 (1987): 327–400; George J. Brooke, "The Wisdom of Matthew's Beatitudes (4QBeat and Mt 5:3–12)," *ScrB* 19 (1989): 35–41; M. Dennis Hamm, *The Beatitudes in Context: What Luke and Matthew Meant* (Zacchaeus Studies: NT; Wilmington, Del.: Glazier, 1990); Benedict T. Viviano, "Beatitudes Found Among Dead Sea Scrolls," *BAR* 18 (1992): 53–55, 66; K. C. Hanson, "How Honorable! How Shameful! A Cultural Analysis of Matthew's Makarisms and Reproaches," *Semeia* 68 (1994): 81–111; David Hellholm, "'Rejoice and Be Glad, for Your Reward is Great in Heaven': An Attempt as Solving the Structural Problem of Matt. 5:11–12," in *Festschrift Günter Wagner* (International Theological Studies: Contributions of Baptist Scholars 1; ed. Faculty of Baptist Theological Seminary Rüschlikon; Bern: P. Lang, 1994), 47–86; Mark Allan Powell, "Matthew's Beatitudes: Reversals and Rewards of the Kingdom," *CBQ* 58 (1996): 460–79; Carl R. Holladay, "The Beatitudes: Jesus' Recipe for Happiness?" in *Between Experience and Interpretation: Engaging the Writings of the New Testament* (eds. Mary F. Foskett and O. Wesley Allen, Jr.; Nashville: Abingdon, 2008), 83–102.

2. For commentary treatments of the Matthean Beatitudes, see W. D. Davies and Dale C. Allison Jr., *The Gospel According to Saint Matthew* (3 vols.; ICC; Edinburgh: T & T Clark, 1988–1997), 1:429–69; Hans D. Betz, *The Sermon on the Mount* (ed. Adela Yarbro Collins;

The Lukan beatitudes (Luke 6:20–26) have a comparable rhetorical function in that they introduce Luke's Sermon on the Plain (Luke 6:20–49), but they are formally distinct from Matthew.[3] Whereas Matthew has nine beatitudes, Luke has four, which (unlike Matthew) are juxtaposed with four corresponding woes or warnings. The existence of these two quite different formulations of beatitudes attributed to Jesus introduces a complex set of interrelated questions, including how they relate to each other, what sources or traditions lie behind the respective formulations, the extent to which each version or individual formulation is traceable to Jesus himself, and how each version relates to the overall literary and theological vision of the Evangelists Matthew and Luke.

Second, even after we acknowledge that the Matthean and Lukan versions of the beatitudes represent two distinct formulations, which must be interpreted in light of the broader theological vision unfolded in their respective Gospels, we must attend to questions of language and translation. While Matthew and Luke draw on common tradition that reflects the ways in which their predecessors spoke and thought about Jesus, each Evangelist gives a distinctive shape to this inherited tradition. This occurs partly through the use of materials to which each alone is privy but also because of each Evangelist's distinctive frame of reference. The most notable example is Matthew's tendency to use the expression "kingdom of heaven," or more literally "the kingdom of the heavens" (*hē basileia tōn ouranōn*) instead of "kingdom of God" (*basileia tou theou*), which is used exclusively in his source, the Gospel of Mark, and also in Luke's Gospel. While it is tempting for interpreters to see these as synonymous, interchangeable expressions, they are nevertheless distinctive. Since Matthew knew Mark's usage, we can assume that he had good reason to use his alternative formulation.[4] When we collapse the two

---

Hermeneia; Minneapolis: Fortress, 1995), 91–153; Ulrich Luz, *Matthew 1–7* (ed. Helmut Koester; trans. James E. Crouch; Hermeneia; Minneapolis: Fortress, 2007); also Alan H. M'Neile, *The Gospel According to St. Matthew* (London: Macmillan, 1915; repr. 1965), 49–55.

3. For commentary treatments of the Lukan Beatitudes, see Joseph A. Fitzmyer, *The Gospel According to Luke* (AB 28; 2 vols.; New York: Doubleday, 1981–85), 1:625–37; C. F. Evans, *Saint Luke* (TPINTC; London: SCM, 1990), 322–33; Betz, *Sermon on the Mount*, 571–89; François Bovon, *Luke 1: A Commentary on the Gospel of Luke 1:1–9:50* (ed. Helmut Koester; trans. Christine M. Thomas; Hermeneia; Minneapolis: Fortress, 2002).

4. M'Neile, *Matthew*, xxiii–xxiv, notes the conventional explanation that "heavens" is substitute language for "God," reflecting the Jewish reverential practice of honoring the divine name by using suitable alternatives. Davies and Allison, *Matthew*, 1:81, note that the expression "kingdom of the heavens" occurs thirty-two times in Matthew, never in Mark and Luke, and nowhere in the LXX or New Testament other than in Matthew; they reckon that it "is to be judged a Semitism in view of rabbinic usage, *malkût šāmayim*," noting Hermann Strack and Paul Billerbeck, *Kommentar zum Neuen Testament aus Talmud und Midrasch* (6 vols.; München: Beck, 1922–1961), 1:172–84. Luz, *Matthew 1–7*, 135, thinks Matthew's choice reflects his community's usage.

formulations, we run the risk of erasing a nuance that Matthew regarded as important.

We need to exercise similar sensitivity to distinctive aspects of each Evangelist's language and thought. "Righteousness" (*dikaiosynē*), for example, which occurs twice in Matthew's beatitudes (Matt 5:6, 10; also repeated in 5:20; 6:1, 33) but is absent in Luke's beatitudes (and Sermon on the Plain), has a particular valence for Matthew, seen not only by its sheer frequency in his Gospel as compared with Luke, but also by how its usage in Matthew is shaped by debates about the continuing relevance of "the law and the prophets" for Matthew's readers. The same applies to Luke's usage of "poor" (*ptōchoi*) and "rich" (*plousios*) as these terms relate to distinctive elements of his depiction of Jesus's teaching.

Perhaps the greatest challenge relating to Matthew and Luke's use of language is how to render the term *makarios*, which both of them employ. Traditionally rendered as "blessed," *makarios* is increasingly translated with the word "happy."[5] While the former is well entrenched within both liturgical and popular usage, the latter is becoming more widely embraced. Some worry that "happy" fails to do justice to the richness and experiential depth connoted by *makarios*, while others insist that "blessed" too narrowly restricts the word's semantic range to religious realms.

Third, what the Matthean and Lukan beatitudes signify about happiness cannot easily be separated from their history of interpretation. Especially in the case of Matthew, the beatitudes have received extensive attention because of the popularity and extraordinary influence of the Sermon on the Mount. As the Sermon on the Mount has fared, so have the beatitudes. To a lesser extent, the Lukan beatitudes have figured in treatments of Luke's Sermon on the Plain. While both the Matthean and Lukan beatitudes are self-contained sets of formulations, which have their own interpretive frames of reference, they are nevertheless smaller sections of a larger literary section—a "sermon." To detach them from their larger literary context inevitably truncates their interpretive horizon.

Because of their popularity, the beatitudes illustrate especially well how different levels or registers of meaning can emerge when a beloved text is read and reread over time. Trying to ascertain what they meant at the time of their composition or editorial redaction is complicated enough. To get at what a single beatitude might have meant when Jesus uttered it requires us to sort through layers of

---

5. KJV, RSV, NIV, NRSV, NJB, among others, render *makarios* as "blessed." NRSV, NJPSV, NETS render *makarios* in Ps 1:1 "happy," whereas RSV renders it "blessed." The difference can be seen in the respective Hermeneia commentaries: Betz opts for "blessed" in translating both the Matthean and Lukan Beatitudes (see his *Sermon on the Mount*, 91 and 571, respectively), as does Bovon (*Luke 1*, 220–21); Luz, however, renders *makarios* "happy" (*Matthew 1–7*, 185). Note also the discussion of the Hebrew term *'asrê* by William P. Brown in the present volume.

tradition, separating later church formulations from his original saying.[6] Even if this proves difficult, we can nevertheless ask what the beatitudes meant to the Evangelist who composed, edited, and included them in his Gospel, or at least to his implied community of readers. Since the beatitudes were known and used quite early by Christian writers, we can also trace how they were used and what they came to mean to different writers in different contexts over time.[7] In some ways, what the beatitudes *have meant* is as critical as *what they originally meant*, either in Jesus's time or at the time of the Evangelist's composition. As it turns out, what they mean now to those who are trying to ascertain biblical perspectives on happiness may be influenced as much by their *received meaning(s)* as by their *original meaning(s)*.

Matthew's first Beatitude illustrates this point. What "poor in spirit" signifies remains one of the most contested interpretive questions in beatitudes scholarship. Without rehearsing all of the interpretive possibilities, we can simply note the recurrent line of interpretation that equates it with humility. Although Matthew uses standard Greek terminology for humility elsewhere in his Gospel, he does not do so in Matt 5:3.[8] Even so, interpreters read "poor in spirit" as a poetic way of expressing humility.[9] Eventually, Matthew's first beatitude was understood to require humility as the first step in the soul's ascent toward heavenly perfection.[10] Since many still read the beatitude this way, it would be easy to assume that Matthew's first beatitude sees a humble spirit as a prerequisite for happiness, and, moreover, that humility orients one to, or prepares one for life in, the kingdom of heaven.

---

6. The tradition-history of the beatitudes has received extensive attention. For one example, see Luz, *Matthew 1–7*, 186–87, who thinks the first three beatitudes preserved in Q (Luke 6:20b–21) are possibly traceable to Jesus.

7. For the reception history of the beatitudes, see Betz, *Sermon on the Mount*, 105–9; and esp. Luz, *Matthew 1–7*, 188–89, 192–202.

8. E.g., Matt 11:19, "For I am ... humble [*tapeinos*] in heart"; Matt 18:4, "Whoever becomes humble [*tapeinoō*] like this child"; also 23:12.

9. See Luz, *Matthew 1–7*, 190–92. On the interpretation of "poor in spirit" in early Christian writings, see Dupont, *Les Béatitudes*, 3:398–419. Best, "Matthew V.3," makes a strong case, based on Qumran parallels, for understanding "poor in spirit" as "faint-hearted," i.e., those lacking courage.

10. See, e.g., Gregory of Nyssa, *Hom. Beat.* 1.84 (translation by Stuart George Hall in *Gregory of Nyssa: Homilies on the Beatitudes: An English Version with Commentary and Supporting Studies: Proceedings of the Eighth International Colloquium on Gregory of Nyssa [Paderborn, 14–18 September 1998]* [eds. Hubertus R. Drobner and Albert Viciano; Supplements to *Vigiliae Christianae* 52; Leiden: Brill, 2000], 27); Augustine, *Sermon on the Mount*, 1.1.3 (translation in *The Preaching of Augustine: "Our Lord's Sermon on the Mount"* [ed. Jaroslav Pelikan; trans. Francine Cardman; The Preacher's Paperback Library 13; Philadelphia: Fortress, 1973], 3); and John Wesley, *Sermon 21*, §I.4 (edition in Albert C. Outler, ed., *The Works of John Wesley: Volume 1: Sermons I [1–33]* [Nashville: Abingdon, 1984], 477).

The significance of the interpretive history of the beatitudes becomes especially clear as they relate to the notion of the kingdom of God. We have already noted the interpretive problem created by Matthew's use of "kingdom of heaven" in contrast to Luke's "kingdom of God." Few questions in Gospel interpretation are as tangled or as intractable as the meaning and significance of the kingdom of God. Since both sets of beatitudes contain this language, it is appropriate to link their respective visions of happiness with this highly provocative expression, however ambiguous or elusive it may be. And yet here too, what the kingdom of heaven/God *has meant* is an inescapable dimension of what the beatitudes might mean now. When the Matthean Jesus promises the "poor in spirit" and "those who are persecuted for righteousness' sake" that the "kingdom of heaven" is theirs, we are bound to ask what precisely they are promised. Is it present or future? Is it theirs to enjoy only in prospect? Or is its reality experienced now, at least in some sense?

In this essay, I will explore these three complicating features of relating the beatitudes to the biblical vision of happiness. First, I identify some of the most pertinent issues that relate to the Matthean and Lukan beatitudes. In particular, I examine how their respective visions of happiness relate to their distinctive literary structure. In the next part of the essay, I explore how the kingdom of heaven/God relates to the vision of blessedness sketched in the beatitudes. Finally, I provide a cursory review of the reception history of the beatitudes through the fifth century in order to show that what the beatitudes *have meant* to different interpreters is a critically important dimension of what they *now mean*. I also give some attention to the relationship between context and meaning, because, as the interpreters' social and political context shifted, so did the way they read the beatitudes.

2. The Matthean and Lukan Beatitudes: A Closer Look

One of the most striking differences between the two New Testament versions of the beatitudes is their formal structure (see Table 6.1). The first eight Matthean beatitudes and the first three Lukan beatitudes exhibit a two-part structure. The first clause is introduced with the plural form of *makarios* followed by a specifically designated group of people introduced by the definite article *hoi*. This is typically translated "blessed" or "happy" are "those who" or "the ones who." The *hoi* is followed by nouns, adjectives functioning substantively, or participles employing vivid language that includes images expressive of lived human experience ("poor, weeping/mourning, hunger and thirst, being persecuted"), qualities embracing both attitudes and behaviors ("meek, merciful, pure in heart"), and concrete actions ("being peacemakers"). While some have tried to structure the

Table 6.1

The Matthean and Lukan Beatitudes Compared	
Matthew 5:1–12 (NRSV)	*Luke 6:20–26 (NRSV)*
Introduction: When Jesus saw the crowds, he went up the mountain; and after he sat down, his disciples came to him. Then he began to speak, and taught them, saying: (5:1–2)	*Introduction*: Then he looked up at his disciples and said (6:20a)
Beatitude 1: Blessed are the poor in spirit, for theirs is the kingdom of heaven. (5:3)	*Beatitude 1:* Blessed are you who are poor, for yours is the kingdom of God. (6:20b)
Beatitude 2: Blessed are those who mourn, for they will be comforted. (5:4)	*Beatitude 3:*[a] Blessed are you who weep now, for you will laugh. (6:21b)
Beatitude 3: Blessed are the meek, for they will inherit the earth. (5:5)	
Beatitude 4: Blessed are those who hunger and thirst for righteousness, for they will be filled. (5:6)	*Beatitude 2:*[b] Blessed are you who are hungry now, for you will be filled. (6:21a)
Beatitude 5: Blessed are the merciful, for they will receive mercy. (5:7)	
Beatitude 6: Blessed are the pure in heart, for they will see God. (5:8)	
Beatitude 7: Blessed are the peace-makers, for they will be called children of God. (5:9)	
Beatitude 8: Blessed are those who are persecuted for righteousness' sake, for theirs is the kingdom of heaven. (5:10)	
Beatitude 9: Blessed are you when people revile you and persecute you and utter all kinds of evil against you falsely on my account. Rejoice and be glad, for your reward is great in heaven, for in the same way they persecuted the prophets who were before you. (5:11–12)	*Beatitude 4:* Blessed are you when people hate you, and when they exclude you, revile you, and defame you on account of the Son of Man. Rejoice in that day and leap for joy, for surely your reward is great in heaven; for that is what their ancestors did to the prophets. (6:22–23)
	Woe 1: But woe to you who are rich, for you have received your consolation. (6:24)

(*continued*)

Table 6.1 (*continued*)

The Matthean and Lukan Beatitudes Compared	
Matthew 5:1–12 (NRSV)	*Luke 6:20–26 (NRSV)*
	Woe 2: Woe to you who are full now, for you will be hungry. (6:25a)
	Woe 3: Woe to you who are laughing now, for you will mourn and weep. (6:25b)
	Woe 4: Woe to you when all speak well of you, for that is what their ancestors did to the false prophets. (6:26)

a. Note that the order of Luke's second and third beatitudes is reversed in this chart to highlight the parallels with the Matthean version.

b. See previous note.

Matthean beatitudes using a scheme of qualities or attitudes singled out in the first four as opposed to activities highlighted in the second four, they defy easy classification. Perhaps most remarkable is how diverse the range of qualities and experiences envisioned in Matthew's eight beatitudes is, and how elusive these beatitudes are.

The second clause in Matthew's beatitudes 1–8 and Luke's beatitudes 1–3 is introduced by the causal particle *hoti*, which is typically translated "for," in the causal sense of "because." As Hans Dieter Betz rightly observes, this second clause establishes the warrant for the makarism in the first clause.[11] How one construes the relationship between the first and second clauses is a critical interpretive decision. Some have seen the grammatical connection between the first and second clauses as an "if/then" relationship, which tends to yield interpretations that understand the first clause as stipulating attitudes or behaviors that are conditions for receiving the stated promise.[12] *If,* for example, one is "poor in spirit," *then* one

---

11. Betz, *Sermon on the Mount,* 110–11.

12. When discussing the two-part sentence structure of the beatitudes, some commentators (e.g., Luz, *Matthew 1–7,* 187–88, 196; Powell, "Matthew's Beatitudes," 465–66, 473, 475) designate the first clause as the protasis and the second clause as the apodosis. While understandable as grammatical shorthand, these labels are inaccurate. Strictly speaking, these are technical designations that apply to conditional sentences in which (usually) the first clause (protasis) introduces a condition and the second clause (apodosis) states the result or consequences of the condition. See Herbert W. Smyth, *Greek Grammar* (Cambridge: Harvard University Press, 1920), § 2280. Grammatically, it is preferable to designate the second part of the sentence as a causal clause introduced by *hoti.* See ibid., § 2240. When BDF § 462 (2) speaks of asyndeton

can receive the kingdom of heaven. *If* one mourns, especially for good reason (say, over one's sins), *then* one will be comforted (by receiving forgiveness). Read in this way, the beatitudes articulate entrance requirements for the kingdom of heaven.[13] But if the grammatical relationship between the clauses is read as "declaration/promise," they tend to be read as the bestowal of grace.[14] Read this way, the first clause, rather than being seen as a prerequisite for some promised reward, extends a gracious offer, both unexpected and unmerited, and in some ways even paradoxical because it seems antithetical to the quality or circumstance that follows. Since the gracious pronouncement of happiness sounds patently unlikely, the second clause immediately follows to justify the pronouncement. It is causal in the sense that it elaborates the cause or reason for making such a seemingly unlikely or even absurd claim. Rather than stipulating entrance requirements for the kingdom, the first clauses are profiling the attitudes and experiences of those already in the kingdom. Rather than being conditions, the blessings expressed in the first clause are benefits, or even rewards, to use language that was anathema to the Reformers. This "declaration/promise" way of reading the beatitudes inverts the "if/then" option. The first clause states the benefit up front. Those who exhibit the named quality or behavior are showered with blessing or happiness, and the reason for this paradoxical bestowal of grace is expressed in the second clause.

This two-part "declaration/promise" structure is worth noting because it distinguishes this set of beatitudes from other makarisms that are often adduced as literary parallels.[15] Rather than bestowing blessing on a named group in a liturgical or even proverbial setting with no further condition or explanation expressed, these Matthean and Lukan formulations declare certain people happy, usually those whose lot or character is ostensibly devoid of happiness, and then reinforce this paradoxical declaration with a reassuring promise.[16]

"almost throughout Mt 5:3–17, not only where there is no connection in thought, but also in spite of such connection," the lack of grammatical connection between each beatitude is in view. They further note that "asyndeton between individual axioms and sayings is very common in the didactic style of the Gospels." The individual formulations themselves are not properly asyndetic because the clauses are connected by *hoti*.

13. See Guelich, "'Entrance Requirements' or Eschatological Blessings?" 415–16, 431–34.

14. Luz, *Matthew 1–7*, 188–89, identifies in the history of interpretation of the beatitudes three major ways of interpreting them: (1) emphasizing the "word of grace" contained in them; (2) understanding them as ethical exhortations; and (3) understanding them as regulations for the life of the community.

15. For discussion of ancient literary parallels, see Betz, *Sermon on the Mount*, 97–105; Davies and Allison, *Matthew*, 1:432–34.

16. Notable biblical examples of the generalized makarism ("Happy are those who …" or "Happy are you …") include Pss 1:1; 128:1–2; Isa 32:20; Deut 33:29; Eccl 10:17; and Sir 14:20–27; 25:7–11. Note also *1 En.* 99:10; *2 Bar* 11:7; *T. Mos.* 10:8; and, from Qumran, 4Q525 (= 4QBeat)

This formalized structure is worth noting since it provides a distinctive angle of vision for understanding happiness within these formulations. In some of the literary parallels, the blessing seems sensible, even straightforward. What distinguishes the Matthean and Lukan beatitudes, by contrast, is the seemingly contradictory claim made in the first clause. Our ordinary expectations are reversed when we hear the poor, or even the spiritually poor, declared happy. Mourning and grieving are not blessed states of mind; they are antithetical to happiness. We normally expect the strong and powerful, not the meek, to possess the land. Hunger and thirst are normally associated with food and water, symbols of survival, the most primitive human instinct. An appetite for righteousness or justice may be a noble human ideal but is more rare than common. To be persecuted for righteousness' sake, that is, to suffer unjustly,[17] would appear to be an experience that is neither blissful nor blessed, certainly not one normally associated with happiness. Or if one takes the Lukan formulations, they are equally paradoxical, perhaps even more so. Being poor, hungry, and sad are antithetical to happiness or blessedness, especially when Luke adds the emphatic "now" to the hunger and sadness (6:21a–b).

In the Matthean beatitudes 5–7, the paradox lies not so much in the inherent contradiction embedded within the first clause as it does between the first and second clauses. We can imagine instinctively that those who show mercy will experience happiness. As their reward, however, we might expect "for they will experience the joy of giving," or some such thing. Instead, by extending mercy they will position themselves to receive mercy. This can easily be perceived as mercy with an agenda—selflessness motivated by selfishness (*do ut des*). Being pure in heart—operating with pure motives—would be a worthy goal among moralists of any persuasion. Then again, being pure in heart would perhaps position one to see God within an intellectual frame of reference in which living a moral life eventuates in union with God. What is surprising here, however, is the common expectation that seeing God is either impossible or lethal, or at least reserved for the rare prophet like Moses who is invited to receive an exceptional divine revelation

---

and also 1QH[a] XXIII.14–15. One of the best examples of the "declaration/promise" formulation is *1 En.* 58:2: "Blessed are you, righteous and elect ones, for glorious is your portion" (cf. similarly Wisd 3:13–14 and Bar 4:4). *2 En.* 52:1–15 elaborates this basic formula with an introductory makarism followed by six pairs of blessings and curses, concluding with a "for" clause introducing the promise. This provides an illuminating formal parallel for the Lukan blessings and woes. New Testament examples of the "declaration/promise" formulation include Matt 13:16; 16:17; Luke 14:14; James 1:12; and Rev 1:3. 1 Pet 4:14 represents a variation of the pattern. Cf. also John 13:17; 1 Pet 3:14; Rev 14:13.

17. To be persecuted for upholding what is right and just means, at least for the one being persecuted, to suffer unjustly.

or for the mystic sequestered in the closet or in a cave praying for a vision of God. Seen against this background, the sixth beatitude opens a wide door for those who wish to see God. The life well lived, devoid of all the things normally associated with an impure heart, opens one's eyes to God. As commentators have often noted, the beatitude about the peacemakers moves from attitude to action. Happiness is not bestowed on those who love peace or even on those who are peaceful themselves but on those who actively make peace. In view is an activist, aggressive stance toward conflict and controversy, which summons those committed to peace not only to seek but also to construct conversations, alliances, relationships, treaties, and political and social structures that have the possibility of achieving meaningful reconciliation. And how might peacemakers experience happiness? We imagine that the answer is by participating in a society or a world in which equilibrium has replaced disequilibrium. Peacemakers become blessed by enjoying the peace they help to restore or achieve. But Matthew's seventh beatitude promises them something else altogether: an unusually high status, what some ancient interpreters saw as the summit of spiritual perfection—becoming God's children. The question this beatitude invites us to probe, then, is the relationship between peacemaking and divine childhood. It asks us to think of peace and those who foster it not in some narrow, exclusively human or social sense, but as an arena in which God stands at the center. So construed, God is present in the quest for peace and peace is seen in terms of divine intention. If it is that which God intends, then those who make it somehow participate in God's own Being. By making peace, they become inseminated by God (cf. 1 John 3:1, 9–12). One might even argue that this beatitude asserts that the instinct for resolving conflict peacefully is divine.

Scholars have observed the close resonance between these and other beatitudes and ancient wisdom traditions. In some respects, they exhibit a proverbial character. Their paraenetic function as advisory, instructive teachings has also been noted. This may account for some of the most conspicuous rhetorical features, such as Matthew's decision to include eight formally identical beatitudes, and the Lukan decision to include an equivalent number although reordered into two pairs of four blessings and woes. Some have seen Matthew's eightfold arrangement as a pedagogical counterpart to the Decalogue. Equally noticeable is the use of alliteration in Matthew's formulation of the first four beatitudes, with the repetition of words beginning with the letter "p."[18] Attention to the oral dimensions of the wording achieves rhetorical effect, especially when they are read

---

18. "Blessed are the poor [*ptōchoi*] in spirit [*pneumati*] . . . those who mourn [*penthountes*] . . . the meek [*praeis*] . . . those who hunger [*peinōntes*]. . . ." See Michaelis, "Die π-Alliteration." The opening lines of Heb 1:1–4, with its burst of "p" sounds, reflects similar rhetorical awareness.

aloud. Another rhetorically intentional choice is the use of "kingdom of heaven" as an inclusio in Matt 5:3, 10. Interpreters have endlessly debated the significance of this, some arguing that the repetition of "kingdom of heaven" in the eighth beatitude makes it a recapitulation of the previous seven. Others have observed that "being persecuted for righteousness' sake" is the price one pays for incorporating the previous seven qualities into one's life. Entry into the kingdom (v. 3) introduces one to a way of life in which the qualities unfolding in the following beatitudes are acquired gradually, culminating in the highest benefits of seeing God and becoming children of God. One's spiritual journey thus begins and ends with the kingdom of heaven.

The paradoxical character of these formulations aligns them more closely with that part of the wisdom tradition associated with riddles or other enigmatic sayings.[19] They are not proverbs in the conventional sense that they express in pithy, memorable form some insight into human life and experience. They are also formally distinct from the subgenre of wisdom sayings normally including parables and similes. They are not parabolic either directly or derivatively. In some respects they resemble the Berakah, the liturgical prayer that is deeply embedded in the Jewish tradition and a standard feature in Jewish prayer books. While some have seen a liturgical context as the setting in which the beatitudes were originally generated, this is a less compelling explanation. Their placement at the beginning of Matthew's and Luke's respective "sermons" underscores their didactic function. Whether the hearers envisioned by the Evangelists are the apostles and Jesus's inner circle of disciples or a much broader audience consisting of "the crowds," and by extension all subsequent readers and hearers of the Gospel, both sets of beatitudes are offered as moral instructions for Jesus's disciples.

3. Happiness and the Kingdom of God

Ulrich Luz has rightly emphasized the thematic prominence of "kingdom of heaven" in the Matthean beatitudes, and their programmatic role in establishing the theological horizon for the whole Sermon on the Mount.[20] The beatitudes introduce in highly rhetorical fashion—carefully placed in the first and eighth positions—the theme of Jesus's ministry (Matt 4:17), which was already announced by John the Baptist (Matt 3:2). In the summary leading up to the Sermon on the Mount, Matthew highlights Jesus's proclamation of the "good news of the kingdom" (*to euangelion tēs basileias*, 4:23), an expression that Jack Dean

---

19. See the essay by Carol A. Newsom in the present volume.

20. Luz, *Matthew 1–7*, 169.

Kingsbury calls "Matthew's own capsule-summary of his work"[21] and that prompts Luz to observe that "Jesus' ethical Sermon on the Mount does not presuppose the gospel of the kingdom—it is the gospel of the kingdom."[22]

Matthew's inclusion of "kingdom of heaven" in his first and eighth beatitudes (Matt 5:3, 10), along with Luke's mention of the "kingdom of God" in his first Beatitude (Luke 6:20), justifies exploring how their respective visions of happiness relate to this highly controversial expression.[23] At the very least, we can infer

---

21. Jack Dean Kingsbury, *Matthew: Structure, Christology, Kingdom* (Philadelphia: Fortress, 1975), 131.

22. Luz, *Matthew 1–7*, 169.

23. For useful orientation to the discussion, see the historical review, beginning with the nineteenth century, in Norman Perrin, *The Kingdom of God in the Teaching of Jesus* (NTL; Philadelphia: Westminster, 1963), and especially the concluding chapter (158–206); Gösta Lundström, *The Kingdom of God in the Teaching of Jesus: A History of Interpretation from the Last Decades of the Nineteenth Century to the Present Day* (Edinburgh: Oliver and Boyd, 1963); Wendell Willis, ed., *The Kingdom of God in 20th-Century Interpretation* (Peabody, MA: Hendrickson, 1987); Dennis C. Duling, "Kingdom of God, Kingdom of Heaven," *ABD* 4:49–69; and Robin Barbour, ed., *The Kingdom of God and Human Society: Essays by Members of the Scripture, Theology, and Society Group* (Edinburgh: T&T Clark, 1993), esp. the essays by Robert Morgan, "From Reimarus to Sanders: the Kingdom of God, Jesus, and the Judaisms of His Day" (80–139); and Mark Chapman, "The Kingdom of God and Ethics: From Ritschl to Liberation Theology" (140–63). Albrecht Ritschl's views are readily accessible in his *Instruction in the Christian Religion*, which is included in Albert T. Swing, *The Theology of Albrecht Ritschl* (London: Longmans, Green, 1901). Part 1 of the *Instruction*, which was translated into English by Alice Mead Swing, is titled "The Doctrine of the Kingdom of God." See also Ritschl's *The Christian Doctrine of Justification and Reconciliation* (trans. H. R. Macintosh and A. B. Macaulay; Edinburgh: T & T Clark, 1902), 30–35, 270–326, 507–22. For appraisals of Ritschl, see Philip Hefner, *Faith and the Vitalities of History: A Theological Study Based on the Work of Albrecht Ritschl* (New York: Harper & Row, 1966); Claude Welch, *Protestant Thought in the Nineteenth Century: Volume 2, 1870–1914* (New Haven: Yale University Press, 1985), 1–30. For Johannes Weiss's critique of Ritschl, see his *Jesus' Proclamation of the Kingdom of God* (Lives of Jesus Series; trans. and ed. Richard H. Hiers and David L. Holland; Philadelphia: Fortress, 1971), with the illuminating introduction by Hiers and Holland (1–54). Albert Schweitzer's view is formulated in his *The Mystery of the Kingdom of God: The Secret of Jesus' Messiahship and Passion* (trans. Walter Lowrie; New York: Macmillan, 1950); also *The Quest of the Historical Jesus* (1st complete edition; ed. John Bowden; Minneapolis: Fortress, 2001), esp. 190–220, 315–54. Schweitzer's more mature views, dating from about 1950, are found in his *Kingdom of God and Primitive Christianity* (ed. Ulrich Neuenschwander; trans. L. A. Garrard; New York: Seabury, 1968). Amos Wilder's contribution to the debate can be found in his *Eschatology and Ethics in the Teaching of Jesus* (rev. ed.; New York: Harper, 1939), esp. 187–214. For Rudolf Otto's views, see *The Kingdom of God and the Son of Man: A Study in the History of Religion* (originally published 1943; new and rev. ed.; trans. Floyd V. Filson and Bertram L. Woolf; Boston: Starr King, 1957); John Bright's influential views are presented in *The Kingdom of God: The Biblical Concept and Its Meaning for the Church* (originally published 1953; Nashville: Abingdon, 1984). Werner G. Kümmel's nuanced position is worked out in *Promise and Fulfillment: The Eschatological Message of Jesus* (SBT 23; London: SCM, 1957; repr. 1966). For C. H. Dodd's "realized eschatology," see *The Parables of the Kingdom* (rev. ed.; New York: Scribner's,

that how they see Jesus's vision of happiness or blessedness is closely, if not inextricably, related to his proclamation of the kingdom. But what precisely is the relationship? Is happiness something his disciples experience only insofar as they look forward to God's future reign, sometime in the distant future, perhaps at the end of time? Do they experience happiness, in other words, as hope? Or is happiness an indispensable element or dimension of God's reign that Jesus grants his disciples now, in their present condition? When linked with God's kingdom, is happiness a present or future state? Does Jesus promise his disciples happiness realized (now) or happiness delayed (later)?

From the perspective of scholarship relating to Jesus's proclamation of the kingdom of God since the mid-nineteenth century, three interpretive options

---

1961), esp. 21–59. George Eldon Ladd's views developed over time, beginning with *Crucial Questions About the Kingdom of God* (Grand Rapids: Eerdmans, 1952); idem, "Kingdom of God—Reign or Realm?" *JBL* 81 (1962): 230–38; and especially idem, *Jesus and the Kingdom: The Eschatology of Biblical Realism* (New York: Harper & Row, 1964), which was updated in idem, *The Presence of the Future: The Eschatology of Biblical Realism* (Grand Rapids: Eerdmans, 1974). See also his *A Theology of the New Testament* (Grand Rapids: Eerdmans, 1974). For Norman Perrin's influential views on the kingdom as a tensive symbol, see *Jesus and the Language of the Kingdom* (Philadelphia: Fortress, 1976), esp. 29–30. For a Roman Catholic perspective, see Rudolf Schnackenburg, *God's Rule and Kingdom* (New York: Herder & Herder, 1963); Helmut Merklein, *Jesu Botschaft von der Gottesherrschaft: Eine Skizze* (SBS 111; Stuttgart: Verlag Katholisches Bibelwerk, 1983); Benedict T. Viviano, *Trinity—Kingdom—Church: Essays in Biblical Theology* (Göttingen: Vandenhoeck & Ruprecht, 2001). For parables as they relate to the kingdom, see Bernard Brandon Scott, *Jesus, Symbol-Maker for the Kingdom* (Philadelphia: Fortress, 1981). Patristic views of eschatology are treated in Brian E. Daley, *The Hope of the Early Church: A Handbook of Patristic Eschatology* (Cambridge: Cambridge University Press, 1991). Also see J. Arthur Baird, *Rediscovering the Power of the Gospels: Jesus' Theology of the Kingdom* (Wooster, Ohio: Iona, 1982); George W. Buchanan, *Jesus: The King and His Kingdom* (Macon: Mercer University Press, 1984); Bruce D. Chilton, *God in Strength: Jesus' Announcement of the Kingdom* (SNTSU; Freistadt: Verlag F. Plöchl, 1979); idem, *The Kingdom of God in the Teaching of Jesus* (IRT; Philadelphia: Fortress, 1984); idem, *Pure Kingdom: Jesus' Vision of God* (Grand Rapids: Eerdmans, 1996); idem, "Kingdom of God, Kingdom of Heaven," *NIDB* 3:512–23; Bruce D. Chilton and J. I. H. McDonald, *Jesus and the Ethics of the Kingdom* (Grand Rapids: Eerdmans, 1987); Dennis Duling, "The Kingdom of God in the Teaching of Jesus," *WW* 2 (1982): 117–26; idem, "Norman Perrin and the Kingdom of God: Review and Response," *JR* 64 (1984): 468–83; John G. Gager, *Kingdom and Community: The Social World of Early Christianity* (Englewood Cliffs, NJ: Prentice-Hall, 1975); Richard H. Hiers, *The Kingdom of God in the Synoptic Tradition* (Gainesville: University of Florida Press, 1970); idem, *The Historical Jesus and the Kingdom of God: Present and Future in the Message and Ministry of Jesus* (University of Florida Humanities Monograph 38; Gainesville: University of Florida Press, 1973); David Hill, "Towards An Understanding of the 'Kingdom of God,'" *IBS* 3 (1981): 62–76; Werner H. Kelber, *The Kingdom in Mark: A New Place and a New Time* (Philadelphia: Fortress, 1974); Karen King, "Kingdom in the Gospel of Thomas," *Foundations and Facets Forum* 3 (1987): 48–97; Günther Klein, "'Reich Gottes' als biblischer Zentralbegriff," *EvT* 30 (1970): 642–70; Halvor Moxnes, *The Economy of the Kingdom: Social Conflict and Economic Relations in Luke's Gospel* (OBT; Philadelphia: Fortress, 1988); Margaret Pamment, "The Kingdom of God According to the First Gospel," *NTS* 27 (1981): 211–32; and Stephen S. Smalley, "Spirit, Kingdom, and Prayer in Luke-Acts," *NovT* 15 (1973): 59–71.

have emerged: the kingdom of God is (i) a future reality, (ii) a present reality, or (iii) a future reality that has already begun. Since each of these options is framed in linear, chronological terms and is formulated in view of the end of time, they have been characterized as different conceptions of eschatology. The kingdom viewed as an essentially future reality, to be ushered in by a messianic figure in a final cataclysm that brings history to a close, is characterized as *unrealized eschatology* (the end is yet to come) or *consistent eschatology* (fixation on the future coming). This view is especially associated with Johannes Weiss and Albert Schweitzer.[24] When viewed as a present reality, either wholly or practically present, primarily in the person of Jesus himself, the kingdom is understood as *realized eschatology*. The chief architect of this position is C. H. Dodd.[25] The mediating position, which acknowledges the presence within the Gospels of texts that speak of the kingdom as both present and future reality, is described as *inaugurated or self-realizing eschatology*. One of the major exponents of this mediating position is Werner G. Kümmel, who employed the language of promise and fulfillment to capture both dimensions.[26]

For all their variety, each of these positions acknowledges the presence of conflicting statements reporting Jesus's proclamation of the kingdom in the Gospels. In Matt 16:28, Jesus speaks of the kingdom as a future reality: "There are some standing here who will not taste death before they see the Son of Man coming in his kingdom."[27] Here the kingdom may be imminent, but it has not yet arrived. In Luke 17:21, however, responding to the Pharisees' question about when to expect the kingdom of God, Jesus asserts, "the kingdom of God is among you." Similarly, in Luke 16:16 Jesus speaks of the kingdom of God, which has been proclaimed

24. Weiss, *Jesus' Proclamation of the Kingdom of God*; Schweitzer, *The Mystery of the Kingdom of God*.

25. Dodd, *Parables*. A version of this position had already been formulated by Ritschl in the nineteenth century, with his insistence that the kingdom of God connotes a moral realm that pertains to life here and now. Adolf von Harnack, *What is Christianity?* (New York: Harper & Row, 1957; originally published in 1900), operated with a similar view, although he saw the kingdom primarily as an inner spiritual reality whose evolutionary development began with Jesus. Otto's *Kingdom of God and the Son of Man* similarly emphasized the realized dimension in Jesus's teaching.

26. Kümmel, *Promise and Fulfillment*. Similar views had been articulated by Rudolf Bultmann in *Jesus and the Word* (trans. Louise P. Smith and Erminie H. Lantero; New York: Scribner's, 1958 [German orig: 1926]); and by Reginald H. Fuller, *The Mission and Achievement of Jesus* (SBT 1/12; London: SCM, 1954). George Eldon Ladd, *Jesus and the Kingdom*, formulated a position that also affirmed both present and future dimensions of the kingdom in Jesus's teaching.

27. Cf. Mark 9:1: "there are some standing here who will not taste death until they see that the kingdom of God has come with power."

since the time of John the Baptist, as that which "everyone tries to enter ... by force." Although the meaning of this enigmatic phrase has eluded scholars, the kingdom is nevertheless seen as a present reality. In reporting the preaching of John the Baptist and Jesus, the Evangelists use similar language. Both Matthew and Luke proclaimed that the kingdom of God/heaven has drawn near (*ēngiken*).[28] The ambiguity of the Greek verb *engizō* allows the translator to accent either its present dimension, thus, "has arrived," or its future aspect, "has drawn near."

The debate about the kingdom of God, which has been pursued vigorously for almost two centuries, has prompted scholars to investigate these exegetical problems at great length, and in great depth. It is not necessary for us to rehearse the exegetical discussions, only to call attention to them as they relate to our discussion of the beatitudes. Especially worth noting is how the language of the beatitudes, in both the Matthean and Lukan versions, exhibits this same ambiguity and attests to the tension between promise and fulfillment, to use Kümmel's formulation.

I wish to argue here that both present and future dimensions are contained within the beatitudes. Jesus's language as reported by Matthew and Luke is evocative rather than prescriptive. This gives it an open-ended rather than definitive quality. This inherent ambiguity has enabled subsequent interpreters to accent one or the other dimension and sometimes both. I will further argue that respecting the fluidity of the language of the beatitudes not only honors the built-in ambiguity, possibly traceable to Jesus himself but certainly attributable to the Evangelists, but also introduces a useful perspective for understanding the vision of happiness encoded in them.

Especially apparent, even in a cursory reading of the Matthean beatitudes, is the intermixing of grammatical tenses. In Matthew's beatitudes 1 and 8 Jesus uses the present tense *estin*, "is," to reassure listeners that the kingdom of heaven belongs to them. But "is" in what sense? Is it *now theirs*, even while he speaks or as later disciples read or hear the Gospel? Or is it *virtually theirs*, impending perhaps but not yet within their reach? Matthew's formulation leaves the question open. But it is also significant that the future tense is not used here. Jesus does not say, "the kingdom of heaven *will be* yours." Instead, "theirs *is* the kingdom of heaven" (Matt 5:3, 10) and "it is yours" (Luke 6:20). This evocative language creates a gap in which the listeners are able to position themselves. They experience hope and expectation by the proximity suggested with this language, and yet they cannot clutch or embrace it as something they fully own or possess.

By contrast, the future tense is used in the second clause of Matthew's beatitudes 2–7: "They *will* be comforted ... they *will* inherit the earth ... they *will* be

28. Matt 3:2; 4:17 (cf. Mark 1:15); 10:7; Luke 10:9, 11.

filled . . . they *will* receive mercy . . . they *will* see God . . . they *will* be called children of God. . . ." Betz insists that each of these six futures should be understood as thoroughly eschatological promises—what the hearers will experience in the future, when the kingdom of God fully comes. These six "promise" clauses, according to Betz, depict "consecutive stages describing the destiny of the righteous in paradise . . . [which present] a greatly abbreviated apocalyptic vision of the world to come."[29]

This way of viewing the six future promises has a neat symmetry. It takes the grammatical futures as true chronological futures: they depict what will happen at a future time. It also recognizes progressive movement from being comforted to becoming children of God, an interpretive move that resonates with patristic exegesis that reads the beatitudes as stages in the soul's mystical ascent to God. This uniform way of reading the six future clauses, however, also flattens them. As later exegetes saw, "they will inherit the earth (or: 'land'; Greek *gē*)" is an unusual way of depicting the promise of heaven. Such a move requires a metaphorical or spiritualized interpretation of *gē* as "promised land" or "heavenly land." For Gregory of Nyssa, the exegetical problem posed by the mention of earth or land is how, if the beatitudes are depicting stages in the soul's ascent toward God, one's first step (beatitude 1) can be heaven, and the next step (beatitude 3) can be earth.[30] Accordingly, *gē* should not be understood as the physical earth below but "the supercelestial land which is in store as the inheritance of those who have lived virtuous lives."[31]

We might ask similar questions of the other promises. Surely those who mourn can experience the comforting words of family and friends, and even the comforting presence of God, now rather than having to wait until they are finally in God's presence at some point in the future. Must those who possess an appetite for righteousness wait until some distant future to be filled? Are we to imagine those who extend mercy not experiencing any reciprocal mercy before they are finally and fully embraced by God's merciful embrace in heaven? Even the rarefied experiences of "seeing God" and becoming "children of God," while perhaps more easily understood as eschatological realities, can surely be realized in some sense on this side of the eschaton.

Recognizing the bivalent quality of each of these promises invites hearers to think of them in multidimensional ways. Even present and future do not

---

29. Betz, *Sermon on the Mount*, 110.

30. In the textual tradition Gregory was using, Beatitude 3, "the meek shall inherit the earth," preceded Beatitude 2.

31. *Hom. Beat.* 2.90 (Hall, *Gregory of Nyssa*, 32).

exhaust the interpretive possibilities for understanding each promise. These temporal categories work as long as they are viewed as points along a chronological and experiential continuum. But there are other conceptual possibilities. Later exegetes who struggled with the possible meanings of "seeing God" were prompted to think of multiple ways in which this could occur. One might see God in the sense of possessing God.[32] One might see God with the heart.[33] Faith might be the lens through which one sees God. "To see [God's] face," Luther suggests, occurs when we "recognize [God] correctly as a gracious and faithful Father, on whom [we] can depend for every good thing. This happens only through faith in Christ."[34] One might even see God by viewing nature, experiencing acts of providential care, or embracing divine teachings and instructions.[35]

Just as the grammatical futures in the second clauses should not be restricted to eschatological blessings, neither should the double reference to kingdom of heaven in Matthew's first and eighth beatitudes be interpreted as a fully present gift because the promise is framed with the grammatical present "is" (*estin*). By framing the promise this way, Matthew locates the promise of the kingdom within an ambiguous, open space. Within the literary framework of Matthew, readers have already experienced this ambiguity in Matthew's formulation of John the Baptist and Jesus's proclamation that the kingdom of heaven "has come near" (Matt 3:2; 4:17). Those who have listened to Jesus's instruction and experienced his healing power, by doing so, have both heard and experienced "the good news of the kingdom" (Matt 4:23). Have they done so actually or only potentially? Matthew leaves the question open.

When the crowds gather to hear Jesus speak from the mountain, the first thing they hear is a series of makarisms bracketed by the promise, "theirs *is* the kingdom of heaven" (Matt 5:3, 10). Within this inclusio they hear six boldly stated future promises. The juxtaposition of present and future tenses is jarring, and this was probably what Matthew intended to achieve. As a rhetorically sensitive interpreter of Jesus's teachings, Matthew expects his readers (and hearers) to allow the present "is" to have a future, unrealized dimension, while at the same time allowing the future "will be" to oscillate between present and future forms of experience. Norman Perrin captures this fluid, even elusive, sense of kingdom

---

32. Gregory of Nyssa, *Hom. Beat.* 6.138.10 (Hall, *Gregory of Nyssa*, 67).

33. Augustine, *Sermon on the Mount* 1.2.8 (Pelikan, *The Preaching of Augustine*, 5–6).

34. Translation from Jaroslav Pelikan, *Luther's Works: Volume 21: The Sermon on the Mount (Sermons) and The Magnificat* (St. Louis: Concordia, 1956), 37.

35. John Wesley, *Sermon 23*, §I.11 (Outler, *Sermons I [1–33]*, 516–17).

by appropriating Philip Wheelwright's interpretive category of "tensive symbol."[36] For Perrin, the kingdom of God is

> a symbol with deep roots in the Jewish consciousness of themselves as the people of God [which] functions within the context of the myth of God active in history on behalf of his people ... [which] by the time of Jesus had come to represent particularly the expectation of a final, eschatological act of God on behalf of his people ... [and which] could be understood and used either as a steno- or as a tensive symbol.[37]

Introducing the kingdom of heaven within the opening section of the Sermon on the Mount, Matthew not only connects Jesus's vision of happiness with the kingdom but also prepares readers to receive further instruction that will illuminate both. Prominently positioned in the Sermon on the Mount is the Lord's Prayer, in which the petition "Your kingdom come" (*elthetō hē basileia sou*) encodes the bivalence, or perhaps even the multivalence, introduced earlier.[38] Here, the imperative form *elthetō* implies an unrealized dimension of God's reign that the petitioner prays will be realized, just as the parallel petition, "Your will be done on earth as it is in heaven" expresses an unrealized hope rather than a state of affairs that has already been achieved. When Jesus further encourages his hearers to "strive first for the kingdom of God and his righteousness," with the assurance that "all these things will be given to you as well" (Matt 6:33), he has in mind all of the material blessings—food and clothing—mentioned earlier in his teaching about anxiety (Matt 6:25–32). Here the kingdom is both means and end. It is the unrealized goal that focuses the disciples' striving, and yet they experience its reality in their strivings. It is theirs in the same ambivalent sense that happiness is promised in the first and eighth Beatitude. It is both reality and promise, and this inherently fluid dimension gives the kingdom its vital force. To use Perrin's language, the kingdom symbolizes something real but never fully exhausts its metaphorical or experiential possibilities.

---

36. Perrin, *Jesus and the Language of the Kingdom*, 29–30. Perrin draws on Philip Wheelwright, *Metaphor and Reality* (Bloomington: Indiana University Press, 1962), who distinguishes between "steno-symbols," which express one-to-one correspondence between the symbol and what is being symbolized (e.g., the mathematical symbol *pi*), and "tensive symbols," which signal "a set of meanings that can neither be exhausted nor adequately expressed by any one referent."

37. Perrin, *Jesus and the Language of the Kingdom*, 32.

38. Augustine, *Sermon on the Mount* 2.11.38, saw Matthew's first seven beatitudes, which he regarded as a self-contained subset recapitulated in the eighth, aligned with the seven petitions in the Lord's Prayer. Convinced that "the sevenfold number of these petitions [in the Lord's Prayer] corresponds to that sevenfold number from which this whole sermon takes its beginning," he links each petition with its respective beatitude.

This tensive dimension of the kingdom is further elaborated in Jesus's sayings and parables. Metaphorical language and images are most suitable for capturing and conveying this elusive yet compelling quality of the kingdom. It is like a seed in that it spawns growth often in unpredictable, surprising ways. What the parable of the sower, along with the many other parables reported in Matthew, accomplishes is to introduce a dazzling array of metaphors that invite readers and hearers to experience the multidimensionality of the kingdom. Its presence is felt with each hearing of the parable, and yet the parables create new possibilities for experiencing it.

This oscillating dimension of the kingdom is captured at the outset in Matthew's formulation of the beatitudes. Jesus's vision of happiness for the disciples is linked with this highly provocative metaphor. This linkage does not render happiness as an evanescent vision but neither does it make it a sure thing. By introducing such a wide range of human emotions and experiences in the first clause, all of which connect directly with lived human experience, Matthew's Jesus locates happiness within the complexity and contradiction common to everyone. By formulating the makarisms paradoxically, he underscores the enigmatic quality of the blessed life. One can experience emotions as draining as poverty, whether absolute (Luke) or spiritual (Matthew), as overwhelming and painful as suffering unjustly, or as lofty as purified hearts and peacemaking, and yet have all of them named as blessings, with the firm assurance in each case that there is ample warrant for doing so. The overarching promise is that the kingdom of heaven belongs to those at every stage of human experience, high or low, and that it is theirs as both promise and fulfillment. It is never theirs to clutch completely, to own or possess wholly, but neither is it a distant hope for which they can only dream as they reflect on the possibility of participating in the rich store of eschatological blessings.

4. Happiness Pursued: What the Beatitudes Have Meant

In the preceding discussion of certain exegetical points, I have already mentioned some of the ways in which Christian interpreters probed the meaning and significance of the beatitudes. In this section I want to extend those comments to consider more broadly how the beatitudes have shaped Christian sensibilities about the blessed or happy life.

The New Testament and Shortly Thereafter

Already in the late first and early second century we hear echoes of the beatitudes. In one sense, their reception history begins already in the New Testament. For example, 1 Pet 4:14, "If you are reviled for the name of Christ, you are blessed," recalls Matt 5:11 and Luke 6:22. With its focused emphasis on suffering, both that of Jesus and of his disciples, the pseudonymous author of 1 Peter could find solace in instructions about "blessed suffering" attributed to Jesus himself. The form of the saying, however, is already altered to an "if/then" structure, which clearly makes this blessedness/happiness a *consequence* or *reward* for suffering. But this form of beatitude in 1 Peter also develops those parts of the Matthean and Lukan beatitudes in which the language shifts to the second person and we find Jesus using a formulation that is more directly consequential: "Blessed are *you* when people revile *you* . . ." (Matt 5:11; cf. Luke 6:22).

References to the beatitudes are sparse and scattered in second-century Christian writers.[39] By the late second and early third century, however, they gain greater prominence in Clement of Alexandria's discussion of martyrdom.[40] Convinced that the Christian life is gnostic in the positive sense that one strives for spiritual perfection through wisdom and understanding mediated by Christ, the soul's Teacher, Clement sees the beatitudes as integral to that process. "The final goal of the beatitudes," writes Judith Kovacs, "is to lead the soul to a state of θεωρία [*theōria*], the pure, direct, lasting contemplation of God."[41] The soul's gradual ascent toward God requires discipline (*askēsis*), which, though rigorous and self-denying, is essentially and finally joyous: "this discipline gives way to love, as intensely loving souls enter the joy of God, and feast on him forever."[42] For Clement, the beatitudes expedite gnostic happiness in the soul's quest for God.

Gregory of Nyssa

Clement's construal of the beatitudes as progressive steps in the Christian pursuit of spiritual perfection becomes more fully developed in the fourth century, most notably in Gregory of Nyssa's Eight Homilies on the beatitudes, which he preached in the 370s. Operating with a sharply defined Platonic cosmology and anthropology, Gregory envisions the individual Christian's moral life along a vertical axis. One lives in the phenomenal or physical world but aspires to move upward to the noumenal or spiritual world. This vertical movement reverses the

---

39. *1 Clem.* 13.2; *Did.* 3.7; Pol. *Phil.* 2.3; *Gos. Thom.* Log. 54, 58, 68, 69; Irenaeus, *Against Heresies* 3.22.1; 4.9.4, 20.5, 33.9; also cf. 3.14.3; *Acts Paul* 3.5–6; *Acts Thom.* 94, 107; *Ep. Apos.* 38, 40; *Vis. Paul* 21.

40. *Strom.* 4.

41. Judith L. Kovacs, "Clement of Alexandria and Gregory of Nyssa on the Beatitudes," in Drobner and Viciano, eds., *Gregory of Nyssa*, 311–29, esp. 321.

42. Kovacs, "Clement of Alexandria," 323.

downward movement of sin, in which the soul "falls" from the heavenly to the earthly world.

Within this intellectual framework, Gregory sees the Matthean beatitudes as steps of a ladder, on which the soul climbs upward toward God. The first seven beatitudes represent ascending stages in the soul's development, while the eighth Beatitude, with its repetition of "kingdom of heaven," recapitulates the previous seven. Accordingly, one begins by becoming "poor in spirit"—that is, by acquiring humility—and progresses toward the higher spiritual levels of seeing God and finally becoming children of God.

Gregory's rhetorical training is clearly evident throughout his exposition. We find several allusions to Plato's Allegory of the Cave, which Gregory sees mirrored in the Christian soul's pursuit of the true light of knowledge. Aristotle's discussion of *eudaimonia* is also reflected both formally and materially in Gregory's exposition.[43] Like Aristotle, Gregory feels compelled to define what he means by happiness or blessedness. It "includes every concept of goodness," and is that "from which nothing answering to good desire is missing."[44] Defined antithetically, it is the opposite of misery, "the wretched experience of painful and undesirable things."[45] Stated positively, however, blessedness

> is the divine itself ... [it is] that unsullied life: the ineffable and inconceivable good, the indescribable beauty, essential grace and wisdom and power, true light, fount of all goodness, authority transcending the universe, sole object of love, always the same, perpetual delight, eternal joy, of which, when one says all that one can, one says nothing worthy.[46]

Attentive to the central importance of the kingdom of heaven in Matthew's version of the beatitudes, Gregory explores the significance of this imagery for understanding Jesus's vision of blessedness. He acknowledges that the heavenly goal toward which the Christian strives is kingly, but in what sense? Since the pursuit essentially becomes a contest with sin in its many forms, the ultimate goal is freedom from sin. Informed by the Stoic view that only the good person is free, Gregory extends the metaphor by proposing kingship as the ultimate form of freedom.

---

43. For more on Aristotle and *eudaimonia*, see the essays by Nathan MacDonald, Jacqueline Lapsley, and Carol A. Newsom in the present volume.

44. *Hom. Beat.* 1.79–80 (Hall, *Gregory of Nyssa*, 24).

45. *Hom. Beat.* 1.80 (Hall, *Gregory of Nyssa*, 24).

46. *Hom. Beat.* 1.80 (Hall, *Gregory of Nyssa*, 24–25).

Now the pinnacle of freedom is self-determination, and the rank of king allows no mastery superior to itself. If therefore the stranger to sin is self-determining, and if it is proper to the kingly state to be sovereign and without superior, it follows that the one who is persecuted by evil is declared blessed, because persecution from that source proclaims his royal rank.[47]

Seen this way, being persecuted for the sake of justice, or as he rephrases it toward the end of his remarks, "for my (Christ's) sake,"[48] can reasonably be connected with the kingdom of heaven as one's ultimate reward. And if persecution, even when experienced in unjust forms, is done for the right reasons and assists the persecuted in distinguishing material baggage from spiritual values, thereby advancing them toward their ultimate destiny, which is unchangeable, permanent, wholly intelligible and nonmaterial, then it qualifies as blessedness or happiness.

Ambrose

Ambrose's exposition of the beatitudes occurs in his *Exposition of the Holy Gospel According to Saint Luke*, which was based on homilies that were given between 377 and 389.[49] Here we see Ambrose's penchant for finding multiple levels of meaning within the biblical text. He moves rather freely from the literal meaning, for which he has little interest, to spiritual, mystical, or allegorical levels of meaning.

In treating the beatitudes, Ambrose insists that the order of the beatitudes, especially in Matthew, must be taken seriously. Being poor (in spirit), whether it symbolizes humility or aversion to physical possessions, constitutes step one. Each successive beatitude represents a progressive step forward (or upward). Although he does not introduce the ladder metaphor, he conceives the beatitudes as instruction for progressive spiritual development.

Ambrose's emphasis on the order of the beatitudes creates a problem: How can the Kingdom of Heaven be the reward for both the first and eighth beatitude?

---

47. *Hom. Beat.* 8.169 (Hall, *Gregory of Nyssa*, 89).

48. *Hom. Beat.* 8.168.15 (Hall, *Gregory of Nyssa*, 89).

49. My analysis is based on Saint Ambrose of Milan, *Exposition of the Holy Gospel According to Saint Luke* (2nd ed.; trans. Theodosia Tomkinson; Etna, CA: Center for Traditionalist Orthodox Studies, 2003); also see Gabriel Tissot, *Ambroise de Milan: Traité sur L'Évangile de S. Luc* (2 vols.; Sources Chrétiennes 45, 52; Paris: Les Éditions du Cerf, 1956–58). See also Johannes Quasten, *Patrology* (4 vols.; Utrecht: Spectrum, 1966–1997), 4:164–65.

"Why is the reward equal for the beginners and the perfect?"[50] One possibility is that the first beatitude should be understood mystically: "the first Kingdom of Heaven is the Apostolic"—that is, departing (being dissolved) and being with Christ (Phil 1:13). Matthew's double mention of the Kingdom of Heaven prompts Ambrose to think of it in two stages: the first Kingdom of the Heavens occurs at one's death (citing 1 Thess 4:17; Dan 12:2), the second Kingdom of the Heavens occurs "after the Resurrection." We should think, then, of "a progress of mansions" (John 14:2–3), as we move through stages of experiencing the Kingdom of Heaven.[51]

One of Ambrose's most interesting exegetical moves is to align both the Matthean and Lukan beatitudes with the four cardinal virtues. He achieves this in several ways. First, he rehearses each beatitude, noting which of the four virtues or which aspect of one of the virtues it tends to cultivate. The one who is poor in spirit is not greedy, the one who weeps is not proud, and so forth. Noticing that there is no one-to-one correlation, he further proposes that "the virtues are interwoven and interlinked, so that he who has one may be seen to have several, and a single virtue befits the Saints."[52] Even so, he finds the four cardinal virtues embedded within the combined set of Matthean and Lukan beatitudes: (1) poor in spirit (Matt 5:3) = temperance (*temperantia*); (2) appetite for righteousness (Matt 5:6) = justice (*iustitia*); (3) weeping/mourning (Luke 6:21) = prudence (*prudentia*); and (4) being reviled and persecuted (Luke 6:22) = fortitude (*fortitudo*). He concludes this synthetic exegesis by observing:

> It is also an attribute of fortitude to conquer anger and to suppress indignation; fortitude, thereby, also strengthens the body, as well as the spirit, and prevents it from being troubled by fear or grief, by which we are often discouraged, as if by evil interpreters. Thus, temperance has purity of heart and spirit, justice has compassion, patience has peace, and fortitude has gentleness.[53]

Ambrose's concern to relate the beatitudes to the four cardinal virtues reflects his appreciation for the Greek and Roman moral tradition. It also shows his awareness of the paraenetic function of the beatitudes within the Christian tradition. Finally, his interweaving of the virtues with beatitudes reflects an

---

50. *Expos. Luke* 5 §60 (Tomkinson, *Exposition of the Holy Gospel According to Saint Luke*, 176).

51. *Expos. Luke* 5 §61 (Tomkinson, *Exposition of the Holy Gospel According to Saint Luke*, 176–77).

52. *Expos. Luke* 5 §63 (Tomkinson, *Exposition of the Holy Gospel According to Saint Luke*, 177).

53. *Expos. Luke* 5 §67–68 (Tomkinson, *Exposition of the Holy Gospel According to Saint Luke*, 178).

Table 6.2

Isa 11:2–3	Matt 5:3–12
1. fear of God	1. humility—"poor in spirit" (Matt 5:3)
2. piety	2. meek (Matt 5:5)
3. knowledge	3. mourn (Matt 5:4)
4. fortitude	4. hunger and thirst for justice (Matt 5:6)
5. counsel	5. merciful (Matt 5:7)
6. understanding	6. pure in heart (Matt 5:8)
7. wisdom	7. peacemakers (Matt 5:9)

Aristotelian awareness that *eudaimonia* cannot be conceived apart from the virtuous life.

Augustine

Our last case study is Augustine, who, writing in the 390s, treated the beatitudes in his exposition on the Sermon on the Mount. Like Gregory, Augustine interprets the beatitudes using the "ascent of the soul" template, but he also introduces some exegetical innovations. We have already noted his alignment of the first seven beatitudes with the seven petitions of the Lord's Prayer. In an equally creative exegetical move, he also coordinates them with the seven gifts of the Holy Spirit, which patristic exegetes had detected in Isa 11:2–3. For each step in the soul's ascent toward perfection expressed in the beatitudes, Augustine finds a corresponding gift of the Spirit, as seen in the following table (Table 6.2).

Augustine's exegetical richness is everywhere evident, but can be illustrated in his exposition of Matt 5:9, "Blessed are the peacemakers."[54] Peace is the absence of contention and conflict. One becomes a peacemaker by overcoming one's passions: "Those who have quieted all the movements of the soul and subjected them to reason (that is, to mind and spirit) and have subdued their carnal desires, are peacemakers within themselves."[55] Through conquest of the passions, we "become a kingdom of God in which everything is so ordered that what is distinctive and superior in [us] rules without resistance those other elements which are common to us and to beasts."[56] This occurs when what is preeminent in us—mind and

---

54. *Sermon on the Mount* 1.2.9 (Pelikan, *The Preaching of Augustine*, 6–7).

55. *Sermon on the Mount* 1.2.9 (Pelikan, *The Preaching of Augustine*, 6).

56. Ibid.

reason—is subject to something higher—truth itself, which is the Son of God. We experience peace when we overcome what is inferior to us by submitting to the One who is superior over us. Jaroslav Pelikan refers to this as Augustine's "great chain of being," in which "all natures are beautiful in their order and by their degrees."[57] Once we grasp this overall order of things, we can then love properly, by loving "all things at their proper level, neither more nor less."[58] Since the "prince of this world" is notorious for upsetting equilibrium, he has no place in such a world. When this peaceable kingdom is established through the moral ordering of the world, whatever persecutions the "prince of the world" inflicts from without only serve to enhance God's glory. His futile efforts only magnify the strength of God's kingdom. This explains the next beatitude (Matt 5:10) that promises the kingdom of heaven to those who suffer persecution for justice's sake.

This cursory review of the reception history of the beatitudes in the first four Christian centuries reveals some of the interpretive trajectories that persisted for centuries. Thomas Aquinas's exposition of the beatitudes in the *Summa Theologiae* draws directly on Ambrose and Augustine, even as it advances their interpretation.[59] Like his predecessors, Thomas spotted many of the paradoxical features of the beatitudes and made strenuous efforts to rationalize them. The stage/step template remains a homiletical trope well into the eighteenth century. This is seen clearly in John Wesley's exposition of the Sermon on the Mount. Albrecht Ritschl's interpretation of the kingdom of God as a moral realm in which the residual effects of justification and reconciliation are gradually worked out represented one way of reading the beatitudes, and the Gospels in general. It accented the present dimension to the virtual exclusion of its future, eschatological dimension. Johannes Weiss and Albert Schweitzer, by contrast, sought to retrieve the eschatological dimension, which, they insisted, had evaporated through centuries of interpretation. This tug of war between competing visions of the kingdom of God continued well into the twentieth century and persists to this day.

5. Conclusions

In spite of their complexity and the numerous exegetical questions presented by the beatitudes, they figure prominently in the New Testament vision of happiness and have continued to figure prominently in New Testament interpretation ever

---

57. *Sermon on the Mount* 1.12.34 (Pelikan, *The Preaching of Augustine*, 38).

58. Pelikan, *The Preaching of Augustine*, xviii.

59. Thomas treats the beatitudes in Question 69, which comes between his treatment of the gifts of the Holy Spirit in Question 68 and the Fruits of the Spirit in Question 70.

since. The Matthean and Lukan beatitudes are by no means the only makarisms in the New Testament, but they are certainly the most conspicuous. Since they occur on the lips of Jesus in two respective sermonic contexts, popular perceptions of happiness and the blessed life in the New Testament invariably gravitate toward them. And rightly so. Their rhetorically balanced, even elegant, formulation has ensured their popularity. But more important than their literary form is their compelling visionary content. Employing utterly realistic, concrete images that connect with everyday experiences, including weeping, hungering, thirsting, and suffering unjustly, but also embracing the hard work of peacemaking, and extending to the higher reaches of spiritual ecstasy that takes the form of seeing God and becoming children of God, the beatitudes have connected with Christians in every time and place. Anchored firmly in life as people experience it and remarkably devoid of mythological symbolism, they also extend promises that reach the deepest levels of human aspiration—being comforted and fed, laughing, finding justice, experiencing mercy, apprehending God, and enjoying filial fellowship with God.

For these reasons, the beatitudes have had resilience through the centuries. We have seen interpreters successively read and reread them within their own contexts, sometimes through gnostic eyes, at other times through dimmer eyes. Given the penetrating persistence of the Greek philosophical tradition from the Presocratics forward, as well as the Greco-Roman moral tradition, interpreters inevitably read the beatitudes through Platonic, Aristotelian, and Stoic lenses, even as they sought assiduously to find intertextual echoes within the broad span of biblical writings. In some cases, this produced profoundly penetrating analyses of happiness and the blessed life, as with Gregory, Ambrose, and Augustine. The texture of their expositions reveals depth rather than naïveté. Even though much in their mystical and allegorical excursions may amuse us, these interpretive efforts were genuine probings toward the blessed life, whether understood as here or hereafter.

7

"We Had to Celebrate and Rejoice!"

HAPPINESS IN THE TOPSY-TURVY
WORLD OF LUKE-ACTS

Joel B. Green

1. A Different Kind of Happiness

At the end of Acts 5, we find a startling observation concerning the apostles. These witnesses to the resurrection of Christ had already been jailed by the high priest and Sadducees for carrying out their work of preaching and healing in public. Having been miraculously released from prison, the apostles obeyed the angel of the Lord and returned to the area of the temple where they engaged in proclamation. This resulted in their being brought before the Sanhedrin, which in turn concluded its deliberations regarding the apostles by silencing them, flogging them, and dismissing them. At this juncture, the narrator, whom I will call Luke, writes of the apostles, "As they left the council, they rejoiced that they were considered worthy to suffer dishonor for the sake of the name" (Acts 5:41, NRSV).[1] Even in the NRSV, the oxymoron is clear, but a less polished translation brings out the emphasis even further: "they were counted worthy enough to have their honor deprived of them." Dishonor suffered for the sake of the name of Christ is honor. Luke thus documents an inversion of values native to the whole of his two-part narrative, the Gospel of Luke and the Acts of the Apostles, or Luke-Acts. Drawing on proleptic intimations of persecution in the Gospel of Luke,[2] Luke identifies these followers of Christ as the embodiment of the words of Jesus spoken earlier in the Gospel:

---

1. Unless otherwise indicated, translations of biblical texts are my own, though I have often had an eye on the CEB.

2. On this motif more generally, see Scott Cunningham, *'Through Many Tribulations': The Theology of Persecution in Luke-Acts* (JNSTSup 142; Sheffield: Sheffield Academic Press, 1997).

Happy are you when people hate you, reject you, insult you, and slander you on account of the Son of Man. Rejoice when that happens! Leap for joy! You have a great reward in heaven. . . . (Luke 6:22–23)[3]

Although Luke's narrative thus bears witness to strange values, this should not surprise us. In another context, the anthropologist Marshall Sahlins observes the plurality of cultures, then draws an important corollary:

Each people knows their own kind of happiness: the culture that is the legacy of their ancestral tradition, transmitted in the distinctive concepts of their ancestral language, and adapted to their specific life conditions. It is by means of this tradition, endowed also with the morality of the community and the notions of the family, that experience is organized, since people do not simply discover the world, they are taught it. They come to it not simply as cognitions but as values.[4]

Sahlins is concerned with the potential imposition of, say, European culture as the universal condition of Homo sapiens. To follow this pattern of thinking, though, is to recognize that what might be identified as "happiness" among one group might be evaluated differently by another. Or, said differently, how or even whether one seeks happiness cannot be universalized.[5]

These initial ruminations frame important windows into Luke's perspective on happiness. First, with the Stoics and against the Epicureans, Luke sees happiness as the effect or byproduct of living in harmony with the way things are. The apostles in Acts 5 did not go in search of happiness, but sought rather to carry out the missionary mandate they had received and so identify themselves as servants of God's kingdom. Nor should it escape us that they did not go in search of the humiliation and beating they sustained at the hands of the Sanhedrin, as though the route to pleasure was through pain. Again, their happiness was a byproduct of their faithful service. Second, Luke has a particular perspective on "the way things are," and thus what it might mean to live, as the Stoics might put it, in harmony with the natural order of things. Luke's perspective would have found a ready home in other New Testament materials, even if its general tenor would undoubtedly have seemed

---

3. For the beatitudes in Luke, see also the essay by Carl R. Holladay in the present volume.

4. Marshall Sahlins, *How "Natives" Think: About Captain Cook, for Example* (Chicago: University of Chicago Press, 1995), 12.

5. This is suggested, too, in B. Grinde, "Happiness in the Perspective of Evolutionary Psychology," *J Happiness St* 3 (2002): 331–54.

strange to those outside the community that followed Christ. Third, as Sahlins's observation might hint, the canons of happiness assumed in Acts 5 belong to the register of the community Luke portrays—in this case, the community over which at this point in the narrative the apostles themselves exercise oversight.

Although the language of happiness is dispersed widely throughout the narrative of Luke-Acts, happiness plays a heightened role at three points: (1) in Luke 1–2, Luke's narrative of birth announcements and celebration, with its anticipations of a new way of construing the world; (2) in Luke 15, a veritable battleground over what constitutes happiness, centered on Jesus's recounting of the parables of the lost sheep, lost coin, and lost son; and (3) in Luke 6, the Sermon on the Plain, where Luke sketches the dispositions of those for whom happiness thus defined is reserved. Some contemporary happiness studies identify happiness in terms of *growth* (intrinsic motivation and progress on the path toward realizing one's life purpose), *integrity* (the internalization and assimilation of one's cultural conventions and practices), and *well-being* (flourishing and contentment).[6] If we assume that kind of typology, then Luke's contribution lies particularly in the context within which happiness thus understood might be cultivated, modulated, and experienced. This context is defined by God's eschatological intervention to bring salvation in all its fullness to all and, then, by the invitation to persons to order their lives accordingly. My identification of Luke's contribution in terms of eschatology does not mean that Luke's narrative is bereft of interest in what we might call the psychological and relational aspects of happiness. It is, rather, that with the advent, death, and exaltation of the Messiah the times have changed, and that humans who orient their lives to the divine purpose disclosed in the Messiah will experience the pleasure and meaningfulness associated with human flourishing within this eschatologically determined world.

2. Joyous Advent (Luke 1–2)

Luke's readers might be forgiven for imagining that, at the turn of the era, the whole Jewish world was characterized not only by oppression under the heavy hand of Rome but also by pervasive anticipation of divine intervention on Israel's behalf. Indeed, in the context of Luke's presentation of John's ministry, the narrator reports that God's people were filled with expectation to the point that everyone wondered whether John might be God's agent of salvation (3:15).

---

6. Cf., e.g., Richard M. Ryan and Edward L. Deci, "On Happiness and Human Potentials: A Review of Research on Hedonic and Eudaimonic Well-Being," *Annu Rev Psychol* 52 (2001): 141–66; Kent C. Berridge and Morten L. Kringelbach, "Affective Neuroscience of Pleasure: Reward in Humans and Animals," *Psychopharmacology* 199 (2008): 457–80.

Historically, both of these images of the Jewish world would be exaggerated in the simplicity with which they portray the complex of contextual factors and responses characteristic of life in the early empire. Nevertheless, this is the world situation as the Third Evangelist has actualized it in the opening of his narrative, and this is the context within which happiness is both foretold and proleptically experienced.

A People in Despair and Anticipation

Luke's portrait of a people in despair is colored with hues both intense and subtle. For example, when Simeon and Anna appear in tandem as male and female prophets, we learn that the one lived in anticipation of the restoration of Israel and the other bore witness to all those longing for Jerusalem's liberation (2:25, 38). Because both are dressed in prophetic garb and are presented as persons of exemplary piety, we are justified in evaluating their perspectives in the most positive light—indeed, in thinking that they represent the very best of Israel's faithfulness. Perhaps even more to the point, Zechariah, whose prophetic speech is Spirit-empowered (1:67), expresses the need for a powerful savior by drawing attention to Israel's need for "salvation from our enemies and from the hand of all who hate us," and anticipating the time when "we would be rescued from the hands of our enemies so that we could serve God without fear, in holiness and righteousness in God's eyes, for as long as we live" (1:71, 74–75). The brush strokes of Mary's Song are perhaps the strongest of all. She interprets the gracious, powerful work of Israel's savior in these terms:

> He has shown strength with his arm.
>> he has scattered those with arrogant dispositions.
> He has pulled the powerful down from their thrones,
>> and lifted up the lowly;
>> he has filled the hungry with good things,
>> and sent the rich away empty-handed. (1:51–53)

Representations of imperial power are never far from the center of Luke's mural, and these provide the immediate backdrop for his representations of Israel's life-setting. For example, Luke devotes more space to the census mandated by Caesar Augustus than to an actual accounting of Jesus's birth. The census is mentioned four times in 2:1–7, hammering home the significance of this registration of persons and property for purposes of enrollment for taxation. Here is a transparent reminder of the concrete reality of the overlordship of Rome, with its demand of tribute as a sign of allegiance to the emperor, which for many stood in conflict with fidelity to the God of Israel. What is more, the angel of the Lord designates Jesus's birth as "good news," associates his birth with earthly peace, and refers to the newborn baby as "Lord" (2:10–14). Granted that each of these terms has precedent in Israel's Scriptures, it is also the case that they are reminiscent of imperial rule. We should think of Luke's exploiting the social, political, and religious depth of these terms against the backdrop of both Roman imperial propaganda and Jewish hope in order to highlight the significance of this child. It is not for nothing that the narrator locates both the births of John and Jesus and the opening of John's ministry within the politics of Rome:

- "In the days of King Herod of Judea . . ." (1:5)
- "In those days Emperor Augustus . . ." (2:1)
- "In the fifteenth year of the reign of Emperor Tiberius, when Pontius Pilate was governor of Judea, Herod was ruler of Galilee, his brother Philip was ruler of the region of Ituraea and Trachonitis, and Lysanias was ruler of Abilene . . ." (3:1)

Within this setting, hope is grounded in God's mercy and memory and focused on divine intervention to set things right. As Mary's Song has it, when God comes to the aid of Israel, God remembers his mercy, "just as he promised to our ancestors, to Abraham and to his descendants forever" (1:54–55).

The Births of John and Jesus: Happy Occasions

In his appearance to the shepherds, the angel of the Lord bears witness to what happiness might look like in the mural of oppression and expectation Luke has painted:

> Do not be afraid! I am bringing good news to you—wonderful, happy news for everyone: Your savior is born today in the city of David; he is Christ the Lord. (2:10–11)

That is, Jesus's birth, and John's before him, signals a world transformation, the consequence of which is the context for renewed happiness.

Given Zechariah and Elizabeth's childlessness, and particularly the shame of childlessness that would have been Elizabeth's lot (1:25), their pregnancy alone is a happy occasion—both for them and for their extended family and friends. Thus, Gabriel announced to Zechariah that he and Elizabeth would have a son and that "he will be a joy and delight" for them (1:14). And on the occasion of John's birth, Elizabeth's "neighbors and relatives celebrated with her because they had heard that the Lord had shown her his great mercy" (1:58). As Gabriel goes on to say, though, the ripple effect of John's birth will extend much further, so that "many people will rejoice at his birth" (1:14). This is because his birth marks the coming of God to set things right, for John's role was to prepare the way of the Lord, to begin the work of the renewal of God's people.

Mary: Exemplar of Happiness

In what are otherwise scenes of joy and celebration, the place Luke carves out for Mary's happiness is especially significant. Joy and happiness are pronounced over her and celebrated by her four times in Luke 1 and once further later in the narrative, in chapter 11. For the sake of convenience, I will take as my point of departure the brief dialogue between Jesus and an unnamed woman from the crowd regarding Mary's status as "the blessed one," found in 11:27–28—a text that brings forward earlier references to Mary in the Gospel. This will allow some insight into how the fresh context generated by the coming of the Savior in Luke 1–2 marks not only a time of celebration but also portends the new order of conventions and values that determine the canons of happiness.

In the midst of Jesus's interaction with those who sought to test him in Luke 11, an unnamed woman interrupts with this declaration: "Happy is the mother who gave birth to you and who nursed you!" (v. 27). Her words bring to the surface conventional values regarding the status and role of women in a near-proverbial way. For example, Petronius had written, "How happy is the mother who gave birth to such a one as you" (Satyricon, 94.1; mid-first century CE).[7] This unnamed woman's announcement is enmeshed with two intertwined perspectives regarding women: (i) that she finds her place in traditional society in terms of her relatedness to her husband; and (ii) that she finds value in childbearing and may be regarded as blessed through being the mother of a son who is granted great honor. This kind of cultural value, whereby honor is obtained through bearing children, is on display in Israel's Scriptures too, such as in the account of the rivalry between Leah and Rachel, for whom steps on the ladder of status and happiness are counted in numbers of pregnancies (Gen 29:31–30:24). The ideal of fecundity and the value for women of bearing children was also largely taken for granted in Rome, not least so as to maintain the family name and to propagate the potency of the empire.[8] Read against such a backdrop, this woman's pronouncement of

---

7. See also Ovid, *Metamorphoses*, 4.320–24; Gen 30:13; 49:25; *2 Apoc. Bar.* 54:10.

8. Cf. Beryl Rawson, "The Roman Family," in *The Family in Ancient Rome: New Perspectives* (ed. Beryl Rawson; Ithaca: Cornell University Press, 1986), 1–57.

happiness seems only fitting and, one might think, marks her as a woman of keen insight into Jesus's character. By referring to his mother in this way, has she not characterized him with high honorifics too?

Jesus's reply, though, moves in a different direction: "Happy rather are those who hear God's word and put it into practice" (11:28). Although it is possible, grammatically, to read his words as a contradiction of the woman's pronouncement,[9] the fact that Elizabeth had spoken similar words, and done so under the inspiration of the Holy Spirit (1:41–42), makes this option doubtful. Neither is it appropriate to imagine that Luke thus narrates Jesus's simple agreement with this woman's assessment.[10] Simply because a statement was made earlier in the narrative by a woman under the guidance of the Spirit does not mean that such a statement is incapable of further nuance. More likely is the view that the words of this woman are not altogether wrong, but need modification.[11] That is, Jesus amends both her pronouncement and the pervasive cultural values to which she gives voice. He engages in cultural criticism, calling into question one of the primary means by which women would have found happiness in Luke's world.

To grasp the depth of this criticism, we might ask on what basis Mary would have been a candidate for this happy pronouncement. Luke has portrayed Mary as one who hears and reflects on the divine word, who embraces it positively, and who proclaims it in the fashion of a prophet (cf. 1:26–38, 46–55; 2:19, 51). Although Jesus's words generalize concerning how anyone might achieve a state of happiness ("happy are those who . . ."), Elizabeth had already declared Mary as happy or blessed on account of her faith (1:45). Taking seriously the criterion Elizabeth and Jesus introduce is important because the alternative has the potential of restricting Mary's happiness (and, with her, that of other women) to her role as mother—that is, to the fruitfulness of her belly and breasts.[12] Jesus's beatitude thus allows no room for conventional notions of happiness in God's economy, for his message works to construct a new world that undermines present conventions.

---

9. E.g., James Malcolm Arlandson (*Women, Class, and Society in Early Christianity: Models from Luke-Acts* [Peabody, MA: Hendrickson, 1997], 123–24) regards the unnamed woman as an outsider, contradicted by Jesus.

10. *Contra* Darrell L. Bock, *Luke* (2 vols.; BECNT 3; Grand Rapids: Baker, 1994–96), 2:1094; M. Philip Scott, "A Note on the Meaning and Translation of Luke 11:28," *ITQ* 41 (1974): 235–50.

11. Cf. *Mary in the New Testament: A Collaborative Assessment by Protestant and Roman Catholic Scholars* (eds. Raymond E. Brown et al.; Philadelphia: Fortress and New York: Paulist, 1978), 171–72.

12. This is noted by Luise Schottroff, *Let the Oppressed Go Free: Feminist Perspectives on the New Testament* (Gender and the Biblical Tradition; Louisville: Westminster John Knox, 1993), 116.

Mary's happiness is not simply the consequence of the promise of mother-hood. What, then, is its basis? To this question, Luke's answer is as profound as it is subtle. Unlike Luke's introduction of other characters in the birth narratives—Zechariah, Elizabeth, Joseph, Simeon, and Anna—in the case of Mary we find no prefatory hints of family pedigree or unassailable character (cf. 1:5–7, 27; 2:4, 25–27, 36–37), both typical measures of social standing in most any world. These are conspicuously absent in the case of Mary. She is presented as a young girl, perhaps twelve or thirteen years old, not yet or only recently having achieved puberty, resident in an insignificant town far removed from the Jewish and Roman centers of power and purity. Her family of origin is never mentioned. She is betrothed to Joseph but has not yet joined his household and, thus, has no claims to his status. In fact, she is not introduced in any way that would com-mend her to us as one particularly noteworthy or deserving of honor. Yet she is granted the highest status allocated anyone within this narrative, an honorable greeting by the archangel of the Lord, and an invitation both to celebrate and to participate in the realization of God's saving purpose. As Mary herself states, God has looked on her lowly position with the result that all generations will recognize her happiness; indeed, in the depths of her inner being, Mary herself knows happiness on account of the Savior God (1:47–48). Here already is the inversion of the social realities of the world Mary occupies. Luke has begun the process of undercutting the conventions of happiness that characterize his world.

In these ways, Luke has begun to cultivate an understanding of happiness con-gruent with the changing of the times announced in these first chapters of his narrative.

3. Earthly Unhappiness—Heavenly Happiness (Luke 15)

Luke 15 presents a tightly organized contrast between two ways of construing the world, documented in the juxtaposition of unhappy Pharisees and legal experts in 15:1–2 and repeated references to happiness throughout the remainder of the chapter (15:5, 6, 7, 9, 10, 23, 24, 29, 32). This last list of texts culminates in a decla-ration of the necessity of happiness when the dead are returned to life and the lost are found: "We had to celebrate and rejoice!" (15:32). The opening of this scene in 15:1–2 makes it clear that the subject of concern is Jesus's table habits, and partic-ularly the question of table companions:

> All the tax collectors and sinners gathered around Jesus to hear him, but the Pharisees and legal experts were grumbling, "This man welcomes sin-ners and eats with them."

In this way Luke introduces yet again the concern that occupies him throughout this larger section of the Gospel, which runs from Luke 13:10–17:10—namely, *Who will participate in the kingdom of God?*

"Will only a few people be saved?" A bystander addresses this question to Jesus during his long journey up to Jerusalem (13:23). Rather than tallying the number of those who would be saved, Jesus focuses instead on the number of those who would be disqualified: "Make every effort to enter through the narrow gate," he replies. "Many, I tell you, will want to enter and won't be able to" (13:24). Ultimately, end-time curiosity about "how many" turns into a call to demonstrate in the present that one is well-suited for future salvation. Jesus's response turns to the end-time meal, when "people will come from east and west, north and south, and sit down to eat in God's kingdom" (13:29). He thus builds on the longstanding notion that the consummation of the kingdom is a great feast (e.g., Isa 25:6–9; 55:1–2; 65:13–14; Zech 1:7). In the world of Luke more generally, meals played a further role. Sharing bread signified acceptance, hospitality entailed the offer of friendship, and people were united in goodwill and camaraderie at the dinner table. The intersection of these ways of understanding meals is striking because Jesus clearly anticipates the inclusion of Gentiles at the end-time banquet, as though Jesus expected that Abraham would extend hospitality even to them. Isaiah had promised as much, observing that, in the end-time, all the nations will exult, "Let us celebrate and rejoice in our salvation" (Isa 25:9).

The combination of table and kingdom resurfaces in Luke 14, where Jesus's teaching on eating habits and dining invitations is interrupted by another on-looker: "Happy are those who will eat bread in God's kingdom!" (14:15). "Yes," we can almost hear Jesus say, "but *who* will eat the kingdom bread?" Who participates in the kingdom of God? This is important because Jesus has just pulled the rug out from under two taken-for-granted aspects of the wider world. The first is the importance of social status and social stratification, the maintenance and broadcasting of one's relative prestige in the community. The second is the gift-and-obligation system that tied together every person—slave or free, male or female, emperor or child—into an intricate web of reciprocal relations. Jesus turned upside down practices tied to these social conventions through his teaching in 14:7–14 about finding one's place at the table and invitation lists. Clearly, Jesus has a different understanding of meals and dining conventions than those shared by his contemporaries. Meals, in his view, were opportunities for the extension of mercy to the hungry and hospitality to the outsider, without reference to the enhancement of one's prestige. They were gifts to be given, without strings attached. In 14:16–24, Jesus goes so far as to relate the story of a wealthy householder who models this instruction by extending hospitality to the blind, the lame, the crippled, and the poor. The wealthy householder does not enhance his prestige, nor does his action provide him with monetary or social reward. Instead, he has embraced an altogether different social order in which the community of God's people is founded in gracious, uncalculating hospitality. Jesus's instruction at the table revolves around the related motifs of table fellowship, celebration with shared meals, and the extension of hospitality. Compared to conventions held by many of his contemporaries, though, his message calls for a tectonic shift in how happiness is measured. As we will see, this shift is itself grounded in his understanding of God's character and purpose. It is not too much to say that Jesus's practices and instruction reflect God's own practices. Jesus urges happiness at a table shared with the poor, the crippled, the blind, the lame—and, indeed, with tax collectors and sinners—because God himself is happy to welcome such people to salvation's banquet table.

Conversion to such ways of thinking, believing, feeling, and behaving is hard, and it is obvious with the beginning of Luke 15 that, thus far, the Pharisees and legal experts have been blind and deaf to Jesus's example and instruction. Hence, they "were grumbling, 'This man welcomes sinners and eats with them'" (v. 2). Here is evidence of Jesus's unequivocal rejection of widespread, contemporary interests and norms. Evident, too, is that Jesus has created a problem for himself. His own practices at the table have begun to shape a community whose existence and openness to the least and left-out of society raise an unflattering, even threatening voice against the attitudes and practices embraced by his adversaries.

Jesus has a lot to answer for, and the parables of Luke 15 are cast as his defense of the nature of his entire ministry. In fact, in the parables of the lost sheep, lost coin, and lost son, Jesus highlights the disposition of his own ministry as the necessary complement to God's own character. To put it differently, Jesus raises the stakes in his encounter with these legal experts and Pharisees. The positive response of tax collectors and sinners as they gather around Jesus constitutes a restoration of the lost that results in heavenly joy and calls for earthly celebration, including feasting at the common table. In welcoming such persons as these social and religious outcasts to the table, Jesus is only giving expression to God's expansive grace and inviting earthbound tables to mirror the divine table. By calling Jesus's behavior into question, then, these legal experts and Pharisees have actually called into question God's character—at least, that is the way Jesus presents things.

There is an obvious parallelism among these three parables, even though the third, concerning the lost son, is more complex. Each follows a threefold pattern: something is lost, what is lost is found, the finding of the lost results is the occasion of heavenly and earthly happiness. Recovery of what was lost leads to joyous repast (see vv. 6, 9, 23–24, 27). It is easy to discern the psychological and relational aspects of happiness in these texts, but we must also see that these are themselves reflections of God's own happiness; in fact, the father elevates such joyous cele-bration to the level of divine necessity (see vv. 7, 10, 32).[13]

Why should Jesus focus in this way on response? Recall that Luke 13–17 repeat-edly underscores the importance of the boundaries of the people of God, with Pharisees, legal experts, the wealthy, and those who act like them excluding those who live on or beyond the social and religious margins of community life. For his part, though, Jesus has repeatedly surprised his audiences by his list of guests. Who will sit down at the table of the kingdom banquet? Not those who assumed that the end-time banquet was included among their just deserts—not the "first," but the "last." Who should one invite to one's luncheons? Not those whose very presence at the table might bolster one's status in the community. Not those capable of recip-rocating with invitations of their own. But the marginal, the crippled, the blind, the lame, and others whose diseased state and low status had relegated them to life beyond the walls of the community. Use what you have to include peripheral folk among your closest friends, Jesus advises, so that you may be welcomed into eternal homes (16:1–9). Care for those like Lazarus—that beggar covered with sores whose hunger and sorry state place him at risk from the rogue dogs that patrol the village streets—and so hear and heed Moses and the prophets (16:19–31).

The father of Jesus's third parable models appropriate response. He looks upon the young man returning to his former household with compassion. His responses are all emblematic of the honorable restoration to the family of this one who had snubbed, abandoned, and cut himself off from them. Running through the middle of the village, kissing the boy again and again as a sign of reconcilia-tion and forgiveness, instructing the servants to dress his son in a manner befit-ting a king, and throwing a feast large enough for the whole village—these behaviors give expression to depth and breadth of heart that can only signal res-toration and reconciliation. Within the Third Gospel, this can only mean that this father has adopted a renewed set of commitments and attitudes grounded in God's own character. His practices of hospitality reflect the very image of God that Jesus has articulated in word and deed throughout the Gospel. Those who believe—those who *really* believe—that God is the gracious Father whose benef-icence is turned toward his people are liberated to give freely even to those who have no claim on our love or care (cf. 12:32–34).

In contrast, the elder son responds with anger and refuses to join the gala. Like the Pharisees and scribes who grumble about Jesus's table fellowship with tax

---

13. In each case, Luke uses the term *dei*, which typically refers to "divine necessity" within the narrative of Luke-Acts. See, already, Hans Conzelmann, *The Theology of St. Luke* (London: SCM, 1960), 151–54; Charles H. Cosgrove, "The Divine Δεῖ in Luke-Acts," *NovT* 26 (1984): 168–90.

collectors and sinners, he stands outside the house and complains. Though he has counted his father's estate as his place of dwelling, he has learned little about his father or from his father. In his behavior toward this fellow, his former brother who had cut himself off from his family so dramatically, he exhibits his own need for revitalization. His commitments have him predisposed in all the wrong ways. Although his behavior makes perfect sense in the world in which he lives, they are markedly out of step with the life-world Jesus's ministry parades.

Jesus, indicted for his receptivity to those who have come near to hear and heed his words, thus responds by asserting the divine necessity of joyous responses to the recovery of the lost. Just as God finds happiness in the discovery and return of what was lost, so do God's people. Like the father of this parable, Jesus recognizes the gravity of receiving as a table intimate the lost who are recovered—whether the lost come in the guise of a son whose behavior has divorced him from his family or of those identified by social and religious conventions as beyond the reach of divine grace. "But when you give a banquet, invite the poor, the crippled, the lame, and the blind. You will be happy! Because they cannot repay you, you will be repaid at the resurrection of the righteous" (14:13–14). "We had to celebrate and rejoice! Your brother was dead but has returned to life! He was lost and has been found" (15:32).

Jesus's parable is cast in the form of a defense, but it is also a challenge and invitation. Will these Pharisees and legal experts embrace this renewed image of God? Will they so identify with God's character and purpose that they are willing to join with sinners at the table? Will they accept as members of God's family those whom God accepts? Will they share God's happiness? Luke tells us neither how the elder son finally responded, nor how the legal experts and Pharisees responded. The parable is open-ended, and so is the invitation.

In Luke 15, then, we find in narrative form a presentation of an order of things that bears immediately on how a people might organize and interpret its experience. Jesus has pulled back the veil on God's character—and, then, for those with ears to hear and eyes to see, he has pulled back the veil on what really is. Happiness is grounded in growing conformity to the character of this God, so that one's inclinations and behaviors are reflections of his. Internalization and assimilation of these dispositions is elemental to the flourishing and contentment associated with kingdom happiness.

Taking seriously the wider context within which Luke 15 appears, we can see how reality as Jesus interprets it is both a sign and foretaste of the eschatological reality, just as table fellowship in the present was for him a sign and foretaste of the kingdom banquet. Literarily and theologically, this is known as "backshadowing." In backshadowing, we have glimpses of a future—in this case, God's future—which casts its shadow back on the present. These give us a sense of God's aims for the future and, in this way, show us what is of real consequence in the present. These visions of the future not only lay a claim on our lives but also materialize around us as we order our lives in accordance with them. The end points the way forward but also draws us forward into it, and in this way the end determines the character of well-being in the present.

This is true in the Third Gospel, as we have seen, but it also extends into the second part of Luke's narrative, the Acts of the Apostles. There we find joy in restoration and health, celebration at a shared table and related expressions of hospitality, and rejoicing at the inclusion of Gentiles among God's people (e.g., Acts 2:46; 3:8–9; 8:8; 13:52; 15:3; 16:34)—all of which are responses congruent with God's own initiative and joy.

4. Happy Dispositions (Luke 6)

Contemporary readers of Luke's series of blessings in 6:20–22 are likely to be reminded of its perhaps more famous cousin, the beatitudes in Jesus's Sermon on the Mount, in Matt 5:3–12.[14] The more immediate framework for grappling with Luke's list is the Lukan narrative itself, which presents two features that distinguish Luke's version from Matthew's. The first is that Luke's version sets out a series of blessings and corresponding woes:

> Jesus raised his eyes to his disciples and said,
> "Happy are you who are poor,
>   because God's kingdom is yours.
> Happy are you who hunger now,
>   because you will be satisfied.
> Happy are you who weep now,
>   because you will laugh.
> Happy are you when people hate you, reject you, insult you, and slander you
>   on account of the Son of Man. Rejoice when that happens! Leap
>   for joy because you have a great reward in heaven. Their ancestors
>   did the same things to the prophets.
> But how terrible for you who are rich,
>   because you have already received your comfort.
> How terrible for you who have plenty now,
>   because you will be hungry.
> How terrible for you who laugh now,
>   because you will weep and cry.

---

14. Again, see the essay by Holladay in the present volume for more on the beatitudes.

How terrible for you when everyone speaks well of you.
Their ancestors did the same things to the false prophets." (Luke 6:20–26)

Reading these blessings ("Happy are you!") alongside their counterparts, the woes ("How terrible for you!") reminds Luke's readers of a relatively stable set of elements that appear throughout the Lukan narrative, by which Luke portrays a topos of reversal. This is the second of the two features that distinguish Luke's version from Matthew's.

Topos refers to a relatively consistent set of motifs that recur in a narrative. In this case, a topos of reversal refers to the transposition of peoples' fortunes as a consequence of the unveiling of God's kingdom in Jesus's mission and message. A list of reversal texts would include, for example, Jesus's instructions regarding table fellowship (14:7–24), the story of the rich man and Lazarus (16:19–31), and the story of the Pharisee and the tax collector (18:9–14). Programmatic in this regard is the reversal proclaimed in Mary's Song (1:46–55):

> He has pulled the powerful down from their thrones
> and lifted up the lowly.
> He has filled the hungry with good things
> and sent the rich away empty-handed. (1:52–53)

Most significant of all, though, would be the reversal sounded in Luke's account of the exaltation of the crucified Jesus (Luke 22–24), summarized in Peter's address in Jerusalem early in Acts: "You rejected the Holy and Righteous One and asked to have a murderer given to you. You put to death the author of life, whom God raised from the dead . . ." (Acts 3:14–15).

For interpretive help, we should also notice how well integrated the language of Luke 6:20–26 is with earlier material in the Third Gospel. Jesus's blessings and woes echo Mary's Song, for example: "happy" (see Luke 1:45, 48; 6:20–22), "hungry" versus "filled" (1:53; 6:21, 25), and "rich" (1:53; 6:24). Likewise, in Jesus's inaugural address (4:18–19), he promised "good news to the poor" while using language similar to his words here at the outset of the Sermon on the Plain. That is, images of salvation declared in Mary's Song to have accompanied Jesus's birth are now repeated and embraced by Jesus as he sets out his understanding of the eschatological reality present in his mission.

Luke's series of blessings is distinguished from its cousin in Matthew 5 in yet one more way. In Matthew, pronouncements are made in the third person: "Happy are those who. . . ." For Luke, however, pronouncements of both happiness and judgment are in the second person: "Happy are you who. . . ." This immediately raises the question, who is the "you" to whom Jesus has addressed these declarations? We might be tempted to say that Jesus's pronouncements of happiness are aimed at his disciples. This is a happy thought (!), of course, but it does not make sense of the fact that Luke gives us no indication at all that one set of pronouncements is aimed at one group, with the other aimed at another. Instead, both blessings and woes seem to be pronounced over *the same people.* How can we make sense of this? Clearly, in this opening to the Sermon on the Plain, Jesus is asking his audience to make a decision. That is, he is calling on his listeners to identify themselves *either* as the poor (the marginal, those who have not and do without, those lacking a good name and the power that comes with it) *or* as the rich (the inner circle, those with power and prestige, the well fed, the secure). He is not asking whether some in his audience *feel* happiness. Happiness is not a fleeting condition based on one's good fortune. Rather, as Jesus defines life's working assumptions and the values that shape day-to-day life before God, he speaks to the dispositions out of which people live their lives. He addresses the patterns of thinking, feeling, behaving, and believing that shape how people experience day-to-day life. Under the category of "happy" he locates the dispositions of those who have embraced life away from the corridors of power and privilege, a life of dependence, a life whose service in God's kingdom has as its corollary misunderstanding, disappointment, and even harassment from those who have not embraced God's kingdom.

In this sense, the blessings and woes in Luke 6 are not so much prescriptive as they are ascriptive. That is, they relate not so much how things ought to be as how things in fact are. They define the life-world disclosed in the coming of Jesus. To be sure, it is a topsy-turvy world when, for example, the poor can be declared "happy" rather than "down on their luck" or even "cursed." But this only underscores the degree to which Jesus's vision of the world is eschatological—not a vision of life relegated to a future bliss, but to the present disclosure of God's kingdom. Jesus's message is thus an invitation to align oneself with the valuation of things characteristic of God's kingdom, and so to embrace ways of being in the world congruent with the end. Accordingly, Jesus's blessings and woes signal a vocation to embody God's salvation, at the same time that they communicate hope to people whose lives are eked out on the frontiers of socioreligious acceptance: the demonized, tax collectors, women, lepers, sinners, and so on. These types are held at arm's length in the status-minded world of everyday life determined by generally recognized social conventions, but in the world disclosed in Jesus's ministry and message, they are not only tolerated but celebrated. What is more, those who appear to live "the happy life" in the present—they are rich, they have plenty, they laugh, they have good reputations—that is, those who measure the goodness of their lives according to the now-outdated order of things—will be caught unawares. As Father Abraham explained to the rich man in Jesus's story, "Child, remember: you received good things during your lifetime, but Lazarus received dreadful things. But now Lazarus is comforted and you are in agony" (16:25).

If we were to expand our search for blessings and woes in the Lukan narrative, what we have begun to see would be highlighted all the more, and our understanding of the nature of the happy life—and its opposite, the life on which judgment is pronounced—would be thickened. Thus, for example, happiness is grounded not in one's rank or one's power, not even in one's power over demons, but in having a share in eternal life (10:17). Happiness is the experience of those whose eyes have been opened to see the significance of Jesus's mission as the disclosure of God's royal rule (10:23–24). Happy are those engaged in the seemingly pedestrian activity of fulfilling their responsibilities in this life, rather than taking advantage of the apparent absence of divine judgment by oppressing or mistreating those under their care (12:37, 38, 43).

Those who practice self-indulgence and give themselves to amassing more for themselves may think they are happy, but in fact they stand under divine judgment (12:15–21; cf. 16:19–31). And those who live their lives to gain recognition from others and so fail to practice God's justice and love—they are the antithesis of happy people (11:42–52). Again, everything depends on how one measures happiness. Good food and plenty of it, fine clothes, a good name in the community, and a secure financial future—who could be happier? In fact, according to conventional standards at work in Luke's world, these were elements of the happy life. That Jesus says the opposite is not an indicator of how out of touch with reality Luke's account might be. It is, rather, an indicator of the degree to which Luke's Gospel draws on and calls for an alternative construal of reality. Salvation has come. Here comes God's kingdom! And nothing can be the same.

5. Conclusion

In this essay I have been concerned especially with the Gospel of Luke, the first half of Luke's two-part narrative. It is here that we find the conditions for happiness most on display. Luke's vocabulary of happiness is diverse, including especially the language of joy, celebration, and blessing. Although this language is scattered through the narrative, happiness comes into particular focus in three sections of the Gospel. In Luke 1–2, the births of John and Jesus are happy occasions that warrant celebration not only for their parents and immediate circle of family and friends, as would be expected, but for all people. As the angel announces to the shepherds after Jesus is born: "I am bringing good news to you—wonderful, happy news for everyone: Your savior is born today in the city of David; he is Christ the Lord" (2:10–11). The times have changed and, with them, what constitutes and cultivates happiness.

The contest over what constitutes and cultivates happiness breaks out into the open most vividly in Luke 15. Here Jesus's pattern of behavior is criticized by Pharisees and legal experts. They are unhappy with Jesus for his table fellowship with such outcasts as tax collectors and sinners. Jesus responds with three parables describing the finding of something lost—a lost sheep, a lost coin, and a lost son. The punch line comes at the end of each of these parables, where Jesus observes that celebration at the table is the appropriate response because it mirrors heavenly celebration. Ought not human happiness to be grounded in and to reflect God's own happiness? Finally, Luke 6:20–26 is the focus point for what I have called "happy dispositions"—that is, the dispositions of those over whom happiness thus defined is pronounced. The particular way that Jesus's message is framed in Luke 6 clarifies the degree to which happiness is a choice. This is not because people go in search of happiness, but rather because God describes as happy those who fully align themselves with God's royal rule revealed in the mission and message of Jesus.

The perspective we have developed underscores the degree to which Luke sees happiness not as the goal of living but as the outcome or byproduct of living in harmony with the way things are. Of course, "the way things are" is itself perspectival and it is clear that not everyone will see it the way Luke does. This is true already within the narrative itself, as Jesus engages his adversaries on questions related to what it might mean genuinely to serve God's kingdom. Luke's contribution, then, lies especially in his narrative articulation of the context within which the happy life might be understood. This context is defined by God's eschatological intervention to bring salvation in all its fullness to all and, then, by the invitation to persons to order their lives accordingly. With Jesus's advent, death, and exaltation the times have changed; those who orient their lives to the divine purpose disclosed in Jesus will experience the pleasure and meaningfulness associated with human flourishing within this eschatologically determined world.

8

"I Have Learned to Be Content"

HAPPINESS ACCORDING TO ST. PAUL

Colleen Shantz

1. Paul's Life: Happiness amidst Suffering

The seven letters written by the Apostle Paul contribute a distinctive perspective to this volume because Paul's is the only straightforwardly personal voice in the canon.[1] The Bible includes first-person forms like the prophetic discourses and many psalms as well as some books written in character (Qoheleth, Song of Songs), but Paul's letters to the various early Christian communities speak more straightforwardly out of a real, particular life than any other book of the Bible. Thus, beyond a simple consideration of what Paul might explicitly teach about happiness, these letters allow a biographical examination of how happiness is shaped and expressed in his life—which in Paul's case was a life that included a good bit of turmoil and hardship. So, when we consider the life of Paul and the "pursuit of happiness," we might well ask: How does one restore happiness when the conditions that foster it are interrupted? In what way can we speak of happiness in the midst of obvious suffering?

In order to benefit as much as possible from the unique perspective afforded by the letters themselves, I will not refer to the book of Acts to (re)construct Paul's circumstances. The value of Acts for the construction of Paul's biography is regularly debated and difficult to settle definitively. One thing, however, is clear:

---

1. More than seven letters in the New Testament bear Paul's name; however, only seven of them are undisputedly accepted as written by Paul: Romans, 1 and 2 Corinthians, Galatians, Philippians, 1 Thessalonians, and Philemon. Colossians, Ephesians, and 2 Thessalonians are held as authentic by some scholars. Others suggest that they were outlined by Paul or written with some degree of input from him. The remaining letters (1 and 2 Timothy and Titus) were likely written in tribute to Paul, but not with his participation.

In Acts, we read the story of Paul as told with the advantage of hindsight. In hindsight many events seem clearer and the course of action that was chosen can appear nearly inevitable after the fact. In real time, the choices are typically much more ambiguous and tentative. Acts provides a theological account that is illustrated by events. By contrast, Paul's letters illustrate the process of trying to find the meaning in events while one is in the midst of them and cannot yet see their outcome. Paul's experience of change (his "call" or "conversion") is an apt example of the contrast between the two sets of writings. The book of Acts describes it three times (Acts 9:3–9; 22:6–11; 26:13–18) with varying details. The details include an extraordinarily bright light and a conversation with the risen Jesus. In contrast to such vivid details, Paul's own description of the revelation of Jesus in the letters is limited to a single sentence:

> But when he who had set me apart before I was born, and had called me through his grace was pleased to reveal his Son in me, that I might preach him among the Gentiles, I did not confer with flesh and blood, nor did I go up to Jerusalem to those who were apostles before me, but I went away into Arabia; and again I returned to Damascus. (Gal 1:15–17)[2]

In fact, it is really just a single phrase within this single clause: "was pleased to reveal his Son in me."

In short, Acts presents a narrative of God's miraculous intervention to change the order of events, while through Paul's letters we can discern the story of a man who, in the midst of difficult, costly, and unexpected events, kept striving to orient himself to God. The two versions are not incompatible; however, the second one has more to teach us about happiness. This latter version of events is especially useful as a window onto happiness for all of us who, like Paul, do not yet know exactly how our own stories will play out.

The present essay makes the case that, despite initial appearances, happiness is very much to the point of Paul's communication with the small groups of Christ-followers. I first outline some of the theorizing about happiness from the fields of cognitive and evolutionary psychology. Evolutionary psychologists argue that a fundamental feature of emotion is its social character. Emotions are socially conditioned and help to maintain the adaptive functioning of social groups. Thus, happiness appears most naturally when shared values and identity are strong and easily accommodated by individuals. Such an understanding suggests that happiness might be in short supply in Paul's life, because in Paul's letters we find evidence of

---

2. Translations are from the RSV, which I have occasionally modified toward the more literal.

profound personal difficulties and loss of social structures. Following on this observation, I explore some of the most relevant barriers to happiness in Paul's life. Finally, I show how Paul's passionate promotion of a new, shared identity and his reinterpretation of the significance of physical suffering effectively prepare the ground for the growth of happiness. Given the extraordinary events of his life, Paul's efforts to restore the conditions for emotional health are a remarkable feature of his correspondence and a signal contribution to the study of the Bible and happiness.

2. Theories of Happiness

Martin E. P. Seligman, a widely respected voice in the field of positive psychology, talks about three kinds of lives that bring people happiness: the pleasurable life, the good life, and the meaningful life.[3] The first of these, the pleasurable life, privileges pleasing experiences and sensations as a source of well-being. In the pleasurable life we focus on being present in the moment and mindful of the gifts that it offers. The second form, the good life, highlights engagement with and pursuit of personal virtues—what Aristotle meant by *eudaimonia*.[4] In this mode, we identify our greatest gifts and structure our lives to pursue and enhance them. The third kind of happy life looks beyond oneself to a cause or purpose that transcends us. The meaningful life is devoted to something that is greater than one's own life.

In an essay titled "Can Happiness Be Taught?" Seligman describes his experience of teaching an annual seminar on happiness to undergraduate students. In the class he not only assigns relevant reading from scientific journals and lectures about the three forms of happy lives and their characteristics, but also requires students to participate in a weekly "real-world homework exercise."[5] So, for example, they practice acts of gratitude, they identify their greatest strengths and intentionally deploy them in difficult or boring situations, and in a single week they do something nice for themselves and something nice for someone else and then compare the respective effects. At the end of the semester students know a lot more about positive psychology. Even more importantly, however, their lives are changed. They regularly reflect on how the course content has contributed to

---

3. See Martin E. P. Seligman, "Can Happiness Be Taught?" *Daedalus* 133 (2004): 80–87; and the fuller examination in his book *Authentic Happiness: Using the New Positive Psychology to Realize Your Potential for Lasting Fulfillment* (New York: Free Press, 2002). Video of Seligman discussing positive psychology can be found online at: www.ted.com/talks/martin_seligman_ on_the_state_of_psychology.html (accessed August 11, 2011).

4. For more on Aristotle and *eudaimonia*, see the essays by Nathan MacDonald and Carol A. Newsom in the present volume.

5. Seligman, "Can Happiness Be Taught?" 81.

the richness of their lives. And they leave the class with new attitudes and practices already incorporated into their lives. So, the obvious answer to Seligman's titular question is yes, happiness can indeed be taught.

While the good or meaningful life is not reducible to emotion—the *feeling* of happiness—the two are related in ways that deserve some consideration. Over the past two decades a number of neuroscientists have probed the relationship between cognition and emotion. Foremost among them, Antonio R. Damasio has studied patients with physical injuries to the regions of their brains that are vital to the processing of emotional inputs (prefrontal and right parietal regions). Quite surprisingly, he found that patients with these sorts of "emotional injuries" could no longer make rationally coherent choices. Although they could perform all the necessary intellectual procedures to understand their options, they consistently chose alternatives that put them at a disadvantage. In Damasio's words, "their ability to tackle the logic of a problem remains intact. Nonetheless, many of their personal and social decisions are irrational, more often disadvantageous . . . than not."[6] Damasio's studies and others like them evidence intriguing interrelationships between reason and emotion.[7] Most significantly, they call into question the old dichotomy that pits affect against cognition; to the contrary, these studies suggest an integrated relationship between the two capacities. As a result, one stream of research conceives of emotions as "appraisal systems" that draw on a variety of human capacities in order to orient attention.[8] Emotions effectively regulate behavior relative to environmental cues and marshal the individual's resources to address the given situation.[9] Emotions are also deeply implicated in the acquisition of new memories. Thus, evolutionary biologists have argued quite convincingly for the survival benefits of emotions as an efficient means to effectively orient individuals in the midst of complex circumstances. In all these ways, emotions are intimately tied to cognition.

---

6. Antonio R. Damasio, *Descartes' Error: Emotion, Reason, and the Human Brain* (New York: Putnam, 1994), 41.

7. See, e.g., Paul Thagard, "The Passionate Scientist: Emotion in Scientific Cognition," in *The Cognitive Basis of Science* (eds. P. Carruthers, S. Stich, and M. Siegal; Cambridge: Cambridge University Press, 2002), 235–50; Joseph P. Forgas, ed., *Handbook of Affect and Social Cognition* (Mahwah, NJ: Lawrence Erlbaum, 2001); and J. LeDoux, *The Emotional Brain* (New York: Simon and Schuster, 1996).

8. Jay Schulkin, *Bodily Sensibility: Intelligent Action* (Series in Affective Science; Oxford: Oxford University Press, 2004), 35–36.

9. Leda Cosmides and John Tooby, "Evolutionary Psychology and the Emotions," in *Handbook of Emotions* (2nd ed.; eds. Michael Lewis and Jeannette M. Haviland-Jones; New York: Guilford, 2000), 91–115, esp. 92. The authors identify capacities spanning anything from intensified perception, to adjustments of "motivational weightings," to retrieval of relevant memories, to alterations in oxygen supply.

A second key feature of emotions is their *social character*. While emotions are universal and even universally recognizable,[10] they are also culturally conditioned.[11] Consider, for example, the feeling of disgust. If you were invited to eat a viscous and slightly gelatinous piece of uncooked flesh, disgust might feel like a wholly natural reflex, free of any conditioning. Yet even such powerful food aversions are inculcated by one's social group. Likewise, anyone who has toilet-trained a toddler will recognize that young children are not naturally put off by the stuff in their diapers. In fact, in their early years children show disgust "solely for bitter tastes, yet by eight to twelve years of age they have adopted the full array of adult disgust triggers in their particular culture."[12] While food and sex are nearly universal stimuli for disgust, revolting comestibles and configurations vary from one culture to another.[13]

This small sampling of information about disgust is the tip of one emotional iceberg. It offers the merest taste of the ways that emotions are universally available, but also socially malleable. Through the profound interconnections of individual neurology and social receptivity, emotions become reflexively connected to the values of the group in ways that make them seem completely inevitable, but of course they are not.

Other studies have demonstrated additional social aspects of affect. For example, the presence of supportive social networks has a significant impact on happiness.[14] Another series of experiments established the socially contagious

10. A great many studies have highlighted the panhuman character of emotion, for instance, through analysis of neonatal facial patterning and cross-cultural studies of recognition of emotion based on facial expression. On the former, see H. Oster, and P. Ekman, "Facial Behavior in Child Development," *Minnesota Symposium on Child Psychology* 11 (1978): 231–76. On the latter, see Nathan Yrizarry, David Matsumoto, Chikako Imai, Kristie Kooken, and Sachiko Takeuchi, "Culture and Emotion," in *Cross-Cultural Topics in Psychology* (2nd ed.; eds. Leonore Loeb Adler and Uwe P. Gielen; Westport, CT: Praeger, 2001), 131–48; and P. Rozin, C. Taylor, L. Ross, G. Bennett, and A. Hejmadi, "General and Specific Emotion Recognition Abilities: Relations among Individual Differences in Recognition of Disgust and Other Emotional Expressions in Facial and Bodily Representations, Obsessive-Compulsive Tendencies, and Disgust Sensitivity," *Cognition and Emotion* 19 (2005): 397–412. While questions continue to be raised about specific points in these studies, the basic claim that some aspects of emotion are panhuman continues to hold.

11. Batja Mesquita discusses the large body of literature that is devoted to documenting cultural differences in the expression of emotion. See Mesquita, "Culture and Emotion: Different Approaches to the Question," in Mayne and Bonanno, eds., *Emotions*, 214–50. She concludes that "emotion potential" (that is, the biological mechanisms of emotion) remains quite consistent across cultures even while "emotional practice" varies (243).

12. Heather Looy, "Embodied and Embedded Morality: Divinity, Identity, and Disgust," *Zygon* 39 (2004): 223.

13. Paul Rozin and April Fallon, "A Perspective on Disgust," *Psychol Rev* 94 (1987): 23–41.

14. Elaine Fox, *Emotion Science: Cognitive and Neuroscientific Approaches to Understanding Human Emotions* (New York: Palgrave Macmillan, 2003), 327.

nature of emotions by demonstrating that merely "listening to another person's emotional expression is sufficient to automatically evoke a congruent mood state in the listener."[15] These and other findings led Dacher Keltner and Jonathan Haidt to suggest that "culture loosens the linkages between emotions and [survival] problems so that cultures find new ways to solve the problems for which emotions evolved, and cultures find new ways of using emotions."[16] Thus, theorists from many subdisciplines agree that emotions are deeply implicated in group identity and the maintenance of social boundaries. Emotional responses are conditioned by our social group and, in turn, help to guard the group's parameters.

So, what social function does happiness, specifically, have? While emotions like disgust are effective in distinguishing outsiders from insiders, happiness seems calibrated for the maintenance of *internal* relations. Keltner and Haidt suggest that "happiness or contentment may signal to the individual her or his general level of social functioning."[17] That is to say that we are most effortlessly happy when we see ourselves mirrored in our friends and most psychologically resilient when we are able to create a coherent worldview that coincides comfortably with that of our social group. In other words, we are happy when we "fit," we are happy when our expectations come to pass, and we are happy when what we have been taught about the way the world should work is reflected in our observations of the way the world really does work. Thus, as a social appraisal system, happiness signals the fit between one's life situation and one's worldview.

Several experiments have probed the ways that emotion, cognition, and social settings work together in the case of happiness. One set of experiments, in particular, considered the role of beliefs in a just world as a factor in positive affect. After assessing the participants' relative degrees of belief in such justice, experimenters introduced subjects to anger-inducing conditions and measured the resulting effects. They found that "the more the subjects believed that the world is just, the less their self-esteem decreased under the threat of anger," and the

---

15. Roland Neumann and Fritz Strack, "'Mood Contagion': The Automatic Transfer of Mood Between Persons," *J Pers Soc Psychol* 79 (2000): 211–23. The authors further specify that "[t]his effect was obtained even though participants were not provided with any verbal or semantic information about the emotion of the target person or an emotion-eliciting situation" (221).

16. Dacher Keltner and Jonathan Haidt, "Social Functions of Emotions," in *Emotions: Current Issues and Future Directions* (eds. Tracy Mayne and George A. Bonanno; New York: Guilford Press, 2001), 193. As Steven Pinker puts it, the whole system is "an assembly of neural circuits cobbled together from older parts of the primate brain and shaped by natural selection to do a job" (*The Blank Slate: The Modern Denial of Human Nature* [London: Penguin, 2002], 270).

17. Keltner and Haidt, "Social Functions of Emotions," 203.

greater effort they exerted to "curb and control angry feelings."[18] The experimenters hypothesize that belief in a just world "endows individuals with the confidence that they will be treated fairly by others and will not fall victim to an unforeseeable disaster."[19] For these reasons, some people find it easier to establish relationships of trust, to invest in the future, to feel less threatened by the actions of others, and to be able to interpret life events coherently and without anxiety. Accompanying these social and psychological advantages, a number of health benefits are correlated with beliefs in a just world. In contrast, participants who lacked such beliefs left the experiments with increased feelings of anger.[20]

Yet these important, internally supportive aspects of happiness can sometimes have a downside. For example, in a series of studies that probed the less functional effects of happiness, the social psychologist Joseph P. Forgas observed that when people feel happy they tend to rely on preexisting ideas and stereotypes rather than judging new situations on the basis of distinctive characteristics. They also tend to be less attentive to the external environment than are people who are experiencing negative moods. In short, many basically happy people tend to see the world in a way that "pre-fits" their worldview, regardless of evidence to the contrary. In another experiment, people who felt happy were found to act with greater self-interest and less focus on fairness than their sadder counterparts.[21] While one must be careful about extrapolating from the experimental conditions to real, lived experience, the work of Forgas and others nevertheless suggests that happiness (and indeed all emotions) needs to be *educated*. Now and then it is actually appropriate to be *unhappy* about the state of affairs.[22] Here, obviously,

---

18. Claudia Dalbert, "Beliefs in a Just World as a Buffer Against Anger," *Social Justice Research* 15 (2002): 123–45 (128), summarizing the results of several different experiments.

19. Ibid., 124.

20. Ibid., 136. The experimental effects were strongest in those persons who sense that the world's justice is meaningfully realized in their own lives rather than merely existing as a general condition. However, given the differences between collectivist and individualist societies, this finding may be culture specific.

21. The former findings (on mood and prejudice) are reported in several articles including Joseph P. Forgas, "Mood and the Perception of Unusual People: Affective Asymmetry in Memory and Social Judgments," *Europ J Soc Psychol* 22 (1992): 531–47; and idem, "On Bad Mood and Peculiar People: Affect and Person Typicality in Impression Formation," *J Pers Soc Psychol* 62 (1992): 863–75. The latter experiments are described in Hui Bing Tan and Joseph P. Forgas, "When Happiness Makes us Selfish, But Sadness Makes Us Fair: Affective Influences on Interpersonal Strategies in the Dictator Game," *J Exper Soc Psychol* 46 (2010): 571–76.

22. Eric G. Wilson makes this point in his book, *Against Happiness: In Praise of Melancholy* (New York: Farrar, Straus and Giroux, 2008). He argues that "negative emotions" frequently generate insight into what is authentically new and genuinely creative, and that they are essential to critique.

Seligman's *three* modes of the happy life are relevant as a corrective to a too facile or overly narrow definition of happiness. Pleasurable events and good feelings are not the only ways to well-being—and indeed not even the most effective, as we will see. So, while happiness plays a significant role in maintaining social values, sometimes those values require significant readjustment.

3. Impediments to Happiness

I now want to consider how this information maps onto Paul's experience. As the section heading suggests, there are plenty of details in Paul's biography that were unlikely to produce happiness, but two passages will suffice as illustrations of the point: Phil 3:4b-8a and 2 Cor 11:21b-29. The former recounts some of the social changes that accompanied Paul's shift into the Christ movement, and the latter describes some experiences of significant pain and austerity, both physical and emotional. Together they illustrate the loss of conditions for happiness even while they hint at the beginnings of its restoration.

Paul writes the letter to the Philippians while he is in prison,[23] apparently awaiting some form of corporal punishment, possibly a death penalty. That context seems to have inspired reflection on the meaning and significance of his life, for in Phil 1:19–26 he deliberates the value of continuing to live: "I am hard pressed between the two. My desire is to depart and be with Christ, for that is far better" (1:23). This is the first of two points in the letter at which Paul takes stock of his life. Later, in chapter three, he considers the profound changes of identity and status that he has endured. Every culture has its distinctive ways to measure the value of a life. In the ancient Mediterranean, human worth was largely coded in terms of honor: the reputation of your family and clan and, if you were a man, your ability to surpass or dominate others. In Phil 3:5–6, Paul lists all of the points on which he had excelled. Some of his honor was ascribed to him by conditions of his birth: his ethnicity (Israel), tribe (Benjamin), and the depth of his heritage to several generations (a Hebrew born of Hebrews).[24] Other details convey the

---

23. The original shape of the letter is disputed. It seems to be ending at 3:1 when in 3:2 Paul abruptly introduces a new topic. Therefore, some argue that two letters have been combined in the canonical form of Philippians. While the reading that I present here is more poignant if written in the context of imprisonment—a context that is explicit only in the first half of the canonical form—the basic information is not altered by the various theories about partitioning. For a study of the question, see Paul A. Holloway, "The Integrity of Philippians," in idem, *Consolation in Philippians: Philosophical Sources and Rhetorical Strategy* (Cambridge: Cambridge University Press, 2001), 7–33. In his thorough review both for and against partitioning, Holloway favors the integrity of the letter in its canonical form.

24. Paul recounts a similar list in 2 Cor 11:22.

honor that Paul acquired by excelling according to cultural norms: practicing the most rigorous form of cultural adherence ("as to the law, a Pharisee"), defending collective honor against the claims made by other groups ("as to zeal, a persecutor of the church"), and applying himself to communal values ("as to righteousness under the law, blameless"). These two verses list all the ingredients for a life of virtue, which counts as a good and happy life in Seligman's terms. Paul's identity was closely matched to that of his social group and his own investment in the group's values was high and successful. Paul had oriented his life around what he perceived to be the highest values available to him. But he recounts these details only in order to reject them: "Whatever gains I had," he writes, "I counted as loss" (3:7). As he repeats that claim, Paul intensifies it with a term of disgust: "I count them as *skubala*," literally: "as crap" (3:8).[25]

Paul's repeated reference to gain and loss in verses 7–8 should not be taken as mere rhetorical flourish. Rather, he is describing a twofold loss: his personal honor and his place within a community that structured his identity. In this passage Paul is not rejecting Judaism, he is rejecting the honor script. He chose a path that would not pay back in public recognition of his accomplishments but, to the contrary, would likely bring dishonor to those who were associated with him. Such a break from cultural norms entails a real cost and hence poses a challenge to happiness. Furthermore, because Paul no longer shared meaningful identity with his group of origin, another of the primary components of happiness was removed from his life. Given such social and cultural isolation, happiness was likely to be elusive.

If Philippians speaks to the loss of social group, the second passage, 2 Corinthians 11, offers a different set of unhappy details. A little background information helps to put this remarkable passage in context. Most students of Paul's epistles agree that 2 Corinthians 10–13 was once an independent letter, and further that it comprises the bulk of a letter that Paul claims to have written in anguish, "with many tears."[26] After Paul first left Corinth he received communication from the house churches there asking for his advice on several matters and

---

25. As is well known, *skubalon* sometimes referred specifically to human excrement. For example, Josephus, Epictetus, and Artemidorus all used it that way. On other occasions, it referred to a more general amalgam of garbage. In the ancient world, all manner of household waste (kitchen scraps, bed pans, dirty water) was thrown from the windows of tenements into the streets below where it mixed with the excrement from pack animals. The resulting potpourri was also called *skubalon* and wise pedestrians kept close to the walls to avoid it.

26. This phrase is used in 2 Cor 2:3–4 to describe a very difficult letter written sometime after 1 Corinthians. Thus, the broad academic consensus holds that 2 Corinthians was originally (at least) two letters: chapters 10–13 represent the earlier letter and chapters 1–7 (with or without chapters 8 and 9) were written later (but prefixed in the final canonical form).

informing him of circumstances in the community. He wrote 1 Corinthians in response to the news and questions. Some time later he paid a second visit to Corinth, which he describes as a "painful visit" (2 Cor 2:1). It appears that Paul was insulted and treated quite badly on that occasion. In response to those troubles Paul wrote 2 Corinthians 10–13 hoping to resolve the difficulties and restore a functioning relationship with the Corinthians. The letter does not mince words. In fact, it represents the very lowest point in his surviving communication with the house churches in Corinth.

Part of the trouble in Corinth was apparently Paul himself. The apostle seems to address the Corinthians' criticisms about his style when he writes that, although his letters might seem "weighty and strong" (2 Cor 10:10a), his presence does not measure up to the same standard (10:1, 10b). Exacerbating the problem, some other apostles who have recently visited Corinth seem to display many of the characteristics that Paul lacked. Paul and his message are being supplanted by these super-apostles (11:5; 12:11). These are among the issues that Paul had to address in the letter if he hoped to redeem his relationship with the church at Corinth.

Thus, in chapter 11 Paul begins an extended contrast between his qualifications and those of the new apostles. If they will boast, so will he (11:16–18). But rather than vying to match virtues on their terms, Paul reverses expectations and begins to report a rather humiliating history. The executive summary includes labors, imprisonments, beatings, and other events that brought him close to death (11:23). Paul then follows with the details of numerous occasions of pain, humiliation, and trauma. He recounts nine occasions of corporal punishment (11:24–25a), some of which would have broken bones and all of which would have left scars and tissue damage. Five separate times Paul's back was scored with the maximum number of lashes allowable in Jewish law. Three times he suffered one of the most severe of Roman punishments short of execution: beating by rod (11:25). Such beating inflicted not only physical injury, but also the deep social damage of humiliation;[27] yet Paul openly admits that he was the victim of this public degradation. In other words, in the course of his work for the "good news" Paul was on the wrong side of the law at least eight times. In addition, in order to support himself in his work as an apostle, he continued to maintain a "day job" working with his hands. Paul then reports the servile conditions related to his manual labor: unsafe travel, hunger, exposure to the elements, and sleep deprivation (11:26–27; see also 1 Cor 4:11–12; 2 Cor 6:5). Yet along with such descriptions, Paul also speaks about the importance of this manual labor (1 Thess 2:9; 1 Cor

---

27. See the detailed discussion of Paul's corporal punishment in Jennifer A. Glancy, "Boasting of Beatings," *JBL* 123 (2004): 99–135.

9:15–18; see also 1 Thess 4:11–12). But even if Paul held ambivalent attitudes about his work,[28] it seems clear that the Corinthians did not think highly of it. At any rate, the *conditions* of Paul's labor would not be honorable in anyone's opinion. Thus, the sum total of the list of his "accomplishments" describes deep humiliation, mistreatment, and loss of status. If Paul is trying to improve the Corinthian opinion of his worth, he has chosen a very unusual way to do it.

Even more to the point for the present study, however, is the question of how Paul coped with so much adversity. Obviously the circumstances of his life are hard to align with belief in a just world. By all evidence, Paul's commitment to the God of Israel remained unwavering throughout his life; however, what evidence could he offer of God's faithfulness in return? He considered himself "blameless" with regard to covenantal requirements so his suffering could hardly be a just punishment for his failings. The long list of Paul's hardships thus stands as a profound challenge to many of the conditions of happiness outlined above. Certainly there was little room to pursue pleasure, and even the virtues Paul tried to embody have not helped his circumstances. Thus, both the pleasurable life and the good life seem largely out of reach for Paul. What is it that kept him from bitterness?

4. Creating the Conditions for Happiness

Alongside these descriptions of social disruption and unjust events, Paul's letters recount their possible remedy. In fact, the letters contain remarkable efforts to shape a meaningful interpretation of the circumstances of his life. Two categories seem particularly important.

First, in a number of passages we find elements of a new social identity—one into which Paul hoped to shape the fledgling communities. Paul, the apostle to the Gentiles, was something of a genius in group formation. These small groups of Christ-followers could form a critical mass of shared values and understanding, which would in turn help to generate the happiness that comes from group cohesion. Second, some of Paul's most moving rhetoric describes a pattern of meaning that turns honor precisely on its head. I will treat each of these two categories in turn.

1. In recent studies of Romans and Galatians, Philip F. Esler employs ethnicity studies to highlight some of Paul's strategies for the construction of a new group identity that could incorporate both Greek and Jewish members.

---

28. Todd D. Still, "Did Paul Loathe Manual Labor? Revisiting the Work of Ronald F. Hock on the Apostle's Tentmaking and Social Class," *JBL* 125 (2006): 781–95.

Cohesive group identity requires more than goodwill to hold it together. Elements like a proper name identifying the group, a "myth of common ancestry," and a shared history and culture provide a structure on which group identity can be fleshed out.[29] Obviously Jews and Gentiles shared none of these details, so, in Rom 9:6–13 Paul sets about instinctively trying to create their equivalent. He begins with the claim that "not all who are descended from Israel belong to Israel" (Rom 9:6b). This is one of the few places that Paul employs the designation "Israel," and he uses it here as the name for the ethnically blended church at Rome. He then proceeds to claim Abraham as the common ancestor of all "the children of the promise" (9:7–8) and to reinterpret the stories of Sarah, Rebecca, and Isaac as stories about God's selection of the young church communities (9:7b-13; cf. Galatians 3).

What Paul is doing here is providing a shared name and shared stories for a new community. It is noteworthy that Romans 9–11 represents the highest density of scriptural references of any part of the Pauline corpus, which further generates a sense of shared heritage. Through these means Paul begins to construct the framework on which a new communal identity can be built. He builds a common story and values that will help to define and maintain in-group relations.

In many ways, Paul is better understood as a pastor than a theologian. This distinction is clear in his persistent and creative efforts to keep the small groups of Christ-followers functioning as communities of care and love. In some texts he offers the famous image of the body of Christ to inspire their sense of their life together (Rom 12:5; 1 Cor 12:12–27). He extols the virtue of love (*agapē*) more than any other virtue and gives extraordinarily varied advice on how to embody it, especially by putting others' good before your own in matters of ethics (Rom 14:15–16; 1 Cor 8:9–13; Gal 5:13–15; Phil 2:1–4). His letters are regularly punctuated with language of affection: he could not bear to be apart from the Thessalonians (1 Thess 2:17–3:1), he remembered how the Galatians would have "plucked out" their eyes for his sake (Gal 4:15), he took on the debt (whether financial or social) of the slave Onesimus as his own (Phlm 18), and so on. In all these ways Paul made the lives and well-being of others an aspect of his own life. Further, in all these ways he attempted to stir greater bonds of kinship and love among the members of the communities. These small groups could provide the social cohesion that was otherwise missing in the urban centers of the early Roman empire.

---

29. Philip F. Esler *Conflict and Identity in Romans: The Social Setting of Paul's Letter* (Minneapolis: Augsburg Fortress, 2003), 43–44. See also idem, "Paul's Contestation of Israel's (Ethnic) Memory of Abraham in Galatians 3," *BTB* 36 (2006): 23–35.

2. Perhaps even more remarkable, however, is the second important category: Paul's effort to articulate a worldview that could make sense of his suffering. A couple of characteristics of this view are especially important. First, Paul remains oriented to the future in a way that places his current difficulties in broader perspective. That orientation depends in part on his sense of the imminent end.[30] Because he believes that God will soon intervene, Paul can exhort those in slavery to live as if they were freed persons of the Lord (1 Cor 7:22) and exhort those who are married to live as if they had no spouse because "the appointed time has grown very short" (1 Cor 7:29).

But more significant still is Paul's sense of participation in the Christological pattern. For example, he describes baptism as the ritual pattern of dying and rising that is replicated in our lives (Rom 6:3–6). Repeatedly, Paul speaks of transformation into Christ's image (e.g., 2 Cor 3:18; Phil 1:20) and extends that pattern to include conforming to his death. In one of his shorter lists of hardships he puts it this way: "persecuted, but not forsaken; struck down, but not destroyed; always carrying in the body the death of Jesus, so that the life of Jesus may also be manifested in our bodies" (2 Cor 4:9–10). Paul's consistent efforts to turn people toward the good of others has already been mentioned, but it is crucial to note that this altruism is central to Paul's sense of dying to self. The Christological pattern of dying and rising convinced Paul that so much of what he feared, especially death itself, had no grip on him. In Philippians, Paul describes his own appropriation of this Christological norm to make sense of the loss of status discussed above. For Paul, the resurrection is immutably linked to death. Dying and rising are necessary and inseparable aspects of God's redemptive action. We attain the resurrection by sharing Christ's sufferings "and becoming like him in his death" (Phil 3:10–11). Paul is so convinced of this truth that dying and rising have become his hermeneutic for all of life, not only for the life to come.

Through this revision of standards Paul creates the conditions for a meaningful life. My description hardly does justice to the depth and insight of Paul's comments. Throughout the letters he demonstrates his commitment to live now for the sake of others and shows how his experiences of humiliation are redeemed by the pattern of Jesus's debasement through crucifixion. In fact, in Paul's new worldview suffering is not merely a means to an end, but an actual participation in the way of Christ that has defeated the powers of death and sin. The standards of triumph and honor have been set on their head by the one who emptied himself of all claim to honor—Jesus Christ.

---

30. For more on happiness and eschatology, see the essay by Greg Carey in the present volume.

If the letter to the Philippians is any indication of Paul's strategies for well-being, they seem to have been extraordinarily effective. As he considers the possibility of violent death, Paul seems able to face it not only resolutely, but, extraordinarily, with what might properly be called happiness.

5. Paul's "Wager"

In the seventeenth century, the French philosopher Blaise Pascal famously articulated the gamble he was willing to take on God. "Pascal's wager," as it came to be known, was his willingness to gamble on the existence of God in the face of insufficient evidence. For Pascal the difficulty of belief inhered in reason's inadequacy; reason alone could not determine God's existence:

> This is what I see and what troubles me. . . . If I saw nothing there which revealed a divinity, I would come to a negative conclusion; if I saw everywhere the signs of a Creator, I would remain peacefully in faith. But, seeing too much to deny and too little to be sure, I am in a state to be pitied; wherefore I have a hundred times wished that if God sustains nature it should testify to Him unequivocally.[31]

Given these circumstances, Pascal decided to risk belief in God. "Pascal's wager" suggests that we lose nothing by living as if there is a God, but could lose everything if we reject the possibility. For him the "everything" was mostly eternal life and on this point he has been criticized by both theologians and atheists alike.

My guess is that Paul might join in some of that critique of Pascal, because, in fact, Paul's sense of faith differs in many ways from that of Pascal. Like Pascal—indeed, like all of us—Paul lacked sufficient information to be absolutely certain of his choice. So perhaps this section would be better called "Paul's investment" rather than his "wager." Paul's "investment" evokes the comparison with Pascal but also distinguishes Paul's life choices from those of the philosopher. Again, like Pascal, Paul did not have enough "evidence" to be absolutely certain about his wager. Indeed, if Paul longed for the pleasurable life, or even the good life, he had much evidence to the contrary. But, unlike Pascal, the wager did cost Paul something, and it was a considerable price: he not only left behind a life of success, but he endured extraordinary hardships because of his choices. Yet Paul was wholehearted in trading in his honor for the uncharted territory of self-giving love. The end of his life demonstrates this point. During much of his ministry Paul was

---

31. Blaise Pascal, *Pascal's Pensées* (trans. Thomas Stearns; New York: E. P. Dutton, 1958), #229.

occupied with collecting funds from the largely Gentile communities to help care for the Jerusalem residents who had suffered famine in the late 40s CE, which only added to the existing difficulties of the Palestinian economy. It appears that while Paul was finally completing the delivery of this nearly decade-long project, he was arrested and eventually died in captivity.

Paul certainly anticipated being united with Christ "in a resurrection like his" (Rom 6:5), but it would not be accurate to describe his choices in terms of a gamble on life after death. Paul lived out of gratitude for the gift (*charis*, "grace") of God. His life was shaped by the discernment that God was active in the world and by his commitment to play his part in that divine work. Paul was investing in a life that was more meaningful because of his commitment to something so much bigger than his own well-being. Paul did not find God for the first time sometime after 30 CE on the "road to Damascus." Given the usual connotation of the word "conversion," we cannot use it as a description for Paul's life: he remained devoted to the same God both before and after Christ was revealed "in him" (Gal 1:16).[32] Perhaps the only change was that Paul somehow learned to live differently in response to his sense of God's benefaction. That sense of grace helped Paul to create communities of love and shared identity and it assisted him in seeing a pattern for living that surpassed and even reversed his prior understanding of success. In so doing, it created joy in the midst of otherwise unbearable hardships. Gratitude became the fuel for all of Paul's unconventional and difficult life—a life that can, despite its hardships, nevertheless be rightfully described as happy.

---

32. In fact, as has long been noted, Paul describes his experience as a *call* to a specific task, not a *conversion* to a new religion (see Krister Stendahl, *Paul Among Jews and Gentiles* [Philadelphia: Fortress, 1979], 7–22). A sympathetic reading of Paul's letters shows that he sees himself consistently oriented to the God of Israel throughout his life. Paul's purpose and his understanding of God's purposes changes, but to call this shift a "conversion" is to wrongly imply a change of religion when in fact there was as yet no other religion to change to. On these distinctions, see Zeba Crook, *Reconceptualising Conversion: Patronage, Loyalty, and Conversion in the Religions of the Ancient Mediterranean* (BZNW 130; Berlin: Walter de Gruyter, 2004).

9

Finding Happiness in Apocalyptic Literature

Greg Carey

1. Happy at the End

Few people associate apocalyptic literature with happiness. Moreover, many assume that apocalyptic happiness amounts to "pie-in-the-sky" escapism. It is true that, in the biblical traditions, it appears that apocalyptic discourse is home to escapist happiness—happiness, that is, in the form of hope for future blessedness. Afterlife hope began to crystallize in Judaism during the second (perhaps third) century BCE, a development Alan F. Segal ties to the emergence of apocalyptic literature.[1] The first clear articulations of concepts such as the resurrection of the dead, a final judgment, and the geography of heaven and hell all occur in apocalyptic discourse. Those otherworldly regions require inhabitants: angels, demons, and the mortals who anticipate an angelic future. All of these receive special attention in the apocalyptic tradition.

From another angle, Darrin M. McMahon has characterized Christianity's distinctive take on happiness as hope for future salvation not from, but through, suffering. Suffering itself, he argues, becomes the path to salvation. Like Segal, McMahon traces this innovation to the apocalyptic tradition. Christian happiness, according to McMahon, is distinguished by its otherworldly quality: "the hope of achieving an end to suffering through suffering itself," especially in the martyr traditions.[2] McMahon acknowledges that early Christianity offered other

---

1. Alan F. Segal, *Life after Death: A History of the Afterlife in Western Religion* (New York: Doubleday, 2004), esp. 282–308, 351–63.

2. Darrin M. McMahon, *Happiness: A History* (New York: Grove, 2006), 93.

goods as well, particularly a community marked by (relative) egalitarianism and mutual support.[3] But its distinguishing feature was an eschatological hope that grew out of the Jewish longing for liberation. Biblical scholars would identify this trajectory with the emergence of protoapocalyptic and apocalyptic literature.[4] McMahon himself places great emphasis on martyrdom's formative influence on Christian happiness, though he is unaware of the martyr consciousness present in Daniel, *1 Enoch*, and some of the Dead Sea Scrolls.

As time passed and apocalyptic expectation perhaps grew more remote, happiness moved closer to the here and now, but always with an eschatological reservation. According to McMahon, Augustine perceived incomplete progress toward happiness this side of heaven, while for medieval Christian mystics heaven broke through a miserable daily life to bring the glory of God into personal experience. Renaissance humanists and reformers articulated the potential for a measure of happiness in this life, reserving "true" happiness for the hereafter. In any case, perfect Christian happiness remained on the other side of death, a boundary that endured throughout the Middle Ages and the Reformation.[5] Apocalyptic literature set the tone, that is, for Western happiness, and its influence continues.

This paper confirms how important and influential apocalyptic texts foreground happiness as a present foretaste of a future blessing. It is well known that some apocalyptic texts regard the present age as thoroughly corrupt. Paul does not stand alone in lamenting "the present evil age" (Gal 1:4). But is that all that can be said? Remarkable diversity characterizes ancient Jewish and Christian apocalyptic discourse, justifying a longer look at the question of happiness in apocalyptic literature. Even futuristic, otherworldly hope takes various forms. Moreover, we might well ask whether and how various apocalyptic texts have contributed to or imagined happiness not only at "the End," but also now, in the present age. Finally, while apocalyptic discourse certainly deals with the problem of suffering, McMahon's claim that apocalyptic happiness places suffering as the *path* to happiness needs a critical assessment. Positive psychology indicates that a sense of identity and commitment are essential to human flourishing, and apocalyptic literature provides such. Apocalyptic literature purports to *reveal* the nature of this world as corrupt and chaotic. It invites believers to adopt a common identity and mission as a faithful minority in the midst of a hostile culture. The

---

3. Ibid., 90.

4. See the discussion in ibid., 80–82, which refers to Third Isaiah (Isaiah 56–66), Ezekiel, Zechariah, and 2 Baruch.

5. Ibid., 96–139.

question that remains, however, is how apocalyptic literature makes one happy (if it does). Put more precisely: How has ancient apocalyptic literature fostered, and how may it still contribute to, the sense of identity and commitment that promotes human flourishing during difficult times?

2. Matters of Definition

Investigating the ways apocalyptic literature portrays human flourishing or happiness is no easy task. It involves two highly contested questions: First, what do we mean by happiness, and, second, how do we define apocalyptic literature?

Defining Happiness

Philosophy has often focused on happiness, and most philosophers have insisted that happiness means more than a mere mood or gift of the affect. Happiness has rather to do with the larger notion of human flourishing. The positive psychology movement, whose influence animates the present volume, identifies an ongoing tension between the hedonic happiness associated with pleasure and the eudaimonic happiness that has more to do with virtue or the fulfillment of human potential.[6]

With Aristotle, the positive psychology movement has largely insisted that happiness requires both a measure of virtue and favorable circumstances that lead to pleasure.[7] Assessing the virtue (or lack of it) in the animated television character Homer Simpson, Raja Halwani remarks that

> enjoying life is not the same as living a flourishing one. A person could indeed enjoy life to the fullest yet not lead a flourishing life. Think of someone who is fully happy spending his life counting blades of grass or collecting bottle-caps, yet who is capable of pursuing worthier goals. No matter how happy that person is [in terms of his subjective mood], no matter how much *he* is enjoying his life, we surely do not want to say of his life that it is well-lived.[8]

---

6. See Carol A. Newsom's essay in this volume; see also Richard Kraut, "Two Conceptions of Happiness," *Philosophical Review* 88 (1979): 167–97.

7. Kraut, "Two Conceptions."

8. Raja Halwani, "Homer and Aristotle," in *The Simpsons and Philosophy: The D'oh! of Homer* (eds. W. Irwin, M. T. Conard, and A. J. Skoble; Chicago: Open Court, 2001), 22; see also Kraut, "Two Conceptions," 179.

As Jonathan Haidt puts it, "*Happiness comes from within, and happiness comes from without.*"[9] That is, happiness depends on one's disposition, but certain kinds of suffering or deprivation can limit one's capacity to live happily.[10]

Accepting wisdom from the broad sweep of human philosophy, along with insight from the positive psychology movement, I assume that happiness corresponds to a combination of virtue and pleasure that together make for human flourishing. While biblical traditions vary in emphasis, I believe this to be the case in biblical literature as well. That said, the task of this paper involves sorting through biblical apocalyptic literature to see exactly what *kinds* of virtues and what *kinds* of circumstances and pleasures are valued in the apocalyptic traditions. Put differently: What is the shape (or shapes) of apocalyptic happiness?

For a book entitled *The Bible and the Pursuit of Happiness*, we might restrict our attention to the classic examples of biblical apocalyptic literature, Daniel and Revelation. However, if our aim involves discerning whether there is anything distinctive to "apocalyptic" happiness, we should also consider apocalyptic discourse more broadly throughout the canon, particularly in the apocalyptic dimensions of the Synoptic Gospels and Paul. We should also look beyond the biblical canon to a few select and highly influential apocalyptic texts that are reflective of apocalyptic tradition writ large.[11]

Defining Apocalyptic Literature

Specialists know that "apocalyptic literature" is an extremely slippery notion. At the risk of oversimplification, apocalyptic literature takes its classic form in the great apocalypses of *1 Enoch* and Daniel. Later literary apocalypses such as *2 Baruch*, *4 Ezra*, Revelation, and the *Shepherd of Hermas* adopted similar literary conventions. From these classic literary works emerged what we might call *apocalyptic discourse*—a flexible set of ideas and literary tropes that spread beyond the apocalypses into popular discourse.[12] Several key ideas mark an apocalyptic outlook:[13]

---

9. Jonathan Haidt, *The Happiness Hypothesis: Finding Modern Truth in Ancient Wisdom* (New York: Basic Books, 2006), 105 (emphasis original).

10. But see Colleen Shantz's essay in the present volume.

11. Though not generically apocalypses, the pseudepigraphal book of *Jubilees* and the *Testaments of the Twelve Patriarchs* played an influential role in both Judaism and emergent apocalyptic literature.

12. I provide a more thorough discussion of apocalyptic discourse and related terms in Greg Carey, *Ultimate Things: An Introduction to Jewish and Christian Apocalyptic Literature* (St. Louis: Chalice Press, 2005), 3–10.

13. Ibid., 6–10. See also Christopher Rowland, "Apocalypticism," in *NIDB* 1:190.

- An apocalyptic outlook ultimately appeals to divinely revealed wisdom concerning an alternative reality. That alternative world may reside in heaven (or hell) or in God's dramatic future intervention to create a new and better world. The literary apocalypses narrate how one mortal has received this wisdom in the form of a vision.

- Apocalyptic discourse regards the present age as so evil and corrupt that the world must endure a period of great crisis (or tribulation) prior to its redemption. Things have gotten so bad that this crisis has already begun or is imminent.

- Apocalyptic discourse expresses a dualistic outlook. Supernatural powers are divided into good and evil, God and the angels versus Satan and the demons. Persons and institutions are either righteous or wicked. With its negative assessment of culture and history, apocalyptic discourse normally describes the righteous as a vulnerable minority.

- In the apocalyptic "story," judgment finally brings the righteous to eternal felicity, while the wicked face condemnation.

Apocalyptic discourse played a central role in the emergence of Christianity. Both Jesus and Paul were heavily motivated by apocalyptic belief, at least in the opinion of most scholars. Indeed, every major layer of the New Testament relies upon apocalyptic discourse—some more heavily than others. As Christopher Rowland puts it, "Apocalypticism was . . . the vehicle whereby the first Christians were able to articulate their deepest convictions about the ultimate significance of Jesus Christ in the divine purposes."[14]

Given this background, it seems that one category from the positive psychology movement holds particular promise for identifying apocalyptic happiness. Jonathan Haidt's discussion of "the uses of adversity" suggests that suffering can provoke reassessment of an individual's life. "Trauma often shatters belief systems and robs people of their sense of meaning."[15] As sages have long observed, such shattering opens the path for healthy adaptation. At the same time, individuals build grand narratives, or life stories, to provide meaning for their experiences and values. Their stories require turning points, often moments of adversity that open the space for growth and new meaning. The most successful stories, in terms of individual happiness, emphasize values such as relationships and intimacy, religion and spirituality, and generativity rather than wealth, status, and achievement.[16]

---

14. Rowland, "Apocalypticism," 1:192.

15. Haidt, *Happiness Hypothesis*, 145.

16. Ibid., esp. 142–45.

Apocalyptic narratives seem to present similar opportunities for the communities that used them. If Stephen D. O'Leary is correct, evil presents one of the basic building blocks of an apocalyptic narrative.[17] All of the grand apocalyptic narratives wrestle with radical evil and how evil challenges a God-oriented outlook. Some of these narratives include a call to turn from one set of values to another set having to do primarily with religion and generativity, and sometimes also with relationships; other apocalyptic narratives simply explain the presence of evil or forecast its eradication. If one objects that this psychological approach is inappropriate to the ancient material, because the apocalypses tend to emphasize collectives rather than individuals, it might be observed that Haidt's own work invokes two collective examples—namely, the two great fires that led to the transformation of both London and Chicago. We might also observe that not all apocalyptic reviews of history are identical: Some call their audiences to new values, whereas others are designed primarily to foster hope.

Moving forward, two framing questions seem appropriate. While they represent alternative approaches to the topic, I wish to hold them in fruitful tension with one another for the time being:

1. Does biblical apocalyptic discourse propose a distinctive outlook on happiness with respect to the virtues and circumstances that make for human well-being?
2. Do we find diverse approaches to happiness within the body of biblical apocalyptic discourse?

3. Framing Apocalyptic Happiness

Apocalyptic literature participates richly in the broad sweep of biblical traditions. Literary apocalypses build upon the reputations of figures such as Enoch, Ezra, Moses, and Baruch. Some apocalyptic texts begin with crucial moments from the larger sacred story. Others amount to retellings of sacred narratives. Still others frame themselves as insertions into biblical "moments." Both Daniel and Revelation profoundly engage with—and reinterpret—scriptural antecedents. While many people think of Revelation as "different" from the rest of the New Testament, sophisticated allusions to scripture occur more frequently in Revelation

---

17. Stephen D. O'Leary, *Arguing the Apocalypse: A Theory of Millennial Rhetoric* (New York: Oxford University Press, 1994), esp. 34–44.

than in any other New Testament book.[18] Indeed, strings of such allusions in Revelation follow scriptural books in sequence; one imagines the author pulling scrolls down from their niches and consulting them from beginning to end.

This "scholarly" (some would prefer "scribal") dimension of apocalyptic discourse implies that apocalyptic happiness would likely bear strong continuity with other Jewish and (where applicable) Christian discourses. As a case in point, we might reflect on a literary form more familiar to readers of biblical literature: the beatitude. A discussion of the larger form of blessing may provide an opening into the question of happiness in ancient Jewish and Christian apocalyptic literature.[19]

Beatitudes occur in a variety of literary contexts, and amidst diverse genres, but their home lies in wisdom discourse.[20] Standard translations sometimes mislead us, however. For example, the NRSV differentiates between the Hebrew word *bārûk* (from the root √*brk*), typically translated as "blessed," and the term *'ašrê*, translated "happy." However, the LXX translates *'ašrê* with *makarios*, a term that the NRSV renders as "blessed" in the New Testament. Whatever the case, the point is simply that Hebrew beatitudes may employ either *bārûk* or *'ašrê*.

Hebrew beatitudes tend to emphasize objective virtues rather than subjective bliss.[21] The first Psalm blesses the one who avoids the path of the ungodly yet rejoices in the law (Ps 1:1–2); the second Psalm blesses all who take refuge in God (Ps 2:12).[22] The book of Proverbs blesses those who attend to wisdom (Prov 3:13; 8:32, 34), along with their children (Prov 20:7). In the Song of Songs, maidens observe the beloved daughter and call her blessed, perhaps because of her beauty (Song 6:9–10). The

---

18. Among a very substantial body of literature, see Gregory K. Beale, *John's Use of the Old Testament in Revelation* (JSNTSup 166; Sheffield: Sheffield Academic Press, 1999); Jon Paulien, *Decoding Revelation's Trumpets: Literary Allusions and Interpretations of Revelation 8:7–12* (AUSSDDS 11; Berrien Springs, MI: Andrews University Press, 1988); idem, "Dreading the Whirlwind: Intertextuality and the Use of the Old Testament in Revelation," *AUSS* 39 (2001): 5–22; Steve Moyise, *The Old Testament in the Book of Revelation* (JSNTSup 115; Sheffield, Sheffield Academic Press, 1995); and the continuing debate between Beale and Moyise in a series of subsequent articles. For a brief introduction to the question, see Moyise, *The Old Testament in the New: An Introduction* (Continuum Biblical Studies Series; New York: Continuum, 2001), 117–27; and Beale, *The Book of Revelation* (NIGTC; Grand Rapids: Eerdmans, 1998), 76–99.

19. See also the essays by William P. Brown and Carl R. Holladay in the present volume.

20. See W. D. Davies and Dale C. Allison, Jr., *The Gospel According to Saint Matthew* (3 vols.; ICC; Edinburgh: T & T Clark, 1988–1997), 1:431–32. See also the essays by Holladay and Newsom in this volume.

21. See the essays by Brown and Newsom in this volume. Loren T. Stuckenbruck suggests that beatitudes accrued an exhortative function during the period of the literary apocalypses (*1 Enoch 91–108* [CEJL; New York: Walter de Gruyter, 2007], 410).

22. For more on the Psalms, see Brown's essay in the present volume.

later Isaiah blesses the one who withholds his hand from evil (Isa 56:2). And Daniel blesses the one who waits, enduring through the 1,335 days of chaos (Dan 12:12).

But biblical happiness also frequently moves from virtue to the fruits and rewards thereof. The happy person in Psalm 1 enjoys stability and prosperity. According to Proverbs, those who find wisdom enjoy long life, riches, honor, pleasantness, and peace (Prov 3:13–18). McMahon may be excused for confusing this-worldly and otherworldly versions of biblical happiness, but his citation of Psalm 128 is right on the mark: the happy life of the one who fears God and walks in God's ways includes all manner of blessings.[23]

The more famous beatitudes of Jesus also participate in this tradition, though with a twist. In the words of W. D. Davies and Dale C. Allison Jr.: beatitudes take on an eschatological tone, "particularly in apocalyptic writings."[24] Indeed, whatever we make of their rhetorical function,[25] several of Jesus's beatitudes in both Matthew and Luke seem to contrast present, undesirable states with an eschatological, divine point of view. That is to say, in both sets of beatitudes God blesses persons who would not appear happy in the sight of their neighbors. People hunger (Luke) because they lack food; they hunger and thirst for righteousness (Matthew) because justice is denied them. But both are blessed, or declared happy, via the beatitude.

Now, what do biblical blessings have to do with happiness? According to Martha C. Nussbaum, Aristotle uses *eudaimon* and *makarion* interchangeably, to indicate the happy person.[26] Thus, the language of blessedness reflects important assumptions about—or arguments for—particular versions of happiness. This is a heuristic rather than a deductive exercise. It assumes that Jewish and Christian apocalyptic literature moves in the stream of broader Jewish discourse—not only Jewish discourse, but Jewish discourse to be sure. It builds upon the insight that blessing in biblical traditions corresponds to the topic of happiness.

Apocalyptic blessedness probably demonstrates a large measure of continuity with this tradition. The burden of proof lies upon us to demonstrate otherwise—or to explore how apocalyptic blessing might be distinctive. We should note that

---

23. McMahon, *Happiness*, 79.

24. Davies and Allison, *Matthew*, 1:432. See also Holladay's essay in this volume.

25. In my view, Matthew's beatitudes serve as an introduction to the Sermon on the Mount, which characterizes Jesus as a teacher. Jesus's blessings both set forth his basic point of view (countercultural and eschatological) and invite the potential audience to find themselves approved by God and addressed by his teaching. As for Luke, I am inclined to agree with Holladay that the beatitudes contribute to the portrayal of Jesus as a prophet (see his essay in the present volume).

26. Martha C. Nussbaum, *The Fragility of Goodness: Luck and Ethics in Greek Tragedy and Philosophy* (rev. ed.; Cambridge: Cambridge University Press, 2001), 329–33. Nussbaum examines contexts in which Aristotle literally switches one word for the other.

important apocalyptic texts such as *1 Enoch*, *4 Ezra*, Revelation, and the *Shepherd of Hermas* feature blessings of one kind or another.[27] Meanwhile, the apocalyptic testaments employ blessing as their basic literary form. At a literary level, in several apocalypses the visionary blesses the audience through a programmatic address. This occurs in the *Epistle of Enoch*, *4 Ezra*, and *2 Baruch*.

At this point, we might draw a few conclusions, against which we may compare apocalyptic happiness.

- Blessedness is not primarily subjective or individualistic. All things being equal, blessedness should lead to an individual's sense of well-being, but blessedness is judged according to publicly articulated values and behaviors. That is, once blessedness is defined, everyone can agree as to whether or not another person is blessed according to that definition.
- Humans have significant agency in the quest for happiness, but some dimensions of blessedness are not up to the individual. One cannot control one's number of offspring, for example, or the sociopolitical circumstances in which one lives.
- Blessedness is not primarily—perhaps not substantially—attitudinal. Instead, blessedness corresponds to favored behavior, to possessing qualities and goods that are highly valued.
- Blessedness invokes a divine perspective.

I suspect this pattern of blessedness might have a great deal in common with *eudaimonia*. Classical philosophical debates concerning *eudaimonia* sought an objective level of excellence, to which others would assent. Acknowledging the power of fate, the ancients nevertheless stressed a free man's capacity to shape his own happiness. While Stoics and Epicureans devoted significant attention to attitudes, they emphasized the priority of practices instead. The Greek and Roman philosophers did not assume a divine perspective, but theories concerning the gods did regulate their notions of happiness.

4. Happiness in Apocalyptic Discourse

From a historical perspective, isolating biblical apocalyptic texts from the broader stream of ancient apocalyptic literature makes no sense. Not only does this move result in the reduction of noncanonical texts as just "background" to canonical

---

27. *1 En.* 1:1; 58:2; 81:4; 82:4 (for these passages see Stuckenbruck, *1 Enoch*, 409); *4 Ezra* 7:45; Revelation 1:3; 14:13; 16:15; 19:9; 20:6; 22:7, 14; and *Shepherd* 6:7; 7:3; 38:9; 51:10; 56:9; 61:1; 101:2; 105:6; 106:3; 107:3.

ones, it also inhibits our ability to situate the canonical texts within a broader flow of Jewish and Christian literature. But, since the present essay has both cultural and theological dimensions, it makes sense to privilege the canonical texts while acknowledging that these developed amidst a much larger conversation.

Clearly, the prospect of future blessing represents the dominant note of apocalyptic happiness. Consider 2 *Baruch* 21:13: "For if only this life exists which everyone possesses here, nothing could be more bitter than this."[28] Several apocalyptic texts thus emphasize heavenly or resurrection bliss (the *Book of the Watchers*, *3 Baruch*, *Apocalypse of Peter*), while others stress the messianic hope come to earth (the *Animal Apocalypse*, *4 Ezra*, *Ascension of Isaiah*). Some prominent texts blend expectation for the transformation of this world with otherworldly hope (as in the *Similitudes of Enoch*, Daniel, *2 Baruch*, and Revelation).

Some scholars have argued that apocalyptic imagery that *seems* otherworldly or heavenly actually functions as a sort of poetry for profoundly this-worldly hope.[29] However, it seems even more likely that many kinds of apocalyptic imagery imply a hope that lies beyond death. Paul insists on a bodily resurrection that involves an incorruptible body (1 Cor 15:42–57) and overcomes death (1 Cor 15:26). Several texts employ angel imagery to describe resurrection life (*1 En.* 104:2; Dan 12:3; Mark 12:25).[30] Revelation envisions a New Jerusalem come to earth, where "Death will be no more"—imagery that makes sense after death and the sea have given up their dead (20:13). Do these images not imply a hope that lies beyond this side of death?[31]

So, future blessing provides the most distinctive contribution of apocalyptic happiness, but more needs to be said. First, the call for future blessing springs from the acute sense of present distress, even oppression here and now. Thus, the *Similitudes* and the *Epistle of Enoch* excoriate "those who build their houses with sin" (*1 En.* 94:6), while the *Shepherd of Hermas* critiques wealth that divides rich

---

28. Where available, translations for Jewish pseudepigraphal works are taken from James H. Charlesworth, ed., *The Old Testament Pseudepigrapha: Volume 1: Apocalyptic Literature and Testaments* (ABRL; New York: Doubleday, 1983).

29. For a prominent example, see N. T. Wright, *The New Testament and the People of God* (Minneapolis: Fortress, 1992), 280–86.

30. Consider also Acts 23:8, which Benedict Viviano renders, "the Sadducees say that there is no resurrection either as an angel (i.e., in the form of an angel) or as a spirit (i.e., in the form of a spirit) but the Pharisees acknowledge them both" ("Sadducees, Angels, and Resurrection [Acts 23:8–9]," *JBL* 111 [1992]: 496–98).

31. Richard Bauckham maintains that, "[t[he earliest Jewish notion of resurrection was that the dead would return from the place of the dead to life on earth" (*The Fate of the Dead: Studies on the Jewish and Christian Apocalypses* [NovTSup 93; Leiden: Brill, 1998], 255). I agree with Bauckham with less confidence than I once did, but the point I am advancing here involves the distinction between a hope that lies beyond death and a hope for transformation on this side of the grave.

from poor (*Shepherd* 17:4–9; 74:1). Major sections of the grand historical apoca-lypses depict the terror imposed by imperial oppressors, along with the hope for their destruction. Daniel, *2 Baruch*, and *4 Ezra* indict Israel for its failure to live out its covenant, while Revelation, the *Shepherd of Hermas*, and the *Apocalypse of Peter* admonish followers of Jesus whose lives are marred by sin. In the face of social injustice, imperial oppression, and communal demoralization, no wonder Ezra laments, "It would have been better for us not to be here than to come here and live in ungodliness, and to suffer and not understand why" (*4 Ezra* 4:12).[32] The future dimension of apocalyptic hope voices a profound engagement with, albeit an alienation from, the present.

Second, despite alienation from the present order, some (but not all) apoca-lyptic traditions offer glimpses of happiness in the present age. *Jubilees*, with its emphasis on cult and calendar, articulates an ordered corporate life in the presence of God. When the people seek God "with all their heart and all their soul," *Jubilees* promises, they will enter "an abundance of peace in righteousness" (*Jub.* 1:15). For *Jubilees*, the proper Sabbath is full of eating, drinking, and blessing God (*Jub.* 2:21). While *Jubilees* envisions a new age on this earth, its basic teachings create space for flourishing in the here and now. Similarly, the Testaments of the Twelve Patriarchs promote a philosophy of virtue, not simply a remote hope. The Testament of Levi enjoins parents to educate their children in the Law, for such persons will gain honor and blessing. "Sow good things in your souls and you will find them in your lives" (*T. Levi* 13:6). After all, nothing can deprive a person of wisdom (*T. Levi* 13:7–9). When the *Shepherd of Hermas* calls for moral virtues such as *egkrateia* ("self-control") and works of mercy, it promises both eternal life and good fortune in this life (*Shepherd* 16:4; 38:9–10; cf. 51:10; 56:1–9; 101:1–2). This makes sense, as the commandments are "good, powerful, cheerful, glorious, and able to save a person's soul" (61:1).[33] In brief, we need not restrict apocalyptic blessing solely to the world to come.

Third, human flourishing requires that people (and presumably, groups) de-velop a sense of narrative identity.[34] To this day apocalyptic discourse excels at pro-viding a sense of meaning by constructing a storyline into which individuals and groups may insert themselves.[35] If anything, this is what the historical apocalypses

32. Unless noted otherwise, all translations from the Bible are derived from the New Revised Standard Version.

33. Translation from Bart D. Ehrman, *The Apostolic Fathers* (2 vols.; LCL 24–25; Cambridge: Harvard University Press, 2003), 2:339.

34. See the essays in Catriona Mackenzie and Kim Adams, eds., *Practical Identity and Narra-tive Agency* (New York: Routledge, 2008); also Haidt, *Happiness Hypothesis*, 142–43.

35. O'Leary, *Arguing the Apocalypse*; and Charles B. Strozier, *Apocalypse: On the Psychology of Fundamentalism in America* (Boston: Beacon Press, 1994).

do best. Ancient apocalypses *reveal* the truth about the present, the nature of empire, and the nature of God, offering their audiences another way to evaluate and engage their circumstances. Consider the climax of the *Animal Apocalypse*:

> Then I kept seeing till one great horn sprouted on one of those sheep, and he opened their eyes, and they had vision in them and their eyes were opened. He cried aloud to the sheep, and all the rams saw him and ran unto him. In spite of this, all those eagles, vultures, ravens, and kites *until now* continue to rip the sheep, swooping down upon them and eating them. As for the sheep, they remain silent; but the rams are lamenting and crying aloud. (*1 En.* 90:9–11; emphasis added)

The key phrase, "until now," indicates the apocalypse's invitation to its audience. It calls them to enter the story (imaginatively) as faithful and vulnerable sheep, exposed to horrific suffering. Despite their vulnerability, these sheep have open eyes; that is, through the help of the apocalypse they perceive the larger reality in which their faithful suffering participates.

The story continues beyond the present into an envisioned future. When the Lord of the sheep returns, he will equip the sheep to make war on their oppressors and vanquish them (*1 En.* 90:17–19). At the conflict's end "all the sheep" enter the (re)new(ed) house built just for them (*1 En.* 90:28–29). However, the blinded sheep—those who do not perceive the truth and do not remain faithful—are cast into a fiery abyss, directly next to the former house. What does it mean to be a seeing sheep, perceiving the ultimate truth, struggling faithfully under great distress, observing the blindness of other sheep and anticipating their judgment? The *Animal Apocalypse* called Jews to "open their eyes" and rally behind Judas Maccabeus in his struggle against the Seleucid Empire. Just as the *Left Behind* novels encourage millenarian Christians to see themselves as a faithful remnant marginalized by menacing cultural forces such as feminism and ecumenism,[36] the *Animal Apocalypse* offered a narrative identity for Jews in their resistance against imperial oppression.

The promise of future happiness, the experience of present blessing, and the construction of narrative identity all contribute to apocalyptic happiness. Yet happiness may not stand as the only—or ultimate—good. Some apocalyptic texts emphasize the joys of right living, while others take a more grim assessment. Almost without exception, apocalyptic texts do not rank one's own individual

---

36. The *Left Behind* series includes sixteen best-selling novels, expanded from an original twelve, by Tim LaHaye and Jerry B. Jenkins (Wheaton, IL: Tyndale House, 1995–2007). The novels dramatically portray the last days according to dispensationalist premillenial theology.

happiness—whether here or in the hereafter—as the ultimate good. Instead, apocalyptic discourse reveals a transcendent reality to which one devotes allegiance. This "apocalyptic gnosis," to borrow a phrase from Carol A. Newsom, sustains hope and motivates fidelity in the present age.[37] Ironically, such allegiance—one might even call it "commitment" or "duty"—contributes an essential resource for happiness under trying circumstances.[38]

5. The Usual Suspects: Apocalyptic Happiness in Daniel and Revelation

The book of Revelation is intensely engaged with Daniel, to the degree that Revelation alludes to Daniel more frequently than to any other scriptural book in proportion to its size.[39] Beyond their identity as the canon's two great apocalypses, these two books share other significant features. Both books explicitly respond to the question of empire by revealing its true character, and both call for faithful, but not violent, resistance to the great empires of their day. In both books such resistance entails distinctive behaviors, including dietary observances and abstention from ruler cults. Both books call for costly commitment in the present and promise eternal blessing in the resurrection age.

Yet the most obvious literary distinction between Daniel and Revelation marks a potential difference in their respective approaches to happiness. Whatever one makes of Daniel's composition history, Daniel makes its point as much in story as in apocalyptic vision. Revelation, on the other hand, is nearly all vision with minimal narrative framework. Daniel begins with six chapters of court legends concerning faithful Jews who abstain from a pagan diet, who continue to pray to the God of Israel despite royal proscription, and who refuse to worship the king. Revelation calls for similar behaviors, including abstention

---

37. Newsom suggested "apocalyptic gnosis" in her review of an earlier draft of this essay. Such an interpretation of apocalyptic discourse is consistent with that of Christopher Rowland, *The Open Heaven: A Study of Apocalyptic in Judaism and Early Christianity* (New York: Crossroad, 1982).

38. See, e.g., Shantz's essay in this volume. On commitment, see Suzanne C. Kobasa, "The Hardy Personality: Toward a Social Psychology of Stress and Health," in *Social Psychology of Health and Illness* (eds. Glenn S. Sanders and Jerry Suls; Hillsdale, NJ: Lawrence Erlbaum Associates, 1982), 3–32, cited in John Yeager, "Faith, Fear, and Motivation—The Back Story of the Stockdale Paradox," *Positive Psychology News Daily*, April 11, 2009, available online at http://positivepsychologynews.com/news/john-yeager/200904111793 (accessed August 12, 2011). Cf. Haidt's notion of "vital engagement" (*Happiness Hypothesis*, 223–26). I use the term "duty" here to connote values to which one subscribes, not externally imposed values.

39. Beale, *The Book of Revelation*, 77.

from "idol-food" (Rev 2:14, 20), "testimony" to the Lamb that can lead to martyrdom (Rev 1:9; 6:9; 12:11, 17; 19:10; 20:4), and refusal to worship the Beast
(Rev 13:8, 15; 14:9–11; 16:2; 20:4). What sets the Daniel stories apart is that they
describe happiness and prosperity for the righteous in the here and now. When
Daniel and his colleagues demonstrate their allegiance to YHWH, not only does
God deliver them from persecution, their bodies thrive and their careers
advance in the midst of such circumstances (see Dan 1:15, 17, 19–20). The stories
of Daniel involve courage in the face of grave threats, but faithfulness in the
midst of such circumstances results in wealth, luxury, and status for Daniel and
his companions.

That said, it is not entirely clear that Daniel commends this here and now
happiness as a viable option for its own audience. The court legends tend to characterize the great kings as buffoons, prone to rapid mood swings and readily subject to manipulation. As we move from the archaic court legends to Daniel's
apocalyptic visions, the portrayal of imperial authorities grows more grim: the
wicked king becomes a menace to God's people. Moreover, luxury, status, and
success hardly define the latter portions of the book of Daniel. The book also
conveys an ascetic sensibility (see Dan 10:2–3), even as it envisions great stress for
its audience. The fourth beast makes war against the holy ones and nearly wears
them out (Dan 7:21, 25); the contemptible king profanes the holy city and its
temple, killing some of the "wise ones" (Dan 11:29–35).[40] Only after divine intervention do the holy ones attain glory (Dan 7:27; 12:3). Thus, the second half of
Daniel displaces the "happy circumstances" we find in the first half of the book. If
Daniel's court legends acknowledge that this-worldly happiness might be possible under difficult circumstances, that hope seems remote by the time we reach
the book's conclusion.

For its part, Revelation seems to reject any such hope altogether. On this side
of the end, Revelation offers its audience neither health nor prosperity; instead, if
offers fictive status, community, and commitment in the midst of suffering. Revelation invites its audience to identify as kings and priests (Rev 1:6; see also 5:10;
12:10; cf. Dan 7:27) who will share in dominion through their endurance and

---

40. Perhaps Daniel 7–12 critiques the legends in chapters 1–6. According to this line of argument, the optimism we find in the court legends cannot withstand the crisis to which Daniel's
apocalyptic visions reply. (I am thankful to Carol A. Newsom for suggesting this to me in her
response to an earlier draft of this paper.) Anathea Portier-Young suggests that the transition
from Aramaic to Hebrew at Dan 7:28 corresponds to a shift in the perspective of Daniel's audience: Daniel's Aramaic sections describe collaboration with imperial powers, while the
Hebrew sections, particularly chapters 8–12, portray a time in which such accommodation is
no longer possible ("Languages of Identity and Obligation: Daniel as a Bilingual Book," *VT* 60
[2010]: 1–18).

persecution (Rev 1:9).[41] Revelation's "happiest" image of its audience may involve the 144,000 who "follow the Lamb wherever he goes" (14:4). As per the discussion above, this image suggests a kind of joy in community and commitment. These 144,000 have been "redeemed from humankind," implying their location in heaven, but their behavior sets an example for John's audience to emulate. Even so, their sort of happiness lies far from that of peace and prosperity.

Like Daniel, Revelation also promotes an "ascetic aesthetic."[42] Revelation voices its critique of Roman imperial commerce through the images of the Beast and the Whore. The figures embody specifically the trappings of luxury and high culture on the grounds that people grow rich through the exploitation of other persons (Rev 13:16–17). Revelation embodies this critique most explicitly in the laments concerning Babylon's destruction. Kings of the earth lament her fall because they have lost a companion with whom they "committed fornication and lived in luxury" (Rev 18:9). Merchants weep because no one purchases their cargo—a list that begins with luxury items and concludes with "slaves—and human lives" (Rev 18:12–13; see also 18:16–17). Sailors wail because seafaring merchants "grew rich by her wealth" (Rev 18:19). Indeed, upon Babylon's fall, cultural pleasures come to an end:

> With such violence Babylon the great city
>   will be thrown down,
>   and will be found no more;
> and the sound of harpists and flutists and trumpeters
>   will be heard in you no more;
> and an artisan of any trade
>   will be found in you no more. . . .
> for your merchants were the magnates of the earth,
>   and all nations were deceived by your sorcery.
> And in you was found the blood of prophets and of saints,
>   and of all who have been slaughtered on earth. (Rev 18:21b-24)

Babylon glitters with gold and purple, she does commerce in fine tastes and scents, and instrumental music fills her streets. While the New Jerusalem also is defined by its opulence, its range of sensory pleasure is much narrower, largely

---

41. I am playing somewhat loosely with the translation here. According to Rev 1:6, Christ "has made us a dominion, priests to his God and Father," while 1:9 identifies the audience as John's siblings and partners "in the persecution, dominion, and endurance that are in Jesus" (my translations).

42. For this language, see Greg Carey, "A Man's Choice: Wealth Imagery and the Two Cities of the Book of Revelation," in *A Feminist Companion to the Apocalypse of John* (eds. Amy-Jill Levine and Maria Mayo Robbins; New York: Continuum, 2009), 147–58.

confined to things cold and hard like precious metals and jewels. Even the gold and jewels that bedeck the Bride, which far exceed Babylon's wealth, convey an ascetic sensitivity: they are "pure" or "clear" (Rev 21:11, 18, 22). The fine garments promised to the Lamb's followers are white, in contrast to the purple worn by Babylon. The Lamb's company features brash trumpets and soothing harps, but one senses a party going on in Babylon with its minstrels, flute players, and trumpets. Where the New Jerusalem has fresh water, Babylon trades in wine. Finally, all the goods Revelation promises to its audience occur in the New Jerusalem, not in this age. Their opulence far outshines Babylon's—and even then they tend to be less soft, less aromatic, less colorful, and less pleasing to the eye than Babylon's luxuries—but in contrast to Daniel, Revelation's hope lies (almost) entirely in the future new world and in the heavenly realms. Even in the end, that is, an ascetic purity defines apocalyptic happiness. Revelation offers commitment, identity, and community, but little by way of pleasure, comfort, or success in this age.

To compare Daniel and Revelation with some noncanonical apocalypses is to explore the diverse potential of apocalyptic discourse, particularly when authors blend apocalyptic topics with nutrients from other discursive streams. Apocalyptic discourse emerges as a distinctive set of imaginative and rhetorical resources within Judaism and Christianity, always in conversation with other traditions.[43] All apocalyptic texts promise future happiness to the faithful, and most construct a narrative identity for their audiences. But while some apocalypses imagine this-worldly happiness, Daniel and Revelation emphasize the age to come.

Moreover, Daniel and Revelation are united in their resistance to the empires of their day. Indeed, this common emphasis on resistance likely accounts for Daniel's heavy influence on Revelation. We might debate whether we think Daniel and Revelation present visions of utopia, but they certainly portray what dystopia looks like. Imperial dystopia renders human flourishing impossible. It generates wealth and power for some at the expense of others. Imperial dystopia is arrogant, boastful, and beastly; it crowds out the worship of God even to the point of occupying holy spaces and making war on God's people. Imperial dystopia implies the drive to dominate and to "cleanse" the world of dissenters.

---

43. Like defining "apocalyptic," explaining the "origins of apocalyptic" is an elusive pursuit. I describe apocalyptic discourse as an identifiable appropriation of particular literary and cosmological commonplaces (*topics*) that can serve a variety of religious and rhetorical ends (see Carey, *Ultimate Things*, 1–18; and also Duane F. Watson, "Introduction," in *The Intertexture of Apocalyptic Discourse in the New Testament* [SBLSymS 14; Atlanta: Society of Biblical Literature, 2002], 1–9). The notion of blending discursive streams in early Christianity is developed in conversation with Vernon K. Robbins and other participants in the Society of Biblical Literature Rhetoric of Religious Antiquity Seminar (see Robbins, *The Invention of Christian Discourse* [Rhetoric of Religious Antiquity; Leiden: Deo, 2009]). Scholars have long noted the resonances between apocalyptic discourse and the wisdom and prophetic streams of ancient Israel and formative Judaism.

In depicting imperial dystopia, Daniel and Revelation implicitly affirm a negative—and partial—view of human happiness. Happiness, in this perspective, requires the absence of idolatry, which is interpreted as imperial arrogance and exploitation. I would not claim that Daniel and Revelation entirely reject empire and imperialism, yet their critiques of empire portray how the drive to domination generates exploitation and arrogance. Freedom—not the modern, individualistic variety, but the freedom to worship God through tangible demonstrations of loyalty—would thus seem to be a necessary condition of apocalyptic happiness.

To sum up: both Daniel and Revelation call for resistance to imperial idolatry and oppression in their cultural contexts. Faithful, persistent resistance defines virtue in both apocalypses. Their critique of the present implies a "negative definition" of happiness, which means that some conditions hinder human flourishing. Both Daniel and Revelation envision a time of great stress and danger for faithful persons, but promise eschatological blessing in the new age. Both apocalypses invest their audiences with great status in the present, a status congruent with their faithful commitment but not evident to eyes outside the community of the faithful. An ascetic sensibility animates both texts. However, Daniel's court legends open the possibility that, under some circumstances, those who resist idolatrous practices may inherit blessings in this age, whereas Revelation imagines no such hope.

6. Beyond the Apocalypses: Happiness in Synoptic and Pauline Apocalyptic Discourse

Interpreters have long noted that an *inaugurated* eschatology dominates the New Testament canon. The Synoptic Gospels (and John too, I would argue) and Paul testify that the kingdom of God has broken into the present evil age, even as this age limps on toward its dissolution. To be sure, eschatology need not be *apocalyptic*: the "day of the LORD" emerges in literature free of specifically apocalyptic topics. Yet resurrection is a thoroughly apocalyptic topic, and New Testament eschatologies are thoroughly and emphatically postresurrection discourses. In other words, the inaugurated eschatologies of the New Testament documents demonstrate heavy apocalyptic influence. Due to constraints of space, I will discuss here only the Synoptic Gospels and the Pauline epistles to illustrate how apocalyptic happiness plays out within the framework of this inaugurated eschatology.[44]

---

44. Dale C. Allison Jr.'s article, "Eschatology of the NT," in *NIDB* 2:294–99 is helpful on this point with regard to terminology. Allison claims that, on the whole, the New Testament espouses a "partially realized" eschatology though his terminology varies. In my view, Allison is describing what scholars have traditionally called an "inaugurated" eschatology.

Synoptic Apocalyptic

The Synoptic Gospels all feature a "little apocalypse" in which Jesus discusses the destruction of the temple and the signs that portend the "completion of the age" (Matt 24:3), "that all these things are about to be accomplished" (Mark 13:4), and "that this is about to take place" (Luke 21:7). In each instance Jesus dissuades the disciples against judging hastily that the final events are upon them, but he also admonishes them to constantly be on the lookout. This eschatological tension—eager anticipation for God's ultimate intervention, along with a sober suspicion of end-time declarations—defines the Synoptics' futuristic outlook. Ultimate happiness resides in the not too distant future, yet engagement with a hostile present is the order for the day.

Scholars have long noted another dimension of Synoptic eschatology, the conviction that in the presence of Jesus, God has already broken into this age.[45] Mark 1:15 and Matthew 4:17 proclaim that God's reign is near, while in Luke, Jesus reads from Isaiah and announces, "Today this scripture has been fulfilled in your hearing" (Luke 4:21). This sentiment underlies the familiar sayings concerning why wedding attendants do not fast when the bridegroom is present, why fresh fabric cannot patch an old garment, and why one does not pour new wine into old wineskins (see Mark 2:19–22). The point is that the presence of Jesus is an eschatological event. We may see it Matthew's way: the blind see, the crippled walk, the lepers are cleansed, the deaf hear, the dead are raised (a crucial apocalyptic trope!), and the poor receive the gospel (Matt 11:5). Or we may adopt Luke's more subdued outlook: "the kingdom of God is among you" (Luke 17:21). However one phrases it, Jesus inaugurates a new age. A very here and now happiness accompanies this moment: Jesus brings healing, liberation, community, and hope. Synoptic happiness participates in the sort of apocalyptic discourse that bears present blessing along with future hope.

One could easily perceive the whole array of Synoptic teachings concerning happiness within this eschatological framework: from the beatitudes, to the lilies in the field, to outrageous purchases of fields and pearls, to the new family of disciples, to the ever-present Lukan banquets, we see how the eruption of the reign of God sets the context for human flourishing in the here and now.[46]

---

45. I set aside for the moment the question of an "apocalyptic Jesus," though I do believe that the historical Jesus was deeply engaged with apocalyptic discourse.

46. For more on the Synoptic Gospels, see the essays by Joel B. Green and Carl R. Holladay in this volume.

Paul and Apocalyptic

As for Paul, conventional wisdom once held that Paul believed in "holding on" until Jesus's return. In this view Paul discouraged attempts to improve one's current state in the present (see 1 Corinthians 7), preferring instead to delay the hope for happiness until the glorious end. Doubtless, Paul was keenly aware that mortal bodies provide great pain and disappointment, and there is no denying the strength of his apocalyptic convictions.[47] Even so, Paul lived in a context in which most people experienced chronic pain, malnutrition, and poverty. Moreover, the popular philosophies of the day reveal that almost everybody—not just Paul—sought strategies to cope with Fate's fickle ways.

On the other hand, Paul testifies to joy in the present, apocalyptic topics often driving his convictions. Important developments in Pauline studies over recent decades overturn the image of an otherworldly, socially passive ("conservative" would be anachronistic) apostle. While virtually every New Testament scholar is aware of these developments, the former portrait still exerts great influence in other theological discipline and in the popular imagination about Paul. A brief summary of these developments is thus in order.

First, there is the matter of authorship. Scholars have long debated Paul's authorship of Colossians, Ephesians, and 2 Thessalonians, with extreme skepticism regarding the Pastoral Epistles. Estimates vary concerning how many scholars assess one epistle or another as likely authentic, though it seems that doubt concerning Pauline authorship of Colossians and Ephesians is on the upswing. Unfortunately, conversations concerning authorship often do not take serious account of Paul's social views.[48] "Wives, be subject to your husbands" (Eph 5:22; Col 3:18) and "Slaves, obey your earthly masters" (Eph 6:5; Col 3:22) still shape our views of Paul. But, take away these six disputed epistles and suddenly it is far from clear that Paul is a social "conservative" on issues such as gender and slavery. Indeed, one can build a stronger case for Paul as a social egalitarian than one can do the same for the historical Jesus. This runs directly counter to the dominant contemporary narrative, in which Jesus transgresses boundaries and blesses people but Paul domesticates the gospel in order to propagate it.

---

47. For more on Paul, see Shantz's essay in the present volume.

48. I say this as a relative outsider to Pauline scholarship. I first encountered the relevance of authorship to a social understanding of Paul in Neil Elliott, *Liberating Paul: The Justice of God and the Politics of the Apostle* (Maryknoll, NY: Orbis, 1994), esp. 20–22. The question is framed provocatively, though I think helpfully, by Marcus Borg and John Dominic Crossan, *The First Paul: Reclaiming the Radical Visionary Behind the Church's Conservative Icon* (San Francisco: HarperSanFrancisco, 2009).

Second, the movement to situate Paul in the context of Roman imperial discourse calls attention to the subversive nature of Paul's Christ language. Romans 13:1–7 continues to perplex interpreters, yet it lies beyond dispute that Paul proclaimed the "messiah" (political title) of "Israel" (a subject people) as "Lord" (an imperial title), "Son of God," and "savior" (acclamations received by emperors) who would return in triumphal procession (an imperial practice). Paul creates and nourishes small sectarian communities called "churches," using a Greek term normally used to indicate the political assembly of free men in a city. Moreover, Paul's messiah had been legitimately executed under imperial authority due to suspicion of sedition. This is not to go so far as to suggest that Paul was a social or political revolutionary; however, if Paul's aim was to avoid trouble, he picked a message and a vocabulary remarkably ill-suited to the project.

A third development brings us to the heart of the matter. Interpreters are now returning to language from which we had formerly shied away, namely, the combination of mysticism, participation, and apocalypticism in Paul's writings. As Jouette M. Bassler puts it, participation in Christ "had a distinctively eschatological component: union with Christ experienced in this world was only a foretaste of the Parousia."[49] Paul's participation language blends with his language of the Spirit. Paul writes that "Christ lives in me" (Gal 2:20), "we have been united with [Christ] in a resurrection like his" (Rom 6:5), and "we ourselves . . . have the first fruits of the Spirit" (Rom 8:23; cf. 1 Cor 15:20). Resurrection discourse, Spirit discourse, participation, and the parousia would seem to come together, as a package.[50]

Moreover, it is precisely the resurrection-Spirit-participation-parousia complex that contributes to happiness in this age. Participation in the risen Christ empowers people to overcome sin (Rom 6:1–15). The Spirit distributes spiritual gifts that animate the one body of Christ (1 Cor 12:4–13; cf. Rom 12:4–8). The presence of the Spirit, marked by participation in Christ, arouses the virtues that enable believers to fulfill the law (Gal 5:22–26). The presence of Christ strengthens Paul to live with joy in the midst of dire circumstances (Phil 4:10–13). In short, the resurrection of Jesus inaugurates a host of present blessings, all of which anticipate the fullness of the resurrection to come. Paul does believe ultimate happiness lies in the future, yet believers taste a strong hint of that blessing in the here and now.

To sum up this section: we have observed that both the Synoptics and Paul's letters reflect an inaugurated eschatology. Both anticipate a fullness of blessing in

---

49. Jouette M. Bassler, *Navigating Paul: An Introduction to Key Theological Concepts* (Louisville: Westminster John Knox, 2007), 44.

50. See Colleen Shantz, *Paul in Ecstasy: The Neurobiology of the Apostle's Life and Thought* (Cambridge: Cambridge University Press, 2009).

the eschatological future, of which believers enjoy a foretaste in the present. The Synoptics locate those present blessings in the arrival of Jesus, who brings community, healing, and joy. Paul attests to the power of Jesus's resurrection, through which believers experience the first fruits of their hope: the presence of the Spirit, spiritual empowerment, charismatic gifts, and joy.

7. Epilogue: Suffering and Apocalyptic Happiness

According to McMahon, the path of suffering sets apart the early Christian vision of happiness as distinctive. This is because Jesus's death and resurrection mark Christianity's definitive symbols. Those symbols mold early Christian piety into a pattern of faithful suffering complemented by the hope of future vindication. Present, faithful suffering is the *path* of early Christian salvation.

For McMahon, the emergence of apocalyptic eschatology poses a necessary condition for the Christian version of happiness. Apocalyptic myths portray end-time crises followed by a final resolution, often depicting the faithful as a suffering minority in an age of corruption. "Unabashedly sensual in its imagined ecstasies," early Christian happiness nevertheless offers a grim view of the here and now.[51]

Our survey of biblical apocalyptic discourse confirms McMahon's basic insights. Apocalyptic discourse did contribute decisively to the picture of happiness in the biblical traditions—and more broadly, to the larger Christian tradition—primarily by promising happiness that lies beyond this age or this life. Moreover, McMahon is correct in his identification of *how* apocalyptic discourse developed this classic vision: it emerged when fidelity could and did lead to suffering, and it provided a compelling response to that problem.

At the same time, McMahon oversimplifies things. Apocalyptic discourse presents a remarkably flexible set of rhetorical and mythological resources. Apocalyptic happiness comes in different flavors. Its diversity includes a spectrum from inaugurated happiness to future-only happiness. It also contributes diverse ways of imagining happiness in the present. Revelation and Daniel stand relatively far toward the otherworldly end of the spectrum. Daniel's court legends, apocalyptic only through their incorporation with the book's vision reports, suggest that God might bless faithfulness in the here and now—but the late Danielic visions indicate great affliction for the saints. The Synoptic Gospels and Paul together depict persecution as the lot of Jesus's followers, though they also maintain that in Christ God has broken into the present with a host of blessings. Finally, every instance of biblical apocalyptic discourse addresses the twin concerns of identity and commitment. That is,

---

51. McMahon, *Happiness*, 95.

apocalyptic discourse constructs a communal narrative for the saints, who under-stand themselves as partners with God and testify to God's work in the world in the face of great opposition. It *reveals* an assessment of the world, the faithful commu-nity, and God—all of which legitimates this storyline. This marks one of the basic signs of human happiness—the sense that one's life is oriented toward a greater, compelling good. This combination of narrative identity and commitment repre-sents apocalyptic happiness.

Then again, suffering, too, plays a major role in biblical apocalyptic traditions. Apocalyptic suffering is not an end in itself, however; rather, it marks a negative interpretation of the current state of affairs, implying that happiness requires the absence of idolatry and oppression. In the apocalyptic traditions one does not seek suffering; one lives and testifies to the truth. Apocalyptic literature promotes happiness by unmasking deception and summoning people to lives of fidelity and purpose.[52]

52. I am indebted to many members of *The Bible and the Pursuit of Happiness* project for their comments, particularly Carol A. Newsom, who provided an insightful response to an earlier version of this chapter. Anathea Portier-Young and Matthew Skinner also contributed valuable suggestions.

PART THREE

Beyond the Bible

CONTINUING THE CONVERSATION INTO
OTHER DISCIPLINES

Introduction to Part III

From its inception, *The Bible and the Pursuit of Happiness* was designed as an interdisciplinary project. So, in order to encourage the biblical essayists to think beyond their own disciplinary boundaries, as well as to exemplify how the biblical materials could have significant impact outside the field of biblical studies proper, three scholars from different fields were invited to the Atlanta conference and asked to offer their expertise, not only during the conference, but also in subsequent written contributions. These essays are collected in Part III. While each responds to the various essays found in Parts I–II, the contributions in Part III are more than "responses." It might be better to call them "projections" because, while each essay demonstrates the significance of the biblical materials to fields beyond biblical studies, each also offers insight into the problem of happiness, and even biblical happiness, from its own disciplinary perspective. It is hoped, then, that the three essays gathered in Part III model an integrative and interdisciplinary way of "continuing the conversation" on biblical happiness.

The first essay is by Ellen T. Charry, the Margaret W. Harmon Professor of Historical and Systematic Theology at Princeton Theological Seminary. Charry considers happiness from a systematic theological perspective. As the name indicates, systematic theology is devoted to the careful (systematic) articulation of all aspects pertaining to God and the life of faith. The Bible has traditionally been understood as a central, if not *the* central, resource for Christian theology, and so it is crucial to see how the biblical materials on happiness "play out" in systematic theology. As Charry notes, for much of Western Christian theological tradition, they do not. But, Charry argues, if Christian doctrine is unable to account for key aspects of the biblical witness on happiness, then something is wrong with the

doctrine, not with the Bible. Unfortunately, Western theology has typically operated with "a narrow and fragile doctrine of terrestrial happiness" that views
human happiness as largely impossible in this life and thus envisions it (solely) as
escape from eternal punishment. "This is a pathology-driven psychology," Charry
argues, "based on God's displeasure with humanity." The similarities here with
positive psychology's critique of the "old" psychology as too disease-based are
obvious, and suggest the need for a "positive theology" alongside positive psychology. Charry begins to offer precisely that by noting the full range of divine
emotion (and the simple *fact* of divine emotion—that is, "passibility") as found in
Scripture. The Bible speaks of God's happiness (see also Terence E. Fretheim's
essay in Part I), not only God's displeasure, but systematic theology's inattention
to this fact has led to a severely reduced view of happiness. In point of fact, part
of what God is happy about is human flourishing, which, in turn, makes God
even happier. Theologically, then, "happiness is the mutual enjoyment of God
and humanity when each fulfills the other." The psychological ramifications of
this "positive theology" perspective should be obvious, and they are dependent,
for Charry, on "the nimbleness of God's psychological repertoire." In brief,
"divine and human happiness must be of a piece." This means, among other
things, that Christians are deputized into God's own "happy project of loving
creation into flourishing."

In the next essay, Thomas G. Long, Bandy Professor of Preaching in the Candler School of Theology and Graduate Division of Religion at Emory University,
considers happiness from the perspective of a practical theologian. Drawing from
several of the biblical essays, especially the papers on the New Testament, Long
highlights the eschatological dimension of biblical happiness—a dimension that
he argues must be kept in constant balance with present concerns because "happiness is an eschatological promise with present-tense implications." This "tensive
balance," as he calls it, means that happiness (flourishing) will be experienced by
those who belong to Christ and yet, insofar as that involves participating in the
pattern of Jesus's own life, it will sometimes take forms that those outside this
faith will not recognize as "happiness." Long goes on to argue that understanding
happiness as an eschatological future that impinges on the present in real and
often difficult ways must inform pastoral practices, including that of preaching.
He takes inspiration at this point from the "Preacher" of Ecclesiastes (see also the
essay by Carol A. Newsom in Part I and, further, the Epilogue), particularly
Qoheleth's emphasis on happiness here and now—in the ordinary, mundane, and
specific rhythms of life that are understood as gifts from God, even if all that is
imperfectly understood. But despite any and all ambiguities and uncertainties,
the life of faith is still going somewhere. For the Christian it is going toward judgment, but, Long reminds us, that judgment turns out to be the crisis of Easter

where so many things—God's wrath, our understandings of happiness, and so on and so forth—are transformed.

The last essay is by Steven J. Sandage, professor of Marriage and Family Studies at Bethel University. Sandage self-identifies as a positive psychologist and, in addition to his teaching post, also has a private practice. His presence at the Atlanta conference was deeply appreciated by the other participants as he contributed numerous insights and "hard data" from the fields of positive psychology and counseling psychology to scholars who generally operate without the benefit of such studies or such empirical data. Sandage's written contribution is brimming with the same gifts, even as it is clear that his own thinking has benefited from the studies of biblical happiness found in Parts I–II. Indeed, it is because of those essays that Sandage argues for what he calls a transformed understanding of happiness (see also the Epilogue). This transformed understanding is at root dialectical, able to face seasons of suffering and unhappiness along with seasons of pure joy. While the latter may be hedonic, the former is certainly *an*hedonic. But even the anhedonic need not be anti-eudaimonic. In fact, "[g]rowth in maturity sometimes emerges from dark nights of trauma, grief, and dysphoria," and even the most difficult of times often prove extremely useful in developing various virtues. Sandage's essay is full of rich insights and research from the psychological literature on happiness, virtue, subjective well-being, and spiritual maturity—all in thoughtful conversation with the biblical materials. In the final analysis, then, his work nicely exemplifies what he calls the "constructive triangulation of disciplinary resources of interpretation in the hermeneutical study of happiness and well-being." Whenever such triangulation takes place, all conversation partners are enriched.

10

The Necessity of Divine Happiness

A RESPONSE FROM SYSTEMATIC THEOLOGY

Ellen T. Charry

IT IS CHALLENGING to respond to biblical material on happiness from a systematic theological perspective. In this essay, I will approach the subject through the doctrine of God. My argument will be that Western theology has a narrow and fragile doctrine of terrestrial happiness as relief from fear of eternal punishment through faith in the forgiveness of sin. This is a pathology-driven psychology based on God's displeasure with humanity. Inattention to the full range of divine emotion has restricted happiness to escaping deserved punishment. Acknowledging God's full-bodied emotional life will enable theology to appreciate God's enjoyment of human flourishing for God's own happiness and to argue that, theologically speaking, happiness is the mutual enjoyment of God and humanity when each fulfills the other.

1. The Systematic Theological Backstory on Happiness

Before responding to the essays on biblical happiness collected in this volume, a prior word on systematic theology is in order.[1] Systematic theology and dogmatics are modern, primarily Protestant enterprises created in response to the epistemological crisis of modernity that required evidence to support truth claims. Theology trembled as the correspondence theory of truth and knowledge no longer inspired confidence. When *empirical evidence* failed to support its claims, theology was hard pressed. As the reliability of received knowledge unraveled,

---

1. In addition to the citations that follow in this section, see further my volume *God and the Art of Happiness* (Grand Rapids: Eerdmans, 2010).

defenders of traditional knowledge sought another theory of truth. They adopted the coherence theory.[2] In the absence of empirical evidence, the coherence theory relied upon *rational evidence*, especially the consistency of the ideas involved in truth claims. In its stronger forms, this rationalist understanding of truth required that conclusions deduced from premises be entailed by the argument being made. Its weaker forms required only that propositions not contradict one another.

In the seventeenth century, Protestant scholasticism, following medieval scholasticism, arose in this context of modern rationalism in order to defend the intelligibility of Christian beliefs and practices. It created dogmatics in Lutheran and Calvinist (Reformed) forms.[3] The dogmatic project was to organize the fundamental dogmas of the Christian tradition—the doctrines of the trinity and incarnation—especially along with the particular theological emphases of Protestant thought, into a clear pattern and to work out detailed arguments within that pattern.

Martin Luther and John Calvin each highlighted a specific doctrine to correct what they took to be the failing of the medieval church. Luther, although not a systematic writer, focused on the doctrine of justification. Calvin, who wrote in a highly organized fashion, focused on the sovereignty of God. Their scions grounded their dogmatic construals on these respective foundations with special attention to what divided them both from Rome and from one another. This privileging of specific doctrines set the stage for later Protestant systematic theology.

Friedrich Schleiermacher pressed coherence in a new direction in the nineteenth century to promote the intelligibility of Christian theology. Like Luther and Calvin, he identified a single doctrinal principle but made it the explicit center that all Christian claims and practices must press. The hope was for a tight system—not just an organized presentation of various theological claims—in which all elements reduce to a single claim. Theological method became especially important for theology of this sort in order to ensure the systematic cogency of the project.

Schleiermacher's principle was that all Christian doctrines promote piety,[4] and Karl Barth, Paul Tillich, and Wolfhart Pannenberg all followed his lead, each selecting a different central point and method to ensure the coherence and

---

2. The coherence theory of truth is generally attributed to John Locke in his *Essay Concerning Human Understanding*, Book 2.

3. Important contributors to this tradition are Martin Chemnitz and John Gerhard, on the Lutheran side, and Jacob Arminius, Hugo Grotius, and François Turretin, on the Calvinist side.

4. See F. D. E. Schleiermacher, *The Christian Faith* (trans. H. R. Mackintosh; Edinburgh: T & T Clark, 1986).

systematic credibility of their system.[5] The systematic nature of their projects led to calling systematic theology a "science," that is a rational science analogous to the natural sciences with compelling methods, foundations, and parameters of its own that could compete in the marketplace of ideas in the modern university.

In sum, modernity spawned both dogmatic- and systematic-theological rationalism. While systematic theology is dogmatic in that it treats the foundational dogmas of the tradition systematically, not all dogmatic theology is systematic because it does not always cohere around a single point. This backstory is important for the present project on biblical conceptions of happiness precisely because happiness has never appeared as a topic, let alone single point of coherence in dogmatic or systematic theology. It is thus not immediately evident how this highly refined form of modern theology can come alongside biblical studies that, in its own backstory, mostly followed the historical and exegetical paths that systematic theology eschewed in favor of its rationalist presentation of truth. This does not mean, however, that systematic theology cannot converse with biblical studies of happiness or any other topic that falls outside its conventional doctrinal rubric, for that matter. It does suggest, however, that one must take care to specify the terms on which such conversation proceeds.

As already indicated above, the systematic theological principle to be pressed in this essay concerns the character of God. The question I wish to explore is whether the theological tradition has adequately understood and appreciated the full range of divine emotion so that it can speak appropriately of divine and human happiness in this life. My argument will be that current openness to divine passibility enables theology to speak cogently of God's genuine enjoyment of creation's flourishing and hence speak cogently of humanity's enjoyment of flourishing.

2. The Dogmatic Theological Backstory on Happiness

While no systematic theology has revolved around happiness, other forms of theology have, albeit infrequently, touched on the subject. Dogmatic theology existed in the patristic age and medieval theologians, beginning with Hugh of Saint Victor (1078–1141), organized dogmatic reflection into a conventional structure as a series of doctrinal themes for easy handling. The structure of such theology most often took the form of exegeting themes of the Nicene Creed with its three articles. One effect of this structure was to separate ideas that had always been discussed

---

5. See, respectively, Karl Barth, *Church Dogmatics* (13 vols.; trans. G. W. Bromiley; Edinburgh: T & T Clark, 1970–1977); Paul Tillich, *Systematic Theology* (3 vols.; Chicago: University of Chicago Press, 1951–1963); and Wolfhart Pannenberg, *Systematic Theology* (2 vols.; Grand Rapids: Eerdmans, 1991–1994).

together, arranging them in different categories so that later systematic theology had to put them back into a coherent pattern. Within this schema, happiness typically fell at the end of the list, under the rubric of eschatology—reflections on "last things," which were generally understood as pertaining to the afterlife.

This "eschatological view" of happiness took its cue from Augustine of Hippo who saw the contingencies of life as so prevalent that he concluded that happiness in this life was an unrealistic expectation. Seeking material goods was striving after false happiness because wealth, health, friends, and power would all eventually be lost. Not only that, but even peace of mind is unstable, for one can control vice and live virtuously at best only fitfully. Permanent happiness will only exist when vice disappears altogether in the heavenly city (*City of God*, 19.27). The only happiness that could endure is happiness in God, for only God is eternal and the human frame too frail not to be distracted from that joy in this life. Augustine thus distinguished terrestrial from celestial happiness and valued the latter over the former because it would endure.

Even celestial happiness is highly restricted territory, however. Happiness is not only restricted to heaven, it is also only for those whom God elects to make up for the number of the rebellious angels led by Lucifer who fell away from God into evil.[6] To press humility before God, Augustine taught that all deserve the wrath of God, yet God elects to save some, not by virtue of their worthiness but simply as an act of mercy on a few: those chosen to replace the number of fallen angels, whose number we know not. Thus, enduring happiness remains primarily a future hope, and not even virtuous living can assure it. It is a scarce commodity and trying for it a mistake, even an audacity.

Medieval eschatology envisioned the Christian afterlife as a hierarchy of locations from hell to heaven with various way stations and intermediate rooms depending on either the quality of one's life or the arbitrary determination of God (depending on how Augustinian the theologian was!). With happiness relegated to the afterlife, concern for terrestrial happiness took a back seat, or perhaps more accurately, never sat in the front seat. Christian eschatology failed to value the happy life. It sought to provide succor and hope in the face of life's hardships and to deter sin so that virtue may be vindicated hereafter with the perfect vision and knowledge of God once human bodies were beyond illness and death.

Focus on the future meant that care for physical and mental well-being were relatively unimportant. The span of life on earth is passing compared with an eternity of bliss or fire. The threat of eternal punishment and the

---

6. Augustine, *City of God*, 22.1. The Lucifer myth derives from Isa 14.12: "How you are fallen from heaven, O Day Star, son of Dawn! How you are cut down to the ground, you who laid the nations low!"

hope of eternal delight struggled to hold Western society together in lawless ages beyond the reach of education, the civilizing power of law, and widespread cultural norms. The theistic sanction sustained society for centuries through fear-driven hope nurtured periodically by art, literature, and itinerant preaching.

With concern for terrestrial well-being off the radar, attention focused on divine displeasure at sins and how they were forgiven. Absolution became salvation and expectation of heavenly reward. Despite Augustine's doctrine of predestination, which moots the value of moral behavior, fear of hell sustained social harmony to the extent that it was sustained in what we formerly called the "Dark Ages." The moral skepticism at the base of Augustine's teaching never captured the medieval imagination that created the penitential system for both short- and long-term hope of absolution, which was, it must be remembered, the chief indication of divine favor.

The need to balance fear with hope underwent a twist with Anselm of Canterbury's *Cur Deus Homo* written to call readers to righteousness while giving hope in the face of inevitable failure.[7] God demands absolute righteousness yet human sin is so dastardly and ubiquitous that simply being human is a capital offense about which we can do nothing. Following Rom 5:6–8, Anselm argued that God the Son voluntarily died in our place to satisfy the demand that sin be punished. That the innocent should die in place of the guilty is not a principle that any moral system but Christianity has ever valorized. While the principle has not been promoted in the raw form that Paul and Anselm have it, Christian agapism has stressed self-sacrifice as the basic Christian moral posture. More on these points later.

Anselm did not go on to argue that Christ's atoning sacrifice morally empowers believers. His influential treatise did not discuss resurrection and the new lease on life that it offers. Failing that, trusting that God forgives one's sins on account of Christ became the core of Western soteriology. Terrestrial happiness in this dogmatic framework would be the joy of relief from guilt and worry. Carrying the theme of divine wrath to the extreme conclusion that being human is a capital crime led theology to pivot around the virtues of humility and gratitude for escaping what one deserves. Western theology became pathology driven. Salvation is the undeserved reprieve from eternal damnation.

The dogmatic theological backstory on happiness is thus that Christian doctrine in this mode narrowed terrestrial happiness to relief from dread of a wrathful punishing God who concluded that humanity is bad news from the Garden of

---

7. Anselm, *Why God Became Man: Cur Deus Homo* (trans. Jasper Hopkins and Herbert Richardson; Queenston, Ontario: E. Mellen Press, 1985).

Eden on. Perhaps a person could be said to be happy as long as he or she can sustain the belief or at least the hope that their sins are forgiven. If salvation is trust in absolution, relief and gratitude constitute the experience of happiness to the extent that there is one. This experience is only as strong as one's faith, however, for it vanishes the moment doubt rears its ugly head. And if faith is a divine gift, not having it or being unable to sustain it over the course of life's vicissitudes leaves only despair. Somewhere along the way, this narrow and fragile vision of happiness from dogmatic theology seeped into systematic theology. It is implied, I would argue, even when it is not explicitly discussed.

As noted above, divine self-emptying in Christ's death carried over into Christian ethics where selflessness and self-sacrifice exemplify the proper Christian posture, following Jesus. The vision of God scowling at us pressed humility as a prized Christian personality trait so that selflessness was the proper imitation of Christ. The Christian is expected to empty herself, eclipse herself for the sake of "the other," just as Jesus did for us. Attending to one's own well-being, be it psychological or physical, is not becoming for a Christian in the light of others' needs. The choice is understood to be a zero sum game in which the last are first and the first last (see Matt 19:30; 20:8, 16; Mark 9:35; 10:31; Luke 13:30). Appeals to the piety of Christian selflessness are often capped with reference to Gal 2:20: "it is no longer I who live, but it is Christ who lives in me."

Just behind this press for humility, hope, gratitude, and relief from dread is a portrayal of God locked in internal combat between the demand for obedience to righteousness and the negative judgment that failure requires, on the one hand, and the call for merciful compassion, on the other. Anselm struggles bravely to find a balance between these two in God's heart. Tilting to the side of judgment means that dread will overpower the sensitive soul. Tilting to the side of mercy threatens to undo the need to submit to the demands of righteousness on which civil society depends for survival. This was especially the case in the eleventh century when the social institutions that impose the rule of law were not in place and obedience to the rule of law was not internalized. Internalizing standards of righteousness and justice in the populace is the burden of education and the family in every age. As a more recent example, we might observe that, in response to Rousseau's self-regulated *Émile*, William Golding pointed out how fragile civilization really is, suggesting that external sanction is needed to quell the savage heart.[8] The theistic sanction served that function well, but risked psychological paralysis for true believers who find themselves caged in

---

8. See William Golding, *Lord of the Flies* (New York: Coward-McCann, 1955); and Jean-Jacques Rousseau, *Émile: Or, Education* (repr. ed.; trans. Barbara Toxley; London: J. M. Dent and Sons, 2010 [French orig: 1762]).

their worst self ("totally depraved") even if they are released from its consequences.

Theologians have long educed the divine pedagogy that they believe will be the most salutary for civil society. Christian formation, though it may appear individualistic, even obsessed with personal salvation, has always been human formation for the common good.[9] Western theologians cast their lot with divine dissatisfaction with humanity with mercy coming just in time to rescue an undeserving humanity—well, at least a slice of undeserving humanity—from infinite and well-deserved punishment for being its worst self.

3. The Tanakh's Story of Happiness

As captivating as this theology has been, doctrinal questions arise. One is whether the accounts are adequately biblical. Another is whether they do justice to the full range of God's pedagogical skills and psychological acumen in dealing with people. I take up the first question here and the second in the next section.

Biblical studies largely eschewed reading dogmatic theology into scripture, focusing instead on reading the theology of the scriptural texts themselves. The essays in this volume recognize the theology of these texts on their own terms. To focus in on a few examples, according to the work of Jacqueline Lapsley, William P. Brown, Carol A. Newsom, and Terence E. Fretheim, the books of Isaiah, Psalms, Proverbs, Ecclesiastes, and other texts scattered across the canon testify to a God who is not driven by anger to bear down on human frailty in order to designate one person as elect and another lost by divine decree.[10] The authors of these biblical texts are shown to not share the negative appraisal of human character that Christian theologians would eventually promote. Quite the contrary! Instead, they urge all to a happy life through measured enjoyment of the good things of this world and the comportment of a morally good life. In most of these texts, material and moral well-being constitute a balanced life.

Jacqueline Lapsley argues that prophetic literature opposes the later Christian agapic ethic with a eudaimonic one that incorporates enjoyment of family, adequate food and drink, and meaningful work on a personal level with the propriety of peaceful and just relations on the communal level established and maintained by obedience to Torah, the teachings of God broadly understood.

---

9. See Ellen T. Charry, *By the Renewing of Your Minds: The Pastoral Function of Christian Doctrine* (New York: Oxford, 1997).

10. The other essays in this volume make the same general point, of course, but I choose to focus on these four as representative of the Tanakh's three parts (Torah, Prophets, and Writings) as well as representative of the present collection of essays as a whole.

"[H]appiness inheres in participation in a community centered on Torah," because the good of the self and other are inextricably bound together.[11] Later Christian self-emptying is not countenanced. "Rather, [happiness in Isaiah] offers a vision of the self deeply and meaningfully connected with other selves, living in a community marked by profound relationship to God and to one another."[12] This prophetic vision of happiness is balanced and down-to-earth compared to the taut Christian teaching that presses to an extreme. While the Christian teaching is that happiness is the result of faith that God will disregard the awful truth about a person, Lapsley concludes that, at least for Isaiah (although it may be a widely shared Israelite perspective), "true happiness *inheres in* the life faithfully lived."[13]

Lapsley notes the absence of any contingency in this vision that would qualify it. Such caution resounds in the Psalter, however, which stresses misery more than happiness, especially through lament. In William P. Brown's essay, despite misfortune and misery, we see that the overriding tone of the Psalter is praise. *'Asrê-* or happy-sayings, sometimes anachronistically referred to as makarisms (from the Greek *makarios*, "fortunate, blessed, happy"),[14] exemplify human flourishing even while knowing misery. Hebrew *'ašrê*, perhaps best translated as "felicitous," highlights divine agency. These verses express gratitude for divine blessings. The happy person is righteous, balancing divine with human agency in response. "Happiness denotes a salutary state of being that is both achieved and granted, received and attained," writes Brown.[15] It is constituted by the fulfillment of desire for worthy goals, and for the psalmists the ultimate goal is God. Wanting rightly leads to the sacred. "To be happy is, in the estimation of Psalms 111–112, to be godly."[16] A happy life combines a pious life with God's ongoing gift of salvation from suffering. Real happiness, Brown concludes, "charts a rocky path through . . . pain, never around it."[17]

Biblical wisdom literature sustains the biblical themes of managing the vicissitudes of life, including negotiating social conflict through acting wisely in order to maximize the good and minimize the bad. In her essay, Carol A. Newsom examines Proverbs and Qoheleth. The former is sanguine that wise living brings

---

11. Jacqueline Lapsley, "A Happy Blend: Isaiah's Vision of Happiness (and Beyond)," 76.

12. Ibid., 79.

13. Ibid., 92.

14. For the New Testament beatitudes, see Carl R. Holladay's essay in this volume as well as the essay by Greg Carey.

15. William P. Brown, "Happiness and Its Discontents in the Psalms," 103.

16. Ibid., 105.

17. Ibid., 115.

well-being at the personal, familial, and social levels. Wisdom need not be garnered through bad experience, but can be passed to the next generation through proper instruction. Wisdom and goodness lead to life while folly and wickedness run to death. Wisdom protects from danger, threat, and instability. Life is assumed to be masterable and a careful life is rewarding. Attunement to the ebb and flow of life bring a sense of serenity across a lifetime.

For its part, the book of Ecclesiastes holds a more skeptical view. Qoheleth sees the absence of a stable order from which one might anticipate positive results. Concerted effort is futile in the face of life's contingencies and so the pursuit of happiness is doomed. The most one can expect is to enjoy momentary pleasure. This "biblical hedonism" stands rather alone in the canon, however. The foundational biblical assumption is that God has made reality good and stable enough that one can exercise some meaningful measure of control over one's life, even though contingency and the suffering that it may bring cannot be foreclosed.

Terence E. Fretheim takes a strikingly fresh approach to the biblical data by looking at God's happiness. Far from the classical view that God is emotionless, Scripture ascribes multiple emotions to God including being happy. Fretheim's approach marks a *novum* for both biblical and theological studies.[18] Citing texts from most of the books examined by the other essays, but also from Job, Jeremiah, Hosea, and Haggai, Fretheim argues that God is happy when his relationship with people thrives and when God enjoys the world and its creatures. "Creation is a joy-filled task and a joy-filled result for both Creator and created—in the beginning, in the ongoing, and in the new creation."[19] Happiness is God's gift to people illustrated by the gift of the woman to the man in Gen 2:19–22. This makes the man happy and this is as God intends. When creatures (both human and nonhuman) flourish as God intended, both they and God rejoice and are happy.

Nothing in the four essays reviewed here supports the later Christian views that terrestrial happiness is not worth hoping for because it is unsustainable or that happiness is limited to relief of dread at the prospect of hell. Moreover, there is no hint here of the wrath of God so often attributed to the Tanakh and that characterizes the Augustinian tradition. Let Marcion rest! Indeed, the Tanakh's openness to both divine and human happiness balances the Anselmian view that God struggles within the divine self to have mercy prevail.[20]

---

18. See also Charry, *God and the Art of Happiness.*

19. Terence E. Fretheim, "God, Creation, and the Pursuit of Happiness," 38.

20. One could compare at this point the one passage in the Talmud, *b. Berakhot* 7a, which states that God himself prays and specifies precisely what it is that God prays: "May it be My Will that My mercy may suppress My anger, and that My mercy may prevail over My [other]

In light of the more positive and homey views in the Tanakh, the dour inclination of Western theology appears at best one-sided, if not distorted. Its portrayal of God as so angry that only death stays the rage betrays a morbid fear of humanity on God's part. God must hold human ferocity in check by threatening punishment, creating dread in the unruly human heart. That dread, in turn, can only be restrained by the hope of undeserved reprieve by dint of the selflessness of God himself.[21] The drama of judgment and mercy fight to the death both within the divine heart in the seamless work of the Father and the Son, and in the soul of every Christian who swings between consolation and desolation, faith and despair.

Over the Christian centuries, God has been portrayed as becoming increasingly disillusioned with the human creatures he set out to enjoy. In the hands of anxious theologians who became ever more cynical about human goodness and more persuaded of the irrefragability of the pernicious side of human nature, God became increasingly hostile, judgmental, and alienated from creation, at least its human element. The Western tradition has thought in binaries: either saint or sinner, either spiritual or carnal, either good or evil, either heaven or hell, either judgment or mercy. This polarization may work well rhetorically but it is not as helpful psychologically.

4. The Continuing Story of Happiness

Questioning the psychological helpfulness of binary thinking leads to the theologically intriguing question of whether the portrayal of God's increasing cynicism about humankind does justice to the nimbleness of God's psychological repertoire. Have other divine emotions and traits been overlooked by the binary polarity of wrath or mercy?

Before proceeding to that discussion, a prior question arises because the very idea of divine emotion is ruled out by the classic doctrine of God. Theologians adopted the Greek philosophical notion of divine perfections—simplicity, impassibility, immutability omnipresence, omnibenevolence, and omnipotence chief among

---

attributes, so that I may deal with my children in the attribute of mercy and, on their behalf, stop short of the limit of strict justice" (for the translation and fuller discussion, see Kimberly Christine Patton, *Religion of the Gods: Ritual, Paradox, and Reflexivity* [Oxford: Oxford University Press, 2009], 249–81, esp. 270–72). *Berakhot* 7a goes on to note that, while God is angry every day (cf. Ps 7:11), God's anger lasts only a moment (cf. Ps 30:5), which is then "defined as one fifty-eight thousand eight hundred and eighty-eighth part of an hour," or six-tenths (.06) of a second (see ibid., 444 n. 96). I thank Brent Strawn for bringing this material to my attention.

21. Admittedly, the Torah portrays divine wrath as unstable and potentially vicious in different instances—for example, Gen 18:20–28 and Exod 32:1–14. I take these to be local incidents that are quite different from the broad Christian generalization that all persons at all times and in all places deserve death by virtue of being human.

them. These assumptions rule out the possibility that God has an emotional life. In this view, God can be neither angry nor compassionate. The divine perfections took their seat at the beginning of most every organized presentation of Christian doctrine since the Middle Ages, but they were in place centuries before.

Classical metaphysics is perhaps best represented in Christian theology by Thomas Aquinas. Aquinas's most famous writing may be the presentation of divine nature as simple, perfect, good, limitless, ubiquitous, immutable, eternal, and supremely one.[22] God cannot experience emotion because that breeches the rules of simplicity and immutability. Yet if God cannot genuinely engage what is not God lest it imply multiplicity in God, what is one to make of a central biblical text on the divine attributes like Exod 34:6–7, which assumes that God has a complex emotional life—loving, being slow to anger, yet punishing severely when needed? Scads of other biblical texts are similarly rendered meaningless or would need to be treated figuratively, including those that depict God as jealous, wrathful, and punishing (e.g., Exod 20:5; 34:14; Deut 4:24; 5:9; 6:15; 32:16, 19, 21; Josh 24:19; Job 36:33; Ps 79:3; Ezek 36:5–6; Joel 2:18; Nah 1:2; Zech 8:2, 14; Matt 3:10, 12; 5:22; 7:19; 13:40, 42; 18:8–9; 25:41; Mark 9:43–49; Luke 3:9, 17; John 15:6); those that portray God as loving and compassionate (e.g., Exod 2:23–25; Deut 7:7–8; Judg 2:18; Ps 72:13; Isa 49:10; 63:9; Hos 1:7; 2:23; 11:1–4; Joel 2.18); and those that testify that Jesus experienced emotions (e.g., Matt 9:36; 14:14; 15:32; 20:34; Mark 6:34; 8:2; Luke 7:13; 19:41; 22:44). If the doctrine of God cannot countenance God's emotional life, there is something wrong with the *doctrine*—it is not fully responsive to the fullness of the biblical witness.

The early theological tradition struggled with the tension between Greek imperturbability and Hebrew passion. In the fourth century, Apollinaris, a priest in Syria, argued that Christ could only be a single person if he were the unity of a human body with the divine Logos. This excluded a human mind or soul from Christ. This position was condemned by the church, which at Chalcedon adopted the doctrine of "hypostatic union"—the claim that Christ was a single person yet composed of two complete natures, one human, one divine, so that the fullness of humanity would include a human soul. This would seem to include a complete emotional life as well. Yet the union was "without confusion, without change, without division, without separation."[23] The qualifications are to protect divine simplicity, immutability, and impassibility. What however, does it mean to be united to something but not affected by it?

---

22. Saint Thomas Aquinas, *Existence and Nature of God (1a.2–11)* (trans. Timothy McDermott; Cambridge: Blackfriars and New York: McGraw-Hill, 1964).

23. These four qualifications ("adverbs") of the hypostatic union were formally adopted at the Council of Chalcedon in 451 CE, perhaps not to explain but at least to describe the orthodox teaching on the unity of the person of Christ.

Abjuring divine emotionality, Chalcedonian norms assign Scripture's attestations to Jesus's experiences of emotion to the human nature to assure that God would not experience emotion. This created a hole between creation and redemption by driving a wedge between God and God's ability to relate to us emotionally. As a result, redemption, while its means were material (the incarnate Son) could not be material but became noetic.[24] Accordingly, salvation was completely spiritualized, separating it—to cite a critical example—from Israel's redemption from Egypt, which was manifestly material. Only with liberation theology did Christian theology begin to reclaim a material vision of redemption. Eschatology drifted into immortality as a nonbodily enjoyment of God where the saints await reunion with their bodies at the second coming of Christ.

The preference for stasis that drove classical theism was tested in the twentieth century when insistence on the *apatheia* of God was shown to be ill-suited to relate to the real world that theists continued to insist God created and loved. Charles Hartshorne's neoclassical dipolar theism argues that God is not monopolar and simple but characterized by complex contrasts—abstract and concrete, absolute and relative, eternal and temporal, infinite and finite, actual and potential—and that these require one another for meaningfulness and for the cogency of cause and effect.[25] That God is both abstract and concrete means that God can engage creation without self-contradiction. Although neoclassical philosophers did not discuss the point, the concrete, relative, finite "pole" of divinity provides for God's emotional life.

The criticism of impassibility struck a chord with Christian theologians because passibility makes sense of the biblical God who is depicted as genuinely engaged with creation to the point of suffering in, with, and through human life itself.[26] Karl Barth recognized the value of the critique and adapted his theology accordingly. In an essay on Barth's critique of classical theism, Don Schweitzer argues that, for Barth, classical theism is a form of idolatry because it poses a

---

24. Of course, the case could be made that even material means of redemption challenged the spiritualizing impact of Greek influence.

25. See Charles Hartshorne, *Reality as Social Process: Studies in Metaphysics and Religion* (Glencoe, IL: Free Press, 1953); and Charles Hartshorne and William L. Reese, eds., *Philosophers Speak of God* (Chicago: University of Chicago Press, 1953).

26. See Paul S. Fiddes, *The Creative Suffering of God* (Oxford: Clarendon, 1988); Terence E. Fretheim, *The Suffering of God: An Old Testament Perspective* (OBT; Philadelphia: Fortress, 1984); Jürgen Moltmann, *The Crucified God: The Cross of Christ as the Foundation and Criticism of Christian Theology* (trans. R. A. Wilson and John Bowden; Minneapolis: Fortress, 1993 [German orig: 1973]); and, earlier, J. K. Mozley, *The Impassibility of God: A Survey of Christian Thought* (Cambridge: Cambridge University Press, 1926).

lifeless God.[27] This is a strong way of putting the neoclassical argument, but Barth is posing God as self-moved being against Aristotle's unmoved mover.

Although coming at the issue from the perspective of revelation rather than metaphysics, Barth is sympathetic to neoclassical theism because it enables theology to account for revelation and divine love. Yet he stops short of its implication that contingency inheres in God because that would curtail divine sovereignty by admitting that the world is meaningful to God. Schweitzer points out that Barth's Reformed insistence on absolute divine sovereignty renders his doctrine of God incoherent because if God's relationships with us do not mean anything to God, if creation does not make a difference to God, then creating becomes an arbitrary act on God's part.[28] If Barth offers no reason why God created simply in order to protect divine transcendence, he has just repeated the problem of classical theism, and his claim that the self-revelation of God is an act of love loses its force.

Going beyond Barth, Jürgen Moltmann, influenced by Luther and Abraham Heschel,[29] carried the suffering of Christ into God in his book *The Crucified God*:

> When the crucified Jesus is called the "image of the invisible God," the meaning is that *this* is God and God is like *this*. God is not greater than he is in this humiliation. God is no more glorious than he is in this self-surrender. God is not more powerful than he is in this helplessness. God is not more divine than he is in this humanity.[30]

While Chalcedon drew a line between the suffering of Christ's humanity and his divinity, Moltmann crossed the line. Here, God suffers and perhaps is even defined by it.

Moltmann went where Barth feared to tread. Christ's suffering is God's own.[31] Theopaschitism (the claim that God suffers) has since become commonplace in our time.[32] One important corollary of the idea, however—namely, that God experiences joy and happiness—has not yet been discussed.

---

27. Don Schweitzer, "Karl Barth's Critique of Classical Theism," *TJT* 18 (2002): 231–44.

28. Ibid., 238–40.

29. See Abraham J. Heschel, *The Prophets* (repr. ed.; New York: Perennial Classics, 2001).

30. Moltmann, *The Crucified God*, 205 (emphasis his).

31. As powerful as Moltmann's work is, it is not without criticism. See, e.g., David A. Scott, "Ethics on a Trinitarian Basis: Moltmann's *The Crucified God*," *AThR* 60 (1978): 166–79.

32. See Ronald Goetz, "The Suffering God: The Rise of a New Orthodoxy," *ChrCent* 103 (1986): 385–89.

This seeming digression from our topic is not a digression at all. In order for systematic theology to speak about the happy life, divine and human happiness must be of a piece. Human happiness cannot be said to displease God for that would mean it was a form of disobedience. Divine happiness cannot be said to harm humanity for that would depict God as sadistic. Rather, admitting that God has a rich emotional life enables one to say that God and people energize and fulfill one another when their flourishing results from appropriate regard for one another. It may not be unusual to suggest that people need God to flourish. It is new, however, to recognize that human flourishing enables God to be the God of a thriving creation that God wants to enjoy to the utmost.

God's ability to celebrate creation's flourishing is essential for us to be able to trust God. Who would obey a remote God to whom our thriving does not matter? Without believing that God is truly invested in creation, hope for humanity's future is foolish. The Exodus and the resurrection indeed strengthen hope in their turn, but if the very nature of God is not to give life and nurture it joyously and carefully from the beginning of time, is God worthy of devotion and obedience? To worship one who holds his transcendence and sovereignty above his love will not earn the trust of those who continually try yet fail to obey what they believe is the way that God would truly have them go. Human frailty is such that we will only obey one we trust utterly. At best, an aloof God is the god of the philosophers and that is not the living God of the biblical matriarchs and patriarchs.

The preceding leads me to follow my beloved teacher, Paul van Buren, who argued that there are good reasons to accept the biblical view that God is an embodied person, indeed the normative person from whom our personal reality derives.[33] A rich emotional life cannot be denied to this God.[34] While there are problems with the view, it is preferable to the alternatives that are incoherent. As van Buren notes, according to Scripture, God's relationship to creation is personal and he adds that we become aware of ourselves as persons from our likeness to God.[35] Without fanfare, van Buren sets before us the view that God norms our

---

33. See Paul M. van Buren, *A Theology of the Jewish-Christian Reality*, Vol. 1: *Discerning the Way* (New York: Seabury, 1980), 102–11.

34. In biblical studies, the main proponent of such a rich divine "interiority" is Walter Brueggemann. Among other works, see his *Theology of the Old Testament: Testimony, Dispute, Advocacy* (Minneapolis: Fortress, 1997). See also Heschel, *The Prophets, passim*; and, more briefly, Brent A. Strawn and Brad D. Strawn, "Prophecy and Psychology," in *Dictionary of the Old Testament: Prophets* (eds. Mark J. Boda and J. Gordon McConville; Downers Grove, IL: IVP Academic, 2012), 610–23.

35. Van Buren, *Discerning the Way*, 102–11. See also J. Richard Middleton, *The Liberating Image: The* Imago Dei *in Genesis 1* (Grand Rapids: Brazos, 2005); and Brent A. Strawn, "Comparative Approaches: History, Theory, and the Image of God," in *Method Matters: Essays on the*

relationships through God's relationship with creation.[36] While we can say little about God's body because it is mostly invisible to us, Scripture's depictions of God's relationally driven insights and actions may perhaps edify our own embodied lives.[37] In what follows, I pursue this line of reasoning.

If, as van Buren suggests, God is the person who norms personhood, God's relationships with creation are those against which we may measure our own and God's actions and decisions for and with creation. Those divine relationships with creation also help us discern and plan what our actions and decisions should strive to be. Let us begin at the point at which Schweitzer noted that Barth stopped: God's reason for creating at all. Schweitzer notes that Barth gives the traditional Reformed reason that creation is "to provide a theater for God's glory."[38] That is, of course, a reason, and it does protect divine transcendence because it is not something that God needs on the rule of divine self-sufficiency. Just as Anselm noted that human sin cannot dishonor God, so human glorification of God cannot truly glorify God if God cannot receive it.

Neither point is compelling. Anselm said that the most human sin can accomplish is to create an aura of disorder in the world, but it cannot dishonor God.[39] By the same token, if glorifying God cannot enhance divine glory because God is perfect glory, what motivation is there for living to that end other than obedience, on the assumption that failing to offer God what God does not need may land us in hell? But if that too is impossible because neither glory nor obedience can affect God, then human life before God is indeed pointless beyond the personal satisfaction of living honorably. In short, theologies that seek a high doctrine of divine sovereignty need to beware of undercutting righteous living. This has been the case ever since the late theology of Augustine of Hippo.

To reckon with the fact that God takes human life seriously presses the point that God's relationship to creation works for and/or on God in some way. If God's creating and continuing to relate to the world means much to God, it may be that the creation is for God's own enjoyment and pleasure. Further, if God is not a sadist, then God's experience of the world matters to God for the sake of

---

Interpretation of the Hebrew Bible in Honor of David L. Petersen (eds. Joel M. LeMon and Kent Harold Richards; SBLRBS 56; Atlanta: Society of Biblical Literature, 2009), 117–42.

36. See also Terence E. Fretheim, *God and World in the Old Testament: A Relational Theology of Creation* (Nashville: Abingdon, 2005).

37. For a recent study of God's body in ancient Israel and its ancient Near Eastern context, see Benjamin D. Sommer, *The Bodies of God and the World of Ancient Israel* (New York: Cambridge University Press, 2011).

38. Schweitzer, "Karl Barth's Critique of Classical Theism," 239.

39. Anselm, *Why God Became Man*, §1.15 (pp. 72–73).

God's own happiness. That is, enjoying the world serves God's pleasure and the enjoyment of God's creativity and love. Engaging us does not chain God to finitude but is for God's own satisfaction. God is internally related to the world because to suggest otherwise plants futility at the base of the human relationship with God. God wants to love us both because God enjoys loving and because by loving us we learn to love well. In this way, God leads us into all truth and joy.

Let us now turn to Scriptural examples of God's emotional versatility that display divine enjoyment and lead us to our own.

5. Probing God's Psychological Probity

That God suffers with creation's groaning for redemption follows not only Paul (Rom 8:22–23), but antecedently Exod 2:23–25, which highlights the divine capacity for compassionate action as God responds to the Israelites' cry for help amidst slavery. Israel's cry reminds God of the covenant with the patriarchs, moving God to rescue Israel. The last clause in Exod 2:25 could be read passively (especially if one followed the lead of the LXX): "and it was known by God." The NRSV translates the clause "God took notice of them," supplying an object to the verb in question, which is usually transitive in Hebrew, but which here lacks an object in the Hebrew text. But this translation is not ideal because the previous verse already indicates that God heard the Israelites' cry. The Hebrew verb used in Exod 2:25 is √yd'; it is typically more intimate than the English word "notice" suggests, and in some contexts connotes sexual intercourse. The verb thus implies God's intimate, emotional engagement with Israel in its suffering. As Deut 7:8 puts it, God simply loves Israel for no apparent reason.

Both Judaism and Christianity seized on this point and have clung to it consistently in various ways. Whether Israel is the Jewish people (as Jews believe) or the church (as Christians believe), both traditions stand on the rock of divine love. If God has no emotional life, and divine love is but a manner of speaking that condescends to the limits of human cognition, then both Jews and Christians hope, pray, and cry out in vain. If God does not truly enjoy loving his creatures, our enjoyment of that love is vacuous and all seems lost.

Compassion is one expression of love. Empathy is another. Fretheim points to the creation of woman as a gift to the first man (Gen 2:21–23) that "happifies" him.[40] But looking at the immediately preceding material in that pericope sheds light on divine empathy. In Gen 2:18, God sees that the human being God has created to enjoy the bountiful garden made for him, is lonely and needs a partner. So God sends the animals and the human establishes a relationship with each by

40. See Fretheim, "God, Creation, and the Pursuit of Happiness," 40–41.

naming them. The human does not complain, but God realizes that this is not adequate. No animal is the right partner. God's first try did not work and so God tries again. This time, one made from the first person's own body turns out to be the perfect partner with the result that the first person realizes himself to be a man and his partner a woman. He rejoices: "at last" this is of myself; this one is right for me.

This brief story, occurring so early in Genesis, indicates that God is not above trial and error. God wants things to be right for God's most sophisticated and beloved human creature. It is telling that God did not get it right the first time. Not that the ambulatory creatures were a mistake—by no means! But God is willing, maybe even eager, to work with the first person until he can celebrate the one who is his own and with whom he can be intimate. Creation is on its way to flourishing. Should God not be delighted in the result and pleased with himself and his work?

God's display of empathy and concern for the first human establishes a positive relationship between them in which they both rejoice. Consider then God's disappointment when the first pair disobeys the single prohibition that was given to them. From God's perspective, eating the fruit is not simply disobeying a rule; it is betrayal of a relationship of trust. God is hurt.[41]

That God anticipates the trial of loneliness in the only creature that images him suggests that God is psychologically attentive and so understands loneliness and empathizes with it. How could it not be so? May we extrapolate from this to suggest that God does not enjoy loneliness or betrayal any more than human creatures would? Scripture does not tell us why God created—might it be to become companioned and thus avoid loneliness just as the creation of woman quelled loneliness for the man?[42] Here we speculate, but the deeply personal portrayal of God in Scripture who experiences empathy, even anguish for creatures, gets hurt, responds to cries of misery, listens to reasoned argument, relents of anger as well as acts on it, and exhibits all manner of parental concern, calls for an expanded appreciation of God's emotional life because creation (including humanity) matters to God.

Even if one considers all the anthropomorphic divine language to be metaphorical in order to protect metaphysical concerns, by speaking so humanly, the

---

41. For divine pathos vis-à-vis human sin, see Fretheim, *The Suffering of God*; and idem, *Creation Untamed: The Bible, God, and Natural Disasters* (Grand Rapids: Baker Academic, 2010).

42. Trinitarian companionship is understood to be outside of time. With creation, God creates and moves into time-space as and perhaps for companionship so that the beauty, wisdom, and goodness that are God may have a new and vigorous form of life. From our side of creation, the dynamism of the trinitarian life sought a new form of companionship, not wanting to be alone, in a manner of speaking.

biblical writers nevertheless invite their readers to think themselves into God's parental place, loving, worrying, getting angry, and being relieved and grateful when the children manage to find their way with considered guidance to the extent that they can accept it.[43]

This psychological (and theological) line of reasoning suggests that God created the world for personal reasons, not that God needed to be glorified or exalted to boost God's self-image against other reputed gods but rather to enjoy God's own ability to love, care for, nourish, and guide those for whom God is responsible. If God created to enjoy himself and for his own delight, creation's flourishing must be a source of divine pleasure.

6. A Happy Conclusion

In sum: humanity's flourishing gives God great satisfaction. On this view, the deep Christian anxiety that one can never please God is turned on its head. It is in flourishing that humankind pleases God, who sees the work of his hands at its optimum. According to Irenaeus, the glory of God is humanity fully alive.[44] By contrast, a perishing creation cannot but distress God. Viewed in this light, divine anger is an expression of disappointment rather than righteous indignation.[45] Judgment and punishment may call people to sober self-assessment; they may not be the best motivators to a godly life, however. Luke 4, for example, notes that Elijah's raising of the son of the Sidonian widow (1 Kgs 17:8–24) and Elisha's curing of Naaman's leprosy (2 Kgs 5:1–15) persuaded these Gentiles to worship the God of Israel. Surely divine encouragement is more effective than punishment (or its threat) in service to creation's flourishing. And if human flourishing is more delightful to God than its perishing (cf. Ezek 18:23; 33:11), theologians would do well to attend to God's and our mutual delight in one another more than to God's displeasure at our failures and our consequent guilt and distress.

This essay has suggested that Western Christian theology must balance its heavy emphasis on divine wrath by turning to biblical sources that offer a more complex picture of God's relationship to creation. The next step in doing that

---

43. See Brent A. Strawn, "'Israel, My Child': The Ethics of a Biblical Metaphor," in *The Child in the Bible* (eds. Marcia Bunge, Terence E. Fretheim, and Beverly R. Gaventa; Grand Rapids: Eerdmans, 2008), 103–40.

44. Irenaeus, *Adversus Haereses*, 4.34.5–7.

45. One of the earliest theologians to distinguish divine disappointment from outrage was Athanasius of Alexandria. See his *On the Incarnation of the Word*, in Athanasius, *Contra Gentes and De Incarnatione* (trans. Robert W. Thompson; OECT; Oxford: Press, 1971), 60–61. For a similar point with reference to the prophets, see Heschel, *The Prophets*, 358–92.

would be to rethink penal substitutionary atonement as God's primary soteriological vehicle—an idea that became common in the second millennium. Unfortunately, Western theology has neglected the soteriological implications of the incarnation itself. That God became human is an act of divine condescension but it is not only that. It is also an act of human elevation. Even if the four adverbs describing Christ's divine-human nature—"without confusion, without change, without division, without separation"—are more descriptive than explanatory, the lifting of human life into the divine life cannot but be the corollary of divine condescension. According to Athanasius, the Word was made human, that we might be made divine.[46] Being carried into the divine life by the Son's becoming human, being placed in the power of his death by baptism, and being made God's field, God's building, and God's temple that is indwelt by God's Spirit (1 Corinthians 3) warrant more than gratitude that Christ stood in our death-deserving place. Being made a participant by baptism and faith in the drama of the salvation of the cosmos that God is about is more than being made right before God. It is all these things but yet still more: It deputizes Christians into God's happy project of loving creation into flourishing.

---

46. Athanasius, *On the Incarnation of the Word*, §54.

A Constructed Happiness

A RESPONSE FROM PRACTICAL THEOLOGY

Thomas G. Long

You probably imagine that philosophy is complicated enough, but let me tell you, this is nothing compared to the hardship of being a good architect. Back when I was building the house for my sister in Vienna I was so exhausted at the end of the day that the only thing I was still able to do was to go every evening to the cinema.

—LUDWIG WITTGENSTEIN[1]

1. The Architecture of Congregational Happiness

In the opening paragraphs of his *The Architecture of Happiness*, cultural critic Alain de Botton pictures a terraced house on a leafy residential street, home to a family of four. It is mid-morning, and a few hours earlier the last member of the family raced out the front door to the day's obligations. Imagining the now silent and unoccupied house almost as a living thing, de Botton writes, "The house gives signs of enjoying the emptiness. It is rearranging itself after the night, clearing its pipes and cracking its joints." The architecture of this house, its arrangement of living spaces and pathways, has influenced and shaped those who live within, and the house itself carries the memory of and bears testimony to the human history that has taken place within its walls. It has, says de Botton, "grown into a knowledgeable witness":

---

1. Horia Marinescu, "Meditatii pe Marginea unei Expozitii Monografice de la Mak, Viena," *Arhitectura* (August–September 2002), translated from Romanian by Aranca Munteanu as "Vienna 1928—Wittgenstein House: Architecture as Reflection," online at www.horia-marinescu.net/texte.php?lang=en&;text=4 (accessed 7/12/2011).

It has been party to early seductions, it has watched homework being written, it has observed swaddled babies freshly arrived from the hospital, it has been surprised in the middle of the night by whispered conferences in the kitchen. . . . It has provided not only physical but psychological sanctuary. It has been a guardian of identity. Over the years, its owners have returned from periods away and, on looking around them, remembered who they were. . . . Although this house may lack solutions to a great many of its occupants' ills, its rooms nevertheless give evidence of a happiness.[2]

Architecture is about more than the pitch of a roof and the placement of walls. It is about making spaces for work, pleasure, and rest, and the crafting of pathways for movement and interaction. Walk into a home, and the floor plan guides one to the heart of activity—perhaps the den, the kitchen, or the backyard pool. Or enter the den of any home and observe what has been designed as the focal point of activity—a large-screen television, a set of bookshelves, or a window overlooking a garden. One can tell what activities take place here and what values are prominent. A house bears "knowledgeable witness" and gives evidence of the joy or sadness, the despair or happiness, the fullness or emptiness of life within.

The New Testament employs the metaphor of a "house" to describe the church. In Heb 3:5–6, the people of God are described as a living house—Moses was faithful *in* the house; Jesus was faithful *over* the house; and confident and hopeful followers of Christ *are* the house. Second John 1:10 warns against permitting any teachers other than those faithful to Christ into the house: "Do not receive into the house or welcome anyone who comes to you and does not bring this teaching." First Peter 2:5 pictures the church as a house undergoing perpetual construction: "[L]ike living stones, let yourselves be built into a spiritual house, to be a holy priesthood, to offer spiritual sacrifices acceptable to God through Jesus Christ."

Indeed, pastors and others who guide religious communities are much like renovation architects, working in response to ever-changing social circumstances in order to fashion congregational environments. Church leaders constantly remodel metaphorical houses of faith so that they gather together people in faithful patterns and provide some semblance of meaningful structure for the wild variety of people and the dizzying mixture of conviction and doubt, courage and petty bickering, acts of love and deeds of betrayal, signs of division and yearnings for unity, truth-telling and deception, birth and death, ecstasy and boredom

2. Alain de Botton, *The Architecture of Happiness* (New York: Vintage, 2008), 1–2.

that constitute routine congregational life. The living architectural designs of congregations, if they are responsive to the ways of the Spirit as it breathes in a particular time and place, bear "knowledgeable witness" to the gospel and provide spaces for people to experience the happiness coherent with the Christian life.

2. *Who We Are, Who We Hope to Be*

How shall the church allow itself, as 1 Peter urges, to be built into a spiritual house? In particular, how shall pastors, preachers, and teachers lead congregations to construct their lives together in such ways that they provide spaces in which people of faith "remember who they are" and fashion themselves into houses that give "evidence of a happiness"? A clue can be found, perhaps, in a key principle of architecture: successful buildings not only provide suitable environments for the activities of the present, they also embody a sense of movement and direction toward people's best dreams for the future. In other words, a well-designed building is an expression not merely of who we are but of who we hope to be.

Take, for example, the open "kitchen-dining-great room" arrangement popular in contemporary American homes. At one level, such a design simply facilitates what actually happens in the space—namely, guests relax on sofas and chairs while continuing to have conversation and company with those preparing food in the kitchen, which is then served at a casual table in the same general space. The configuration nicely accommodates who we are and what we do. But it also signifies who we would like to be: open, friendly, informal, nonpompous, accessible people, with no secrets or closed doors, whose lives are well-integrated and who generously welcome others into the center of our lives. The virtues of the space are generated by and point toward its *telos*; or, to put it theologically, the meals served in this space are aimed toward a hoped-for and more perfect banquet. The moments of happiness discovered around hearth and table are drawn forward by a dream of a full happiness not yet achieved. In secular dress, the arrangement of the space for present practices reveals an eschatology.

Several of the essays in this volume describe the biblical understanding of happiness as just such a tensive balance between present practice and yet-to-be-realized hope:

1. Carl R. Holladay, in his exploration of Jesus's beatitudes, as found in variant forms in Matthew and Luke, notes that "since the mid-nineteenth century, three interpretive options have emerged: the kingdom of God is (i) a future reality, (ii)

a present reality, or (iii) a future reality that has already begun."[3] Holladay argues "that both present and future dimensions are contained within the beatitudes" and points out that Jesus's language in both versions of the beatitudes "is evocative rather than prescriptive," which "gives it an open-ended rather than definitive quality."[4] The inherent ambiguity about whether the beatitudes are about the present or the future has, Holladay says, lured some interpreters "to accent one or the other dimension and sometimes both."[5] Holladay, however, claims,

> that respecting the fluidity of the language of the beatitudes not only honors the built-in ambiguity, possibly traceable to Jesus himself but certainly attributable to the Evangelists, but also introduces a useful perspective for understanding the vision of happiness encoded in them.[6]

Looking, for example, at the mingling of present and future tenses in Matthew's version of the Beatitudes, Holladay observes,

> The juxtaposition of present and future tenses is jarring, and this was probably what Matthew intended to achieve. As a rhetorically sensitive interpreter of Jesus' teachings, Matthew expects his readers (and hearers) to allow the present "is" to have a future, unrealized dimension, while at the same time allowing the future "will be" to oscillate between present and future forms of experience.[7]

Jesus's beatitudes refer to the enigmatic symbol, the kingdom of God, but in doing so, they are occupied with the concerns of everyday life. "By introducing such a wide range of human emotions and experiences," Holladay writes,

> all of which connect directly with lived human experience, Matthew's Jesus locates happiness within the complexity and contradiction common to everyone. . . . The overarching promise is that the kingdom of heaven belongs to those at every stage of human experience, high or low, and that it is theirs as both promise and fulfillment. It is never theirs to clutch

---

3. See Carl R. Holladay, "The Beatitudes: Happiness and the Kingdom of God," 154–55.

4. Ibid., 156.

5. Ibid.

6. Ibid.

7. Ibid., 158.

completely, to own or possess wholly, but neither is it a distant hope for which they can only dream as they reflect on the possibility of participating in the rich store of eschatological blessings.[8]

2. Colleen Shantz, who addresses the epistles of Paul, recognizes that Paul can perhaps be better understood as a pastor than as a systematic theologian. As such, his principal goal was comprised of "persistent and creative efforts to keep the small groups of Christ-followers functioning as communities of care and love."[9] To put this in the terms of our architectural metaphor, Paul was a congregational architect whose aim was to design the ecclesial house so that the life within was characterized by the pattern of Christ. In order to do this, Paul sometimes called upon compelling structural images, such as the church as "the body of Christ," or upon environmental virtues, especially *agape* love, or upon the power of his personal relationship with the congregation.

However, even more remarkable, according to Shantz, is Paul's articulation of an eschatological worldview that shapes the present congregational practices and customs. Paul, she says, is

> oriented to the future in a way that places his current difficulties in broader perspective. That orientation depends in part on his sense of the imminent end. Because he believes that God will soon intervene Paul can exhort those in slavery to live as if they were freed persons of the Lord (1 Cor 7:22) and exhort those who are married to live as if they had no spouse because "the appointed time has grown very short" (1 Cor 7:29).[10]

A key component of this eschatology is the idea of the dying and rising Christ, which, Shantz argues, becomes for Paul the master pattern for congregational life. By shaping their lives according to this pattern, the faithful participate in the life of Christ now and also in Christ's ultimate eschatological triumph to come. This allows current hardships not to destroy the possibility of happiness but, to the contrary, to enhance it because they are signs of participation in the very life of Christ. The faithful, like Paul, are "persecuted, but not forsaken; struck down, but not destroyed; always carrying in the body the death of Jesus, so that the life

---

8. Ibid., 160.

9. See Colleen Shantz, "'I Have Learned to Be Content': Happiness according to St. Paul," 198.

10. Ibid., 199.

of Jesus may also be manifested in our bodies" (2 Cor 4:9–10). For Paul, Shantz claims, "dying and rising have become his hermeneutic for all of life, not only for the life to come."[11] Paul can face even the prospect of his own death "with what might properly be called happiness."[12]

3. Greg Carey explores biblical apocalyptic literature and finds that, for the apocalyptic writers, "happiness comes in different flavors" involving "a spectrum from inaugurated happiness to future-only happiness."[13] On one end (the other-worldly side) of that spectrum stand books like Revelation and Daniel, which see happiness essentially in terms of resistance, saying no to the imperial oppressive demands. Here the blessings of God, promised to those who remain faithful, reside essentially in the eschatological future, visible on the horizon but just barely evident in the present experience of suffering. On the other end (the more this-worldly side) of the spectrum are the apocalyptic strands in the synoptic Gospels and Paul, which, Carey says, share with Revelation and Daniel a portrait of "persecution as the lot of Jesus's followers,"[14] but they are relatively more positive about how the blessings of that future may be experienced in the present. "[I]n Christ," he says, "God has broken into the present with a host of blessings."[15]

Regardless of where it falls on the spectrum, Carey argues, biblical apocalyptic discourse:

> addresses the twin concerns of identity and commitment. That is, apocalyptic discourse constructs a communal narrative for the saints, who understand themselves as partners with God and testify to God's work in the world in the face of great opposition. . . . This marks one of the basic signs of human happiness—the sense that one's life is oriented toward a greater, compelling good.[16]

In each of these three essays on New Testament approaches to the theme of happiness there is an insistence that, for the New Testament writers, happiness is

---

11. Ibid.

12. Ibid., 200.

13. See Greg Carey "Finding Happiness in Apocalyptic Literature," 223.

14. Ibid.

15. Ibid.

16. Ibid., 223–24.

an eschatological promise with present-tense implications.[17] For those who belong to Christ, happiness or blessedness is experienced in the present, but because this happiness involves participating in the pattern of Jesus's own life, it sometimes takes forms not recognizable as "happiness" to those outside. In the beatitudes, for example, happiness in the present tense can look like "hungering," "weeping," or "being persecuted"; in Paul, happiness can take shape as carrying the death of Jesus in one's body; and in the apocalyptic literature, happiness looks for all the world like the weak futilely resisting the powerful. All of these actions and emotions can be called "blessedness" or "happiness" because they anticipate, participate in, and, to some degree, already manifest the eschatological triumph glimpsed at Easter. In other words, the house of faith is marked by happiness not only because of what happens inside it—indeed life inside is often hard, demanding, and salted with suffering—but also and primarily because of where it is heading, because of its *eschaton*, because of its *telos*.

3. *The Architectural Challenge*

So how do these New Testament visions of happiness translate into the tasks of pastoral ministry? In one sense, like all architecture, the pastoral task is a matter of balancing dreams and pragmatic realities, the imagination of what might be placed in tension with the constraints of the probable and the possible. A house too beautiful to live in, for example, a house whose sterile perfection mocks human messiness, mediocrity, and frailty, often generates not inspiration but condemnation, the sad recognition that life can never be this way.[18] On the other hand, a house with no beauty to lift the eye and spirit, a house whose design simply reinforces the disorganization and chaos of everyday life, often demoralizes its inhabitants.

The balance is delicate. Imagine a couple on a house-hunting expedition. If they view a home with a spacious and hospitable basement family room, they are invited to imagine themselves and their children enjoying this space. They lean toward an ideal future, picturing the family pleasantly gathered around a Scrabble board on frequent game nights, background music gaily sounding from the home theater system, and cans of refreshing soda fetched from the convenient wet bar. At best, such ideal imaginings provide grace and gratitude for those moments, however rare, of actual family communion. They are not barriers to happiness, but guides to it. At worst, though, the images collide violently with the facts and become dispiriting, despoiled by fragmented schedules and the centrifugal forces of contemporary family life.

---

17. Though I have not cited it, Joel B. Green's essay in this volume also attests to this thematic.

18. De Botton, *The Architecture of Happiness*, 147.

The same is true about congregational life. Overly idealized pictures of ecclesial life lead only to astonished and bitter cries of betrayal when the inevitable failure happens, when church treasurers abscond with the offerings, congregations divide in toxic feuds, or priests compromise their vows. Wrongly preached and taught, the snapshot of the early church in Acts 2:43–47—full of awe and wonder, sharing all their possessions, eating meals together with gladness and generosity, growing dramatically in numbers, and admired by all—can lead to discouragement when contrasted with the typical, beleaguered local congregation. Only when this text is preached for what it is—an eschatological "seeing through" to the blessings that shimmer amid the foibles and frailties of ordinary worship, service, and fellowship—can it serve to help congregations discover the messianic banquet in an event as mundane as a Wednesday night supper.

On the other hand, to imagine congregational life exclusively in noneschatological, this-worldly terms runs a similar risk of discouragement. If the church is lauded only for what it provides in the present tense—whether that be service, fellowship, or spiritual contentment—that leads ultimately to the church becoming simply one more human agency for good, and not a very compelling or efficient one at that. The Parable of the Unfaithful Slave (Matt 24:45–51) depicts a church whose eschatological expectation has gone slack ("My master is delayed . . ."), which leads to the results all too familiar to worn-out church bureaucrats and burned-out clergy: violence and stupor.

The pastoral architect, then, must preach with utter candor and honesty about the broken nature of the community that fills the house and with an equally confident word about the journey of hope on which the broken and halting church nevertheless travels.

Surprisingly, there may be some guidance in the book of Ecclesiastes for the pastoral architect who wishes to design an ecclesial house occupied by real people but one whose architecture presses its residents forward toward God's good future, a house of hope to be inhabited by real and flawed people.[19] I say surprisingly, because Qoheleth, the narrator of Ecclesiastes, is widely considered to be scripture's most skeptical voice. Commentator James L. Crenshaw, who confesses to a fascination with Ecclesiastes "perhaps because he makes my own skepticism appear solidly biblical,"[20] sums up Qoheleth's message as follows:

Wisdom's claim to secure one's existence is patently false. No discernable principle of order exists, no heavenly guarantor rewards good conduct and

---

19. For more on Ecclesiastes, see also Carol A. Newsom's essay in the present volume.

20. James L. Crenshaw, *Ecclesiastes: A Commentary* (OTL; Philadelphia: Westminster, 1987), 53.

punishes evil deeds. . . . Since death cancels every imagined gain, rendering life under the sun absurd, one should enjoy a woman, wine, and food before old age and death end even these fleeting pleasures.[21]

Ecclesiastes begins with Qoheleth engaging in a guerilla assault on the temple of traditional Hebrew wisdom and declaring the whole enterprise null and void. The first chapter consists of a kind of anticommencement address in which the speaker, wearing all of the requisite academic regalia, declares the whole aim of education, the acquisition of wisdom, to be "vanity," "wearisome," and "a chasing after wind" (see Eccl 1:12–18; cf. 1:8).

In chapter 2, and here is where it gets interesting for our purposes, Qoheleth, disgustedly ripping off his robes of wisdom and declaring himself free of traditional constraints on faithful knowledge, engages in a free-wheeling quest for meaning and happiness, a pursuit that leads him to take four deliberative steps:

First, Qoheleth decides to give sheer personal contentment a try, "a test of pleasure" (Eccl 2:1) as he describes it. He cheers his body with wine; he sets out to accomplish great works and to reap the rewards of large houses with vineyards, gardens, and parks; he assembles a household of servants and gathers around him works of art and music, plus the pleasures of beautiful women (Eccl 2:3–8).

Initially this first step appears to the contemporary reader as a sign of debauchery—Qoheleth as a 1960s-era Hugh Hefner giving reign to every fleshly impulse. Commentator Craig G. Bartholomew, however, reminds us that Qoheleth's "experiment with pleasure was sophisticated and wide ranging," so that Qoheleth here is less like Hugh Hefner and more like what the sages imagined of Solomon.[22] In this first step, Qoheleth wonders if making for himself a life like that of the truly wise Solomon would, in and of itself, generate happiness. This is less about giving in to fleshly desire and more about assembling a lifestyle conducive to contentment. Maybe wisdom can be found in the Chevy pickup, the NASCAR tickets, the Tim McGraw albums, the Bud Light, and the vacation at Myrtle Beach; or perhaps it is the organic garden, the Volvo, the Brandenburg Concertos, the California Chardonnay, and the subscription to the *New Yorker*.

But, either way, this experiment with a pleasurable lifestyle ends in failure for Qoheleth: "Then I considered all that my hands had done and the toil I had spent in doing it, and again, all was vanity and a chasing after wind, and there was nothing to be gained under the sun" (Eccl 2:11). The problem with the "test of pleasure" was not that it did not yield pleasure; in fact, it did. It was, rather, that

---

21. Ibid., 28.

22. Craig G. Bartholomew, *Ecclesiastes* (BCOTWP; Grand Rapids: Baker Academic, 2009), 132.

it led to nothing; it was going nowhere, a chasing after the fickle and ever-shifting wind.

So, in a second step, Qoheleth picks up his old textbooks, but this time not as a young student of wisdom, but as one with some real life experience. Wisdom is no longer rote learning, but the testing of tradition over against the foolishness one sees all around in the world. In a way, Qoheleth at this stage is like the young couple who come back to church after their first child is born, seeking now a life with a future, with some meaning and direction.

But this renewed encounter with traditional wisdom also fails Qoheleth. Yes, wisdom is of great value, especially over against folly, and yes, wisdom has some direction and movement toward a life of meaning. Unlike sheer pleasure, wisdom is going somewhere. But when Qoheleth looked down the corridor of the future, (still) standing at the end was death, the great leveler. Everybody dies: sages and fools, winners and losers, Nobel Peace Prize winners and ne'er-do-wells. "What happens to the fool will happen to me also," Qoheleth discerns (Eccl 2:15). So what's the use? One may be a wise person, one may be a fool; a thousand years from now, who will remember or care? "So I hated life," groans Qoheleth (Eccl 2:17).

Despising life, Qoheleth takes a third step: he turns and gives "my heart up to despair" (Eccl 2:20). This does not mean that Qoheleth became emotionally depressed. Qoheleth *chooses* despair, which means it is less about a psychological state into which he fell and more about an existential choice, reminiscent of Sartre, to live courageously without illusions. Life is going nowhere except toward death, neither wisdom nor folly count in the long run, there is no enduring meaning in seeking pleasure, no "greater power" is out there to reward the righteous and punish the wicked, and the real challenge, one that Qoheleth seems to take on, is simply getting out of bed every morning in a world without hope.

But such a choice leads also finally to a dead end, in this case a life marked by restlessness and anxiety. "Even at night their [mortals'] minds do not rest" (Eccl 2:23). So this realization leads Qoheleth to a dramatic statement, one that some commentators mistakenly view as merely a summary of despair, but one that actually constitutes a new departure, his fourth and decisive step. "There is nothing better for mortals than to eat and drink, and find enjoyment in their toil. This also, I saw, is from the hand of God" (Eccl 2:24).

At first the phrase "eat and drink, and find enjoyment" seems to go full circle and to return to the pleasure-seeking of the first step, as if Qoheleth were saying, "I've tried it all and nothing works; might as well go back to a life-style of self-centered pleasure." But as William P. Brown has seen, Qoheleth is not merely circling back to where he started. He has rather had a personal, and I would say somewhat theological, change of heart. All through the first three steps, Qoheleth has been grasping after life's meaning, chasing after true meaning. But all of this chasing has shown him only that he has been pursuing the wind. But now he gives up grasping, chasing, and pursuing and begins, in a cautious, realistic, and doggedly honest way, to view life as a gift, even a gift from God. As Brown says,

> As Qoheleth comes to realize, joy is not a means to a greater, vainglorious end. The true pleasures are the most mundane. They are the "simple gifts." Whereas Qoheleth found his life is a constant state of ceaseless activity and accomplishment, of making, building, planting, and gathering ([Eccl 2:]4–8)—the all-consuming and self-aggrandizing labors of any oriental despot—he now discovers what is ultimately worthwhile: the task of *receiving*. Neither achieved nor planned, neither grasped nor produced, the gifts of true pleasure are simply received from God.[23]

There is value here for the Christian pastor when Ecclesiastes shows where happiness and deep meaning are *not* to be found: in a self-centered lifestyle of pleasure, in a competitive grasping for wisdom, or in a bravely skeptical leaning forward into the winds of hopelessness and absurdity. The main value of Ecclesiastes, however, lies in its astonishing claim about where happiness *is* to be found: in eating, drinking, and labor; at the table and in the field; in the ordinary, everyday rhythms of life, received as a gift from the hand of God.

This, then, should be a major theme of Christian preaching: happiness and blessing are not found in the ways the world seeks them, in grasping life and squeezing the juice out of it; but they are also not found in the places where religious seekers often look, in a world-denying spirituality that disdains the mundane in favor of the pure and holy.[24] The spiritual "thin place" is not in Iona or Nepal, but at *that* particular table with *this* spouse and *these* children, and making peace with *those* pesky neighbors, and doing *this* job, and living out the messiness of ordinary life in a workaday world. To eat and drink and labor—*this* is the temple where happiness is possible and where the holy has chosen to dwell.

At the close of Ecclesiastes, another voice, more traditional, inserts itself and speaks a final word: "The end of the matter; all has been heard. Fear God and keep his commandments" (Eccl 12:13). Some readers hear this as a corrective, a sternly parental proclamation that the skepticism of Qoheleth has been given enough rope, and the parent has come to tie a knot, to call a halt to the skepticism, and to

---

23. William P. Brown, *Ecclesiastes* (Interpretation; Louisville: John Knox, 2000), 37 (his emphasis).

24. See also Jacqueline Lapsley's and Ellen T. Charry's essays in the present volume.

reaffirm the verities of wisdom. As Crenshaw comments, the affirmations of this new voice are "alien to anything Qohelet has said thus far."[25]

But that is true only if "eat, drink and find enjoyment in toil from the hand of God" is opposed to "fear God and keep God's commandments." I would like to argue instead that it is likelier that the former is how the latter sounds when uttered by one who tried in vain to grab life's gusto and then found true wisdom not in grasping but in opening one's hands to receive God's good gifts amidst this ambiguous life.

This is not to say that Qoheleth has become Thomas Merton or that Ecclesiastes turns into *Chicken Soup for the Soul*. He retains his sharp edges and his clear-eyed assault on rosy piety; he begins his treatise "vanity of vanities," and he ends it with the same words (Eccl 12:8). This also is not to say that the author of the epilogue has nothing to add, because that voice does insist on the truth of eschatology: "For God will bring every deed into judgment . . ." (Eccl 12:14). For the pastoral architect, though, the materialism of Qoheleth can remind us of the insistently incarnational character of the gospel. The wispy Logos, the elusive and spiritual Mystery, became flesh and dwelt among us, rendering sacred the messy places and encounters that make up everyday life in the household. So eat, drink, and labor . . . *and* fear God and keep the commandments. But the eschatological afterword of Ecclesiastes would remind us that eating and drinking with Jesus is more than pleasure—it is a life full of ambiguity, but one that is nevertheless *going somewhere*. To eat and drink with Jesus is to be fed, but it is also "to show forth his death" and the sufferings of those who follow him. To labor in the name of Jesus is to find joy, but it is also to carry a cross. This life is one of happiness only because it is headed toward judgment, toward the crisis. But it is the crisis of Easter, and the wrath of God we fear turns out to be, as Paul Ricoeur said, "only the sadness of love."[26] And the sufferings of those who follow Christ are not, as Qoheleth feared, rendered vain by death, but validated by the triumph of life in Christ.

It is this conception of blessing, this tensive relationship between everyday happiness and satisfaction and the ultimate fulfillment of the gospel promise in God's good time, that allowed Martin Luther King Jr. to describe himself as "happy" on the last night of his life, in the midst of a perilous crusade for civil rights that had brought him not to a mountaintop retreat, but to a garbage worker's strike in Memphis:

---

25. Crenshaw, *Ecclesiastes*, 192.

26. Paul Ricoeur, *The Symbolism of Evil* (New York: Harper and Row, 1967), 67.

Well, I don't know what will happen now. We've got some difficult days ahead. But it really doesn't matter with me now, because I've been to the mountaintop.

And I don't mind.

Like anybody, I would like to live a long life. Longevity has its place. But I'm not concerned about that now. I just want to do God's will. And He's allowed me to go up to the mountain. And I've looked over. And I've seen the Promised Land. I may not get there with you. But I want you to know tonight, that we, as a people, will get to the promised land!

And so I'm happy, tonight. I'm not worried about anything. I'm not fearing any man! Mine eyes have seen the glory of the coming of the Lord!![27]

---

27. Martin Luther King Jr., "I've Been to the Mountaintop," a speech delivered April 3, 1968 at Mason Temple, Memphis, TN; online at www.americanrhetoric.com/speeches/mlkivebeento-themountaintop.htm (accessed 7/12/2011).

The Transformation of Happiness

A RESPONSE FROM COUNSELING PSYCHOLOGY

Steven J. Sandage

> *If we were to ask the question: "What is human life's chief concern?" one of the answers we should receive would be: "It is happiness." How to gain, how to keep, how to recover happiness, is in fact for most men [and women] at all times the secret motive of all they do, and of all they are willing to endure.*
>
> —WILLIAM JAMES[1]

1. The Varieties of Religious Happiness

The essays in Parts I and II of this volume have studied the biblical drama of happiness, a complex and multifaceted story that truly reveals a *variety of religious experiences*, to borrow from William James's classic title. There is a promise of happiness, the loss of happiness, and eventually the redemption and reorientation of happiness. Like any complicated drama, the Bible depicts the vicissitudes of happiness and well-being in human communities marked by love, war, romance, political struggle, family conflict, crime, and even apocalypse. One of my initial reflections after reading the essays of my colleagues in this volume is that the Bible, read as a whole, calls for *transformation in the pursuit of happiness.*

The positive psychology movement represents something of a transformation in the field of psychology and offers excellent resources for integration with

---

1. William James, *The Varieties of Religious Experience: A Study in Human Nature* (New York: Modern Library, 1958), 76.

biblical scholarship in the study of happiness. Arguably there has always been a stream of psychology focused on empirical research into positive aspects of human growth and meaning, at least as far back as the work of William James and other psychologists of religion of that era. However, during the twentieth century, psychology developed largely as a clinical discipline with a focus on the diagnosis and effective treatment of psychopathology. Martin E. P. Seligman has pointed out that the field of psychology was quite successful during this time in constructing empirically supported therapies for a variety of mental disorders, which alleviated suffering and restored certain levels of well-being to many who had previously been marginalized.[2] Seligman helped to organize and empower the emerging field of positive psychology and heralded a greater focus on character strengths and virtues, human flourishing, and questions of *the good life*. There is now a wealth of empirical data on many of the biblical connections between happiness, virtues, and spirituality suggested in the preceding chapters. As a psychologist teaching at a theological seminary, I see the rich potential for rapprochement between biblical and psychological studies in understanding and even transforming human happiness. In this chapter, I will outline some questions and points for possible integration in advancing this field of study. As a practicing therapist, I will also highlight some applications for psychotherapy and pastoral counseling.

2. Whose Happiness? Which Well-Being?

Psychologists and other social scientists will often approach complex topics like happiness and well-being with the priorities of acknowledging (a) individual differences, (b) cultural diversity, and (c) the importance of operational definitions. This leads to questions like "whose happiness are we considering?" and "which definitions of happiness or well-being are we using?"[3]

Individual Differences

The field of personality psychology has identified significant individual differences in happiness or subjective well-being. Subjective well-being is typically

---

2. Martin E. P. Seligman, *Authentic Happiness: Using the New Positive Psychology to Realize Your Potential for Lasting Fulfillment* (New York: Free Press, 2002).

3. This language as well as the title for this section is obviously an adaptation from Alasdair MacIntyre, *Whose Justice? Which Rationality?* (Notre Dame: University of Notre Dame Press, 1989). MacIntyre's book similarly explores the challenges of diversity in traditions and definitions, but with relation to justice, not happiness proper.

defined as the feeling of satisfaction with one's life. A room full of people will usually show vast differences in subjective well-being, particularly if measured across days or weeks rather than a single moment. A stadium might be filled with happy fans when the home team is winning, but if we measured the subjective well-being of the visiting team fans or anyone in the postgame parking jam we would begin to see personality differences emerge. Some would cope with the loss or the traffic stress and remain fairly happy while others would show prominent dysphoria. If we measured the entire group the day after the game, the variance in happiness levels would likely be even more complex.

David Lykken and Auke Tellegen's widely cited behavioral genetics study has suggested that, while happiness levels differ considerably across individuals, happiness tends to be quite stable within a given individual over time.[4] Their research based on twin studies found the genetic heritability of happiness was about 50 percent at participants' initial assessment, but nearly 80 percent of the variance was due to heritability when participants completed measures a decade later. Lykken and Tellegen offered the provocative conclusion that each person has a genetically derived and stable set point of happiness and that "trying to be happier [may be] as futile as trying to be taller."[5] Since then, researchers have shown that estimations of the stability of happiness depend, in part, on a number of methodological issues and that long-term levels of subjective well-being can change significantly in relation to contextual circumstances.[6] Yet most of this research showing greater instability in happiness identifies downward trends in subjective well-being due to stressors such as divorce, widowhood, unemployment, or disability. There is, of course, ample research showing psychotherapy can effectively treat depression and many other mental health problems that impair happiness; however, outcome measures have typically focused on symptoms of distress rather than indicators of positive well-being. Overall, research in this area serves to raise a vital point for any discussion of happiness—we are not all "dealt the same hand" when it comes to happiness, either through genetics or life circumstances. Ontological hermeneutical philosophy reminds us of the *thrownness* of human life, as each of us finds ourselves emerging out of certain contexts into which we were initially

---

4. David Lykken and Auke Tellegen, "Happiness is a Stochastic Phenomenon," *Psychol Sci* 7 (1996): 186–89.

5. Ibid, 189.

6. Richard E. Lucas, "Adaptation and the Set-Point Model of Subjective Well-Being: Does Happiness Change After Major Life Events?" *Curr Dir Psychol Sci* 16 (2007): 75–79; Richard E. Lucas and M. Brent Donnellan, "How Stable is Happiness? Using the STARTS Model to Estimate the Stability of Life Satisfaction," *J Res Pers* 41 (2007): 1091–98. It is also worth noting that longitudinal studies of happiness in the field of personality have often not accounted for the potential effects of therapeutic interventions.

thrown.[7] Even if we choose to be hopeful about the potential for positive transformations in human happiness, we will be wise to also face human finitude and the reality that achieving happiness is typically not an easy goal.

William James was aware of individual differences in happiness among two "religious temperaments" he identified—the healthy-minded and the sick soul. James said those with a healthy-minded religious temperament are "organically weighted on the side of cheer and fatally forbidden to linger, as those of the opposite temperament linger, over the darker aspects of the universe."[8] The healthy-minded prefer a religious focus on beauty, goodness, and universal progress while tending to exclude evil from their "field of vision."[9] In biblical terms, the healthy-minded are rarely inclined to practice lament. In contrast, those with a sick soul form of religious temperament view sin, evil, and loss as unavoidable and believe that meaning in life depends upon honestly lamenting injustice and suffering. James, who was particularly interested in conversion and spiritual transformation, thought the healthy-minded fit with a "once-born" form of natural religion without an internal need for crisis or dramatic transformation. However, sick souls will experience a divided sense of self and the felt need to be "twice-born" through a religious experience of deliverance and redemption to heal the internal splits. They will not overcome melancholy or achieve happiness without an intense, deep transformation. James's phenomenological studies led him to believe that religion "often transforms the most intolerable misery into the profoundest and most enduring happiness."[10] James was himself a sick soul who considered this more complex or existential outlook to potentially open pathways to "the deepest levels of truth."[11]

Contemporary psychologists of religion would tend to broaden the typologies of religion and personality well beyond James's two types. Yet the overarching point is an important one. Religious experience is mediated by psychological (and sociocultural) structures. Personality traits, such as extraversion or neuroticism, will influence interpretations of spiritual and religious experience and even theological views such as Christology.[12] This is why some people gravitate toward

---

7. See Martin Heidegger, *Being and Time* (trans. John Macquarrie and Edward Robinson; London: SCM, 1962).

8. James, *The Varieties of Religious Experience*, 79.

9. Ibid., 83.

10. Ibid., 146.

11. Ibid., 138.

12. Ralph Piedmont, Joseph Williams, and Joseph Ciarrochi, "Personality Correlates of One's Image of Jesus: Historiographic Analysis using the Five-Factor Model of Personality," *J Psychol Theol* 25 (1997): 364–73.

meditating on psalms of praise while seeming to ignore or avoid the book of Job or psalms of lament. Those with James's sick soul temperament might find comfort in the latter and feel miserable trying to read or sing the former. In his essay in the present volume, Terence E. Fretheim alludes to this dynamic indirectly by raising the possibility that many theologians may miss God's emotionality in the biblical text through the influence of gender stereotypes and the fact that "[o]ur culture seems to be much more comfortable with a left-brain God and a male God."[13] We all "bring" our personalities to the task of interpreting scripture and spiritual experience.

Based on a relational perspective, my colleagues and I have defined spirituality as "ways of relating to the sacred."[14] Psychologically speaking, humans relate to the sacred through neurobiological templates shaped by relational experiences. Attachment researchers describe internal working models of relationship that can be characterized along a continuum of emotional security-insecurity.[15] A secure style of attachment with others and with God tends to be positively associated with well-being and relational trust, which integrates nicely with Fretheim's insights about relational spirituality in the Old Testament. Such individuals tend to be internally committed to their faith and to hold warm, loving images of God. In contrast, individuals with insecure styles of attachment tend to hold more distant or unstable images of God that can parallel certain struggles in their interpersonal relationships. Insecurely attached styles of relational spirituality involve internal barriers to the trust and intimacy that enhance spiritual well-being and happiness.

The empirical research to date suggests that, on average, "happiness is greater for those who are more religious, however this is assessed, though the effect is often small."[16] Measures of individual religiosity tend to correlate positively with well-being and mental and physical health variables, and this is particularly true when religiosity measures assess intrinsic motivations and commitments, or tap

---

13. See Terence E. Fretheim, "God, Creation, and the Pursuit of Happiness," 37.

14. F. LeRon Shults and Steven J. Sandage, *Transforming Spirituality: Integrating Theology and Psychology* (Grand Rapids: Baker Academic, 2006), 161; Steven J. Sandage, Mary L. Jensen, and Dan Jass, "Relational Spirituality and Transformation: Risking Intimacy and Alterity," *JSFSC* 1 (2008): 182–206.

15. Lee A. Kirkpatrick, *Attachment, Evolution, and the Psychology of Religion* (New York: Guilford, 2005). Most of the attachment and religion research is based on samples within theistic religious traditions.

16. Michael Argyle, "Causes and Correlates of Happiness," in *Well-Being: The Foundations of Hedonic Psychology* (eds. Daniel Kahneman, Edward Diener, and Norbert Schwarz; New York: Russell Sage Foundation, 1999), 365.

into social support elements of religiosity.[17] These findings fit with the emphasis on spiritual internalization and community in Luke-Acts described by Joel B. Green.[18] In fact, longitudinal research with seminary students has found that increases in intrinsic faith predict increases in both spiritual well-being and active faith involvement over time.[19] Conversely, a relational spirituality based on extrinsic conformity tends to show a limited or negative correlation with authentic well-being.

But a simple look at the empirical correlations between religiosity and happiness risks a "tyranny of the positive attitude" and overlooking the "virtues of negativity," a prophetic critique of the positive psychology movement offered by Barbara S. Held.[20] Held draws on William James to point out that negative or unhappy experiences in life can sometimes be meaningful. Furthermore, undisciplined valorization of optimism and positivity can serve to stigmatize those who are not happy, either due to temperament or situation. This can also obscure empirical evidence that many pessimists learn to function in adaptive ways. Moreover, there is limited research on negative spiritual or religious experiences, such as spiritual abuse, in which social systems associated with the sacred directly contribute to the unhappiness of some persons. Arguably, this is an area in which social scientists have neglected realities about which the Bible is painfully clear. As Carol A. Newsom points out, the wisdom of Qoheleth reveals that the pursuit of happiness is sometimes doomed, or at least severely limited, in certain contexts, and human finitude means we do not have the level of control over happiness we might like.[21] Greg Carey offers a similar point based on Apocalyptic literature: "Humans have significant agency in the quest for happiness, but some dimensions of blessedness are not up to the individual. One cannot control one's number of offspring, for example, or the sociopolitical circumstances in which one lives."[22] Those of us in the contemporary field of positive psychology would do well to heed the humility and dialectical wisdom offered by this ancient wisdom.

---

17. Lisa Miller and Brien S. Kelley, "Relationships of Religiosity and Spirituality with Mental Health and Psychopathology," in *Handbook of the Psychology of Religion and Spirituality* (eds. Raymond F. Paloutzian and Crystal L. Park; New York: Guilford, 2005), 460–78.

18. See the essay by Joel B. Green in the present volume.

19. Ian T. Williamson and Steven J. Sandage, "Longitudinal Analyses of Religious and Spiritual Development Among Seminary Students," *MHRC* 12 (2009): 787–801.

20. Barbara S. Held, "The Negative Side of Positive Psychology," *J Humanist Psychol* 44 (2004): 9–46.

21. See Carol A. Newsom's essay in the present volume. Note also Thomas G. Long's reflections on Qoheleth in his essay, also in this volume.

22. See Greg Carey, "Finding Happiness in Apocalyptic Literature," 211.

Cultural Diversity

Positive psychologists have differed on the question of whether concepts such as happiness, well-being, and virtue are best viewed as universal or culturally specific. Some researchers have employed an *etic* approach that emphasizes universal definitions and taxonomies of virtue,[23] while others have argued for an *emic* perspective with sensitivity to cultural and contextual dynamics that can influence differing construals of value-laden notions like well-being or virtue.[24] Certainly, collectivistic cultures typically define well-being more communally than individualistic cultures, and some cross-cultural variations in subjective well-being have emerged in empirical research.[25] For example, self-esteem has been a stronger predictor of subjective well-being in individualistic cultures than collectivistic ones, while the opposite pattern has been shown for relational harmony. Positive emotions are a strong predictor of happiness across numerous cultures, which suggests some dimensions of happiness may be relatively universal while others (e.g., self-other configurations) are more contextually shaped.

Indigenous positive psychology represents an emerging multicultural framework that promotes culturally sensitive research and practice by integrating the methodological strengths of both etic and emic perspectives.[26] This approach involves attention to indigenous or culturally particular understandings of a concept while also limiting premature transcultural applications of psychological theories and methods. Once indigenous understandings have been identified and appropriate measures developed, empirical testing can elaborate the web of associations and meaning. For example, Samuel M. Y. Ho and Mike W. L. Cheung suggested that Chinese people tend to use metaphors and symbols to communicate happiness, including a hexagram that represents either a lake or a smiling

---

23. Katherine Dahlsgaard, Christopher Peterson, and Martin E. P. Seligman, "Shared Virtue: The Convergence of Valued Human Strengths across Culture and History," *Rev Gen Psychol* 9 (2005): 203–13.

24. Jennifer Teramoto Pedrotti, Lisa M. Edwards, and Shane J. Lopez, "Positive Psychology within a Cultural Context," in *Oxford Handbook of Positive Psychology* (2nd ed.; eds. Shane J. Lopez and C. R. Snyder; New York: Oxford University Press, 2011), 49–57; Steven J. Sandage, Kaye V. Cook, Peter C. Hill, Brad D. Strawn, and Kevin S. Reimer, "Hermeneutics and Psychology: A Review and Dialectical Model," *Rev Gen Psychol* 12 (2008): 344–64.

25. Carol D. Ryff and Burton Singer, "The Contours of Positive Human Health," *Psychol Inq* 9 (1998): 1–28; Robert W. Lent, "Toward a Unifying Theoretical and Practical Perspective on Well-Being and Psychosocial Adjustment," *J Couns Psychol* 51 (2004): 482–509.

26. Uichol Kim, Kuo-Shu Yang, and Kwang-Kuo Hwang, eds., *Indigenous and Cultural Psychology: Understanding People in Context* (New York: Springer, 2006); Steven J. Sandage and Merrishia S. Naicker, "Indigenous Positive Psychology," in *The Encyclopedia of Positive Psychology* (2 vols.; ed. Shane J. Lopez; Oxford: Wiley-Blackwell, 2009), 1:514–17.

face.[27] This is a metaphor of relational harmony and the basic idea "you are happy and therefore I am happy." Ho and Cheung developed a measure of interpersonal subjective well-being based on this indigenous concept of happiness and confirmed a two-factor model of interpersonal and intrapersonal subjective well-being among the Chinese. This approach highlights an alternative to imposing western measures of happiness onto other cultural contexts and parallels the benefits of contextual models of hermeneutics and theology.

Sociocultural differences in social justice also serve to problematize the topic of happiness, as raised in many of the exegetical chapters in this volume. While large increases in wealth do not seem to increase happiness, economic factors do relate to emotional well-being as it can be hard to be happy while fighting against poverty.[28] Racism, sexism, and other forms of systemic oppression also work against the well-being of nondominant groups. As Newsom suggests, social justice concerns raise important and often-neglected questions for both positive psychology and faith communities about institutional or organizational dynamics and well-being. Subjective happiness might be maintained by privileged groups by avoidance of facing the unhappiness of others in one's community. This takes us back to the question above: Whose happiness does a particular social system protect? Flipped around: Whose happiness is neglected or abused? And the most systemic questions explore the interlocking or reciprocal dynamics—for example, is happiness gained for some (groups) *by* neglecting or abusing the happiness of others (other groups)?

Table 12.1   Philosophical and Psychological Views of Well-Being[a]

Philosophical View of Well-Being	Primary Goal of Health	Primary Goal of Spiritual Formation	Example of Psychological Researcher
Hedonic	Adjustment	Spiritual Well-Being	Ed Diener
Eudaimonic	Virtue	Spiritual Maturity	Carol Ryff

a. Adapted from Shults and Sandage, *Transforming Spirituality*; Lent, "Toward a Unifying Theoretical and Practical Perspective."

---

27. Samuel M. Y. Ho and Mike W. L. Cheung, "Using the Combined Etic-Emic Approach to Develop a Measurement of Interpersonal Subjective Well-Being in Chinese Populations," in *Oxford Handbook of Methods in Positive Psychology* (eds. Anthony D. Ong and Manfred H. M. van Dulmen; New York: Oxford University Press, 2007), 139–52.

28. Lingxin Hao and Richard W. Johnson, "Economic, Cultural, and Social Origins of Emotional Well-Being: Comparison of Immigrants and Natives at Midlife," *Res Aging* 22 (2000): 599–629.

Definitions of Well-Being

The different definitions of happiness or well-being have been thematized in this volume through engagement with contemporary discussions of the contrast between *hedonic* and *eudaimonic* views of well-being. Table 12.1 is adapted from other sources and summarizes some corollaries of these views.[29] Hedonic views of well-being emphasize positive emotions, the absence of negative emotions, and subjective life satisfaction. Eudaimonic views of well-being emphasize developmental growth, life purpose, the pursuit of meaning, and self-actualization. While hedonic views orient toward health goals of adjustment or balance, eudaimonic views are more teleological and integrate health with the development of virtues. From a eudaimonic perspective, happiness and well-being are typically by-products of meaningful growth and engagement with life.[30] Positive psychologists who study well-being often differ in the implicit view of well-being they are using. Ed Diener's work on subjective well-being reflects the hedonic view and Carol D. Ryff's research on psychological well-being is eudaimonic.[31] There is empirical support for the notion of two latent factors of well-being, which could be labeled happiness and meaning (or growth), and these essentially map onto the hedonic and eudaimonic categories.[32]

In a parallel fashion, some models of spiritual formation and popular literature on spirituality emphasize an ultimate goal of spiritual well-being or feeling good about one's spirituality. Such hedonic approaches to spirituality might reflect socioeconomic privilege, as can be seen in many of the beautiful pictures of spas and gardens in the magazine *Spirituality & Health*. Or, as Newsom suggests based on Qoheleth, hedonic spirituality might represent a form of social resistance by living in the moment when systemic oppression limits opportunities for self-actualization.[33] In contrast, other models of spiritual formation are eudaimonic in orienting toward a goal of spiritual maturity. Maturity-based models of spiritual formation will tend to promote a view in which spiritual well-being

---

29. Lent, "Toward a Unifying Theoretical and Practical Perspective," 482–509; Shults and Sandage, *Transforming Spirituality*.

30. Richard M. Ryan and Edward L. Deci, "On Happiness and Human Potentials: A Review of Research on Hedonic and Eudaimonic Well-Being," *Annu Rev Psychol* 52 (2001): 141–66.

31. See, e.g., Ed Diener, *The Science of Well-Being: The Collected Works of Ed Diener* (New York: Springer Science and Business Media, 2009); and Carol D. Ryff and Burton H. Singer, "Know Thyself and Become What You Are: A Eudaimonic Approach to Psychological Well-Being," *J Happiness St* 9 (2008): 13–39.

32. Lent, "Toward a Unifying Theoretical and Practical Perspective," 486.

33. See Newsom's essay in the present volume.

must somehow be integrated with (i) relational growth in community, and (ii) engagement in social justice concerns. This point is raised implicitly in many of the preceding chapters on the different biblical visions of happiness. The developmental orientation of eudaimonic or maturity-based models also suggests the need for periodic transformations or growth in the meaning and practice of happiness as trials are faced and contexts change. Moreover, virtues become integrative constructs in such models. That is, virtues serve to integrate personal and relational well-being in ways that ultimately benefit self and the wider community.

3. Well-Being and Virtue

Virtues have been defined in the psychological literature as dispositions or embodied traits of character that promote personal, relational, and communal well-being. In terms of the psychological state-trait distinction, virtues are relatively stable traits of personality rather than more acute subjective states. Virtues are character qualities that promote resilience in the face of suffering while also potentially serving to prevent some risks of suffering. For example, a person with high levels of self-control may tend to enjoy greater stability in work and relationships than the person characterized by extremes of impulsivity. At the same time, some virtues may emerge from growth during periods of suffering. Those who are high in mature forms of compassion and forgiveness may have developed those virtues through significant disappointments or relational injuries, and those virtues may become useful in cultivating future well-being and relational commitments. This understanding seems to generally fit with the biblical connections between virtue and happiness suggested in many of the essays in this volume.

The field of positive psychology has generated considerable data linking many of the virtues with measures of health, happiness, and well-being. For example, there is now a vast empirical literature on interpersonal forgiveness suggesting dispositional forgivingness is positively correlated with many indices of health and well-being.[34] As the beatitudes teach, there appears to often be a blessedness for those who work toward peace, at least in comparison to those who work toward revenge.[35] Hope, a virtue highlighted in the exegetical chapters by William P. Brown and Jacqueline Lapsley, has also been extensively

---

34. See Everett L. Worthington, Jr., ed., *Handbook of Forgiveness* (New York: Routledge, 2005).

35. For more on the beatitudes, see the essay by Carl R. Holladay in the present volume.

investigated in the research of C. R. Snyder and others.[36] Dispositional hope is not only associated with higher levels of well-being but also many other positive outcomes ranging from academic success to recovery from traumatic injuries. Gratitude (and appreciation for gifts) is another virtue mentioned by biblical exegetes in this volume and is also a disposition that has been widely studied by positive psychologists in recent years. Dispositional gratitude is not only positively associated with health and well-being but with numerous measures of generous, prosocial behavior.[37] As a concept, gratitude represents fertile ground for interdisciplinary integration involving the themes of appreciating gifts (spiritual and material) and reciprocal generosity in relationships. Studies have also found positive correlations between forgiveness, gratitude, and hope, suggesting there is often the interweaving of virtuous dispositions as suggested by Carl R. Holladay in his contribution to the present collection.

Generativity also emerged as an explicit or implicit theme across several of the exegetical chapters. Erik Erikson defined psychosocial generativity as "the concern in establishing and guiding the next generation" and linked it with the virtue of caring.[38] It was Erikson's genius to see the interlocking or systemic benefits when adults' need to make a lasting contribution lines up with the younger generation's need for care and guidance. This is consistent with Lapsley's linkage of hope and generativity in Isaiah's vision of happiness: "sons and daughters are the very best hope for the future—their flourishing is a major component of happiness in this life."[39]

Generativity can also be integrated with the biblical theme of *bearing fruit*. Empirical studies have found generativity to be positively correlated with well-being, and my colleagues and I found generativity goals to be positively correlated with dispositional gratitude and intrinsic faith among a sample of seminary students.[40] Some results have also been suggestive that generativity may be related

---

36. See the essays by William P. Brown and Jacqueline Lapsley in this volume and C. R. Snyder, ed. *Handbook of Hope: Theory, Measures, and Applications* (San Diego: Academic Press, 2000).

37. Robert A. Emmons and Michael E. McCullough, eds., *The Psychology of Gratitude* (New York: Oxford University Press, 2004).

38. Erik H. Erikson, *Childhood and Society* (2nd ed.; New York: Norton, 1964), 267.

39. See Jacqueline Lapsley, "A Happy Blend: Isaiah's Vision of Happiness (and Beyond)," 91.

40. See Steven J. Sandage, Peter C. Hill, and Deanne C. Vaubel, "Generativity, Relational Spirituality, Gratitude, and Mental Health: Relationships and Pathways," *Int J Psychol Relig* 21 (2011): 1–16.

to processes of transformation or profound change. For example, there is evidence that self-reported experiences of transformation can be associated with an increased valuing of generosity and self-giving.[41] The narrative psychology research of Dan P. McAdams and his colleagues has demonstrated that transformation is a common theme in the life stories of highly generative adults.[42] Those who score high on scales of generativity tend to narrate their life stories by highlighting *redemption sequences*, which are scenes in which bad events eventually have good outcomes (e.g., growth, meaning, revitalization, enlightenment, etc.).[43] The bad event is redeemed through a personal transformation that ultimately leads to good things for self and a desire to benefit others. This, too, fits with Carey's biblical insight about the importance of narrative identity in providing a sense of meaningful happiness.[44] Generativity may prove to be a key concept for integrating biblical and psychological understandings of how "the good life" eventually requires a transformation in how we find happiness with movement toward meaningful care for others.

Some virtues show a more robust positive correlation with well-being than do other virtues, at least when using a hedonic view based on subjective well-being. Nansook Park, Christopher Peterson, and Martin E. P. Seligman surveyed a large sample of US citizens with self-ratings of twenty-four different virtues and satisfaction with life.[45] The top ten virtues in terms of a positive correlation with happiness were (in order): hope, zest, gratitude, curiosity, love, perspective/wisdom, persistence, self-regulation, spirituality, and forgiveness. The virtue with the lowest correlation with life satisfaction was modesty/humility, and this correlation was actually negligible in terms of statistical significance. This could suggest the virtue of hope is a better pathway to happiness than is humility; however, this type of correlational research design does not allow inferences of causality. These considerations also necessitate the questions raised earlier about definitions of well-being and the place of eudaimonic maturity. Virtues such as humility and justice may not show strong correlations with hedonic measures of well-being,

---

41. William R. Miller and Janet C'de Baca, *Quantum Change: When Epiphanies and Sudden Insights Transform Ordinary Lives* (New York: Guilford, 2001).

42. Dan P. McAdams and Regina L. Logan, "What is generativity?" in *The Generative Society: Caring for Future Generations* (eds. Ed de St. Aubin, Dan P. McAdams, and Tae-Chang Kim; Washington, DC: American Psychological Association, 2004), 15–31.

43. Dan P. McAdams, *The Redemptive Self: Stories Americans Live By* (New York: Oxford University Press, 2006).

44. See Carey's essay in the present volume.

45. Nansook Park, Christopher Peterson, and Martin E. P. Seligman, "Strengths of Character and Well-Being," *J Soc Clin Psychol* 23 (2004): 603–19.

perhaps due to the possibility that they are often developed through challenging processes of suffering. Yet the development of interwoven virtues suggests that spiritual maturity might involve a complex constellation of virtues: for example, the mature capacity to hold together hope *and* humility or forgiveness *with* justice.[46] This raises the question of how one defines spiritual maturity and its association with well-being.

4. Well-being and Maturity

Spiritual well-being and spiritual maturity are somewhat differing goals.[47] While the empirical psychological literature on spirituality has risen markedly in recent decades, most of the research has focused on spiritual well-being rather than spiritual maturity. This is probably due to a variety of factors, including the simple fact that maturity is a more complex and value-laden concept to define and measure. Definitions of maturity necessarily involve ideals of optimal functioning and these ideals tap into the influences of cultural and religious traditions. For those who value or even enjoy contextual and emic perspectives, this is to be expected. However, this works against using generic or etic definitions of spirituality that can be efficiently employed across groups.

My colleagues and I have suggested an integrative rapprochement between (i) spiritual well-being and the biblical concept of *shalom* and (ii) spiritual maturity and the biblical concept of *teleios*.[48] The multidimensional Hebrew concept of *shalom* is a highly relational and covenantal vision of well-being in relation to God and neighbor. *Shalom* connoted not only peaceful flourishing for one's own community but also included a wider sociopolitical commitment to justice.[49] The biblical prophets considered systemic injustice a violation of *shalom* and warned against the happiness of pseudo-peace. The Greek concept of *teleios* is consistent with *shalom* and also implies wholeness, completeness, and maturity. It is a teleological or eudaimonic-like goal that one grows toward. In the New Testament, this involves the types of endurance and perseverance psychologists would now associate with resilience.

---

46. On the integration of hope and humility, see Josef Pieper, *On Hope* (trans. M. F. McCarthy; San Francisco: Ignatius, 1986); on forgiveness and justice, see Everett L. Worthington, Jr., *A Just Forgiveness: Responsible Healing without Excusing Injustice* (Downers Grove, IL: InterVarsity Press, 2009).

47. Shults and Sandage, *Transforming Spirituality*.

48. Sandage, Jensen, and Jass, "Relational Spirituality and Transformation."

49. For a biblical treatment, see Walter Brueggemann, *Peace* (St. Louis: Chalice, 2001).

The differentiation of spiritual well-being and maturity can assist in navigating some of the conceptual challenges of integrating happiness and spiritual formation. On the one hand, high levels of self-reported spiritual well-being and happiness cannot necessarily be equated with spiritual maturity. Those who are high in spiritual grandiosity or narcissism may feel very close to God, even superior to others. In fact, extreme narcissists are often optimistic and typically report positive mood states, but this may come with severe limitations in relational or intercultural maturity. Keith J. Edwards and Todd W. Hall have developed a sophisticated measure of "illusory spiritual health," a tendency to self-report high levels of spirituality that defensively masks emotional difficulties.[50] This involves the use of impression management and significant defense mechanisms to avoid underlying pain and psychological vulnerability, which leads to a variety of relational problems and reactivity to disappointment. Richard Beck's notion of "defensive theology" also describes a religious orientation that functions to defend against a sense of vulnerability and mortality by minimizing existential complexity and maintaining a sense of personal specialness through divine protection.[51] In contrast, Beck defined existential religion as "a faith that is willing to sit with or even embrace the confusions, doubts, and anxieties of belief" and hypothesized that a defensive religious orientation would correlate with in-group bias while existential religion would not due to this underlying spiritual narcissism and need to feel special.[52] In an experimental study, Beck had Christian undergraduate students rate the authors of two basically equivalent essays, one pro-Christian and one pro-Buddhist with several adjectives (e.g., "honest," "arrogant," "likable," "insensitive"). Those high in defensive theology tended to show an in-group bias, while existential participants tended to rate in-group and out-group targets as equally capable. This suggests those with strongly defensive forms of religious faith may use bias against out-group members to protect a sense of spiritually privileged status, possibly as a defensive or exclusionary form of pursuing happiness.

On the other hand, low levels of spiritual well-being do not mean a person is spiritually immature. Some who would fit James's sick soul description struggle

---

50. Keith J. Edwards and Todd W. Hall, "Illusory Spiritual Health: The Role of Defensiveness in Understanding and Assessing Spiritual Health," in *Spiritual Formation, Counseling, and Psychotherapy* (eds. Todd W. Hall and Mark R. McMinn; Hauppauge, NY: Nova Sciences Publishers, 2003), 261–75.

51. Richard Beck, "Defensive versus Existential Religion: Is Religious Defensiveness Predictive of Worldview Defense?" *J Psychol Theol* 34 (2006): 142–52.

52. Ibid., 144.

with significant levels of spiritual instability, fear, and self-contempt that work against spiritual well-being. Our research with seminary students has found that such spiritual instability is negatively associated with emotional well-being and interpersonal forgiveness while also associated with higher levels of mental health symptoms.[53] Spiritual instability can be associated with symptoms of borderline personality disorder and severe emotional dysregulation due to a history of trauma or abuse. Unhealthy forms of "spiritual selflessness" may also lead to compulsivity and a type of suffering servant complex, or what may represent a fear of the vulnerability inherent in happiness and enjoyment. Forms of emotional suffering such as depression, anxiety, and other mental health problems should also not be minimized. In some cases, spiritual maturity might be facilitated by directly treating mental health problems that impede well-being and happiness, yet I occasionally see clients in my clinical practice who worry that investing in therapy or medication might be compromising their faith in God's power to heal. This often reflects extremes of dualistic theology that do not resonate with the holistic or integrated view of personhood in the Bible or the biblical legitimacy of enjoying life.[54]

Overall, what is needed is a dialectical perspective that recognizes that seasons of unhappiness or dark nights of the soul are not necessarily a sign of sin—an obvious lesson from the book of Job, for example, or the psalmic laments—and therefore should not be stigmatized. Growth in maturity sometimes emerges from dark nights of trauma, grief, and dysphoria.[55] Pain in and of itself does not create maturity, however. Research has found those with high levels of maturity *and* happiness tend to (i) seek new meaning and more complex understandings of life that can arise from difficult experiences and (ii) value growth in relational understanding.[56] They seek to learn from difficult experiences rather than simply dwelling in pain. Spiritual maturity is also consistent with the development of healthy capacities for coping with stress and recovering well-being after periods of struggle. Psychologists use the term "self-regulation" to describe the capacity to manage or self-soothe the stress of anxiety and other challenging emotions in

53. Steven J. Sandage and Peter J. Jankowski, "Forgiveness, Spiritual Instability, Mental Health Symptoms, and Well-Being: Mediation Effects of Differentiation of Self," *Psychol Relig Spir* 2 (2010): 168–80.

54. See Lapsley's essay in the present volume.

55. See Gerald G. May, *The Dark Night of the Soul: A Psychiatrist Explores the Connection Between Darkness and Spiritual Growth* (San Francisco: HarperSanFrancisco, 2004).

56. Jack J. Bauer, Dan P. McAdams, and April R. Sakaeda, "Interpreting the Good Life: Growth Memories in the Lives of Mature, Happy People," *J Pers Soc Psychol* 88 (2005): 203–17.

order to regain a sense of emotional equilibrium and well-being. This does not imply avoiding stress, nor does self-regulation mean human coping apart from God. Rather, embracing the eudaimonic challenges of growth can require mature forms of relational spirituality and coping (e.g., meditative prayer, engaging in authentic community) that help self-regulate anxiety and restore well-being while undergoing transformative processes.

5. Differentiation of Self and Mature Happiness

These proposed connections between relational spirituality, self-regulation, and maturity necessitate an integrative conceptualization of spiritual formation and human development. Differentiation of Self is a relational notion that is useful for conceptualizing spiritual maturity and mature expressions of the pursuit of happiness.[57] The concept of Differentiation of Self was first articulated by family systems theorist Murray Bowen based on evolutionary biology to refer to the mature capacity to balance (i) thoughts and feelings, and (ii) connection and independence in relationships.[58] Bowen suggested that Differentiation of Self, being applicable at both individual and family system levels, involves an ability to self-regulate anxiety and to maintain one's sense of self whether in close proximity to, or distant from, others. Highly differentiated persons have capacities for self-soothing but are also not ashamed to seek help when needed.[59] They also tend to be good at containing projections and differentiating their own internal experiences from those of others, which facilitates accurate perspective-taking. In the language of Romans, differentiation involves the ability to "rejoice with those who rejoice" and "weep with those who weep" (Rom 12:15).

Bowen developed this understanding based on his clinical observations of the relational dynamics between patients with mental illness and their families as they lived together in an inpatient unit. He was among a group of seminal theorists who shifted the clinical focus from pathology *within* the individual to also consider dysfunctional relational interactions *between* individuals in a given family or social system. This systems view is closer to the communal worldview throughout the Bible and the systemic awareness mentioned in many of the essays in this

---

57. Brian D. Majerus and Steven J. Sandage, "Differentiation of Self and Christian Spiritual Maturity: Social Science and Theological Integration," *J Psychol Theol* 38 (2010): 41–51.

58. See Michael E. Kerr and Murray Bowen, *Family Evaluation: An Approach Based on Bowen Theory* (New York: Norton, 1988).

59. This resonates with the integration of hope and help in the Psalms, as described in Brown's chapter in the present volume.

volume than is the individualistic focus of much of the contemporary medical system in North America.

Systems that are low in differentiation tend to be vulnerable to psychosocial problems and reduced well-being, and those systems are also susceptible to maintaining dysfunctional patterns of coping. Scapegoating is one such pattern in which a family system unconsciously colludes to blame a particular family member for all the family problems. The unhappiness and struggles of the scapegoated person serve the systemic function of reducing anxiety and maintaining a certain level of pseudo well-being for other family members (i.e., "I'm not the one with the problems"). This is obviously paralleled in larger social systems that unjustly scapegoat certain groups to maintain the well-being of privileged groups. Highly differentiated systems tend to promote greater resilience and relational fairness for all as differences are accepted without overwhelming anxiety and there is a healthier balance of closeness and respect for boundaries.

Differentiation of Self has been applied to the challenges of religious leadership and congregational life in the pastoral care literature.[60] Spiritual leaders are at risk for burnout and compromised well-being without healthy levels of Differentiation of Self. Moreover, the systemic tensions or challenges of congregational life parallel those of family systems. Over time, it is impossible for everyone to be happy in either family or congregational systems. Poorly differentiated spiritual leaders tend toward the extremes of either (i) emotional fusion and the belief it is their responsibility to "make everyone happy," or (ii) emotional cutoff and a lack of responsiveness to feedback about unhappiness in the congregation. Both extremes put the leader at risk for unhappy outcomes (e.g., burnout or being fired) and prove ineffective for healthy leadership and pastoral care.

Integrative theorists have also applied Differentiation of Self in relation to couples and family dynamics as an expression of healthy human development.[61] Relational systems high in differentiation maintain well-being not by avoiding all conflict but through underlying dynamics of covenant, grace, intimacy, and empowerment. In contrast, relational systems low in differentiation

---

60. Edwin H. Friedman, *Generation to Generation: Family Processes in Church and Synagogue* (New York: Guilford, 1985); Ronald W. Richardson, *Becoming a Healthier Pastor: Family Systems Theory and the Pastor's Own Family* (Minneapolis: Fortress, 2005); Peter L. Steinke, *Congregational Leadership in Anxious Times: Being Calm and Courageous No Matter What* (Herndon, VA: Alban Institute, 2006).

61. Jack O. Balswick, Pamela Ebstyne King, and Kevin S. Reimer, *The Reciprocating Self: Human Development in Theological Perspective* (Downers Grove, IL: InterVarsity Press, 2005); Jack O. Balswick and Judith K. Balswick, *The Family: A Christian Perspective on the Contemporary Home* (3rd ed.; Grand Rapids: Baker Academic, 2007).

tend to engage in power and control struggles that perpetuate unforgiveness and relational distance. When stress levels exceed the differentiation capacities of a couple or family system there is a high risk for dissolution as chronic anxiety and unhappiness are hard to sustain. Theologically, the Trinity can be understood as the ultimate exemplar of differentiated relationality—distinct Persons who always exist in intimate and cooperative relationship.[62] Trinitarian differentiation has been suggested as the divine grounding for a relational model of spiritual maturity.[63]

Empirical research on Differentiation of Self has greatly increased in the past decade, most notably through the work of Elizabeth A. Skowron.[64] Studies have found Differentiation of Self to be positively correlated with well-being for both genders, across most of the lifespan, and for a diverse range of ethnic groups.[65] Differentiation of Self has also been associated with higher levels of marital adjustment and intergenerational intimacy, as well as with reduced risk for interpersonal problems and child abuse. These salutary correlates of Differentiation of Self appear to be due to the combination of *intra*personal (i.e., self-regulation) and *inter*personal (i.e., balancing connection and autonomy) dimensions of Differentiation of Self as a concept.

Several studies have yielded empirical results connecting Differentiation of Self to other spiritual maturity factors evident from the exegetical chapters of this volume. Differentiation of Self has been positively correlated with virtues such as dispositional hope,[66] forgiveness,[67] gratitude,[68] and self-control,[69] as well as with a

---

62. See, e.g., Miroslav Volf, *After Our Likeness: The Church as the Image of the Trinity* (Grand Rapids: Eerdmans, 1998).

63. Sandage, Jensen, and Jass, "Relational Spirituality and Transformation."

64. See, e.g., Elizabeth A. Skowron, Krystal L. Stanley, and Michael D. Shapiro, "A Longitudinal Perspective on Differentiation of Self, Interpersonal and Psychological Well-Being in Young Adulthood," *Contemp Fam Ther* 31 (2009): 3–18.

65. For an overview of this research, see Majerus and Sandage, "Differentiation of Self and Christian Spiritual Maturity: Social Science and Theological Integration."

66. Ian Williamson, Steven J. Sandage, and Richard M. Lee, "How Social Connectedness Affects Guilt and Shame: Mediated by Hope and Differentiation of Self," *Pers Indiv Differ* 43 (2007): 2159–70.

67. Sandage and Jankowski, "Forgiveness, Spiritual Instability, Mental Health Symptoms, and Well-Being."

68. Steven J. Sandage and Mark G. Harden, "Relational Spirituality, Differentiation of Self, and Virtue as Predictors of Intercultural Development," *MHRC* 14 (2011): 819–38.

69. Elizabeth A. Skowron, Sarah E. Holmes, and Ronald M. Sabatelli, "Deconstructing Differentiation: Self Regulation, Interdependent Relating, and Well-Being in Adulthood," *Contemp Fam Ther* 25 (2003): 111–29.

measure of spiritual maturity.[70] Some may conflate Differentiation of Self with individuation, yet the latter is a more individualistic notion that emphasizes interpersonal separation and becoming one's own person. Conversely, Differentiation of Self is a dialectical notion that expresses a balance of capacities for community and solitude. There is some initial empirical evidence that Differentiation of Self is positively correlated with intercultural development or the capacity to relate effectively across cultural differences.[71] This requires the type of contextual sensitivity that Green mentions in his essay on Luke-Acts.[72] Those high in Differentiation of Self can be expected to have a solid sense of narrative identity, yet the narrative is likely to be inclusive enough to allow for the happiness of outgroup members. In contrast, those with lower levels of Differentiation of Self may strongly identify with more exclusionary and ethnocentric narratives that maximize their own happiness while also promising punishment for outsiders.

David Schnarch has related Differentiation of Self to growth through crucibles of transformation, with crucibles referring to developmental processes of intensified anxiety that can catalyze growth toward greater relational maturity.[73] In the language of contemplative spirituality, crucible processes are like dark nights of the soul. Those who are growing in Differentiation of Self find ways to tolerate the dark nights of pain and ambiguity that are often necessary for growth. At low levels of Differentiation of Self, it may take a severe crisis to provoke transformative change since the person may resist any increased anxiety or reduction in hedonic well-being. For example, severe alcoholics often require a significant intervention to break through defenses and mobilize change because intrinsic motivation can be low. Over time, those with high levels of Differentiation of Self will require less intensity or crisis to catalyze necessary change. The person begins to tolerate temporary reductions of happiness if they serve anticipated gains in well-being. Among adults, this can involve facing existential issues of finitude and loss in order to make constructive choices about life priorities. Narrative psychologists have found those with high levels of ego development (similar to Differentiation of Self) tend to view negative experiences as transformative in gaining new understandings.[74] These

---

70. Peter J. Jankowski and Marsha Vaughn, "Differentiation of Self and Spirituality: Empirical Explorations," *Couns Val* 53 (2009): 82–96.

71. Sandage and Harden "Relational Spirituality, Differentiation of Self, and Virtue."

72. See Green's essay in the present volume.

73. David Schnarch, *Intimacy and Desire: Awaken the Passion in Your Relationship* (New York: Beufort Books, 2009).

74. Jack J. Bauer, Dan P. McAdams, and Jennifer L. Pals, "Narrative Identity and Eudaimonic Well-Being," *J Happiness St* 9 (2008): 81–104.

differentiation- and narrative-based models of transformation resonate particularly well with (i) Brown's essay on the Psalter's vision of pilgrimage toward a new orientation of transformed happiness following disorientation and (ii) Colleen Shantz's insights on Paul's cruciform transformation of happiness through finding meaning in Christ-like suffering.[75]

6. Future Directions and Integrative Applications

In this final section, I will summarize some future directions for interdisciplinary scholarship on happiness that occur to me as a psychologist, as well as some applications for the fields of psychology and pastoral care.

Hermeneutics of Happiness

Biblical studies and psychology are both hermeneutical disciplines that involve interpreting data. I believe the essays in this volume suggest the tremendous advantages of a constructive triangulation of disciplinary resources of interpretation in the hermeneutical study of happiness and well-being. Biblical studies can provide a rich understanding of sacred traditions and teachings about happiness, virtue, and the good life. For positive psychologists, this could deepen appreciation for the spiritual dimensions of the definitions and theoretical understandings of happiness and virtue and thus lead to more robust measures for scientific research. The biblical scholars in this volume also show the sensitivity to differing social contexts and situations that can temper tendencies among some psychologists to overgeneralize or universalize models. Once interdisciplinary models and measures are developed, they can be empirically tested to validate integrative understandings. Some of the recent research on interpersonal forgiveness and well-being generally fits this integrative approach.[76]

Interdisciplinary integration can also serve to overcome several concerns that are shared by many in biblical studies and psychology. First, scholars in both disciplines often lament an uncritical popularization of their disciplines in ways that compromise quality and substance. A trip to any large bookstore is likely to reveal many popular books on happiness-related topics in both the religion and self-help sections—books that lack much scholarly grounding. Triangulating disciplines will not completely prevent this problem but may contribute to quality work with wider

---

75. See the essays by Brown and Colleen Shantz in the present volume.

76. Sandage and Jankowski, "Forgiveness, Spiritual Instability, Mental Health Symptoms, and Well-Being"; Worthington, *A Just Forgiveness*.

applications across multiple fields. Second, biblical scholars and psychologists are likely to share an interest in the authentic embodiment of virtues and well-being. It is fair to say the Bible strongly emphasizes authentic spirituality and virtue, and psychologists tend to want to move beyond immature defenses and extrinsic conformity toward true authenticity. Although far from perfect, empirical psychology has developed many research strategies that are useful in getting closer to authentic measures of the virtues. Finally, biblical scholarship can be particularly useful for identifying misuses and misinterpretations of sacred texts in ways that impede mature happiness. As a practicing therapist, I find it quite helpful to be able to dialogue with biblical scholars and theologians when clients justify certain pathogenic stances in life based on questionable interpretations of the Bible.

"Reoriented" Happiness

The essays in this volume also suggest the need for a reoriented form of happiness. By "reoriented," I mean a transformed type of happiness and well-being that includes the capacities to honestly face the disorienting realities of suffering and injustice in the world. In faith communities, this means making space for the practice of lament and grief. It also means acknowledging that spiritual struggles and doubt might be spiritually formative. Suffering should not be idealized, however, and there is a great need for faith communities to collaborate with mental health professionals in treating and supporting those who are struggling, as well as to assist with suicide prevention. Topics like depression and suicide still carry too much stigma. Relational maturity and wisdom for these difficult situations does not necessarily come naturally, so there is an ever-present need for training in lay counseling and healthy relationships more generally. Faith communities with substantial numbers of people who can "sit with Job" will have good relational resources for fostering reoriented happiness.

Maturing Happiness

Another area for future interdisciplinary research is understanding the processes by which people move toward reoriented happiness and posttraumatic growth and well-being. Scholars across disciplines might collaborate in investigating mediators of change and narrative turning points. There is a growing literature in the area of spirituality and health (or well-being), and scholars and practitioners are working toward identifying spiritual practices and virtues that actually contribute to well-being.[77] This body of empirical research could be likened paradigmatically to

---

77. For a summary, see Shults and Sandage, *Transforming Spirituality*.

the practical wisdom and eudaimonic orientation of Proverbs. This eudaimonic approach means emphasizing happiness or well-being as legitimate goals that are typically best achieved through meaningful engagement with life and relationships. The corresponding integrative approaches to virtue and well-being can allow leaders in faith communities to teach virtue and well-being practices that have biblical and empirical validity rather than relying on idealized notions or platitudes. Finally, the pursuit of a mature approach to happiness could involve engaging a topic we have largely neglected in this volume—namely, sexuality. While sex is often construed as purely hedonic, a more integrative and eudaimonic perspective could frame sexuality as a formative domain for both pleasure and meaningful growth in maturity and relational intimacy. Clinically, I have found many of my religious clients who are working on sexual growth have a hard time finding eudaimonic sexuality resources in their faith communities that go beyond prohibitions.

Intercultural Happiness

An integrative theme mentioned above from both biblical studies and some streams of psychology is the need for interculturally sensitive and socially just orientations toward happiness. This involves questioning ways in which systems such as families, schools, workplaces, or congregations can become more interculturally sensitive and attentive to disparities in equity. Intercultural development is an individual differences factor that ranges along a continuum from ethnocentric to interculturally competent. There are assessment tools and training resources available to help individuals and organizations with this process, which can also be integrated with spiritual formation and maturity.[78] Those who are higher in intercultural and spiritual maturity tend to enjoy learning about diversity and engaging in diverse relationships despite the stress that is sometimes involved. In contrast, those who are lower in intercultural and spiritual development tend to view diversity as a problem that gets in the way of personal happiness.

There are significant social justice issues at stake in the level of intercultural sensitivity of an organization. For example, Thao N. Le and his colleagues found empirical evidence that the multicultural sensitivity of schools was associated with the subjective happiness of minority and immigrant youth.[79] As someone

---

78. Mitchell R. Hammer, Milton J. Bennett, and Richard Wiseman, "Measuring Intercultural Sensitivity: The Intercultural Development Inventory," *Int J Intercult Rel* 27 (2003): 421–43; Sandage, Jensen, and Jass, "Relational Spirituality and Transformation."

79. Thao N. Le, Mary H. Lai, and Judy Wallen, "Multiculturalism and Subjective Happiness as Mediated by Cultural and Relational Variables," *Cult Div Ethn Min Psychol* 15 (2009): 303–13.

who does cultural diversity training in schools, it is clear to me that the level of cultural sensitivity of educators greatly impacts the learning process. Teachers or school staff who hold prejudice or even a more simple lack of intercultural understanding are likely to be ineffective (or even punitive) with students who differ from their cultural orientation. If we consider the growing diversity of populations in the United States and many parts of the world combined with the importance of education in relation to many happiness factors, this becomes a key social justice issue. And a similar level of importance could be extended to the need for intercultural sensitivity in many other systems (e.g., church congregations). Faith communities are frequently involved in missions and service projects across cultural differences, and a lack of intercultural sensitivity is harmful to such efforts. Spiritual leaders and therapy practitioners who lack intercultural competence will also be ineffective in promoting well-being across cultural differences.

Eudaimonic Psychotherapy, Counseling, and Happiness

Finally, I offer a few comments about eudaimonic implications for psychotherapy and pastoral counseling: First, the developmental virtue orientation of *eudaimonia* would start with highlighting an emphasis on the personal formation, Differentiation of Self, and well-being of the therapist or counselor. This would fit with what is sometimes called the "self of the therapist" in the marriage and family therapy field. The psychoanalytic traditions also place great emphasis on analysts doing personal work in therapy and attending to countertransference in an ongoing fashion. Therapists or counselors who are burned out or who lack personal and cultural self-awareness will have limited effectiveness and even be at risk of ethical violations.

Second, the complex biblical and psychological landscape related to happiness can highlight the need for differentiated wisdom in appreciating meaningful individual and contextual differences. In literary terms, people may "read" their life stories through differing genres and may need differing genres, so to speak, in sparking transformation. Personality differences and various diversity factors suggest counselors and therapists be attuned to differing pathways toward transformation. Some clients may appreciate approaches that parallel the optimistic practical wisdom of Proverbs while other clients may need to lament. In my view, a eudaimonic approach to counseling and therapy is not represented by trying to be explicitly eudaimonic all the time but involves a flexible posture with high tolerance for anxiety and ambiguity. It involves a deep belief that meaning can eventually be found in life along with a phenomenological orientation toward the process of discovery. This fits with an appreciation for the reality that transformative change in crucibles of happiness is often nonlinear with things frequently getting worse before they get better.

Finally, the interdisciplinary reflections I have offered in this response have highlighted relational factors as central to mature forms of well-being based on both biblical scholarship and empirical research. From a differentiation-based perspective, relational dynamics are a key source of transformation. While some clients may benefit from learning structured spiritual and psychological practices to enhance well-being, there will always be some type of relational dynamics at play in counseling and therapy. Those who have deeper intrapsychic barriers to happiness may present the greatest interpersonal challenges and also have the greatest need for a corrective relational experience.[80]

80. Some of the research described in this chapter was supported by a grant from the Fetzer Institute (#2266).

EPILOGUE

The Triumph of Life

TOWARDS A BIBLICAL THEOLOGY OF HAPPINESS

Brent A. Strawn

O, for that blessed happiness of the ancients!
—PHILO OF BYBLOS[1]

1. Life Finds a Way

In the Michael Crichton novel-turned-movie *Jurassic Park*, the chaos theorist Dr. Ian Malcolm (played by Jeff Goldblum), in response to the stunning news that newly reconstituted but sterilized dinosaurs are unexpectedly reproducing, remarks: "I'm simply saying that life, uh ... finds a way." To which he adds: "If there is one thing the history of evolution has taught us it's that life will not be contained. Life breaks free, expands to new territory, and crashes through barriers, painfully, maybe even dangerously."[2]

"Life finds a way ..." In *Jurassic Park* that means that what was once considered contained and controlled—even dead, insofar as it was sterilized and unable to propagate—struggles against containment, control, and death, and somehow transcends all that, all within the realm of finitude, to be sure. What, then, of human happiness—also a finite reality—and specifically human happiness within the

---

1. τῆς μακαριζομένης ἐκείνης τῶν παλαιῶν εὐδαιμονίας. Philo of Byblos, as preserved in Eusebius, *Praeparatio Evangelica* (*PE* 1.10.30); the translation is from Harold W. Attridge and Robert A. Oden, Jr., *Philo of Byblos, the Phoenician History: Introduction, Critical Text, Translation, Notes* (CBQMS 9; Washington, DC: Catholic Biblical Association of America, 1981), 55.

2. *Jurassic Park*, directed by Steven Spielberg, 1993, Universal Pictures. For the novel version, see Michael Crichton, *Jurassic Park* (New York: Ballentine, 1990), 159: "Life breaks free. Life expands to new territories. Painfully, perhaps even dangerously. But life finds a way."

bounds of the Bible, a finite collection of books and traditions despite its sacred status in several of the world's major religions? Do these, too, somehow transcend their limitations? Despite containment, control, and death—not to mention other human "finitudes" like pain, disease, sickness, hurt, loss, and so forth—does life, here understood as the good and happy life, somehow "find a way"?

The essays in this collection clearly suggest as much. Each one is sober-eyed, reflecting the sober-eyed nature of so much of Scripture itself. Both "happiness and its discontents," to cite the title of William P. Brown's essay on the Psalms, live together in the Bible.[3] Indeed, during the Atlanta conference that gave rise to the present collection there was more than one chuckle over whether there would be much to say at all about happiness and the Bible, simply because the Bible's contributions to darker realities are equally if not more well-known, especially by professional biblical scholars, even if these aren't as well-known or as fully appreciated by many "lay" readers.[4] But despite the laughs—which may have just been nerves as the participants worried if they would have enough to say to fill out an essay—the contributors to this volume dug in, did their homework, and, most importantly, have not fudged the data. Yes, there are exceedingly bleak statements about human life reflected in the Bible—some of which are simply *descriptive* (e.g., John 16:33: "In this world, you will have trouble . . ."; NIV), though some are admittedly *prescriptive* (e.g., Luke 9:23: "If any want to become my followers, let them deny themselves and take up their cross daily and follow me")—but there is also happiness, in both the hedonic and eudaimonic senses, mixed together, in "a happy blend," to evoke the title of Jacqueline Lapsley's essay.

How do these two—the truly bleak and the truly happy (including the two major differentiations of happiness, the hedonic and eudaimonic)—go together? How do they live together in the pages of the Bible and in the theology that is described there and the theology that draws its inspiration from there?[5] Must one

---

3. In addition to Brown's essay in the present volume, note J. Clinton McCann Jr., "The Shape of Book I of the Psalter and the Shape of Human Happiness," in *The Book of Psalms: Composition and Reception* (eds. Peter W. Flint and Patrick D. Miller Jr.; VTSup 99; Leiden: Brill, 2005), 340–48.

4. Cf. R. Norman Whybray, *The Good Life in the Old Testament* (London: T & T Clark, 2002), 2: "This topic [the good life] may appear bizarre and at best of secondary importance compared with the more 'spiritual' Old Testament concerns; but this is to underestimate the extent to which the ancient Israelites were affected in their daily lives by a longing for a more satisfactory mode of life." Whybray acknowledges that "much of the history of Israel recorded in the Old Testament is a tale of woe rather than of joy," but argues nevertheless that the good life is a "major topic of the Old Testament," adding that it "has been neglected in recent Old Testament study, and deserves more intense research" (291).

5. "Biblical theology" is typically defined as either descriptive (theology *in* the Bible) or prescriptive (theology *based on* the Bible), or, sometimes, both.

constantly deny one of these, whether the bleak or the happy, in favor of the other? If so, it hardly seems accurate to say that denying one (whichever one it may be) is in order "to be true" to the other, because both are present and operative in the Bible. One can only "be true" to the larger complex, that is, if one is true to *both*. But to put an even finer point on it, the real question is this: Must one deny the bleak in order to be "biblically happy"? The authors of the preceding essays, and indeed the collection taken as a whole, vigorously deny any such "splitting off," but one wonders if more popular and syrupy sweet articulations of happiness and the Bible are not successful precisely because they ignore its darker corners.[6] But surely such ignorance will not do—not if the goal is a robustly biblical articulation of the happy life. As Ellen T. Charry put it with reference to problematic theological articulations of happiness, if a doctrine is "not fully responsive to the fullness of the biblical witness," then "there is something wrong with the *doctrine*."[7] What then?

In the course of the preceding essays, several authors have touched on what Steven J. Sandage has helpfully termed a "reoriented form of happiness." Sandage defines this reoriented happiness as "a transformed type of happiness and well-being that includes the capacities to honestly face the disorienting realities of suffering and injustice in the world."[8] In this Epilogue I wish to build from and add to my colleagues' work in this regard, combining it with Dr. Malcolm's insight that "life finds a way." As indicated by my title, I will characterize the notion of transformed or reoriented happiness—or what might be called the dynamic of sober-eyed happiness—as "the triumph of life." I will illustrate this triumph of life in the Bible via three case studies (§2): (1) the shape of the lament psalms and the Psalter as a whole, (2) the shape of the Hebrew Bible; and (3) the shape of the Christian Bible, comprising both the Old and New Testaments.[9] Together these

---

6. Cf. the intriguing essay by W. Sibley Towner that empirically demonstrates the lack of lament language in the hymnals of several major US denominations: "'Without Our Aid He Did Us Make': Singing the Meaning of the Psalms," in *A God So Near: Essays on Old Testament Theology in Honor of Patrick D. Miller* (eds. Brent A. Strawn and Nancy R. Bowen; Winona Lake: Eisenbrauns, 2004), 17–34. Cf. more generally Keith J. Edwards and Todd W. Hall, "Illusory Spiritual Health: The Role of Defensiveness in Understanding and Assessing Spiritual Health," in *Spiritual Formation, Counseling, and Psychotherapy* (eds. Todd W. Hall and Mark R. McMinn; Hauppauge, NY: Nova Sciences Publishers, 2003), 261–75.

7. Ellen T. Charry, "The Necessity of Divine Happiness: A Response from Systematic Theology," 239.

8. Steven J. Sandage, "The Transformation of Happiness: A Response from Counseling Psychology," 283. Sandage's remarks are inspired by reflection on all of the essays in this volume, which thus essentially concur on the point, but see especially the essays by Jacqueline Lapsley, Joel B. Green, and Colleen Shantz.

9. For practical purposes I do not treat the apocryphal/deutero-canonical books here, leaving that to future research.

three vignettes that showcase the triumph of life in the Bible provide one entrée into a larger, more encompassing topic: a biblical theology of happiness.[10] Certainly, given the importance and thickness of the topic of happiness—not to mention the importance of the Bible in so many religious understandings of happiness—other ways into a biblical theology of happiness can be envisioned and should be pursued in future work. That granted, this initial probe also suggests something crucial about the notion of the "pursuit" of happiness—a point I consider after the case studies (§3). In closing, I return to the issues that opened this volume and prompted its study, namely the pollution and meaning of happiness, especially in the Bible (§4), before offering some final remarks on what the present book has taught us regarding "The Bible and Happiness" (§5).

2. The Triumph of Life
The Shape of the Psalms and Psalter

It is a well known and oft-discussed phenomenon that the individual lament psalms—virtually without exception[11]—shift abruptly in a change that is typically described as a movement from petition to praise. Since the individual lament

---

10. Whybray's posthumously published work, *The Good Life in the Old Testament*, is suggestive on this score but is different than what I propose here. He defines the good life as "a life of entire contentment with things as they are, the desire for which is a common feature of human mentality." While that definition could immediately be challenged by the positive psychology literature, Whybray helpfully glosses it by means of a minimal list of twelve "component features": security, a land to live in, some degree of power, adequate food and sustenance, a long life, wealth and material prosperity (which are the "natural consequence of a virtuous life lived under divine blessing"), family, justice, a body of laws, the quality of mind known as wisdom, pleasure, and trust in God (4–6). He then proceeds to discuss this list (or as many of its elements as occur) in each of the books of the Old Testament with the odd exception of Obadiah, Nahum, Zephaniah, and Habakkuk. These latter are excluded, according to Whybray, because "they do not contain information about the good life" (xi). But surely books like Obadiah and Nahum have strong contributions to make to the element of justice, at least, which is a feature of the good life by Whybray's own admission.

11. The famous exception is Psalm 88 (cf. also the book of Lamentations). See further below, and, for a recent study, David M. Howard, Jr., "Psalm 88 and the Rhetoric of Lament," in *My Words Are Lovely: Studies in the Rhetoric of the Psalms* (eds. Robert L. Foster and David M. Howard, Jr.; LHBOTS 467; New York: T & T Clark, 2008), 132–46. For now, however, it might be said that this one exception stereotypically "proves the rule." That said, a few psalms witness different correlations of lament and praise, including the precisely opposite movement, going from praise to lament. See the recent study by Federico G. Villanueva, *The 'Uncertainty of a Hearing': A Study of the Sudden Change of Mood in the Psalms of Lament* (VTSup 121; Leiden: Brill, 2008). Even so, as Villanueva notes, the movement from lament to praise "is the most common in the individual lament psalms" (43).

psalm is the most frequently attested type of psalm in the Psalter, examples are
not hard to find, and readers of the Psalms are likely familiar with this "sudden
change of mood," even if they have not thought of it using that precise phrase.
The following three texts are thus merely illustrative and representative of many
others (the turning point has been italicized):

> O LORD, how many are my foes!
>   Many are rising against me. . . .
> *But you, O LORD, are a shield around me,*
>   my glory, and the one who lifts up my head.
> I cry aloud to the LORD,
>   and he answers me from his holy hill. (Ps 3:1–2)

> I am weary with my moaning;
>   every night I flood my bed with tears;
>   I drench my couch with my weeping.
> My eyes waste away because of grief;
>   they grow weak because of all my foes.
> *Depart from me, all you workers of evil,*
>   *for the LORD has heard the sound of my weeping. (Ps 6:6–8)*

> But you, O LORD, do not be far away!
>   O my help, come quickly to my aid!
> Deliver my soul from the sword,
>   my life from the power of the dog!
>   Save me from the mouth of the lion!
> *From the horns of the wild oxen you have rescued me.*
> I will tell of your name to my brothers and sisters;
>   in the midst of the congregation I will praise you. (Ps 22:19–22)

While this movement from petition to praise is well known, it is still not fully
understood. Many different theories explaining the shift have been offered, with none
commanding complete consensus.[12] The most frequently encountered explanation
was popularized by Joachim Begrich in 1934, though it dates still earlier to the work

---

12. For recent reviews, see LeAnn Snow Flesher, "Rapid Change of Mood: Oracles of Salvation, Certainty of a Hearing, or Rhetorical Play?" in Foster and Howard, eds., *My Words Are Lovely*, 33–45; Beat Weber, "Zum sogenannten 'Stimmungsumschwung' in Psalm 13," in Flint and Miller, eds., *The Book of Psalms*, 116–38; Sung-Hun Lee, "Lament and the Joy of Salvation in the Lament Psalms," in Flint and Miller, eds., *The Book of Psalms*, 224–47; and Villanueva, *The 'Uncertainty of a Hearing'*, esp. 2–27.

of Friedrich Küchler in 1918.[13] This explanation posits that the psalmist received some sort of "good word" after voicing their lament, most likely from a priest in the temple, to which the psalmist then responded with a vow of praise. Such "good words"— more technically: "oracles of salvation"—are found scattered around the Old Testament, especially in the latter parts of Isaiah (see, e.g., Isa 41:8–10), and one notes a transaction similar to the one proposed for the lament psalms in 1 Samuel 1, where the barren Hannah pours out her soul before the LORD (1 Sam 1:15–16). Combining the words that the priest Eli says to Hannah after learning of her plight in that text with the words of the individual lament Psalm 13, the following script can be offered:

Psalmist:

> How long, O LORD? Will you forget me forever?
>> How long will you hide your face from me?
> How long must I bear pain in my soul,
>> and have sorrow in my heart all day long?
> How long shall my enemy be exalted over me?
> Consider and answer me, O LORD my God!
>> Give light to my eyes, or I will sleep the sleep of death,
> and my enemy will say, "I have prevailed";
>> my foes will rejoice because I am shaken. (Ps 13:1–4)

Priest:

> Go in peace, and may the God of Israel grant the petition you have made to him. (1 Sam 1:17; NRSV adapted)

Psalmist:

> But I trusted in your steadfast love;
>> my heart shall rejoice in your salvation.
> I will sing to the LORD,
>> because he has dealt bountifully with me. (Ps 13:5–6)

This is a very nice reconstruction indeed—and a perfectly sensible one—but the main problem is that we lack clear evidence that the psalmists received such

---

13. See Joachim Begrich, "Das priesterliche Heilsorakel," *ZAW* 52 (1934): 81–92; reprinted in idem, *Gesammelte Studien zum Alten Testament* (ed. Walther Zimmerli; Theologische Bücherei 21; München: Chr. Kaiser, 1964), 217–31; and, for the earlier essay, Friedrich Küchler, "Das priesterliche Orakel in Israel und Juda," in *Abhandlungen zur semitischen Relgionskunde und Sprachwissenschaft: Wolf Wilhelm Grafen von Baudissin zum 26. September 1917* (eds. Wilhelm Frankenberg and Friedrich Küchler; BZAW 33; Giessen: Alfred Töpelmann, 1918), 285–301.

oracles of salvation in this fashion or on a regular basis such that the reconstruction can be viewed as probable or the explanation certain.[14] Many of the psalms, moreover, may well reflect *non*cultic settings—prayer at home, that is, not in the temple—and so one must reckon with the absence of a priestly official and thus the lack of a "priestly oracle," at least in a highly formalized liturgical context like that of the temple.

One is tempted, then, if not required, to think of other options. Again, many have been offered and these have run the gamut from dealing with the *cause* of the shift to its *function* to its *nature*,[15] and they have employed everything from *theological* to *psychological* to *rhetorical* understandings.[16] Many of these options are not mutually exclusive and may be profitably combined.[17] Indeed, in the case of the lament psalms it seems that the theological and psychological, at the very least, must be combined since *the psalmist him- or herself* (i.e., the "I" of the psalm in question) is clearly affected by and transformed in the praying of the psalm; but that transformation is effected at least in part by *theological data*, which is to say the predications about God that are made in the psalm, as well as by the *theological context*, which is to say that this is prayer—invocation and plea to God by one who believes that God can, should, and ultimately will do something about one's dire straits. Moreover, the fact that this sort of prayer is dominated by petition and plea indicates that the *rhetorical*, too, is an essential element of the picture.

Whatever solution is adopted, my main point here is that, as they now stand, the lament psalms attest to a remarkable movement *through pain unto happiness*.[18] Perhaps that movement was caused *externally*: perhaps a priest said the right words at just the right moment. Perhaps the movement happened *internally*: the psalmists "worked through" their grief, not around it, and in the process were

---

14. Ps 12:5 is often cited as a possible oracle, though this is heavily debated and by no means certain. Moreover, even if it is such an oracle, the example is isolated and there is no indication that a priest is the one who spoke it. Note also Ps 60:6–9, though this, too, is not said to have been spoken by a priest per se and it occurs in a communal (not individual) lament.

15. This language is from Villanueva, *The 'Uncertainty of a Hearing'*, 5–27.

16. For a rhetorical approach, see Flesher, "Rapid Change of Mood," though the idea antedates Flesher and is present to some degree at least already in Gunkel's work on the Psalms.

17. Oddly, much recent work on the shift from lament to praise eschews combinatory approaches and explicitly disavows psychological insights. Both developments are unfortunate.

18. Cf. the thoughtful work by Kristin M. Swenson, *Living Through Pain: Psalms and the Search for Wholeness* (Waco, TX: Baylor University Press, 2005).

transformed.[19] Perhaps *both* took place.[20] Whatever the case, it is likely, if 1 Samuel 1 is any indication, that even in a formal liturgical transaction, the immediate circumstances of a petitioner were unchanged. Hannah, after all, had to return to normal life with her husband Elkanah and her "rival," Peninnah, who irritated and provoked her because of her childlessness (see 1 Sam 1:2, 5–7)—even after the reassuring words from Eli. And even if Hannah's conception was immediate (cf. 1 Sam 1:20), there were still the months of pregnancy to wait through and worry about, not to mention the birth itself.

While we lack narrative settings for the psalms, it is not hard to imagine that a similar situation obtains there. It is not likely, that is, that the psalmists' external circumstances were immediately changed and that this is what led to their altered outlook on life—one now dominated by gratitude, hope, and praise (all marks of the flourishing life according to eudaimonic understandings),[21] whereas before it was marked by incessant lament and despair. Rather, it seems more likely that something else, something interior or intrinsic to the psalmist has changed—even if that was prompted by some exterior reality, say an external word. Somehow, someway, in the midst of lament and despair, life has "found a way." Life has triumphed, despite and in spite of pain and grief.[22]

This same movement—from petition to praise or, for our purposes, from death to life or from suffering to happiness—seems to mark not only the individual lament psalms, but indeed the book of Psalms as a whole. Scholars have noticed that the majority of laments are found in the first half of the book, while the majority of the hymns of praise cluster in the second half, thus tracing out the shift from lament to praise in the Psalter itself.[23] One should be careful not to

---

19. See Brad D. Strawn and Brent A. Strawn, "The Shift from Lament to Praise: A Psychodynamic Phenomenon" (forthcoming).

20. The combination of external and internal aspects resonates with the happiness literature. Cf., e.g., Jonathan Haidt, *The Happiness Hypothesis: Finding Modern Truth in Ancient Wisdom* (New York: Basic, 2006), *passim*, e.g., xii: "Happiness comes from within, and happiness comes from without."

21. See the Introduction and note also William P. Brown, "Happiness and Its Discontents in the Psalms," 108: "In praise, happiness is consummated."

22. With other scholars, I think it is better to think of this as a tension or process rather than a once-for-all sort of victory. See the discussion in Weber, "Zum sogenannten 'Stimmungsumschwung' in Psalm 13," 116–38; Bernd Janowski, *Konfliktgespräche mit Gott: Eine Anthropologie der Psalmen* (3rd ed.; Neukirchen-Vluyn: Neukirchener Verlag, 2003), 75–84; and Villaneuva, *The 'Uncertainty of a Hearing'*, 22. See further below.

23. Cf. Walter Brueggemann, "Bounded by Obedience and Praise: The Psalms as Canon," *JSOT* 50 (1991): 63–92, reprinted in idem, *The Psalms and the Life of Faith* (ed. Patrick D. Miller; Minneapolis: Fortress, 1995), 189–213. See also Walter Brueggemann and Patrick D. Miller, "Psalm 73 as a Canonical Marker," *JSOT* 72 (1996): 45–56.

overdo this canonical movement, however.[24] While the final form of the book of Psalms appears to reflect a high degree of intentional editorial shaping, scholars continue to debate the details of all that.[25] More to the point, one shouldn't imagine that the first part of the Psalter is devoid of praise or the latter entirely free of lament. That is patently *not* the case. Indeed, the one lament that refuses to end in praise, Psalm 88, is found in the latter half of the Psalms, and the last individual lament is Psalm 143, which comes very late in the game indeed.

Even so, the movement at the book level toward praise is clear. The "contrary evidence" does not disprove the case so much as underscore the point I am trying to make—namely, that the shift toward hope, confidence, praise, and the like is not simplistic, but truly hard fought and painfully won. This is a "triumph" of life, yes, but one achieved only after a protracted struggle; it is by no means and by no stretch of the imagination an easy victory. So, while it is true that Psalm 88 does not end in praise, it is also the case that it is not the final psalm. Many more psalms are in the queue, and as one reads them one makes the journey of the ups and downs of faith and life with the psalmists and in the Psalms until one culminates, finally, in unbounded praise:

> Let every living thing praise the LORD
> Praise the LORD! (Ps 150:6; CEB)

Life is, then, "underway" in the psalms and in the Psalter.[26] But even the finale of Psalm 150, as climactic as it is, shouldn't be overdone. The faithful may never

---

24. See the cautions of Villaneuva, *The 'Uncertainty of a Hearing'*; as well as Harry P. Nasuti, "The Interpretive Significance of Sequence and Selection in the Book of Psalms," in Flint and Miller, eds., *The Book of Psalms*, 311–39. Similarly, Norman Whybray, *Reading the Psalms as a Book* (JSOTSup 222; Sheffield: Sheffield Academic Press, 1996), *passim*, though he acknowledges the general movement, and thus believes that "this rather loose application of the notion of 'progression' in the flow of the Psalter" has some plausibility (85; cf. 35, 121–22).

25. See J. Clinton McCann, Jr., ed., *The Shape and Shaping of the Psalter* (JSOTSup 159; Sheffield: JSOT Press, 1993); and, for a strongly contrarian perspective, Whybray, *Reading the Psalms as a Book*.

26. Cf. Claus Westermann, *Praise and Lament in the Psalms* (trans. Keith R. Crim and Richard N. Soulen; Atlanta: John Knox, 1981 [German orig: 1965]), 75: "The cry to God is . . . never one-dimensional, without tension. It is always somewhere in the middle between petition and praise. By nature it cannot be *mere* petition or lament, but is always underway from supplication to praise"; and Walter Brueggemann, *The Message of the Psalms: A Theological Commentary* (Minneapolis: Augsburg, 1984), 20: "*two decisive moves of faith* . . . are always underway"—one being the move from orientation to disorientation, and the other from disorientation to new orientation.

get to Psalm 150 or, even if they do, may never say it at full ease.[27] As Brown reminds us in his essay in the present collection, only the wicked enjoy a life free of pain in the Psalms (see Ps 73:3–5, 12).[28] So it is that "the journey from Psalm 1 to Psalm 150, from joyful obedience to ecstatic praise, proceeds in fits and starts, with wild oscillations between despair and joy—a veritable rollercoaster ride of emotions. The cultivation of happiness is somehow found amid these bipolar swings in the Psalter."[29] This is just another way of saying, with Dr. Malcolm, that "life . . . finds a way."

It is of utmost importance here to say that this stunning and paradigmatic shift from lament to praise, whether that is found in the individual lament psalms or the Psalter as a whole is not the result of simply "switching the mental channel" from negativity to positivity or "reprogramming" the mental computer, as some "happiologists" like Joel Osteen would have it.[30] That kind of advice no doubt means well—and one can hardly debate the benefits of positive habits (including cognitive therapies) that have been empirically tied to the life of happiness[31]—but

---

27. See Brent A. Strawn, "Psalm 150," in *Psalms for Preaching and Worship: A Lectionary Commentary* (eds. Roger E. Van Harn and Brent A. Strawn; Grand Rapids: Eerdmans, 2009), 376–81, esp. 381; also Villanueva, *The 'Uncertainty of a Hearing'*, 256: "Restoration and deliverance do occur, but it is not always immediate. For some it may take months, for others years, and even a lifetime." In a note he adds: "For some, the restoration may never come in this side of eternity" (256 n. 27).

28. See Brown's essay in the present volume, to which one might profitably add Tal Ben-Shahar, *Being Happy: You Don't Have to Be Perfect to Lead a Richer, Happier Life* (New York: McGraw Hill, 2010), 15: "the only people who don't experience . . . normal unpleasant feelings" like envy or anger, disappointment or sadness, fear or anxiety, "are psychopaths. And the dead."

29. Brown, "Happiness and its Discontents in the Psalms," 105.

30. See Joel Osteen, *Your Best Life Now: 7 Steps to Living at Your Full Potential* (New York: FaithWords, 2004), *passim*, but esp. 113–20, 144–45. John Piper, *Desiring God: Meditations of a Christian Hedonist* (Colorado Springs, CO: Multnomah, 2003), has a chapter on suffering (253–88), but it is almost exclusively devoted to religious persecution. I find Rick Warren's work far better than Osteen's and Piper's, especially on issues of suffering and hardship (e.g., *The Purpose Driven Life: What On Earth Am I Here For?* [Grand Rapids: Zondervan, 2002], 107–13, 193–208)—though I do not agree with all of it. For "happiology," and how it differs from positive psychology, see Christopher Peterson, *A Primer in Positive Psychology* (Oxford: Oxford University Press, 2006), 7–8; for the differences between positive psychology and positive thinking, see Sarah Lewis, *Positive Psychology at Work: How Positive Leadership and Appreciative Inquiry Create Inspiring Organizations* (Oxford and Malden, MA: Wiley-Blackwell, 2011), 2–6. See further below on how happiness studies and positive psychology need not be Pollyannaish.

31. See, e.g., Peterson, *A Primer in Positive Psychology*, 107–36; Haidt, *The Happiness Hypothesis*, 23–44. Note that Ben-Shahar argues that the purpose of cognitive therapy is "to restore a sense of realism by getting rid of distorted thinking" (*Being Happy*, 144). The sense of realism is precisely what seems to be missing from many purveyors of positive thinking who prefer to think instead in terms of *creating* reality.

this profound shift in the psalms is *definitely not* the result of the psalmist's pull-ing up on her mental "bootstraps." Neither are the psalms interested in the power of positive thinking or the power of faith words, or the like. Instead, it is impera-tive to remember that what caused this shift in the individual laments, the func-tion of that shift, and its precise nature remain highly debated topics—in part because we simply do not know or understand all that. That means, among other things, but certainly at the very least, that the matter cannot be reduced simply to "changing your thinking." Quite to the contrary, "life finds a way" and "shift hap-pens," whether at the level of the poems themselves or the Psalter as a whole, and when it does, it is resolutely *theological*. In the words of the old hymn, "something happened"—what that was, we do not know and cannot say for sure, or at least we cannot know it or speak of it outside the realm and language of faith—"and now I know, He touched me and made me whole."[32] Or, as Brown puts it in the present collection: "The Psalms . . . suggest . . . a dynamic of happiness that finds a way *through* misery rather than around it. . . . Happiness is false if it is not reached through the lived experience of affliction and deprivation, if it does not signal a process and transformation."[33] This lived experience, this process and transformation, is precisely the triumph of life.

Again, I believe the happiologists mean well, but they are surely peddling a polluted happiness at this point—one that reckons with a God that is far too small (despite the big talk about God's "control," "favor," and so forth),[34] in part because their polluted happiness overestimates human ability and the power of

---

32. Cf. Brent A. Strawn, "The Psalms: Types, Functions, and Poetics for Proclamation," in Van Harn and Strawn, eds., *Psalms for Preaching and Worship*, 15–17. Brueggemann describes the movement as an unprecedented theological *novum*, in a nutshell, the Gospel (*Message of the Psalms*, 20–23). One might compare, as Brueggemann himself does, the accent on unprece-dented newness in the idea of resurrection, on which see further Kevin J. Madigan and Jon D. Levenson, *Resurrection: The Power of God for Christians and Jews* (New Haven: Yale Univer-sity Press, 2008); and Jon D. Levenson, *Resurrection and the Restoration of Israel: The Ultimate Victory of the God of Life* (New Haven: Yale University Press, 2006).

33. Brown, "Happiness and its Discontents in the Psalms," 108. Cf. Swenson, *Living Through Pain*, 6: "The psalmists do not deny, downplay, or dismiss honest reactions to the problem of pain. They tell them, wrestle with them in conversation with God and others, and they move through them. That the psalmists do not pontificate on answers to the problem of pain, but rather move through aspects of the experience, dignifies the process itself. That the psalmists' difficult words are canonized in sacred texts suggests that such dynamic wrestling has a place, even in a 'godly' life."

34. For the ambiguity and "deeply unfortunate" nature of theological "control" language, es-pecially with reference to God's "absolute" control, see Terence E. Fretheim, *Creation Untamed: The Bible, God, and Natural Disasters* (Grand Rapids: Baker Academic, 2010), 62.

positive thinking, at least according to the witness of the Psalms.[35] But not only according to the witness of the Psalms, as important as that is; also according to the witness of experience: thousands of people are clinically depressed and it is not simply a matter of switching mental channels.[36] Cognitive behaviorism certainly has its place and its many correct uses, but Osteen is no psychotherapist, and neither is he hawking (primarily) a psychological product. More to the point, though, is the fact that the triumph of life in the Psalms is not a matter of changing but of *being changed* (again, the crucial points are italicized):

> I cry aloud to the LORD,
>> and *he answers me* from the his holy hill. (Ps 3:4)

> Depart from me, all you workers of evil,
>> *for the LORD has heard* the sound of my weeping.
> *The LORD has heard* my supplication;
>> *the LORD accepts* my prayer. (Ps 6:8–9)

> I will sing to the LORD,
>> *because he has dealt bountifully with me.* (Ps 13:6)

> From the horns of the wild oxen *you [LORD] have rescued me.* (Ps 22:21b)

> O LORD my God, I cried to you for help,
>> and *you have helped* me.
> O LORD, *you brought up* my soul from Sheol,
>> *restored* me to life from among those gone down to the Pit. (Ps 30:2–3).

> I waited patiently for the LORD;
>> *he inclined* to me *and heard* my cry.
> He drew me up from the desolate pit,
>> out of the miry bog,
> *and set* my feet upon a rock,
>> *making* my steps secure. (Ps 40:1–2)

---

35. Another deficiency, equally as serious, is the underestimation of the importance of human obedience. For the crucial role that covenantal faithfulness plays in biblical happiness, see the essays by MacDonald, Lapsley, and Green in the present volume, as well as Ellen T. Charry, *God and the Art of Happiness* (Grand Rapids: Eerdmans, 2010), *passim*, esp. 215, 252.

36. I mean here the truly clinically depressed, not those who are medicated for unhappiness that is not clinical—a point that rightly concerns Ronald W. Dworkin, *Artificial Happiness: The Dark Side of the New Happy Class* (New York: Carrol and Graf, 2006). For a profound theological treatment of mental illness, see Kathryn Greene-McCreight, *Darkness Is My Only Companion: A Christian Response to Mental Illness* (Grand Rapids: Brazos, 2006).

To be sure, these passages always contain an *object* of the verbal change—the "me" or "my" of the psalmist or her focus (prayer, supplication, feet, soul, etc.)—but the *Subject* is invariably other: it is the LORD who does these things. These changes are wrought *ab extra*, from the outside, by God, even as they are manifested internally, by the psalmists themselves, in their words, and—if their words are trustworthy in addition to being lovely—in their subsequent lives, affect, and flourishing. Still further *contra* happiologists of whatever stripe, the shift that comes in the lament psalms and the book of Psalms is no Pollyanna-type. It does not ignore, squelch, split-off, or deny the real pain and real suffering of life— some of which, it should be noted, stems from the psalmists themselves (their sin, for instance) by their own testimony, but much of which comes from their enemies and from God—but rather moves through it.[37]

There is no new life, the psalmists and the Psalms assert, via cover-up and denial, but only through deep honesty about sin and suffering. And while it is true that some people luxuriate overmuch in past tragedy until they are locked in and can't escape, the Bible as a whole witnesses to the importance of bad memories that forever fix God's saving activity in the mind, life, and heart (see, e.g., Exod 20:2; Deut 9:7–10:22; Psalm 30). So while Osteen and others apparently want people to "change channels" whenever their minds flutter to a bad memory, the psalmists would want people to linger—as they themselves did—because they know that morning joy (mourning joy?) only comes after a night full of tears (cf. Ps 30:5b).[38]

---

37. This speaks to Villanueva's concern over what he sees as a "stubborn bent, especially among Western scholars, to impose the one-way linear movement lament-praise on every psalm where the two elements are present" (*The 'Uncertainty of a Hearing'*, 28). While Villanueva's work shows clearly that there are, indeed, other configurations of lament and praise in the Psalms, I am not convinced that the scholarly problem as such is "Western." Proof of my point may be found in Villanueva's misreading of Brueggemann as always favoring praise over lament. One citation from Brueggemann's work will suffice, though his larger corpus makes the point repeatedly: "Israel does not sustain that unencumbered singing very long. Israel repeatedly goes back into the heart of the Psalter where the drama of suffering and hope, the conversation of alienation and gratitude, and the practice of candor and lyric are to be pursued again. It is in the heart of the Psalter, not at its extreme edges of simple obedience and guileless doxology, where Israel mostly lives" ("Bounded by Obedience and Praise," 213). Said differently, attention to movement need not involve a correlate underemphasizing of lament, the "downside" of life, the negative, and so forth. Such underemphasis is possible, but hardly necessary.

38. Cf. George H. Pollock's idea of "mourning-liberation": "The basic insight is that parts of the self that once were, or that one hoped might be, are no longer possible. With the working out of the mourning of the changed self, lost other, unfulfilled aspirations, as well as feelings about reality losses and changes, there is an increasing ability to face reality as it is and as it can be. 'Liberation' from the past allows the unattainable to occur" ("Aging and Aged: Development or Pathology," in *The Course of Life: Psychoanalytic Contributions Toward Understanding Personality Development*, Vol. 3: *Adulthood and the Aging Process* [eds. Stanley I. Greenspan and George H. Pollock; Rockville, MD: National Institute of Mental Health (U.S.) Mental Health Studies and Reports Branch, 1981], 549–85 (576). Further, Pollock, *The Mourning-Liberation Process* (2 vols.; Madison, CT: International Universities Press, 1989).

The points I have made here about the lament psalms and the Psalter as a whole find their correlates in much of the positive psychology literature that has also struggled against Pollyanna popularizations. Any positive psychologist worth her salt will tell you, however, that the happy life only exists because of and in interrelationship with pain.[39]

The Shape of the Hebrew Bible

Although I do not have the space to demonstrate it fully here, the triumph of life that is seen in the lament psalms and the book of Psalms can be traced throughout the Hebrew Bible on at least three levels.[40] It is found, first of all, in *specific books*, as already demonstrated in the case of the Psalter. In her contribution to the present volume, Lapsley notes a very similar dynamic in the book of Ezekiel, the canonical shape of which, she says, "*points toward happiness.*"[41] About halfway through Ezekiel, the book takes a decisive shift toward a future that is hope-filled, culminating in an extended vision of a restored Israel and a new city named "the LORD is there" with a life-giving river that streams from the temple where God is present and from which God promises never to depart (see Ezekiel 40–48; esp. 43:5, 7, 9; 44:1–2; 47:1–12; 48:35).

Second, the triumph of life is also found in *larger complexes* within the Bible, not just in its constituent books. In his contribution, Nathan MacDonald notes

---

39. Ed Diener, "Positive Psychology: Past, Present, and Future," in *Oxford Handbook of Positive Psychology* (2nd ed.; eds. Shane J. Lopez and C. R. Snyder; New York: Oxford University Press, 2011), 10: "In fact, positive psychologists do not ignore what is negative in the human condition.... Instead, positive psychologists ... tackle problems while focusing on the positive in their approach to problems." See also Martin E. P. Seligman, *Authentic Happiness: Using the New Positive Psychology to Realize Your Potential for Lasting Fulfillment* (New York: Free Press, 2002), 56–57; Haidt, *The Happiness Hypothesis*, 135–53; Peterson, *A Primer in Positive Psychology*, 9, 12–15, 19, 96, 305–6; Tal Ben-Shahar, *Even Happier: A Gratitude Journal for Daily Joy and Lasting Fulfillment* (New York: McGraw Hill, 2010), 25; and idem, *Being Happy*, 18–19.

40. At this point I am particularly discussing the organization or "flow" of the Bible in its Hebrew form and signal that by the nomenclature "Hebrew Bible." However, insofar as the points are not dependent solely on a linear reading of the texts in question (see further below), I believe they can also stand—*mutatis mutandis*—for the ordering of the books in English versions of the Old Testament, which goes back, to some degree at least, to the Greek Septuagint (LXX). In ancient times, of course, the precise order of the biblical books was often subject to a good bit of variation. For the Hebrew and Greek evidence, see, respectively: Christian D. Ginsburg, *Introduction to the Massoretico-Critical Edition of the Hebrew Bible* (repr. ed.; New York: Ktav, 1966), 1–8; and H. B. Swete, *Introduction to the Old Testament in Greek* (repr. ed.; Peabody, MA: Hendrickson, 1989 [orig. 1900]), 197–230.

41. See Jacqueline Lapsley, "A Happy Blend: Isaiah's Vision of Happiness (and Beyond)," 91 (her emphasis).

the teleological shape of the current form of the Pentateuch. It is open-ended and unfinished, as it were, insofar as the long-promised land is not yet taken as Deuteronomy closes. This shows that happiness involves an orientation to the future and that God's people are, in many ways, *on their way* to happiness. This is so, not in denial of, but nevertheless in spite of, the very real *un*happiness that is often found in the Torah.

Third and finally, the triumph of life can be seen in the overall flow of the Hebrew Bible.[42] What is seen, that is, at the level of the basic canonical unit (the biblical book) and in larger complexes of such units (e.g., the Pentateuch), can also be tracked at the highest level of the canon itself. The Hebrew Bible is tripartite, consisting of Torah, Prophets, and Writings (Kethubim). The triumph of life in the *Torah* has already been discussed. In the case of the *Prophets*, which are divided into the Former (Joshua-Kings) and Latter (Isaiah, Jeremiah, Ezekiel, and the book of the twelve minor prophets) Prophets, the case might be more difficult to establish, but is not impossible. Here I briefly sketch two ideas.

1. The first is that the *Former Prophets*, often called the Deuteronomistic History given their seeming dependence upon the book of Deuteronomy, stretch from the taking of the land (Joshua) to the loss of that land (2 Kings). One might be hard pressed, then, to see the deleterious turn of events that ends the book of Kings as "the triumph of life." While that observation stands, scholars have nevertheless long noticed hopeful elements within the Former Prophets. For some scholars, such elements may be as small as the release of King Jehoiachin from his Babylonian imprisonment (2 Kgs 25:27–30); for others it might be the possibility of repentance that is manifested in key ways throughout the Former Prophets.[43] The former may be a slender hope indeed, but may nevertheless suggest that a new life back in the land is possible, despite the destruction and despair of exile.[44] The latter may suggest that it is never too late for repentance—even after

---

42. Cf. Whybray, *The Good Life in the Old Testament*, 1, 288, 299, on how the final form of the Bible was designed by its editors to encourage their readers, offering hope after times of serious suffering.

43. See, e.g., the classic studies by Gerhard von Rad ("The Deuteronomic Theology of History in 1 and 2 Kings," in *From Genesis to Chronicles: Explorations in Old Testament Theology* [ed. K. C. Hanson; Minneapolis: Fortress, 2005], 154–66); and Hans Walter Wolff ("The Kerygma of the Deuteronomic Historical Work," in Walter Brueggemann and Hans Walter Wolff, *The Vitality of Old Testament Traditions* [2nd ed.; Atlanta: John Knox, 1982], 83–100), respectively.

44. That such a hope is more than implied seems confirmed by the subsequent history of Israel and what takes place in the so-called "restoration" period detailed in Ezra-Nehemiah.

disobedience—and that such repentance sometimes works. Still further, the Latter Prophets can be slotted, as it were, back into the movement of the Former Prophets. When this is done, they add their own complex interweaving of death and life, judgment and hope into the mix—this is the second idea that needs to be sketched.

2. It has often been noted that the *Latter Prophets* seem to have been schematically arranged so that—painting here with a broad brush—even the most judgmental of prophetic books ends with oracles of salvation and hope. Such a dynamic was noted in Ezekiel above, but it can also be traced in Isaiah and Jeremiah, Hosea and Amos, Micah and so on. Despite the blood and iron of God's wrath and judgment that one often finds in the Latter Prophets, there is also the lavender, even roses, of hope, including the hope for and experience of God's mercy and forgiveness.[45] Somehow, despite death and destruction—the barriers Dr. Malcolm mentions—whatever their nature or origin, life breaks free and finds a way.

And what of the *Writings*? This material is harder to characterize, at least in part because these books do not hold together as a larger complex like the Torah and the Former/Latter Prophets do. That said, no less than three books from the Kethubim have been treated in the present volume (Proverbs, Qoheleth, and Psalms), which demonstrates that these books, too, have something to say about the flourishing life. Further, while the precise ordering of the biblical books seems to have been in flux for some time, it is noteworthy that, at least in several important manuscripts and according to the Talmud (*b. B. Bat.* 14b), the Hebrew Bible ends with Chronicles.[46] Chronicles begins at the beginning, with a long genealogical section that picks up at the start of Genesis with Adam and sons (1 Chronicles 1–8). But then it jumps to the Judean exile (1 Chr 9:1) before returning to Saul, briefly (1 Chr 9:35–10:14), then David, extensively (1 Chr 11:1–29:30), before then chronicling more concisely those who succeeded David in the southern kingdom (2 Chronicles 1–35). The very last chapter of the book, 2 Chronicles 36, recounts the fall of Jerusalem and the exile, which are also described in 2 Kings

---

45. The imagery comes from Julius Wellhausen's remarks on the ending of Amos. See his *Skizzen und Vorarbeiten 5: Die kleinen Propheten übersetzt und erklärt* (3rd ed.; Berlin: Reimer, 1898), 96: "Rosen und Lavendel statt Blut und Eisen."

46. See Ginsburg, *Introduction to the Massoretico-Critical Edition of the Hebrew Bible*, 1–8, esp. 6–8. Of the eight different orderings Ginsburg presents, five (representing sixteen manuscripts) end with Chronicles. The other three (representing six manuscripts) end with Ezra-Nehemiah and, somewhat curiously, put Chronicles first.

25. What is intriguing, however, is the material the Chronicler includes that 2 Kings does not. As mentioned above, 2 Kings 25 ends with the release of the deposed and exiled Jehoiachin from a Babylonian prison cell, but 2 Chronicles 36 does not mention this event at all, but instead ends with King Cyrus of Persia's proclamation that the Judean exiles could go free, back to Judah and Jerusalem:

> In the first year of King Cyrus of Persia, in fulfillment of the word of the LORD spoken by Jeremiah, the LORD stirred up the spirit of King Cyrus of Persia so that he sent a herald throughout all his kingdom and also declared in a written edict: "Thus says King Cyrus of Persia: The LORD, the God of heaven, has given me all the kingdoms of the earth, and he has charged me to build him a house at Jerusalem, which is in Judah. Whoever is among you of all his people, may the LORD his God be with him! Let him go up!" (2 Chr 36:22–23).

And that is how not only the Writings, but the entire Hebrew Bible ends—not with the slender hope of 2 Kings 25, but with the LORD's direct agency, "stirring up" the leader of the world's then-superpower, in accordance with a prior word of one of the greatest of Israel's prophets, to allow a return to the center: to Judah, to Jerusalem, to the temple, to the LORD, the God of heaven himself. Life has found a way—because God has found a way, let it be underscored—which is all the more remarkable in light of the destruction and years of desolation, which Chronicles makes clear also came about to fulfill Jeremiah's words (2 Chr 36:21).

The Shape of the Christian Bible

The shape of the Christian Bible, too, reflects the triumph of life. The points noted for the Hebrew Bible also stand in the main for the Old Testament. The latter has a different order, however, ending not with 2 Chronicles 36, but with the Latter Prophets, particularly with the Book of the Twelve with their accent on the "Day of the LORD." Even more specifically, the English Old Testament ends with the book of Malachi and its promise of the sending of Elijah "before the great and terrible day of the LORD comes" so that YHWH "will not come and strike the land with a curse" (Mal 4:5–6). The effect of this ordering is like the ending of the teleologically shaped Torah, and it is a small hop, skip, and jump indeed from Malachi 4 to the Gospels; to John the Baptist, who is identified with Elijah's "spirit and power" (Luke 1:17) and whom Jesus calls the "Elijah who is to come" (Matt 11:14; cf. 17:13; John 1:21); and to Jesus himself, whom others call Elijah (Matt 16:14; Mark 8:28; Luke 9:19) and who appears with that great prophet in the Transfiguration (Matt 17:1–8; Mark 9:2–8; Luke 9:28–36).

As for the New Testament proper, everyone knows of the triumph of life that is Easter Sunday. And yet there is no resurrection without the crucifixion on "Good Friday"—which is a dark and subtle use of the adjective "good" to be sure! And yet Sunday comes, despite the death on Friday. Then, after resurrection, come the ascension and the explosion of the early church according to Acts. That success does not come without cost: problems, persecution, even death beset the apostles at every turn, but the triumph of life that has taken place in Jesus's life, ministry, and death allows them to flourish despite terror all around.[47] In Paul's words:

> We are hard pressed on every side, but not crushed; perplexed, but not in despair; persecuted, but not abandoned; struck down, but not destroyed. We always carry around in our body the death of Jesus, so that the life of Jesus may also be revealed in our body. For we who are alive are always being given over to death for Jesus' sake, so that his life may be revealed in our mortal body. So then, death is at work in us, but life is at work in you. (2 Cor 4:8–12; NIV)

One sees here the interweaving of life and death, death and life, but it is the latter order that wins out in the end and for the (good of the) many.

After Acts, the New Testament breaks from its narrative flow and shifts to Paul's letters, which fold back onto the story of the early Christian communities, not unlike how the Latter Prophets fold back into the Former. Paul's corpus, as well as the Catholic letters, is full of the mundane realities of life: people to greet, problems to fix, collections to take up, details to arrange, advice to give, and so on and so forth. And yet, despite the mundane realities, and despite the delay of the Christ's return, there is still happiness and flourishing, which includes people to greet, problems to fix, collections to take up, details to arrange, advice to give, and so on and so forth! Moreover, even in the midst of the harshest realities, like prison and the threat of violent death, Paul's epistles contain verses like "Rejoice in the Lord always; again I will say, Rejoice!" (Phil 4:4). Somehow, someway, the triumph of life happened to Paul—in his own life, even in his own body—despite his carrying around Jesus's death in that selfsame life and body.[48]

Finally, we come to the Apocalypse of John, a work irrefutably oriented to the final *telos* and thus to future happiness.[49] Here, too, there is significant suffering,

---

47. See the essays by Joel B. Green and Carl R. Holladay in the present volume.

48. See Colleen Shantz's essay in the present volume.

49. See Greg Carey's contribution to the present volume.

even trauma, but also what must be considered—from the perspective of the full sweep of the Christian Bible—the ultimate triumph of life: the giving of the new heaven, the new earth, and the new Jerusalem—which comes down to earth, let it be noted, and where tears, death, mourning, crying, and pain will be no more (Rev 21:1–4). The triumph of life here is apocalyptic, to be sure, but it includes the aquatic and arboreal in its vision: the thirsty receive water "as a gift from the spring of the water of life" (Rev 21:6); and on either side of this river of life-giving water is "the tree of life . . . and the leaves of the tree are for the healing of the nations" (Rev 22:2). The images evoke the end of Ezekiel and the beginning of Genesis, respectively, with all their associations, on the one hand, with the "pre-lapsarian" paradise that was lost (Genesis), and, on the other, with the "post-lapsarian" paradise that was promised (Ezekiel).

Again, let me be clear: None of this comes without price. The triumph of life in the New Testament, too, is a hard-fought victory, not a given and definitely no easy result. Even so, despite and in spite of any and all trouble, pain, finitude, death, you name it, life "finds a way."

Much more could be said about the individual biblical books, the respective testaments, and the flow of the canon(s) as a whole. While that work cannot be done here, I wish to make two important interpretive points before taking leave of the triumph of life in the Bible.

The Question of Sequence

The first point is that tracing the triumph of life in the Bible need not be restricted solely to some sort of linear reading of the Bible as a grand narrative. Such an approach to the "story" of the Bible is common in both popular and professional circles, and there is much to commend it. In my judgment, the narrative approach, while helpful in many ways, is not yet a comprehensive or definitive one.[50] Much of the Bible is not narrative, after all, and one is hard pressed to read it straight through as one would a novel—even as a modern or postmodern novel, which often play with time and sequencing in atypical ways.[51] The four Gospels tell a repetitive story, albeit one with (not insignificant) differences and nuances, and even though Acts continues that "narrative" (particularly that of Luke),

---

50. For what follows, see further Brent A. Strawn, "Lyric Poetry," in *Dictionary of the Old Testament: Wisdom, Poetry and Writings* (eds. Tremper Longman III and Peter Enns; Downers Grove: IVP Academic, 2008), 437–46.

51. See Mieke Bal, *Narratology: Introduction to the Theory of Narrative* (3rd ed.; Toronto: University of Toronto Press, 2009), esp. 77–98, 214–19.

everything that follows thereafter does not—neither in terms of the plot nor in terms of the genre (where no more narrative is to be found). Similar points could be made of the Old Testament/Hebrew Bible.

Calling the whole Bible, then, or even just one of its testaments "a story" or "narrative" is thus something of an imposition. The rough juxtaposition of books we find in the Bible, often with no clear connection between them, is much more akin to lyric poetry than it is a coherent narrative. Calling the Bible "a poem" or, better, "a poetic sequence" is surely no less an imposition than calling it a "story" or a "narrative," but the poetic option has some distinct advantages. For our purposes, a primary help would be that the triumph of life does not need to be seen—and indeed *should not* be seen—as an inevitable result, the automatic march of progress, as it were.[52] The triumph of life needn't be seen and shouldn't be seen as "triumphalism," especially of the worst sort. Rather, in the warp and woof of the Bible's "poetry," we see happiness emerging within and among the mundane aspects of life—yes, even amidst its decidedly *un*happy moments of tragedy, suffering, and the like. So, to return to an earlier point, while Psalm 88 may not be the last psalm in the Psalter, one needn't read the Psalms solely or only in order, nor all the way through.[53] Sometimes one might stay with Psalm 88 for

---

52. Nasuti, "The Interpretive Significance of Sequence and Selection," 313, defines a sequential arrangement as "one distinguished by linear movement in a given direction. The order of the elements cannot be reversed without affecting the meaning of the whole." While this is largely true, lyric sequences, insofar as they are comprised of lyric poems, and thus mirror the workings of lyric poetry, are comprised of both centripetal and centrifugal structures that complicate, if not resist, any sort of simplistic understanding of "linear" movement. See further Strawn, "Lyric Poetry," 437–46; F. W. Dobbs-Allsopp, "The Psalms and Lyric Verse," in *The Evolution of Rationality: Interdisciplinary Essays in Honor of J. Wentzel van Huyssteen* (ed. F. LeRon Shults; Grand Rapids: Eerdmans, 2006), 346–79; and Katie M. Heffelfinger, *I Am Large, I Contain Multitudes: Lyric Cohesion and Conflict in Second Isaiah* (BIS 105; Leiden: Brill, 2011). To be sure, with any "sequence" it is important to guard against devaluation of earlier compositions (e.g., the lament psalms in the first half of the Psalter) as only or merely preliminary to the supposedly superior compositions that follow in the sequence (cf. Villanueva, *The Uncertainty of a Hearing*, 19, 253; Nasuti, "The Interpretive Significance of Sequence and Selection," 323). In my judgment, however, a poetic sequence as opposed to a narrative one is innately better suited for addressing precisely such a concern. In fact, as Nasuti shows from the history of interpretation (*viz.*, Gregory of Nyssa's *Commentary on the Inscriptions of the Psalms*), it is, in fact, possible to read the Psalms as a sequence—even as a developmental sequence that fosters a virtuous life—without necessarily devaluing early psalms (324–27).

53. See further Nasuti, "The Interpretive Significance of Sequence and Selection," *passim*, but esp. 334: "Because the 'life settings' of different readers are not the same, even readers who discern the same sequence in the Psalter may find themselves at different points of standing within that sequence. Indeed, the same reader will almost certainly have a different point of standing at different times of his/her own life. Since the path to holiness is seldom a smooth and steady ascent, [the] reader rarely leaves behind certain psalms once and for all."

some time—or Psalm 150 for that matter. Either way, the individual psalms and the individual books, traditions, units, and so on of the Bible are still there, engaging us in the process of the triumph of life. That process is not simplistic, nor is it simplistically linear. Thinking the Bible-as-poetry rather than as forward-driven-narrative helps with that.

A nonlinear approach is true not only for much of the Bible but for much of life—and indeed the two mirror each other at this point. In his essay in this volume, Sandage speaks of "the reality that transformative change in crucibles of happiness is often non-linear with things often getting worse before they get better."[54] Here again one thinks of Psalm 88 or its next-door neighbor, Psalm 89, which isn't much better—not, at least, if one is hoping for syrupy sweet (pseudo)happiness. Both poems are a long way from either Psalm 1 or Psalm 150.

Fitting Some Parts (for example, Job and James)

The second interpretive point I wish to make is that tracing the triumph of life in the Bible writ large, especially with the help of positive psychology and the work of the authors in this volume, might help us make sense of those parts of the Bible that don't quite seem to fit the theme of happiness.[55] I've already addressed this issue in various ways above as well as in the Introduction. For one thing, the problem may be in how we define "happiness": simply put it isn't always (or for very long) syrupy sweet. For another thing, the triumph of life—or, in fuller terms, "the good, happy, flourishing life"—is never far removed from other, less triumphant, less positive, and more negative aspects of life. The poem that is a truly happy life (whether that is found in the Bible or in a human life) is a complex, multifaceted, and many-colored thing—and it is not always "beautiful." Not in any simplistic sense at any rate.

But my main point here is to echo an observation made by MacDonald in his essay—namely, that happiness is a hermeneutical issue. It is a *lens*. The present

---

54. Sandage, "The Transformation of Happiness: A Response from Counseling Psychology," 285.

55. Sandage makes a similar point in his brief mention of sexuality—a topic that is neglected in this volume but that certainly belongs in discussions of happiness generally (hedonically and eudaimonically understood), and in discussions of happiness and the Bible (one need think only of the Song of Songs).

volume did not have time or space to address all of the Bible or its parts. More work remains to be done. Such work, and the hermeneutical lens of happiness discussed here, will afford new light on passages that are crucial to the study of happiness—even if they remain difficult—which have not been addressed in the present collection. As indication of how future research might proceed, I mention two examples:

1. First, we might consider Job. Certainly the book, its content, structure, and themes are too complex to receive adequate treatment here. It is enough to make a few observations that may be generative of further work. One of these is that Claus Westermann has argued that the book as a whole is structured along the lines of the lament form.[56] Although not all would agree,[57] and one must guard against any overly simplistic analysis given the generic complexity of Job,[58] the broad contours Westermann notes are suggestive. If he is right, it means, among other things, that the only way to emerge on the other side of tragedy, as Job does—whether that is in the poetic, wisdom dialogue (see Job 40:3–5; 42:1–6) or in the prosaic frame's epilogue (see Job 42:10–17)—is by means of the lament and the "going through" of the tragedy. At the same time, Westermann's work on Job, especially when coupled with his work on praise and lament in the Psalms, also suggests that Job *does* in fact emerge on the other side of his lament and tragedy.

This means not only that the book of Job is yet another instance of the triumph of life in the Bible, but also that Job, even posttragedy Job, could correctly be called "happy."[59] Carol A. Newsom's work on Job is particularly helpful at

---

56. Claus Westermann, *The Structure of the Book of Job: A Form-Critical Analysis* (trans. Charles A. Muenchow; Philadelphia: Fortress, 1981 [German orig.: 1977]).

57. See, e.g., Villaneuva's remarks, though without reference to Westermann (*The 'Uncertainty of a Hearing'*, 258).

58. See Carol A. Newsom, *The Book of Job: A Contest of Moral Imaginations* (Oxford: Oxford University Press, 2003), esp. 3–31.

59. One might note here the notion of and literature on posttraumatic growth (PTG) in positive psychology. Ben-Shahar, *Even Happier*, 103, describes PTG as taking place when a loss transforms someone in "profound ways—they appreciate life more, their relationships improve, and they become more resilient." See more extensively Christopher G. Davis and Susan Nolen-Hoeksema, "Making Sense of Loss, Perceiving Benefits, and Posttraumatic Growth," in *Oxford Handbook of Positive Psychology* (2nd ed.; eds. Shane J. Lopez and C. R. Snyder; New York: Oxford University Press, 2011), 641–49; also Haidt, *The Happiness Hypothesis*, 136–41.

this point.[60] Newsom contrasts the moral imagination suggested by Job's final summation and defense in chapters 29–31 with the moral imagination suggested in the God speeches found in chapters 38–41. The difference between the two "indicate[s] that there is something flawed in Job's moral and religious understanding."[61] By means of different images, metaphors, patterns, and the like, the God speeches present Job with an alternative way of organizing his world. Among other things, that reorganization involves models of relationality that are marked by "nondependence and nondomination."[62]

We cannot know, of course, on the basis of the text, how all that affected "the real (character) Job," but Newsom makes a strong case that Job may well have "understood the context and motivation of his deeds quite differently," afterwards:

> I doubt that he cared much any more for gestures of deference. It probably did not matter to him as it once had whether the distressed blessed him for his help or not. Above all, I suspect that he looked on society's outcasts with rather different eyes. Indeed, it was Job's seeing, as he himself observes, that was most radically altered (42:5). The horizon of his vision and the patterns he discerned were different. We do know three details from the end of the story that suggest this difference in his life. Job received his brothers and sisters when they came to him; he no longer had to experience his suffering as rejection. Also, although he knew how fragile life could be, he was again willing to participate in the goodness of creation by giving birth, with his wife, to ten more children. Finally and most intriguingly, he gave his daughters an inheritance along with his sons, a gesture that would lessen their dependence in a patriarchal world.[63]

This is very much "a posttragic epilogue to the whole book," but it is also "one in which the goodness of life in all its fragility is embraced."[64] Seen in this

---

60. I draw here particularly from Carol A. Newsom, "The Moral Sense of Nature: Ethics in the Light of God's Speech to Job," *PSB* 15 (1994): 9–27. Newsom puts matters differently in her larger study (*The Book of Job*, esp. 234–58), but I consider both studies, at least for present purposes, as ultimately complementary.

61. Newsom, "The Moral Sense of Nature," 15.

62. Ibid., 25.

63. Ibid., 27.

64. Newsom, *The Book of Job*, 257. Cf. above on posttraumatic growth (PTG).

way, the end of the book of Job—and the book as a whole—is not only a witness to the triumph of life, it can also be said to be a witness to a *happy life*, with Job, who dies "old and full of days" (Job 42:17),[65] aptly called "a happy man."[66]

2. Surely, this would be a thick use of the term "happy" but it would be a use altogether in line with the points made throughout this volume as well as with the notion of the triumph of life outlined above. Such a thick use, to continue in this same vein, seems to me the only way to make sense of other passages pertaining to the study of happiness that are particularly in danger of thin and/or polluted (mis)understandings. And so, as a second example, I cite the well-known text from James 1:

> My brothers and sisters, whenever you face trials [*peirasmos*] of any kind, consider it nothing but joy [*pasan charan*], because you know that the testing of your faith produces endurance; and let endurance have its full effect, so that you may be mature and complete, lacking in nothing. (James 1:2–4)

---

65. The notion that one can only be judged happy after their death goes back at least to Solon's remark to King Croesus recounted in Herodotus's *Histories*, 1.32 (see further the Introduction to the present volume): "You seem to be very wealthy, and you rule over many people, but I cannot yet tell you the answer you asked for until I learn how you have ended your life" (translation from Robert B. Strassler, ed., *The Landmark Herodotus: The Histories* [New York: Pantheon Books, 2007], 20). At several points, Aristotle speaks of the necessity of a "full term of years" for the exercise of one's faculties in accordance with excellence or virtue (i.e., to live a happy life; he explicitly considers Solon's statement in *Nicomachean Ethics*, 1.10 [1100a–1101a]; cf. also 10.8 [1179a]). He remarks: "one day or a short time does not make someone blessed and happy" (*Nicomachean Ethics*, 1.7 [1098a]; the translation is from Robert C. Bartlett and Susan D. Collins, *Aristotle's Nicomachean Ethics* [Chicago: University of Chicago, 2011], 13; cf. also 1.9 [1100a]; 10.7 [1177b]). He also states that the happy person "would not be unstable and subject to reversals . . . for he will not be easily moved from happiness, and then not by any random misfortunes but only by great and numerous ones. And as a result of such things he would not become happy again in a short time; but, if in fact he does, he will do so in the completion of some lengthy period of time during which he comes to attain great and noble things" (1.10 [1101a]; Bartlett and Collins, *Aristotle's Nicomachean Ethics*, 20). In this light, the comment about the duration of Job's life in 42:17 takes on increased significance.

66. Cf. Newsom (*The Book of Job*, 258) where she reflects on whether or not "tragic Job" can be said to laugh. Newsom highlights the enigmatic and intriguing information about Job's daughters' names that are related to beauty (Jemimah, "dove"), sensuous beauty (Keziah, "cinnamon"), and even erotic beauty (Keren-happuch, "horn of eye shadow"). "Such playful names are a form of laughter—not heedless or anarchic laughter—but human and therefore tragic laughter." Note also Whybray's reflections on Job (*The Good Life in the Old Testament*, 137–41).

Only a rich definition of happiness, in the eudaimonic sense, can make sense of such a text, not to mention the many others in the New Testament that are like it (e.g., Rom 5:2–5; 2 Cor 6:10; 1 Thess 5:16–18; 1 Pet 1:6–7).[67] Trials and testing, especially of the kind that are likely to produce stamina, are rarely of the pleasurable kind (one thinks of marathon training). But this text is not about subjective well-being—and certainly not in hedonic mode—but about *spiritual maturity*.[68] And it is *only* (let that qualification be triply underscored!) the spiritually mature that are able to *interpret* (note: "*consider* it [*hē geomai*] joy" not "*experience* it") such trials as a matter of "joy," "grace" (*charis*), or "happiness." But that is just another way to say that the truly happy life, the flourishing life in all its fullness, is never removed from real life in all its fullness, and that such fullness experiences real pain as well as pleasure. And yet, despite all that, life "finds a way" because, in no small part, it is *on its way*.[69] In Sandage's words, "the Bible, read as a whole, calls for *transformation in the pursuit of happiness*."[70]

---

67. Aristotle says something quite similar in *Nicomachean Ethics*, 1.10 (1100b): "The happy man, then, as we define him, will have this required property of permanence, and all through life will preserve his character; for he will be occupied continually, or with the least possible interruption, in excellent deeds and excellent speculations; and whatever his fortune be, he will take it in the noblest fashion, and bear himself always and in all things suitably, since he is truly good and 'foursquare without a flaw'" (the translation here is from Aristotle, *Nicomachean Ethics* [trans. F. E. Peters; repr. ed.; New York: Barnes and Noble, 2004], 17).

68. See further Sandage's essay in the present volume and Gerald G. May, *The Dark Night of the Soul: A Psychiatrist Explores the Connection Between Darkness and Spiritual Growth* (San Francisco: HarperSanFrancisco, 2004). Note also Charry, *God and the Art of Happiness*, *passim*, but esp. 254–55: "Happiness is a realizing eschatology: it is the intensification of spiritual maturity in which happiness expands and deepens as people become spiritually stronger and better able to contribute to their own and the world's well-being."

69. See Peter Davids for the eschatological nature of the joy-amidst-suffering theme in James (also Romans 5, 1 Peter 1, the Beatitudes, etc.): "[T]he reason why an eschatological perspective produces joy" is because "the test produces the virtue of ὑπομονή [*hypomonē*, 'endurance, perseverance, patience']" (*The Epistle of James: A Commentary on the Greek Text* [NIGTC; Grand Rapids: Eerdmans, 1986], 68). In chapter 5, James calls "blessed" (*makarizō*) those who have endured (*hypomenō*) and explicitly mentions the endurance of Job (5:11), though most scholars believe he is alluding to the pseudepigraphical *Testament of Job*, not the canonical book of Job. James 5:11 also mentions the "purpose [*telos*] of the Lord," apparently with the sense of the result of God's work "as known from the story of Job, i.e., blessing. As in the case of Job, the Christian can expect ultimate good. . . . Thus, as the example of Job shows, if one is patient enough the time will come (i.e. in the parousia) when the good end of the Lord will appear" (Davids, *The Epistle of James*, 188).

70. Sandage, "The Transformation of Happiness: A Response from Counseling Psychology," 263.

Only a deeply transformed understanding of "happiness"—a term so carelessly used, so poorly defined, and so deeply polluted in our context—can make sense of Job and James. The "pursuit" of that kind of transformed happiness must now be addressed.

3. On the "Pursuit" of Happiness

In the Introduction to this book, I discussed the work of Arthur M. Schlesinger, which demonstrated that the popular understanding of the phrase "the pursuit of happiness" from the Declaration of Independence is erroneous.[71] Historically, that phrase meant the *obtaining* and *practicing* of happiness or the happy life, not simply the *quest* or *seeking* of pleasurable experience. Schlesinger's work is helpful, not only because it clarifies the meaning of the phrase in the Declaration, but also because it shows how words and phrases can become polluted, or, to put a more friendly face on it (though not necessarily its results), how they can drift semantically. Be that as it may, what can we say now, at the end of this book, about "the pursuit of happiness"?

Perhaps, in light of the triumph of life motif and the struggle that is implied in that notion, we might want to say, against Schlesinger but with the folk understanding of "pursuit" in the Declaration of Independence, that happiness in the Bible *is*, in fact, a real seeking and striving toward happiness. If so, we should be quick to point out that this needn't be interpreted agonistically, and it certainly isn't a zero-sum game.[72] There is enough happiness to go around, especially because this is a thick, eudaimonic kind of happiness that does not exist apart from the hard realities of life, and it is not primarily a hedonic kind of happiness based on limited resources ideally suited for only certain kinds of pleasures. Even so, life finds a way precisely in crashing through barriers, "painfully, maybe even dangerously" (again Dr. Malcolm), and so pursuing this kind of happiness is to embark on the long hard road of maturity. The sages of Proverbs knew that.[73] So did Paul.[74] In this sense, then, happiness *is* a kind of pursuit,

---

71. Arthur M. Schlesinger, "The Lost Meaning of 'The Pursuit of Happiness,'" *The William and Mary Quarterly* 31 (1964): 325–27.

72. See Nathan MacDonald's essay in the present volume.

73. See Newsom's essay in the present volume.

74. See Shantz's essay in the present volume, especially her comment that "Paul lived out of gratitude for the gift (*charis*, 'grace') of God. . . . Paul was investing in a life that was more meaningful because of his commitment to something so much bigger than his own well-being" ("'I Have Learned to Be Content': Happiness According to St. Paul," 201).

an *ethos* or *habitus*.[75] "Happiness is a choice," on the other hand, sounds far too simplistic.[76]

There is another reason why "choosing happiness" isn't quite right. It is this: happiness in the Bible isn't so much a quest—though neither is it correct to say it is an unalienable right, a la the Declaration—so much as it is a *gift*. A *divine gift*. Happiness, in the Bible, involves God.[77] It is hard to escape that biblical fact—and the importance of religion to the flourishing life has not gone unnoticed in positive psychology.[78]

---

75. Cf. Charry, *God and the Art of Happiness*, 252: "insight and clarity follow from, rather than motivate, habits formed by practice.... Healing is learned by enacting healing behavior, not first by talking and thinking about healing as an outcome. This is the apprenticeship model and also the way children acquire language."

76. This is the title of the final chapter in Osteen, *Your Best Life Now*, 269–81, and is the title of Barry Neil Kaufman's book, *Happiness Is a Choice* (New York: Fawcett, 1991). Many of the "pop" happiness books that emphasize attitude seem to overstress choice. See, e.g., Gretchen Rubin, *The Happiness Project: Or, Why I Spent a Year Trying to Sing in the Morning, Clean My Closets, Fight Right, Read Aristotle, and Generally Have More Fun* (New York: HarperCollins, 2009). This is not to say choice is not involved at all, whether in positive psychology research or in the Bible. For the former, see Peterson, *A Primer in Positive Psychology*, 97: "Happiness is not solely the product of will, but will is a component at least insofar as it leads us to do things that will result in more versus less happiness." Later, Peterson states that it is not just volitional activity that matters, but "*sustained* volitional activity" (100; his emphasis). For the role of choice in biblical happiness, see the essays by Green and Carey in the present volume. In his essay, Thomas G. Long notes that Qoheleth is said to choose despair, not happiness.

77. See Charry, *God and the Art of Happiness*, *passim*, esp. 275: "The vision of happiness proposed here is theologically qualified"; Whybray, *The Good Life in the Old Testament*, *passim*, but esp. 6, 141, 159, 288; Nasuti, "The Interpretive Significance of Sequence and Selection," 326–27; and McCann, "The Shape of Book I of the Psalter and the Shape of Human Happiness," 340–48, who describes the Psalms as "'A Declaration of *Dependence*'—dependence first upon God and then upon other human beings" (347). Aristotle acknowledges divine giftedness of happiness as well: "Now, if there is in fact anything that is a gift of the gods to human beings, it is reasonable that happiness is god given, and it especially among the human concerns insofar as it is the best of them" (*Nicomachean Ethics*, 1.9 [1099b]; Bartlett and Collins, *Aristotle's Nicomachean Ethics*, 17). The very etymology of Greek *eudaimon* also suggests a religious connection, since it is composed of *eu*, meaning "good" or "well," and *daimon*, meaning "divinity" or "spirit." "To be *eudaimon* is therefore to be living in a way that is well-favored by a god" (Richard Kraut, "Aristotle's Ethics," in *Stanford Encyclopedia of Philosophy*, last modified March 29, 2010, http://plato.stanford.edu/entries/aristotle-ethics/, accessed September 2, 2011). Aristotle himself does not treat the etymology of *eudaimon*.

78. The happiness literature notes that religion increases people's happiness, though the effect is often moderate. See, e.g., Seligman, *Authentic Happiness*, 59–61; Haidt, *The Happiness Hypothesis*, 181–211; Richard Layard, *Happiness: Lessons from a New Science* (New York: Penguin, 2005), 9, 193–94; Peterson, *A Primer in Positive Psychology*, 6, 92–94, 310 n. 3; and Ed Diener and Robert Biswas-Diener, *Happiness: Unlocking the Mysteries of Psychological Wealth* (Malden, MA: Blackwell, 2008), 112–26. Sonja Lyubomirsky, *The How of Happiness: A Scientific Approach to Getting the Life You Want* (New York: Penguin, 2008), 229–39, includes "practicing religion and spirituality" as one of her happiness activities. Spirituality is also on the "top ten" list of virtues (coming in at number nine) that have been positively correlated with subjective well-being in positive psychology research. See Nansook Park, Christopher Peterson, and Martin E. P. Seligman, "Strengths of Character and Well-Being," *J Soc Clin Psychol* 23 (2004): 603–19.

In the Bible, God is happy, and God's happiness affects and infects the rest of the non-God world, humans included.[79] And, to return to the Torah for a moment, we see that the external circumstances of the happy life—what Aristotle called the "furniture of fortune"[80]—are not the result of luck after all, but are rather the gifts of God: wealth, lots of kids, good kids, living to a ripe old age, having a good reputation, receiving honor, and so on.[81]

For his part, that crotchety old preacher Qoheleth seems to have been quite comfortable with the notion of luck, or what he calls "fate" (מקרה from √qrh):[82]

> Again I saw that under the sun the race is not to the swift, nor the battle to the strong, nor bread to the wise, nor riches to the intelligent, nor favor to the skillful; but time and chance happen to them all. For no one can anticipate the time of disaster. Like fish taken in a cruel net, and like birds caught in a snare, so mortals are snared at a time of calamity, when it suddenly falls upon them. (Eccl 9:11–12; cf. 2:14–15; 3:19–20; 9:2–3)

Time and chance "happen" (√qrh), and it is only God who knows why ... or when for that matter—as Qoheleth himself observes in 3:1–15 and 7:14. But this is the same Qoheleth who says (and he may say this for the very same reason) that one must enjoy what one has from God, whenever, that is, one has something to enjoy in the first place, and whenever one has the chance to enjoy it. And what one has is often the simple pleasures of life, though these are no less divine in origin and the same judgment holds true for partaking of them: It is "God's gift that all should eat and drink and take pleasure in all their toil" (3:13; cf. 2:24–25; 5:18–20). So, to quote Newsom, "What chance brings one's way should be enjoyed to the fullest—but without any sense of claim upon it. All that one can bring to the situation is receptivity."[83]

---

79. See Terence Fretheim's essay in the present volume; also Charry, *God and the Art of Happiness*, 202, 275, and her essay in the present volume.

80. Aristotle, *Nicomachean Ethics*, 1.8 (1099a); the translation here is that of Peters, *Nicomachean Ethics*, 14.

81. Cf. Aristotle, *Rhetoric*, 1.5 (1360b); see further MacDonald's essay in the present volume.

82. For a thorough study, see Peter Machinist, "Fate, *miqreh*, and Reason: Some Reflections on Qohelet and Biblical Thought," in *Solving Riddles and Untying Knots: Biblical, Epigraphic, and Semitic Studies in Honor of Jonas C. Greenfield* (eds. Ziony Zevit, Seymour Gitin, and Michael Sokoloff; Winona Lake: Eisenbrauns, 1995), 159–75.

83. Carol A. Newsom, "Positive Psychology and Ancient Israelite Wisdom," 133. See also Thomas G. Long's essay in the present volume.

Receptivity. Not choice and not pursuit. A different writer, Simone Weil, in a very different context puts it not altogether differently: "We do not obtain the most precious gifts by going in search of them but by waiting for them. Man cannot discover them by his own powers, and if he sets out to seek for them he will find in their place counterfeits of which he will be unable to discern the falsity."[84]

4. "Happiness," Again: On Word Pollution and Pidginization

Weil's mention of counterfeits, along with our inability to recognize them for what they are, brings us full circle to the problem of the Bible and happiness with which this book began. In the Introduction, following Walker Percy's remarks about the pollution of "love," I raised the possibility that "happiness," too, has been ruined by misuse and ill-definition. "Beware of people who go around talking about happiness," I suspect Percy would say, "especially if they are thumping a Bible!" And especially if they aren't crystal clear about what kind of happiness, exactly, they are pursuing. There are, after all, different definitions. Some are better than others.

The path through this collection of essays, with its unexpected twists and turns, insights and delights, shows that maybe the matter isn't quite as simple as defining a word, however. Maybe it isn't a matter of exchanging one simplistic-but-polluted definition of happiness for another, perhaps-more-complex-but-purified, one. As we have seen, some aspects of the "pollution" of "happiness," if it is accurate to speak in this way, are ancient indeed; they are hardly new pathologies. And we have also seen that to define "happiness" in its best, fullest, purest form is going to take some time and real effort. Even so, Weil's point stands: counterfeits to the best gifts—and happiness is the best of the lot, according to Aristotle—are legion and it is often hard to distinguish the real McCoy from the knock-off brand, price tags notwithstanding. Aristotle put it correctly if overly bluntly with reference to happiness and how it is understood by the masses: "For the drawing of precise distinctions does not belong to the many."[85]

In conclusion, I'd like to borrow once more from linguistics, but shift the metaphor from "word pollution" (or semantic drift) to the phenomena of

---

84. Simone Weil, "On the Right Use of School Studies with a View to the Love of God," in *Waiting for God* (trans. Emma Craufurd; New York: Harper Perennial Modern Classics, 2009), 57–66 (62).

85. Aristotle, *Nicomachean Ethics*, 10.1 (1172b); Bartlett and Collins, *Aristotle's Nicomachean Ethics*, 210.

pidginization and creolization, and consider the Bible and happiness in their light.[86]

Pidgins are greatly abbreviated languages that usually arise to facilitate the bare minimum of communicative needs among people who don't share a common language but who must nevertheless interact for some reason, either due to trade, living along highly-traveled areas, colonization, and/or the like. Pidgins are primarily based on one language—that of the dominant group (the superstrate)—but they typically mix in bits of other languages along the way (substrates) and develop constructions of their own. What is crucial to note, regardless, is that everything is simplified in a pidgin: the phonology, syntax, and lexicon of the original, base languages are radically reduced.

If a pidgin survives long enough—especially in those cases where the children of parents who speak a pidgin acquire the pidgin as their first language—it can become a creole. Creoles, especially once they enjoy "native" speakers, quickly take on a life of their own. They develop more complex syntactical constructions and add more vocabulary items. Eventually, then, a creole will be indistinguishable from any other "full" language. The only way to know the difference would be if one knew the history of the creole's development.[87] That said, it remains the case that the creole is quite distinguishable and obviously at significant remove from the original languages that contributed to the pidgin that was, in turn, the creole's immediate ancestor.

The linguistic phenomena of pidgins/pidginization and creoles/creolization is instructive here because, after coming to grips with the fuller visions of happiness found in the Bible and in positive psychology, so much of what passes for popular happiness—religious or not—looks not only like word pollution but like a linguistic pidgin. It simply lacks the depth, the richness, the variety, and, most importantly, the nuance of the original, full language. To focus on popular religious happiness, one sees immediately how little of that is about the *triumph of life*, and the struggle that somehow, someway, with God's help, moves from lament to praise (all the while encompassing that lament even if and as it is reframed). Instead, so much popular religious happiness seems to be about success, glory, favor. All shine, no sweat. In more theological terms: it's a theology of

---

86. For more on these linguistic subjects, see Jean Aitchison, *Lingusitics* (6th ed.; Chicago: Teach Yourself, 2003), 128–30; John McWhorter, *The Power of Babel: A Natural History of Language* (New York: Perennial, 2001), 131–76; and Hans Henrich Hock, *Principles of Historical Linguistics* (2nd ed.; Berlin: Mouton de Gruyter, 1991), 512–29. For religion as analyzable like a language, cf. Claude Lévi-Strauss, *Structural Anthropology* (trans. Clair Jacobson and Brook Grundfest Schoepf; New York: Basic, 1963).

87. Hock, *Principles of Historical Linguistics*, 527.

glory with no theology of the cross.[88] But without the sweat, without the cross, without the lament, the struggle, the triumph of life, and so forth, "religious (pseudo)happiness" is at best just a pidgin, a very thin happiness indeed, a rich truth greatly reduced.

We might press this analogy further and try to identify the original, dominant (superstrate) language of this pidgin. Is it the Bible, which is no doubt what many of the religiously (pseudo)happy would claim (though without admitting its pidginized form)? Hardly. The Bible is far too rich and thick on the concept (and problem) of human flourishing to let someone really believe that they could and should pray for more and more and more, especially when that more is constantly and consistently refracted through anecdotes about money, power, prestige, job promotion, and so on and so forth[89]—especially if said person is a Christian, whose Lord taught them to pray for "daily bread" (Matt 6:11), which is definitely *not more* than enough, but *just enough*: just enough for the day.[90] No, the dominant language of this pidginized-happiness isn't the Bible so much as the commercial consumerist capitalism of the First World with a few stock lexical items thrown in from the Bible, exactly as one expects with a pidgin.[91] In fact, since the pidgin has been around a while now—at least since 1952 and Norman Vincent Peale's *Power of Positive Thinking*, but in truth long before that—it seems like it would be more accurate to call it not a pidgin but a creole. It now has "native speakers" who have grown up knowing only the pidgin-now-turned-creole, which is thus well on its way to developing into a full language, with new syntactical

---

88. See the still seminal essay by Ernst Käsemann, "The Saving Significance of the Death of Jesus in Paul," in *Perspectives on Paul* (trans. Margaret Kohl; repr. ed.; Mifflintown, PA: Sigler, 1996 [German original 1969]), 32–59.

89. Again, see Osteen, *Your Best Life Now*, *passim*, but esp. x, 11, 41.

90. The meaning and translation of "daily bread" is debated, but most scholars agree that it means bread enough for the current day (or for the next day). Either way, the relationship of "daily bread" to the story of the manna in Exodus 16 should not be missed. The latter, too, is enough only for just one day (or two days in preparation for the Sabbath); hoarding it only made it spoil.

91. Cf. Eric G. Wilson's remarks about North American Protestant Christianity (*Against Happiness: In Praise of Melancholy* [New York: Farrar, Straus and Giroux, 2008], 19–21, 52–56), who calls Christian denominations "basically happiness companies" (20); Dworkin's remarks on religion in America (*Artificial Happiness*, 286–93); and Charry, *God and the Art of Happiness*, xii, who speaks of the need "to reclaim Christianity's offering of happiness from secular captivity." In some ways the linguistic situation as I metaphorize it here is more akin to "trade jargons" than pidgins proper, though the two are related (see Hock, *Principles of Historical Linguistics*, 522–23).

constructions and lexical items, all the while remaining dependent on its linguistic superstrate. It is *that* language—certainly not the Bible—that thinks in terms of never-ending economic growth (such that economic downturns are the closest thing to apocalyptic scenarios "happy" consumers can imagine), never-ending consumption, never-ending plastic and technology and pleasure.

But biblical happiness—*real* happiness—isn't just about pleasure, more money, job promotions, stuff. It is about well-being, flourishing, the life well-lived. That includes pleasure, to be sure, and other facilitating factors. It must! As the essays in this volume demonstrate, the Bible knows of a "happy blend" of hedonic and eudaimonic perspectives on happiness.[92] But the *blending* is absolutely crucial. Indeed, given the topsy-turvy nature of so much of what happens in the Bible, it might be better to speak not solely of blending but of a "hierarchy of happinesses"—or at least a predominance of certain ingredients in the happy concoction. Newsom puts this helpfully in her essay when she speaks of hedonism and eudaimonism both occurring in the Bible but "within an encompassing eudaimonic framework."[93]

These sorts of nuances are crucial but they are only known from and available in the original "language," the high dialect of Scripture, not in the pidgin and not in the creole. When there is no "happy blend," no encompassing eudaimonic framework but only plastic (pseudo)happiness marked by the syrupy sweet, the real estate success, the hedonically egoistical, the perfect parking spot, and the like, something has gone seriously wrong. A radical reduction has taken place. We have a pidgin on our hands, if not a creole. Either way, we can be sure that what we do not have is biblical happiness.

Is there any hope for reversing the situation? Perhaps, though linguists point out that, even when de-creolization happens, it is typically the case in such scenarios that the creole is eventually and entirely subsumed by the linguistic superstrate—a sobering and problematic proposition in the analogy entertained here. That is to say, speakers do not simply rid themselves of the creole and go back to its predecessor—the pidgin—let alone to the pidgin's constituent languages, especially the nondominant (substrate) one that contributed, though only just a bit, to the pidgin in the first place. Religious (pseudo)happiness, that is, if de-creolized may just become part and parcel of the dominant language of First

---

92. See the contributions by Lapsley, Newsom, and Charry in the present volume. See also Charry, *God and the Art of Happiness*, xii on the crucial link between piety and pleasure.

93. Newsom, "Positive Psychology and Ancient Israelite Wisdom," 135. Given the importance of sociality to happiness, maybe we should expand the statement to "an encompassing eudaimonic framework embedded in positive institutions."

World commercial consumerist capitalism, completely absorbed by the latter and no longer distinguishable from it in the least. Indeed, in many circles that seems exactly to be what has taken place. That is a sobering diagnosis that offers little hope for recapturing the meaning and significance of happiness in the Bible.

Going back behind the creole to the pidgin, and behind the pidgin to the full, rich language of the Bible and its visions of happiness will thus be very hard work indeed, the virtual equivalent to saving a dying language.[94] Many speakers simply won't be able to do it. Many won't *want* to do it because the difficulties involved in learning a new (old) language, not to mention maintaining it, will prove to be "a lesser option than the world of tall buildings," if not, in fact, ultimately "incompatible with the upward mobility they seek."[95]

Before concluding this linguistic metaphor of happiness as having been pidginized and/or creolized, let me add that the metaphor helps to explain two important points. The first point is that not everything that the pseudo-happy say, whether they are religious or not, is wrong. The pidgin/creole still retains at least some lexical stock that goes back to the fuller more articulate visions of happiness, whether those are found in the Bible or elsewhere. So it is that there is much that is right in the writings of the happiologists, though their accent betrays their true tongue. But this first point should come as no real surprise: if the history of Christian doctrine has anything to teach us, it is that the difference between orthodoxy and heterodoxy was often very slight indeed—sometimes as minor as a dipthong[96]—and the heretics in question rarely "meant bad." In our case, the difference is thus one between (authentic) happiness and (pseudo) happiology.[97]

The second point is that understanding pseudo-happiness as a pidgin/creole allows one to recognize and concur with the important critiques of happiness (or perhaps better of happiology) by people like Eric G. Wilson, Ronald W. Dworkin,

---

94. On language death, see McWhorter, *The Power of Babel*, 253–86; Hock, *Principles of Historical Linguistics*, 530–31; K. David Harrison, *The Last Speakers: The Quest to Save the World's Most Endangered Languages* (Washington, DC: National Geographic Society, 2010); and, more extensively, David Crystal, *Language Death* (Cambridge: Cambridge University Press, 2000; and Nancy C. Dorian, ed., *Investigating Obsolescence: Studies in Language Contraction and Death* (Cambridge: Cambridge University Press, 1989).

95. McWhorter, *The Power of Babel*, 271. Note his further sociolinguistic reflections on 273–74.

96. I allude here to the distinction between *homoousios* (same essence) vs. *homoiousios* (similar essence) in the debates over Christ's divinity.

97. Or, analogously, consider clichés, which, while trite, are nevertheless rarely completely at odds from the more significant truths they trivialize.

Barbara S. Held, Julie K. Norem, and others.[98] These critiques, insofar as they are against pseudo-happiness, whether that is manifested in ill-definition (word pollution) or worse (pidgin/creole), are spot on. The full language of happiness includes the pain with the pleasure, the hedonic along with the eudaimonic, the negative and the positive. The happy critics are thus right, but not really with reference to the full language so much as its pidginized bastard. When these critics level their critiques against authentic happiness, however, even against the very possibility of such, they are misguided and guilty of another kind of (opposite) pidginization.[99] Only the full dialect can prevent against the real errors of the happiologists, on the one hand, and those of the melancholists, on the other.

One final linguistic remark: The full dialect needn't be as difficult to learn as Russian or Akkadian. My four-year-old son's picture Bible speaks of "Israel's hard and happy history."[100] Quite right! But only if we realize that "hard and happy" in that formulation is a hendiadys.

5. Final Thoughts on the Bible and Happiness

What have we learned, in the end, about "The Bible and Happiness?" Quite a lot it would seem. Among other things, we have seen that it takes time and hard work to unpack the meaning of "happiness," its relationship to the Bible (i.e., the meaning and significance of the "and"), and how the Bible, in turn, contributes to ancient and contemporary notions of happiness. Patricia Walsh's comments on well-being are apropos at this point:

> any adequate conception of a good life *cannot* be limited to either a narrowly moral, or a non-moral, account. It will be a highly complex account,

---

98. Wilson, *Against Happiness*; Dworkin, *Artificial Happiness*; Barbara S. Held, "The Negative Side of Positive Psychology," *J Humanist Psychol* 44 (2004): 9–46; and Julie K. Norem, *The Positive Power of Negative Thinking: Using Defensive Pessimism to Harness Anxiety and Perform at Your Peak* (New York: Basic, 2001).

99. Cf. Wilson, *Against Happiness*, 82–83, though, in my judgment, Wilson himself comes perilously close to such a reverse pidginization in his (ironically) overly optimistic, generous, and "best case" presentation of melancholia. Wilson's sporadic references to balance, harmony, concord, or dynamic unity between the melancholy and the happy are far better and more accurate (see, e.g., 33, 76, 82–83, 94, 148–49). Despite the fact that he takes issue with it, Dworkin's thoughts on religion and happiness (*Artificial Happiness*, 286–93) seem to reflect a fully pidginized view (not to mention some misunderstandings regarding religion, science, and their interrelation).

100. David Helm and Gail Schoonmaker, *The Big Picture Story Bible* (Wheaton, IL: Crossway, 2004), 411.

akin to the answer a parent might give when asked "What sort of life do you wish for your children?," with all the intricacies such an answer would involve.[101]

A highly complex account indeed—far more complex than Tom Cruise's comment (cited in the Introduction) that his children, "You know, enjoy their jobs." Cruise's comment, which I take to be indicative of a large number of people, needs significant nuance and expansion, if not, in fact, (re)education.[102]

We have also seen that the Bible can help in the study of happiness as that is known in positive psychology and vice versa. The insights from the Bible collected here support key aspects of the study of happiness in positive psychology, and, if they do not add to those aspects substantively (which in my opinion they certainly do), at the very least they round out some that have been less or underdeveloped.[103] Insights from positive psychology, in turn, have cast new light on enigmatic texts from the Bible as well as on biblical passages that are well known but often misunderstood or misused (e.g., 1 Thess 5:16–18: "Rejoice always, pray without ceasing, give thanks in all circumstances; for this is the will of God in Christ Jesus for you"). Still further, the "science" that is the contemporary study of happiness lends hard data—real teeth, as it were—to what is too often in biblical studies an ethereal or theoretical discussion of reified "texts" or "traditions." One can imagine a number of intriguing and productive studies at the interface of happiness studies, especially cross-cultural ones, and the study of ancient texts, especially the Bible.[104]

Finally, the study of the Bible, on the one hand, and positive psychology on the other, has revealed that much of what has passed as happiness—whether in religion or not—has been polluted, a pidginized version, if not, in fact, a full creole. Together, then, the biblical materials and the findings of positive psychology suggest a fuller and far richer definition of authentic happiness. Maybe the problem of happiness isn't solely one of word pollution, but if it is, the combination of the Bible and positive psychology is helpful in our attempt to correctly

---

101. Patricia Walsh, "Well-being," in *The Oxford Companion to Philosophy* (2nd ed.; ed. Ted Honderich; Oxford: Oxford University Press, 2005), 955–56 (955; her emphasis).

102. See Shantz's essay on the education of emotions like happiness.

103. Esp. the notion of positive institutions. See the essays by Newsom and Sandage in this volume.

104. Robert Williamson Jr., "Death and Symbolic Immortality in Second Temple Wisdom Instructions" (PhD diss., Emory University, 2011), which appropriates psychological research on terror management theory and applies it to Hebrew Bible, is an instructive example of this kind of "empirical biblical studies" approach.

redefine the term. Maybe the problem is instead one of pidginization/creolization, but if it is, again, the combination of the Bible and positive psychology is helpful in our attempt to recapture the original dialect that is necessary for authentic happiness or, to continue the linguistic metaphor, to revive the true but endangered language of happiness.

That true, original language of happiness is, according to several of the essays in this volume, God's mother tongue. God is happy, Fretheim says, and necessarily so, Charry adds. Divine happiness, moreover, is directly related to the happiness—the flourishing—of the human and nonhuman worlds. The biblical authors knew this, even without the insights of positive psychology, though we can be very happy that the insights of the latter are helping us, with fresh eyes and a new hermeneutical lens, to begin to recapture the full language of happiness found in those ancient writings. "O, for that blessed happiness of the ancients" indeed!

A Biblical Lexicon of Happiness[1]

Michael J. Chan

Introduction

To take up "happiness" as an object of theological inquiry is to partake in a centuries-old debate concerned with human joy, flourishing, well-being, and fulfillment. The study of happiness by biblical scholars and theologians is only in its infancy, however—the essays in the present collection as notable exceptions to the rule.[2] While a good number of dictionary articles survey biblical terms, images, and concepts related to joy, the concept of happiness has never received a broad-sweeping lexical analysis that encompasses

---

1. I would like to thank several people for their help in bringing this "lexicon of happiness" to its present form. First, Brent Strawn provided both generous encouragement and invaluable feedback on the lexicon's structure, layout, and theory. Second, this listing would not exist without my former teacher, Terry Fretheim, who first proposed that it be included in the volume. Finally, Audrey DiPalma provided me with excellent, detailed editorial feedback.

2. Over the last hundred years, only a small number of studies have taken up various aspects of happiness in biblical literature. In addition to the literature cited in the essays in this volume, see, for example, Eilis Gideon Gulin, *Die Freude im Neuen Testament* (Helsinki: Helsinki Druckerei-A.G. der Finnischen Literatur-Gesellschaft, 1932–36); Paul Humbert, "*Laetari et exultare* dans le vocabulaire religieux de l'ancien Testament," *RHPR* 22 (1942): 185–214; Wolfgang Nauck, "Freude im Leiden: Zum Problem einer urchristlichen Verfolgungstradition," *ZNW* 46 (1955): 68–80; Günter Mansfeld, "Der Ruf zur Freude im Alten Testament" (PhD diss., Heidelberg, 1966); Eckart Otto and Tim Schramm. *Festival and Joy* (Biblical Encounters Series; Nashville: Abingdon, 1980); William G. Morrice, *Joy in the New Testament* (Grand Rapids: Eerdmans, 1984); Gary A. Anderson, *A Time to Mourn, A Time to Dance: The Expression of Grief and Joy in Israelite Religion* (Pennsylvania: Pennsylvania State University Press, 1991); William P. Brown, "Joy and the Art of Cosmic Maintenance: An Ecology of Play in Psalm 104," in *"And God Saw That it Was Good": Essays on Creation and God in Honor of Terence E. Fretheim* (Word and World Supplement Series 5; Saint Paul: Luther Seminary, 2006), 23–32; and Eduard Lohse, *Freude des Glaubens: Die Freude im Neuen Testament* (Göttingen: Vandenhoeck & Ruprect, 2007). With only a few exceptions, most contemporary scholarship on biblical joy focuses on human joy, whereas the bibliography related to divine joy is unfortunately very sparse.

both the Hebrew Bible/Old Testament (OT)[3] and the New Testament (NT).[4] Ellen T. Charry's recently published work, *God and the Art of Happiness*, is perhaps the most significant contemporary theological reflection on the topic, although other authors such as John Piper have made significant contributions to the discussion on a more popular level.[5]

The collection of lexemes and texts from the OT and the NT gathered in this Appendix provides readers with the raw data needed to probe how the biblical texts might contribute to contemporary discussions on happiness.[6] But how does one determine the

---

3. Since HB is used elsewhere in this appendix to designate "heavenly beings," I default to the Christian designation OT (Old Testament) to avoid confusion when speaking of the text corpus proper.

4. Clinton E. Arnold, "Joy," in *ABD* 3:1022–23; the following entries in Leland Ryken, James C. Wilhoit, and Tremper Longman III, eds., *Dictionary of Biblical Imagery* (Downers Grove: InterVarsity Press, 1998): "Abundance" (5–7), "Blessing and Blessedness" (98–99), "Good Life, the" (342–43), "Happiness" (363–64), "Joy" (464–66), "Prosperity" (674–76); Jouette M. Bassler, "Joy," in *HarperCollins Bible Dictionary* (eds. P. J. Achtemeier et al.; 2nd ed.; San Francisco: HarperSanFrancisco, 1996), 548–49; Evelina Volkmann, "Freude," in *Calwer Bibellexikon* (eds. O. Betz et al.; 2 vols.; Stuttgart: Calwer, 2003), 1:377; Friedmann Eißler, "Glück," in *Calwer Bibellexikon*, 1:452; Carole R. Fontaine, "Happiness," in *NIDB* 2:734; Eunny Lee, "Joy," in *NIDB* 3:417–18; Claudia Janssen and Rainer Kessler, "Glück," in *Sozialgeschichtliches Wörterbuch zur Bibel* (eds. Frank Crüsemann et al.; Gütersloh: Gütersloher, 2009), 219–20. For individual terms, the major theological dictionaries should be consulted as well.

5. Ellen T. Charry, *God and the Art of Happiness* (Grand Rapids: Eerdmans, 2010). While "mainline" theologians often ignore developments within Evangelical theology, several evangelical writers should not be ignored as resources for theological reflection on happiness. See, e.g., John Piper's work, the most relevant of which are *Desiring God: Meditations of a Christian Hedonist* (Sisters, OR: Multnomah, 1996); and idem and David Cochran Heath, *The Dangerous Duty of Delight: The Glorified God and the Satisfied Soul*, available online at: www.desiringgod.org/ResourceLibrary/OnlineBooks/ByTitle/1730_The_Dangerous_Duty_of_Delight_Sample/ (accessed 7/27/2011). Other well-known Evangelical and Pentecostal/charismatic authors have dealt with this topic as well, again, on a more popular level: Billy Graham, *The Secret of Happiness: Jesus' Teaching on Happiness as Expressed in the Beatitudes* (Garden City: Doubleday, 1955); David Martyn Lloyd-Jones, *The Path to True Happiness* (Grand Rapids: Baker, 1999); John MacArther, *The Beatitudes: The Only Way to Happiness* (Chicago: Moody, 1998); and Joyce Meyer, *The Secret to True Happiness: Enjoy Today, Embrace Tomorrow* (New York: Faith Words, 2008).

6. While this list has sought to be as broad and comprehensive as current tools permit, there are undoubtedly terms and texts that have been overlooked in the process. An additional limitation is this study's exclusive attention to *lexical* evidence, which leaves unaddressed images and metaphors that represent or allude to happiness or joy but do not use terminology directly related to happiness. For instance, the phrase "each under his own vine and under his own fig tree" (1 Kgs 5:5; cf. Micah 4:4; Zech 3:10), while undoubtedly an image of the "good life," does not turn up in a search for the main lexemes relating to happiness. One way of filling these gaps is to supplement the current list with the entries provided in Ryken, Wilhoit, and Longman, eds., *Dictionary of Biblical Imagery*. Visual evidence from the ancient world is another resource that promises to add texture to a study of happiness in the Bible. Othmar Keel's seminal work with iconography in the Psalms, for instance, contains a number of iconographic sources related to "Thanks and Praise." See his *Symbolism of the Biblical World: Ancient Near Eastern Iconography and the Book of Psalms* (trans. T. J. Hallett; repr. ed.; Winona Lake: Eisenbrauns, 1997), 314–18.

relevance of a given biblical lexeme to the admittedly slippery and polyvalent English word "happiness"? This appendix takes a maximalist approach to the issue.[7] The choice to use a broad approach reflects my sensitivity to two problems: (1) the difficulty of defining happiness in the English language; and (2) the problems that arise when one attempts to find resonant concepts in the vocabulary of ancient cultures.[8] The decision to associate a given Hebrew, Aramaic, or Greek term with "happiness" was thus based on the presence of *plausible conceptual intersections*, rather than direct or synonymous correspondences between the source languages and the target language (English). Generally speaking, the lexemes presented here are related to the larger domain of positive "attitudes," "emotions," "dispositions," and "states of affairs."[9] Associated subdomains include, "acceptability," "celebration," "cheer," "contentment," "delight," "gratefulness/gratitude," "joy," "pleasure," "praise," "rejoicing," "satisfaction," "thankfulness," and "well-being."[10] The reader will also notice that the lists include terms referring to activities, behaviors, and practices that are associated with joy and happiness (e.g., חגג/ḥgg: "celebrate, hold a festival, keep a pilgrimage"). The decision to include activities, behaviors, and practices associated with happiness acknowledges that, for many cultures, sentiment and performance are often inseparably linked. That is to say, many cultures do not view joyful behavior merely as an epiphenomenal *expression* of a subjective emotional state, as is the case in many Western countries.[11] One example must suffice: in the OT, both

---

7. A number of caveats will show up throughout this lexicon. One important one, however, is that conjectures made by either lexica or critical versions of the biblical text have been omitted. For instance, both *HALOT* and *BHS* suggest that in Isa 3:10, ʾimrû should be emended to ʾašrê. For obvious reasons, speculative conjectures like this have not been included.

8. This problem is particularly notable in America, where the notion of the "pursuit of happiness" is written into the United States Declaration of Independence, thus making happiness not only "the quintessential American emotion" (Nicole Eustace, "Happiness," in *Encyclopedia of the New American Nation* [ed. Paul Finkelman; 2 vols.; Detroit: Charles Schribner's Sons, 2006], 2:145) but also a closely guarded societal value and even a legal right.

9. This is a modified version of the domain, "Attitudes and Emotions," which can be found in Johannes P. Louw and Eugene A. Nida, eds., *Greek-English Lexicon of the New Testament: Based on Semantic Domains* (2 vols.; 2nd ed.; New York: United Bible Societies, 1989), 1:288.

10. One problem with this larger, "maximalist" approach is that, alongside the verses that are applicable, one also encounters a significant number of verses that are not applicable to the study of happiness. For instance, the substantives associated with the root √ʾwr often simply refer to "light" or some variant thereto (e.g., Gen 1:3, 4, etc.). However, light is also used figuratively to describe the face of a joyful person (see, e.g., Job 29:4; Ps 4:7). Various methods have been employed to reduce the number of irrelevant citations, all of which are discussed in greater detail below and in the footnotes. Nevertheless, the reader will still have to make interpretive decisions regarding a given verse's appropriateness to the topic of happiness. This approach risks the frustration of the reader, but has the advantage of including the maximum number of references, including those that might be ambiguous or susceptible to different interpretations.

11. For a discussion of performed joy in light of anthropological categories, see Anderson, *A Time to Mourn, A Time to Dance*, 1–18.

"love" and "joy" can be commanded in legal contexts, which suggests that something more than just internal (and subjective) affect states are in mind—or, perhaps better, in practice.[12]

Due to the sheer number of lexemes and verses, the raw data are divided into two large lexical sets (Set 1 and Set 2). Set 1 collects all the lexemes determined to be relevant to the study of happiness in the Bible. Each lexeme is accompanied by a list of verses indicating where the lexeme is found. When the subject of the lexeme can be determined— that is, when it is a finite verb, an infinitive with a suffixed pronoun as its subject (applicable only to Hebrew and Aramaic), or a participle—a code is provided indicating the subject or associated noun/pronoun. The goal of Set 1 is to provide a wide-angle shot of the lexical landscape as it relates to happiness.

Set 2 is more focused, presenting *only* those lexemes and verses where a subject can be identified (again, this applies only to verses containing a finite verb, an infinitive construct with a suffixed pronoun functioning as a subject [applicable only to Hebrew and Aramaic], or a participle). The goal of this list is to identify characters—human, divine, creational, and otherwise—that act, bring about, are characterized by, or are acted upon in ways related to happiness. So, while Set 1 presents the fullest possible range of data, Set 2 collects all *identifiable subjects* from the first listing in a more selective presentation. Readers who are primarily interested in *who* or *what* is happy in the Bible will therefore want to begin with Set 2.

It will prove useful to further describe each Set in turn along with a few worked examples.

Set 1: Set 1 is organized according to the alphabetical ordering of the lexemes— first OT, then NT, with the former divided into Hebrew and Aramaic terms. Each lexeme is accompanied by a list of verse citations, which, in the case of the OT, follows the versification found in *Biblia Hebraica Stuttgartensia* (*BHS*).[13] If the instance in question reveals a subject—that is, it is a finite verb, an infinitive construct with a suffixed personal pronoun functioning as a subject (applicable only to Hebrew and Aramaic), or a participle—a letter indicating the class or identity of the subject, pronoun, or semantically associated noun is included ("C = creation"; "D = deity"; "HB = heavenly being";[14]

---

12. For a discussion of commanded "love," see William L. Moran, "Ancient Near Eastern Background of the Love of God in Deuteronomy," *CBQ* 25 (1963): 77–87; but also Jacqueline E. Lapsley, "Feeling Our Way: Love for God in Deuteronomy," *CBQ* 65 (2003): 350–69. For a discussion of "joy," see Anderson, *A Time to Mourn*, 14.

13. The verse numbers in some English Bible translations differ from the numbering found in *BHS*, especially, though not exclusively, in the book of Psalms. Since the OT terms are here taken from the Hebrew and Aramaic texts, it seemed best to use *BHS*'s versification.

14. Demonic characters in the NT, including Satan, are included in this category.

"H = human";[15] "J = Jesus"; "I/AI = inanimate/abstract item"). Subjects that do not fit well into these categories or that need clarification are given a parenthetical description in place of a letter (e.g., "Jerusalem").

The following two examples illustrate how entries in Set 1 are presented:

Example 1. ἀρέσκω/*areskō*—"please"
   Gal 1:10 (2x: H).

The citation is from the NT book of Galatians, and this particular verse contains two occurrences of the verb. Only one subject designation (H = human), however, is included in the parenthesis[16] because only one of the two occurrences of the verb has a subject; the other (*areskein*) is an infinitive, which has no subject.

Example 2. גיל/*gyl*—Qal: "rejoice"
   Joel 1:16.

In this verse, *gyl* does not have a subject since it is a substantive (i.e., a noun). So, the text is cited without parenthetical notations.

In the case of the OT, the lexemes are listed according to root, as they are in the still-standard one-volume lexicon by Brown, Driver, and Briggs (BDB).[17] For example, the noun *rāṣôn* ("pleasure, will, desire, favor") is listed under *rṣh* I.[18] With a number of exceptions, personal names associated with a given term are also listed under their associated root since biblical names—especially names in the OT—are frequently symbolic

---

15. The H (human) and D (divine) subject categories include idioms that refer metonymically to body parts or components as subjects. For example, Acts 2:26 describes the rejoicing (*ēgalliasato*) of both the tongue (*glōssa*) and heart (*kardia*). Psalm 67:2 refers to the shining of God's face ("may he shine his face [*yāʾēr pānāyw*] on us"). These idioms clearly refer to an expression of surprise or joy on the part of the one whose eyes or face is the verbal subject; therefore, I have included such idioms beneath the D and H subject categories. Additionally, collective terms that seem to refer to human expressions of joy are included under the H category as well. For example, when Ps 68:33 refers to the rejoicing of kingdoms (*mamlĕkôt hāʾāreṣ šîrû lēʾlōhîm zammĕrû ʾădonāy*), this study assumes that "kingdom" refers collectively to its inhabitants.

16. Occasionally the subject of a given verb is uncertain. This is especially true in certain psalms, where calls to praise can apply to both human (H) and creational (C) subjects. In such cases, the possible identifications will be separated with a slash; so, e.g., C/H, which would signify "creation or human."

17. For the convenience of readers who cannot read the script of the original languages, transliterations are included with each lexeme.

18. When there are multiple entries for a given root, the numbering found in the standard multivolume dictionary by Ludwig Koehler, Walter Baumgartner, and Johann Jakob Stamm, *The Hebrew and Aramaic Lexicon of the Old Testament* (trans. and ed. M. E. J. Richardson; 5 vols.; Leiden: Brill, 1994–1999), hereafter *HALOT*, will be used, as illustrated in the citation of *rṣh* I.

and are often constructed around the author's understanding of a given lexeme (see, e.g., Gen 4:1; 5:29; 17:5, 15; 41:45; Exod 2:10; Isa 8:1–4; Dan 1:7).[19]

Unlike the Hebrew and Aramaic lexemes, the Greek lexemes are not listed according to a root. Rather, Greek lexicography typically distinguishes between verbal and nonverbal forms of a word, a practice that is followed here. For example, the reader will find different entries for the noun ἀγαλλίασις, –εως, ἡ/*agalliasis, –eōs, hē* ("extreme joy") and the related verb, ἀγαλλιάω/*agalliaō* ("be extremely joyful").

The English glosses of Hebrew and Aramaic terms are primarily based on the multivolume lexicon by Ludwig Koehler and Walter Baumgartner (*HALOT*); the Greek glosses are mainly based on the semantic lexicon of the New Testament by Johannes Louw and Eugene Nida.[20] These glosses are not comprehensive definitions but were selected because of their associations with happiness more generally. For the finer nuances of a given lexeme, the reader will have to consult these lexica and other resources. As a result, for polysemic terminology, glosses that are unrelated to happiness have been excluded. For example, the Greek word χάρις/*charis*, while certainly embracing meanings associated with happiness ("thankfulness, gratitude, etc."; see, e.g., 1 Tim 1:12; 2 Tim 1:3), also has a wide range of other meanings that have little to do with happiness (e.g., "grace"; see Acts 11:23; 13:43; Rom 5:2; Eph 4:29). Furthermore, for the OT, irrelevant stems are also not listed. For example, *ṭôb* in the Qal can mean "be pleasant, delightful, joyful, glad." In the Hiphil, however, it typically means, "act rightly" and deals with the appropriate nature of a given act. Thus, in the case of this word, a gloss for the Qal is provided, but one for the Hiphil is excluded. This explains why Esth 1:10 is cited in the lists below, but 2 Kgs 10:30 is not—namely, because Esth 1:10 uses *ṭôb* (Qal) to describe the merry inebriation of King Ahasuerus ("On the seventh day, when the heart of the king *was merry* [*ṭôb*] because of wine . . ."), while 2 Kgs 10:30 uses *ṭôb* in the Hiphil to evaluate Jehu's mission against the house of Ahab ("because you have *done rightly* [*hĕṭîbōtā*]"; cf. also 1 Kgs 8:18; 2 Chr 6:8). As a general rule, then, the lexical lists have been streamlined to present the reader with as little irrelevant textual data as is possible, while still casting the net as widely as possible.

---

19. See Jeffrey H. Tigay, *You Shall Have No Other Gods: Israelite Religion in the Light of Hebrew Inscriptions* (HSS 31; Atlanta: Scholars Press, 1986); Jeaneane D. Fowler, *Theophoric Personal Names in Ancient Hebrew: A Comparative Study* (JSOTSup 49; Sheffield: JSOT Press, 1988); Richard S. Hess, *Studies in the Perosnal Names of Genesis 1–11* (AOAT 234; Kevelaer: Verlag Butzon & Bercker and Neukirchen-Vluyn: Neukirchiner Verlag, 1993); Karen Radner, *Die Macht des Namens: Altorientalischen Strategien zur Selbsterhaltung* (Santag 8; Wiesbaden: Harrassowitz, 2005); Francis I. Andersen and Richard S. Hess, *Names in the Study of Biblical History: David, Yhwh Names, and the Role of Personal Names* (Buried History Monograph 2; Melbourne: Australian Institute of Archaeology, 2007); and Timothy M. Willis, "Name, Naming," *NIDB* 4:217–19.

20. On some occasions, it was necessary to consult other lexica, especially when a lexeme's definition is disputed. For example, in the case of עלס/ *'ls*, *HALOT* splits the verb into I עלס/ *'ls* ("to taste something; to sample together") and II עלס/ *'ls* ("to become agitated or vivacious"). In an earlier edition of the same lexicon, however (see Ludwig Koehler and Walter Baumgartner, *Lexicon in Veteris Testamenti* [2 vols.; Leiden: Brill, 1985]), the term was not divided in two and was defined simply as "enjoy."

Set 2: As indicated above, Set 2 focuses on instances where the subject of the happiness language can be identified. Again, this applies to verses containing finite verbs, infinitive constructs with suffixed pronouns functioning as a subject (applicable only to Hebrew and Aramaic), and participles. Generally speaking, this more specialized set addresses the following questions: Who/what is happy in the Bible? Who/what makes a person/thing happy in the Bible? Who/what is made happy in the Bible? Set 2 is organized according to the subject categories utilized in Set 1; so C = creation; D = deity; H = human; HB = heavenly being; J = Jesus; I/AI = inanimate/abstract item. Each subject or associated substantive functions as a heading. The relevant lexemes and verse citations are then placed under the subject headings and are ordered as they are in Set 1—that is, the OT and NT lexemes are separated from one another, and the lexemes are alphabetically listed (Hebrew first, then Aramaic for OT). In contrast to this practice, the miscellaneous subjects (i.e., those given a full parenthetical descriptor, not a code, in Set 1) are mixed together, whether Hebrew, Aramaic, or Greek, whether OT or NT, in one integrated presentation. The following example is illustrative:

Example 3. C = Creation
    פצח I/*psḥ* I—Qal: "be cheerful, happy, serene, break forth"
        Ps 98:4; Isa 14:7; 44:23; 49:13; 55:12.

The subject category is C (Creation) and the lexeme is פצח I/*psḥ* I. The verses listed here indicate where creation is the subject of a finite verb, represented by a pronoun that is attached to an infinitive, or associated with a participle. In Isa 44:23, for example, the hills and forests break forth into song ("Shout for joy, O mountains, O forests with all your trees!"). So, in this case (and others like it), the prophet treats creation as a subject capable of joyful expression.[21]

Set 1
Old Testament Lexemes (Hebrew)

אור/*'wr*—Qal: "become, be light, shine"; Niphal: "to be lit up"; Hiphil: "make the countenance shine, make the face shine."[22]

Gen 1:3 (2x), 4 (2x), 5, 15, 17, 18; 44:3 (C); Exod 10:23; 13:21; 14:20 (C); 25:37 (I/AI); Num 6:25 (D); 8:2 (I/AI); Judg 16:2; 19:26; 1 Sam 14:27 (H), 29 (H), 36; 25:34, 36; 29:10

---

21. See further the essays by Terence E. Fretheim and William P. Brown in the present volume.

22. References to the city of "Ur" (*'ûr*), "stall" (*'urwāh*), and the plant mallow (*'ōrōt*) have been removed from this list due to their lack of relevance to the topic of happiness. All references to *mĕ'ōr* ("luminary, lamp"), have been removed as well, except Prov 15:30, which is clearly associated with human joy.

(impersonal subject);[23] 2 Sam 2:32 (impersonal subject); 17:22; 23:4; 2 Kgs 7:9; 1 Chr 11:35; Ezra 9:8; Neh 8:3; 9:12,19; Esth 8:16; Job 3:9, 16, 20; 12:22, 25; 17:12; 18:5, 6, 18; 22:28; 24:13, 14, 16; 25:3; 26:10; 28:11; 29:3, 24; 30:26; 31:26; 33:28, 30 (2x); 36:30, 32; 37:3, 11, 15, 21; 38:15, 19, 24; 41:10, 24 (C); Pss 4:7; 13:4 (D); 18:29 (D); 19:9 (precepts of Yahweh); 27:1; 31:17 (D); 36:10 (2x); 37:6; 38:11; 43:3; 44:4; 49:20; 56:14; 67:2 (D); 76:5 (D); 77:19 (C); 78:14; 80:4 (D), 8 (D), 20 (D); 89:16; 97:4 (C), 11; 104:2; 105:39; 112:4; 118:27 (D); 119:105, 130 (I/AI),135 (D); 136:7; 139:11, 12 (2x: C); 148:3; Prov 4:18 (2x: path of the righteous); 6:23; 13:9; 15:30; 16:15; 29:13 (D); Eccl 2:13; 8:1 (Wisdom); 11:7; 12:2; Isa 2:5; 5:20 (2x), 30; 9:1 (2x); 10:17; 13:10 (2x); 18:4; 24:15; 27:11 (H); 30:26 (4x); 31:9; 42:6, 16; 44:16; 45:7; 47:14; 49:6; 50:11; 51:4; 58:8, 10; 59:9; 60:1 (2x; Jerusalem), 3, 19 (3x; C), 20; Jer 4:23; 13:16; 25:10; 31:35 (2x); Lam 3:2; Ezek 5:2; 32:7 (2x: C), 8; 43:2 (C); Dan 9:17 (D); Hos 6:5; Amos 5:18, 20; 8:8, 9; Micah 2:1; 7:8, 9; Hab 3:4, 11; Zeph 3:5; Zech 14:6, 7; Mal 1:10 (H).

אשׁר II/ *'šr* II—Piel: "pronounce happy"; Pual: "be blessed"

    Gen 30:13 (3x: H); 35:26; 46:17; 49:20; Exod 1:4; Num 1:13, 40, 41; 2:27 (2x); 7:72; 10:26; 13:13; 26:44, 46, 47; 34:27; Deut 27:13; 33:24 (2x), 29; Josh 17:7, 10, 11; 19:24, 31, 34; 21:6, 30; Judg 1:31, 32; 5:17; 7:23; 1 Kgs 4:16; 10:8; 1 Chr 2:2; 6:47, 59; 7:30, 40; 12:37; 2 Chr 9:7; 30:11; Job 5:17; 29:11 (H); Pss 1:1; 2:12; 32:1, 2; 33:12; 34:9; 40:5; 41:2, 3 (H); 65:5; 72:17 (H); 84:5, 6, 13; 89:16; 94:12; 106:3; 112:1; 119:1, 2; 127:5; 128:1, 2; 144:15 (2x); 146:5; Prov 3:13,18 (H); 8:32, 34; 14:21; 16:20; 20:7; 28:14; 29:18; 31:28 (H); Cant 6:9 (H); Isa 1:17 (H); 30:18; 56:2; Ezek 48:2, 3, 34; Dan 12:12; Mal 3:12 (H), 15.

בלג/*blg*—Hiphil: "brighten up/cheer up"

    1 Chr 24:14; Neh 10:9; 12:5, 18; Job 9:27 (H); 10:20 (H); Ps 39:14 (H); Jer 8:18; Amos 5:9 (D).

ברך II/*brk* II—Qal: "praised, be blessed"; Niphal: "wish oneself a blessing"; Piel: "bless"; Pual: "be blessed, praised"; Hithpael: "bless each other, bless oneself"

    Gen 1:22 (D), 28 (D); 2:3 (D); 5:2 (D); 9:1 (D), 26 (D); 12:2 (2x: D), 3 (3x: D, H, H); 14:19 (2x: H, H), 20 (D); 17:16 (2x: D, D), 20 (D); 18:18 (H); 22:17 (2x: D), 18 (H); 24:1 (D), 27 (D), 31 (H), 35 (D), 48 (H), 60 (H); 25:11 (D); 26:3 (D), 4 (H), 12 (D), 24 (H), 29 (H); 27:4 (H), 7 (H), 10 (H),12, 19 (H), 23 (H), 25 (H), 27 (2x: H, D), 29 (2x: H, H), 30, 31 (H), 33 (2x: H, H), 34 (H), 35, 36 (2x), 38 (2x: H), 41 (2x: H); 28:1 (H), 3 (D), 4, 6 (2x: H,

---

23. In English, the impersonal subject is typically identified by the pronoun "it," as, e.g., in the sentences, "*It* is raining" or "*It* is sometimes said." The impersonal pronoun is common in Deuteronomy with respect to the root *ytb* (e.g., "so that it may go well with you . . ."; see, e.g., Deut 6:18; 12:25). For the impersonal subject, see Andrew Radford, *Syntax: A Minimalist Introduction* (Cambridge: Cambridge University Press, 1997), 262.

H), 14 (H); 30:27 (D), 30 (D); 32:1 (H), 27 (HB?),[24] 30 (HB?); 33:11; 35:9 (D); 39:5 (2x: D); 47:7 (H), 10 (H); 48:3 (D), 9 (H), 15 (H), 16 (HB), 20 (2x: H, H); 49:25 (4x: D), 26 (2x), 28 (3x: H, H); Exod 12:32 (H); 18:10 (D); 20:11 (D), 24 (D); 23:25 (D); 32:29; 39:43 (H); Lev 9:22 (H), 23 (H); 25:21; Num 6:23 (H), 24 (D), 27 (D); 22:6 (2x: H, H),12 (H); 23:11 (2x: H), 20 (2x: D), 25 (2x: H); 24:1, 9 (2x:, H, H), 10 (2x: H); Deut 1:11 (D); 2:7 (D); 7:13 (2x: D, D), 14 (H); 8:10 (H); 10:8; 11:26, 27, 29; 12:7 (D), 15; 14:24 (D), 29 (D); 15:4 (2x: D), 6 (D), 10 (D), 14 (D), 18 (D); 16:10 (D), 15 (D), 17; 21:5; 23:6, 21 (D); 24:13 (H), 19 (D); 26:15 (D); 27:12; 28:2, 3 (2x: H, H), 4 (fruit of the womb), 5 (I/AI), 6 (2x: H, H), 8 (2x: D), 12; 29:18 (H); 30:1, 16 (D), 19; 33:1 (2x: H), 11 (D), 13 (C), 20 (D), 23, 24 (H); Josh 8:33, 34; 14:13 (H); 15:19; 17:14 (D); 22:6 (H), 7 (H), 33 (H); 24:10 (2x: H); Judg 1:15; 5:2 (H), 9 (H), 24 (2x: H, H); 13:24 (D); 17:2 (H); Ruth 2:4 (D), 19 (H), 20 (H); 3:10 (H); 4:14 (D); 1 Sam 2:20 (H); 9:13 (H); 13:10; 15:13 (H); 23:21 (H); 25:14, 27, 32 (D), 33 (2x: prudence, H), 39 (D); 26:25 (H); 30:26; 2 Sam 2:5 (H); 6:11 (D), 12 (D), 18 (H), 20; 7:29 (3x: D, I/AI); 8:10; 13:25 (H); 14:22 (H); 18:28 (D); 19:40 (H); 21:3 (H); 22:47 (D); 1 Kgs 1:47, 48 (D); 2:45 (H); 5:21 (D); 8:14 (H), 15 (D), 55 (H), 56 (D), 66 (H); 10:9 (D); 21:10 (H), 13 (H); 2 Kgs 4:29 (2x: H, H); 5:15; 10:15 (H); 18:31; 1 Chr 4:10 (2x: D); 12:3; 13:14 (D); 16:2 (H), 36 (D), 43; 17:27 (3x: D, D); 18:10; 23:13; 26:5 (D); 29:10 (2x: H, D), 20 (2x: H, H); 2 Chr 2:11 (D); 6:3 (H), 4 (D); 9:8 (D); 20:26 (2x: H); 30:27 (H); 31:8 (H), 10 (D); Ezra 7:27 (D); Neh 8:6 (H); 9:5 (3x: H, D); 11:2 (H); 13:2; Job 1:5 (H), 10 (D), 11 (H), 21 (D); 2:5 (H), 9 (H); 29:13; 31:20 (H); 32:2, 6; 42:12 (D); Pss 3:9; 5:13 (D); 10:3 (H); 16:7 (H); 18:47 (D); 21:4, 7; 24:5; 26:12 (H); 28:6 (D), 9 (D); 29:11 (D); 31:22 (D); 34:2 (H); 37:22 (H), 26; 41:14 (D); 45:3 (D); 49:19 (H); 62:5 (H); 63:5 (H); 65:11 (D); 66:8 (H), 20 (D); 67:2 (D), 7 (D), 8 (D); 68:20 (D), 27 (H), 36 (D); 72:15 (H), 17 (H), 18 (D), 19 (D); 84:7; 89:53 (D); 96:2 (H); 100:4 (H); 103:1 (H), 2 (H), 20 (HB), 21 (HB), 22 (2x: C/H, H); 104:1 (H), 35 (H); 106:48 (D); 107:38 (D); 109:17, 28 (D); 112:2 (H); 113:2 (D); 115:12 (3x: D, D, D), 13 (D), 15 (H), 18 (H); 118:26 (H, H); 119:12 (D); 124:6 (D); 128:4 (H), 5 (D); 129:8 (2x: H); 132:15 (2x: D); 133:3; 134:1 (H), 2 (H), 3 (D); 135:19 (2x: H, H), 20 (2x: H, H), 21 (D); 144:1 (D); 145:1 (H), 2 (H),10 (H), 21 (C); 147:13 (D); Prov 3:33 (D); 5:18 (I/AI: figurative); 10:6, 7, 22; 11:11, 25, 26; 20:21 (I/AI); 22:9 (H); 27:14 (H); 28:20; 30:11 (H); Isa 19:24, 25 (2x: D, H); 36:16; 44:3; 51:2 (D); 61:9 (D); 65:8, 16 (2x: H, H), 23 (H); 66:3 (H); Jer 4:2 (H); 17:7 (H); 20:14 (day of birth); 31:23 (D); Ezek 3:12 (D); 34:26 (2x); 44:30; Joel 2:14; Hag 2:19 (D); Zech 8:13; 11:5 (D); Mal 2:2; 3:10.

בשׂר/*bśr*—Piel: "bring good news"; Hithpael: "receive good news"
    1 Sam 4:17 (H); 31:9; 2 Sam 1:20 (H); 4:10 (H); 18:19 (H), 20 (3x: H, H), 22, 25, 26 (H), 27, 31 (H); 1 Kgs 1:42 (H); 2 Kgs 7:9; 1 Chr 10:9 (H); 16:23 (H); Pss 68:12 (H); 96:2 (H); Isa 40:9 (2x: Zion); 41:27 (H); 52:7 (2x: H, H); 60:6 (H); 61:1; Jer 20:15 (H); Nah 2:1 (H).

---

24. The precise identification of the being with whom Jacob wrestles, divine or human, is uncertain. See the discussions in Gordon J. Wenham, *Genesis 16–50* (WBC 2; Dallas: Word Books, 1994), 283–304; Nahum M. Sarna, *Genesis* (The JPS Torah Commentary; Philadelphia: The Jewish Publication Society, 1989), 403–404.

גִּיל/*gyl*—Qal: "rejoice"

1 Chr 16:31 (C); Job 3:22; Pss 2:11 (H); 9:15 (H); 13:5 (H), 6 (H); 14:7 (H); 16:9 (H); 21:2 (H); 31:8 (H); 32:11 (H); 35:9 (H); 43:4; 45:16; 48:12 (towns of Judah [*běnôt yěhûdāh*; literally, "daughters of Judah"]); 51:10 (crushed bones); 53:7 (H); 65:13; 89:17 (H); 96:11 (C); 97:1 (C), 8 (towns of Judah [*běnôt yěhûdāh*; literally, "daughters of Judah"]); 118:24 (H); 149:2 (H); Prov 2:14 (H); 23:24 (2x: H), 25 (H); 24:17 (H); Cant 1:4 (H); Isa 9:2 (H); 16:10; 25:9 (H); 29:19 (H); 35:1 (C), 2 (2x: C); 41:16 (H); 49:13 (C); 61:10 (H); 65:18 (H), 19 (D); 66:10 (H); Jer 48:33; Dan 1:10; Hos 9:1; 10:5 (H); Joel 1:16; 2:21 (C), 23 (H); Hab 1:15 (H); 3:18 (H); Zeph 3:17 (D); Zech 9:9 (Daughter of Zion);[25] 10:7 (H).

הלל II/*hll* II—Piel: "praise"; Pual: "be praised"; Hithpael: "boast, pride oneself"

Gen 12:15 (H); Lev 19:24; Deut 10:21; 26:19; Judg 9:27; 12:13, 15; 16:24 (H); 2 Sam 14:25; 22:4 (D); 1 Kgs 20:11 (H); 1 Chr 1:2; 1 Chr 4:16; 16:4, 10 (H), 25 (D), 35, 36 (H); 23:5 (2x: H), 30; 25:3; 29:13 (H); 2 Chr 5:13 (2x); 7:6; 8:14; 20:19, 21 (H), 22; 23:12 (H), 13; 29:12, 30 (2x: H); 30:21 (H); 31:2; Ezra 3:10, 11 (2x); Neh 5:13 (H); 9:5; 11:4, 17; 12:24, 46; Pss 9:15; 10:3 (H); 18:4 (D); 22:4, 23 (H), 24 (H), 26, 27 (H); 33:1; 34:2, 3 (H); 35:18 (H), 28; 40:4; 44:9 (H); 48:2 (D), 11; 49:7 (H); 51:17; 52:3 (H); 56:5 (H), 11 (2x: H, H); 63:6 (H), 12 (H); 64:11 (H); 65:2; 66:2, 8; 69:31 (H), 35 (C); 71:6, 8, 14; 74:21 (H); 78:4, 63 (H); 79:13; 84:5 (H/C); 96:4 (D); 97:7 (H); 100:4 (2x); 102:19 (H), 22; 104:35 (H); 105:3 (H), 45 (H); 106:1 (H), 2, 5, 12, 47, 48 (H); 107:32 (H); 109:1, 30 (H); 111:1 (H), 10; 112:1 (H); 113:1 (3x: H, H, H,), 3 (D), 9 (H); 115:17 (H), 18 (H); 116:19 (H); 117:1 (H), 2 (H); 119:164 (H), 171, 175 (H); 135:1 (3x: H, H, H), 3 (H), 21 (H); 145:1, 2 (H), 3 (D), 21; 146:1 (2x: H, H), 2 (H), 10 (H); 147:1 (2x: H),12 (Zion), 20 (H); 148:1 (3x: HB, HB, HB), 2 (2x: HB, HB), 3 (2x: C, C), 4 (C), 5 (C), 7 (C), 13 (H), 14 (H); 149:1 (H), 3 (H), 9 (H); 150:1 (3x: H, H, H), 2 (2x: H, H), 3 (2x: H, H), 4 (2x: H, H), 5 (2x: H, H), 6 (C);[26] Prov 12:8 (H); 20:14 (H); 25:14 (H); 27:1 (H), 2 (H), 21; 28:4 (H); 31:28 (H), 30 (H), 31 (deeds); Cant 6:9 (H); Isa 38:18 (death); 41:16 (H); 42:8, 10, 12; 43:21; 45:25 (H); 48:9; 60:6, 18; 61:3, 11; 62:7, 9 (H); 63:7; 64:10 (H); Jer 4:2 (H); 9:22 (3x; H, H, H), 23 (2x; H, H); 13:11; 17:14; 20:13 (H); 31:7 (H); 33:9; 48:2; 49:4 (H), 25; 51:41; Ezek 26:17 (Tyre); Joel 2:26 (H); Hab 3:3; Zeph 3:19, 20.

---

25. All references to the "Daughter of Zion" are included under the "Jerusalem/Zion" category.

26. The subjects of the imperatival verbs in Psalm 150 are often ambiguous, especially when read in light of the last verse, which calls on *all creation* to praise God (see v. 6). Iconographic evidence indicates that singing and even instrument playing was not limited to the human world, at least in the imaginations of some ANE artists and scribes. See Brent A. Strawn and Joel M. LeMon, "'Everything That Has Breath': Animal praise in Psalm 150:6 in the light of ancient Near Eastern iconography," in *Bilder als Quellen/Images as Sources: Studies on ancient Near Eastern artefacts and the Bible inspired by the work of Othmar Keel* (eds. S. Bickel, S. Schroer, R. Schurte, and C. Uehlinger; OBO Sonderband; Fribourg: Academic Press and Göttingen: Vandenhoeck & Ruprecht, 2007), 451–85 and Pls. XXXIII–XXXIV. The same sort of ambiguity may exist in other Psalms (particularly those in Book IV of the Psalter) where an unspecified audience is called upon to praise (see, e.g., Pss 96:1; 147:1).

זמר I/*zmr* I—Piel: "sing, praise"

Judg 5:3 (H); 2 Sam 22:50 (H); 23:1; 1 Chr 16:9 (H); Job 35:10; Pss 3:1; 4:1; 5:1; 6:1; 7:18 (H); 8:1; 9:1, 3 (H), 12 (H); 12:1; 13:1; 15:1; 18:50 (H); 19:1; 20:1; 21:1; 21:14 (H); 22:1; 23:1; 24:1; 27:6 (H); 29:1; 30:1, 5 (H), 13 (H); 31:1; 33:2 (H); 38:1; 39:1; 40:1; 41:1; 47:1, 7 (4x: H, H, H, H), 8 (H); 48:1; 49:1; 50:1; 51:1; 57:8 (H), 10 (H); 59:18 (H); 61:9 (H); 62:1; 63:1; 64:1; 65:1; 66:1, 2 (H), 4 (2x; H, H); 67:1; 68:1, 5 (H), 33 (H); 71:22 (H), 23 (H); 73:1; 75:1, 10 (H); 76:1; 77:1; 79:1; 80:1; 81:3; 82:1; 83:1; 84:1; 85:1; 87:1; 88:1; 92:1, 2; 95:2; 98:1, 4 (C), 5 (2x: H); 100:1; 101:1 (2x: H); 104:33 (H); 105:2 (H); 108:1, 2 (H), 4 (H); 109:1; 110:1; 119:54; 135:3 (H); 138:1 (H); 139:1; 140:1; 141:1; 143:1; 144:9 (H); 146:2 (H); 147:1, 7 (H); 149:3 (H); Cant 2:12; Isa 12:5 (H); 24:16; 25:5; 51:3; Amos 5:23.

חגג/*ḥgg*—Qal: "leap, walk in procession, celebrate"

Gen 46:16; Exod 5:1 (H); 10:9; 12:14 (2x: H, H); 13:6; 23:14 (H), 15, 16 (2x), 18; 32:5; 34:18; 34:22 (2x), 25; Lev 23:6, 34, 39 (2x: H), 41 (3x: H, H); Num 26:15 (2x); 28:17; 29:12 (2x: H); Deut 16:10, 13, 14, 15 (H), 16 (3x); 31:10; Judg 21:19; 1 Sam 30:16 (H); 2 Sam 3:4; 1 Kgs 1:5, 11; 2:13; 8:2, 65; 12:32 (2x), 33; 1 Chr 3:2; 6:15; 2 Chr 5:3; 7:8, 9; 8:13 (3x); 30:13, 21; 35:17; Ezra 3:4; 5:1; 6:14, 22; Neh 8:14, 18; Pss 42:5 (H); 81:4; 107:27 (H); 118:27; Isa 29:1; 30:29; Ezek 45:17, 21, 23, 25; 46:11; Hos 2:13; 9:5; Amos 5:21; 8:10; Nah 2:1 (2x; H); Hag 1:1, 3, 12, 13; Hag 2:1, 10, 13, 14, 20; Zech 14:16 (2x), 18 (2x), 19 (2x); Mal 2:3.

חדה I/*ḥdh* I—Qal: "rejoice"; Piel: "make joyful, cheer"

Exod 18:9 (H); 1 Chr 5:24; 16:27; 24:20; 27:30; Neh 8:10; Job 3:6 (night); Ps 21:7 (D).

חול/*ḥwl*—Qal: "dance round dances"; Pilpel: "dance round dances"

Gen 10:23; Judg 21:21; 2 Sam 3:29 (guilt); 1 Chr 1:17; Ps 87:7 (H); Jer 4:19 (H); 23:19 (C); 30:23 (C); Lam 4:6 (H); Ezek 30:16 (2x: H); Hos 11:6 (I/AI).

חמד/*ḥmd*—Qal: "desire, take pleasure in"; Niphal: "desirable"; Piel: "fiercely desire"

Gen 2:9 (C); 3:6 (C); 27:15; 36:26; Exod 20:17 (2x: H, H); 34:24 (H); Deut 5:21 (H); 7:25 (H); Josh 7:21 (H); 1 Sam 9:20; 1 Kgs 20:6; 2 Chr 21:20; 32:27; 36:10, 19; Ezra 8:27; Job 20:20 (I/AI); Pss 19:11 (the judgments of Yahweh); 39:12 (I/AI); 68:17 (D); 106:24; Prov 1:22 (H); 6:25 (H); 12:12 (H); 21:20 (I/AI); Cant 2:3 (H); 5:16; Isa 1:29 (H); 2:16; 27:2; 32:12; 44:9 (I/AI); 53:2 (H); 64:10; Jer 3:19; 12:10; 25:34; Lam 1:7, 10, 11; 2:4; Ezek 23:6, 12, 23; 24:16, 21, 25; 26:12; Dan 9:23; 10:3, 11, 19; 11:8, 37, 38, 43; Hos 9:6, 16; 13:15; Joel 4:5; Amos 5:11; Micah 2:2 (H); Nah 2:10; Hag 2:7; Zech 7:14.

חפץ I/*ḥpṣ* I—Qal: "take pleasure in, desire, delight in"

Gen 34:19 (H); Num 14:8 (D); Deut 21:14 (H); 25:7 (H), 8 (H); Judg 13:23 (D); Ruth 3:13 (H); 1 Sam 2:25 (D); 15:22; 18:22 (H), 25; 19:1 (H); 2 Sam 15:26 (D); 20:11 (H); 22:20 (D); 23:5; 24:3 (H); 1 Kgs 5:22, 23, 24; 9:1 (H), 11; 10:9 (D), 13; 13:33; 21:6; 2 Kgs 21:1; 1 Chr 28:9; 2 Chr 9:8 (D), 12; Neh 1:11; Esth 2:14 (H); 6:6 (2x: H, H), 7 (H), 9 (2x: H, H), 11 (H); Job 9:3 (H); 13:3 (H); 21:14 (H), 21; 22:3; 31:16; 33:32 (H); Pss 1:2; 5:5; 16:3; 18:20 (D); 22:9

(D); 34:13; 35:27 (2x); 37:23 (D); 40:7 (D), 9 (H), 15; 41:12 (D); 51:8 (D), 18 (D), 21 (D); 68:31 (H); 70:3; 73:25 (H); 107:30; 109:17 (H); 111:2; 112:1 (H); 115:3 (D); 119:35 (H); 135:6 (D); 147:10 (D); Prov 3:15; 8:11; 18:2 (H); 21:1 (D); 31:13; Eccl 3:1, 17; 5:3, 7; 8:3 (H), 6; 12:1, 10; Cant 2:7 (love); 3:5 (love); 8:4 (love); Isa 1:11 (D); 13:17 (H); 42:21 (D); 44:28; 46:10; 48:14; 53:10 (2x: D); 54:12; 55:11 (D); 56:4 (D); 58:2 (2x: H, H), 3, 13 (2x); 62:4 (2x: D); 65:12 (D); 66:3 (H), 4 (D); Jer 6:10 (H); 9:23 (D); 22:28; 42:22 (H); 48:38; Ezek 18:23 (2x: D), 32 (D); 33:11 (D); Hos 6:6 (D); 8:8; Jon 1:14 (D); Micah 7:18; Mal 1:10; 2:17 (D); 3:1, 12.

טוב/*ṭwb*—Qal: "be pleasant, delightful, joyful, glad"

Gen 1:4, 10, 12, 18, 21, 25, 31; 2:9 (2x), 12, 17, 18; 3:5, 6, 22; 6:2; 15:15; 16:6; 18:7; 19:8; 20:15; 24:10, 16, 50; 25:8; 26:7, 29; 27:9; 29:19; 30:20; 31:24, 29; 40:16; 41:5, 22, 24, 26 (2x), 35; 44:4; 45:18, 20, 23; 49:15; 50:20; Exod 2:2; 3:8; 14:12; 18:9, 17; 33:19; Lev 27:10 (2x), 12, 14, 33; Num 10:29, 32; 11:18 (impersonal subject); 13:19; 14:3, 7; 24:1 (impersonal subject), 5 (I/AI), 13; 36:6; Deut 1:14, 25, 35, 39; 3:25 (2x); 4:21, 22; 5:33 (impersonal subject); 6:10, 11, 18 (2x), 24; 8:7, 10, 12; 9:6; 10:13; 11:17; 12:28; 15:16 (impersonal subject); 19:13; 23:7, 17; 26:11; 28:11, 12, 47; 30:9 (2x), 15; Josh 7:21; 9:25; 21:45; 23:13, 14, 15 (2x), 16; Judg 8:2, 32, 35; 9:2, 11, 16; 10:15; 11:3, 5, 25 (2x: H); 15:2; 16:25 (H); 18:9, 19; 19:24; Ruth 2:22; 3:13; 4:15; 1 Sam 1:8, 23; 2:24, 26 (H); 3:18; 8:14, 16; 9:2 (2x), 10; 11:10; 12:23; 14:3, 36, 40; 15:9, 22, 28; 16:12, 16, 23; 19:4 (2x); 20:7, 12; 22:9, 11, 12, 20; 24:18, 19, 20; 25:3, 8, 15, 21, 30, 36 (H); 26:16; 27:1; 29:6 (2x), 9; 2 Sam 2:6; 3:13, 19 (impersonal subject), 36 (deeds); 7:28; 8:17; 10:6, 8, 12; 11:2; 13:22, 28; 14:17, 32; 15:3, 26 (impersonal subject); 17:7, 14 (2x); 18:3, 27 (2x); 19:19, 28, 36, 38 (impersonal subject), 39; 24:22; 1 Kgs 1:6, 42; 2:18, 32, 38, 42; 3:9; 8:36, 56, 66 (2x); 10:7; 12:7; 14:13, 15; 15:18; 18:24; 19:4; 20:3; 21:2 (2x); 22:8, 13 (2x), 18; 2 Kgs 2:19; 3:19 (2x), 25 (2x); 5:12; 8:9; 10:3, 5; 20:3, 13, 19; 25:28; 1 Chr 4:40; 5:33, 34, 37, 38; 6:37; 8:11; 9:11; 13:2; 16:34; 17:26; 18:16; 19:13; 21:23; 28:8; 29:28; 2 Chr 3:5, 8; 5:13; 6:27, 41; 7:3, 10 (2x); 10:7 (2x); 12:12; 14:1; 18:7, 12 (2x), 17; 19:3, 11; 21:13; 24:16; 30:18, 22; 31:20; Ezra 2:60; 3:11; 4:7; 7:2, 9; 8:18, 22, 27; 9:12 (2x); Neh 2:5, 7, 8, 10 (2x), 18 (2x), 19; 3:35; 4:1; 5:9, 19; 6:1, 12, 14, 17 (2x), 19 (2x); 7:62; 9:13, 20, 25 (2x), 35, 36; 11:11; 13:4, 7, 8, 31; Esth 1:10, 11, 19; 2:2, 3, 7, 9; 3:9, 11; 5:4, 8, 9; 7:3, 9; 8:5 (2x), 8, 17; 9:13, 19, 22; 10:3; Job 2:10; 7:7; 9:25; 10:3; 13:9; 20:21; 21:13, 16, 25; 22:18, 21; 30:26; 34:4; 36:11; Pss 4:7; 14:1, 3; 16:2; 21:4; 23:6; 25:7, 8, 13; 27:13; 31:20; 34:9, 11, 13, 15; 35:12; 36:5; 37:3, 16, 27; 38:21 (2x); 39:3; 45:2; 52:5, 11; 53:2, 4; 54:8; 63:4; 65:5, 12; 68:11; 69:17; 73:1, 28; 84:11, 12; 85:13; 86:5, 17; 92:2; 100:5; 103:5; 104:28; 106:1, 5; 107:1, 9; 109:5, 21; 111:10; 112:5; 118:1, 8, 9, 29; 119:39, 65, 66, 68, 71 (impersonal subject), 72, 122; 122:9; 125:4; 128:2, 5; 133:1, 2; 135:3; 136:1; 143:10; 145:7, 9; 147:1; Prov 2:9, 20; 3:4, 14, 27; 4:2; 8:11, 19; 11:10, 23, 27; 12:2, 9, 14, 25; 13:2, 15, 21, 22; 14:14, 19, 22; 15:3, 15, 16, 17, 23, 30; 16:8, 16, 19, 20, 29, 32; 17:1, 13, 20, 26; 18:5, 22; 19:1, 2, 8, 22; 20:23; 21:9, 19; 22:1, 9; 24:13, 23, 25; 25:7, 24, 25, 27; 27:5, 10; 28:6, 10, 21; 31:12, 18; Eccl 2:1, 3, 24 (2x), 26 (2x); 3:12, 13, 22; 4:3, 6, 8, 9 (2x), 13; 5:4, 10, 17 (2x); 6:3 (2x), 6, 9, 12; 7:1 (2x), 2, 3, 5, 8 (2x), 10, 11, 14 (2x), 18, 20, 26; 8:12, 13, 15; 9:2 (2x), 4, 7, 16, 18 (2x); 11:6, 7; 12:14; Cant 1:2, 3; 4:10 (love); 7:10; Isa 1:19; 3:10; 5:9, 20 (2x); 7:6, 15, 16; 38:3; 39:2, 8; 41:7; 52:7; 55:2; 56:5; 63:7; 65:2, 14; Jer 2:7; 5:25; 6:16, 20; 8:15; 12:6; 14:11, 19; 15:11; 17:6; 18:10, 20 (2x); 21:10; 22:15, 16; 24:2, 3 (2x), 5 (2x), 6; 26:14; 29:10, 32; 31:12, 14; 32:39, 42; 33:9 (2x), 11, 14; 39:16; 40:4 (2x); 42:6; 44:17, 27; 52:32; Lam 3:17, 25,

26, 27, 38; 4:1, 9; Ezek 17:8; 18:18; 20:25; 24:4; 31:16; 34:14 (2x), 18; 36:31; Dan 1:4, 15; Hos 2:9; 3:5; 4:13; 8:3; 10:1, 11; 14:3; Joel 4:5; Amos 5:14, 15; 6:2; 9:4; Jon 4:3, 8; Micah 1:12; 3:2; 6:8; 7:4; Nah 1:7; 3:4; Zech 1:13, 17; 6:10, 14; 8:19; 9:17; 11:12; Mal 2:17.

יטב/*yṭb*—Qal: "be well, pleasing"; Hiphil: "treat well, graciously, do good; make things go well for"

Gen 4:7 (2x: H, H); 12:13 (impersonal subject), 16; (impersonal subject); 32:10 (D), 13 (2x: D); 34:18 (words); 36:39; 40:14 (impersonal subject); 41:37 (plan); 45:16 (news); 47:6, 11; Exod 1:20 (D); 22:4 (2x); 30:7 (H); Lev 5:4; 10:19 (ritual activity), 20 (explanation/report); Num 10:29 (H), 32 (2x: D, H); 33:33, 34; Deut 1:23 (plan/idea); 4:40 (impersonal subject); 5:16 (impersonal subject), 28 (H), 29 (impersonal subject); 6:3 (impersonal subject), 18 (impersonal subject); 8:16; 9:21; 10:7; 12:25 (impersonal subject), 28 (impersonal subject); 13:15; 17:4; 18:17 (H); 19:18; 22:7 (impersonal subject); 27:8; 28:63; 30:5 (D); Josh 22:30 (words), 33 (report); 24:20 (D); Judg 17:13 (D); 18:20 (H); Judg 19:6 (H), 9 (H), 22 (H); Ruth 3:1 (impersonal subject), 7 (H), 10 (H); 1 Sam 2:32 (D); 15:9, 15; 16:17 (H); 18:5 (the placement of David over all the soldiers); 20:13 (impersonal subject); 24:5 (impersonal subject); 25:31 (D); 2 Sam 3:36 (impersonal subject); 18:4 (impersonal subject); 1 Kgs 1:47 (D); 3:10 (request); 21:7 (H); 2 Kgs 9:30 (H); 11:18; 21:19; 25:24 (impersonal subject); 1 Chr 1:50; Neh 2:5 (H), 6 (idea); 6:10; Esth 1:21 (idea); 2:4 (2x: H, idea), 9 (H); 5:14 (idea); Job 24:21 (H); Pss 33:3 (H); 36:4; 49:19 (H); 51:20 (D); 69:32 (praise); 119:68 (D); 125:4 (D); Prov 15:2 (the tongue of the wise), 13 (a joyful heart); 17:22 (a joyful heart); 30:29 (2x: C/H); Eccl 7:3 (H); 11:9 (H); Isa 1:17; 23:16 (H); 41:23 (D); Jer 1:12 (H); 2:33 (H); 4:22; 7:3 (H), 5 (2x: H), 23 (impersonal subject); 10:5; 13:23; 18:10, 11 (H); 26:13 (H); 32:40 (D), 41; 35:15 (H); 38:20 (impersonal subject); 40:9 (impersonal subject); 42:6 (impersonal subject); Ezek 33:32 (H); Hos 10:1 (H); Jon 4:4, 9 (2x); Micah 2:7 (words); 7:3; Nah 3:8 (Nineveh); Zeph 1:12 (D); Zech 8:15.

כשר/*kšr*—Qal: "be proper, pleasing"; Hiphil: "bring success"

Esth 8:5 (idea); Ps 68:7; Eccl 2:21; 4:4; 5:10; 10:10; 11:6 (sowing).

לעב/*lʿb*—Hiphil: "make jest at"

2 Chr 36:16 (H).

נעם I/*nʿm* I—Qal: "be pleasant, lovely; be a delight for"

Gen 4:22; 46:21; 49:15 (C); Num 26:40 (3x); Josh 15:41; Judg 4:6, 12; 5:1, 12; Ruth 1:2, 3, 8, 11, 19, 20, 21, 22; 2:1, 2, 6, 20 (2x), 22; 3:1; 4:3, 5, 9, 14, 16, 17; 1 Sam 14:50; 25:43; 27:3; 30:5; 2 Sam 1:23, 26 (H); 2:2; 3:2; 23:1; 1 Kgs 14:21, 31; 2 Kgs 5:1, 2, 6, 9, 11, 17, 20, 21 (2x), 23, 27; 1 Chr 3:1; 4:15; 8:4, 7; 11:46; 2 Chr 12:13; Job 36:11; Pss 16:6, 11; 27:4; 81:3; 90:17; 133:1; 135:3; 141:4, 6 (words); 147:1; Prov 2:10 (knowledge); 3:17; 9:17 (I/AI); 15:26; 16:24; 22:18; 23:8; 24:4, 25 (impersonal subject); Cant 1:16; 7:7 (H); Isa 17:10; Ezek 32:19 (H); Zech 11:7, 10.

סלד/*sld*—Piel: "jump for joy"

1 Chr 2:30; Job 6:10 (H).

עדן I/ '*dn* I—Hithpael: "to live a life of luxury, let things go well"

    Gen 2:8, 10, 15; 3:23, 24; 4:16; 18:12; 49:20; 2 Sam 1:24; 23:8; 2 Kgs 19:12; 1 Chr 11:42; 2 Chr 17:14; 29:12; 31:15; Ezra 2:15; 8:6; Neh 7:20; 9:25 (H); 10:17; Job 38:31; Ps 36:9; Prov 29:17; Eccl 4:2, 3; Isa 37:12; 47:8; 51:3; Jer 51:34; Lam 4:5; Ezek 27:23; 28:13; 31:9, 16, 18 (2x); 36:35; Joel 2:3; Amos 1:5.

עלז/ '*lz*—Qal: "rejoice, exult"

    2 Sam 1:20 (H); Pss 28:7 (H); 60:8 (H); 68:5 (H); 94:3 (H); 96:12 (C); 108:8 (H); 149:5 (H); Prov 23:16 (H); Isa 5:14; 13:3; 22:2; 23:7, 12; 24:8; 32:13; Jer 11:15 (H); 15:17 (H); 50:11 (H); 51:39 (H); Hab 3:18 (H); Zeph 2:15; 3:11, 14 (Daughter of Jerusalem).

עלס I/ '*ls* I—Qal: "enjoy a thing"; Hithpael: "enjoy each other"

    Job 20:18 (H); Prov 7:18 (H).

עלץ/ '*lṣ*—Qal: "rejoice, exult"

    1 Sam 2:1 (H); 1 Chr 16:32 (C); Pss 5:12 (H); 9:3 (H); 25:2 (H); 68:4 (H); Prov 11:10 (H); 28:12; Hab 3:14.

ענג/ '*ng*—Hithpael: "take delight, pleasure in; make merry, be content"

    Deut 28:54, 56 (2x); Job 22:26 (H); 27:10 (H); Ps 37:4 (H), 11 (H); Prov 19:10; Eccl 2:8; Cant 7:7; Isa 13:22; 47:1; 55:2 (H); 57:4 (H); 58:13, 14 (H); 66:11 (H); Jer 6:2 (Daughter of Zion); Micah 1:16; 2:9.

ערב III/ '*rb* III—Qal: "be pleasing"

    Ps 104:34 (prayer); Prov 3:24 (sleep); 13:19 (realized desire); 20:17; Cant 2:14; Jer 6:20 (I/AI); 31:26 (sleep); Ezek 16:37 (H); Mal 3:4 (I/AI).

פוש/*pwš*—Qal: "paw the ground (playfully?)"

    Jer 50:11 (H); Hab 1:8 (C); Mal 3:20 (H).

פזז II/*pzz* II—Piel: "leap (with joy?)"

    2 Sam 6:16 (H)

פצח I/*psḥ* I—Qal: "be cheerful, happy, serene"

    Ps 98:4 (C/H); Isa 14:7 (C/H); 44:23 (C); 49:13 (C); 52:9 (ruins of Jerusalem); 54:1 (H); 55:12 (C).

צחק/*ṣḥq*—Qal: "laugh"; Piel: "sport, play, jest"[27]

    Gen 17:17 (H); 18:12 (H), 13 (H), 15 (2x: H, H); 19:14 (H); 21:6 (2x: H), 9 (H); 26:8 (H); 39:14, 17; Exod 32:6; Judg 16:25 (H); Ezek 23:32.

---

27. The name "Isaac" (*yiṣḥāq*) is clearly related to *ṣḥq*, a point explicitly made in Gen 21:6 ("Then Sarah said, God has made laughter [*ṣěḥōq*] for me; everyone who hears will laugh [*yiṣḥaq*] with me"). To save space, however, references to Isaac have been omitted from this list, especially since the laughter motif is rarely evident or at work in the instances of the proper name.

רוח/*rwḥ*—Qal: "feel relieved, easy"; Hiphil: "smell, enjoy"[28]

Gen 8:21 (D); 27:27 (H); 32:17; Exod 8:11; 30:38; Lev 26:31 (D); Deut 4:28 (D); Judg 16:9 (I/AI); 1 Sam 16:23 (I/AI); 26:19 (D); Esth 4:14; Job 32:20 (speaking); 39:25 (C); Ps 115:6 (idols); Isa 11:3 (H); Lam 3:56; Ezek 20:41; Hos 14:7; Amos 5:21 (D).

רוע/*rw'*—Hiphil: "shout in joy, cheer"; Polal: "a shout is uttered"; Hithpolal: "shout in triumph"

Exod 32:17; Lev 23:24; 25:9; Num 10:5, 6 (2x), 7 (H), 9 (H); Num 10:5, 6 (2x); 23:21; 29:1; 31:6; Josh 6:5 (2x: H), 10 (3x: H, H, H), 16 (H), 20 (3x: H, H); Judg 7:21 (H); 15:14 (H); 1 Sam 4:5 (2x: H), 6 (2x); 10:24 (H); 17:20 (H), 52 (H); 2 Sam 6:15; 1 Chr 15:28; 2 Chr 13:12 (2x), 15 (2x: H); 15:14; Ezra 3:11 (2x: H), 12, 13 (3x: H); Job 8:21; 30:5 (H); 33:26; 36:33; 38:7 (HB); 39:25; Pss 27:6; 33:3; 41:12 (H); 47:2 (H), 6; 60:10 (H); 65:14 (C); 66:1 (C/H); 81:2 (H); 89:16; 95:1 (H), 2 (H); 98:4 (C/H), 6 (C/H); 100:1 (C/H); 108:10 (H); 150:5; Isa 15:4 (H); 16:10 (H); 42:13 (D); 44:23 (C); Jer 4:19; 20:16; 49:2; 50:15 (H); Ezek 21:27; Hos 5:8 (H); Joel 2:1 (H); Amos 1:14; 2:2; Micah 4:9 (2x: Jerusalem); Zeph 1:16; 3:14 (H); Zech 9:9 (Daughter of Jerusalem).

רנן/*rnn*—Qal: "jubilate, give a cry of joy"; Piel: "give a ringing cry in joy"; Pual: "cry for joy"; Hiphil: "cause to cry for joy"

Lev 9:24 (H); Deut 32:43 (H); 1 Kgs 8:28; 22:36; 1 Chr 4:20; 16:33 (C); 2 Chr 6:19; 20:22; Job 3:7; 20:5; 29:13 (H); 38:7; Pss 5:12 (H); 17:1; 20:6 (H); 30:6; 32:7, 11 (H); 33:1 (H); 35:27 (H); 42:5; 47:2; 51:16 (H); 59:17 (H); 61:2; 63:6, 8 (H); 65:9 (D); 67:5 (H); 71:23 (H); 81:2 (H); 84:3 (H); 88:3; 89:13 (C); 90:14 (H); 92:5 (H); 95:1 (H); 96:12 (C); 98:4 (C/H), 8 (C); 100:2; 105:43; 106:44; 107:22; 118:15; 119:169; 126:2, 5, 6; 132:9 (H), 16 (2x: H); 142:7; 145:7 (H); 149:5 (H); Prov 1:20 (Wisdom); 8:3 (Wisdom); 11:10; 29:6 (H); Isa 12:6 (H); 14:7; 16:10 (impersonal subject); 24:14 (H); 26:19 (the dead); 35:2, 6 (H), 10; 42:11 (H); 43:14; 44:23 (2x: C); 48:20; 49:13 (2x: C); 51:11; 52:8 (H), 9 (ruins of Jerusalem); 54:1 (2x: barren one); 55:12; 61:7 (H); 65:14 (H); Jer 7:16; 11:14; 14:12; 31:7 (H), 12 (H); 51:48 (C); Lam 2:19 (H); Zeph 3:14 (Daughter of Zion), 17; Zech 2:14 (Daughter of Zion).

רצה I/*rṣh* I—Qal: "be pleased with, be favorable to"; Niphal: "be treated as favored"; Hithpael: "make oneself favored with"

Gen 33:10 (H); 49:6; Exod 28:38; Lev 1:3, 4 (I/AI); 7:18 (I/AI); 19:5, 7 (I/AI); 22:19, 20, 21, 23 (I/AI), 25 (I/AI), 27 (I/AI), 29; 23:11; Num 26:33; 27:1; 36:11; Deut 33:11 (D), 16, 23, 24 (H); Josh 12:24; 17:3; 1 Sam 29:4 (H); 2 Sam 24:23 (D); 1 Kgs 14:17; 15:21, 33; 16:6, 8, 9 (2x), 15, 17, 23; 2 Kgs 15:14, 16; 1 Chr 7:39; 28:4 (D); 29:3 (H), 17 (D); 2 Chr 10:7 (H);

---

28. The substantives, *rûaḥ* ("wind, breath, spirit, etc.") and *rêaḥ* ("smell") have been omitted from this list. While both are etymologically related to *rwḥ* (see H.-J. Fabry, "רוּחַ," in *TDOT* 13:367–8), neither seems related to concepts of happiness.

15:15; Ezra 10:11; Neh 9:24, 37; Esth 1:8; 9:5; 10:3 (H); Job 33:26 (D); 34:9 (H); Pss 5:13; 19:15; 30:6, 8; 40:9, 14 (D); 44:4 (D); 49:14 (H); 50:18 (H); 51:18 (D), 20; 62:5 (H); 69:14; 77:8; 85:2 (D); 89:18; 102:15 (H); 103:21; 106:4; 119:108 (D); 143:10; 145:16, 19; 147:10 (D), 11 (D); 149:4 (D); Prov 3:12 (H); 8:35; 10:32; 11:1, 20, 27; 12:2, 22; 14:9, 35; 15:8; 16:7, 13, 15; 18:22; 19:12; 23:26 (H); Eccl 9:7 (D); Cant 6:4; Isa 42:1 (D); 49:8; 56:7; 58:5; 60:7, 10; 61:2; Jer 6:20; 14:10 (D), 12 (D); Ezek 20:40 (D), 41 (D); Dan 8:4; 11:3, 16, 36; Hos 8:13 (D); Amos 5:22 (D); Micah 6:7 (D); Hag 1:8 (D); Mal 1:8 (H), 10 (D), 13 (D); 2:13.

רקד/*rqd*—Qal: "skip about"; Piel: "dance"; Hiphil: "cause to skip about"

   1 Chr 15:29 (H); Job 21:11 (H); Pss 29:6 (D); 114:4 (C), 6 (C); Eccl 3:4; Isa 13:21 (C); Joel 2:5 (H); Nah 3:2 (I/AI).

שבע/*śb'*—Qal: "be sated"; Niphal: "sated"; Piel: "satisfy a person"; Hiphil: "satisfy"

   Gen 25:8; 35:29; 41:29, 30, 31, 34, 47, 53; Exod 16:3, 8, 12 (H); Lev 25:19; 26:5, 26 (H); Deut 6:11 (H); 8:10 (H), 12 (H); 11:15 (H); 14:29 (H); 23:25; 26:12 (H); 31:20 (H); 33:23; Ruth 2:14 (H), 18; 1 Sam 2:5; 1 Chr 23:1 (H); 29:28; 2 Chr 24:15 (H); 31:10; Neh 9:25 (H); Job 7:4 (H); 9:18 (D); 10:15; 14:1; 19:22 (H); 27:14 (H); 31:31 (H); 38:27; 42:17; Pss 16:11; 17:14 (H), 15 (H); 22:27 (H); 37:19 (H); 59:16 (H); 63:6 (H); 65:5 (H); 78:25, 29 (H); 81:17 (D); 88:4 (H); 90:14 (D); 91:16 (D); 103:5 (D); 104:13 (C), 16 (C), 28 (C/H); 105:40 (D); 107:9 (D); 123:3 (H), 4 (H); 132:15 (D); 145:16 (D); 147:14 (D); Prov 1:31 (H); 3:10; 5:10 (H); 12:11 (H), 14 (H); 13:25; 14:14 (H); 18:20 (2x: H, H); 19:23; 20:13 (H); 25:16 (H), 17 (H); 27:7, 20 (2x: Sheol and Abaddon/H); 28:19 (2x: H, H); 30:9 (H), 15 (three insatiable things), 16 (C), 22 (H); Eccl 1:8 (H); 4:8 (H); 5:9 (H), 11; 6:3 (H); Isa 1:11 (D); 9:19 (H); 23:18; 44:16 (H); 53:11 (H); 55:2; 56:11; 58:10 (H), 11 (D); 66:11 (H); Jer 5:7 (D); 31:14 (H); 44:17 (H); 46:10 (I/AI); 50:10 (H), 19 (H); Lam 3:15 (D), 30 (H); 5:6; Ezek 7:19 (H); 16:28 (2x: Jerusalem, Jerusalem), 29 (Jerusalem), 49; 27:33 (Tyre); 32:4 (D); 39:19, 20 (C); Hos 4:10 (H); 13:6 (2x: H, H); Joel 2:19 (H), 26; Amos 4:8 (H); Micah 6:14 (H); Hab 2:5 (H), 16 (H); Hag 1:6.

שוש/*śwś*—Qal: "rejoice, display joy"

   Deut 28:63 (2x: D, D); 30:9 (2x: D); Esth 8:16, 17; Job 3:22 (H); 8:19; 39:21 (C); Pss 19:6 (C); 35:9 (H); 40:17 (H); 45:8; 48:3; 51:10, 14; 68:4 (H); 70:5 (H); 105:43; 119:14 (H), 111, 162 (H); Isa 12:3; 22:13; 24:8 (2x), 11; 32:13, 14; 35:1 (C), 10; 51:3, 11; 60:15; 61:3, 10 (2x: H); 62:5 (2x: D); 64:4 (H); 65:18 (2x: H), 19 (D); 66:10 (2x: H), 14 (H); Jer 7:34; 15:16; 16:9; 25:10; 31:13; 32:41 (D); 33:9, 11; 49:25; Lam 1:21 (H); 2:15; 4:21 (Daughter of Edom); 5:15; Ezek 21:15 (H?); 24:25; Hos 2:13; Joel 1:12; Zeph 3:17 (D); Zech 8:19.

שחק/*śḥq*—Qal: "play, amuse, laugh, entertain"; Piel: "be merry, play with, make merry, dance"

   Judg 16:25 (H), 27; 1 Sam 18:7 (H); 2 Sam 2:14 (H); 6:5 (H), 21 (H); 1 Chr 13:8 (H); 15:29 (H); 2 Chr 30:10 (H); Job 5:22 (H); 8:21 (H); 12:4 (2x); 29:24 (H); 30:1 (H); 39:7 (C), 18 (C), 22 (C); 40:20 (C), 29 (H); 41:21 (C); Pss 2:4 (D); 37:13 (D); 52:8 (H); 59:9 (D); 104:26; 126:2; Prov 1:26 (Wisdom); 8:30 (Wisdom), 31 (Wisdom); 10:23; 14:13;

26:19 (H); 29:9 (H); 31:25 (H); Eccl 2:2; 3:4; 7:3, 6; 10:19; Jer 15:17 (H); 20:7; 30:19 (H); 31:4 (H); 48:26, 27, 39; Lam 1:7 (H); 3:14; Hab 1:10 (2x: H); Zech 8:5 (H).

שׂמח/*śmḥ*—Qal: "rejoice"; Piel: "cause to rejoice, gladden"; Hiphil: "cause to rejoice"
Gen 31:27; Exod 4:14 (H); Lev 23:40 (H); Num 10:10; Deut 12:7 (H), 12 (H), 18 (H); 14:26 (H); 16:11 (H), 14, 15; 24:5 (H); 26:11 (H); 27:7 (H); 28:47; 33:18 (H); Judg 9:13 (I/AI), 19 (2x: H, H); 16:23; 19:3 (H); 1 Sam 2:1 (H); 6:13 (H); 11:9 (H), 15 (H); 18:6; 19:5 (H); 2 Sam 1:20 (H); 6:12; 1 Kgs 1:40 (2x), 45; 4:20; 5:21 (H); 8:66; 2 Kgs 11:14, 20 (H); 1 Chr 12:41; 15:16, 25; 16:10 (H), 31 (C); 29:9 (3x: H, H), 17, 22; 2 Chr 6:41 (H); 7:10; 15:15 (H); 20:27 (2x: D); 23:13, 18, 21 (H); 24:10 (H); 29:30, 36 (H); 30:21, 23, 25 (H), 26; Ezra 3:12, 13; 6:22 (2x: D); Neh 8:12, 17; 12:27, 43 (5x: H, D, H), 44; Esth 5:9, 14; 8:15 (H), 16, 17; 9:17, 18, 19, 22 (2x); Job 3:22; 20:5; 21:12 (H); 22:19 (H); 31:25 (H), 29 (H); Pss 4:8; 5:12 (H); 9:3 (H); 14:7 (H); 16:9 (H), 11; 19:9 (precepts); 21:2 (H), 7; 30:2 (D), 12; 31:8 (H); 32:11 (H); 33:21 (H); 34:3 (H); 35:15 (H), 19 (H), 24 (H), 26, 27 (H); 38:17 (H); 40:17 (H); 43:4; 45:9 (I/AI), 16; 46:5 (streams); 48:12 (Zion); 51:10; 53:7 (H); 58:11 (H); 63:12 (H); 64:11 (H); 66:6 (H); 67:5 (H); 68:4 (2x: H); 69:33 (H); 70:5 (H); 85:7 (H); 86:4 (D); 89:43 (D); 90:14 (H), 15 (D); 92:5 (D); 96:11 (C); 97:1 (C/H), 8 (Zion), 11, 12 (H); 100:2; 104:15 (I/AI), 31 (D), 34 (H); 105:3 (H), 38 (H); 106:5 (2x); 107:30 (H), 42 (H); 109:28 (H); 113:9; 118:24 (H); 119:74 (H); 122:1 (H); 126:3; 137:3, 6; 149:2 (H); Prov 2:14; 5:18 (H); 10:1 (H), 28; 12:20, 25 (a good word); 13:9 (the light of the righteous); 14:10, 13; 15:13, 20 (H), 21, 23, 30 (brightness of eyes); 17:5, 21 (H), 22; 21:15, 17; 23:15 (H), 24 (H), 25 (H); 24:17 (H); 27:9 (I/AI), 11 (H); 29:2 (H), 3 (H), 6 (H); Eccl 2:1, 2, 10 (2x), 26; 3:12, 22 (H); 4:16 (H); 5:18, 19; 7:4; 8:15 (2x); 9:7; 10:19 (I/AI); 11:8 (H), 9 (H); Cant 1:4 (H); 3:11; Isa 9:2 (3x: H), 16 (D); 14:8 (C), 29 (H); 16:10; 22:13; 24:7, 11; 25:9 (H); 29:19; 30:29; 35:10 (2x); 39:2 (H); 51:3, 11 (2x); 55:12; 56:7 (D); 61:7; 65:13 (H); 66:5, 10 (H); Jer 7:34; 15:16; 16:9; 20:15 (2x: H); 25:10; 31:7, 13 (2x: H, D); 33:11; 41:13 (H); 48:33; 50:11 (H); Lam 2:17 (D); 4:21 (Daughter of Edom); Ezek 7:12 (H); 25:6 (H); 35:14, 15; 36:5 (H); Hos 7:3 (H); 9:1 (H); Joel 1:16; 2:21 (C), 23 (H); Amos 6:13; Obad 12 (H); Jon 4:6 (2x: H); Micah 7:8 (H); Hab 1:15 (H); Zeph 3:14 (Daughter of Jerusalem), 17; Zech 2:14 (Daughter of Zion); 4:10 (seven eyes of the LORD); 8:19; 10:7 (H).

שׁבח I/*šbḥ*I—Piel: "praise, laud, congratulate"; Hithpael: "boast of"
1 Chr 16:35; Pss 63:4 (H); 106:47; 117:1 (H); 145:4 (H); 147:12 (Jerusalem); Eccl 4:2; 8:15 (H).

שׁיר/*šyr*—Qal: "sing"; Hophal: "be sung"; Polel: "burst into song"
Gen 31:27; Exod 15:1 (3x: H, H), 21 (H); Num 21:17 (2x: H); Deut 31:19 (2x), 21, 22, 30; 32:44; Judg 5:1 (H), 3 (H), 12; 1 Sam 18:6; 2 Sam 19:36 (2x: H, H); 22:1; 1 Kgs 5:12; 10:12 (H); 1 Chr 6:16, 17, 18 (H); 9:33 (H); 13:8; 15:16 (2x: H), 19 (H), 27 (2x: H, H); 16:9 (H), 23 (C/H), 42; 25:6, 7; 2 Chr 5:12 (H), 13 (2x: H); 7:6 (H); 9:11 (H); 20:21 (H); 23:13 (2x: H), 18; 29:27, 28 (2x: song); 34:12; 35:15, 25 (2x: H, H); Ezra 2:41 (H), 65 (2x: H, H), 70 (H); 7:7 (H); 10:24 (H); Neh 7:1 (H), 44 (H), 67 (2x: H, H), 72 (H); 10:29 (H), 40 (H); 11:22 (H), 23 (H); 12:27, 28 (H), 29 (H), 36, 42 (H), 45 (H), 46 (2x: H), 47 (H); 13:5 (H), 10 (H); Job

36:24 (H); Pss 7:1 (H); 13:6 (H); 18:1; 21:14 (H); 27:6 (H); 28:7; 30:1; 33:3 (2x: H); 40:4; 42:9; 45:1; 46:1; 48:1; 57:8 (H); 59:17 (H); 65:1, 14 (C); 66:1; 67:1; 68:1, 5 (H), 26 (H), 33 (H); 69:31; 75:1; 76:1; 83:1; 87:1, 7; 88:1; 89:2 (H); 92:1; 96:1 (3x: C/H, C/H), 2 (C/H); 98:1 (2x: H); 101:1 (H); 104:33 (H); 105:2 (H); 106:12 (H); 108:1, 2 (H); 120:1; 121:1; 122:1; 123:1; 124:1; 125:1; 126:1; 127:1; 128:1; 129:1; 130:1; 131:1; 132:1; 133:1; 134:1; 137:3 (3x: H), 4 (2x: H); 138:5 (H); 144:9 (2x: H); 149:1 (2x: H); Prov 25:20 (2x: H); Eccl 2:8 (2x: H, H); 7:5; 12:4; Cant 1:1 (2x); Isa 5:1 (2x: H); 23:15, 16; 24:9; 26:1 (2x: song); 30:29; 42:10 (2x: H); Jer 20:13 (H); Ezek 26:13; 33:32; 40:44 (H); Amos 5:23; 6:5; 8:3, 10; Zeph 2:14 (C).

שלם/*šlm*—Qal: "be completed, finished, happy"[29]

Gen 14:18; 15:15, 16; 26:29, 31; 28:21; 29:6 (2x); 33:18; 34:21; 37:4, 14 (2x); 41:16; 43:23, 27 (2x), 28; 44:17; 46:24; Exod 4:18; 18:7, 23; 20:24; 24:5; 29:28; 32:6; Lev 3:1, 3, 6, 9; 4:10, 26, 31, 35; 6:5; 7:11, 13, 14, 15, 18, 20, 21, 29 (2x), 32, 33, 34, 37; 9:4, 18, 22; 10:14; 17:5; 19:5; 22:21; 23:19; 24:11; Num 1:6; 2:12; 6:14, 17, 18, 26; 7:17, 23, 29, 35, 36, 41 (2x), 47, 53, 59, 65, 71, 77, 83, 88; 10:10, 19; 15:8; 25:12; 26:49 (2x); 29:39; 34:27; Deut 2:26; 20:10, 11; 23:7; 25:15 (2x); 27:6, 7; 29:18; 32:35; Josh 8:31 (2x); 9:15; 10:21; 22:23, 27; Judg 4:17; 6:23, 24; 8:9; 11:13, 31; 18:6, 15; 19:20; 20:26; 21:4, 13; Ruth 2:12; 1 Sam 1:17; 7:14; 10:4, 8; 11:15; 13:9; 16:4, 5; 17:18, 22; 20:7, 13, 21, 42; 25:5, 6 (3x), 35; 29:7; 30:21; 2 Sam 3:21, 22, 23; 6:17, 18; 8:10; 11:7 (3x); 15:9, 27; 17:3; 18:28, 29, 32; 19:25, 31; 20:9, 19 (H); 24:25; 1 Kgs 2:5, 6, 13 (2x), 33; 3:15; 5:4, 26; 6:7; 7:51 (work); 8:61, 63, 64 (2x); 9:25; 11:4; 15:3, 14; 20:18; 22:17, 27, 28; 2 Kgs 4:23, 26 (4x); 5:19, 21, 22; 9:11, 17, 18 (2x), 19 (2x), 22 (2x), 31; 10:13; 15:10, 13, 14, 15; 16:13; 20:3, 19; 21:19; 22:3, 14, 20; 1 Chr 2:40, 41; 3:15, 19 (2x); 4:25; 5:13, 38, 39; 7:13; 8:17; 9:7, 8, 11, 12 (2x), 17 (2x), 19, 31; 12:18, 19 (3x), 39; 16:1, 2; 18:10; 21:26; 22:9; 23:9, 18; 24:22 (2x); 26:1, 2, 9, 14, 25, 26, 28; 28:9; 29:9, 19; 2 Chr 5:1 (work); 7:7; 8:16; 11:20; 15:5, 17; 16:9; 18:16, 26, 27; 19:1, 9; 25:2; 28:12 (2x); 29:35; 30:22; 31:2; 33:16; 34:12, 22, 28; Ezra 2:42; 7:2; 8:10, 16; 9:12; 10:15, 24, 29, 41, 42; Neh 3:4, 6, 12, 30 (2x); 6:15 (I/AI),18; 7:45; 8:4; 10:8, 21; 11:7, 11, 13; 12:13, 16, 25, 33; Esth 2:11; 9:30; 10:3; Job 5:24; 9:4 (H); 15:21; 21:9; 22:21 (H); 25:2; Pss 4:9; 7:5 (H); 28:3; 29:11; 34:15; 35:20, 27; 37:11, 37; 38:4; 41:10; 55:19, 21; 69:23; 72:3, 7; 73:3; 76:3; 85:9, 11; 119:165; 120:6, 7; 122:6, 7, 8; 125:5; 128:6; 147:14; Prov 3:2, 17; 7:14; 11:1; 12:20; Eccl 3:8; Cant 8:10; Isa 9:5, 6; 26:3 (2x), 12; 27:5 (2x); 32:17, 18; 33:7; 34:8; 38:3, 17; 39:8; 41:3; 42:19; 45:7; 48:18, 22; 52:7; 53:5; 54:10, 13; 55:12; 57:2, 19 (2x), 21; 59:8 (2x); 60:17, 20 (days of mourning); 66:12; Jer 4:10; 6:14 (3x); 8:11 (3x), 15; 9:7; 12:5, 12; 13:19; 14:13, 19; 15:5; 16:5; 20:10; 22:11; 23:17; 25:37; 28:9; 29:7 (3x), 11; 30:5; 32:7; 33:6, 9; 34:5; 35:4; 36:14, 26; 38:1, 4, 22; 43:12; Lam 3:17; Ezek 7:25; 13:10 (2x), 16 (2x); 34:25; 37:26; 43:27; 45:15, 17; 46:2, 12 (2x); Dan 10:19; Hos 10:14; Amos 1:6, 9; 5:22; Obad 7; Micah 3:5; 5:4; Nah 1:12; 2:1; Hag 2:9; Zech 6:13; 8:10, 12, 16, 19; 9:10; Mal 2:5, 6.

---

29. *šillûm* ("retaliation, vengeance; compensation, payment") and *šalmōnîm* ("bribes") have been excluded from this list, due to their lack of relevance. Additionally, to save the reader from having to sort through all of the references to *šelōmōh* ("Solomon"), *yĕrûšālēm/yĕrûšālayim* ("Jerusalem"), and *'abšālôm* ("Absalom"), these proper nouns have also been excluded, though their etymological connections to the root √*šlm* should be noted.

שׁעע II/*šʿʿ*—Pilpel: "take delight in"; Pulpel: "be played with, be fondled"; Hithpalpel: "take pleasure in, delight in"

Pss 94:19 (assurances); 119:16 (H), 24, 47 (H), 70 (H), 77, 92, 143, 174; Prov 8:30, 31; Isa 5:7; 11:8 (H); 66:12 (H); Jer 31:20.

Old Testament Lexemes (Aramaic)

ברך II/*brk* II—Peal: "bless"; Pael: "bless"
Dan 2:19 (H), 20 (the name of God); 3:28 (D); 4:31 (H).

הדר/*hdr*—Pael: "glorify"
Dan 4:27, 31 (H), 33, 34 (H); 5:18, 23 (H).

חדה/*ḥdh*—"be joyful" (only attested nominally)
Ezra 6:16.

טאב/*ṭʾb*—Peal: "be good, pleasing, glad"
Ezra 5:17; Dan 2:32; 6:24 (impersonal subject).

יטב/*yṭb*—Peal: "it is pleasing"
Ezra 7:18 (impersonal subject).

צבה/*ṣbh*—Peal: "be pleased"
Dan 4:14 (D), 22 (D), 29 (D), 32 (D); 5:19 (4x: H, H, H, H), 21 (D); 7:19 (H).

רים/*rym*—Polel: "praise"[30]
Dan 4:34 (H).

רען/*rʿn*—"flourish, be fortunate, happy" (only attested nominally)
Dan 4:1.

שׁבח/*šbḥ*—Pael: "praise"
Dan 2:23 (H); 4:31 (H), 34 (H); 5:4 (H); 5:23 (H).

שׁלם/*šlm*—Peal: "be complete, peaceful, be well"[31]
Dan 3:31; 6:26; Ezra 4:7; 4:17; 5:7.

שׁפר/*špr*—Peal: "please"
Dan 3:32 (impersonal subject); 4:9, 18, 24 (counsel); 6:2 (impersonal subject).

---

30. The derived substantive (*rûm*) has to do with height (see, e.g., Ezra 6:3; Dan 3:1) and has been excluded from this list.

31. In biblical Aramaic, the verbal form of *šlm* is typically used to speak of the completion of an action (e.g., Ezra 5:16; Dan 5:26) or can even refer to the delivery of objects (Ezra 7:19). The substantive, *šĕlām*, however, is frequently used as a greeting that wishes for the welfare of the recipient. Therefore, only references to the substantive are included in this list.

New Testament Lexemes (Greek)

ἀγαλλίασις, -εως, ἡ/*agalliasis, -eōs, hē*—"extreme joy"
Luke 1:14, 44; Acts 2:46; Heb 1:9; Jude 1:24.

ἀγαλλιάω/*agalliaō*—"be extremely joyful"
Matt 5:12 (H); Luke 1:47 (H); 10:21 (J); John 5:35; 8:56 (H); Acts 2:26 (H); 16:34 (H); 1 Pet 1:6 (H), 8 (H); 4:13 (H); Rev 19:7 (H/HB?).

ἀγαπάω/*agapaō*—"love, show love, take pleasure in"
Matt 5:43 (H), 44 (H), 46 (2x: H, H); 6:24 (H); 19:19 (H); 22:37 (H), 39 (H); Mark 10:21 (J); 12:30 (H), 31 (H), 33 (2x); Luke 6:27 (H), 32 (4x: H, H, H, H), 35 (H); 7:5 (H), 42 (H), 47 (2x: H, H); 10:27 (H); 11:43 (H); 16:13 (H); John 3:16 (D), 19 (H), 35 (D); 8:42 (H); 10:17 (D); 11:5 (J); 12:43 (H); 13:1 (2x: J, J), 23 (J), 34 (3x: H, J, H); 14:15 (H), 21 (4x: H, H, H, J), 23 (2x: H, D), 24 (H), 28 (H), 31 (J); 15:9 (2x: D, J), 12 (2x: H, J), 17 (H); 17:23 (2x: D, D), 24 (D), 26 (D); 19:26 (J); 21:7 (J), 15 (H), 16 (H), 20 (J); Rom 8:28 (H), 37 (D/J); 9:13 (D), 25 (2x: H, H); 13:8 (2x: H), 9 (H); 1 Cor 2:9 (H); 8:3 (H); 2 Cor 9:7 (D); 11:11 (H); 12:15 (2x: H, H); Gal 2:20 (J); 5:14 (H); Eph 1:6 (J); 2:4 (D); 5:2 (J), 25 (2x: H, J), 28 (3x: H, H), 33 (H); 6:24 (H); Col 3:12 (H), 19 (H); 1 Thess 1:4 (H); 4:9; 2 Thess 2:13 (H), 16 (D); 2 Tim 4:8 (H), 10 (H); Heb 1:9 (J); 12:6 (D); James 1:12 (H); 2:5 (H), 8 (H); 1 Pet 1:8 (H), 22 (H); 2:17 (H); 3:10; 2 Pet 2:15 (H); 1 John 2:10 (H), 15 (2x: H, H); 3:10 (H), 11 (H), 14 (2x: H, H), 18 (H), 23 (H); 4:7 (2x: H, H), 8 (H), 10 (2x: H, D), 11 (2x: D), 12 (H), 19 (2x: H, D), 20 (3x: H, H), 21 (2x: H, H); 5:1 (2x: H, H), 2 (2x: H, H); 2 John 1:1 (H), 5 (H); 3 John 1:1 (H); Jude 1:1 (H); Rev 1:5 (J); 3:9 (J); 12:11 (H); 20:9 (I/AI).

ἀνάψυξις, -εως, ἡ/*anapsyxis, -eōs, hē*—"relief, encouragement"
Acts 3:20.

ἀναψύχω/*anapsychō*—"encourage"
2 Tim 1:16 (H).

ἀνθρωπάρεσκος, -ον/*anthrōpareskos, -on*—"one who tries to please people"
Eph 6:6; Col 3:22.

ἀπόδεκτος, -ον/*apodektos, -on*—"pleasing, acceptable"
1 Tim 2:3; 5:4.

ἀπόλαυσις, -εως, ἡ/*apolausis, -eōs, hē*—"enjoyment"
1 Tim 6:17; Heb 11:25.

ἀρεσκεία, -ας/*areskeia, -as*—"means of favor"
Col 1:10.

ἀρέσκω/*areskō*—"please"

Matt 14:6 (H); Mark 6:22 (H); Acts 6:5 (an idea); Rom 8:8; 15:1, 2 (H), 3 (J); 1 Cor 7:32 (H), 33 (H), 34 (H); 10:33 (H); Gal 1:10 (2x: H); 1 Thess 2:4 (H), 15 (H); 4:1; 2 Tim 2:4 (H).

ἀρεστός, -ή, -όν/*arestos*, -ē, -on—"pleasing, proper"

John 8:29; Acts 6:2; 12:3; 1 John 3:22.

ἀρκέω/*arkeō*—"be satisfied"

Matt 25:9 (impersonal subject); Luke 3:14 (H); John 6:7 (I/AI); 14:8 (impersonal subject); 2 Cor 12:9 (grace); 1 Tim 6:8 (H); Heb 13:5 (H); 3 John 1:10 (H).

ἀσμένως/*asmenōs*—"gladly"

Acts 21:17.

ἀσπάζομαι/*aspazomai*—"greet, be happy about, welcome"

Matt 5:47 (H); 10:12 (H); Mark 9:15 (H); 15:18; Luke 1:40 (H); 10:4 (H); Acts 18:22 (H); 20:1 (H); 21:7 (H), 19 (H); 25:13 (H); Rom 16:3 (H), 5 (H), 6 (H), 7 (H), 8 (H), 9 (H), 10 (2x: H, H), 11 (2x: H, H), 12 (2x: H, H), 13 (H), 14 (H), 15 (H), 16 (2x: H, H), 21 (H), 22 (H), 23 (2x: H, H); 1 Cor 16:19 (2x: H, H), 20 (2x: H, H); 2 Cor 13:12 (2x: H, H); Phil 4:21 (2x: H, H), 22 (H); Col 4:10 (H), 12 (H), 14 (H), 15 (H); 1 Thess 5:26 (H); 2 Tim 4:19 (H), 21 (H); Titus 3:15 (2x: H, H); Phlm 1:23 (H); Heb 11:13 (H); 13:24 (2x: H, H); 1 Pet 5:13 (H), 14 (H); 2 John 1:13 (H); 3 John 1:15 (2x: H, H).

αὐτάρκεια, -ας, ἡ/*autarkeia*, -as, hē—"contentment, adequacy"

2 Cor 9:8; 1 Tim 6:6.

αὐτάρκης, -ες/*autarkēs*, -es—"content"

Phil 4:11.

γελάω/*gelaō*—"laugh"

Luke 6:21 (H), 25 (H).

γέλως, -ωτος, ὁ/*gelōs*, -ōtos, ho—"laughter"

James 4:9.

δεκτός, -ή, -όν/*dektos*, -ē, -on—"pleasing, welcomed, appropriate"

Luke 4:19, 24; Acts 10:35; 2 Cor 6:2; Phil 4:18.

ἐμπίπλημι/*empiplēmi*—"to satisfy"

Luke 1:53 (D); 6:25 (H); John 6:12 (H); Acts 14:17 (D); Rom 15:24 (H).

εὐαρεστέω/*euaresteō*—"to please, to be pleased, to cause pleasure"

Heb 11:5, 6; 13:16 (D).

εὐάρεστος, -ον/*euarestos*, -on—"pleasing"

Rom 12:1, 2; 14:18; 2 Cor 5:9; Eph 5:10; Phil 4:18; Col 3:20; Titus 2:9; Heb 13:21.

εὐαρέστως/*euarestōs*—"pleasing"
Heb 12:28.

εὐδοκέω/*eudokeō*—"be pleased with, enjoy, prefer"
Matt 3:17 (D); 12:18 (D); 17:5 (D); Mark 1:11 (D); Luke 3:22 (D); 12:32 (D); Rom 15:26 (H), 27 (H); 1 Cor 1:21 (D); 10:5 (D); 2 Cor 5:8 (H); 12:10 (H); Gal 1:15 (D); Col 1:19 (D); 1 Thess 2:8 (H); 3:1 (H); 2 Thess 2:12 (H); Heb 10:6 (D), 8 (D), 38 (D); 2 Pet 1:17 (D).

εὐδοκία, –ας, ἡ/*eudokia, –as, hē*—"what pleases, desire"
Matt 11:26; Luke 2:14; 10:21; Rom 10:1; Eph 1:5, 9; Phil 1:15; 2:13; 2 Thess 1:11.

εὐθυμέω/*euthymeō*—"be encouraged"
Acts 27:22, 25 (H); James 5:13 (H).

εὔθυμος, –ον/*euthymos, –on*—"encouraged"
Acts 27:36.

εὐθύμως/*euthymōs*—"cheerfully"
Acts 24:10.

εὐπρόσδεκτος, –ον/*euprosdektos, –on*—"quite pleasing, truly favorable"
Rom 15:16, 31; 2 Cor 6:2; 8:12; 1 Pet 2:5.

εὐφραίνω/*euphrainō*—"make glad"
Luke 12:19 (H); 15:23 (H), 24, 29 (H), 32; 16:19 (H); Acts 2:26 (H); 7:41 (H); Rom 15:10 (H); 2 Cor 2:2 (H); Gal 4:27 (H); Rev 11:10 (H); 12:12 (C); 18:20 (C).

εὐφροσύνη, –ης, ἡ/*euphrosynē, –ēs, hē*—"joyfulness"
Acts 2:28; 14:17.

εὐχαριστέω/*eucharisteō*—"thank, be thankful"
Matt 15:36 (J); 26:27 (J); Mark 8:6 (J); 14:23 (J); Luke 17:16 (H); 18:11 (H); 22:17 (J), 19 (J); John 6:11 (J), 23 (J); 11:41 (J); Acts 27:35 (H); 28:15 (H); Rom 1:8 (H), 21 (H); 14:6 (2x: H, H); 16:4 (H);1 Cor 1:4 (H), 14 (H); 10:30 (H); 11:24 (J); 14:17 (H), 18 (H); 2 Cor 1:11 (thanks); Eph 1:16 (H); 5:20 (H); Phil 1:3 (H); Col 1:3 (H), 12 (H); 3:17 (H); 1 Thess 1:2 (H); 2:13 (H); 5:18 (H); 2 Thess 1:3; 2:13; Phlm 1:4 (H); Rev 11:17 (H).

εὐχαριστία, –ας, ἡ/*eucharistia, –as, hē*— "gratitude, thankfulness"
Acts 24:3; 1 Cor 14:16; 2 Cor 4:15; 9:11-12; Eph 5:4; Phil 4:6; Col. 2:7; 4:2; 1 Thess. 3:9; 1 Tim 2:1; 4:3-4; Rev 4:9; 7:12.

εὐχάριστος, –ον/*eucharistos, –on*—"thankful, thanking"
Col 3:15.

εὐψυχέω/*eupsycheō*—"be encouraged"
Phil 2:19 (H).

ἡδέως/*hēdeōs*—"gladly"
   Mark 6:20; 12:37; 2 Cor 11:19; 12:9, 15.

ἡδονή, –ῆς, ἡ/*hēdonē, –ēs, hē*—"pleasure, passion"
   Luke 8:14; Tit 3:3; James 4:1, 3; 2 Pet 2:13.

θέλω/*thelō*—"purpose, be of an opinion, desire, enjoy"
   Matt 1:19 (H); 2:18 (H); 5:40 (H), 42 (H); 7:12 (H); 8:2 (J), 3 (J); 9:13 (D); 11:14
(H); 12:7 (D), 38 (H); 13:28 (H); 14:5 (H); 15:28 (H), 32 (J); 16:24 (H), 25 (H); 17:4 (J),
12 (H); 18:23 (H), 30 (H); 19:17 (H), 21 (H); 20:14 (H), 15 (H), 21 (H), 26 (H), 27 (H),
32 (H); 21:29 (H); 22:3 (H); 23:4 (H), 37 (2x: J, H); 26:15 (H), 17 (J), 39 (J); 27:15 (H),
17 (H), 21 (H), 34 (J), 43 (D); Mark 1:40 (J), 41 (J); 3:13 (J); 6:19 (H), 22 (H), 25 (H),
26 (H), 48 (J); 7:24 (J); 8:34 (H), 35 (H); 9:13 (H), 30 (J), 35 (H); 10:35 (H), 36 (H), 43
(H), 44 (H), 51 (H); 12:38 (H); 14:7 (H), 12 (J), 36 (J); 15:9 (H), 12 (H); Luke 1:62 (H);
4:6 (HB); 5:12 (J), 13 (J), 39 (H); 6:31 (H); 8:20 (H); 9:23 (H), 24 (H), 54 (J); 10:24
(H), 29 (H); 12:49 (J); 13:31 (H), 34 (2x: J, H); 14:28 (H); 15:28 (H); 16:26 (H); 18:4
(H), 13 (H), 41 (H); 19:14 (H), 27 (H); 20:46 (H); 22:9 (J); 23:8 (H), 20 (H); John 1:43
(J); 3:8 (wind); 5:6 (H), 21 (J), 35 (H), 40 (H); 6:11 (H), 21 (H), 67 (H); 7:1 (J), 17 (H),
44 (H); 8:44 (H); 9:27 (2x: H, H); 12:21 (H); 15:7 (H); 16:19 (H); 17:24 (J); 21:18 (2x:
H, H), 22 (J), 23 (J); Acts 2:12 (tongues); 7:28 (H), 39 (H); 10:10 (H); 14:13 (H); 16:3
(H); 17:18 (H), 20 (strange things); 18:21 (D); 19:33 (H); 24:27 (H); 25:9 (2x: H, H);
26:5 (H); Rom 1:13 (H); 7:15 (H), 16 (H), 18, 19 (2x: H, H), 20 (H), 21 (H); 9:16 (H), 18
(2x: D, D), 22 (D); 11:25 (H); 13:3 (H); 16:19 (H); 1 Cor 4:19 (D), 21 (H); 7:7 (H), 32
(H), 36 (H), 39 (H); 10:1 (H), 20 (H), 27 (H); 11:3 (H); 12:1 (H), 18 (D); 14:5 (H), 19
(H), 35 (H); 15:38 (D); 16:7 (H); 2 Cor 1:8 (H); 5:4 (H); 8:10, 11; 11:12 (H); 12:6 (H), 20
(2x: H, H); Gal 1:7 (H); 3:2 (H); 4:9 (H), 17 (H), 20 (H), 21 (H); 5:17 (H); 6:12 (H), 13
(H); Phil 2:13; Col 1:27 (D); 2:1 (H), 18 (H); 1 Thess 2:18 (H); 4:13 (H); 2 Thess 3:10 (H);
1 Tim 1:7 (H); 2:4 (D); 5:11 (H); 2 Tim 3:12 (H); Phlm 1:14 (H); Heb 10:5 (D), 8 (D);
12:17 (H); 13:18 (H); James 2:20 (H); 4:15 (D); 1 Pet 3:10 (H), 17 (God's will); 2 Pet 3:5
(H); 3 John 1:13 (H); Rev 2:21 (H); 11:5 (2x: H, H), 6 (two witnesses); 22:17 (H).

ἱλαρός, –ά, –όν/*hilaros, –a, –on*—"happy"
   2 Cor 9:7.

ἱλαρότης, –ητος, ἡ/*hilarotēs, –ētos, hē*—"happiness"
   Rom 12:8.

κορέννυμι/*korennymi*—"be content, have enough"
   Acts 27:38 (H); 1 Cor 4:8 (H).

μακαρίζω/*makarizō*—"regard as happy"
   Luke 1:48 (H); James 5:11 (H).

μακάριος, –α, –ον/*makarios, –a, –on*—"happy"
   Matt 5:3, 4, 5, 6, 7, 8, 9, 10, 11; 11:6; 13:16; 16:17; 24:46; Luke 1:45; 6:20, 21 (2x), 22; 7:23; 10:23; 11:27, 28; 12:37, 38, 43; 14:14, 15; 23:29; John 13:17; 20:29; Acts 20:35; 26:2; Rom 4:7, 8; 14:22; 1 Cor 7:40; 1 Tim 1:11; 6:15; Titus 2:13; James 1:12, 25; 1 Pet 3:14; 4:14; Rev 1:3; 14:13; 16:15; 19:9; 20:6; 22:7, 14.

μακαρισμός, –οῦ, ὁ/*makarismos, –ou, ho*—"happiness"
   Rom 4:6, 9; Gal 4:15.

παρακαλέω/*parakaleō*—"encourage"
   Matt 2:18; 5:4 (H); 8:5 (H), 31 (HB), 34 (H); 14:36 (H); 18:29 (H), 32 (H); 26:53; Mark 1:40 (H); 5:10 (HB), 12 (HB), 17, 18 (H), 23 (H); 6:56 (H); 7:32 (H); 8:22 (H); Luke 3:18 (H); 7:4 (H); 8:31 (HB), 32 (HB), 41 (H); 15:28 (H); 16:25 (H); Acts 2:40 (H); 8:31 (H); 9:38 (H); 11:23 (H); 13:42 (H); 14:22 (H); 15:32 (H); 16:9 (H), 15 (H), 39 (H), 40 (H); 19:31 (H); 20:1 (H), 2 (H), 12 (H); 21:12 (H); 24:4 (H); 25:2 (H); 27:33 (H), 34 (H); 28:14 (H), 20 (H); Rom 12:1 (H), 8 (H); 15:30 (H); 16:17 (H); 1 Cor 1:10 (H); 4:13 (H), 16 (H); 14:31 (H); 16:12 (H), 15 (H); 2 Cor 1:4 (3x: D, H), 6 (H); 2:7, 8 (H); 5:20 (D); 6:1 (H); 7:6 (2x: D, D), 7 (H), 13 (H); 8:6; 9:5; 10:1 (H); 12:8 (H), 18 (H); 13:11 (H); Eph 4:1 (H); 6:22 (H); Phil 4:2 (2x: H, H); Col 2:2 (H); 4:8 (H); 1 Thess 2:12 (H); 3:2, 7 (H); 4:1 (H), 10 (H), 18 (H); 5:11 (H), 14 (H); 2 Thess 2:17 (D/J); 3:12 (H); 1 Tim 1:3 (H); 2:1 (H); 5:1 (H); 6:2 (H); 2 Tim 4:2 (H); Titus 1:9; 2:6 (H), 15 (H); Phlm 1:9 (H), 10 (H); Heb 3:13 (H); 10:25 (H); 13:19 (H), 22 (H); 1 Pet 2:11 (H); 5:1 (H), 12 (H); Jude 1:3 (H).

παράκλησις, –εως, ἡ/*paraklēsis, –eōs, hē*—"encouragement, earnest request"
   Luke 2:25; 6:24; Acts 4:36; 9:31; 13:15; 15:31; Rom 12:8; 15:4, 5; 1 Cor 14:3; 2 Cor 1:3, 4, 5, 6 (2x), 7; 2 Cor 7:4, 7, 13; 8:4, 17; Phil 2:1; 1 Thess 2:3; 2 Thess 2:16; 1 Tim 4:13; Phlm 1:7; Heb 6:18; 12:5; 13:22.

προσφιλής, –ές/*prosphilēs, –es*—"pleasing"
   Phil 4:8.

σκιρτάω/*skirtaō*—"jump for joy, be extremely joyful"
   Luke 1:41 (H), 44 (H); 6:23 (H).

συγχαίρω/*synchairō*—"rejoice with"
   Luke 1:58 (H); 15:6 (H), 9 (H); 1 Cor 12:26 (member of the body); 13:6 (love); Phil 2:17 (H), 18 (H).

συμπαρακαλέω/*symparakaleō*—"be encouraged together"
   Rom 1:12.

συνήδομαι/*synēdomai*—"rejoice in"
   Rom 7:22 (H).

φιλάγαθος, -ον/*philagathos*, -on—"liking what is good"
    Titus 1:8.

φιλέω/*phileō*—"love, like, kiss"
    Matt 6:5 (H); 10:37 (2x: H, H); 23:6 (H); 26:48 (H); Mark 14:44 (H); Luke 20:46 (H); 22:47; John 5:20 (D); 11:3 (J), 36 (J); 12:25 (H); 15:19 (the world); 16:27 (2x: D, H); 20:2 (J); 21:15 (H), 16 (H), 17 (3x: H, H, H); 1 Cor 16:22 (H); Titus 3:15 (H); Rev 3:19 (J); 22:15 (H).

φιλήδονος, -ον/*philēdonos*, -on—"loving pleasure"
    2 Tim 3:4.

χαίρω/*chairō*—"rejoice, greetings"
    Matt 2:10 (H); 5:12 (H); 18:13 (H); 26:49;*[32] 27:29*; 28:9*; Mark 14:11 (H); 15:18*; Luke 1:14 (H), 28*; 6:23 (H); 10:20 (2x: H, H); 13:17 (H); 15:5 (H), 32; 19:6 (H), 37 (H); 22:5 (H); 23:8 (H); John 3:29 (H); 4:36 (H); 8:56 (H); 11:15 (J); 14:28 (H); 16:20 (the world), 22 (H); 19:3*; 20:20 (H); Acts 5:41 (H); 8:39 (H); 11:23 (H); 13:48 (H); 15:23, 31 (H); 23:26; Rom 12:12 (H), 15 (2x: H); 16:19 (H); 1 Cor 7:30 (2x: H, H); 13:6 (love); 16:17 (H); 2 Cor 2:3; 6:10 (H); 7:7, 9 (H), 13 (H), 16 (H); 13:9 (H), 11 (H); Phil 1:18 (2x: H, H); 2:17 (H), 18 (H), 28 (H); 3:1 (H); 4:4 (2x: H, H), 10 (H); Col 1:24 (H); 2:5 (H); 1 Thess 3:9 (H); 5:16 (H); James 1:1; 1 Pet 4:13 (2x: H, H); 2 John 1:4 (H), 10, 11; 3 John 1:3 (H); Rev 11:10 (H); 19:7 (H/HB?).

χαρά, -ᾶς, ἡ/*chara*, -as, hē—"gladness, reason for gladness"
    Matt 2:10; 13:20, 44; 25:21, 23; 28:8; Mark 4:16; Luke 1:14; 2:10; 8:13; 10:17; 15:7, 10; 24:41, 52; John 3:29 (2x); 15:11 (2x); 16:20, 21, 22, 24; 17:13; Acts 8:8; 12:14; 13:52; 15:3; Rom 14:17; 15:13, 32; 2 Cor 1:24; 2:3; 7:4, 13; 8:2; Gal 5:22; Phil 1:4, 25; 2:2,29; 4:1; Col 1:11; 1 Thess 1:6; 2:19, 20; 3:9; 2 Tim 1:4; Phlm 1:7; Heb 10:34; 12:2,11; 13:17; James 1:2; 4:9; 1 Pet 1:8; 1 John 1:4; 2 John 1:12; 3 John 1:4.

χάρις, -ιτος, ἡ/*charis*, -itos, hē—"kindness, gift, thanks, good will"
    Luke 1:30; 2:40, 52; 4:22; 6:32, 33, 34; 17:9; John 1:14, 16 (2x), 17; Acts 2:47; 4:33; 6:8; 7:10, 46; 11:23; 13:43; 14:3, 26; 15:11, 40; 18:27; 20:24, 32; 24:27; 25:3, 9; Rom 1:5, 7; 3:24; 4:4, 16; 5:2, 15 (2x), 17, 20, 21; 6:1, 14, 15, 17; 7:25; 11:5, 6 (3x); 12:3, 6; 15:15; 16:20; 1 Cor 1:3, 4; 3:10; 10:30; 15:10 (3x), 57; 16:3, 23; 2 Cor 1:2, 12, 15; 2:14; 4:15; 6:1; 8:1, 4, 6, 7, 9, 16, 19; 9:8, 14, 15; 12:9; 13:13; Gal 1:3, 6, 15; 2:9, 21; 5:4; 6:18; Eph 1:2, 6, 7; 2:5, 7, 8; 3:2,7,

---

32. The terms *chaire* and *chairete*, which are typically translated as "greetings" or "hail," are technically imperatives ("rejoice") that developed into an idiomatic greeting (see also Matt 27:29; 28:9; John 19:3, etc.). Henceforth, this formal greeting will be marked with an asterisk (*) but no subject will be assigned.

8; 4:7, 29; 6:24; Phil 1:2, 7; 4:23; Col 1:2, 6; 3:16; 4:6, 18; 1 Thess 1:1; 5:28; 2 Thess 1:2, 12; 2:16; 3:18; 1 Tim 1:2, 12, 14; 6:21; 2 Tim 1:2, 3, 9; 2:1; 4:22; Titus 1:4; 2:11; 3:7, 15; Phlm 1:3, 25; Heb 2:9; 4:16 (2x); 10:29; 12:15, 28; 13:9, 25; James 4:6 (2x); 1 Pet 1:2, 10, 13; 2:19, 20; 3:7; 4:10; 5:5, 10, 12; 2 Pet 1:2; 3:18; 2 John 1:3; Jude 1:4; Rev 1:4; 22:21.

χορτάζω/*chortazō*—"eat one's fill, be content"

Matt 5:6 (H); 14:20 (H); 15:33, 37 (H); Mark 6:42 (H); 7:27; 8:4, 8 (H); Luke 6:21 (H); 9:17 (H); 15:16; 16:21; John 6:26 (H); Phil 4:12; James 2:16 (H); Rev 19:21 (C).

ψάλλω/*psallō*—"sing, sing praise"

Rom 15:9 (H); 1 Cor 14:15 (2x: H, H); Eph 5:19 (H); James 5:13 (H).

ψαλμός,-οῦ,ὁ/*psalmos, -ou, ho*—"song of praise, psalm"

Luke 20:42; 24:44; Acts 1:20; 13:33; 1 Cor 14:26; Eph 5:19; Col 3:16.

Set 2[33]
Creation (= C)

1. Old Testament Lexemes (Hebrew)

a. אור/ '*wr*—"become, be light, shine; to be lit up; make the countenance shine, make the face shine"

Gen 44:3; Exod 14:20; Job 41:24; Pss 77:19; 97:4; 139:12; Prov 4:18; Isa 60:19; Ezek 32:7; 43:2.

b. ברך II/*brk* II—"praised, be blessed; wish oneself a blessing; bless; bless each other; bless oneself"

Deut 33:13; Ps 103:22; 145:21.

c. גיל/*gyl*—"rejoice"

1 Chr 16:31; Pss 96:11; 97:1; Isa 35:1, 2; 49:13; Joel 2:21; Pss 69:35; 84:5.

d. חול/*ḥwl*—"dance round dances"

Jer 23:19; 30:23.

e. הלל II/*hll* II—"praise; be praised; boast oneself"

Ps 148:3, 4, 5, 7; 150:6.

f. זמר I/*zmr* I—"sing, praise"

Ps 98:4, 5.

---

33. In Set 2, the references to verbal stems (e.g., Qal, Piel, etc.) have been removed. For full documentation, see Set 1.

g. חמד/*ḥmd*—"desire, take pleasure in; desirable; fiercely desire"
Gen 2:9; 3:6.

h. יטב/*yṭb*—"be well, pleasing; treat well, graciously, do good; make things go well for"
Prov 30:29.

i. נעם/*n ʿm*—"be pleasant, lovely; be a delight for"
Gen 49:15.

j. עלז/ *ʿlz*—"rejoice, exult"
Ps 96:12.

k. עלץ/ *ʿlṣ*—"rejoice, exult"
1 Chr 16:32.

l. פוש/*pwš*—"paw the ground (playfully?)"
Hab 1:8.

m. פצח I/*pṣḥ*I—"be cheerful, happy, serene"
Ps 98:4; Isa 14:7; 44:23; 49:13; 55:12.

n. רוח/*rwḥ*—"feel relieved, easy; smell, enjoy"
Job 39:25.

o. רוע/*rwʿ*—"shout in joy, cheer; a shout is uttered; shout in triumph"
Pss 65:14; 66:1; 98:4, 6; 100:1; Isa 44:23.

p. רנן/*rnn*—"jubilate, give a cry of joy; give a ringing cry in joy; cry for joy; cause to cry for joy"
1 Chr 16:33; Pss 89:13; 96:12; 98:4, 8; Isa 44:23; 49:13; Jer 51:48.

q. רקד/*rqd*—"skip about; dance; cause to skip about"
Pss 114:4, 6; Isa 13:21.

r. שבע/*śbʿ*—"be sated; sated; satisfy a person; satisfy"
Ps 104:13, 16, 28; Prov 30:16; Ezek 39:20.

s. שוש/*śwś*—"rejoice, display joy"
Job 39:21; Ps 19:6; Isa 35:1.

t. שחק/*śḥq*—"play, amuse, laugh, entertain; be merry, play with, make merry, dance"
Job 39:7, 18, 22; 40:20; 41:21.

u. שמח/*śmḥ*—"rejoice; cause to rejoice, gladden; cause to rejoice"
1 Chr 16:31; Pss 96:11; 97:1; Isa 14:8; Joel 2:21.

v. שׁיר/*šyr*—"sing; be sung; burst into song"

    1 Chr 16:23; Pss 65:14; 96:1, 2; Zeph 2:14.

2. New Testament Lexemes (Greek)

a. εὐφραίνω/*euphrainō*—"make glad"

    Rev 12:12; 18:20.

b. χορτάζω/*chortazō*—"eat one's fill, be content"

    Rev 19:21.

Deity (= D)

1. Old Testament Lexemes (Hebrew)

a. אור/*'wr*—"become, be light, shine; to be lit up; make the countenance shine, make the face shine"

    Num 6:25; Pss 13:4; 18:29; 31:17; 67:2; 76:5; 80:4, 8, 20; 118:27; 119:135; Prov 29:13; Dan 9:17.

b. בלג/*blg*—"brighten up/cheer up"

    Amos 5:9.

c. ברך II/*brk* II—"praised, be blessed; wish oneself a blessing; bless; bless each other, bless oneself"

    Gen 1:22, 28; 2:3; 5:2; 9:1, 26; 12:2, 3; 14:20; 17:16, 20; 22:17; 24:1, 27, 35; 25:11; 26:3, 12, 24; 27:27; 28:3; 30:27, 30; 35:9; 39:5; 48:3; 49:25; Exod 18:10; 20:11, 24; 23:25; Num 6:24, 27; 23:20; Deut 1:11; 2:7; 7:13; 12:7; 14:24, 29; 15:4, 6, 10, 14, 18; 16:10, 15; 23:21; 24:19; 26:15; 28:8; 30:16; 33:11, 20; Josh 17:14; Judg 13:24; Ruth 2:4; 4:14; 1 Sam 25:32, 39; 2 Sam 6:11, 12; 7:29; 18:28; 22:47; 1 Kgs 1:48; 5:21; 8:15, 56; 10:9; 1 Chr 4:10; 13:14; 16:36; 17:27; 26:5; 29:10; 2 Chr 2:11; 6:4; 9:8; 31:10; Ezra 7:27; Neh 9:5; Job 1:10, 21; Job 42:12; Pss 5:13; 18:47; 28:6, 9; 29:11; 31:22; 41:14; 45:3; 65:11; 66:20; 67:2, 7, 8; 68:20, 36; 72:18, 19; 89:53; 106:48; 107:38; 109:28; 113:2; 115:12, 13; 119:12; 124:6; 128:5; 132:15; 134:3; 135:21; 144:1; 147:13; Prov 3:33; Isa 19:25; 51:2; 61:9; Jer 31:23; Ezek 3:12; Hag 2:19; Zech 11:5; Zeph 3:17.

d. גיל/*gyl*—"rejoice"

    Isa 65:19; Zeph 3:17.

e. הלל II/*hll* II—"praise; be praised; boast, pride oneself"

    2 Sam 22:4; 1 Chr 16:25; Pss 18:4; 48:2; 96:4; 113:3; 145:3.

f. חדה I/*ḥdh* I—"rejoice; make joyful, cheer"

    Ps 21:7.

g. חמד/*ḥmd*—"desire, take pleasure in; desirable; fiercely desire"
Ps 68:17.

h. חפץ I/*ḥpṣ* I—"take pleasure in, desire, delight in"
Num 14:8; Judg 13:23; 1 Sam 2:25; 2 Sam 15:26; 22:20; 1 Kgs 10:9; 2 Chr 9:8; Pss 18:20; 22:9; 37:23; 40:7; 41:12; 51:8, 18, 21; 115:3; 135:6; 147:10; Prov 21:1; Isa 1:11; 42:21; 53:10; 55:11; 56:4; 62:4; 65:12; 66:4; Jer 9:23; Ezek 18:23, 32; 33:11; Hos 6:6; Jon 1:14; Mal 2:17.

i. יטב/*yṭb*—"be well, pleasing; treat well, graciously, do good, make things go well for"
Gen 32:10, 13; Exod 1:20; Num 10:32; Deut 30:5; Josh 24:20; Judg 17:13; 1 Sam 25:31; 1 Kgs 1:47; Pss 51:20; 119:68; 125:4; Isa 41:23; Jer 32:40; Zeph 1:12.

j. רוח/*rwḥ*—"feel relieved, easy; smell, enjoy"
Gen 8:21; Lev 26:31; Deut 4:28; 1 Sam 26:19; Amos 5:21.

k. רוע/*rw'*—"shout in joy, cheer; a shout is uttered; shout in triumph"
Isa 42:13.

l. רנן/*rnn*—"jubilate, give a cry of joy; give a ringing cry in joy; cry for joy; cause to cry for joy"
Ps 65:9.

m. רצה I/*rṣh* I—"be pleased with, be favorable to; be treated as favored; make oneself favored with"
Deut 33:11; 2 Sam 24:23; 1 Chr 28:4; 29:17; Job 33:26; Pss 40:14; 44:4; 51:18; 85:2; 119:108; 147:10, 11; 149:4; Eccl 9:7; Isa 42:1; Jer 14:10, 12; Ezek 20:40, 41; Hos 8:13; Amos 5:22; Micah 6:7; Hag 1:8; Mal 1:10, 13.

n. רקד/*rqd*—"skip about; dance; cause to skip about"
Ps 29:6.

o. שבע/*śb'*—"be sated; sated; satisfy a person; satisfy"
Job 9:18; Pss 81:17; 90:14; 91:16; 103:5; 105:40; 107:9; 132:15; 145:16; 147:14; Isa 1:11; 58:11; Jer 5:7; Lam 3:15; Ezek 32:4.

p. שוש/*śwś*—"rejoice, display joy"
Deut 28:63; 30:9; Isa 62:5; 65:19; Jer 32:41; Zeph 3:17.

q. שחק/*śḥq*—"play, amuse, laugh, entertain; be merry, play with, make merry, dance"
Pss 2:4; 37:13; 59:9.

r. שמח/*śmḥ*—"rejoice; cause to rejoice, gladden; cause to rejoice"
2 Chr 20:27; Ezra 6:22; Neh 12:43; Pss 30:2; 86:4; 89:43; 90:15; 92:5; 104:31; Isa 9:16; 56:7; Jer 31:13; Lam 2:17.

2. Old Testament Lexemes (Aramaic)

a. ברך II/*brk* II—"bless"
   Dan 3:28.

b. צבה/*ṣbh*—"be pleased"
   Dan 4:14, 22, 29, 32; 5:21.

3. New Testament Lexemes (Greek)

a. ἀγαπάω/*agapaō*—"love, show love, take pleasure in"
   John 3:16, 35; 10:17; 14:23; 15:9; 17:23, 24, 26; Rom 8:37; 9:13; 2 Cor 9:7; Eph 2:4; 2 Thess 2:16; Heb 12:6; 1 John 4:10, 11, 19.

b. ἐμπίπλημι/*empiplēmi*—"to satisfy"
   Luke 1:53; Acts 14:17.

c. εὐαρεστέω/*euaresteō*—"to please, to be pleased, to cause pleasure"
   Heb 13:16.

d. εὐδοκέω/*eudokeō*—"be pleased with, enjoy, prefer"
   Matt 3:17; 12:18; 17:5; Mark 1:11; Luke 3:22; 12:32; 1 Cor 1:21; 10:5; Gal 1:15; Heb 10:6, 8, 38; 2 Pet 1:17.

e. θέλω/*thelō*—"purpose, be of an opinion, desire, enjoy"
   Matt 9:13; 12:7; 27:43; Acts 18:21; Rom 9:18, 22; 1 Cor 4:19; 12:18; 15:38; Col 1:27; 1 Tim 2:4; Heb 10:5, 8; James 4:15.

f. παρακαλέω/*parakaleō*—"encourage"
   2 Cor 1:4; 5:20; 7:6; 2 Thess 2:17.

g. φιλέω/*phileō*—"love, like, kiss"
   John 5:20; 16:27.

Heavenly Being (= HB)

1. Old Testament Lexemes (Hebrew)

a. ברך II/*brk* II—"praised, be blessed; wish oneself a blessing; bless; bless each other, bless oneself"
   Gen 32:27, 30; 48:16; Ps 103:20, 21.

b. הלל II/*hll* II—"praise; be praised; boast, pride oneself"
   Ps 148:1, 2.

c. רוע/*rwʿ*—"shout in joy, cheer; a shout is uttered; shout in triumph"
   Job 38:7.

2. New Testament Lexemes (Greek)

a. ἀγαλλιάω/*agalliaō*—"be extremely joyful"
   Rev 19:7.

b. θέλω/*thelō*—"purpose, be of an opinion, desire, enjoy"
   Luke 4:6.

c. παρακαλέω/*parakaleō*—"encourage"
   Matt 8:31; Mark 5:10, 12; Luke 8:31, 32.

d. χαίρω/*chairō*—"rejoice, greetings"
   Rev 19:7.

Human (= H)

1. Old Testament Lexemes (Hebrew)

a. אור/ *'wr*—"become, be light, shine; to be lit up; make the countenance shine, make the face shine"
   1 Sam 14:27, 29; Isa 27:11; Mal 1:10.

b. אשר II/ *'šr* II—"pronounce happy; be blessed"
   Gen 30:13; Job 29:11; Pss 41:3; 72:17; Prov 3:18; Cant 6:9; Isa 1:17; Mal 3:12, 15.

c. בלג/*blg*—"brighten up, cheer up"
   Job 9:27; 10:20; Ps 39:14.

d. ברך II/*brk* II—"praised, be blessed; wish oneself a blessing; bless; bless each other, bless oneself"
   Gen 12:3; 14:19; 18:18; 22:18; 24:31, 48, 60; 26:4, 29; 27:4, 7, 10, 19, 23, 25, 27, 29, 31, 33, 34, 38, 41; 28:1, 6, 14; 32:1; 47:7, 10; 48:9, 15, 20 (2x: H, H); 49:28; Exod 12:32; 39:43; Lev 9:22, 23; Num 6:23; 22:6, 22:12; 23:11, 25; 24:9, 10; Deut 7:14; 8:10; 24:13; 28:3, 6; 29:18; 33:1, 24; Josh 14:13; 22:6, 7, 33; 24:10; Judg 5:2, 9, 24; 17:2; Ruth 2:19, 20; 3:10; 1 Sam 2:20; 9:13; 15:13; 23:21; 25:33; 26:25; 2 Sam 2:5; 6:18; 13:25; 14:22; 19:40; 21:3; 1 Kgs 2:45; 8:14, 55, 66; 21:10, 13; 2 Kgs 4:29; 10:15; 1 Chr 16:2; 29:10, 20; 2 Chr 6:3; 20:26; 30:27; 31:8; Neh 8:6; 9:5; 11:2; Job 1:5, 11; 2:5, 9; 31:20; Pss 10:3; 16:7; 26:12; 34:2; 37:22; 49:19; 62:5; 63:5; 66:8; 68:27; 72:15, 17; 96:2; 100:4; 103:1, 2, 22; 104:1, 35; 112:2; 115:15, 18; 118:26; 128:4; 129:8; 134:1, 2; 135:19, 20; 145:1, 2, 10; Prov 22:9; 27:14; 30:11; Isa 19:25; 65:16, 23; 66:3; Jer 4:2; 17:7.

e. בשר/*bśr*—"bring good news; receive good news"
   1 Sam 4:17; 2 Sam 1:20; 4:10; 18:19, 20, 26, 31; 1 Kgs 1:42; 1 Chr 16:23; Pss 68:12; 96:2; Isa 40:9; 41:27; 52:7; 60:6; Jer 20:15; Nah 2:1.

f. גיל/*gyl*—"rejoice"

    Pss 2:11; 9:15; 13:5, 6; 14:7; 16:9; 21:2; 31:8; 32:11; 35:9; 53:7; 89:17; 118:24; 149:2; Prov 2:14; 23:24, 25; 24:17; Cant 1:4; Isa 9:2; 25:9; 29:19; 41:16; 61:10; 65:18; 66:10; Hos 10:5; Joel 2:23; Hab 1:15; 3:18; Zech 10:7.

g. הלל II/*hll* II—"praise; be praised; boast, pride oneself"

    Gen 12:15; Judg 16:24; 1 Kgs 20:11; 1 Chr 16:10, 36; 23:5; 29:13; 2 Chr 20:21; 23:12; 29:30; 30:21; Neh 5:13; Pss 10:3; 22:23, 24, 27; 34:3; 35:18; 44:9; 49:7; 52:3; 56:5, 11; 63:6, 12; 64:11; 69:31; 74:21; 78:63; 84:5; 97:7; 102:19; 104:35; 104:35; 105:3, 45; 106:1, 48; 107:32; 109:1, 30; 111:1; 112:1; 113:1, 9; 115:17, 18; 116:19; 117:1, 2; 119:164, 175; 135:1, 3, 21; 145:2; 146:1, 2, 10; 147:1, 20; 148:13, 14; 149:1, 3, 9; 150:1, 2, 3, 4, 5; Prov 12:8; 20:14; 25:14; 27:1, 2; 28:4; 31:28, 30; Cant 6:9; Isa 41:16; 45:25; 62:9; 64:10; Jer 4:2; 9:22, 23; 20:13; 31:7; 49:4; Joel 2:26.

h. זמר I/*zmr* I—"sing, praise"

    Judg 5:3; 2 Sam 22:50; 1 Chr 16:9; Pss 7:18; 9:3, 12; 18:50; 21:14; 27:6; 30:5, 13; 33:2; 47:7, 8; 57:8, 10; 59:18; 61:9; 66:2, 4; 68:5, 33; 71:22, 23; 75:10; 98:5; 101:1; 104:33; 105:2; 108:2, 4; 135:3; 138:1; 144:9; 146:2; 147:7; 149:3; Isa 12:5.

i. חגג/*ḥgg*—"leap, walk in procession, celebrate"

    Exod 5:1; 12:14; 23:14; Lev 23:39, 41; Num 29:12; Deut 16:15; 1 Sam 30:16; Pss 42:5; 107:27; Nah 2:1.

j. חדה I/*ḥdh* I—"rejoice; make joyful, cheer"

    Exod 18:9.

k. חול/*ḥwl*—"dance round dances"

    Ps 87:7; Jer 4:19; Lam 4:6; Ezek 30:16.

l. חמד/*ḥmd*—"desire, take pleasure in; desirable; fiercely desire"

    Exod 20:17; 34:24; Deut 5:21; 7:25; Josh 7:21; Prov 1:22; 6:25; 12:12; Cant 2:3; Isa 1:29; 53:2; Micah 2:2.

m. חפץ I/*ḥpṣ* I—"take pleasure in, desire, delight in"

    Gen 34:19; Deut 21:14; 25:7, 8; Ruth 3:13; 1 Sam 18:22; 19:1; 2 Sam 20:11; 24:3; 1 Kgs 9:1; Esth 2:14; 6:6, 7, 9, 11; Job 9:3; 13:3; 21:14; 33:32; Pss 40:9; 68:31; 73:25; 109:17; 112:1; 119:35; Prov 18:2; Eccl 8:3; Isa 13:17; 58:2; 66:3; Jer 6:10; 42:22.

n. טוב/*ṭwb*—"be pleasant, delightful, joyful, glad"

    Judg 11:25; 16:25; 1 Sam 2:26; 25:36; 2 Sam 15:26; 19:38.

o. יטב/*yṭb*—"be well, pleasing; treat well, graciously, do good, make things go well for"

    Gen 4:7; Exod 30:7; Num 10:29, 32; 5:28; 18:17; Judg 18:20; 19:6, 9, 22; Ruth 3:7, 10; 1 Sam 16:17; 1 Kgs 21:7; 2 Kgs 9:30; Neh 2:5; Esth 2:4, 9; Job 24:21; Pss 33:3; 49:19; Prov

15:2; 30:29; Eccl 7:3; 11:9; Isa 23:16; Jer 1:12; 2:33; 7:3, 5; 18:11; 26:13; 35:15; Ezek 33:32; Hos 10:1.

p. לעב/*lʿb*—"make jest at"
2 Chr 36:16.

q. נעם/*nʿm*—"be pleasant, lovely; be a delight for"
2 Sam 1:26; Cant 7:7; Ezek 32:19.

r. סלד/*sld*—"jump for joy"
Job 6:10.

s. עדן I/ *ʿdn* I—"to live a life of luxury, let things go well"
Neh 9:25.

t. עלז/ *ʿlz*—"rejoice, exult"
2 Sam 1:20; Pss 28:7; 60:8; 68:5; 94:3; 108:8; 149:5; Prov 23:16; Jer 11:15; 15:17; 50:11; 51:39; Hab 3:18.

u. עלס I/ *ʿls* I—"enjoy a thing; enjoy each other"
Job 20:18; Prov 7:18.

v. עלץ/ *ʿlṣ*—"rejoice, exult"
1 Sam 2:1; Pss 5:12; 9:3; 25:2; 68:4; Prov 11:10.

w. ענג/ *ʿng*—"take delight, pleasure in; make merry, be content"
Job 22:26; 27:10; Ps 37:4, 11; Isa 55:2; 57:4; 58:14; 66:11.

x. ערב III/ *ʿrb* III—"be pleasing"
Ezek 16:37.

y. פוש/*pwš*—"paw the ground (playfully?)"
Jer 50:11; Mal 3:20.

z. פזז II/*pzz* II—"leap (with joy?)"
2 Sam 6:16.

aa. פצח I/*pṣḥ* I—"be cheerful, happy, serene"
Ps 98:4; Isa 14:7; 54:1.

bb. צחק/*ṣḥq*—"laugh; sport, play, jest"
Gen 17:17; 18:12, 13, 15; 19:14; 21:6, 9; 26:8; Judg 16:25.

cc. רוח/*rwḥ*—"feel relieved, easy; smell, enjoy"
Gen 27:27; Isa 11:3.

dd. רוע/*rw'*—"shout in joy, cheer; a shout is uttered; shout in triumph"

Num 10:7, 9; Josh 6:5, 10, 16, 20; Judg 7:21; 15:14; 1 Sam 4:5; 10:24; 17:20, 52; 2 Chr 13:15; Ezra 3:11, 13; Job 30:5; Pss 41:12; 47:2; 60:10; 66:1; 81:2; 95:1, 2; 98:4, 6; 100:1; 108:10; Isa 15:4; 16:10; Jer 50:15; Hos 5:8; Joel 2:1; Zeph 3:14.

ee. רנן/*rnn*—"jubilate, give a cry of joy; give a ringing cry in joy; cry for joy; cause to cry for joy"

Lev 9:24; Deut 32:43; Job 29:13; Pss 5:12; 20:6; 32:11; 33:1; 35:27; 51:16; 59:17; 63:8; 67:5; 71:23; 81:2; 84:3; 90:14; 92:5; 95:1; 98:4; 132:9, 16; 145:7; 149:5; Prov 29:6; Isa 12:6; 24:14; 35:6; 42:11; 52:8; 61:7; 65:14; Jer 31:7, 12; Lam 2:19.

ff. רצה I/*rṣh* I—"be pleased with, be favorable to; be treated as favored; make oneself favored with"

Gen 33:10; Deut 33:24; 1 Sam 29:4; 1 Chr 29:3; 2 Chr 10:7; Esth 10:3; Job 34:9; Pss 49:14; 50:18; 62:5; 102:15; Prov 3:12; 23:26; Mal 1:8.

gg. רקד/*rqd*—"skip about; dance; cause to skip about"

1 Chr 15:29; Job 21:11; Joel 2:5.

hh. שבע/*śb'*—"be sate; sated; satisfy a person; satisfy"

Exod 16:12; Lev 26:26; Deut 6:11; 8:10, 12; 11:15; 14:29; 26:12; 31:20; Ruth 2:14; 1 Chr 23:1; 2 Chr 24:15; Neh 9:25; Job 7:4; 19:22; 27:14; 31:31; Pss 17:14, 15; 22:27; 37:19; 59:16; 63:6; 65:5; 78:29; 88:4; 104:28; 123:3, 4; Prov 1:31; 5:10; 12:11, 14; 14:14; 18:20; 20:13; 25:16, 17; 27:20; 28:19; 30:9, 22; Eccl 1:8; 4:8; 5:9; 6:3; Isa 9:19; 44:16; 53:11; 58:10; 66:11; Jer 31:14; 44:17; 50:10, 19; Lam 3:30; Ezek 7:19; Hos 4:10; 13:6; Joel 2:19; Amos 4:8; Micah 6:14; Hab 2:5, 16.

ii. שוש/*śwś*—"rejoice, display joy"

Job 3:22; Pss 35:9; 40:17; 68:4; 70:5; 119:14, 162; Isa 61:10; 64:4; 65:18; 66:10, 14; Lam 1:21; Ezek 21:15(?).

jj. שחק/*śḥq*—"play, amuse, laugh, entertain; be merry, play with, make merry, dance"

Judg 16:25; 1 Sam 18:7; 2 Sam 2:14; 6:5, 21; 1 Chr 13:8; 15:29; 2 Chr 30:10; Job 5:22; 29:24; 30:1; 40:29; Ps 52:8; Prov 26:19; 29:9; 31:25; Jer 15:17; 30:19; 31:4; Lam 1:7; Hab 1:10; Zech 8:5.

kk. שמח/*śmḥ*—"rejoice; cause to rejoice, gladden; cause to rejoice"

Exod 4:14; Lev 23:40; Deut 12:7, 12, 18; 14:26; 16:11, 14; 24:5; 26:11; 27:7; 33:18; Judg 9:19; 19:3; 1 Sam 2:1; 6:13; 11:9, 15; 19:5; 2 Sam 1:20; 1 Kgs 5:21; 2 Kgs 11:20; 1 Chr 16:10; 29:9; 2 Chr 6:41; 15:15; 23:21; 24:10; 29:36; 30:25; 12:43; Esth 8:15; Job 21:12; 22:19; 31:25, 29; Pss 5:12; 9:3; 14:7; 16:9; 21:2; 31:8; 32:11; 33:21; 34:3; 35:15, 19, 24, 27; 38:17; 40:17; 53:7; 58:11; 63:12; 64:11; 66:6; 67:5; 68:4; 69:33; 70:5; 85:7; 90:14; 97:1, 12; 104:34; 105:3, 38; 107:30, 42; 109:28; 118:24; 119:74; 122:1; 149:2; Prov 5:18; 10:1; 15:20; 17:21; 23:15, 24,

25; 24:17; Prov 27:11; 29:2, 3, 6; Eccl 3:22; 4:16; 11:8, 9; Cant 1:4; Isa 9:2; 14:29; 25:9; 39:2; 65:13; 66:10; Jer 20:15; 31:13; 41:13; 50:11; Ezek 7:12; 25:6; Hos 7:3; 9:1; Joel 2:23; Obad 12; Jon 4:6; Micah 7:8; Hab 1:15; Zech 10:7.

ll. שׁבח I/*šbḥ* I—"praise, laud, congratulate; boast of"

Pss 63:4; 117:1; 145:4; Eccl 8:15.

mm. שׁיר/*šyr*—"sing; be sung; burst into song"

Exod 15:1, 21; Num 21:17; Judg 5:1, 3; 2 Sam 19:36; 1 Kgs 10:12; 1 Chr 6:18; 9:33; 15:16, 19, 27; 16:9, 23; 2 Chr 5:12, 13; 9:11; 20:21; 23:13; 35:25; Ezra 2:41, 65, 70; 7:7; 10:24; Neh 7:1, 44, 67, 72; 10:29, 40; 11:22, 23; 12:28, 29, 42, 45, 46, 47; 13:5, 10; Job 36:24; Pss 7:1; 13:6; 21:14; 27:6; 33:3; 57:8; 59:17; 68:5, 26, 33; 89:2; 96:1, 2; 98:1; 101:1; 104:33; 105:2; 106:12; 108:2; 137:3, 4; 138:5; 144:9; 149:1; Prov 25:20; Eccl 2:8; Isa 5:1; 42:10; Jer 20:13; Ezek 40:44.

nn. שׁלם/*šlm*—"be completed, finished, happy"

2 Sam 20:19; Job 9:4; 22:21; Ps 7:5.

oo. שׁעע II/*šʿʿ*—"take delight in; be played with, be fondled; take pleasure in, delight in"

Ps 119:16, 47, 70; Isa 11:8; 66:12.

2. Old Testament Lexemes (Aramaic)

a. ברך II/*brk* II—"bless"

Dan 2:19; 4:31.

b. הדר/*hdr*—"glorify"

Dan 4:31, 34; 5:23.

c. צבה/*ṣbh*—"be pleased"

Dan 5:19; 7:19.

d. רים/*rym*—"praise"

Dan 4:34.

e. שׁבח/*šbḥ*—"praise"

Dan 2:23; 4:31, 34; 5:4, 23.

3. New Testament Lexemes (Greek)

a. ἀγαλλιάω/*agalliaō*—"be extremely joyful"

Matt 5:12; Luke 1:47; John 8:56; Acts 2:26; 16:34; 1 Pet 1:6, 8; 4:13; Rev 19:7.

b. ἀγαπάω/*agapaō*—"love, show love, take pleasure in"

Matt 5:43, 44, 46; 6:24; 19:19; 22:37, 39; Mark 12:30, 31; Luke 6:27, 32, 35; 7:5, 42, 47; 10:27; 11:43; 16:13; John 3:19; 8:42; 12:43; 13:34; 14:15, 21, 23, 24, 28; 15:12, 17; 21:15, 16; Rom 8:28; 9:25; 13:8, 9; 1 Cor 2:9; 8:3; 2 Cor 11:11; 12:15; Gal 5:14; Eph 5:25, 28, 33; 6:24; Col 3:12, 19; 1 Thess 1:4; 2 Thess 2:13; 2 Tim 4:8, 10; James 1:12; 2:5, 8; 1 Pet 1:8, 22; 2:17; 2 Pet 2:15; 1 John 2:10, 15; 3:10, 11, 14, 18, 23; 4:7, 8, 10, 12, 19, 20, 21; 5:1, 2; 2 John 1:1, 5; 3 John 1:1; Jude 1:1; Rev 12:11.

c. ἀναψύχω/*anapsychō*—"encourage"

2 Tim 1:16.

d. ἀρέσκω/*areskō*—"please"

Matt 14:6; Mark 6:22; Rom 15:2; 1 Cor 7:32, 33, 34; 10:33; Gal 1:10; 1 Thess 2:4, 15; 2 Tim 2:4.

e. ἀρκέω/*arkeō*—"be satisfied"

Luke 3:14; 1 Tim 6:8; Heb 13:5; 3 John 1:10.

f. ἀσπάζομαι/*aspazomai*—"greet, be happy about, welcome"

Matt 5:47; 10:12; Mark 9:15; Luke 1:40; 10:4; Acts 18:22; 20:1; 21:7, 19; 25:13; Rom 16:3, 5, 6, 7, 8, 9, 10, 11, 12, 13, 14, 15, 16, 21, 22, 23; 1 Cor 16:19, 20; 2 Cor 13:12; Phil 4:21, 22; Col 4:10, 12, 14, 15; 1 Thess 5:26; 2 Tim 4:19, 21; Titus 3:15; Phlm 1:23; Heb 11:13; 13:24; 1 Pet 5:13, 14; 2 John 1:13; 3 John 1:15.

g. γελάω/*gelaō*—"laugh"

Luke 6:21, 25.

h. ἐμπίπλημι/*empiplēmi*—"to satisfy"

Luke 6:25; John 6:12; Rom 15:24.

i. εὐδοκέω/*eudokeō*—"be pleased with, enjoy, prefer"

Rom 15:26, 27; 2 Cor 5:8; 12:10; 1 Thess 2:8; 3:1; 2 Thess 2:12.

j. εὐθυμέω/*euthymeō*—"be encouraged"

Acts 27:25; James 5:13.

k. εὐφραίνω/*euphrainō*—"make glad"

Luke 12:19; 15:23, 29; 16:19; Acts 2:26; 7:41; Rom 15:10; 2 Cor 2:2; Gal 4:27; Rev 11:10.

l. εὐχαριστέω/*eucharisteō*—"thank, be thankful"

Luke 17:16; 18:11; Acts 27:35; 28:15; Rom 1:8, 21; 14:6; 16:4; 1 Cor 1:4, 14; 10:30; 14:17, 18; Eph 1:16; 5:20; Phil 1:3; Col 1:3, 12; 3:17; 1 Thess 1:2; 2:13; 5:18; Phlm 1:4; Rev 11:17.

m. εὐψυχέω/*eupsycheō*—"be encouraged"

Phil 2:19.

n. θέλω/*thelō*—"purpose, be of an opinion, desire, enjoy"

Matt 1:19; 2:18; 5:40, 42; 7:12; 11:14; 12:38; 13:28; 14:5; 15:28; 16:24, 25; 17:12; 18:23, 30; 19:17, 21; 20:14, 15, 21, 26, 27, 32; 21:29; 22:3; 23:4, 37; 26:15; 27:15, 17, 21, 34; Mark 6:19, 22, 25, 26; 8:34, 35; 9:13, 35; 10:35, 36, 43, 44, 51; 12:38; 14:7; 15:9, 12; Luke 1:62; 5:39; 6:31; 8:20; 9:23, 24; 10:24, 29; 13:31, 34; 14:28; 15:28; 16:26; 18:4, 13, 41; 19:14, 27; 20:46; 23:8, 20; John 5:6, 35, 40; 6:11, 21, 67; 7:17, 44; 8:44; 9:27; 12:21; 15:7; 16:19; 21:18; Acts 7:28, 39; 10:10; 14:13; 16:3; 17:18; 19:33; 24:27; 25:9; 26:5; Rom 1:13; 7:15, 16, 19, 20, 21; 9:16; 11:25; 13:3; 16:19; 1 Cor 4:21; 7:7, 32, 36, 39; 10:1, 20, 27; 11:3; 12:1; 14:5, 19, 35; 16:7; 2 Cor 1:8; 5:4; 11:12; 12:6, 20; Gal 1:7; 3:2; 4:9, 17, 20, 21; 5:17; 6:12, 13; Col 2:1, 18; 1 Thess 2:18; 4:13; 2 Thess 3:10; 1 Tim 1:7; 5:11; 2 Tim 3:12; Phlm 1:14; Heb 12:17; 13:18; James 2:20; 1 Pet 3:10; 2 Pet 3:5; 3 John 1:13; Rev 2:21; 11:5; 22:17.

o. κορέννυμι/*korennymi*—"be content, have enough"

Acts 27:38; 1 Cor 4:8.

p. μακαρίζω/*makarizō*—"regard as happy"

Luke 1:48; James 5:11.

q. παρακαλέω/*parakaleō*—"encourage"

Matt 5:4; 8:5, 34; 14:36; 18:29, 32; Mark 1:40; 5:18, 23; 6:56; 7:32; 8:22; Luke 3:18; 7:4; 8:41; 15:28; 16:25; Acts 2:40; 8:31; 9:38; 11:23; 13:42; 14:22; 15:32; 16:9, 15, 39, 40; 19:31; 20:1, 2, 12; 21:12; 24:4; 25:2; 27:33, 34; 28:14, 20; Rom 12:1, 8; 15:30; 16:17; 1 Cor 1:10; 4:13, 16; 14:31; 16:12, 15; 2 Cor 1:4, 6; 2:8; 6:1; 7:7, 13; 10:1; 12:8, 18; 13:11; Eph 4:1; 6:22; Phil 4:2; Col 2:2; 4:8; 1 Thess 2:12; 3:7; 4:1, 10, 18; 5:11, 14; 2 Thess 3:12; 1 Tim 1:3; 2:1; 5:1; 6:2; 2 Tim 4:2; Titus 2:6, 15; Phlm 1:9, 10; Heb 3:13; 10:25; 13:19, 22; 1 Pet 2:11; 5:1, 12; Jude 1:3.

r. σκιρτάω/*skirtaō*—"jump for joy, be extremely joyful"

Luke 1:41, 44; 6:23.

s. συγχαίρω/*synchairō*—"rejoice with"

Luke 1:58; 15:6, 9; Phil 2:17, 18.

t. συνήδομαι/*synēdomai*—"rejoice in"

Rom 7:22.

u. φιλέω/*phileō*—"love, like, kiss"

Matt 6:5; 10:37; 23:6; 26:48; Mark 14:44; Luke 20:46; John 12:25; 16:27; 21:15, 16, 17; 1 Cor 16:22; Titus 3:15; Rev 22:15.

v. χαίρω/*chairō*—"rejoice, greetings"

Matt 2:10; 5:12; 18:13; Mark 14:11; Luke 1:14; 6:23; 10:20; 13:17; 15:5; 19:6, 37; 22:5; 23:8; John 3:29; 4:36; 8:56; 14:28; 16:22; 20:20; Acts 5:41; 8:39; 11:23; 13:48; 15:31; Rom 12:12, 15; 16:19; 1 Cor 7:30; 16:17; 2 Cor 6:10; 7:9, 13, 16; 13:9, 11; Phil 1:18; 2:17, 18, 28; 3:1; 4:4, 10; Col 1:24; 2:5; 1 Thess 3:9; 5:16; 1 Pet 4:13; 2 John 1:4; 3 John 1:3; Rev 11:10; 19:7.

w. χορτάζω/*chortazō*—"eat one's fill, be content"
  Matt 5:6; 14:20; Mark 6:42; 8:8; Luke 6:21; 9:17; John 6:26; James 2:16.

x. ψάλλω/*psallō*—"sing, sing praise"
  Rom 15:9; 1 Cor 14:15; Eph 5:19; James 5:13.

Jesus (= J)[34]

a. ἀγαλλιάω/*agalliaō*—"be extremely joyful"
  Luke 10:21.

b. ἀγαπάω/*agapaō*—"love, show love, take pleasure in"
  Mark 10:21; John 11:5; 13:1, 23, 34; 14:21, 31; 15:9, 12; 19:26; 21:7, 20; Rom 8:37; Gal 2:20; Eph 1:6; 5:2, 25; Heb 1:9; Rev 1:5; 3:9.

c. ἀρέσκω/*areskō*—"please"
  Rom 15:3.

d. εὐχαριστέω/*eucharisteō*—"thank, be thankful"
  Matt 15:36; 26:27; Mark 8:6; 14:23; Luke 22:17, 19; John 6:11, 23; 11:41; 1 Cor 11:24.

e. θέλω/*thelō*—"purpose, be of an opinion, desire, enjoy"
  Matt 8:2, 3; 15:32; 17:4; 23:37; 26:17, 39; 27:34; Mark 1:40, 41; 3:13; 6:48; 7:24; 9:30; 14:12, 36; Luke 5:12, 13; 9:54; 12:49; 13:34; 22:9; John 1:43; 5:21; 7:1; 17:24; 21:22, 23.

f. παρακαλέω/*parakaleō*—"encourage"
  2 Thess 2:17.

g. φιλέω/*phileō*—"love, like, kiss"
  John 11:3, 36; 20:2; Rev 3:19.

h. χαίρω/*chairō*—"rejoice, greetings"
  John 11:15.

Inanimate/Abstract Item (= I/AI)

1. Old Testament Lexemes (Hebrew)

a. אור/ *'wr*—"become, be light, shine; to be lit up; make the countenance shine, make the face shine"
  Exod 25:37; Num 8:2; Ps 119:130.

---

34. Obviously this category applies only to NT (Greek) texts.

b. ברך II/*brk* II—"praised, be blessed; wish oneself a blessing; bless; bless each other, bless oneself"

Deut 28:5; 2 Sam 7:29; Prov 5:18; 20:21.

c. חול/*ḥwl*—"dance round dances"

Hos 11:6.

d. חמד/*ḥmd*—"desire, take pleasure in; desirable; fiercely desire"

Job 20:20; Ps 39:12; Prov 21:20; Isa 44:9.

e. טוב/*ṭwb*—"be pleasant, delightful, joyful, glad"

Num 24:5.

f. נעם/*n ʿm*—"be pleasant, lovely; be a delight for"

Prov 9:17.

g. ערב III/*ʿrb* III—"be pleasing"

Jer 6:20; Mal 3:4.

h. רוח/*rwḥ*—"feel relieved, easy; smell, enjoy"

Judg 16:9; 1 Sam 16:23.

i. רצה I/*rṣh* I—"be pleased with, be favorable to; be treated as favored; make oneself favored with"

Lev 1:4; 7:18; 19:7; 22:23, 25, 27.

j. רקד/*rqd*—"skip about; dance; cause to skip about"

Nah 3:2.

k. שבע/*śb ʿ*—"be sated; sated; satisfy a person; satisfy"

Jer 46:10.

l. שמח/*śmḥ*—"rejoice; cause to rejoice, gladden; cause to rejoice"

Judg 9:13; Pss 45:9; 104:15; Prov 27:9; Eccl 10:19.

m. שלם/*šlm*—"be completed, finished, happy"

Neh 6:15.

2. *New Testament Lexemes (Greek)*

a. ἀγαπάω/*agapaō*—"love, show love, take pleasure in"

Rev 20:9.

b. ἀρκέω/*arkeō*—"be satisfied"

John 6:7.

Miscellaneous[35]

a. assurances

שׁעע II/*šʿʿ*—"take delight in; be played with, be fondled; take pleasure in, delight in"
  Ps 94:19.

b. barren one

רנן/*rnn*—"jubilate, give a cry of joy; give a ringing cry in joy; cry for joy; cause to cry for joy"
  Isa 54:1.

c. brightness of eyes

שׂמח/*śmḥ* —"rejoice; cause to rejoice, gladden; cause to rejoice"
  Prov 15:30.

d. counsel (Aramaic)

שׁפר/*špr*—"please"
  Dan 4:24.

e. crushed bones

גיל/*gyl*—"rejoice"
  Ps 51:10.

f. Daughter of Edom

  1. שׂושׂ/*śwś*—"rejoice, display joy"
    Lam 4:21.

  2. שׂמח/*śmḥ*—"rejoice; cause to rejoice, gladden; cause to rejoice"
    Lam 4:21.

g. day of birth

ברך II/*brk* II—"praised, be blessed; wish oneself a blessing; bless; bless each other, bless oneself"
  Jer 20:14.

---

35. For this category, the different languages/text corpora have been intermixed into one alphabetical listing. Only in the case of the Aramaic lexemes is the language identified to avoid possible confusion for English-only readers.

h. days of mourning

שלם/*šlm*—"be completed, finished, happy"
Isa 60:20.

i. dead, the

רנן/*rnn*—"jubilate, give a cry of joy; give a ringing cry in joy; cry for joy; cause to cry for joy"
Isa 26:19.

j. death

הלל II/*hll* II—"praise; be praised; boast, pride oneself"
Isa 38:18.

k. deeds

1. הלל II/*hll* II—"praise; be praised; boast, pride oneself"
Prov 31:31.

2. טוב/*twb*—"be pleasant, delightful, joyful, glad"
2 Sam 3:36.

l. explanation(s)/idea(s)/information/news/plan(s)/report(s)/word(s)

1. יטב/*ytb*—"be well, pleasing; treat well, graciously, do good; make things go well for"
Gen 34:18; 41:37; 45:16; Lev 10:20; Deut 1:23; Josh 22:30, 33; Neh 2:6; Esth 1:21; 2:4; 5:14; Micah 2:7.

2. כשר/*kšr*—"be proper, pleasing; bring success"
Esth 8:5.

3. נעם/*n'm*—"be pleasant, lovely; be a delight for"
Ps 141:6.

4. שׂמח/*śmḥ*—"rejoice; cause to rejoice, gladden; cause to rejoice"
Prov 12:25.

m. fruit of the womb

ברך II/*brk* II—"praised, be blessed; wish oneself a blessing; bless; bless each other, bless oneself"
Deut 28:4.

n. God's will

θέλω/*thelō*—"purpose, be of an opinion, desire, enjoy"
    1 Pet 3:17.

o. grace

ἀρκέω/*arkeō*—"be satisfied"
    2 Cor 12:9.

p. guilt

חול/*ḥwl*—"dance round dances"
    2 Sam 3:29.

q. idea, an → see also explanation(s)/idea(s)/information/news/plan(s)/report(s)/word(s)

ἀρέσκω/*areskō*—"please"
    Acts 6:5.

r. idols

רוח/*rwḥ*—"feel relieved, easy; smell, enjoy"
    Ps 115:6.

s. impersonal subject

    1. אור/*'wr*—"become, be light, shine; to be lit up; make the countenance shine, make the face shine"
        1 Sam 29:10; 2 Sam 2:32.

    2. טאב/*ṭ'b*—"be good, pleasing, glad" (Aramaic)
        Dan 6:24.

    3. טוב/*ṭwb*—"be pleasant, delightful, joyful, glad"
        Num 11:18; 24:1; Deut 5:33; 15:16; 2 Sam 3:19; Ps 119:71.

    4a. יטב/*yṭb*—"be well, pleasing; treat well, graciously, do good; make things go well for"
        Gen 12:13, 16; 40:14; Deut 4:40; 5:16, 29; 6:3, 18; 12:25, 28; 22:7; Ruth 3:1; 1 Sam 2:32; 20:13; 24:5; 2 Sam 3:36; 18:4; 2 Kgs 25:24; Jer 7:23; 38:20; 40:9; 42:6.

    4b. יטב/*yṭb*—"it is pleasing" (Aramaic)
        Ezra 7:18.

5. נעם/*n'm*—"be pleasant, lovely; be a delight for"
Prov 24:25.

6. רנן/*rnn*—"jubilate, give a cry of joy; give a ringing cry in joy; cry for joy; cause to cry for joy"
Isa 16:10.

7. שפר/*špr*—"please" (Aramaic)
Dan 3:32; 6:2.

8. ἀρκέω/*arkeō*—"be satisfied"
Matt 25:9; John 14:8.

9. εὐδοκέω/*eudokeō*—"be pleased with, enjoy, prefer"
Col 1:19.

t. information → see explanation(s)/idea(s)/information/news/plan(s)/report(s)/word(s)

u. Jerusalem/Zion

1. אור/*'wr*—"become, be light, shine; to be lit up; make the countenance shine, make the face shine"
Isa 60:1; Ps 147:12.

2. גיל/*gyl*—"rejoice"
Zech 9:9.

3. עלז/*'lz*—"rejoice, exult"
Zeph 3:14.

4. ענג/*'ng*—"take delight, pleasure in; make merry, be content"
Jer 6:2.

5. רוע/*rw'*—"shout in joy, cheer; a shout is uttered; shout in triumph"
Micah 4:9; Zech 9:9.

6. רנן/*rnn*—"jubilate, give a cry of joy; give a ringing cry in joy; cry for joy; cause to cry for joy"
Zeph 3:14; Zech 2:14.

7. שבע/*śb'*—"be sated; sated; satisfy a person; satisfy"
Ezek 16:28, 29.

8. שׂמח/*śmḥ*—"rejoice; cause to rejoice, gladden; cause to rejoice"
   Pss 48:12; 97:8; Zeph 3:14; Zech 2:14.

9. שׁבח I/*šbḥ* I—"praise, laud, congratulate; boast of"
   Ps 147:12.

v. joyful heart, a

יטב/*yṭb*—"be well, pleasing; treat well, graciously, do good; make things go well for"
Prov 15:13; 17:22.

w. judgments of Yahweh

חמד/*ḥmd*—"desire, take pleasure in; desirable; fiercely desire"
Ps 19:11.

x. knowledge

נעם/*n ʿm*—"be pleasant, lovely; be a delight for"
Prov 2:10.

y. light of the Righteous, the

שׂמח/*śmḥ*—"rejoice; cause to rejoice, gladden; cause to rejoice"
Prov 13:9.

z. love

1. חפץ I/*ḥpṣ* I—"take pleasure in, desire, delight in"
   Cant 2:7; 3:5; 8:4.

2. טוב/*ṭwb*—"be pleasant, delightful, joyful, glad"
   Cant 4:10.

3. συγχαίρω/*synchairō*—"rejoice with"
   1 Cor 13:6.

aa. member of the body

συγχαίρω/*synchairō*—"rejoice with"
1 Cor 12:26.

bb. name of God, the (Aramaic)

ברך II/*brk* II—"bless"
Dan 2:20.

cc. news → see explanation(s)/idea(s)/information/news/plan(s)/report(s)/word(s) dd. night

חדה I/*ḥdh* I—"rejoice; make joyful, cheer"

Job 3:6.

ee. Nineveh

יטב/*yṭb*—"be well, pleasing; treat well, graciously, do good; make things go well for"

Nah 3:8.

ff. placement of David over all the soldiers, the

יטב/*yṭb*—"be well, pleasing; treat well, graciously, do good; make things go well for"

1 Sam 18:5.

gg. plan → see explanation(s)/idea(s)/information/news/plan(s)/report(s)/word(s)

hh. praise

יטב/*yṭb*—"be well, pleasing; treat well, graciously, do good; make things go well for"

Ps 69:32.

ii. prayer

ערב III/ *'rb* III—"be pleasing"

Ps 104:34.

jj. precepts

1. אור/ *'wr*—"become, be light, shine; to be lit up; make the countenance shine, make the face shine"

Ps 19:9.

2. שׂמח/*śmḥ*—"rejoice; cause to rejoice, gladden; cause to rejoice"

Ps 19:9.

kk. prudence

ברך II/*brk* II—"praised, be blessed; wish oneself a blessing; bless; bless each other, bless oneself"

1 Sam 25:33.

ll. realized desire

ערב III/ *'rb* III—"be pleasing"

Prov 13:19.

mm. report → see explanation(s)/idea(s)/information/news/plan(s)/report(s)/word(s) nn. request

יטב/*yṭb*—"be well, pleasing; treat well, graciously, do good; make things go well for"
   1 Kgs 3:10.

oo. ritual activity

יטב/*yṭb*—"be well, pleasing; treat well, graciously, do good; make things go well for"
   Lev 10:19.

pp. ruins of Jerusalem

   1. פצח I/*pṣḥ* I—"be cheerful, happy, serene"
      Isa 52:9.

   2. רנן/*rnn*—"jubilate, give a cry of joy; give a ringing cry in joy; cry for joy; cause to
cry for joy"
      Isa 52:9.

qq. seven eyes of Yahweh, the

שׂמח/*śmḥ*—"rejoice; cause to rejoice, gladden; cause to rejoice"
   Zech 4:10.

rr. Sheol and Abaddon

שׂבע/*śbʿ*—"be sated; sated; satisfy a person; satisfy"
   Prov 27:20.

ss. sleep

ערב III/*ʿrb* III—"be pleasing"
   Prov 3:24; Jer 31:26.

tt. song

שׁיר/*šyr*—"sing; be sung; burst into song"
   2 Chr 29:28; Isa 26:1.

uu. sowing

כשׁר/*kšr*—"be proper, pleasing; bring success"
   Eccl 11:6.

vv. streams

שׂמח/*śmḥ*—"rejoice; cause to rejoice, gladden; cause to rejoice"
   Ps 46:5.

ww. "three insatiable things"

שׂבע/*śb'*—"be sated; sated; satisfy a person; satisfy"
   Prov 30:15.

xx. speaking

רוח/*rwḥ*—"feel relieved, easy; smell, enjoy"
   Job 32:20.

yy. strange things

θέλω/*thelō*—"purpose, be of an opinion, desire, enjoy"
   Acts 17:20.

zz. thanks

εὐχαριστέω/*eucharisteō*—"thank, be thankful"
   2 Cor 1:11.

aaa. tongues

θέλω/*thelō*—"purpose, be of an opinion, desire, enjoy"
   Acts 2:12.

bbb. towns of Judah

גיל/*gyl*—"rejoice"
   Pss 48:12; 97:8.

ccc. two witnesses

θέλω/*thelō*—"purpose, be of an opinion, desire, enjoy"
   Rev 11:6.

ddd. Tyre

   1. הלל II/*hll* II—"praise; be praised; boast, pride oneself"
      Ezek 26:17.

   2. שׂבע/*śb'*—"be sated; sated; satisfy a person; satisfy"
      Ezek 27:33.

eee. wind

θέλω/*thelō*—"purpose, be of an opinion, desire, enjoy"
     John 3:8.

fff. Wisdom

     1. אור/ *'wr*—"become, be light, shine; to be lit up; make the countenance shine,
make the face shine"
          Eccl 8:1.

     2. רנן/*rnn*—"jubilate, give a cry of joy; give a ringing cry in joy; cry for joy; cause to
cry for joy"
          Prov 1:20; 8:3.

     3. שׂחק/*śḥq*—"play, amuse, laugh, entertain; be merry, play with, make merry, dance"
          Prov 1:26; 8:30, 31.

ggg. words → see explanation(s)/idea(s)/information/news/plan(s)/report(s)/word(s)

hhh. work

שׁלם/*šlm*—"be completed, finished, happy"
     1 Kgs 7:51; 2 Chr 5:1.

iii. world, the

     1. φιλέω/*phileō*—"love, like, kiss"
          John 15:19.

     2. χαίρω/*chairō*—"rejoice, greetings"
          John 16:20.

Bibliography

Achor, Shawn. *The Happiness Advantage: The Seven Principles of Positive Psychology that Fuel Success and Performance at Work*. New York: Crown, 2010.

Achtemeier, Elizabeth. *The Community and Message of Isaiah 56–66*. Minneapolis: Augsburg, 1982.

Agouridès, S. "La tradition des béatitudes chez Matthieu et Luc." In *Mélanges bibliques en hommage au R.P. Béda Rigaux*, edited by A. Descamps and A. de Halleux, 9–27. Gembloux: Duculot, 1970.

Aitchison, Jean. *Lingusitics*. 6th ed. Chicago: Teach Yourself, 2003.

Allison, Dale C., Jr. "Eschatology of the NT." In *The New Interpreter's Dictionary of the Bible*, edited by Katharine Doob Sakenfeld, et al., 2:294–99. 5 volumes. Nashville: Abingdon, 2006–2009.

Ambrose of Milan. *Exposition of the Holy Gospel According to Saint Luke*. 2nd edition. Translated by Theodosia Tomkinson. Etna, CA: Center for Traditionalist Orthodox Studies, 2003.

Andersen, Francis I., and Richard S. Hess. *Names in the Study of Biblical History: David, Yhwh Names, and the Role of Personal Names*. Buried History Monograph 2. Melbourne: Australian Institute of Archaeology, 2007.

Anderson, Gary A. *A Time to Mourn, A Time to Dance: The Expression of Grief and Joy in Israelite Religion*. Pennsylvania: Pennsylvania State University Press, 1991.

Anderson, Ken. *Little Book of Where to Find it in the Bible: The Ultimate A to Z Resource Fully Illustrated, Hundreds of Contemporary Topics, For Users of KJV, NIV, NKJV, CEV, LB, NRSV, and Other Popular Translations*. Nashville: Thomas Nelson, 2001.

Annas, Julia. *The Morality of Happiness*. New York: Oxford University Press, 1993.

Anselm. *Why God Became Man: Cur Deus Homo*. Translated by Jasper Hopkins and Herbert Richardson. Queenston, Ontario: E. Mellen Press, 1985.

Aquinas, Thomas. *Existence and Nature of God (1a.2–11)*. Translated by Timothy McDermott. Cambridge: Blackfriars and New York: McGraw-Hill, 1964.

Argyle, Michael. "Causes and Correlates of Happiness." In *Well-Being: The Foundations of Hedonic Psychology*, edited by Daniel Kahneman, Edward Diener, and Norbert Schwarz, 353–73. New York: Russell Sage Foundation, 1999.

———. *The Psychology of Happiness*. 2nd edition. New York: Routledge, 2001.

Aristotle. *Nicomachean Ethics*. Translated by F. E. Peters. Reprint edition. New York: Barnes and Noble, 2004.

Arlandson, James Malcolm. *Women, Class, and Society in Early Christianity: Models from Luke-Acts*. Peabody, MA: Hendrickson, 1997.

Arnold, Clinton E. "Joy." In *The Anchor Bible Dictionary*, edited by David Noel Freedman, et al., 3:1022–23. 6 volumes. New York: Doubleday, 1992.

Athanasius. *Contra Gentes and De Incarnatione*. Translated by Robert W. Thompson. Oxford Early Christian Texts. Oxford: Oxford University Press, 1971.

Attridge, Harold W., and Robert A. Oden, Jr. *Philo of Byblos, the Phoenician History: Introduction, Critical Text, Translation, Notes*. Catholic Biblical Quarterly Monograph Series 9. Washington, DC: Catholic Biblical Association of America, 1981.

Audi, Robert, ed. *The Cambridge Dictionary of Philosophy*. 2nd edition. Cambridge: Cambridge University Press, 1999.

Auld, A. Graeme. "Creation and Land: Sources and Exegesis." In *Joshua Retold: Synoptic Perspectives*, 63–68. Old Testament Studies. Edinburgh: T & T Clark, 1998.

Baird, J. Arthur. *Rediscovering the Power of the Gospels: Jesus' Theology of the Kingdom*. Wooster, Ohio: Iona, 1982.

Baird, Julia. "Blacks Are Getting Happier: Whites Are Not, Ask Your Mother Why." *Newsweek* (September 6, 2010): 20.

Bal, Mieke. *Narratology: Introduction to the Theory of Narrative*. 3rd edition. Toronto: University of Toronto Press, 2009.

Balentine, Samuel E. *The Torah's Vision of Worship*. Overtures to Biblical Theology. Minneapolis: Fortress, 1999.

Balswick, Jack O., and Judith K. Balswick. *The Family: A Christian Perspective on the Contemporary Home*. 3rd edition. Grand Rapids: Baker Academic, 2007.

Balswick, Jack O., Pamela Ebstyne King, and Kevin S. Reimer. *The Reciprocating Self: Human Development in Theological Perspective*. Downers Grove, IL: InterVarsity Press, 2005.

Baltzer, Klaus. *Deutero-Isaiah: A Commentary on Isaiah 40–55*. Translated by M. Kohl. Edited by Peter Machinist. Hermeneia. Minneapolis: Fortress, 2001.

Barbour, Robin, ed. *The Kingdom of God and Human Society: Essays by Members of the Scripture, Theology, and Society Group*. Edinburgh: T & T Clark, 1993.

Barr, James. *The Semantics of Biblical Language*. London: Oxford University Press, 1961.

Barth, Karl. *Church Dogmatics*. 13 volumes. Translated by G.W. Bromiley. Edinburgh: T & T Clark, 1970–1977.

Bartholomew, Craig G. *Ecclesiastes*. Baker Commentary on the Old Testament Wisdom and Psalms. Grand Rapids: Baker Academic, 2009.

Bartlett, Robert C., and Susan D. Collins. *Aristotle's Nicomachean Ethics*. Chicago: University of Chicago, 2011.

Barton, John. "Ethics in the Book of Isaiah." In *Writing and Reading the Scroll of Isaiah: Studies of an Interpretive Tradition*, edited by C. Broyles and C. Evans, 1:67–77. 2 volumes. Vetus Testamentum Supplements 70. Brill: Leiden, 1997.

Bass, Dorothy C. and Craig Dykstra, eds. *For Life Abundant: Practical Theology, Theological Education, and Christian Ministry*. Grand Rapids: Eerdmans, 2008.

Bassler, Jouette M. "Joy." In *HarperCollins Bible Dictionary*, edited by P. J. Achtemeier et al., 548–49. 2nd edition. San Francisco: HarperSanFrancisco, 1996.

———. *Navigating Paul: An Introduction to Key Theological Concepts*. Louisville: Westminster John Knox, 2007.

Bauckham, Richard. *The Fate of the Dead: Studies on the Jewish and Christian Apocalypses*. Novum Testamentum Supplements 93. Leiden: Brill, 1998.

Bauer, Jack J., Dan P. McAdams, and Jennifer L. Pals. "Narrative Identity and Eudaimonic Well-Being." *Journal of Happiness Studies* 9 (2008): 81–104.

Bauer, Jack J., Dan P. McAdams, and April R. Sakaeda. "Interpreting the Good Life: Growth Memories in the Lives of Mature, Happy People." *Journal of Personality and Social Psychology* 88 (2005): 203–17.

Beale, Gregory K. *The Book of Revelation*. New International Greek Text Commentary. Grand Rapids: Eerdmans, 1998.

———. *John's Use of the Old Testament in Revelation*. Journal for the Study of the New Testament Supplement Series 166. Sheffield: Sheffield Academic Press, 1999.

Beck, Richard. "Defensive versus Existential Religion: Is Religious Defensiveness Predictive of Worldview Defense?" *Journal of Psychology and Theology* 34 (2006): 142–52.

Begrich, Joachim. "Das priesterliche Heilsorakel." *Zeitschrift für die alttestamentliche Wissenschaft* 52 (1934): 81–92.

———. *Gesammelte Studien zum Alten Testament*. Edited by Walther Zimmerli. Theologische Bücherei 21. München: Chr. Kaiser, 1964.

Beierwaltes, Werner. *Regio Beatitudinis: Augustine's Concept of Happiness*. Villanova: Augustinian Institute, Villanova University, 1981.

Bekoff, Marc. *The Emotional Lives of Animals: A Leading Scientist Explores Animal Joy, Sorrow, and Empathy—and Why They Matter*. Novato, CA: New World Library, 2007.

Ben-Shahar, Tal. *Happier: Learn the Secrets to Daily Joy and Lasting Fulfillment*. New York: McGraw-Hill, 2007.

———. *Being Happy: You Don't Have to Be Perfect to Lead a Richer, Happier Life*. New York: McGraw Hill, 2010.

———. *Even Happier: A Gratitude Journal for Daily Joy and Lasting Fulfillment*. New York: McGraw Hill, 2010.

Berridge, Kent C., and Morten L. Kringelbach. "Affective Neuroscience of Pleasure: Reward in Humans and Animals." *Psychopharmacology* 199 (2008): 457–80.

Best, Ernest. "Matthew V.3." *New Testament Studies* 7 (1960–1961): 255–58.

Betz, Hans D. "The Beatitudes of the Sermon on the Mount (Matt. 5:3–12): Observations on Their Literary Form and Theological Significance." In *Essays on the Sermon on the Mount*, 17–36. Translated by L. L. Welborn. Philadelphia: Fortress, 1985.

———. *The Sermon on the Mount*. Edited by Adela Yarbro Collins. Hermeneia. Minneapolis: Fortress, 1995.

Biswas-Diener, Robert. *Practicing Positive Psychology Coaching: Assessment, Activities, and Strategies for Success*. Hoboken, NJ: John Wiley and Sons, 2010.

Biswas-Diener, Robert, and Ben Dean. *Positive Psychology Coaching: Putting the Science of Happiness to Work for Your Clients*. Hoboken, NJ: John Wiley and Sons, 2007.

Black Dog Institute. "Fact Sheet: Happiness." Online at www.blackdoginstitute.org.au/docs/Happiness.pdf. Accessed September 23, 2011.

Blenkinsopp, Joseph. *Isaiah 56–66: A New Translation with Introduction and Commentary*. Anchor Bible 19B. New York: Doubleday, 2003.

Bock, Darrell L. *Luke*. 2 volumes. Baker Exegetical Commentary on the New Testament 3. Grand Rapids: Baker, 1994–96.

Borg, Marcus, and John Dominic Crossan. *The First Paul: Reclaiming the Radical Visionary Behind the Church's Conservative Icon*. San Francisco: HarperSanFrancisco, 2009.

Bovon, François. *Luke 1: A Commentary on the Gospel of Luke 1:1–9:50*. Translated by Christine M. Thomas. Edited by Helmut Koester. Hermeneia. Minneapolis: Fortress, 2002.

Braude, William G. *The Midrash on Psalms*. 2 volumes. Yale Judaica Series 13. New Haven: Yale University Press, 1959.

Braumann, G. "Zum traditionsgeschichtlichen Problem der Seligpreisungen Mt V 3–12." *Novum Testamentum* 4 (1960): 253–60.

Brichto, Herbert Chanan. "Kin, Cult, Land and Afterlife—A Biblical Complex." *Hebrew Union College Annual* 44 (1973): 1–54.

Bright, John. *The Kingdom of God: The Biblical Concept and Its Meaning for the Church*. Nashville: Abingdon, 1984 (original edition 1953).

Broer, Ingo. *Die Seligpreisungen der Bergpredigt: Studien zu ihrer Überlieferung und Interpretation*. Bonner biblische Beiträge 61. Bonn: Peter Hanstein, 1986.

Brooke, George J. "The Wisdom of Matthew's Beatitudes (4QBeat and Mt 5:3–12)." *Scripture Bulletin* 19 (1989): 35–41.

Brown, Raymond E. *An Introduction to the New Testament*. Anchor Bible Reference Library. New York: Doubleday, 1997.

Brown, Raymond E., et al., eds. *Mary in the New Testament: A Collaborative Assessment by Protestant and Roman Catholic Scholars*. Philadelphia: Fortress and New York: Paulist, 1978.

Brown, William P. *The Ethos of the Cosmos: The Genesis of Moral Imagination in the Bible*. Grand Rapids: Eerdmans, 1999.

———. *Ecclesiastes*. Interpretation. Louisville: John Knox, 2000.

———. *Seeing the Psalms: A Theology of Metaphor*. Louisville: Westminster John Knox, 2002.

———. "Joy and the Art of Cosmic Maintenance: An Ecology of Play in Psalm 104." In *"And God Saw That It Was Good": Essays on Creation in God in Honor of Terence E. Fretheim*, edited by F. Gaiser and M. Throntveit, 23–32. Word and World Supplement Series 5. St. Paul: Luther Seminary, 2006.

Brueggemann, Walter. "The Formfulness of Grief." *Interpretation* 31 (1977): 263–75.

———. "Psalms and the Life of Faith: A Suggested Typology of Function," *Journal for the Study of the Old Testament* 17 (1980): 3–32.

———. *The Message of the Psalms: A Theological Commentary*. Augsburg Old Testament Studies. Minneapolis: Augsburg, 1984.

———. "Bounded by Obedience and Praise: The Psalms as Canon." *Journal for the Study of the Old Testament* 50 (1991): 63–92

———. "Praise and the Psalms: A Politics of Glad Abandonment," *The Hymn* 43/3 (1992): 14–19; 43/4(1992): 14–18.

———. *The Psalms and the Life of Faith*. Edited by Patrick D. Miller. Minneapolis: Fortress, 1995.

———. *Theology of the Old Testament: Testimony, Dispute, Advocacy*. Minneapolis: Fortress, 1997.

———. *Peace*. St. Louis: Chalice, 2001.

Brueggemann, Walter, and Patrick D. Miller. "Psalm 73 as a Canonical Marker." *Journal for the Study of the Old Testament* 72 (1996): 45–56.

Buchanan, George W. "Matthean Beatitudes and Traditional Promises." In *New Synoptic Studies*, edited by William R. Farmer, 161–84. Macon: Mercer University Press, 1983.

———. *Jesus: The King and His Kingdom*. Macon: Mercer University Press, 1984.

Bultmann, Rudolf. *Jesus and the Word*. Translated by Louise P. Smith and Erminie H. Lantero. New York: Scribner's, 1958 (German original 1926).

Buzy, Denis. "Béatitudes." In *Dictionnaire de Spiritualité* 1 (1937): 1298–1310.

Callahan, Sidney. *Called to Happiness: Where Faith and Psychology Meet*. Maryknoll: Orbis, 2011.

Campbell, Edward F. *Ruth: A New Translation with Introduction, Notes, and Commentary*. Anchor Bible 7. New York: Doubleday, 1975.

Carey, Greg. *Ultimate Things: An Introduction to Jewish and Christian Apocalyptic Literature*. St. Louis: Chalice Press, 2005.

———. "A Man's Choice: Wealth Imagery and the Two Cities of the Book of Revelation." In *A Feminist Companion to the Apocalypse of John*, edited by Amy-Jill Levine and Maria Mayo Robbins, 147–58. New York: Continuum, 2009.

Carr, David M. "Passion for God: A Center in Biblical Theology." *Horizons in Biblical Theology* 23 (2001): 1–24.

Chadwick, Henry. *Saint Augustine: Confessions*. Oxford: Oxford University Press, 1991.

Chapman, Mark. "The Kingdom of God and Ethics: From Ritschl to Liberation Theology." In *The Kingdom of God and Human Society: Essays by Members of the Scripture, Theology, and Society Group*, edited by Robin Barbour, 140–63. Edinburgh: T & T Clark, 1993.

Charlesworth, James H., ed. *The Old Testament Pseudepigrapha, Volume 1: Apocalyptic Literature and Testaments*. Anchor Bible Reference Library. New York: Doubleday, 1983.

Charry, Ellen T. *By the Renewing of Your Minds: The Pastoral Function of Christian Doctrine*. New York: Oxford, 1997.

———. *God and the Art of Happiness*. Grand Rapids: Eerdmans, 2010.

Childs, Brevard S. *Isaiah*. Old Testament Library. Louisville: Westminster John Knox, 2001.

Chilton, Bruce D. *God in Strength: Jesus' Announcement of the Kingdom*. Studien zum Neuen Testament und seiner Umwelt. Freistadt: Verlag F. Plöchl, 1979.

———. *Pure Kingdom: Jesus' Vision of God*. Grand Rapids: Eerdmans, 1996.

———. "Kingdom of God, Kingdom of Heaven." In *The New Interpreter's Dictionary of the Bible*, edited by Katharine Doob Sakenfeld, et al., 3:512–23. 5 volumes. Nashville: Abingdon, 2006–2009.

Chilton, Bruce D., ed. *The Kingdom of God in the Teaching of Jesus*. Issues in Religion and Theology 5. Philadelphia: Fortress, 1984.

Chilton, Bruce D., and J. I. H. McDonald. *Jesus and the Ethics of the Kingdom*. Grand Rapids: Eerdmans, 1987.

Chittister, Joan. *Happiness*. Grand Rapids: Eerdmans, 2011.

Clines, David J.A. *The Theme of the Pentateuch*. 2nd edition. Sheffield: Sheffield Academic Press, 1997.

Conoley, Collie Wyatt, and Jane Close Conoley. *Positive Psychology and Family Therapy: Creative Techniques and Practical Tools for Guiding Change and Enhancing Growth*. Hoboken, NJ: John Wiley and Sons, 2009.

Conzelmann, Hans. *The Theology of St. Luke*. London: SCM, 1960.

Cosgrove, Charles H. "The Divine Δεῖ in Luke-Acts." *Novum Testamentum* 26 (1984): 168–90.

Cosmides, Leda, and John Tooby. "Evolutionary Psychology and the Emotions." In *Handbook of Emotions*, edited by Michael Lewis and Jeannette M. Haviland-Jones, 91–115. 2nd edition. New York: Guilford, 2000.

Cottone, Robert Rocco. *Toward a Positive Psychology of Religion: Belief Science in the Postmodern Era*. Winchester, UK: O-Books, 2011.

Creach, Jerome. *Yahweh as Refuge and the Editing of the Hebrew Psalter*. Journal for the Study of the Old Testament Supplement Series 217. Sheffield: Sheffield Academic Press, 1996.

Crenshaw, James L. *Ecclesiastes: A Commentary*. Old Testament Library. Philadelphia: Westminster, 1987.

Crichton, Michael. *Jurassic Park*. New York: Ballentine, 1990.

Crook, Zeba. *Reconceptualising Conversion: Patronage, Loyalty, and Conversion in the Religions of the Ancient Mediterranean*. Beiheft zur Zeitschrift für die neutestamentliche Wissenschaft 130. Berlin: Walter de Gruyter, 2004.

Crystal, David. *Language Death*. Cambridge: Cambridge University Press, 2000.

Csikszentmihalyi, Mihaly. "If we are so rich, why aren't we happy?" *American Psychologist* 54 (1999): 821–27.

Cunningham, Scott. *'Through Many Tribulations': The Theology of Persecution in Luke-Acts*. Journal for the Study of the New Testament Supplement Series 142. Sheffield: Sheffield Academic Press, 1997.

Dahlsgaard, Katherine, Christopher Peterson, and Martin E. P. Seligman. "Shared Virtue: The Convergence of Valued Human Strengths across Culture and History." *Review of General Psychology* 9 (2005): 203–13.

Dalbert, Claudia. "Beliefs in a Just World as a Buffer Against Anger." *Social Justice Research* 15 (2002): 123–45.

Daley, Brian E. *The Hope of the Early Church: A Handbook of Patristic Eschatology*. Cambridge: Cambridge University Press, 1991.

Damasio, Antonio R. *Descartes' Error: Emotion, Reason, and the Human Brain*. New York: Putnam, 1994.

Davids, Peter. *The Epistle of James: A Commentary on the Greek Text*. New International Greek Testament Commentary. Grand Rapids: Eerdmans, 1986.

Davies, W. D., and Dale C. Allison, Jr. *The Gospel According to Saint Matthew*. 3 volumes. International Critical Commentary. Edinburgh: T & T Clark, 1988–1997.

Davis, Christopher G., and Susan Nolen-Hoeksema. "Making Sense of Loss, Perceiving Benefits, and Posttraumatic Growth." In *Oxford Handbook of Positive Psychology*, 641–49. 2nd edition. Edited by Shane J. Lopez and C.R. Snyder. New York: Oxford University Press, 2011.

Davis, Ellen F. *Proverbs, Ecclesiastes, and the Song of Songs*. Westminster Bible Companion. Louisville: Westminster John Knox, 2000.

———. *Scripture, Culture, and Agriculture: An Agrarian Reading of the Bible*. New York: Cambridge University Press, 2009.

De Botton, Alain. *The Architecture of Happiness*. New York: Vintage, 2008.

deClaissée-Walford, Nancy L. *Introduction to the Psalms: A Song from Ancient Israel*. St. Louis: Chalice, 2004.

———. "Tree of Knowledge, Tree of Life." In *The New Interpreter's Dictionary of the Bible*, edited by Katharine Doob Sakenfeld, et al., 5:660–61. 5 volumes. Nashville: Abingdon, 2006–2009.

Devereux, David Trent. "Eudaimonism." In *The Cambridge Dictionary of Philosophy*, 291. 2nd edition. Edited by Robert Audi. Cambridge: Cambridge University Press, 1999.

Diagnostic and Statistical Manual of Mental Disorders (4th ed., text revision; Arlington, VA: American Psychiatric Association, 2000).

Diener, Ed. *The Science of Well-Being: The Collected Works of Ed Diener*. New York: Springer Science and Business Media, 2009.

———. "Positive Psychology: Past, Present, and Future." In *Oxford Handbook of Positive Psychology*, 7–11. 2nd edition. Edited by Shane J. Lopez and C. R. Snyder. New York: Oxford University Press, 2011.

Diener, Ed, and Robert Biswas-Diener. *Happiness: Unlocking the Mysteries of Psychological Wealth*. Malden, MA: Blackwell, 2008.

Diener, Ed, Richard E. Lucas, and Shigehiro Oishi. "Subjective Well-Being: The Science of Happiness and Life Satisfaction." In *Handbook of Positive Psychology*, edited by C. R. Snyder and S. J. Lopez, 63–73. New York: Oxford University Press, 2002.

Dobbs-Allsopp, F.W. "The Psalms and Lyric Verse." In *The Evolution of Rationality: Interdisciplinary Essays in Honor of J. Wentzel van Huyssteen*, 346–79. Edited by F. LeRon Shults. Grand Rapids: Eerdmans, 2006.

Dodd, C.H. *The Parables of the Kingdom*. Revised edition. New York: Scribner's, 1961.

———. "The Beatitudes: A Form-Critical Study." In *More New Testament Studies*, 1–10. Manchester: Manchester University Press, 1968.

Donaldson, Stewart I., Mihaly Csikszentmihalyi, and Jeanne Nakamura, eds. *Applied Positive Psychology: Improving Everyday Life, Health, Schools, Work, and Society*. New York: Routledge, 2011.

Dorian, Nancy C., ed. *Investigating Obsolescence: Studies in Language Contraction and Death*. Cambridge: Cambridge University Press, 1989.

Downing, F. Gerald. "Honor." In *The New Interpreter's Dictionary of the Bible*, edited by Katharine Doob Sakenfeld, et al., 2:884–85. 5 volumes. Nashville: Abingdon, 2006–2009.

Drobner, Hubertus R., and Albert Viciano, eds. *Gregory of Nyssa: Homilies on the Beatitudes: An English Version with Commentary and Supporting Studies: Proceedings of the Eighth International Colloquium on Gregory of Nyssa (Paderborn, September 14–18, 1998)*. Supplements to Vigiliae Christianae 52. Leiden: Brill, 2000.

Duling, Dennis. "The Kingdom of God in the Teaching of Jesus." *Word and World* 2 (1982): 117–26.

———. "Norman Perrin and the Kingdom of God: Review and Response." *Journal of Religion* 64 (1984): 468–83.

———. "Kingdom of God, Kingdom of Heaven." In *The Anchor Bible Dictionary*, edited by David Noel Freedman, et al., 4:49–69. 6 volumes. New York: Doubleday, 1992.

Dupont, Jacques. *Les Béatitudes*. 3 volumes. Volume 1, 2nd edition, Bruges: Abbaye de Saint-André, 1958. Volume 2, Paris: Gabalda, 1969. Volume 3, Paris: Gabalda, 1973.

Dworkin, Ronald W. *Artificial Happiness: The Dark Side of the New Happy Class*. New York: Carroll & Graf, 2006.

Edwards, Keith J., and Todd W. Hall. "Illusory Spiritual Health: The Role of Defensiveness in Understanding and Assessing Spiritual Health." In *Spiritual Formation, Counseling, and Psychotherapy*, edited by Todd W. Hall and Mark R. McMinn, 261–75. Hauppauge, NY: Nova Sciences Publishers, 2003.

Ehrman, Bart D. *The Apostolic Fathers*. 2 volumes. Loeb Classical Library 24–25. Cambridge, MA: Harvard University Press, 2003.

Eichrodt, Walther. *Theology of the Old Testament*. 2 volumes. Old Testament Library. Philadelphia: Westminster, 1961.

Eißler, Friedmann. "Glück." In *Calwer Bibellexikon*, edited by O. Betz et al., 1:452. 2 volumes. Stuttgart: Calwer, 2003.

Elliott, Neil. *Liberating Paul: The Justice of God and the Politics of the Apostle*. Maryknoll, NY: Orbis, 1994.

Emmons, Robert A., and Michael E. McCullough, eds. *The Psychology of Gratitude*. New York: Oxford University Press, 2004.

Erikson, Erik H. *Childhood and Society*. 2nd edition. New York: Norton, 1964.

Esler, Philip F. *Conflict and Identity in Romans: The Social Setting of Paul's Letter*. Minneapolis: Augsburg Fortress, 2003.

———. "Paul's Contestation of Israel's (Ethnic) Memory of Abraham in Galatians 3." *Biblical Theology Bulletin* 36 (2006): 23–35.

Eustace, Nicole. "Happiness." In *Encyclopedia of the New American Nation*, edited by Paul Finkelman, 2:145. 2 volumes. Detroit: Charles Scribner's Sons, 2006.

Evans, C.F. *Saint Luke*. TPI New Testament Commentaries. London: SCM, 1990.

Fabry, H.-J. "רוח." In *Theological Dictionary of the Old Testament*, edited by G. Johannes Botterweck, et al., 13:367–68. 15 volumes. Translated by J. T. Willis et al.; Grand Rapids: Eerdmans, 1974–2006.

Fiddes, Paul S. *The Creative Suffering of God*. Oxford: Clarendon, 1988.

Fitzmyer, Joseph A. *The Gospel According to Luke*. 2 volumes. Anchor Bible 28. New York: Doubleday, 1981–85.

Flesher, LeAnn Snow. "Rapid Change of Mood: Oracles of Salvation, Certainty of a Hearing, or Rhetorical Play?" In *My Words Are Lovely: Studies in the Rhetoric of the Psalms*, 33–45. Edited by Robert L. Foster and David M. Howard, Jr. Library of Hebrew Bible/Old Testament Studies 467. New York: T & T Clark, 2008.

Flint, Peter W. *The Dead Sea Psalms Scrolls and the Book of Psalms*. Studies on the Texts of the Desert of Judah 17. Leiden: Brill, 1997.

Flint, Peter W., and Patrick D. Miller, Jr. *The Book of Psalms: Composition and Reception*. Supplements to Vetus Testamentum 99. Leiden: Brill, 2005.

Flusser, David. "Blessed are the Poor in Spirit . . ." *Israel Exploration Journal* 10 (1960): 1–13.

———. "Some Notes on the Beatitudes (Matt 5:3–12, Luke 6:20–26)." *Immanuel* 8 (1978): 37–47.

Fontaine, Carole R. "Happiness." In *The New Interpreter's Dictionary of the Bible*, edited by Katharine Doob Sakenfeld, et al., 2:734. 5 volumes. Nashville: Abingdon, 2006–2009.

Forgas, Joseph P. "Mood and the Perception of Unusual People: Affective Asymmetry in Memory and Social Judgments." *European Journal of Social Psychology* 22 (1992): 531–47.

———. "On Bad Mood and Peculiar People: Affect and Person Typicality in Impression Formation." *Journal of Personality and Social Psychology* 62 (1992): 863–75.

Forgas, Joseph P., ed. *Handbook of Affect and Social Cognition*. Mahwah, NJ: Lawrence Erlbaum, 2001.

Foster, Robert L., and David M. Howard, Jr., eds. *My Words Are Lovely: Studies in the Rhetoric of the Psalms*. Library of Hebrew Bible/Old Testament Studies 467. New York: T & T Clark, 2008.

Fowler, Jeaneane D. *Theophoric Personal Names in Ancient Hebrew: A Comparative Study*. Journal for the Study of the Old Testament Supplement Series 49. Sheffield: JSOT Press, 1988.

Fox, Elaine. *Emotion Science: Cognitive and Neuroscientific Approaches to Understanding Human Emotions*. New York: Palgrave Macmillan, 2003.

Fox, Michael V. *Proverbs 1–9: A New Translation with Introduction and Commentary*. Anchor Bible 18A. New York: Doubleday, 2000.

Frankenmölle, Hubert. "Die Makarismen (Mt 5,1–12; Lk 6,20–23): Motive und Umfang der redaktionellen Komposition." *Biblische Zeitschrift* 15 (1971): 52–75.

Franklin, Samuel S. *The Psychology of Happiness: A Good Human Life*. Cambridge: Cambridge University Press, 2010.

Fretheim, Terence E. *The Suffering of God: An Old Testament Perspective*. Overtures to Biblical Theology. Philadelphia: Fortress, 1984.

———. "Nature's Praise of God in the Psalms." *Ex Auditu* 3 (1987): 16–30.

———. "Christology and the Old Testament." In *Who Do You Say That I Am? Essays on Christology*, edited by Mark A. Powell and David Bauer, 201–15. Louisville: Westminster John Knox, 2000.

———. *Jeremiah*. Macon: Smyth & Helwys, 2002.

———. *God and World in the Old Testament: A Relational Theology of Creation*. Nashville: Abingdon, 2005.

———. *Creation Untamed: The Bible, God, and Natural Disasters*. Grand Rapids: Baker Academic, 2010.

Friedman, Edwin H. *Generation to Generation: Family Processes in Church and Synagogue*. New York: Guilford, 1985.

Fuller, Reginald H. *The Mission and Achievement of Jesus*. Studies in Biblical Theology 1/12. London: SCM, 1954.

Gager, John G. *Kingdom and Community: The Social World of Early Christianity*. Englewood Cliffs, NJ: Prentice-Hall, 1975.

Gentry, W. Doyle. *Happiness for Dummies*. Hoboken, NJ: Wiley, 2008.

Gertz, Jan. "Antibabylonische Polemik im priesterlichen Schöpfungsbericht?" *Zeitschrift für Theologie und Kirke* 106 (2009): 137–55.

Gilbert, Daniel. *Stumbling on Happiness*. New York: Vintage, 2006.

Ginsburg, Christian D. *Introduction to the Massoretico-Critical Edition of the Hebrew Bible*. Reprint edition. New York: Ktav, 1966.

Glancy, Jennifer A. "Boasting of Beatings." *Journal of Biblical Literature* 123 (2004): 99–135.

Goetz, Ronald. "The Suffering God: The Rise of a New Orthodoxy." *Christian Century* 103 (1986): 385–89.

Golding, William. *Lord of the Flies.* New York: Coward-McCann, 1955.

Goldingay, John. *Isaiah.* NIBC. Peabody, MA: Hendrickson, 2001.

Gosling, J. C. B. "Hedonism." In *The Oxford Companion to Philosophy*, 363–64. 2nd edition. Edited by Ted Honderich. Oxford: Oxford University Press, 2005.

Graham, Billy. *The Secret of Happiness: Jesus' Teaching on Happiness as Expressed in the Beatitudes.* Garden City: Doubleday, 1955.

Greene-McCreight, Kathryn. *Darkness Is My Only Companion: A Christian Response to Mental Illness.* Grand Rapids: Brazos, 2006.

Griffin, Susan. *Pornography and Silence: Culture's Revenge against Nature.* New York: Harper & Row, 1981.

Grinde, B. "Happiness in the Perspective of Evolutionary Psychology." *Journal of Happiness Studies* 3 (2002): 331–54.

Gruber, Mayer I. *Aspects of Nonverbal Communication in the Ancient Near East.* 2 volumes. Studia Pohl 12. Rome: Biblical Institute Press, 1980.

Guelich, Robert. "The Matthean Beatitudes: 'Entrance Requirements' or Eschatological Blessings?" *Journal of Biblical Literature* 95 (1976): 415–34.

———. *The Sermon on the Mount: A Foundation for Understanding.* Waco: Word, 1982.

Gulin, Eilis Gideon. *Die Freude im Neuen Testament.* Helsinki: Helsinki Druckerei-A.G. der Finnischen Literatur-Gesellschaft, 1932–36.

Gunkel, Hermann. *Die Psalmen.* 5th edition. Göttingen: Vandenhoeck & Ruprecht, 1968.

Haidt, Jonathan. *The Happiness Hypothesis: Finding Modern Truth in Ancient Wisdom.* New York: Basic Books, 2006.

Halwani, Raja. "Homer and Aristotle." In *The Simpsons and Philosophy: The D'oh! of Homer*, edited by W. Irwin, M. T. Conard, and A. J. Skoble, 7–24. Chicago: Open Court, 2001.

Hamm, M. Dennis. *The Beatitudes in Context: What Luke and Matthew Meant.* Zacchaeus Studies: NT. Wilmington, Delaware: Glazier, 1990.

Hammer, Mitchell R., Milton J. Bennett, and Richard Wiseman. "Measuring Intercultural Sensitivity: The Intercultural Development Inventory." *International Journal of Intercultural Relations* 27 (2003): 421–43.

Hanson, K. C. "How Honorable! How Shameful! A Cultural Analysis of Matthew's Makarisms and Reproaches." *Semeia* 68 (1994): 81–111.

Hao, Lingxin, and Richard W. Johnson. "Economic, Cultural, and Social Origins of Emotional Well-Being: Comparison of Immigrants and Natives at Midlife." *Research on Aging* 22 (2000): 599–629.

Harnack, Adolf von. *What is Christianity?* New York: Harper & Row, 1957 (German original 1900).

Harrison, K. David. *The Last Speakers: The Quest to Save the World's Most Endangered Languages.* Washington, DC: National Geographic Society, 2010.

Hartshorne, Charles. *Reality as Social Process: Studies in Metaphysics and Religion.* Glencoe, IL: Free Press, 1953.

Hartshorne, Charles, and William L. Reese, eds. *Philosophers Speak of God.* Chicago: University of Chicago Press, 1953.

Hauck, F., and G. Bertram. "*makarios* ktl." In *Theological Dictionary of the New Testament,* edited by G. Kittel and G. Friedrich, 4:362–70. 10 volumes. Translated by G. W. Bromiley. Grand Rapids: Eerdmans: 1964–1976.

Heffelfinger, Katie M. *I Am Large, I Contain Multitudes: Lyric Cohesion and Conflict in Second Isaiah.* Biblical Interpretation Series 105. Leiden: Brill, 2011.

Hefner, Philip. *Faith and the Vitalities of History: A Theological Study Based on the Work of Albrecht Ritschl.* New York: Harper & Row, 1966.

Heidegger, Martin. *Being and Time.* Translated by John Macquarrie and Edward Robinson. London: SCM, 1962.

Heim, Knut M. *Like Grapes of Gold Set in Silver: An Interpretation of Proverbial Clusters in Proverbs 10:1–22:16.* Beihefte zur Zeitschrift für die alttestamentliche Wissenschaft 273. Berlin: Walter de Gruyter, 2001.

Held, Barbara S. "The Negative Side of Positive Psychology." *Journal of Humanistic Psychology* 44 (2004): 9–46.

Hellholm, David. "'Rejoice and Be Glad, for Your Reward is Great in Heaven': An Attempt as Solving the Structural Problem of Matt. 5:11–12." In *Festschrift Günter Wagner,* 47–86. International Theological Studies: Contributions of Baptist Scholars 1. Edited by the Faculty of Baptist Theological Seminary Rüschlikon. Bern: P. Lang, 1994.

Helm, David, and Gail Schoonmaker. *The Big Picture Story Bible.* Wheaton, IL: Crossway, 2004.

Hengel, Martin. *Judaism and Hellenism: Studies in Their Encounter in Palestine during the Early Hellenistic Period.* 2 volumes. Translated by John Bowden. Philadelphia: Fortress, 1981.

———. "Zur matthäischen Bergpredigt und ihrem jüdischen Hintergrund." *Theologische Rundschau* 52 (1987): 327–400.

Hermisson, H.-J. "Observations on the Creation Theology in Wisdom." In *Creation in the Old Testament,* edited by Bernhard W. Anderson. Issues in Religion and Theology 6. Philadelphia: Fortress, 1984.

Heschel, Abraham J. *The Prophets.* Reprint edition. New York: Perennial Classics, 2001.

Hess, Richard S. *Studies in the Personal Names of Genesis 1–11.* Alter Orient und Altes Testament 234. Kevelaer: Verlag Butzon & Bercker and Neukirchen-Vluyn: Neukirchiner Verlag, 1993.

Hiers, Richard H. *The Kingdom of God in the Synoptic Tradition.* Gainesville: University of Florida Press, 1970.

————. *The Historical Jesus and the Kingdom of God: Present and Future in the Message and Ministry of Jesus.* University of Florida Humanities Monograph 38. Gainesville: University of Florida Press, 1973.

Hill, David. "Towards An Understanding of the 'Kingdom of God.'" *Irish Biblical Studies* 3 (1981): 62–76.

Hillers, Delbert R. "Study of Psalm 148." *Catholic Biblical Quarterly* 40 (1978): 322–34.

His Holiness the Dalai Lama and Howard C. Cutler. *The Art of Happiness: A Handbook of Living.* New York: Riverhead Books, 2009 (original: 1998).

Ho, Samuel M. Y., and Mike W. L. Cheung. "Using the Combined Etic-Emic Approach to Develop a Measurement of Interpersonal Subjective Well-Being in Chinese Populations." In *Oxford Handbook of Methods in Positive Psychology*, edited by Anthony D. Ong and Manfred H. M. van Dulmen, 139–52. New York: Oxford University Press, 2007.

Hock, Hans Henrich. *Principles of Historical Linguistics.* 2nd edition. Berlin: Mouton de Gruyter, 1991.

Holladay, Carl R. "The Beatitudes: Jesus' Recipe for Happiness?" In *Between Experience and Interpretation: Engaging the Writings of the New Testament*, edited by Mary F. Foskett and O. Wesley Allen, Jr., 83–102. Nashville: Abingdon, 2008.

Holloway, Paul A. *Consolation in Philippians: Philosophical Sources and Rhetorical Strategy.* Cambridge: Cambridge University Press, 2001.

Honderich, Ted., ed. *The Oxford Companion to Philosophy.* 2nd edition. Oxford: Oxford University Press, 2005.

Howard, David M., Jr. "Psalm 88 and the Rhetoric of Lament." In *My Words Are Lovely: Studies in the Rhetoric of the Psalms*, 132–46. Edited by Robert L. Foster and David M. Howard, Jr. Library of Hebrew Bible/Old Testament Studies 467. New York: T & T Clark, 2008.

Huang, Peter H., and Jeremy A. Blumenthal. "Positive Institutions, Law, and Policy." In *Oxford Handbook of Positive Psychology*, 589–97. Edited by C. R. Snyder and Shane J. Lopez. Oxford: Oxford University Press, 2009.

Huppert, Felicia A. "A Population Approach to Positive Psychology: The Potential for Population Interventions to Promote Well-Being and Prevent Disorder." In *Positive Psychology in Practice*, 693–709. Edited by P. Alex Linley and Stephen Joseph. Hoboken, NJ: Wiley, 2004.

Huppert, Felicia, Nick Baylis, and Barry Keverne, eds. *The Science of Wellbeing.* Oxford: Oxford University Press, 2006.

Humbert, Paul. "Laetari et exultare dans le vocabulaire religieux de l'ancien Testament." *Revue d'histoire et de philosophie religieuses* 22 (1942): 185–214.

Hvidberg, F. F. *Weeping and Laughter in the Old Testament: A Study of Canaanite-Israelite Religion.* Leiden: Brill, 1962.

Jackson, Bernard. *Wisdom Laws: A Study of the Mishpatim of Exodus 21:1–22:16.* Oxford: Oxford University Press, 2006.

James, William. *The Varieties of Religious Experience: A Study in Human Nature*. New York: Modern Library, 1958.

Jankowski, Peter J., and Marsha Vaughn. "Differentiation of Self and Spirituality: Empirical Explorations." *Counseling and Values* 53 (2009): 82–96.

Janowski, Bernd. *Konfliktgespräche mit Gott: Eine Anthropologie der Psalmen*. 3rd edition. Neukirchen-Vluyn: Neukirchener Verlag, 2003.

Janssen, Claudia, and Rainer Kessler. "Glück." In *Sozialgeschichtliches Wörterbuch zur Bibel*, edited by Frank Crüsemann et al., 219–20. Gütersloh: Gütersloher, 2009.

Janzen, Waldemar. "'Ašrê in the Old Testament." *Harvard Theological Review* 58 (1965): 215–26.

Jobling, David. "Wealth." In *The New Interpreter's Dictionary of the Bible*, edited by Katharine Doob Sakenfeld, et al., 5:826–27. 5 volumes. Nashville: Abingdon, 2006–2009.

Kähler, Christoph. "Studien zur Form-und Traditions-geschichte der biblischen Makarismen." 2 volumes. PhD diss., Jena, 1974.

Kahneman, Daniel, Edward Diener, and Norbert Schwarz, eds. *Well-Being: The Foundations of Hedonic Psychology*. New York: Russell Sage Foundation, 1999.

Kaminsky, Joel. *Yet I Loved Jacob: Reclaiming the Biblical Concept of Election*. Nashville: Abingdon, 2007.

Käsemann, Ernst. "The Saving Significance of the Death of Jesus in Paul." In *Perspectives on Paul*, 32–59. Translated by Margaret Kohl. Reprint edition. Mifflintown, PA: Sigler, 1996 (German original 1969).

Käser, Walter. "Beobachtungen zum alttestamentlichen Makarismus." *Zeitschrift für die alttestamentliche Wissenschaft* 82 (1970): 225–50.

Kaufman, Barry Neil. *Happiness Is a Choice*. New York: Fawcett, 1991.

Kayatz, Christa. *Studien zu Proverbien 1–9*. Wissenschaftliche Monographien zum Alten und Neuen Testament 22. Neukirchen-Vluyn: Neukirchener Verlag, 1966.

Keel, Othmar. *Symbolism of the Biblical World: Ancient Near Eastern Iconography and the Book of Psalms*. Translated by T. J. Hallett. Reprint edition. Winona Lake: Eisenbrauns, 1997.

Kelber, Werner H. *The Kingdom in Mark: A New Place and a New Time*. Philadelphia: Fortress, 1974.

Keltner, Dacher, and Jonathan Haidt. "Social Functions of Emotions." In *Emotions: Current Issues and Future Directions*, edited by Tracy Mayne and George A. Bonanno, 192–213. New York: Guilford Press, 2001.

Kennedy, George A. *Aristotle: On Rhetoric: A Theory of Civic Discourse*. 2nd edition. New York: Oxford University Press, 2007.

Kerr, Michael E., and Murray Bowen. *Family Evaluation: An Approach Based on Bowen Theory*. New York: Norton, 1988.

Keyes, Corey L. M., and Jonathan Haidt, eds. *Flourishing: Positive Psychology and the Life Well-Lived*. Washington, DC: American Psychological Association, 2003.

Kieffer, R. "Wisdom and Blessing in the Beatitudes of St. Matthew and St. Luke." In *Studia evangelica 6: Papers Presented to the Fourth International Congress on New Testament Studies held at Oxford, 1969*, edited by Elizabeth A. Livingstone, 291–95. Texte und Untersuchungen zur Geschichte der altchristlichen Literatur 112. Berlin: Akademie-Verlag, 1973.

——. "Weisheit und Segen als Grundmotive der Seligpreisungen bei Mattäus und Lukas." In *Theologie aus dem Norden*, edited by A. Fuchs, 29–43. Studien zum Neuen Testament und seiner Umwelt. Linz: Studien zum Neuen Testament und seiner Umwelt, 1977.

Kim, Uichol, Kuo-Shu Yang, and Kwang-Kuo Hwang, eds. *Indigenous and Cultural Psychology: Understanding People in Context*. New York: Springer, 2006.

King, Karen. "Kingdom in the Gospel of Thomas." *Foundations and Facets Forum* 3 (1987): 48–97.

King, Martin Luther, Jr. "I've Been to the Mountaintop." Accessed July 12, 2011. www.americanrhetoric.com/speeches/mlkivebeentothemountaintop.htm.

Kingsbury, Jack Dean. *Matthew: Structure, Christology, Kingdom*. Philadelphia: Fortress, 1975.

Kirkpatrick, Lee A. *Attachment, Evolution, and the Psychology of Religion*. New York: Guilford, 2005.

Klein, Günther. "'Reich Gottes' als biblischer Zentralbegriff." *Evangelische Theologie* 30 (1970): 642–70.

Klein, Stefan. *The Science of Happiness: How Our Brains Make Us Happy—and What We Can Do to Get Happier*. Translated by Stephen Lehmann. Philadelphia: Da Capo, 2006 (German original: 2002).

Kobasa, Suzanne C. "The Hardy Personality: Toward a Social Psychology of Stress and Health." In *Social Psychology of Health and Illness*, edited by Glenn S. Sanders and Jerry Suls, 3–32. Hillsdale, NJ: Lawrence Erlbaum Associates, 1982.

Koehler, Ludwig, and Walter Baumgartner. *Lexicon in Veteris Testamenti*. 2 volumes. Leiden: Brill, 1985.

Koehler, Ludwig, Walter Baumgartner, and Johann Jakob Stamm. *The Hebrew and Aramaic Lexicon of the Old Testament*. Translated and edited by M. E. J. Richardson. 5 volumes. Leiden: Brill, 1994–1999.

Kovacs, Judith L. "Clement of Alexandria and Gregory of Nyssa on the Beatitudes." In *Gregory of Nyssa: Homilies on the Beatitudes: An English Version with Commentary and Supporting Studies: Proceedings of the Eighth International Colloquium on Gregory of Nyssa (Paderborn, September 14–18, 1998)*, edited by Hubertus R. Drobner and Albert Viciano, 311–29. Supplements to Vigiliae Christianae 52. Leiden: Brill, 2000.

Kraut, Richard. "Two Conceptions of Happiness." *The Philosophical Review* 88 (1979): 167–97.

——. *Aristotle on the Human Good*. Princeton: Princeton University Press, 1989.

———. "Aristotle's Ethics." In *The Stanford Encyclopedia of Philosophy*. Last modified March 29, 2010. http://plato.stanford.edu/entries/aristotle-ethics/. Accessed September 2, 2011.

Krüger, Thomas. *Qoheleth: A Commentary*. Translated by O. C. Dean, Jr. Edited by Klaus Baltzer. Hermeneia. Minneapolis: Fortress Press, 2004.

Küchler, Friedrich. "Das priesterliche Orakel in Israel und Juda." In *Abhandlungen zur semitischen Relgionskunde und Sprachwissenschaft: Wolf Wilhelm Grafen von Baudissin zum 26. September 1917*, 285–301. Edited by Wilhelm Frankenberg and Friedrich Küchler. Beihefte zur Zeitschrift für die alttestamentliche Wissenschaft 33. Giessen: Alfred Töpelmann, 1918.

Kümmel, Werner G. *Promise and Fulfillment: The Eschatological Message of Jesus*. Studies in Biblical Theology 23. London: SCM, 1966 (original edition 1957).

Ladd, George Eldon. *Crucial Questions About the Kingdom of God*. Grand Rapids: Eerdmans, 1952.

———. "Kingdom of God—Reign or Realm?" *Journal of Biblical Literature* 81 (1962): 230–38.

———. *Jesus and the Kingdom: The Eschatology of Biblical Realism*. New York: Harper & Row, 1964.

———. *A Theology of the New Testament*. Grand Rapids: Eerdmans, 1974.

———. *The Presence of the Future: The Eschatology of Biblical Realism*. Grand Rapids: Eerdmans, 1974.

Lapsley, Jacqueline. "Feeling Our Way: Love for God in Deuteronomy." *Catholic Biblical Quarterly* 65 (2003): 350–69.

———. "Doors Thrown Open and Waters Gushing Forth: Mark, Ezekiel, and the Architecture of Hope." In *The Ending of Mark and the Ends of God: Essays in Memory of Donald Harrisville Juel*, edited by Beverly Roberts Gaventa and Patrick D. Miller, 139–53. Louisville: Westminster John Knox, 2005.

Layard, Richard. *Happiness: Lessons from a New Science*. New York: Penguin, 2005.

Le, Thao N., Mary H. Lai, and Judy Wallen. "Multiculturalism and Subjective Happiness as Mediated by Cultural and Relational Variables." *Cultural Diversity and Ethnic Minority Psychology* 15 (2009): 303–13.

LeDoux, J. *The Emotional Brain*. New York: Simon and Schuster, 1996.

Lee, Eunny P. *The Vitality of Enjoyment in Qoheleth's Theological Rhetoric*. Beihefte zur Zeitschrift für die alttestamentliche Wissenschaft 353. Berlin: Walter de Gruyter, 2005.

———. "Joy." In *The New Interpreter's Dictionary of the Bible*, edited by Katharine Doob Sakenfeld, et al., 3:417–18. 5 volumes. Nashville: Abingdon, 2006–2009.

Lee, Sung-Hun. "Lament and the Joy of Salvation in the Lament Psalms." In *The Book of Psalms: Composition and Reception*, 224–47. Edited by Peter W. Flint and Patrick D. Miller, Jr. Supplements to Vetus Testamentum 99. Leiden: Brill, 2005.

Leimon, Averil, and Gladeana McMahon. *Positive Psychology for Dummies*. Chichester: John Wiley and Sons, 2009.

Lent, Robert W. "Toward a Unifying Theoretical and Practical Perspective on Well-Being and Psychosocial Adjustment." *Journal of Counseling Psychology* 51 (2004): 482–509.

Levenson, Jon D. *Creation and the Persistence of Evil: The Jewish Drama of Divine Omnipotence.* 2nd edition. Princeton: Princeton University Press, 1994 (original edition 1988).

———. *Resurrection and the Restoration of Israel: The Ultimate Victory of the God of Life.* New Haven: Yale University Press, 2006.

Lévi-Strauss, Claude. *Structural Anthropology.* Translated by Clair Jacobson and Brook Grundfest Schoepf. New York: Basic, 1963.

Lewis, Sarah. *Positive Psychology at Work: How Positive Leadership and Appreciative Inquiry Create Inspiring Organizations.* Oxford and Malden, MA: Wiley-Blackwell, 2011.

Linley, P. Alex, and Stephen Joseph, eds. *Positive Psychology in Practice.* Hoboken, NJ: Wiley, 2004.

Linley, P. Alex, Susan Harrington, and Nicola Garcea, eds. *Oxford Handbook of Positive Psychology and Work.* Oxford: Oxford University Press, 2010.

Lipiński, Edward. "Marcismes et Psaumes de congratulation." *Revue Biblique* 75 (1968): 321–67.

Lloyd-Jones, David Martyn. *The Path to True Happiness.* Grand Rapids: Baker, 1999.

Lohfink, Norbert. *Theology of the Pentateuch: Themes of the Priestly Narrative and Deuteronomy.* Translated by Linda M. Maloney. Minneapolis: Fortress, 1994.

Lohr, Joel N. *Chosen and Unchosen: Conceptions of Election in the Pentateuch and Jewish-Christian Interpretation.* Siphrut 2. Winona Lake: Eisenbrauns, 2009.

Lohse, Eduard. *Freude des Glaubens: Die Freude im Neuen Testament.* Göttingen: Vandenhoeck & Ruprect, 2007.

Löning, Karl, and Erich Zenger. *To Begin with, God Created . . . : Biblical Theologies of Creation.* Collegeville, MN: Liturgical, 2000.

Looy, Heather. "Embodied and Embedded Morality: Divinity, Identity, and Disgust." *Zygon* 39 (2004): 219–35.

Lopez, Shane J., ed. *The Encyclopedia of Positive Psychology.* 2 volumes. Malden, MA: Wiley-Blackwell, 2009.

Lopez, Shane J., and C. R. Snyder, eds. *Oxford Handbook of Positive Psychology.* 2nd edition. New York: Oxford University Press, 2011.

Louw, Johannes P., and Eugene A. Nida, eds. *Greek-English Lexicon of the New Testament: Based on Semantic Domains.* 2nd edition. 2 volumes. New York: United Bible Societies, 1989.

Lucas, Richard E. "Adaptation and the Set-Point Model of Subjective Well-Being: Does Happiness Change After Major Life Events?" *Current Directions in Psychological Science* 16 (2007): 75–79.

Lucas, Richard E., and M. Brent Donnellan. "How Stable is Happiness? Using the STARTS Model to Estimate the Stability of Life Satisfaction." *Journal of Research in Personality* 41 (2007): 1091–98.

Lundström, Gösta. *The Kingdom of God in the Teaching of Jesus: A History of Interpretation from the Last Decades of the Nineteenth Century to the Present Day*. Edinburgh: Oliver and Boyd, 1963.

Luz, Ulrich. *Matthew 1–7*. Translated by James E. Crouch. Edited by Helmut Koester. Hermeneia. Minneapolis: Fortress, 2007.

Lykken, David, and Auke Tellegen. "Happiness is a Stochastic Phenomenon." *Psychological Science* 7 (1996): 186–89.

Lyubomirsky, Sonja. *The How of Happiness: A Scientific Approach to Getting the Life You Want*. New York: Penguin, 2008.

Maahs, Charles H. "The Makarisms in the New Testament: A Comparative Religions and Form Critical Investigation." PhD diss, Tübingen, 1965.

MacArthur, John. *The Beatitudes: The Only Way to Happiness*. Chicago: Moody, 1998.

MacDonald, Nathan. *Not Bread Alone: The Uses of Food in the Old Testament*. Oxford: Oxford University Press, 2008.

Machinist, Peter. "Fate, *miqreh*, and Reason: Some Reflections on Qohelet and Biblical Thought." In *Solving Riddles and Untying Knots: Biblical, Epigraphic, and Semitic Studies in Honor of Jonas C. Greenfield*, 159–75. Edited by Ziony Zevit, Seymour Gitin, and Michael Sokoloff; Winona Lake: Eisenbrauns, 1995.

MacIntyre, Alasdair. *Whose Justice? Which Rationality?* Notre Dame: University of Notre Dame Press, 1989.

Mackenzie, Catriona, and Kim Adams, eds. *Practical Identity and Narrative Agency*. New York: Routledge, 2008.

Madigan, Kevin J., and Jon D. Levenson. *Resurrection: The Power of God for Christians and Jews*. New Haven: Yale University Press, 2008.

Majerus, Brian D., and Steven J. Sandage. "Differentiation of Self and Christian Spiritual Maturity: Social Science and Theological Integration." *Journal of Psychology and Theology* 38 (2010): 41–51.

Mansfeld, Günter. "Der Ruf zur Freude im Alten Testament." PhD diss., Heidelberg, 1966.

Marinescu, Horia. "Vienna 1928—Wittgenstein House: Architecture as Reflection." Translated by Aranca Munteanu. Accessed July 12, 2001. www.horia-marinescu.net/texte.php?lang=en&;text=4. Romanian original: "Meditatii pe Marginea unei Expozitii Monografice de la Mak, Viena." Arhitectura (August–September 2002).

Marlow, Hilary. *Biblical Prophets and Contemporary Environmental Ethics: Re-Reading Amos, Hosea, and First Isaiah*. Oxford: Oxford University Press, 2009.

Mason, Michelle, and Valerie Tiberius. "Aristotle." In *The Encyclopedia of Positive Psychology*, 1:63–64. 2 volumes. Edited by Shane J. Lopez. Malden, MA: Wiley-Blackwell, 2009.

May, Gerald G. *The Dark Night of the Soul: A Psychiatrist Explores the Connection Between Darkness and Spiritual Growth*. San Francisco: HarperSanFrancisco, 2004.

Mayne, Tracy, and George A. Bonanno, eds. *Emotions: Current Issues and Future Directions*. New York: Guilford Press, 2001.

Mays, James L. *Psalms*. Interpretation. Louisville: John Knox, 1994.

———. *Preaching and Teaching the Psalms*. Edited by Patrick D. Miller and Gene M. Tucker. Louisville: Westminster John Knox, 2006.

McAdams, Dan P. *The Redemptive Self: Stories Americans Live By*. New York: Oxford University Press, 2006.

McAdams, Dan P., and Regina L. Logan. "What is generativity?" In *The Generative Society: Caring for Future Generations*, edited by Ed de St. Aubin, Dan P. McAdams, and Tae-Chang Kim, 15–31. Washington, DC: American Psychological Association, 2004.

McBride, S. Dean, Jr. "Divine Protocol: Genesis 1:1–2:3 as Prologue to the Pentateuch." In *The God Who Creates: Essays in Honor of W. Sibley Towner*, edited by William P. Brown and S. Dean McBride Jr., 3–41. Grand Rapids: Eerdmans, 2000.

McCann, J. Clinton, Jr. "The Shape of Book I of the Psalter and the Shape of Human Happiness." In *The Book of Psalms: Composition and Reception*, edited by Peter W. Flint and Patrick D. Miller, 340–48. Vetus Testamentum Supplements 99. Leiden: Brill, 2005.

McCann, J. Clinton, Jr., ed. *The Shape and Shaping of the Psalter*. Journal for the Study of the Old Testament Supplement Series 159. Sheffield: JSOT Press, 1993.

McCown, Chester S. "The Beatitudes in the Light of Ancient Ideals." *Journal of Biblical Literature* 46 (1927): 50–61.

McEleney, Neil J. "The Beatitudes of the Sermon on the Mount/Plain." *Catholic Biblical Quarterly* 43 (1981): 1–13.

McMahon, Darrin M. *Happiness: A History*. New York: Grove, 2006.

McWhorter, John. *The Power of Babel: A Natural History of Language*. New York: Perennial, 2001.

Merklein, Helmut. *Jesu Botschaft von der Gottesherrschaft: Eine Skizze*. Stuttgarter Bibelstudien 111. Stuttgart: Verlag Katholisches Bibelwerk, 1983.

Mesquita, Batja. "Culture and Emotion: Different Approaches to the Question." In *Emotions: Current Issues and Future Directions*, edited by Tracy Mayne and George A. Bonanno, 214–50. New York: Guilford Press, 2001.

Meyer, Joyce. *The Secret to True Happiness: Enjoy Today, Embrace Tomorrow*. New York: FaithWords, 2008.

Michaelis, Christine. "Die π-Alliteration der Subjektsworte der ersten 4 Seligpreisungen in Mt v 3–6 und ihre Bedeutung für den Aufbau der Seligpreisungen bei Mt., Lk., und in Q." *Novum Testamentum* 10 (1968): 148–61.

Middleton, J. Richard. *The Liberating Image: The Imago Dei in Genesis 1*. Grand Rapids: Brazos, 2005.

Mieder, Wolfgang. *Proverbs: A Handbook*. Westpoint, CT: Greenwood Press, 2004.

Milgrom, Jacob. *Leviticus: A Book of Ritual and Ethics*. Continental Commentaries. Minneapolis: Fortress, 2004.

Miller, Lisa, and Brien S. Kelley. "Relationships of Religiosity and Spirituality with Mental Health and Psychopathology." In *Handbook of the Psychology of Religion and Spirituality*, edited by Raymond F. Paloutzian and Crystal L. Park, 460–78. New York: Guilford, 2005.

Miller, Patrick D., Jr. *Genesis 1–11: Studies in Structure and Theme.* Journal for the Study of the Old Testament Supplement Series 8. Sheffield: JSOT Press, 1978.

———. "Syntax and Theology in Genesis XII 3a." *Vetus Testamentum* 34 (1984): 472–76.

———. "God's Other Stories: On the Margins of Deuteronomic Theology." In *Realia Dei: Essays in Archaeology and Biblical Interpretation in Honor of Edward F. Campbell Jr. at His Retirement*, edited by Prescott H. Williams, Jr. and Theodore Hiebert, 185–94. Atlanta: Scholars Press, 1999.

———. *Israelite Religion and Biblical Theology: Collected Essays.* Journal for the Study of the Old Testament Supplement Series 267. Sheffield: Sheffield Academic Press, 2000.

———. "The Good Neighborhood: Identity and Community Through the Commandments." In *Character and Scripture: Moral Formation, Community, and Biblical Interpretation*, edited by William P. Brown, 55–72. Grand Rapids: Eerdmans, 2002.

———. "A Strange Kind of Monotheism." In *Theology Today: Reflections on the Bible and Contemporary Life*, 44–46. Louisville: Westminster John Knox, 2006.

Miller, William R., and Janet C'de Baca. *Quantum Change: When Epiphanies and Sudden Insights Transform Ordinary Lives.* New York: Guilford, 2001.

M'Neile, Alan H. *The Gospel According to St. Matthew.* Reprint edition. London: Macmillan, 1965 (original edition 1915).

Moberly, R. W. L. *The Old Testament of the Old Testament: Patriarchal Narratives and Mosaic Yahwism.* Overtures to Biblical Theology. Minneapolis: Fortress, 1992.

———. *The Theology of the Book of Genesis.* Old Testament Theology. Cambridge: Cambridge University Press, 2009.

Moltmann, Jürgen. *The Crucified God: The Cross of Christ as the Foundation and Criticism of Christian Theology.* Translated by R. A. Wilson and John Bowden. Minneapolis: Fortress, 1993 (German original 1973).

Montmarquet, James A. "Hedonism." In *The Cambridge Dictionary of Philosophy*, 364–65. 2nd edition. Edited by Robert Audi. Cambridge: Cambridge University Press, 1999.

Moran, William L. "The Ancient Near Eastern Background of the Love of God in Deuteronomy." *Catholic Biblical Quarterly* 25 (1963): 77–87.

Morgan, Robert. "From Reimarus to Sanders: the Kingdom of God, Jesus, and the Judaisms of His Day." In *The Kingdom of God and Human Society: Essays by Members of the Scripture, Theology, and Society Group*, edited by Robin Barbour, 80–139. Edinburgh: T & T Clark, 1993.

Morrice, William G. *Joy in the New Testament.* Grand Rapids: Eerdmans, 1984.

Morris, John. *God Wants You Happy: From Self-Help to God's Help.* New York: Harper One, 2011.

Moxnes, Halvor. *The Economy of the Kingdom: Social Conflict and Economic Relations in Luke's Gospel*. Overtures to Biblical Theology. Philadelphia: Fortress, 1988.

Moyise, Steve. *The Old Testament in the Book of Revelation*. Journal for the Study of the New Testament Supplement Series 115. Sheffield, Sheffield Academic Press, 1995.

———. *The Old Testament in the New: An Introduction*. Continuum Biblical Studies Series. New York: Continuum, 2001.

Mozley, J. K. *The Impassibility of God: A Survey of Christian Thought*. Cambridge: Cambridge University Press, 1926.

Murphy, Roland E. *Ecclesiastes*. Word Biblical Commentary 23A. Dallas, TX: Word, 1992.

———. *Proverbs*. Word Biblical Commentary 22. Nashville: Thomas Nelson, 1998.

Myers, David G. *The Pursuit of Happiness: Discovering the Pathway to Fulfillment, Well-Being, and Enduring Personal Joy*. New York: Avon, 1992.

———. "Human Connections and the Good Life: Balancing Individuality and Community in Public Policy." In *Positive Psychology in Practice*, 641–57. Edited by P. Alex Linley and Stephen Joseph. Hoboken, NJ: Wiley, 2004.

Nasuti, Harry P. "The Interpretive Significance of Sequence and Selection in the Book of Psalms." In *The Book of Psalms: Composition and Reception*, 311–39. Edited by Peter W. Flint and Patrick D. Miller, Jr. Supplements to Vetus Testamentum 99. Leiden: Brill, 2005.

Nauck, Wolfgang. "Freude im Leiden: Zum Problem einer urchristlichen Verfolgungstradition." *Zeitschrift für die neutestamentliche Wissenschaft* 46 (1955): 68–80.

Neumann, Roland, and Fritz Strack. "'Mood Contagion': The Automatic Transfer of Mood Between Persons." *Journal of Personality and Social Psychology* 79 (2000): 211–23.

Newman, Barclay M. "Some Translational Notes on the Beatitudes. Matthew 5.1–12." *The Bible Translator* 26 (1975): 106–20.

Newsom, Carol A. "The Moral Sense of Nature: Ethics in the Light of God's Speech to Job." *Princeton Seminary Bulletin* 15 (1994): 9–27.

———. *The Book of Job: A Contest of Moral Imaginations*. New York: Oxford University Press, 2003.

Niemiec, Ryan M., and Danny Wedding. *Positive Psychology at the Movies: Using Films to Build Virtues and Character Strengths*. Cambridge, MA: Hogrefe and Huber, 2008.

Niskanen, Paul. "The Poetics of Adam: The Creation of *'adam* in the image of *'elohim*." *Journal of Biblical Literature* 128 (2009): 417–36.

Norem, Julie K. *The Positive Power of Negative Thinking: Using Defensive Pessimism to Harness Anxiety and Perform at Your Peak*. New York: Basic, 2001.

Norman, Richard J. "Happiness." In *The Oxford Companion to Philosophy*, 358–59. 2nd edition. Edited by Ted Honderich. Oxford: Oxford University Press, 2005.

Nussbaum, Martha C. *The Fragility of Goodness: Luck and Ethics in Greek Tragedy and Philosophy*. Revised edition. Cambridge: Cambridge University Press, 2001 (original edition 1987).

O'Leary, Stephen D. *Arguing the Apocalypse: A Theory of Millennial Rhetoric*. New York: Oxford University Press, 1994.

Ong, Anthony D., and Manfred H. M. van Dulmen, eds. *Oxford Handbook of Methods in Positive Psychology*. New York: Oxford University Press, 2007.

Osteen, Joel. *Your Best Life Now: 7 Steps to Living at Your Full Potential*. New York: FaithWords, 2004.

———. *Every Day a Friday: How to Be Happier 7 Days a Week*. New York: FaithWords, 2011.

Oster, H., and P. Ekman. "Facial Behavior in Child Development." *Minnesota Symposium on Child Psychology* 11 (1978): 231–76.

Otto, Eckart, and Tim Schramm. *Festival and Joy*. Biblical Encounters Series. Nashville: Abingdon, 1980.

Otto, Rudolf. *The Kingdom of God and the Son of Man: A Study in the History of Religion*. Revised edition. Translated by Floyd V. Filson and Bertram L. Woolf. Boston: Starr King, 1957 (original edition 1943).

Outler, Albert C., ed. *The Works of John Wesley: Volume 1: Sermons I (1–33)*. Nashville: Abingdon, 1984.

The Oxford English Dictionary. 2nd edition. 20 volumes. Oxford: Clarendon, 1989. Online version June 2011.

Pakaluk, Michael. *Aristotle's Nicomachean Ethics: An Introduction*. Cambridge: Cambridge University Press, 2005.

Paloutzian, Raymond F., and Crystal L. Park, eds. *Handbook of the Psychology of Religion and Spirituality*. New York: Guilford, 2005.

Palsgrave, John. *Lesclarcissement de la langue francoyse*. 1st ed. London: J. Haukyns, 1530.

Pamment, Margaret. "The Kingdom of God According to the First Gospel." *New Testament Studies* 27 (1981): 211–32.

Pannenberg, Wolfhart. *Systematic Theology*. 2 volumes. Grand Rapids: Eerdmans, 1991–1994.

Park, Nansook, Christopher Peterson, and Martin E. P. Seligman. "Strengths of Character and Well-Being." *Journal of Social and Clinical Psychology* 23 (2004): 603–19.

Parrish, V. Steven. *A Story of the Psalms: Conversation, Canon, and Congregation*. Collegeville, MN: Liturgical Press, 2003.

Pascal, Blaise. *Pascal's Pensées*. Translated by Thomas Stearns. New York: E. P. Dutton, 1958.

Patton, Kimberly Christine. *Religion of the Gods: Ritual, Paradox, and Reflexivity*. Oxford: Oxford University Press, 2009.

Paulien, Jon. *Decoding Revelation's Trumpets: Literary Allusions and Interpretations of Revelation 8:7–12*. Andrews University Seminary Doctoral Dissertation Series 11. Berrien Springs, MI: Andrews University Press, 1988.

———. "Dreading the Whirlwind: Intertextuality and the Use of the Old Testament in Revelation," *Andrews University Seminary Studies* 39 (2001): 5–22.

Pavot, William, and Ed Diener. "Findings on Subjective Well-Being: Applications to Public Policy, Clinical Interventions, and Education." In *Positive Psychology in Practice*, 679–92. Edited by P. Alex Linley and Stephen Joseph. Hoboken, NJ: Wiley, 2004.

Peale, Norman Vincent. *The Power of Positive Thinking*. New York: Fireside, 2003 (original: 1952).

Pedrotti, Jennifer Teramoto, Lisa M. Edwards, and Shane J. Lopez. "Positive Psychology within a Cultural Context." In *Oxford Handbook of Positive Psychology*, edited by Shane J. Lopez and C. R. Snyder, 49–57. 2nd edition. New York: Oxford University Press, 2011.

Pelikan, Jaroslav. *Luther's Works*, Volume 21: *The Sermon on the Mount (Sermons) and The Magnificat*. St. Louis: Concordia, 1956.

Pelikan, Jaroslav, ed. *The Preaching of Augustine: "Our Lord's Sermon on the Mount."* Translated by Francine Cardman. The Preacher's Paperback Library 13. Philadelphia: Fortress, 1973.

Percy, Ernst. *Die Botschaft Jesu: Eine traditions-kritische und exegetische Untersuchung*. Lunds universitets årsskrift, n.f. Avdeeling 1, 49.5. Lund: Gleerup, 1953.

Percy, Walker. *Lost in the Cosmos: The Last Self-Help Book*. New York: Picador, 1983.

Perdue, Leo G. *Wisdom and Creation: The Theology of Wisdom Literature*. Nashville: Abingdon, 1994.

Perrin, Norman. *The Kingdom of God in the Teaching of Jesus*. New Testament Library. Philadelphia: Westminster, 1963.

———. *Jesus and the Language of the Kingdom*. Philadelphia: Fortress, 1976.

Peterson, Christopher. *A Primer in Positive Psychology*. New York: Oxford University Press, 2006.

Peterson, Christopher, and Martin E. P. Seligman. *Character Strengths and Virtues: A Handbook and Classification*. New York: Oxford University Press, 2004.

Petersen, David L. "Genesis and Family Values." *Journal of Biblical Literature* 124 (2005): 5–23.

Piedmont, Ralph, Joseph Williams, and Joseph Ciarrochi. "Personality Correlates of One's Image of Jesus: Historiographic Analysis using the Five-Factor Model of Personality." *Journal of Psychology and Theology* 25 (1997): 364–73.

Pieper, Josef. *On Hope*. Translated by M. F. McCarthy. San Francisco: Ignatius, 1986.

Pinker, Steven. *The Blank Slate: The Modern Denial of Human Nature*. London: Penguin, 2002.

Piper, John. *Desiring God: Meditations of a Christian Hedonist*. Colorado Springs, CO: Multnomah, 2003 (earlier edition, Sisters, OR: Multnomah, 1996).

Piper, John, and David Cochran Heath. *The Dangerous Duty of Delight: The Glorified God and the Satisfied Soul*. Accessed July 27, 2011. www.desiringgod.org/ResourceLibrary /OnlineBooks/ByTitle/1730_The_Dangerous_Duty_of_Delight_Sample/.

Pollock, George H. "Aging and Aged: Development or Pathology." In *The Course of Life: Psychoanalytic Contributions Toward Understanding Personality Development*, Volume 3: *Adulthood and the Aging Process*, 549–85. Edited by Stanley I. Greenspan and George H. Pollock. Rockville, MD: National Institute of Mental Health (US) Mental Health Studies and Reports Branch, 1981).

———. *The Mourning-Liberation Process*. 2 volumes. Madison, CT: International Universities Press, 1989.

Portier-Young, Anathea. "Languages of Identity and Obligation: Daniel as a Bilingual Book." *Vetus Testamentum* 60 (2010): 1–18.

Powell, Mark Allan. "Matthew's Beatitudes: Reversals and Rewards of the Kingdom." *Catholic Biblical Quarterly* 58 (1996): 460–79.

Quasten, Johannes. *Patrology*. 4 volumes. Utrecht: Spectrum, 1966–1997.

Rad, Gerhard von. *Wisdom in Israel*. Translated by James D. Martin. Nashville: Abingdon, 1972 (German original 1970).

———. "The Deuteronomic Theology of History in 1 and 2 Kings." In *From Genesis to Chronicles: Explorations in Old Testament Theology*, 154–66. Edited by K. C. Hanson. Minneapolis: Fortress, 2005.

Radford, Andrew. *Syntax: A Minimalist Introduction*. Cambridge: Cambridge University Press, 1997.

Radner, Karen. *Die Macht des Namens: Altorientalischen Strategien zur Selbsterhaltung*. Santag 8. Wiesbaden: Harrassowitz, 2005.

Rawson, Beryl. "The Roman Family." In *The Family in Ancient Rome: New Perspectives*, edited by Beryl Rawson, 1–57. Ithaca: Cornell University Press, 1986.

Richardson, Ronald W. *Becoming a Healthier Pastor: Family Systems Theory and the Pastor's Own Family*. Minneapolis: Fortress, 2005.

Ricoeur, Paul. *The Symbolism of Evil*. New York: Harper and Row, 1967.

———. *The Rule of Metaphor: Multi-Disciplinary Studies of the Creation of Meaning in Language*. Translated by R. Czerny et al. Toronto: University of Toronto Press, 1977.

Rife, J. Merle. "Matthew's Beatitudes and the Septuagint." In *Studies in the History and Text of the New Testament in Honor of Kenneth Willis Clark*, edited by Boyd L. Daniels and M. Jack Suggs, 107–12. Salt Lake City, UT: University of Utah Press, 1967.

Ringgren, Helmer. *Word and Wisdom: Studies in the Hypostatization of Divine Qualities and Functions in the Ancient Near East*. Lund: Ohlssons, 1947.

Ritschl, Albrecht. *The Christian Doctrine of Justification and Reconciliation*. Translated by H. R. Macintosh and A. B. Macaulay. Edinburgh: T & T Clark, 1902.

Robbins, Vernon K. *The Invention of Christian Discourse*. Rhetoric of Religious Antiquity. Leiden: Deo, 2009.

Robinson, H. Wheeler. *Inspiration and Revelation in the Old Testament*. Oxford: Clarendon, 1946.

Rousseau, Jean-Jacques. *Émile: Or, Education*. Translated by Barbara Toxley. Reprint edition. London: J. M. Dent and Sons, 2010 (French original 1762).

Rowland, Christopher. *The Open Heaven: A Study of Apocalyptic in Judaism and Early Christianity*. New York: Crossroad, 1982.

———. "Apocalypticism." In *The New Interpreter's Dictionary of the Bible*, edited by Katharine Doob Sakenfeld, et al., 1:190. 5 volumes. Nashville: Abingdon, 2006–2009.

Rozin, Paul, and April Fallon. "A Perspective on Disgust." *Psychology Review* 94 (1987): 23–41.

Rozin, P., C. Taylor, L. Ross, G. Bennett, and A. Hejmadi. "General and Specific Emotion Recognition Abilities: Relations among Individual Differences in Recognition of Disgust and Other Emotional Expressions in Facial and Bodily Representations, Obsessive-Compulsive Tendencies, and Disgust Sensitivity." *Cognition and Emotion* 19 (2005): 397–412.

Rubin, Gretchen. *The Happiness Project: Or, Why I Spent a Year Trying to Sing in the Morning, Clean My Closets, Fight Right, Read Aristotle, and Generally Have More Fun*. New York: HarperCollins, 2009.

Ryan, Richard M., and Edward L. Deci. "On Happiness and Human Potentials: A Review of Research on Hedonic and Eudaimonic Well-Being." *Annual Review of Psychology* 52 (2001): 141–66.

Ryff, Carol D., and Burton H. Singer. "The Contours of Positive Human Health." *Psychological Inquiry* 9 (1998): 1–28.

Ryff, Carol D., and Burton H. Singer. "Know Thyself and Become What You Are: A Eudaimonic Approach to Psychological Well-Being." *Journal of Happiness Studies* 9 (2008): 13–39.

Ryken, Leland, James C. Wilhoit, and Tremper Longman III, eds. *Dictionary of Biblical Imagery*. Downers Grove, IL: InterVarsity Press, 1998.

Sahlins, Marshall. *How "Natives" Think: About Captain Cook, for Example*. Chicago: University of Chicago Press, 1995.

Sandage, Steven J., and Mark G. Harden. "Relational Spirituality, Differentiation of Self, and Virtue as Predictors of Intercultural Development." *Mental Health, Religion, and Culture* 14 (2011): 819–38.

Sandage, Steven J., and Peter J. Jankowski. "Forgiveness, Spiritual Instability, Mental Health Symptoms, and Well-Being: Mediation Effects of Differentiation of Self." *Psychology of Religion and Spirituality* 2 (2010): 168–80.

Sandage, Steven J., and Merrishia S. Naicker. "Indigenous Positive Psychology." In *The Encyclopedia of Positive Psychology*, edited by Shane J. Lopez, 1:514–17. 2 volumes. Oxford: Wiley-Blackwell, 2009.

Sandage, Steven J., Mary L. Jensen, and Dan Jass. "Relational Spirituality and Transformation: Risking Intimacy and Alterity." *Journal of Spiritual Formation and Soul Care* 1 (2008): 182–206.

Sandage, Steven J., Peter C. Hill, and Deanne C. Vaubel. "Generativity, Relational Spirituality, Gratitude, and Mental Health: Relationships and Pathways." *International Journal for the Psychology of Religion* 21 (2011): 1–16.

Sandage, Steven J., Kaye V. Cook, Peter C. Hill, Brad D. Strawn, and Kevin S. Reimer. "Hermeneutics and Psychology: A Review and Dialectical Model." *Review of General Psychology* 12 (2008): 344–64.

Sandoval, Timothy J. *The Discourse of Wealth and Poverty in the Book of Proverbs*. Biblical Interpretation Series 77. Leiden: Brill, 2006.

Sarna, Nahum M. *Genesis*. The JPS Torah Commentary. Philadelphia: The Jewish Publication Society, 1989.

Schifferdecker, Kathryn. *Out of the Whirlwind: Creation Theology in the Book of Job*. Harvard Theological Studies. Cambridge, MA: Harvard Divinity School, 2008.

Schleiermacher, F. D. E. *The Christian Faith*. Translated by H. R. Mackintosh. Edinburgh: T & T Clark, 1986.

Schlesinger, Arthur M. "The Lost Meaning of 'The Pursuit of Happiness.'" *The William and Mary Quarterly* 31 (1964): 325–27.

Schloss, Jeffrey P. "From Evolution to Eschatology." In *Resurrection: Theological and Scientific Assessments*, edited by Ted Peters, et al., 59–86. Grand Rapids: Eerdmans, 2002.

Schnackenburg, Rudolf. *God's Rule and Kingdom*. New York: Herder & Herder, 1963.

Schnarch, David. *Intimacy and Desire: Awaken the Passion in Your Relationship*. New York: Beufort Books, 2009.

———. "Die Seligpreisung der Friedensstifter (Mt 5,9) im mattäischen Kontext." *Biblische Zeitschrift* 26 (1982): 161–78.

Schottroff, Luise. *Let the Oppressed Go Free: Feminist Perspectives on the New Testament*. Gender and the Biblical Tradition. Louisville: Westminster John Knox, 1993.

Schulkin, Jay. *Bodily Sensibility: Intelligent Action*. Series in Affective Science. Oxford: Oxford University Press, 2004.

Schwarz, G. "'Ihnen gehört das Himmelreich'? (Matthäus V.3)." *New Testament Studies* 23 (1977): 341–43.

Schweitzer, Albert. *The Mystery of the Kingdom of God: The Secret of Jesus' Messiahship and Passion*. Translated by Walter Lowrie. New York: Macmillan, 1950.

———. *Kingdom of God and Primitive Christianity*. Translated by L. A. Garrard. Edited by Ulrich Neuenschwander. New York: Seabury, 1968.

———. *The Quest of the Historical Jesus*. 1st complete edition. Edited by John Bowden. Minneapolis: Fortress, 2001.

Schweitzer, Don. "Karl Barth's Critique of Classical Theism." *Toronto Journal of Theology* 18 (2002): 231–44.

Schweizer, Eduard. "Formgeschichtliches zu den Seligpreisungen Jesu." *New Testament Studies* 19 (1973): 121–26.

Scott, Bernard Brandon. *Jesus, Symbol-Maker for the Kingdom*. Philadelphia: Fortress, 1981.

Scott, David A. "Ethics on a Trinitarian Basis: Moltmann's *The Crucified God*." *Anglican Theological Review* 60 (1978): 166–79.

Scott, M. Philip. "A Note on the Meaning and Translation of Luke 11:28." *Irish Theological Quarterly* 41 (1974): 235–50.

Segal, Alan F. *Life after Death: A History of the Afterlife in Western Religion.* New York: Doubleday, 2004.

Seligman, Martin E. P. *Authentic Happiness: Using the New Positive Psychology to Realize Your Potential for Lasting Fulfillment.* New York: Simon and Schuster, 2002.

———. "Can Happiness Be Taught?" *Daedalus* 133 (2004): 80–87.

———. *Flourish: A Visionary New Understanding of Happiness and Well-being.* New York: Free Press, 2011.

Seow, Choon-Leong. *Ecclesiastes: A New Translation with Introduction and Commentary.* Anchor Bible 18C. New York: Doubleday, 1997.

Shults, F. LeRon, and Steven J. Sandage. *Transforming Spirituality: Integrating Theology and Psychology.* Grand Rapids: Baker Academic, 2006.

Skowron, Elizabeth A., Sarah E. Holmes, and Ronald M. Sabatelli. "Deconstructing Differentiation: Self Regulation, Interdependent Relating, and Well-Being in Adulthood." *Contemporary Family Therapy* 25 (2003): 111–29.

Skowron, Elizabeth A., Krystal L. Stanley, and Michael D. Shapiro. "A Longitudinal Perspective on Differentiation of Self, Interpersonal and Psychological Well-Being in Young Adulthood." *Contemporary Family Therapy* 31 (2009): 3–18.

Smalley, Stephen S. "Spirit, Kingdom, and Prayer in Luke-Acts." *Novum Testamentum* 15 (1973): 59–71.

Smyth, Herbert W. *Greek Grammar.* Cambridge, MA: Harvard University Press, 1920.

Snyder, C. R., ed. *Handbook of Hope: Theory, Measures, and Applications.* San Diego: Academic Press, 2000.

Snyder, C. R., and Shane J. Lopez, *Oxford Handbook of Positive Psychology.* 2nd edition. Oxford: Oxford University Press, 2009.

Snyder, C. R., Shane J. Lopez, and Jennifer Teramoto Pedrotti. *Positive Psychology: The Scientific and Practical Explorations of Human Strengths.* 2nd edition. Los Angeles: Sage, 2011.

Solzhenitsyn, Aleksandr. *Cancer Ward.* New York: Noonday, 2001.

Sommer, Benjamin D. *The Bodies of God and the World of Ancient Israel.* New York: Cambridge University Press, 2009 (paperback edition 2011).

Stadelmann, Luis I. J. *The Hebrew Conception of the World.* Analecta biblica 39. Rome: Pontifical Biblical Institute, 1970.

Steck, Odil Hannes. "Beobachtungen zur Anlage von Jes 65–66." *Biblische Notizen* 38/39 (1987): 103–16.

———. "Der neue Himmel und die neue Erde: Beobachtungen zur Rezeption von Gen 1–3 in Jes 65, 16b–25." In *Studies in the Book of Isaiah: Festschrift Willem A. M. Beuken,* edited by J. van Ruiten, M. Vervenne, 349–65. Bibliotheca Ephemeridum theologicarum Lovaniensium 132. Leuven: Leuven University Press, 1997.

Steinke, Peter L. *Congregational Leadership in Anxious Times: Being Calm and Courageous No Matter What.* Herndon, VA: Alban Institute, 2006.

Stendahl, Krister. *Paul Among Jews and Gentiles.* Philadelphia: Fortress, 1979.

Still, Todd D. "Did Paul Loathe Manual Labor? Revisiting the Work of Ronald F. Hock on the Apostle's Tentmaking and Social Class." *Journal of Biblical Literature* 125 (2006): 781–95.

Strack, Hermann, and Paul Billerbeck. *Kommentar zum Neuen Testament aus Talmud und Midrasch.* 6 volumes. München: Beck, 1922–1961.

Strassler, Robert B., ed. *The Landmark Herodotus: The Histories.* New York: Pantheon Books, 2007.

Strawn, Brad D., and Brent A. Strawn. "The Shift from Lament to Praise: A Psychodynamic Phenomenon" (forthcoming).

Strawn, Brent A. "And These Three Are One: A Trinitarian Critique of Christological Approaches to the Old Testament." *Perspectives in Religious Studies* 31 (2004): 191–210.

———. *What Is Stronger than a Lion? Leonine Image and Metaphor in the Hebrew Bible and the Ancient Near East.* Orbis biblicus et orientalis 212. Fribourg: Academic Press and Göttingen: Vandenhoeck & Ruprecht, 2005.

———. "'Israel, My Child': The Ethics of a Biblical Metaphor." In *The Child in the Bible*, edited by Marcia Bunge, Terence E. Fretheim, and Beverly R. Gaventa, 103–40. Grand Rapids: Eerdmans, 2008.

———. "Lyric Poetry." In *Dictionary of the Old Testament: Wisdom, Poetry and Writings*, 437–46. Edited by Tremper Longman III and Peter Enns. Downers Grove: IVP Academic, 2008.

———. "Comparative Approaches: History, Theory, and the Image of God." In *Method Matters: Essays on the Interpretation of the Hebrew Bible in Honor of David L. Petersen*, edited by Joel M. LeMon and Kent Harold Richards, 117–42. Society of Biblical Literature Resources for Biblical Studies 56. Atlanta: Society of Biblical Literature, 2009.

———. "Deuteronomy." In *Theological Bible Commentary*, edited by Gail R. O'Day and David L. Petersen, 63–76. Louisville: Westminster John Knox, 2009.

———. "Psalm 1." In *Psalms for Preaching and Worship: A Lectionary Commentary*, edited by Roger E. Van Harn and Brent A. Strawn, 50–55. Grand Rapids: Eerdmans, 2009.

———. "Psalm 150." In *Psalms for Preaching and Worship: A Lectionary Commentary*, 376–81. Edited by Roger E. Van Harn and Brent A. Strawn. Grand Rapids: Eerdmans, 2009.

———. "The Psalms: Types, Functions, and Poetics for Proclamation." In *Psalms for Preaching and Worship: A Lectionary Commentary*, 3–40. Edited by Roger E. Van Harn and Brent A. Strawn. Grand Rapids: Eerdmans, 2009.

Strawn, Brent A., and Joel M. LeMon. "'Everything That Has Breath': Animal praise in Psalm 150:6 in the light of ancient Near Eastern iconography." In *Bilder als Quellen/Images as*

Sources: Studies on ancient Near Eastern artefacts and the Bible inspired by the work of Othmar Keel, edited by S. Bickel, S. Schroer, R. Schurte, and C. Uehlinger, 451–85 and Pls. XXXIII-XXXIV. Orbis biblicus et orientalis Sonderband. Fribourg: Academic Press and Göttingen: Vandenhoeck & Ruprecht, 2007.

Strawn, Brent A., and Brad D. Strawn. "Prophecy and Psychology." In *Dictionary of the Old Testament: Prophets*, 610–23. Edited by Mark J. Boda and J. Gordon McConville. Downers Grove, IL: IVP Academic, 2012.

Strecker, Georg. "Die Makarismen der Bergpredigt." *New Testament Studies* 17 (1971): 255–75.

———. *Die Bergpredigt: Ein exegetischer Kommentar*. Göttingen: Vandenhoeck & Ruprecht, 1984.

Strozier, Charles B. *Apocalypse: On the Psychology of Fundamentalism in America*. Boston: Beacon Press, 1994.

Stuckenbruck, Loren T. *1 Enoch 91–108*. Commentaries on Early Jewish Literature. New York: Walter de Gruyter, 2007.

Swenson, Kristin M. *Living Through Pain: Psalms and the Search for Wholeness*. Waco, TX: Baylor University Press, 2005.

Swete, H.B. *Introduction to the Old Testament in Greek*. Reprint edition. Peabody, MA: Hendrickson, 1989 (orig: 1900)

Swing, Albert T. *The Theology of Albrecht Ritschl*. London: Longmans, Green, 1901.

Tan, Hui Bing, and Joseph P. Forgas. "When Happiness Makes us Selfish, But Sadness Makes Us Fair: Affective Influences on Interpersonal Strategies in the Dictator Game." *Journal of Experimental Social Psychology* 46 (2010): 571–76.

Tanner, Beth LaNeel. *The Book of Psalms through the Lens of Intertextuality*. Studies in Biblical Literature 26. New York: Peter Lang, 2001.

Taylor, Charles. *Sources of the Self: The Making of the Modern Identity*. Cambridge, MA: Harvard University Press, 1992.

Thagard, Paul. "The Passionate Scientist: Emotion in Scientific Cognition." In *The Cognitive Basis of Science*, edited by P. Carruthers, S. Stich, and M. Siegal, 235–50. Cambridge: Cambridge University Press, 2002.

Tiberius, Valerie, and Michelle Mason. "Eudaimonia." In *The Encyclopedia of Positive Psychology*, 1:351–55. 2 volumes. Edited by Shane J. Lopez. Malden, MA: Wiley-Blackwell, 2009.

Tigay, Jeffrey H. *You Shall Have No Other Gods: Israelite Religion in the Light of Hebrew Inscriptions*. Harvard Semitic Studies 31. Atlanta: Scholars Press, 1986.

Tillich, Paul. *Systematic Theology*. 3 volumes. Chicago: University of Chicago Press, 1951–1963.

Tissot, Gabriel. *Ambroise de Milan: Traité sur L'Évangile de S. Luc*. 2 volumes. Sources Chrétiennes 45, 52. Paris: Les Éditions du Cerf, 1956–58.

Towner, W. Sibley. "'Without Our Aid He Did Us Make': Singing the Meaning of the Psalms." In *A God So Near: Essays on Old Testament Theology in Honor of Patrick*

D. Miller, 17–34. Edited by Brent A. Strawn and Nancy R. Bowen. Winona Lake: Eisenbrauns, 2004.

Tuckett, Christopher M. "The Beatitudes: A Source-Critical Study; with a Reply by Michael M. Goulder." *Novum Testamentum* 25 (1983): 193–216.

Vanier, Jean. *Happiness: A Guide to the Good Life, Aristotle for the New Century*. Translated by Kathryn Spink. New York: Arcade, 2002.

Van Buren, Paul M. *A Theology of the Jewish-Christian Reality*, Volume 1: *Discerning the Way*. New York: Seabury, 1980.

Van Harn, Roger E., and Brent A. Strawn, eds. *Psalms for Preaching and Worship: A Lectionary Commentary*. Grand Rapids: Eerdmans, 2009.

Van Leeuwen, Raymond C. "The Book of Proverbs." In *The New Interpreter's Bible*, edited by Leander E. Keck et al., 5:19–264. 12 volumes. Nashville: Abingdon, 1994–2004.

——. "Form Criticism, Wisdom, and Psalms 111–112." In *The Changing Face of Form Criticism for the Twenty-First Century*, edited by Marvin A. Sweeney and Ehud Ben Zvi, 71–81. Grand Rapids: Eerdmans, 2003.

Van Ruiten, J. T. A. G. M. "The Intertextual Relationship between Isaiah 65:25 and Isaiah 11:6–9." In *The Scriptures and the Scrolls*, edited by F. García Martínez, A. Hilhorst, and C. J. Labuschchagne, 31–42. Vetus Testamentum Supplements 49. Leiden: Brill, 1992.

Veenhoven, Ruut. "Happiness as a Public Policy Aim: The Greatest Happiness Principle." In, *Positive Psychology in Practice*, 658–78. Edited by P. Alex Linley and Stephen Joseph. Hoboken, NJ: Wiley, 2004.

Villanueva, Federico G. *The 'Uncertainty of a Hearing': A Study of the Sudden Change of Mood in the Psalms of Lament*. Supplements to Vetus Testamentum 121. Leiden: Brill, 2008.

Viviano, Benedict T. "Beatitudes Found Among Dead Sea Scrolls." *Biblical Archaeology Review* 18 (1992): 53–55, 66.

——. "Sadducees, Angels, and Resurrection (Acts 23:8–9)." *Journal of Biblical Literature* 111 (1992): 496–98.

——. *Trinity—Kingdom—Church: Essays in Biblical Theology*. Göttingen: Vandenhoeck & Ruprecht, 2001.

Volf, Miroslav. *After Our Likeness: The Church as the Image of the Trinity*. Grand Rapids: Eerdmans, 1998.

Volkmann, Evelina. "Freude." In *Calwer Bibellexikon*, edited by O. Betz et al., 1:377. 2 volumes. Stuttgart: Calwer, 2003.

Wallis, Claudia. "The New Science of Happiness." *Time* (Sunday, January 9, 2005). Online at www.time.com/time/magazine/article/0,9171,1015902,00.html. Accessed September 20, 2011.

Walsh, Patricia. "Well-being." In *The Oxford Companion to Philosophy*, 955–56. 2nd edition. Edited by Ted Honderich. Oxford: Oxford University Press, 2005.

Walter, Nikolaus. "Die Bearbeitung der Seligpreisungen durch Matthäus." In *Studia evangelica IV-V: Papers Presented to the Third International Congress on New Testament Studies Held at Christ Church, Oxford, 1965*, edited by F. L. Cross, 1:246–58. 2 volumes. Texte und Untersuchungen zur Geschichte der altchristlichen Literatur 102–103. Berlin: Akademie-Verlag, 1968.

Wang, Stephen. "Aquinas on Human Happiness and the Natural Desire for God." *New Blackfriars* 88 (2007): 322–34.

Warren, Rick. *The Purpose Driven Life: What On Earth Am I Here For?* Grand Rapids: Zondervan, 2002.

Watson, David. "Positive Affectivity: The Disposition to Experience Pleasurable Emotional States." In *Handbook of Positive Psychology*, edited by C. R. Snyder and S. J. Lopez, 106–19. New York: Oxford University Press, 2002.

Watson, Duane F. "Introduction." In *The Intertexture of Apocalyptic Discourse in the New Testament*, edited by Duane F. Watson, 1–9. Society of Biblical Literature Symposium Series 14. Atlanta: Society of Biblical Literature, 2002.

Weber, Beat. "Zum sogenannten 'Stimmungsumschwung' in Psalm 13." In *The Book of Psalms: Composition and Reception*, 116–38. Edited by Peter W. Flint and Patrick D. Miller, Jr. Supplements to Vetus Testamentum 99. Leiden: Brill, 2005.

Weder, Hans. *Die 'Rede der Rede': Ein Auslegung der Bergpredigt Heute*. Zurich: Theologischer Verlag, 1985.

Weil, Simone. "On the Right Use of School Studies with a View to the Love of God." In *Waiting for God*, 57–66. Translated by Emma Craufurd. New York: Harper Perennial Modern Classics, 2009.

Weinberg, Steven. *Dreams of a Final Theory*. New York: Pantheon Books, 1992.

Weiss, Johannes. *Jesus' Proclamation of the Kingdom of God*. Translated and edited by Richard H. Hiers and David L. Holland. Lives of Jesus Series. Philadelphia: Fortress, 1971.

Welch, Claude. *Protestant Thought in the Nineteenth Century: Volume 2, 1870–1914*. New Haven: Yale University Press, 1985.

Wellhausen, Julius. *Skizzen und Vorarbeiten 5: Die kleinen Propheten übersetzt und erklärt*. 3rd edition. Berlin: Reimer, 1898.

Wenham, Gordon J. *Genesis 16–50*. Word Biblical Commentary 2. Dallas: Word Books, 1994.

Westermann, Claus. *Isaiah 40–66: A Commentary*. Old Testament Library. Philadelphia: Westminster, 1969.

———. *Praise and Lament in the Psalms*. Translated by Keith R. Crim and Richard N. Soulen. Atlanta: John Knox, 1981 (German original: 1965).

———. *The Structure of the Book of Job: A Form-Critical Analysis*. Translated by Charles A. Muenchow. Philadelphia: Fortress, 1981 (German original: 1977).

———. *Genesis 1–11*. Translated by John J. Scullion. Continental Commentaries. Minneapolis: Augsburg, 1984.

Wheelwright, Philip. *Metaphor and Reality*. Bloomington: Indiana University Press, 1962.

White, Nicholas. *A Brief History of Happiness*. Malden, MA: Blackwell, 2006.

Whybray, R. Norman. *Reading the Psalms as a Book*. Journal for the Study of the Old Testament Supplement Series 222. Sheffield: Sheffield Academic Press, 1996.

———. *The Good Life in the Old Testament*. London: T & T Clark, 2002.

Wilder, Amos. *Eschatology and Ethics in the Teaching of Jesus*. Revised edition. New York: Harper, 1939.

Williamson, Ian T., and Steven J. Sandage. "Longitudinal Analyses of Religious and Spiritual Development Among Seminary Students." *Mental Health, Religion, and Culture* 12 (2009): 787–801.

Williamson, Ian T., Steven J. Sandage, and Richard M. Lee. "How Social Connectedness Affects Guilt and Shame: Mediated by Hope and Differentiation of Self." *Personality and Individual Differences* 43 (2007): 2159–70.

Williamson, Robert, Jr. "Death and Symbolic Immortality in Second Temple Wisdom Instructions." PhD diss., Emory University, 2011.

Willis, Timothy M. "Name, Naming." In *The New Interpreter's Dictionary of the Bible*, edited by Katharine Doob Sakenfeld, et al., 4:217–19. 5 volumes. Nashville: Abingdon, 2006–2009.

Willis, Wendell, ed. *The Kingdom of God in 20th-Century Interpretation*. Peabody, MA: Hendrickson, 1987.

Wilson, Eric G. *Against Happiness: In Praise of Melancholy*. New York: Farrar, Straus, and Giroux, 2008.

Wilson, Gerald H. *The Editing of the Hebrew Psalter*. Society of Biblical Literature Dissertation Series 76. Chico, CA: Scholars Press, 1985.

Winnicott, D. W. *The Maturational Processes and the Facilitating Environment: Studies in the Theory of Emotional Development*. London: Karnac and the Institute of Psycho-Analysis, 2004 (original 1965).

———. *Playing and Reality*. London: Routledge, 2005 (original edition 1971).

Wolff, Hans Walter. "The Kerygma of the Deuteronomic Historical Work." In *Walter Brueggemann and Hans Walter Wolff, The Vitality of Old Testament Traditions*, 83–100. 2nd edition. Atlanta: John Knox, 1982.

Worthington, Everett L., Jr. *A Just Forgiveness: Responsible Healing without Excusing Injustice*. Downers Grove, IL: InterVarsity Press, 2009.

Worthington, Everett L., Jr., ed. *Handbook of Forgiveness*. New York: Routledge, 2005.

Wright, Addison G. "'For Everything There is a Season': The Structure and Meaning of the Fourteen Opposites (Ecclesiastes 3,2–8)." In *De la Tôrah au Messie: Mélanges Henri Cazelles*, edited by J. Dore et al., 321–28. Paris: Desclée, 1981.

Wright, G. Ernest. *The Old Testament Against Its Environment*. Studies in Biblical Theology 2. London: SCM, 1950.

Wright, N. T. *The New Testament and the People of God*. Minneapolis: Fortress, 1992.

Yeager, John. "Faith, Fear, and Motivation—The Back Story of the Stockdale Paradox." *Positive Psychology News Daily* (April 11, 2009). Accessed August 12, 2011. http://positivepsychologynews.com/news/john-yeager/200904111793.

Yee, Gale. "The Theology of Creation in Proverbs 8:22–31." In *Creation in the Biblical Traditions*, edited by Richard J. Clifford and John J. Collins, 85–96. Catholic Biblical Quarterly Monograph Series. Washington, DC: Catholic Biblical Association, 1992.

Yoder, Christine Roy. *Wisdom as a Woman of Substance: A Socioeconomic Reading of Proverbs 1–9 and 31:10–31*. Beihefte zur Zeitschrift für die alttestamentliche Wissenschaft 304. Berlin: Walter de Gruyter, 2000.

———. "The Woman of Substance (*'ēšet ḥayil*): A Socioeconomic Reading of Proverbs 31:10–31." *Journal of Biblical Literature* 122 (2003): 427–47.

Yrizarry, Nathan, David Matsumoto, Chikako Imai, Kristie Kooken, and Sachiko Takeuchi. "Culture and Emotion." In *Cross-Cultural Topics in Psychology*, edited by Leonore Loeb Adler and Uwe P. Gielen, 131–48. 2nd edition. Westport, CT: Praeger, 2001.

Zimmerli, Walter. "Zwillingspsalmen." In *Studien zur alttestamentlichen Theologie und Prophetie: Gesammelte Aufsätze 2*, 263–67. Theolgische Bücherei 51. Munich: Kaiser, 1974.

———. "Die Seligpreisungen der Bergpredigt und das Alte Testament." In *Donum Gentilicium: New Testament Studies in Honour of David Daube*, edited by E. Bammel, C. K. Barrett, and W. D. Davies, 8–26. Oxford: Clarendon, 1978.

Index of Biblical and Other Ancient Sources

Note that biblical references in the index follow the ordering of the Christian Old Testament. The Appendix has not been indexed for biblical citations.

Index of Modern Authors